OPENING UP THE BIBLE

Opening Up
the Bible

David Jackman

Hodder & Stoughton
LONDON SYDNEY AUCKLAND

First published in Great Britain in 2000 as *I Believe in the Bible*

This edition first published in 2003

The right of David Jackman to be identified as the Author
of the Work has been asserted by him in accordance with the
Copyright, Designs and Patents Act 1988.

10 9 8 7 6 5 4 3 2 1

British Library Cataloguing in Publication Data
A record for this book is available from the British Library

ISBN 0 340 86175 4

Typeset in Ehrhardt by Avon DataSet Ltd,
Bidford-on-Avon, Warwickshire

Printed and bound in Great Britain by
Bookmarque Ltd, Croydon, Surrey

The paper and board used in this paperback are natural recyclable
products made from wood grown in sustainable forests.
The manufacturing processes conform to the environmental
regulations of the country of origin.

Hodder and Stoughton
A Division of Hodder Headline Ltd
338 Euston Road
London NW1 3BH
www.madaboutbooks.com

Contents

Editor's Preface   vii
Acknowledgments   ix

Introduction   xi
1 The Bible at the Start of the Twenty-First   15
   Century
2 The Bible's Own Story   28
3 The Bible's Own Testimony   51
4 Can We Trust the Bible's Reliability?   74
5 And What Does It Really Mean?   95
6 So How Do We Unpack the Old Testament?   111
7 But How Does the Old Relate to the New?   139
8 So How Do We Unpack the New Testament?   159
9 How Can I Hear God Speaking in the Bible?   188
10 Is There Anybody Out There Listening?   215

Bibliography   238

Editor's preface

When I was originally planning this book as part of the new 'I Believe' series, David Jackman was the obvious author to approach with an invitation to tackle the subject of the Bible itself. He exercises a widely appreciated Bible teaching ministry and, as Director of the Cornhill Training Course, is hard at work preparing Bible teachers and preachers for the next generation. He is therefore no stranger to the challenge of helping Christians tackle the questions and controversies that surround the Bible.

As you will soon see from what he has written, David brings a combination of intellectual rigour and passionate enthusiasm to his subject. Here is someone who really does believe in the Bible! I'm delighted at the way his gentle and persuasive manner comes across so clearly as he shows how to make sense of this ancient book and apply it to the issues we face in the modern world. For David Jackman, the Bible is far more than a fascinating book from long ago: it's how we hear God speak today. Keep reading and let him show you how!

David Stone

Acknowledgments

I should like to thank the Proclamation Trust for study leave to enable me to do much of the writing of the text, and the students of the Cornhill Training Course, by whom many of its ideas and examples have been tested and clarified over the years. My warmest thanks are due to Nancy Olsen, whose keyboard skills converted my hieroglyphics into successive drafts of a readable manuscript, and to Annabel Robson and David Moloney for their editorial support and help. To my colleague Doug Johnson and my daughter, Philly Simpkin, who read the first draft, many thanks are due for their helpful suggestions, and to my wife Heather, whose love and support, as always, enabled me to start, continue and complete the project, I owe my deepest thanks and gratitude.

Introduction

'Of making many books there is no end.' The words of the writer of the Bible book of Ecclesiastes certainly have a contemporary ring about them. However, the purpose of this particular book is to encourage the reader to read the greatest book of all, of which God himself is the author. The Bible, still the world's best-seller, is probably found in more copies, editions and translations than any other text which has ever been published, and yet in spite of its availability it remains unknown – a closed book – to so many people today.

Most of my adult working life has centred on this book, ever since I first tried to explain one of its texts, as a raw and somewhat nervous student, to a supportive and hugely tolerant little congregation in a rural chapel, nearly forty years ago now. My great passion is still to understand the contents of this amazing book, so as to seek to live it out and share its truth and light with others. As a Christian pastor and teacher, it has been my privilege to open the Bible and try to explain its meaning, several times a week, in a great variety of contexts, to all sorts of people, believing and sceptical, around the world. I have been able to put the Bible to the test and I have never found it to fail. Wherever you go, whatever the culture, the Bible speaks to the basic needs of the human heart and mind with an immediate relevance and a penetrating power, which can only be explained by its divine origin. 'Men spoke from God as they were carried along by the Holy Spirit' (2 Peter 1:21).

I believe in the Bible because it is God's book, articulating in human language the mind of the God who made us for relationship with himself. It is through the pages of the Bible that we come to know his character and to understand his ways. It is here that we encounter God in person, as we meet Jesus Christ, the central focus of the whole revelation, and are called to repent of our rebellious autonomy by acknowledging God as God, in our own personal lives. The Bible is not a book about God; it is God speaking to us, in a directly engaging way, teaching, rebuking, correcting, training and equipping us to live rightly in his world now, in preparation for the life of the world to come.

Like all good gifts, the Bible can be abused, and has often been misused by those whose own agenda is to distort its message and destroy its credibility. It is often said that you can make the Bible mean anything you want it to. But that is only true if the basic rules by which we understand and interpret any document are ignored or infringed. Of course, if a sentence is lifted entirely out of its setting and then made to stand on its own as an absolute statement, the Bible can be made to say some strange things. 'There is no God' is a straight quote from Psalm 14:1, but look at it in its context! Playing childish games like that with the Bible is the worst sort of trivialisation. And yet the Bible remains a closed book to millions of people for a variety of reasons which are almost as trivial. The tragedy is that so many of the answers to the dilemmas of our contemporary world are contained within its pages, and yet lie there unknown and ignored. It is as if medical researchers were to discover a cure for cancer, write it up in a widely circulated textbook, distribute it to every hospital and health centre around the world, and then for the precious information to remain unread on the bookshelf, as people continued to die of the disease. If we were told that God was going to make a television broadcast after the evening news tonight, most of us would plan to be in, or at the very least to have the video set. We would be interested to know what he would say. But he has already told us all we need to know to bring us to eternal life, and the book lies unopened and unread.

The purpose of this book is to encourage you into reading the Bible for yourself, whether or not you have tried it before. They say that you can eat an elephant if you tackle it slice by slice. So the aim of these pages is to make the Bible more accessible, by seeing how its great variety keeps returning to, and underlining, its central story. Its goal is to give confidence in handling the Bible well, practising the principles of good understanding and interpretation, so that its message becomes clear and compelling. We may not always like what we discover, because the Bible has a way of getting under the skin, challenging our comfort zones and questioning our dearly held opinions. But that is what we most need if our lives are going to be changed and renewed. However, it is perhaps true that this book should come with a 'health warning', because reading and understanding the Bible is a high-risk activity. What we do with what we discover can have eternal implications, because we never walk away from an encounter with God in the Bible unchanged. Either our hearts are softened, as we accept what he says to us, through faith and practical action in obedience, or they are hardened, as we refuse his revelation and reject his demands. The Bible will not allow anyone who reads it seriously to remain neutral.

'I believe in the Bible' is not just a credal statement; it expresses the passion which motivates my life and ministry. When Martin Luther was accused of being obsessed with the Bible and totally prejudiced in its favour, he didn't deny the fact. Rather, he retorted that it was natural for anyone to be prejudiced in favour of his own mother, affirming that it was through the Bible he was brought to birth – to the new life in Christ, which is being born again. That is the experience of every Bible-believing Christian. The Spirit of God still uses the Word of God to produce the people of God. Those who belong to that community affirm that all they believe comes from God's revelation in the Holy Scriptures. They are supremely those who believe in the Bible.

Chapter 1

The Bible at the Start of the Twenty-First Century

It was an ordinary afternoon at the school gate, as the cars pulled up and the pushchairs were wheeled across the zebra crossing. But Alison had a mission in the couple of minutes before the children began to stream out. She had got to know Christine quite well during the term and had enjoyed the snatched conversations they often had together. Now was the time to ask her to the Bible study on investigating Christianity which she and some other mums at the Church were planning to start. She grabbed her courage with both hands and launched out into the invitation. Christine's response was hardly enthusiastic. 'The Bible? You mean you actually spend your time reading that old-fashioned stuff? I can only remember bits of it from school in RE lessons – all that fusty, musty language, people slaughtering one another or committing adultery, and those weird, out-of-date explanations about how the world began. Anyway, science disproved it all long ago, and it's all been rewritten and changed down the centuries. I really don't have time to waste on all that rubbish. I'm just too busy with the children.'

The debate round the table in the students' union bar was getting more heated. 'No, Dan, I don't want to come and read the Bible with you and your friends,' Matt was almost shouting. 'I tried to read it once and it didn't make any sense. Anyway, didn't you listen to that lecture this morning? A literary text doesn't have a "meaning". It's just black marks on white paper. It's just a place where the ideas of the author are expressed. I'll relate to it one way, and you another, and Kate another. It's only what you want it to be. You want your Bible to mean something to boost your predetermined religious ideas, and that's fine for you. Sure! You can have your Bible study circle, but don't try to force your ideas on me, because at the end of the day the Bible is just an ancient text from a totally archaic culture. I'm twenty-first-century man, mate, not neolithic!'

Julia and Andy slowly realised that they were facing a dead end. The circles their relationship had been going round in for two years or more had become a downward spiral and they were facing break-up. They had tried so hard and invested so much in one another. They'd had their good times and neither of them really wanted to face the future alone, but they couldn't face it together, either. 'Someone at work today asked whether we'd ever looked at the Bible,' Julia ventured. 'Supposed to give us some uplift, direction even – full of good advice, that sort of thing.' Andy stopped stirring his coffee and looked up. 'Yeah, right! But where would you even start? I tried it once, but it doesn't have a subject index, does it, and none of it seems to make sense or fit together, and what on earth have all those incomprehensible names got to do with us? Anyway, we're not the religious sort, are we? That's not what we need right now!'

Three different, but negative, views of the book that is still, by all the figures, the world's best-seller. We could all multiply the scenarios from our own personal experience, because to most people, at the beginning of the twenty-first century, the Bible is quite simply a closed book. For many it's a black, forbidding book, speaking in a language 'which thou dost no longer use in conversation with thy friends', consigned to the mists of antiquity. To others, it's a slippery collection of mutually contradictory ideas that can be made to mean almost anything, and then be pressed into the service of almost any cause. For some, it's a glorious part of our cultural heritage, along with Shakespeare and Dr Johnson – the flowering of the English language, a profound influence on the minds and imaginations of generations long since forgotten. To most, it has nothing to say to life today, because it deals in certainties and absolutes which no longer command any credibility. Its ethos is more the quill pen than information technology. To a few, it is the living and enduring Word of God, the means by which the eternal creator of the world, everything and everyone in it, continues to reveal his purposes and character to human beings, created to know their deepest fulfilment and satisfaction in a personal relationship with him.

I believe in the Bible. It is a book written in time, unfolding eternity. It could not be more relevant and is never out of date, because it reveals the unchanging character of the God who is there. Its divine truth still transforms human life and experience, and it is available in easy-to-read, accurate, modern translations in every bookshop in the land. But the Bible does need to be unlocked, and all too often we lack the time and patience to unpack its treasures carefully enough. We pick it up and, rather like a lucky-dip at the village fête, hope to pull out something of value with the minimum amount of effort. We are like the eager five-year-old returning from her first day at school, bitterly complaining that she hasn't learned how to read yet. What we need to do is to make a start!

Let's do that by exploding two myths about the Bible, which commonly deter the contemporary explorer at the very outset of the process. The first is that it is an advanced religious textbook, accessible only to the experts after years of study in Semitic languages or the more abstruse areas of philosophy and theology. On the contrary, if you can read a newspaper, you can read the Bible, particularly if it is in one of the excellent contemporary English translations. It has been said that, like the ocean, the Bible is shallow enough for a toddler to paddle in and deep enough for an elephant to drown in. Through its pages, we are introduced to otherwise unimaginable spiritual depths, mysteries which were kept hidden in God's providence but which have now been revealed. But it is neither obscure nor mysterious in its essential contents.

The second myth is that its historical antiquity makes it remote from our everyday, contemporary life. Its historical particularity seems to distance it irretrievably from our world. But the Bible is full of human life. On every page we encounter real people who have the same concerns and struggles, the same problems and opportunities, as we do. Their cultural clothing is different, but we would be blind not to see beyond such superficial distinctives to their essential humanity, which is common to ours. We are not in a fairy-tale world, nor are we bound up in a cultural time-warp, when we read the pages of the Bible. We are among flesh and blood like our own, facing a common experience of what it is to be human, in the real world, and exploring the possibilities of knowing the God of eternity in the midst of time.

The Bible's claims

But why a book, and what is this phenomenon we call 'the Holy Bible'? To answer these initial questions, we need to step outside of the immediate picture in order to pose some issues which are even more fundamental. For example, what is the ultimate ground for believing anything about anything? How do we come to the practical judgments we make in everyday life as to what is true or false, right or wrong, what works or doesn't work? Or, to express the issue more abstractly, what grounds of authority do we look for in making decisions about what we believe or how we behave?

In the practical affairs of everyday life, we recognise the authority of fact, established by proof, which becomes a conditioning factor in every aspect of our lives and experience. The law of gravity is an example of an observable and constant physical phenomenon, which I am powerless to contradict, either by argument or will-power. It is a fact that if I jump from the top of a high-rise building I shall fall to the earth, irrespective of what I may have persuaded myself, in my own mind, as to the likely outcome of the event. If the action takes place, the consequence follows, and both are facts. They can be proved by visible evidence and tangible results. There can be plenty of argument about how and why the event happened, but the fact that it did happen cannot be denied. The radar speed trap, the police cameras, the video clip are all automatically accepted as corroboration of past events. Arguments can and do happen about interpretation, but they only happen because there are facts and events about which to argue. The Bible has many claims to this sort of factual authority.

But there are very many areas of human thought and expression where facts need to be interpreted if their full significance is to be appreciated. Our opinions and subsequent actions will probably be based on the degree of authority, or credibility, we attribute to a particular explanation or interpretation. In such areas, we may utilise a whole range of criteria by which to make our assessment. How *do* we come to our value judgments? It may be on the basis of what the majority think, so that the opinion survey percentages become the arbiter of what is acceptable and what is not. Or we may decide to go with what the experts say, even though different schools of equally well-qualified people may fundamentally contradict one another's findings. Perhaps we revert to what we were taught at school, or by our parents, – 'well, my mum always used to say . . .' – and it becomes a dictum which influences our thinking, almost without our realising it.

The problem with all such criteria is that they are limited in scope and transient in relevance, because they are conditioned by our humanness. For example, in the recent discussion about the lowering of the age of consent for homosexual activity, the percentages of the public approving or disapproving the various proposed changes have swung wildly backwards and forwards over a period of time and according to different polls. But if the 50 per cent who wanted reform at one time have been reduced to 25 per cent a few months later, does that affect the rights or wrongs of the issue either way? It may provide a more or less accurate barometer of public opinion, but it has no authoritative comment to make in the area of morality. Existentialist philosophers throughout the second half of the twentieth century consistently pointed out that right and wrong, truth and error can only be meaningful concepts if they are grounded in a divine being, outside of and distinct from our human relativism. Jean-Paul Sartre's dictum, that finite man is meaningless without an infinite reference point, recognises the reality that human beings cannot attribute meaning in life without an authority external to ourselves, greater than we are, consistent and unchanging, by which moral absolutes can be declared and upheld. This is the authority which the Bible claims to be able to mediate.

Let's spend a short time understanding the logic of the claim. If the only ground for Truth (with a capital 'T') as a given absolute lies in a divine being whose attributes are infinite and eternal, then the most important quest any of us can be involved in is to discover whether such a God actually exists. This is the quest for an ultimate authority. But how could we ever discover such a reality with any certainty? Clearly, such a 'God' could not be expressed as a mathematical formula, however complex, or be available for our examination like the data of a scientific experiment. Such a being must be, by definition, far beyond human analysis and even imagination, because of our finitude. Any 'deity' that could be encompassed within the framework of a human mind, however brilliant, has thereby forfeited the title of 'god'. So the long quest by humankind either to discover God or even to create our own deity is doomed to failure. We have neither the mental nor the spiritual capacities to achieve the goal. Indeed, the Bible recognised the dilemma centuries ago, in one of its earliest books, when it asked the rhetorical questions, 'Can you fathom the mysteries of God? Can you probe the limits of the Almighty? They are higher than the heavens – what can you do? They are deeper than the depths of the grave – what can you know?' (Job 11:7–8).

At this point, we must not miss an important clue in the Bible itself. It is that nowhere in the sixty-six books, which constitute the Bible as we have it, is the existence of God argued or proved on a philosophical basis. The Church has sometimes attempted the task, with arguments about the unmoved Mover, or that just as a watch is inexplicable without a watch-maker, so a complex universe requires an infinite creator. But the Bible's own method is to state God's existence and point to the evidence of his words and actions. In other words, the Bible's claim to ultimate authority lies in its declaration that God has chosen to reveal himself by what he does and what he says, and that its own pages are the authoritative record of that self-disclosure. 'Proofs' will always be inadequate, because God's reality transcends the greatest human intellect. The God of the Bible is not the sum total of our best thoughts and most insightful notions about him. God would remain for ever hidden from human perception and completely unknowable had he not chosen to make himself known, and to do that in terms which his human creation can understand, because they are the same currency of words and actions by which we make ourselves known to one another.

The human parallels are both clear and helpful. We have all had the galling experience of trying to get to know someone only to be met with a brick wall of resistance. Of course, we each have the right to reveal, or conceal, our thoughts, words and actions from others. Indeed, the measure of depth in our interpersonal relationships is largely the extent to which we are happy to disclose ourselves to another person, marriage being the prime example. But while relationships among equals are conducted on the basis of mutual disclosure, the same is not true of relationships with superiors. There the measure of relating is determined by the condescension of the higher to the lower. The first-year schoolboy does not bowl along to the headmaster's office for a chat whenever the whim takes him. The subject cannot demand access to his or her monarch. The greater has to stoop to the lesser, if any relationship between them is to exist at all. How much more, then, must this be the case between the infinite, yet personal, God who is the creator of the universe and his finite, human creatures? To imagine that we could saunter into his presence, with our hands in our pockets, or could put him through our computers and come up with a comprehensive analysis, is simply an indicator of our human arrogance. The only hope that finite human beings have of relating to the infinite is if he condescends to reveal himself to us. The only way that morally flawed people can relate to a God of perfection is if he discloses himself on terms that can bridge the chasm between us. Again, it is the Bible's claim to do just that, which constitutes a unique authority.

Alternative authorities

There are, of course, many rival claims of authority within the broad field of religious belief systems. Even within Christianity itself, different emphases have emerged, and at root these account for the many divisions, along denominational lines, which church history has sadly witnessed. However, all Christians would agree that all authority within creation rightly belongs to the creator. As Daniel told King Nebuchadnezzar, we must 'acknowledge that the Most High is sovereign over the kingdoms of men and gives them to anyone he wishes' and that 'Heaven rules' (Daniel 4:25–6). Again, 'His dominion is an eternal dominion; his kingdom endures from generation to generation . . . He does as he pleases with the powers of heaven and the peoples of the earth' (Daniel 4:34–5). The question is how that authority is mediated to us.

For some, it is through the Church and its traditions. The Bible is seen as the product of the believing community, which is therefore superior to it. The interpretation of a book that would otherwise be dead therefore becomes the primary task, and only then can it become a source of authority. The properly appointed officers of the Church become the custodians and arbiters of truth, by whom the Bible's message is interpreted and applied. The Thirty-Nine Articles of the Church of England recognise an important place for tradition in the life of the Church, but add the rider: so long as it 'be not repugnant to the Word of God', recognising that the Church is subsidiary, as an authority, to the Bible. The authors of the Reformation formularies recalled the charges Jesus himself laid at the door of the traditionalists of his own day, the Pharisees, when he accused them of elevating their traditional practices above the teaching of the Old Testament. 'You have let go of the commands of God and are holding on to the traditions of men' he told them (Mark 7:8). And again, 'You have a fine way of setting aside the commands of God in order to observe your own traditions . . . Thus you nullify the word of God by your tradition that you have handed down' (Mark 7:9, 13). Jesus is criticising tradition as the ultimate authority because it actually takes us back to a human base, which is inevitably flawed and inadequate.

The same weakness must be identified in the exaltation of human reason to the position of ultimate authority. The Bible then becomes *an* authority, but acceptable only in so far as it accords with what seems reasonable. It is argued that, after all, the Bible is a book produced by human authors, who were themselves inevitably conditioned by their culture, language and thought-forms. To give them an authority beyond that of a witness to developing religious experience would be naïve and misleading. Once again, this view internalises the ultimate authority to that of our own wisdom and knowledge, both of which are notoriously subjective and ephemeral. Bible writers claim much more for their writings, though in the relativism of our own times the authority of what seems reasonable is culturally very attractive. In the end, of course, we lose any concept of unchanging truth or absolute standards, so that the Bible itself is relativised and shorn of its divine power and authority.

But perhaps the most popular authority base for twenty-first-century people is that of personal experience. We have become suspicious of being overly dependent on reason and sceptical about the effects of warring schools of rationalism within our world. The experience of the twentieth-century mass murderers such as Hitler, Stalin and Mao, all in the name of rationality, has produced a sense of vulnerability within human beings which has contributed to a headlong retreat from all externally informed authority systems. Whether religious, political, academic or parental, authority *per se* is no longer trusted and now subjected to the most rigorous examination. Indeed, one might argue that the defining characteristic of our post-modern, contemporary culture is the repudiation of the very concept of objective authority, in favour of personal autonomy and individual creativity. 'Just do it!' has become more than a sales pitch; it embodies a culture. If it feels good, it *is* good. If it's OK for you, then do it your way. The only restriction is that it shouldn't inhibit me from enjoying what's OK for me.

In such a context, the message of the Bible takes on authority only when I decide personally to agree with it. Its record of how prophets and apostles met with God in the past may or may not reverberate with my experience, but it is that experience which becomes the ground of my personal being. What I feel and experience emotionally therefore becomes more real, more significant to me, as a living human being, than what I think, or read, of what others have written. There is an immediacy, a 'nowness', to the authority of experience, which becomes all-controlling. The Bible may be a useful foil, or even a plumb-line by which to evaluate experience in a wider, deeper context, but it can also be restrictive and inhibiting. Why should God commit himself to words spoken yesterday, if he is the living God of today? Who is to say that he cannot reveal himself equally through current dreams and visions, trances and altered states of consciousness, prophecies and inspired utterances? The real issue is not so much whether there is an authority that can be imposed upon resistant human minds and consciences. The history of the past century is full of examples of that sort of totalitarianism, the misery it generates and the seeds of its own inevitable decline which it always sows. The new century may well witness a reaction against such structures and a resistance to all sorts of control. The real issue is whether there is an authority which can win the recognition and submission of human beings, voluntarily and gladly. Is there a liberating source of truth and reality which can provide a foundation for life to be fulfilling and a dynamic to transform human nature? That is what the Bible claims to offer, as an objective, gracious and eternal reality.

How the Bible works

Why should we be willing to believe it? The answers relate to both reason and experience, to both the tradition of the past and the daily challenge of the future. We need, at this point, however, to return to the concept of our personal relationships depending on words and actions, by which we reveal ourselves to one another.

Human relationships of trust and confidence can only develop through mutual self-disclosure, which comes through words and actions. Both are needed. We may say that actions speak louder than words, but they do not speak as clearly and informatively. Indeed, the very development of language and the nuances of vocabulary, within different cultures, are evidence of a deep human striving for precision and focus, for communication that is unmistakable and therefore understood. If that is the way human beings relate, why should we not expect an infinite, yet personal, creator to relate to those made in his own image in exactly the same way?

The Bible is the self-revelation of this personal God, in the particularities of time and space, to real people in history, by his actions and his explanatory words. Both are vital. The actions are the necessary proof of the reality of the divine purposes and power. Without them, the words would be merely philosophical and theoretical. But the words are equally vital, to predict or explain the meaning of God's activity, as it reveals his character and purposes, to the recipients of revelation. He is not a miming but a speaking God. Sometimes the actions are on a grand scale, such as Noah's flood, or the exodus of the nation of Israel, or the Babylonian exile. Often, they are very detailed and personal, as when the shepherd-boy David is anointed to be king, or when the prophet Elijah crumbles into depression. But at the heart of every biblical event, God is the prime mover, the chief actor and the divine author, whose script explains the action. The way the Bible works has often been summarised in the form of the following equation:

EVENT + EXPLANATION = REVELATION

One of the clearest Bible passages to explain and illustrate this methodology comes in the short second letter written by the apostle Peter, as he faced imminent martyrdom, to encourage his fellow-Christians to stand firm in their faith, in spite of fierce persecution. He wants them to have confidence in the authenticity and reliability of the message of the good news about Jesus Christ, which he and the other apostles have been faithfully preaching and for which they intend to die, rather than deny its truth. Peter writes:

> So I will always remind you of these things, even though you know them and are firmly established in the truth you now have. I think it is right to refresh your memory as long as I live in the tent of this body, because I know that I will soon put it aside, as our Lord Jesus Christ has made clear to me. And I will make every effort to see that after my departure you will always be able to remember these things. We did not follow cleverly invented stories when we told you about the power and coming of our Lord Jesus Christ, but we were eye-witnesses of his majesty. For he received honour and glory from God the Father when the voice came to him from the Majestic Glory, saying, 'This is my Son, whom I love; with him I am well pleased.' We ourselves heard this voice that came from heaven when we were

with him on the sacred mountain. (2 Peter 1:12–18)

As a Bible writer, Peter claims to have witnessed the truth of God's self-revelation in two striking ways. He is referring to the event described in the gospels as the transfiguration of Christ (Matthew 17:1–8), when, for a brief moment, Peter, James and John were made overwhelmingly aware of the transcendent glory and divine splendour of the Son of God. They were 'eye-witnesses of his majesty' (2 Peter 1:16). It was an event they would never forget, demonstrating to them beyond all doubt the divine character of the master they loved and served. But they were also ear-witnesses of the explan-ation, equally divine. 'We ourselves heard this voice that came from heaven . . .' (v. 18). The voice explained the meaning of the event, together culminating in the divine revelation, 'This is my Son, whom I love; with him I am well pleased' (v. 17). That is how the Bible always works. God is its hero on every page. He is the one who acts and speaks, to disclose himself to finite, sinful people.

It is one of the great distinctives of the God revealed in the Bible that he is a speaking God, and this helps to explain why the Bible itself, as a written record of God's words, is so central and indispensable to the Christian faith. The God of the Bible stands in stark contrast to the idols of the pagan world, as Psalm 115 so ruthlessly points out. Such idols may be of silver and gold, but they are 'made by the hands of men. They have mouths but cannot speak, eyes, but they cannot see; they have ears but cannot hear, noses, but they cannot smell . . . nor can they utter a sound with their throats' (vv. 4–7). But the God of the Bible does speak and see and hear. Indeed, nothing else would ever have come into existence if he did not. For it is by his word that creation exists and at every point where that created order is least like him, it is the Word of the living God which bridges the gap.

The Bible begins with the creation of the cosmos, according to the will and power of God. But it is no accident that paragraph after paragraph of that majestic overture to the whole Bible begins 'and God said, "Let there be . . ." and there was . . .' (Genesis 1:3, 6, 9, 11, 14, 20, 24, 26). The mind of God is articulated in the Word of God, which becomes the executive agent by which his will is carried out. When God speaks, it is done, and the rest of the Bible never lets us forget it. To quote but two examples, one from each testament: 'By the word of the LORD were the heavens made, their starry host by the breath of his mouth . . . For he spoke, and it came to be; he commanded, and it stood firm' (Psalm 33:6, 9). Or, in the New Testament letter to the Hebrews, 'By faith we understand that the universe was formed at God's command, so that what is seen was not made out of what was visible' (Hebrews 11:3). Because the world is not self-generated, but created by the word of God, the world will never be able to be explained coherently and consistently by its own terms or framework of visible reference, but only by the revelation of God in the words he has spoken. Those words are in themselves our ultimate authority, because they constitute the revelation of the otherwise unknown character and purposes of the invisible, infinite God. We shall deal with this more fully when we explore the Bible's own story in Chapter 3, but all the way through the sixty-six books which make up the whole of the Scriptures, the same principle holds good. Human beings rightly understand and relate to God only through his Word. Often this is a word of promise, which needs to be believed and acted on. Frequently, it is a word of command, to be obeyed, or a warning to be heeded, or a propositional statement to be understood and applied.

The Bible's relevance

But there is one important further link to establish, and that is to us today. When we begin to understand why the Bible has been given to us and how it works, the problem of its alleged 'remoteness' and questions about its relevance to contemporary life start to find their answers. For the God who spoke once in the particular words of every Bible verse is unchanging in his character and settled in his will. What he once said, he is still saying. We do not have to make the Bible relevant (what an absurdly arrogant idea!); it is 'the living and enduring word of God' and 'the word of the Lord stands for ever' (1 Peter 1:23, 25). We have to work hard at understanding its message both within its own context and in our own, but we do not have to discover some elusive interpretative key, because God is interpreting himself to us and the keys to understanding are all within the text, if we will only give ourselves to it. All that God asks of us is a humble spirit, an attentive mind and a willingness to put into action whatever he reveals to us. 'For the word of God is living and active. Sharper than any double-edged sword, it penetrates even to dividing soul and spirit, joints and marrow; it judges the thoughts and attitudes of the heart' (Hebrews 4:12).

So we can see that the answers to our opening scenarios do in fact lie in this much-neglected best-seller. It will introduce Julia and Andy to the God who made them and provide them with the Maker's handbook on personal relationships. That won't be comfortable at first. There will be some harsh realities to face in their own selfishness and ingrained wrong thinking. But the Bible won't moralise, or set them on a course of relational-improvement therapy. It doesn't just deal with alleviating symptoms; it has a much more radical solution, as we shall see. Christine will need to lose her prejudices, founded on half-remembered, immature judgments and half-digested popular excuses for not bothering. Far from finding that science has 'disproved' the Bible, she could discover that God's self-revelation has always been way ahead of our human understanding, and rather than assuming the biblical text to be distorted and unreliable, she might do a little research and find out how reliable the contemporary translations of these well-established ancient documents really are. And if Matt could lay aside his presuppositions for a moment to see that no one can actually live in a world where words are meaningless, he might discover in the Bible the God who gave him his mind, and who is the only one who will be able to satisfy his hunger, which is deeper than the intellect and more enduring than a slick argument. It would be such a tragedy to miss life's greatest adventure, in getting to know God, because of pride or prejudice about a book which has been his channel of communication to countless multitudes of people over two millennia.

To remind you
- The Bible is not a religious textbook, but a book about real people, like us, living in the real world. It communicates (pp. 16–17).
- The Bible claims the authority of factual accuracy, but does not set out to prove it, so much as to demonstrate it by revelation (pp. 18–19).
- If an infinite yet personal God can be known, it must be by self-revelation, since our finite human minds could not discover or comprehend the infinite (pp. 19–23).
- God reveals himself in the Bible by acting in human history and explaining his actions in authoritative interpretation (pp. 23–5).
- The God of the Bible is supremely the speaking God who accomplishes his will through his word (pp. 25–6).
- What God once said, he is still saying, since his nature is eternal. So there is no doubt about the Bible's relevance in the new millennium (pp. 26–7).

Chapter 2

The Bible's Own Story

IT TOOK SOME time for Christine to overcome her prejudice, but eventually, partly because of Alison's gentle persistence and partly out of sheer curiosity, she decided to visit the Bible study and discussion group, 'just this once' as she told herself. She was pleasantly surprised. They seemed a normal enough group of people. Even her husband, Rob, would have had to admit that they were not obviously religious maniacs, or even eccentric. There was no hocus-pocus, no manipulative techniques, no artificial 'atmosphere' – just a bunch of ordinary people, each with a copy of the same book in their hands, talking about what they understood it to mean – and what they didn't, or couldn't, understand. It was intriguing. The Bibles were all in the same contemporary language translation and, mercifully, the pages were numbered, so that even a complete novice like Christine could find her way around. People seemed to speak genuinely and in a down-to-earth way about how what was in the book related to their everyday lives, at work and at home, so that Christine felt much less embarrassed and much more involved than she had ever expected to be.

But one of her most lasting impressions was of the sheer size of the Bible. It was rather like facing the complete works of William Shakespeare. At least that had only one author. But who wrote the Bible? And when? Someone in the group had said its composition spanned a thousand years or more. But when you think how much human knowledge develops during a millennium, doesn't that mean that it must be full of contradictions, that the later must have displaced the earlier? And who was it who pulled all these different authors and topics together and decided to call them 'the Holy Bible'? The group had been discussing from a book called 'John' or 'the gospel of John', as they called it. But who was John? And what was the gospel? And how did he fit in with all the other sixty-five books that made up the Bible library?

Christine's questions will be familiar enough to anyone who has tried seriously to get some grip on the Bible as an entity. Because it is a collection of sixty-six books written over a long period of time, probably as much as 1,600 years, and because these books are not always arranged chronologically, nor do they seem on the surface necessarily to relate to one another, many an explorer of the Bible has quickly got lost in the jungle and given up. Some have begun enthusiastically to read their way through, only to get bogged down irremediably in Leviticus (book three). Others have 'picked 'n' mixed' their way through their own selection of biblical texts, but never seen how the whole fits together, and are therefore conscious of huge 'black holes' of biblical material, into which they have not yet had the courage, or energy, to plunge. All of us who read the Bible need to have some awareness of its organising principles, its unifying themes, so that we develop some map references, or marker-points, by which to plot our passage into its interior. That is the purpose of this chapter.

The Bible library

Opening a Bible in modern English at the page entitled 'Contents', one immediately recognises it to be a book of two halves. Within the longer, first section, known as the Old Testament, there are thirty-nine books, followed by the twenty-seven books which comprise the New Testament. The first documents were written during the time of Moses, the first great leader of the Hebrew people (fifteenth century BC), while the latest date from the end of the first century AD, or as it is increasingly designated, the Common Era. This method of dating in itself presents us with the most significant key to understanding not only the millennia of human history, but also the message of the Bible itself. It centres on Jesus Christ. The Old Testament predates his coming, preparing the way and explaining the focus of God's purposes for all humanity in the 'Messiah', God's specially appointed and unique revealer, ruler and rescuer. The New describes and explains his life, death, resurrection and all that flows from these great events for the potential benefit of all people, in every place, at every time, and indeed throughout eternity. Jesus Christ is the centre and focus of the entire Bible.

However, that may not be immediately obvious to the new reader. Returning to the contents page, we discover that our English translations of the Old Testament follow a simple three-part division, based on the Greek translation of the original Hebrew, known as the Septuagint, which itself dates from at least 200 years before Christ. Broadly speaking, Genesis to Esther are historical books, Job to Song of Songs books of wisdom and poetry, and Isaiah to Malachi books of prophecy. But the original Hebrew order is rather more instructive. Following a three-fold pattern, it divides the material into the law, the prophets and the writings.

Genesis, Exodus, Leviticus, Numbers and Deuteronomy, often called the books of Moses, constitute the first main section of the library. Sometimes also called the Pentateuch ('five scrolls'), the best title is the Hebrew word *Torah*, usually translated 'law', but having the sense not so much of an inflexible and impersonal moral code as of a father giving his children 'teaching' and 'instruction', as a foundation for their living. These are the five foundation stones on which the whole of the rest of the Bible is built, by way of explanation and application.

The next long section (the prophets) is subdivided into two, the former and the latter. The former prophets are the books of Joshua, Judges, 1 and 2 Samuel and 1 and 2 Kings. They are historical books with a great deal of narrative, factual account, concerning the history of the nation of Israel. But they are 'prophets' because the history is explained from God's perspective, and as such it is used to present God's authoritative word to his people. The interest of the authors is never merely historicist, but overtly theological. The latter prophets are equally preachers of God's truth to his people, though they reflect on Israel's past and present experience in the light of God's future plans, including both judgment and rescue. Of these, there are three major, or longer, prophets – Isaiah, Jeremiah and Ezekiel – and twelve minor prophets, so called because they are shorter, not less important – Hosea, Joel, Amos, Obadiah, Jonah, Micah, Nahum, Habakkuk, Zephaniah, Haggai, Zechariah and Malachi.

To class all the remaining Old Testament books as 'the writings' may seem a 'catch-all' solution to the problem of unifying what seem to be quite different books. But, in fact, there are two types of material here which can very legitimately be grouped together. The books of Job, Proverbs, Ecclesiastes, Song of Songs and some of the Psalms constitute what is called the 'wisdom literature', in which the principles of God's self-revelation and will are applied to the circumstances of everyday life. The remaining books largely cover the history of the people of Israel at the time when they were carried into exile in Babylon, their eventual restoration and the rebuilding that followed.

Such divisions provide useful handles for dealing with large amounts of biblical material, through which otherwise we might not easily see our way. But before we turn to the New Testament, it is important to look beyond the classifications and structures, to see the story which progressively unfolds through this first half of the Bible. In doing this, we begin to move from description to understanding. For it is one coherent story. Every Christmas Eve, the service of nine lessons and carols from King's College, Cambridge, is broadcast around the English-speaking world, and marks for many the beginning of Christmas. The 'Bidding Prayer' bids, or invites, the congregation, in these words: 'Let us read and mark in Holy Scripture the tale of the loving purposes of God from the first days of our disobedience unto the glorious redemption brought us by this holy child.' And the lessons begin in Genesis chapter 3. For the story of the Old Testament is the story of God's grace, reaching out in rescue to a lost humanity. Let me explain.

The seed-bed of the Bible

It has sometimes been said that the Bible's division into two could be best expressed as Genesis chapters 1 to 11, and the rest! The point which is being rightly made is that the first eleven chapters are the seed-bed of the whole Bible. They act as a sort of spring-board for all that follows. The story starts with God. 'In the beginning God created the heavens and the earth' (Genesis 1:1). That creation expresses not only God's unfathomable wisdom and incalculable power, but also reflects his essential nature of perfection: 'It was very good' (Genesis 1:31). At its climax is a creature, made for a personal relationship with God, to act as God's agent in governing and tending the whole created order – a human being, or, to be precise, two human beings. 'Male and female he created them' (Genesis 1:26–8).

What is created on the grandest scale in Genesis 1 seems almost domestic by comparison in Genesis 2, where the focus shifts to the relationship with God for which Adam and Eve are designed. It is a relationship of great fulfilment and freedom and yet there is a necessary structure, within which alone the freedom can be enjoyed and continue. God has to be recognised and honoured as God. That is the fundamental 'given' of the world as he has made it. What he says has to be obeyed. So although human beings are created in God's image, with the amazing potential to be able to love, worship and serve him, they are not to usurp God's authority, or seek to dethrone God by using their own very considerable autonomy to rebel against his rightful rule. Yet, that is exactly what happens. God's one prohibition, 'You must not eat from the tree of the knowledge of good and evil' (Genesis 2:17), is ignored. The meaning clearly is that to seek the knowledge of good and evil would be an attempt to be 'like God' (Genesis 3:5), no longer dependent on him, no longer recognising him as creator, but exalting oneself as a God-substitute. So the disobedience of Adam and Eve begins the long unending trail of human rebellion against God and consequent alienation from him. 'Sin' (a word the Bible will use many times) enters the scene, the relationship of loving trust and dependence is shattered and God acts in righteous judgment against the offenders by expelling them from his presence in Eden, and so from the tree of life. Death, not immediate in the physical sense but nonetheless real and inevitable, becomes the lot of humankind. Disintegration of human relationships swiftly follows, so that by chapter 4 the first murder has taken place, as Cain kills his brother, Abel (vv. 1–8). Work becomes toil, as human beings struggle with an environment which has become hostile because its creator has been rejected.

> To Adam he said, 'Because you listened to your wife and ate from the tree about which I commanded you, "You must not eat of it," Cursed is the ground because of you; through painful toil you will eat of it all the days of your life. It will produce thorns and thistles for you, and you will eat the plants of the field. By the sweat of your brow you will eat your food until you return to the ground, since from it you were taken; for dust you are and to dust you will return.' (Genesis 3:17–19)

Here, then, is the seed-bed of the rest of the Bible's story. By chapter 6, when Noah is introduced, the situation has reached the point of desperation.

The LORD saw how great man's wickedness on the earth had become, and that every inclination of the thoughts of his heart was only evil all the time. The LORD was grieved that he had made man on the earth, and his heart was filled with pain. So the LORD said, 'I will wipe mankind, whom I have created, from the face of the earth – men and animals, and creatures that move along the ground, and birds of the air – for I am grieved that I have made them.' (Genesis 6:5–7)

Everything seems bleak and hopeless, but at that very point God steps in, and a new sequence begins. He selects a man, called Noah, not in the first place because he was inherently more righteous than his rebellious contemporaries, but in order to show his grace to him. A new biblical concept is introduced – that of 'grace', which is God's unmerited favour and goodness to those who do not deserve it in the least. God's grace found Noah and made of him a righteous man (Genesis 6:8–9). The point is made in the text by the Hebrew term often translated in English as 'generations'. It is inserted at the beginning of verse 9 and could be translated literally 'This is what was generated by that'. So, to paraphrase, God's grace found Noah and this is what was generated by that – Noah became a righteous man. That was God's doing, not Noah's, and it becomes a paradigm of the way God will go on dealing with his fallen, rebellious human creatures throughout the whole Bible story.

Another new concept, also introduced at this point, is that of 'covenant'. 'I am going to bring floodwaters on the earth to destroy all life under the heavens, every creature that has the breath of life in it. Everything on earth will perish. But I will establish my covenant with you, and you will enter the ark – you and your sons and your wife and your sons' wives with you' (Genesis 6:17–18). God determines freely, out of sheer mercy, to rescue Noah and his family from the judgment of the flood which is about to destroy that entire generation. It is as though he will start again with Noah. The covenant is the free promise of God to carry out what he has said he will do, rescuing the recipient of his mercy, by his own initiative and power. Noah has to build the ark, but God shuts (and eventually opens) the door, so that the God who sends his judgment to consume evil also preserves his chosen one, by covenant grace. Nor is this unjust in any way. Noah is not rescued because he is righteous, or else the Bible's pattern would mean that we have by our own works and efforts somehow to attempt to make ourselves acceptable to God. Noah is a sinner like all the rest, and he undergoes the experience of the flood like all the rest, but the grace of God provides him and his family with a protection from God's righteous wrath in the form of the ark, and this means of salvation carries him through the judgment, into the new world beyond.

When the waters recede, God formalises his covenant with Noah, his family and all living creatures. 'Never again will all life be cut off by the waters of a flood; never again will there be a flood to destroy the earth' (Genesis 9:11). Moreover, he gives Noah a sign as proof of his covenant promises, 'my rainbow in the clouds', investing it with the covenant significance that the promise will never be broken. It looks like a wonderful new beginning, and it is a great step forward in understanding God's plan for humanity, but the infection of sin and rebellion has not been expunged from human nature. Noah and his sons may father a new human race, but all the old signs of rebellion reappear too soon and culminate in the ultimate act of human defiance we call the tower of Babel, recorded in Genesis 11.

> Now the whole world had one language and a common speech. As men moved eastward, they found a plain in Shinar and settled there. They said to each other, 'Come, let's make bricks and bake them thoroughly.' They used brick instead of stone, and bitumen for mortar. Then they said, 'Come, let us build ourselves a city, with a tower that reaches to the heavens, so that we may make a name for ourselves and not be scattered over the face of the whole earth.' But the LORD came down to see the city and the tower that the men were building. The LORD said, 'If as one people speaking the same language they have begun to do this, then nothing they plan to do will be impossible for them. Come, let us go down and confuse their language so they will not understand each other.' So the LORD scattered them from there over all the earth, and they stopped building the city. That is why it was called Babel – because there the LORD confused the language of the whole world. From there the LORD scattered them over the face of the whole earth. (Genesis 11:1–9)

Once again, the motivation is human pride and self-assertion.

Building technology has developed. We can preserve ourselves by our own techniques and skills. We will climb up to the heavens. Not only do we not need God, we can challenge his very right to rule. So the fall and the flood are followed by the third great judgment – the scattering, with its confusion of languages, its destruction of relationships and fragmentation of human society. Human beings cannot set up their own independent kingdom, because they remain God's creatures living in God's world, and that inescapable bottom-line means that all our rebellion will ultimately blow up in our faces.

This, then, is the dilemma which the first eleven chapters of the Bible articulate so clearly and pose so challengingly. If human nature is corrupted by sin and rebellion, so that any relationship with a holy and righteous God becomes an impossibility, is there any hope for the human race? Can the effects of sin ever be undone? Can a just God ever accept an unjust person into relationship with himself? Could life shared with God, in an environment of perfection such as Eden had been, ever be on the agenda again? By way of answer, chapter 12 begins, 'The LORD had said to Abram, "Leave your country, your people and your father's household and go to the land I will show you" ' (v. 1). It is in Abraham that the solution begins to take shape. And the shape it takes is that of promise and fulfilment – covenant grace.

Covenant community

The Abraham story revolves entirely around the covenant promises and becomes the pattern on which the whole of the biblical enterprise operates. So what did God promise? First, that Abraham's descendants will become a great nation.

> I will make you into a great nation and I will bless you; I will make your name great, and you will be a blessing. (Genesis 12:2)

> I will make your offspring like the dust of the earth, so that if anyone could count the dust, then your offspring could be counted. (Genesis 13:16)

> He took him outside and said, 'Look at the heavens and count the stars – if indeed you can count them.' Then he said to him, 'So shall your offspring be.' (Genesis 15:5)

The angel added, 'I will so increase your descendants that they will be too numerous to count.' (Genesis 16:10)

Abraham will surely become a great and powerful nation, and all nations on earth will be blessed through him. (Genesis 18:18)

Here we have the beginnings of the nation of Israel, which becomes such a key actor in the drama that is the unfolding of God's purposes. It was because of God's direct promises to Abraham that Israel existed, as the focus of his blessing. In the place of the curse, so graphically worked out in chapters 1–11, God now promises its opposite, and the call of Abraham and his family to a new beginning is integral to the plan. Second, the great nation will be given a land, Canaan, the land of promise, in which to live.

The LORD appeared to Abram and said, 'To your offspring I will give this land.' So he built an altar there to the LORD, who had appeared to him. (Genesis 12:7)

The LORD said to Abram after Lot had parted from him, 'Lift up your eyes from where you are and look north and south, east and west. All the land that you see I will give to you and your offspring for ever. (Genesis 13:14–15)

On that day the LORD made a covenant with Abram and said, 'To your descendants I give this land, from the river of Egypt to the great river, the Euphrates.' (Genesis 15:18)

The whole land of Canaan, where you are now an alien, I will give as an everlasting possession to you and your descendants after you; and I will be their God. (Genesis 17:8)

While this will not be Eden restored, nevertheless the land will be a place of rest where God's blessing will be enjoyed in prosperity and security. This good and pleasant land will be given to God's people as a tangible manifestation of his grace towards them. But this is no narrowly nationalistic blessing, reserved merely for the children of Abraham. 'All peoples on earth' are to enter into God's blessing through Abraham and his descendants. The universal problem of humanity will find a universal solution, but it begins with the particularity of the one man, to whom God gives both a command ('leave your country') and a promise ('go to the land I will show you'). That becomes the pattern for the story which the rest of the Bible is written to tell.

In the course of the rest of Genesis, the family becomes the nation. The promised son of Abraham and Sarah, Isaac, is eventually born, by supernatural intervention, when both parents are in old age, as though to confirm that with God nothing is impossible, especially when the fulfilment of his promise is involved. Of Isaac's twin sons, Jacob (renamed Israel), the younger and the heir of the promised blessing, himself becomes the father of twelve sons, who become the clan-heads of the emerging nation. But though the nation is being formed, they as yet have no land; indeed, they are in Egypt as slave labourers for the Pharaoh. Their present land is a place of suffering and slavery, but God has not forgotten his covenant promise. At the start of the Exodus narrative, he affirms, 'I have come down to rescue them from the hand of the Egyptians and to bring them up out of that land into a good and spacious land, a land flowing with milk and honey' (Exodus 3:8). Raising up Moses as his chosen leader, God delivers the children of Israel, through plagues and passover, bringing them out of Egypt, through the sea, into the desert and eventually on to the land of Canaan. Central to this part of the story is their meeting with God the deliverer at Mount Sinai, where the ten commandments are given as a summary of God's character and a charter, along with many other laws, of their developing relationship with him. The people enter into covenant with God to be his obedient children. 'We will do everything the LORD has said; we will obey' (Exodus 24:7). They have already been designated by God as 'my firstborn son' (4:22), 'my treasured possession . . . a kingdom of priests and a holy nation' (19:5–6). Now they are to live in the enjoyment of God's rescuing grace and travel to the land of promise to receive the fulness of God's covenant blessings.

It seems as though the answer may have been found in the newly redeemed and constituted covenant community that is Israel. Perhaps this will be God's master-plan to bring rebellious humanity back into a right relationship with him. But the optimism is very short-lived. Only days after God has appeared to them on Mount Sinai they are fashioning a golden calf and worshipping man-made idols. Their progress through the desert is sustained on God's part by daily food and drink, protection from enemies, guidance and direction, but on Israel's part it is characterised by grumbling and discontent, fear, disobedience and downright unbelief. Because they are unwilling to trust God to bring them into the land and rather complain to him that he has brought them out of Egypt to kill them in the desert, they are condemned to remain out of the land for forty years, until that generation which had experienced so much of God's deliverance, but failed to trust his grace, has died. The tragedy is that while God is patiently and persistently fulfilling his promises, Israel is equally persistently unfaithful and unbelieving. The old pattern has re-asserted itself. Whatever the blessings God's covenant mercy has brought, men and women still seem to respond with sin and rebellion.

And for the rest of the Old Testament there is no real change. From generation to generation, the same dilemma is presented. Under Joshua the people enter and occupy the promised land, but the book of Judges records the recurring downward spirals of rebellion against God and his covenant.

Then the Israelites did evil in the eyes of the LORD and served the Baals. They forsook the LORD, the God of their fathers, who had brought them out of Egypt. They followed and worshipped various gods of the peoples around them. They provoked the LORD to anger because they forsook him and served Baal and the Ashtoreths. In his anger against Israel the LORD handed them over to raiders who plundered them. He sold them to their enemies all around, whom they were no longer able to resist. Whenever Israel went out to fight, the hand of the LORD was against them to defeat them, just as he had sworn to them. They were in great distress. Then the LORD raised up judges, who saved them out of the hands of these raiders. Yet they would not listen to their judges but prostituted themselves to other gods and worshipped them. Unlike their fathers, they quickly turned from the way in which their fathers had walked, the way of obedience to the LORD's commands. Whenever the LORD raised up a judge for them, he was with the judge and saved them out of the hands of their enemies as long as the judge lived; for the LORD had compassion on them as they groaned under those who oppressed and afflicted them. But when the judge died, the people returned to ways even more corrupt than those of their fathers, following other gods and serving and worshipping them. They refused to give up their evil practices and stubborn ways. (Judges 2:11–19)

As the nation was degenerating into civil war and facing break-up, the cry arose for a king who would unify them, 'such as all the other nations have' (1 Samuel 8:5). This was in itself a confession of their failure and persistent unfaithfulness. God had marked them out as different from all the other nations in that he was their king, but the people's idolatry and disobedience to his Torah were effectively a rejection of the LORD as their ruler. And yet the amazing motif running through the whole Old Testament story is that God never gave up on Israel. When they were faithless, he was always faithful. None of his covenant promises were forgotten or unfulfilled. Constantly, in situations of great need, God intervened on behalf of his disobedient people. During their early centuries in the land he raised up a succession of deliverers ('judges') who defeated their enemies and provided times of stability and prosperity. Yet the story of Judges is that each human rescuer seems more flawed than the one before, and no one is able to arrest the downward spiral. The establishment of the monarchy seems to offer a better hope. The creation of a dynastic succession should provide security and strong able government, but because it is actually the old Adam pattern of refusing to let God be God, it is inevitably doomed. The very first king, Saul, begins his reign by disobediently taking to himself the function of priest as well as ruler, and almost before his rule has commenced, the prophet Samuel is telling him, 'Your kingdom will not endure . . . because you have not kept the LORD's command' (1 Samuel 13:14).

The hope of a king

Yet God continues to be gracious. Saul is succeeded by David and then by his son, Solomon, and from many standpoints a new golden age seems to have begun. David captures the city of Jerusalem and makes it his capital (2 Samuel 5). He begins to conquer his enemies, and Israel grows in prosperity and security. In many ways he is the deliverer of his people, a ruler of military prowess, but a man 'after God's own heart', with a deep dependence on God and awareness of his promises and commands. David's psalms reveal just how deep and intimate his relationship with God was. But this is not only a relationship with great benefits for the king, as an individual. 'David knew that the LORD had established him as king over Israel and had exalted his kingdom for the sake of his people Israel' (2 Samuel 5:12).

Another key development in David's reign centres on his desire to build a temple in Jerusalem, to house the ark of the covenant, the tangible symbol of God's presence among his people. 'Here I am, living in a palace of cedar, while the ark of God remains in a tent' (2 Samuel 7:2). But God refuses the warrior-king permission to do this. That will be the role of his son. Instead, God promises to build David a house, a royal dynasty, but with the most amazing addition that this throne will be 'for ever'.

> I declare to you that the LORD will build a house for you: When your days are over and you go to be with your fathers, I will raise up your offspring to succeed you, one of your own sons, and I will establish his kingdom. He is the one who will build a house for me, and I will establish his throne for ever. I will be his father, and he will be my son. I will never take my love away from him, as I took it away from your predecessor. I will set him over my house and my kingdom for ever; his throne will be established for ever. (1 Chronicles 17:10b–14)

Here is another major milestone in the Old Testament story, comparable in importance to those initial covenant promises made to Abraham. Through David's dynasty, God's people will find rest and peace, they will enjoy God's land and live in relationship with him. From this new covenanted promise there developed the recognition of the king as God's 'son' (v. 13), in a sense replacing the failed firstborn son, Israel, and summing up in his own person all that God had intended the nation to be. Coupled to this unseen personal relationship between the king and God was the visible, objective recognition of the ruler in his 'anointing'. In Psalm 2, for example, the king is referred to as God's 'Anointed One' (v. 2) who is his 'Son' (v. 7). The significance of this for the whole Bible is that the Hebrew term for 'anointed one' is *Messiah*, which translates, in Greek, to the word *Christos* – Christ. As the monarchy is established, something of the larger long-term purposes of God is coming into focus.

But even here, as before, the human protagonists are severely flawed. David, the anointed one, becomes an adulterer and a murderer.

His son, Solomon, universally famous for his God-given wisdom, saw his kingdom expand in size and prosperity beyond Israel's wildest dreams in the opening years of his reign. The temple was built and magnificently furnished, not only to provide Israel with a focus of God's presence and a means by which they might make atonement for their sins so as to experience his forgiveness, but also to be a blessing to all the nations of the world. Solomon's consecration prayer at the temple's completion asks that as foreigners come to observe its splendour 'all the peoples of the earth may know your name [that is, God's character] and fear you' (1 Kings 8:43). But Solomon's serial adultery with 'many foreign women' led him away from the exclusive worship of the God whose temple he had built, into all sorts of idolatry, which, as ever, generated God's righteous judgment (1 Kings 11).

As a direct result, on Solomon's death the kingdom was divided. His son, Rehoboam, ruled only over the tribe of Judah, known from now on as the southern kingdom. The rest of the tribes appointed Jeroboam as their king and developed an alternative nation-state, based in Samaria, ignoring the temple in Jerusalem and setting up their own 'shrines' in Dan and Bethel. Such forbidden, idolatrous worship could only bring about disaster (1 Kings 13:33–4), and the rest of the history of the northern kingdom, Israel, is full of the evidence. Kings are replaced by violent usurpers, the worship of pagan idols increases, until gradually the kingdom of Israel slides away from any recognisable identity as God's covenant nation, virtually indistinguishable from its idolatrous neighbours.

Yet still God was merciful. He sent the prophets, most notably Amos and Hosea, to proclaim and apply his covenant instructions to a faithless renegade nation. Their preaching made it abundantly clear that a cataclysmic judgment of God was about to fall on this rebellion and that the northern kingdom would be destroyed and its people scattered. In time this event happened, with the fall of Samaria to the Assyrian army after a three-year siege, and the deportation of many of the Israelites to Nineveh. 'All this took place because the Israelites had sinned against the LORD their God . . . they worshipped other gods and followed the practices of the nations . . .' (2 Kings 17:7–8). The remaining tribe of Judah proved ultimately to be no better. Though the record of their kings was not the unbroken disaster-line that the north suffered, the southern kingdom was mainly governed by idolatrous successors to David. Eventually, after sending more prophets, such as Micah and Isaiah, God's decree of judgment was activated against Judah, and after a long campaign which devastated the country, the city of Jerusalem fell to the Babylonian army and many of her citizens were exiled.

Is that to be the end of the story? What about the promises to Abraham and to David? What, especially, about the Davidic dynasty and the kingdom that would be 'for ever'? Just as Adam and Eve had broken God's laws and forfeited God's place, so now Israel, Abraham's descendants, 'my firstborn son', has trampled on God's word and forfeited the land. Even her kings, anointed for a special role and relationship with God, have proved to be tarnished, sinful individuals, sharing the common disease of a heart that turns away from God's will to do its own. So the monarchy, which had seemed it might be the answer and had offered so much, lies shattered and the kingdom is destroyed. Is there no way forward? Is the whole human race always to be bound in to the same depressing pattern of wonderful promises ultimately unfulfilled, because of wilful rebellion?

New beginnings

But God is still merciful. Even as the prophets thunder their message of inescapable judgment, they also affirm the continuation of God's covenant promises and purposes. Israel has certainly suffered for her faithlessness, but God will not go back on his word. Their enjoyment of God's covenant blessings depended on their faithful fulfilment of their covenant obligations, in obedience to his instructions. But the failure of Israel to be the people he intended did not signal the failure of God's purposes. Beyond the exile there will be restoration. The people will be restored to the land and the structures of the theocracy will be rebuilt. There will be a new temple and a rebuilding of Jerusalem. The theme rings with unmistakable clarity through Isaiah, Jeremiah and Ezekiel. But there is an additional ingredient of huge significance. The root problem of human nature and its wretched propensity to sinful rebellion will be dealt with by God. Just listen to his promises.

'The time is coming,' declares the LORD, 'when I will make a new covenant with the house of Israel and with the house of Judah. It will not be like the covenant I made with their forefathers when I took them by the hand to lead them out of Egypt, because they broke my covenant, though I was a husband to them,' declares the LORD. 'This is the covenant that I will make with the house of Israel after that time,' declares the LORD. 'I will put my law in their minds and write it on their hearts. I will be their God, and they will be my people. No longer will a man teach his neighbour, or a man his brother, saying, "Know the LORD," because they will all know me, from the least of them to the greatest,' declares the LORD. 'For I will forgive their wickedness and will remember their sins no more.' (Jeremiah 31:31–4)

For I will take you out of the nations; I will gather you from all the countries and bring you back into your own land. I will sprinkle clean water on you, and you will be clean; I will cleanse you from all your impurities and from all your idols. I will give you a new heart and put a new spirit in you; I will remove from you your heart of stone and give you a heart of flesh. And I will put my Spirit in you and move you to follow my decrees and be careful to keep my laws. You will live in the land I gave to your forefathers; you will be my people, and I will be your God. (Ezekiel 36:24–8)

My servant David will be king over them, and they will all have one shepherd. They will follow my laws and be careful to keep my decrees. They will live in the land I gave to my servant Jacob, the land where your fathers lived. They and their children and their children's children will live there for ever, and David my servant will be their prince for ever. I will make a covenant of peace with them; it will be an everlasting covenant. I will establish them and increase their numbers, and I will put my sanctuary among them for ever. My dwelling-place will be with them; I will be their God, and they will be my people. (Ezekiel 37:24–7)

Clearly, the best is yet to be! But when, and how? In time, the Babylonian empire fell to the Persians whose leader, Cyrus, decreed the return of all exiled people to their homelands. Though many of the Jews had thoroughly assimilated into Babylonian culture, a large number did return, and over the century that followed they struggled to rebuild the temple, the city of Jerusalem and its defences. The books of Ezra and Nehemiah tell the story, and the prophecies of

Haggai, Zechariah and Malachi date from this period. But these were clearly not the great days which the major prophets had promised. The mere physical restoration of Israel to the land could not deal with the spiritual problems, which were the root of all their troubles. So, when the Old Testament ends, we are still left looking forward, with increasing longing. When will God activate his plan to deal with human sinfulness and its effects? When will the Messiah come, who will truly fulfil the qualities of 'anointed one' and 'son of God'? Where will the eternal kingdom, foreshadowed in the Davidic monarchy come to fruition? All these great Old Testament ideals are still crying out for fulfilment at the end of Malachi, and then for four centuries, as far as God's self-revelation is concerned, there is silence. Successive armies invade and conquer. The 'remnant' of Israelites who continue to believe God's word and obey his commands seems to shrink from generation to generation. But the hope of 'Messiah' is kept alive, and from time to time the tide of expectation runs high, until one day a young man, dressed like the prophet Elijah, in clothes of camel's hair, begins to preach by the Jordan river, 'Repent, for the kingdom of heaven [God's kingly rule] is near' (Matthew 3:1–6). The new day has dawned. The new testament is beginning.

As we turn to the New Testament, one point is now abundantly clear, namely that the page which the translators and publishers customarily place between the Old and the New has no business to be there. At least, that is so if ever it misleads us into separating the two halves of the Bible, to the extent of forgetting that they constitute one integrated whole. The Bible is one book in its great story-line, from Genesis to Revelation. Sadly, that has often been ignored, and specialists in Old and New Testaments have pursued their studies in separation if not mistrust of one another. But our brief survey of the Old Testament has surely prepared us to see the New as its completion and fulfilment, just as the New's own unique message is down-sized and almost trivialised, without relating it to the Old.

The coming of Jesus

So it is not by accident that the New Testament begins with four gospels (Matthew, Mark, Luke and John) or four presentations of one and the same gospel, or 'good news', in the birth, life, death and resurrection of Jesus Christ. Here are eye-witness accounts, carefully researched and brought together with theological coherence, committing to writing what would have been the orally preserved and proclaimed truths of who Jesus was, what he said and did, and what it all meant. John defines his purpose 'that you may believe that Jesus is the Christ, the Son of God, and that by believing you may have life in his name' (John 20:31). Luke writes 'an orderly account', based on his own careful research and investigation, 'of the things that have been fulfilled among us, just as they were handed down to us by those who from the first were eye-witnesses . . . so that you may know the certainty of the things you have been taught (Luke 1:1–4). Here are the events and their explanations which constitute the unique and perfect self-revelation of God in his Son, Jesus Christ. Indeed, the agenda of the four evangelists is to demonstrate for ever, beyond all doubt or contradiction, how the person and the work of Jesus are the fulfilment of all that the Old Testament promised.

The gospels are not primarily biographies, at least in the contemporary meaning of the term, though they have a good deal of biographical detail. Rather, a seemingly disproportionate amount of their time is taken up with the events of the last week of Jesus' life, in his death and resurrection. It is easy for us to pass over the uniqueness of this approach. There is no description of his physical appearance. Huge tracts of his short life (about thirty-three years) are omitted. The focus is clearly on the events by which God's long-awaited promises were being fulfilled and particularly on the specific patterns of the Old Testament Scriptures coming to completion in Christ. Listen to Jesus' own testimony.

Do not think that I have come to abolish the Law or the Prophets; I have not come to abolish them but to fulfil them. (Matthew 5:17)

He said to them, 'How foolish you are, and how slow of heart to believe all that the prophets have spoken! Did not the Christ have to suffer these things and then enter his glory?' And beginning with Moses and all the Prophets, he explained to them what was said in all the Scriptures concerning himself . . . He said to them, 'This is what I told you while I was still with you: Everything must be fulfilled that is written about me in the Law of Moses, the Prophets and the Psalms.' Then he opened their minds so they could understand the Scriptures. He told them, 'This is what is written: The Christ will suffer and rise from the dead on the third day, and repentance and forgiveness of sins will be preached in his name to all nations, beginning at Jerusalem.' (Luke 24:25–7, 44–7)

'My sheep listen to my voice; I know them, and they follow me. I give them eternal life, and they shall never perish; no-one can snatch them out of my hand. My Father, who has given them to me, is greater than all; no-one can snatch them out of my Father's hand. I and the Father are one.' (John 10:27–30)

It is the characteristic of the good shepherd that he 'lays down his life for the sheep' (John 10:11) and it is to his death on the cross that each of the four gospels inexorably moves us. Again, Jesus' own testimony is striking. Take, for example, his saying in Mark 10:45, 'For even the Son of Man did not come to be served, but to serve, and to give his life as a ransom for many.' In context, he is clearly claiming to be the Son of Man, an Old Testament title, dating from Daniel's vision of a human figure led into God's presence and given 'authority, glory and sovereign power; all peoples, nations and men of every language worshipped him. His dominion is an everlasting dominion that will not pass away, and his kingdom is one that will never be destroyed' (Daniel 7:14). Jesus is claiming to be that figure of eternal and universal regal authority. But look at the way in which the authority is to be exercised. This king conquers by serving his subjects, even to the point of offering up his own life as a ransom price, in order to set them free from their captivity. The cross is the means by which this freedom will be achieved, just as the mysterious figure of the 'suffering servant' in Isaiah's prophecy was 'pierced for our transgressions, he was crushed for our iniquities; the punishment that brought us peace was upon him, and by his wounds we are healed' (Isaiah 53:5). To bring the universal king and the suffering servant together was God's master-stroke through the cross of Jesus. It was a voluntary death – 'No one takes it from me but I lay it down of my own accord' (John 10:18). In this way God's immeasurable love for humanity was revealed. But it was supremely an atoning death – 'This is my blood of the [new] covenant, which is poured out for many for the forgiveness of sins' (Matthew 26:28). Because through Christ's sacrifice God's reconciling purposes finally found their fulfilment, he was able to die with a shout of triumph, 'Finished!' (John 19:30). The acceptance of his substitutionary death in the place of the sins of the world is vividly highlighted by the gospel writers when they tell us that the curtain in the Jerusalem temple, a huge heavily woven barrier which prevented the worshipper from entering into the presence of God, symbolised by the 'holy of holies', was torn in two, from the top to the bottom. This was so manifestly a divine action and so deeply significant that it became a visual enactment of what Christ's death had just achieved. It was the means by which God had removed the barrier separating himself, in all his holiness, from sinful human beings, so that in the death of his Son he was declaring to all the world, 'You can come in now.' This is the gospel of Christ.

The other great sign of the efficacy of Jesus' death and consequently the beginning of a new creation is, of course, his resurrection from the tomb on Easter morning. Good Friday and Easter Day for ever belong together. A dead Messiah would be no guarantee of an effective work, but as his followers were soon proclaiming, 'God raised him from the dead, freeing him from the agony of death, because it was impossible for death to keep its hold on him' (Acts 2:24). Jesus and the resurrection became the focus and content of the earliest Christian proclamation, and that unique historical event has marked out the 'gospel' as distinctive from all other religious beliefs and ideologies ever since. The gospel writers are very specific in their accounts of the empty tomb and the many encounters of his disciples with the risen Christ, in person, so that on these two great factual foundations our own understanding and personal relationship with the living Lord Jesus can be solidly grounded. For, as Paul expressed it, 'if Christ has not been raised, our preaching is useless and so is your faith' (1 Corinthians 15:14).

The spreading gospel

Such world-changing events had not only to be believed and entered into through a personal response to God of repentance and faith, but also proclaimed to all the nations. Now at last they all could experience the blessing promised so long ago to Abraham. Through his seed Jesus, Jews and Gentiles can alike enter into peace with God, know the forgiveness of sins, enjoy a deep personal relationship with their creator and begin to realise their destiny as God's own people. This is the agenda which the rest of the New Testament books are dedicated to pursuing. Apart from the Acts of the Apostles, written as a sequel to his gospel by Luke, and the book of Revelation, with which the

Bible ends, all the rest are in the form of letters (epistles) dealing with the life and problems of the early Churches, groups of Christians meeting in a particular locality. Often the area or city of those being addressed provides the title for the letter, to the Romans, to the Galatians, and so on. Sometimes an individual addressee gives his name to the book – Timothy or Titus – and sometimes the author, James, Peter, John.

Many of the epistles divide clearly into doctrinal and practical issues, theology and ethics, or what Christians believe and how they should then live. These two strands are always much more carefully interwoven than such a generalisation might suggest. However, it remains true that the practical issues raised both by the developing theological understanding of the gospel and by the invasion of un-orthodox and distorting teaching from both Judaistic and Gentile sources, largely generated and therefore govern the content of the apostolic writings. Monumental in scale among them is the work of the apostle Paul, once Saul of Tarsus, 'a Hebrew of Hebrews', arrested by the risen Christ as he travelled to Damascus to persecute Christ-ians, and reshaped as Christ's bondslave, commissioned to be his apostle, the evangelist to the nations. Not only is the scope of Paul's missionary endeavours mind-boggling, but the breadth and depth of his theological understanding and reflection are magisterial. To Paul, Peter and John particularly we owe our informed understanding of who Christ really is, what he accomplished, his present provision in the gift of the Holy Spirit to all his people and his future plans and purposes. The outworking of these realities in godly living now is always stressed, not least in the light of the fact that there is still one last stage of the cosmic drama to be completed.

For the Christ who rose from the dead and ascended to heaven will come again, in power and great glory, in the fulness of his divine majesty, to bring in his eternal kingdom. This is expressed by the familiar New Testament term 'the last days', used to describe the period of time, in which the Church has always had to live, between Christ's ascension and his return. 'This same Jesus, who has been taken from you into heaven, will come back in the same way you have seen him go into heaven' (Acts 1:11). These are the last days, because the whole of God's covenant plan is now complete, except for Christ's return to wind up human history. This reflects the tension expressed in Jesus' own teaching when he spoke of the kingdom of God, or of the heavens, having broken into the world of time and space history, in his incarnation; the kingdom is already here because Jesus is, but not yet in its fulness, because Christ is not yet revealed as universal judge and king. Similarly, the blessings of Christ's kingly rule belong to his disciples here and now, but only in a measure, since we do not yet in this world know the full release from sin, suffering or death, which will be fully ours in the life of the world to come. Rather like Old Testament believers waiting for the Messiah to appear, Christians are also a waiting people, but for Jesus' return. It is to that focus that the book of Revelation directs us, with its analysis of human history and its motivational visions of the heavenly kingdom, the destruction of all evil and the permanence of Christ's eternal reign. In that sense, contemporary Christians are still in the uncompleted chapter of the Bible's story, waiting for all that we have already begun to experience in Christ to become fully and eternally our own.

That, in all too brief summary, is the Bible's 'big picture', its meta-narrative, as we might call it today. But only a moment's reflection is needed to underscore that the story is not presented as a textbook of historical information, to be remembered or memorised, but as an invitation to enter into a relationship of faith with its central character, the present-tense God, our ruler, rescuer and judge, who has promised and fulfilled his great plan to bring men and women back to himself, through Jesus. Biblical truth is never merely propositional, but relational. It requires a response. When God came, in the person of Jesus Christ, he came as a preacher, summoning his hearers to repent and believe the good news of his kingly rule (Mark 1:14–15). How do we rightly relate to the promises of God and the God who makes the promises? By believing the promises and building our lives on his trustworthy, unchanging character. That was how it all started with the covenant man, Abraham, who 'believed the LORD and he credited it to him as righteousness' (Genesis 15:6). That is how the New Testament apostles expect us to respond to the word of the gospel, for it is only that content which can generate true belief. But where you have the Biblical word producing faith in God, through his Son, Jesus Christ, there you have the essence of Biblical Christianity and the continuing outworking of the Bible's own story.

To remind you

- The Bible is itself a library of sixty-six books, divided into several 'genres' or types of literature, written over many centuries (pp. 28–31).

- Its first eleven chapters (Genesis 1–11) are a 'seed-bed' for all that follows, showing human rebellion and God's reaction in both righteous wrath and delivering grace (pp. 31–3).

- A key concept introduced is that of 'covenant' – God makes and keeps his promises (pp. 33–5).

- Beginning with a man (Abraham) he creates a family and eventually a nation as the focus of his grace, but human rebellion persists (pp. 35–9).

- The provision of a king cannot solve the problem of rebellion and eventually the prophets predict the loss of land and nationhood (pp. 39–42).

- Beyond the exile, God promises a new start that will deal with the problem of sin, in the person of the Messiah (pp. 42–4).

- With the coming of Christ the exile ends and the kingdom of God breaks in on human history. By his death on the cross and his resurrection from the dead, Christ provides forgiveness for sins and eternal life for all who trust in him. This is the good news (pp. 44–7).

- This gospel has spread throughout the world and down through history. Just one event remains for the completion of God's purposes, which is the second coming of Christ (pp. 47–9).

Chapter 3

The Bible's Own Testimony

'YOU SEE, ONE of the biggest problems you Christians have is that you're all so incredibly gullible.' Matt was warming to a favourite theme. 'Take this commitment to the Bible, for example. You base your whole life on a book that's as old as the hills, but when you're asked why, you don't have any real evidence. It's like a journey on the Circle line. You assume there is a God, that he is wanting to speak to us in words and that the Bible is the true and reliable record of what he has revealed. Why? Because the Bible says it is. Well, it would, wouldn't it?'

'Yes, but hold on a minute,' Dan butted in. 'All arguments are going to be circular in that sense whenever they deal with the ultimate meaning of life, the universe and everything, because they are bound to go beyond the limits of what you can see or prove. Your starting point, Matt, is to try to explain the world without any reference to the "God-hypothesis", but that ties into your *own* circle. So, by assuming there is no God, you interpret your data to "prove" that he doesn't exist. After all, if the word "God" does have any meaning, any reality behind it, then, by definition, only God can demonstrate his true nature to human beings, because we are finite in our understanding and so vastly inferior to him. Only God can break into our little circles of human logic and show us something of the infinite. Ultimately, the only way that can be done must involve words, and the only person who could tell us they are his words is God.'

'Well, I see what you're driving at,' Matt grudgingly admitted, 'but I'd still want some hard evidence before I waste my time reading the Bible.'

'OK. So where shall we start? Archaeology has proved the Bible's historical accuracy over and over again. Or what about the Bible's principles of behaviour which have been the solid foundation of our civilisation for centuries? Then, you can't discount millions of Christians, down the centuries and from all over the world, who have put the Bible's claims to the test and found them to be true. It's not lack of evidence that is the problem, so much as our own unwillingness to submit to any authority other than ourselves. You can go on asking for more evidence until the cows come home. Your danger, Matt, is that you don't want to go into the water until you've learned to swim. But it doesn't work like that. There's a lot of truth in what G. K. Chesterton said, that it was not that Christianity had been tried and found wanting, but that, for most people, it had been found difficult and not tried. Why don't you try the Bible for yourself? All you have to lose is your prejudice!'

'No,' Matt shook his head, and then with a grin, 'you never know, I might be convinced!'

The question of the Bible's authority is of central importance to the whole issue of believing its message. At one level, it is true that the Bible is a book like any other. If you can read a newspaper, you can read the Bible. But at the level of process, something additional is going on, because in the Bible we hear God speaking to us, which is what it consistently claims for itself. When reading a paper or a book, we have been trained to read critically. We look for coherence, logic, evidence, argument. The same approach is entirely appropriate for the Bible, and Christians should never advocate a switch-off of their critical faculties. If the Bible is God's unchanging truth then it must be able to stand up to the most rigorous critical analysis, provided presuppositions from outside the Bible are not being employed to produce a destructive circular argument. But Bible readers of any consistency and application soon discover another process in operation. We may begin by applying our critical faculties to the biblical text, making our judgments as to its credibility or acceptability. Yet it is not long before we find the text itself sitting in judgment on us and our categories, exposing our weaknesses and shortcomings, facing us with our sin and rebellion, posing pressing issues about our relationship with God which are ultimately inescapable. Such a book hardly needs to be defended. As Charles Spurgeon, one of the greatest British preachers of the nineteenth century, commented, you might as well defend a lion. All you do is let it loose!

In his stimulating book, *Working the Angles* (1987, published by

W. M. Eerdmans, Grand Rapids, USA), Eugene Peterson has a chapter on learning to listen to God, through the Bible. His thesis is that we are in danger of being turned, by our culture, into 'cool analysts' rather than 'passionate hearers', because reading is a much less demanding activity than listening. We are in charge of the text; we can pull out whenever we want to. The book can be shut, the newspaper discarded. But a conversation has a much higher level of demand. It requires a response, often in actions as well as words. What makes Bible reading so challenging is the personal address of the voice of God, to which we need to tune in and listen, for that is how its authority and truth are conveyed. The Bible is not a religious treasury of memorable quotations or purple passages, to be used for our delectation or to select what we want out of them. It is the urgent, conversational voice of the living God, inviting us into relationship, probing our innermost thoughts and values, prompting us to stop and reflect, to consider our ways, to learn to live in the light of eternity. Our danger is that because all this is in book form for us, printed and bound like any other on our shelves, we treat it merely as we would any other book. We pick it up, look at it, use it even, for our comfort or inspiration, but we do not listen long enough, or hard enough, to meet the person who is speaking through its pages, or to enter the relationship of love to which we are being invited. We need to let the Bible speak for itself, for what Scripture is saying, God is saying.

What then is the Bible's testimony about itself? A number of semi-technical terms are commonly used to summarise this and it will be best to explore each of them in turn, since they do constitute a logical progression.

Let the Bible speak

It is usual to begin by speaking about the *authority* of the Bible. In a post-modern culture, the word will inevitably convey negative content and be liable to rejection before it has been examined. But separating the idea from any sub-biblical concept of authoritarianism, we can see that we are talking about a 'givenness' which the Bible both discloses and has within itself, by virtue of its origin. There is an 'authority' to the way things are in the created order, which we may rebel against, but cannot overturn. As I write, considerable parts of the world are about to witness a major eclipse of the sun, total in some areas. The newspapers are full of warnings about the danger of looking at the sun's eclipse even through special lenses, let alone with the naked eye, supported by tragic cases of those who have been blinded in very few seconds. That is a 'given', an authority. I may not like it. I can choose to ignore it, but I will blind myself. In an age like ours, so dedicated to pushing back the boundaries of individual freedom as far as we possibly can, it may appear irksome, but nothing changes the reality. Natural laws (as we call them) covering the use of electricity, or gravity, or food hygiene are simply the observed, inevitable properties of the world as we have it. We learn to live our lives within the parameters of the physical order. Why should the creator not build the same patterns of 'givenness' into the spiritual and eternal realities he has chosen to reveal?

It is just that sort of *spiritual* authority which is inherent in the Bible's claim to be the Word of God. Here is one of its clearest, most classic statements.

> The holy Scriptures . . . are able to make you wise for salvation through faith in Christ Jesus. All Scripture is God-breathed and is useful for teaching, rebuking, correcting and training in righteousness, so that the man of God may be thoroughly equipped for every good work. (2 Timothy 3:15–17)

Paul, writing to Timothy, is, of course, thinking of the Old Testament which his young colleague had been taught from childhood, but what he says is equally true of the New. How his writings were recognised as having similar authority we shall examine in Chapter 4. However, orthodox Christian belief has always held to the view that the whole Bible is 'God's Word written' (Article 20 of the Thirty-Nine Articles – the credal statement of the Church of England at the time of the Reformation). Perhaps the clearest contemporary statement of this position is made in 'The Chicago Statement on Biblical Hermeneutics', emanating from the consultations of leading evangelical church leaders and theologians in North America. Article I states, 'We affirm that the normative authority of Holy Scripture is the authority of God Himself, and is attested by Jesus Christ, the Lord of the Church. We deny the legitimacy of separating the authority of Christ from the authority of Scripture or of opposing the one to the other.'

Closely linked to the idea of authority is that of *inspiration*, a term used in older translations of this passage to translate 'God-breathed', which is preferable as it is the literal rendering of the Greek. The words of Scripture carry authority, the right to rule our lives, because they are the expression of the mind and will of God, 'breathed out' in human vocabulary. Paul has no small-print exclusion clauses. He speaks of 'all Scripture'. Everything that God says is true, and the mark of being a Christian is submitting to that truth and so recognising his authority as creator and Lord. Obedience to the word of Scripture is therefore a hallmark of discipleship. However, it is common to want to reduce this element of biblical authority by drawing attention to the fallibility of the human channels through which it is mediated, whether authors or interpreters. How can an infallible divine word be conveyed by human beings who are themselves morally flawed, intellectually limited and the prisoners of a language and culture that are time-bound? The danger of such an attitude is that it will inevitably exalt human reason above the Bible's own words, so that we end up with a subjective assessment as to what we can bring ourselves to believe. In practice this often seems to work out as acceptance that God is loving but not our judge, that heaven exists but not hell, and Jesus was a fine moral example and an inspirational teacher, but not God in human form, fully human and fully divine. This last denial reflects the inability of its proponents to believe that the Bible could be God's words through human writers, at one and the same time. But why should that not be so? In his penetrating little book, *God Has Spoken* (1965, Hodder & Stoughton), Dr J. I. Packer makes the point this way.

The Bible is not only man's word, but God's also; not merely a record of revelation, but a written revelation in its own right, God's own witness to Himself in the form of human witnesses to Him. Accordingly, the authority of the Scriptures rests, not simply on their worth as an historical source, a testament of religion, and a means of uplift, real though this is, but primarily and essentially on the fact that they came to us from the mouth of God. (p. 72)

To believe in the Bible in this way is clearly to affirm one's faith in the supernatural. But that is neither irrational nor unreasonable. Nor is it to capitulate to subjectivism, which is actually what the critics of this conviction tend to do. Because much of what the Bible teaches confronts and challenges our culture, it is tempting for the critic to decide what cannot be accepted, and then go looking for internal textual 'evidence' that will enable the plain meaning of the Bible to be changed. Usually its new 'meaning' will correspond with the critic's subjective contemporary views, and in this way the voice of God is silenced. We know that in the area of scientific investigation, careful observation and experimentation are the essential foundations of any hypothesis. Wishful thinking and subjective preferences have no place in scientific endeavour. But biblical theology, once the 'queen of the sciences', is no more governed by subjective wish than is chemistry. The difference is that in science the investigator moves towards the object of knowledge, whereas in theology the religious 'object' (God himself) moves towards us, determining the character and expression of the revelation of truth which is inherent in his own nature. We are back to the concept of self-disclosure and the subsequent invitation to a personal response in terms of a relationship with him. The authority principle of the Bible is the living God in self-revelation, which is neither subjectively determined nor authoritarian, but infinite and personal. So, a Christian is subject to the final authority of God himself, revealed supremely in Jesus Christ, and mediated by 'all Scripture'. This prevents us from thinking of 'inspiration' as merely a heightening of human consciousness within the Bible authors, as we might refer to a great composer or artist generally as 'inspired'. If that were so, we would have to sort the more inspired from the less, and we would be back to the limited human authorities of reason, emotion, or even prejudice. The apostle Peter makes the point with trenchant clarity.

> Above all, you must understand that no prophecy of Scripture came about by the prophet's own interpretation. For prophecy never had its origin in the will of man, but men spoke from God as they were carried along by the Holy Spirit. (2 Peter 1:20–1)

In summary, we have seen that without self-revelation God would be unknowable. Having created humankind in his own image, able to think abstractly and with highly developed language skills, God determined to convey his self-revelation through a variety of human channels over a period of years. But his revelatory work is always related to his redemptive plan (see Chapter 2) since the human dilemma is not so much one of finite ignorance as of moral guilt. God's revelation centres then on what human beings need to know of his character and their need, and how the one has met the other, in his great rescue plan to undo the effects of sinful rebellion and bring men and women back into a loving, personal relationship with their creator. Both the key to the plan and its fulfilment lie in Jesus Christ, 'the radiance of God's glory and the exact representation of his being' (Hebrews 1:3). The Bible is the record of this self-revelatory message from God, with his one integrated plan being pursued throughout the one revelation. Because this is so central to God's purposes and activated by supernatural power, the resulting testimony is undistorted, reliable truth for all people, at all times, and reveals, in comprehensible human language, as much of the knowledge of God as we can understand or need to know.

It is a derivative of this high view of Scripture to describe the Bible further as *inerrant*, though this has been an area of prolonged and sometimes acrimonious debate over the last several decades. There is an extensive literature on the whole subject and this is not the place to attempt to do justice to all the arguments. Discussion has often centred on so-called contradictions or apparently conflicting records of events in the Bible. How can both be true? And if the Bible is found to err in its historical or cosmological details, how can it maintain its divine authority? One way of dealing with the issue is to reduce the scope of the Bible's authority range. Thus the Lausanne Declaration in the 1970s spoke of the Bible as 'reliable in all that it genuinely affirms and authoritative for guidance in doctrine and behaviour', while earlier Vatican II had pronounced that the Bible teaches 'firmly, faithfully and without error that truth which God wanted put into the sacred writings for the sake of our salvation'. Such statements allow room for mistakes to have occurred in areas which do not have an impact on the major doctrines of the faith. If it is agreed, however, that God's providential and supernatural over-ruling has prevented the distortion of his message in such essential areas, why could such care not also extend to its entire contents? Indeed, if it does not, what guarantees of its veracity can we claim?

Frequently, it is assumed that the Bible is 'full of contradictions' but they become notoriously difficult to find and generally come down to such issues as whether one or two angels were present at Christ's tomb, or whether a blind beggar was healed by Jesus on his way in or out of Jericho. In these and similar cases harmonisation of the accounts is perfectly possible and even reasonable. An error is a false statement which is presented as true, yet to prove that such exists would require us to be certain that we have a correct understanding, that we possess all the knowledge needed to come to a judgment and that no further light can possibly be thrown on the issue by further research or discovery. But it is precisely the incompleteness of our knowledge and the inadequacies of our interpretations which constitute the problem. To prejudge unsolved difficulties as errors is equivalent to insisting that the current absence of a solution means that no solution is possible. The discussion then lies more in the area of presuppositions. We cannot understand how Jesus could be both God and man: we rightly speak of the great mystery of the incarnation. But if we accept its reality we have no problem in accepting also his life of moral perfection and sinless righteousness. We do not charge the Bible writers with error or exaggeration because the one is the corollary of the other. In the same way, if the Bible is the Word of God, how can it be anything other than true and inerrant in every word? And, indeed, every word does matter. For meaning does not exist in isolated words, but in their grouping together in phrases, sentences and paragraphs. We all know how the addition or removal of one word, or its relocation in a different position in a sentence, can substantially change the meaning of that sentence. So, when we speak of the 'verbal inspiration' of Scripture, we mean that every word is 'God-breathed', that each word has a vital, constituent part to play in its own unit of meaning, and that God's sovereign control extends as much to the details of each verse as to the grand themes of the Bible's books. To return to the Chicago Statement, we find at Article XX the following, helpful summary. 'We affirm that since God is the author of all truth, all truths, biblical and extra-biblical, are consistent and cohere, and that the Bible speaks truth when it touches on matters pertaining to nature, history, or anything else.'

These general affirmations we have been considering are, however, all derived from the Bible's own testimony about itself, and to that we must return. In Chapter 2 we saw how Christ is himself the centre and pivot of the whole story. It is not for nothing that John describes him as 'the Word made flesh' (John 1:14). So it is to the infallible Christ that we must turn for a true understanding of the nature of the Scriptures. Indeed, it is in the light of my allegiance to Jesus Christ as Lord that I believe in the inspiration, infallibility and inerrancy of the Scriptures. Yet I have been brought to that conviction through their own self-authenticating power and through the gracious illumination of the Holy Spirit. Bible readers come to Bible convictions as they experience Bible truth.

Jesus and the Old Testament

There is no doubt that Jesus fully accepted the Old Testament's claim, which occurs hundreds of times throughout its pages, 'This is what the LORD says . . .' He had a comprehensive knowledge of those Scriptures, quoting and referring to them constantly and with ease. For Jesus, whatever the Scriptures said settled the argument. The gospels include direct reference by Jesus to Genesis, Exodus, Leviticus, Numbers, Deuteronomy, Samuel, Kings, Chronicles, Psalms, Isaiah, Jeremiah, Daniel, Hosea, Joel, Micah, Zechariah and Malachi – at least! Each time the message is clear. Scripture is totally authoritative because what it says God says. Constantly, he recognised Old Testament Scripture as the 'Word of God'. A key and representative passage occurs in Mark 7 (paralleled in Matthew 15).

The Pharisees and some of the teachers of the law who had come from Jerusalem gathered round Jesus and saw some of his disciples eating food with hands that were 'unclean', that is, unwashed. (The Pharisees and all the Jews do not eat unless they give their hands a ceremonial washing, holding to the tradition of the elders. When they come from the market-place they do not eat unless they wash. And they observe many other traditions, such as the washing of cups, pitchers and kettles.) So the Pharisees and teachers of the law asked Jesus, 'Why don't your disciples live according to the tradition of the elders instead of eating their food with "unclean" hands?' He replied, 'Isaiah was right when he prophesied about you hypocrites; as it is written: "These people honour me with their lips, but their hearts are far from me. They worship me in vain; their teachings are but rules taught by men." You have let go of the commands of God and are holding on to the traditions of men.' And he said to them: 'You have a fine way of setting aside the commands of God in order to observe your own traditions! For Moses said, "Honour your father and your mother," and, "Anyone who curses his father or mother must be put to death." But you say that if a man says to his father or mother: "Whatever help you might otherwise have received from me is Corban" (that is, a gift devoted to God), then you no longer let him do anything for his father or mother. Thus you nullify the word of God by your tradition that you have handed down. And you do many things like that.' (Mark 7:1–13)

Jesus is in dialogue with the religious leaders of Israel, as so often in the gospels. This time the issue under discussion is that of ritual purification before meals. His disciples have been accused of less than satisfactory practices of holiness, but Jesus turns the tables on his opponents by scrutinising their lives for a much deeper, internal sanctity. They imagine that they have the right to set aside one of God's commands (the fifth of his ten 'words' or commandments in Exodus 20) and find a way around its demands (vv. 9–13). For Jesus, the words of Moses are the commands of God. The written Scriptures must therefore constitute the supreme authority over all religious traditions, however important or impressive their proponents may seem to be, and however venerable a pedigree they may be able to present. Similarly, using Isaiah's prophecy (29:13), Jesus elevates God's Word over all human teaching and all the structures of institutionalised religion. Without submission to that authority, religious teachers are 'blind guides', whose work cannot be authorised by the heavenly Father (Matthew 15:13–14). Without detailed obedience to his written instructions in Scripture, any professed worship of God is in fact 'in vain' (v. 7).

Nor is this merely an isolated instance. In John 10:34, in another argument with the Jews, Jesus bases his case on one word used in Psalm 82:6 which he refers to both as 'your Law' and 'the word of God'. For Jesus there was no problem with dual authorship, for he was convinced of their divine inspiration and consequent authority and infallibility. Either we must dismiss his attitude as being conditioned by the prevailing fashions of his day and so fallible, which in effect is to deny his full deity, or we recognise that above every other man who ever lived he alone knew how that word was given and its true authority. If Jesus Christ is truly Lord, then his attitude to the Old Testament Scriptures must be followed by his contemporary disciples. It is significant too that for Jesus those Scriptures are to be reverenced in their entirety. We are not at liberty to pick and choose, or to base our beliefs on single proof texts without setting them in the context of the whole revelation. This brief quotation from the closing days of Jesus' earthly life provides an excellent example of this very important principle.

While the Pharisees were gathered together, Jesus asked them, 'What do you think about the Christ? Whose son is he?' 'The son of David,' they replied. He said to them, 'How is it then that David, speaking by the Spirit, calls him "Lord"? For he says, "The Lord said to my Lord: Sit at my right hand until I put your enemies under your feet." If then David calls him "Lord", how can he be his son?' No-one could say a word in reply, and from that day on no-one dared to ask him any more questions. (Matthew 22:41–6)

The Pharisees are only partly right. In all the discussion about Jesus' identity and whether or not he might be the promised Messiah, the Pharisees, who greatly revered the Scriptures, made the point that he would be David's son, born into the tribe of Judah, as Jesus was in Bethlehem, David's home town. But what they had not come to terms with was the reference from Psalm 110:1 to the Messiah as also being David's 'lord', that is having a divine nature. One Scripture is not to be set against another, but Scripture is to be used to interpret Scripture since its single divine authorship predisposes the careful reader to harmonising what seem to be contradictions, or at least to holding both together with equal conviction. Had they done so they would not have been so keen to dismiss his claims and hound him to the cross.

Similarly in Mark 12:18–27, Jesus is dialoguing with the Sadducees on the subject of the resurrection, in which they did not believe.

Then the Sadducees, who say there is no resurrection, came to him with a question. 'Teacher,' they said, 'Moses wrote for us that if a man's brother dies and leaves a wife but no children, the man must marry the widow and have children for his brother. Now there were seven brothers. The first one married and died without leaving any children. The second one married the widow, but he also died, leaving no child. It was the same with the third. In fact, none of the seven left any children. Last of all, the woman died too. At the resurrection whose wife will she be, since the seven were married to her?' Jesus replied, 'Are you not in error because you do not know the Scriptures or the power of God? When the dead rise, they will neither marry nor be given in marriage; they will be like the angels in heaven. Now about the dead rising – have you not read in the book of Moses, in the account of the bush, how God said to him, "I am the God of Abraham, the God of Isaac, and the God of Jacob"? He is not the God of the dead, but of the living. You are badly mistaken!'

They take as their text Deuteronomy 25:5–6.

If brothers are living together and one of them dies without a son, his widow must not marry outside the family. Her husband's brother shall take her and marry her and fulfil the duty of a brother-in-law to her. The first son she bears shall carry on the name of the dead brother so that his name will not be blotted out from Israel.

Their point, that in theory a man might have married a number of wives, is being used to rubbish the idea of a resurrection. But Jesus rounds on them with a stinging rebuke for their facetious confidence. 'Are you not in error, because you do not know the Scriptures or the power of God?' (Mark 12:24). The Scripture concerned is Exodus 3:6, in which God declares himself to be the God of Abraham, Isaac and Jacob, who must therefore be living beyond this world, proving that there is life beyond death. Jesus argues that *all* the biblical evidence must be weighed and considered, and that as this is done it will be found to be coherent and increasingly illuminating, which is actually the experience of every serious Bible student.

In his personal earthly life, the human Jesus used the Old Testament Scriptures to discover God's purpose and to determine his conduct. As he faced the cross he saw the details of his coming betrayal, passion, death and resurrection as the fulfilment of Old Testament prophecy (Matthew 26:24, 31, 53–6). Indeed, these events are in themselves a demonstration of the Old Testament's reliability since their fulfilment was beyond Christ's 'engineering'. So much that others did to him, over which he had no human influence, had already been predicted. Evidence of the way in which Old Testament principles controlled his whole thinking and subsequent life-style often comes almost incidentally, as when, in response to the Pharisees' criticism of his 'eating with sinners', he quotes Hosea 6:6, 'I desire mercy, not sacrifice', going beyond the narrow, more precise meaning of the words in their original context to a broader, more basic truth, which they clearly illustrate.

But perhaps the strongest and most impressive way in which Jesus confirms the authority and infallibility of the Old Testament Scriptures is his constant linking of himself to them, since it is through knowing them that we can come to know him. We can take one example from the many cited during his ministry. Much of the debate in John's gospel settles on the issue of Christ's personal identity, but Jesus again accuses his religious opponents of blindness because they do not recognise how he fulfils the prophecies and promises. 'You diligently study the Scriptures,' Jesus says, 'because you think that by them you possess eternal life. These are the Scriptures that testify about me, yet you refuse to come to me to have life' (John 5:39–40). Again, he challenges them. 'If you [really] believed Moses, you would believe me, for he wrote about me. But since you do not believe what he wrote, how are you going to believe what I say?' (John 5:46–7). Theoretically their belief in the truth of the Old Testament was impeccable, but they refused to see its fulfilment in Christ and so they revealed a practical unbelief. Frequently Jesus drew attention to the testimony of the Old Testament as to his identity and its explanation of his mission. He is the fulfilment of the Passover lamb by whose death God's people are liberated (Exodus 12), and the brass serpent bringing healing and life to all who obeyed Moses to look and live (Numbers 21). Most profoundly of all, he is the suffering servant of the Lord (Isaiah 53) by whose wounds we are healed. We cannot therefore separate Jesus from the Old Testament witness to him. We shall not worship him as we ought if we do not accept its authoritative divinely-given testimony to his person and work.

Moreover, the risen Christ goes out of his way to make exactly this point to his disciples before his ascension. The Scriptures are to remain as the authoritative rule and guide of the new community, the Church, he came to build. What could have been more 'natural', or supernatural, than for the risen Christ to demonstrate his continuing identity to his, at first, agnostic disciples by power displays of miraculous energy and effect? But the final chapter of Luke's gospel goes out of its way to show the opposite. How does Jesus convince his doubting disciples that he really has conquered death, has risen in power and is Lord of the universe? Luke tells us twice. To the two travelling from Jerusalem to Emmaus, the stranger who joined them seemed to demonstrate no supernatural appearance or character, but he explained his resurrection, demonstrating its inevitability from the Scriptures. ' "How foolish you are, and how slow of heart to believe all that the prophets have spoken! Did not the Christ have to suffer these things and then enter his glory?" And beginning with Moses and all the Prophets, he explained to them what was said in all the Scriptures concerning himself' (Luke 24:25–7). It may seem at first that he was taking them on a 'loop-line', when he might have revealed himself directly to them, but that is to miss his purpose. For all the future centuries of the Church, the pattern was being set. We meet the Lord Jesus in the written Word, and without the Book we shall never understand him. Unless the Scriptures determine the real character of the true Christ, and unless we humbly allow the Holy Spirit to be our teacher through them, we shall always be vulnerable to re-creating a false Christ of our own imagination, and being deluded by the echo of our own thoughts, rather than knowing the certainty of his self-revelation. The scholar George Tyrell said of the nineteenth-century critics who embarked on a quest for the 'Jesus of history' that they looked into the well of history and came up with a Jesus who was but a reflection of themselves. It is only by submitting to the Jesus of Scripture that we can enter into the true experience of his rescue and rule. Luke makes the point a second time when Jesus appears on Easter evening, to his bewildered disciples in the upper room. 'He said to them, "This is what I told you while I was still with you: Everything must be fulfilled that is written about me in the Law of Moses, the Prophets, and the Psalms." Then he opened their minds so they could understand the Scriptures. He told them, "This is what is written . . ." ' (Luke 24:44–6). It may sound more immediately convincing and impressive when someone says, 'I don't need to go back to the Bible, I have an encounter with the living Christ. My authority is that dynamic personal relationship with God, into which Jesus has brought me, not an impersonal book.' But the inescapable biblical truth is that the risen Christ taught his disciples to understand and proclaim the good news of all that he had achieved only through the written Scripture, since that is his chosen channel of self-revelation.

Jesus and the New Testament

But what about the New Testament? We have just been quoting extensively from the gospels to establish Christ's own attitude to the Old Testament. What about their own authenticity? Did Jesus have anything to say about that? Again, the answer is strongly positive. We saw earlier that the New Testament was written in order to guarantee continuing accurate records of the events of Jesus' life, death and resurrection, for succeeding generations, as the apostles began to die. What had been oral testimony was committed to writing, and with the events ran the explanations of them, as the apostolic theology deepened and strengthened, both by reflection and through experience of the gospel impacting alien cultures. But Jesus had already made provision for all this. John records his words to the disciples.

I have much more to say to you, more than you can now bear. But when he, the Spirit of truth, comes, he will guide you into all truth. He will not speak on his own; he will speak only what he hears, and he will tell you what is yet to come. He will bring glory to me by taking from what is mine and making it known to you. All that belongs to the Father is mine. That is why I said the Spirit will take from what is mine and make it known to you. (John 16:12–15)

Clearly, this is a very wonderful promise, but limited to the apostolic circle. It is not to be understood that Christians in any succeeding generation will be miraculously led into understanding everything about everything through the Holy Spirit. Nor does it mean that in our day we receive direct, authoritative revelation which should be preserved and bound into the covers of the Bible, because it is universally and infallibly true, as Scripture is. But it is a great promise that the Holy Spirit, given to all Christians from the day of Pentecost onwards (Acts 2:1–4, 38–9), would inspire the closest followers of Jesus to understand and apply the benefits of Christ's teaching and work and so to be able to preach the gospel authoritatively and with confidence throughout the world. The same supernatural activity, which inspired and empowered the prophets of the Old, would be active in the writing of the New Testament, as a divine gift. That is what John 14:26 clearly promises. 'But the Counsellor, the Holy Spirit, whom the Father will send in my name, will teach you all things and will remind you of everything I have said to you.' Again, it is a promise to the apostles, who were the personally commissioned witnesses of the risen Christ, and the result is the sure and certain testimony, which is our New Testament. It explains why apostolic authority was such an important touchstone in the early Church and how this affected the recognition of individual books of the New Testament as holy Scripture. But more of that in the next chapter. What is significant to note is that by the time the apostle Peter wrote his second letter (probably in the 60s AD), the apostle Paul's letters were already circulating with Scriptural authority. 'Our dear brother Paul also wrote to you with the wisdom that God gave him . . . His letters contain some things that are hard to understand, which ignorant and unstable people distort, as they do the other Scriptures, to their own destruction' (2 Peter 3:15–16). If Paul, who had not been one of the original twelve, was already recognised as writing Scripture, it is hardly surprising that Peter, John or Matthew and others within their immediate circle should be acknowledged as having been divinely inspired in their writings.

This special status of the apostles in the early Church, undergirding the authority of the New Testament writings, can be traced back to Christ's own commission. 'Apostle' (*apostolos*) simply means someone who is sent. 'Missionary' is the English term derived from the equivalent Latin. As early as Mark 3:14, we are told that Jesus appointed twelve, 'designating them apostles that they might be with him and that he might send them out to preach and to have authority to drive out demons'. Though Judas Iscariot was removed from their number by his suicide, following Christ's betrayal, Matthias was added in his place (Acts 1:15–26). But a further apostle, Paul, commissioned and sent by the risen Lord to the Gentile world, in a sense eclipsed them all. From time to time in his letters, particularly in Galatians and 1 and 2 Corinthians, there is a discussion and major defence of his apostleship. Clearly it was under considerable criticism, since as Paul himself admits he was not part of the original group. But he argues fervently that his apostleship is no less authoritative or divinely commissioned. 'For I am the least of the apostles and do not even deserve to be called an apostle because I persecuted the Church of God. But by the grace of God I am what I am, and his grace to me was not without effect' (1 Corinthians 15:9–10). If the mark of the apostle is a direct meeting with the risen Christ and a personal commissioning, then Paul's credentials are impeccable. 'Am I not an apostle? Have I not seen Jesus our Lord? Are you not the result of my work in the Lord? . . . For you are the seal of my apostleship in the Lord,' he tells the Corinthian Church he founded (1 Corinthians 9:1–2). Again, speaking of the evidences for his claim in his ministry among them at Corinth, he affirmed, 'The things that mark an apostle – signs, wonders and miracles – were done among you with great perseverance' (2 Corinthians 12:12).

The reason it all matters so much is because, in Christ's purposes, the apostles were to be the foundation of the whole future Church. They became this, Paul explains, by being the custodians of the revelation of the gospel, through the Holy Spirit's revelation, as we saw Jesus promise in John's gospel. They are therefore the first gift of the ascended Christ to his Church (Ephesians 2:20, 3:5, 4:11) and, as such, their testimony becomes the foundation for the future building, with Christ himself as the chief cornerstone. They are the eyewitnesses who became the authoritative preachers and, for some, writers of the gospel word. This view was not a later accommodation to Paul, but a central ingredient of early church life from the beginning. It is already clearly established in Peter's thinking when he preaches the gospel for the first time to Gentiles, in the house of Cornelius, the Roman centurion, at Caesarea. The apostles see themselves as specially chosen and accredited witnesses, whose responsibility is to proclaim that in Christ all the promises of forgiveness made by the prophets have been fulfilled, and since he is also the judge of all, the rescue he offers is certain and sure.

> God raised him from the dead on the third day and caused him to be seen. He was not seen by all the people, but by witnesses whom God had already chosen – by us who ate and drank with him after he rose from the dead. He commanded us to preach to the people and to testify that he is the one whom God appointed as judge of the living and the dead. All the prophets testify about him that everyone who believes in him receives forgiveness of sins through his name. (Acts 10:40–3)

Not surprisingly, therefore, the apostles regarded their teaching as having Christ's authority in the Church, not by virtue of their office or any kind of label, but because of their inspiration by the Holy Spirit. Paul reminds the Corinthians of 'the gospel I preached to you' and affirms, 'by this gospel you are saved . . . for what I received I passed on to you' (1 Corinthians 15:1–3). For him it was of primary importance that this was the special gift of God to him. 'I want you to know, brothers, that the gospel I preached is not something that man made up. I did not receive it from any man, nor was I taught it; rather, I received it by revelation from Jesus Christ' (Galatians 1:11–12). When he eventually visited the Jerusalem church, 'they saw that I had been entrusted with the task of preaching the gospel to the Gentiles, just as Peter had been to the Jews' (Galatians 2:7). It was the same gospel, with the same Christ-given authority.

The logical inference is that they expected this authoritative teaching to be read aloud when the groups of Christians met together, just as the Old Testament Scriptures were read aloud in the Jewish synagogue. 'After this letter has been read to you, see that it is also read in the church of the Laodiceans' (Colossians 4:16). 'I charge you before the Lord to have this letter read to all the brothers' (1 Thessalonians 5:27). So, it came about that what we know as the Old and New Testaments were immediately placed together as having the same divine authority. This was not something which the Church gave to the Bible, rather it was the Bible, the word of God's truth in the gospel, which gave birth and life to the Church. Peter joins the two together when he writes, 'I want you to recall the words spoken in the past by the holy prophets and the command given by our Lord and Saviour through your apostles' (2 Peter 3:2). Paul makes the same conjunction when he quotes the law (Deuteronomy 25:4) and the gospel (Luke 10:7) in the same verse. 'For the Scripture says, "Do not muzzle the ox while it is treading out the grain" and "The worker deserves his wages" ' (1 Timothy 5:18). Both are equally designated 'Scripture', so that both are equally authoritative.

Modern views of the Bible

This, then, is the Bible's self-testimony, which represented original, orthodox Christian belief down the centuries, and still does. Rediscovered during the Protestant reformation of the sixteenth century, the watchword '*Sola Scriptura*' swept across much of Europe and on into the New World. It was ironic, however, that the fruit of this new understanding, in terms of scientific investigation and the consequent exaltation of the faculty of human reason in the Enlightenment, was to provide its greatest challenge over the last four centuries. If Psalm 111:2 was true, 'Great are the works of the LORD; they are pondered by all who delight in them', then the Christian motivation to modern science was rooted in revelation. But what if the human 'pondering' took on a greater authority and delight than the 'works of the Lord', and what if it developed its own autonomy and rival authority to the word written? It was only a small step for the Cambridge Platonists to affirm, 'To follow reason is to follow God', for in all our investigations humankind would simply be thinking God's thoughts after him. Certainly God had revealed himself and his truth to the apostles, but would he not do so to anyone who lived according to reason? The Bible could illuminate and confirm new discoveries of truth, but the apostles no longer had a monopoly on revelation.

From there, it was only another small enough step to affirm that Reason (now capitalised and personified) is the undoubted Word of God, or that the spiritual understanding of the reasonable (enlightened) man is a more sure guide to truth than Scripture. Evidence that the apostles were mistaken was produced. Had they not wrongly expected Christ's imminent return? Were they not children of their times, with all the limitations that implied? Were there not serious differences between Peter and Paul, between Jewish and Gentile Christianity? Such questions as these have clear internal answers within the Bible. We are to live every day ready for Christ's coming and eagerly awaiting the fulness of his kingdom. The supernatural works of the Holy Spirit over-ruled the inevitable human fallibility of the biblical writers. The New Testament demonstrates a wonderful unity in the authentic gospel, so that no one author needs to be set against another.

But by now theology was the 'queen of the sciences', whose purpose was to discover the historical process by which the religious ideas of the Bible were formed, and as a result the reconstruction of the history of New Testament Christianity became the arbiter of what is true and what could therefore be believed. Apostolic theology was accounted for in terms of a cultural expression of a particular religious faith, which borrowed from, and reacted to, the surrounding climate of religious ideas and beliefs. Anti-supernatural assumptions became more blatant. The miracles were superstition, myths designed to teach religious truth, but without any historical foundation. The resurrection was not a literal event. It would no longer do to proclaim unequivocally the deity of the Lord Jesus Christ. Relentlessly, as these expressions of doubt and unbelief dominated higher theological education, based on a culturally fashionable denial of the supernatural (as an unsubstantiated presupposition), it became only too clear that the so-called 'higher criticism' inevitably undermined the theological and moral value of the Bible.

As the critics saw the implicit destruction of Christian culture in their denigration of the Bible, an existential methodology was developed to hold on to what was regarded as religiously important, even though in their understanding it no longer had any basis in objective, historical fact. Jesus may not have fed the multitude miraculously with bread and fish, but the eternal truth remained that compassion and active charity towards the under-privileged is a godlike quality. In such a scheme we have an explanation without any event. Of course, it is a nonsense. If the events did not occur, then there is not the slightest guarantee that what they are alleged to teach has any lasting objective validity either. Not surprisingly, the history of the twentieth century was of the churches of the Western world being emptied because the supernatural Christ of the New Testament was rejected. Not destroyed – for none of these arguments was unanswerable, and indeed throughout the long process, Bible-believing scholars have developed their skills of understanding and interpretation to give an even greater confidence than ever before in God's written Word – but despised and rejected, as being out of tune with the intellectual fashions of the age, and the process continues. As with the religious leaders of his day, Jesus 'came to that which was his own, but his own did not receive him. Yet to all who received him, to those who believed in his name, he gave the right to become children of God' (John 1:11–12).

Of course, this is not to say that the development of close, analytical critical studies of the Bible has been entirely negative. There is much of immense value that has been learned from exploring how the Bible writers put their work together, their sources and the forms used. These are well-developed tools which have their usefulness. What is dangerous is the unproven presuppositions which insist on approaching the Bible, scissors in hand, to reduce and ultimately destroy. Then we are left with conscience, or more often personal opinion, as the final arbiter of belief, and truth no longer exists. The Bible becomes a closed book, the province of the critical expert alone, and the voice of the living God is silenced. Instead we have the voice of our own subjective reaction, a notoriously fickle and unreliable guide, since we are usually the prisoners of the spirit of the age to a much greater extent than we are prepared to admit. 'This is what the Lord says . . .' has been transmuted into 'I like to believe that . . .'

Most of us in the Western world are familiar with the 'Bible minus' approach I have just been describing, but it is less common to realise that there is an equally dangerous virus attacking healthy orthodox Christian faith, which we might identify as the 'Bible plus'. Subtracting from the Bible is only one way of denying its authority. Certainly the history of the last hundred years, with its bewildering multiplication of cults and sects, confirms that the Bible can be distorted and ultimately rejected by adding another parallel authority alongside it, to which equal credence is given. So the Bible *plus* the Book of Mormon, or the teachings of Mary Baker Eddy, or the words of some new contemporary prophet, such as a David Koresh, become the new base of authority.

At first, it all sounds so reasonable. It is simply an attempt to bring the application up to date, to make the Bible more relevant to a new cultural context. But very soon the new authority begins to re-interpret the plain teaching of Scripture by adding so-called 'fresh revelation' direct from God, and the written Word, having been considered insufficient, is quickly undermined. 'You may go to the Bible for what God was saying yesterday,' we are told, 'but the prophet is needed to hear what God is saying today.' That is the quick route to disaster. Once another human authority is added to Scripture, its unique truth claims will soon be reinterpreted, redefined and ultimately dismissed.

For this reason, I think it is right to express concern about the contemporary emphasis on 'prophecy' in some Christian circles. At root, it is the sufficiency of the Bible which is at stake. The Church has rarely been without those who have claimed to speak directly from God, but such claims are not to be accepted uncritically. When Christians say, 'the Lord told me', with regard to decisions being made, what do they actually mean? In practice, they are often speaking of an inner conviction about a course of action, formed through study of the Scriptures, prayer and consultation with others. But it would be unwise to assume that all such convictions are automatically the work of the Holy Spirit. Sincerity is not in itself a proof of reality, since the smallest amount of self-knowledge tells us that we can all be sincere, but sincerely wrong!

The sufficiency of the Bible

The only truly objective test we have is the word which God has already spoken in the Scriptures. Any Christian who claims a word, insight or vision from God must be willing for it to be submitted to the primary revelation of the Bible, for what God has once said he is still saying. His Word is eternal, and because it is Truth it is obviously non-contradictory. So, if any so-called 'prophecy' is truly from God it will be able to be confirmed by the message of Scripture. If that is so, then we could have derived its content from Scripture anyway, so that what is happening is in no sense the receiving of fresh revelation, but a new focus on, or better comprehension of, the specific revelation already given. In my own view, the appropriate biblical description of this ministry is exhortation or teaching, rather than prophecy. Indeed, once we accept the sufficiency of the written Scriptures, it follows that the gift of prophecy, in its narrow biblical sense of direct revelation, will no longer function. We still need to be guided in all our decision-making by the Holy Spirit, but the tool he uses is the Word he has already inspired, of which Christ is the great centre and theme. He is *the* Word of God to man, totally sufficient in every way, and any other words must be assessed by the standard of whether they exalt the Lord Jesus and reflect his glorious character. But the only way we know about him, with divinely revealed certainty, is through the written record of revelation, the Bible.

This is what is meant when Bible commentators refer to the 'sufficiency' of Scripture. Biblical Christianity affirms not only that God *can* speak to man, whom he has made in his own image, but that he has so spoken. This word has been committed to writing, because it has continuing application and binding authority for every generation and because God's intention is that his message should be preserved and proclaimed. It is a complete word, coming to its fulness and culmination in the 'Word made flesh', who is God's last word to man – Jesus Christ (Hebrews 1:1–2). Beyond Christ, God has nothing more to say. The apostolic record of that revelation forms the authoritative and inspired New Testament. So the God who reveals himself in nature by his works reveals those same truths in Scripture by his written Word.

Therefore, we have in the Bible the total revelation which God has designed to provide the rule of faith and practice in the Church, until Christ returns and human history ends. Its sufficiency means that nothing can be added to it or subtracted from it. It is God's truth, the whole truth and nothing but the truth! Accordingly, nothing is to be imposed on the consciences of God's people, whether as truth or duty, if it is not taught in the Bible. The people of God are bound by nothing but the Word of God.

A corollary of this is what the Reformers called the 'perspicuity' of Scripture. By this they meant that the Bible is a plain book, intelligible to all. It is not the preserve of a priestly or scholarly caste. Every Christian must therefore study the Word of God, in dependence on the illumination and guidance of the Spirit of God. All that is needed for salvation and godly living is sufficiently plain in the Scripture to be understood by all (2 Peter 1:3–4). The teaching of gifted leaders in the churches, in matters of interpretation, is of course to be heeded, but the principle of individual judgment, under the sovereign rule of the Holy Spirit, is central to biblical Christianity. It is because ultimately we all have to answer to God for ourselves that we are commanded to search the Scriptures. They are addressed not to a special clan of church leaders, but to all believers ('the saints'). Always the apostles appeal to the authority of the inspired word, not that of individual teachers, however good or godly. We are to weigh our understanding and interpretation of Scripture with others, and not to lean on our own wisdom. But, in the end, we all have to believe and act on what we have discovered. That is why we need, and have, a sufficient Bible.

To remind you

- When we let the Bible speak, we discover it claims a spiritual authority, deriving from divine inspiration and leading to its inerrancy (pp. 52–9).
- The witness of the gospels to Jesus' own view of the Old Testament is that he gave it supreme authority as the Word of God. Further, he claimed the fulfilment of its prophecies and promises in his own person and ministry (pp. 59–64).
- The authority of the New Testament derives from Christ's commissioning of the apostles as the authoritative communicators of the gospel (pp. 64–8).
- Views of the Bible's authority have changed since the Reformation due to the elevation of the principle of reason over that of revelation (pp. 68–71).
- The Bible is therefore the sufficient Word of God to the Church in all generations and we must neither subtract from it nor add to it. What we need to do is to understand it and apply it (pp. 71–3).

Chapter 4

Can We Trust the Bible's Reliability?

JULIA AND ANDY travelled home from the supper party in silence. They had responded to Julia's work colleague's invitation to go round to her home for a special evening, 'just looking' at the Christian faith. Assured that it wouldn't be a pressurised sales-pitch, they had agreed, with a good deal of reluctance. After all, they had never thought seriously about Christianity, or imagined it could have any relevance whatever to their lives. They knew they needed some help, but from *that* source? It was all very unlikely. It had been an intriguing experience. The food had been good and the other guests seemed friendly enough. There had been a short talk in which basically it became clear that the Bible was the key source to understanding the whole thing. Andy's memories of hearing it read at school assemblies and never being able to make much of it came flooding back. But now here they were, driving back, with Julia clutching a Bible which her friend had pressed into her hand as they left. 'Do read it,' she'd said, 'it will really help you to understand.'

Andy had been fielding all the objections to the whole bizarre process which had been filling his mind, as he drove. Eventually, he broke the silence. 'But, I mean it's just not that easy, is it? It's all very well saying "do read it", but it's not like any other book, is it? Is it really going to be worthwhile taking time to understand it? I mean, where did it come from? Who wrote it? How did it all get put together? And how do we know it hasn't been altered and changed beyond recognition from its original format? You know, it's not like just dipping into some ancient document, out of interest, just to see what people thought in those days. Those people tonight, they really take it seriously; even base their lives on it, don't they? I mean that can't be normal, can it?'

Julia sighed. 'Well, they all looked pretty normal to me,' she replied. 'Perhaps there are perfectly good answers to those questions, only we just haven't ever thought about it. Surely it's worth finding out, isn't it? We don't want to walk away from it all, just because it's different, do we?'

Any serious reader of the Bible is going to come up with questions similar to those Andy was grappling with. We are dealing, after all, with very ancient documents of which the original manuscripts have long since disappeared. Those documents are being read in translation, but nearly two millennia stretch between us and the latest of the originals. The reliability of both the text and the translation is of paramount importance. Moreover, given the wide range of authorship, how did these sixty-six books and no others come to be regarded as the authoritative 'word of God written'? They are important issues for us to tackle.

At first sight, a new explorer of the Bible, in English, might decide that the nearest equivalent to it in his experience is a literary anthology. In fact, the Bible has sometimes been marketed as 'designed to be read as literature'. The older English translations, with their rich vocabulary, majestic sentences and vivid turns of phrase, represent some of the most memorable images of the emerging English language and in turn had a major formative influence on its development. But as we have seen, the quality of literary composition is not the criterion by which the Bible was assembled. In fact, it was not compiled by any anthologist, although it is the most remarkable collection of writings. The late Professor F. F. Bruce put the point well in his title *The Books and the Parchments* (1950, Pickering & Inglis).

If we enquire into the circumstances under which the various Biblical documents were written, we find that they were written at intervals over a span of nearly 1500 years . . . The writers themselves were a heterogeneous number of people, not only separated from each other by hundreds of years and hundreds of miles, but belonging to the most diverse walks of life. In their ranks we have kings, herdsmen, soldiers, legislators, fishermen, statesmen, courtiers, priests and prophets, a tentmaking Rabbi and a Gentile physician . . . The writings themselves belong to a great variety of literary types. They include history, law (civil, criminal, ethical, ritual, sanitary), religious poetry, didactic treatises, lyric poetry, parable and allegory, biography, personal correspondence, personal memoirs and diaries, in addition to the distinctively Biblical types of prophecy and apocalyptic. (p. 87)

Yet the amazing and unique quality of the Bible's composition is that it simply grew. No one ever compiled it; no committee ever decreed its contents. Councils of the Church later affirmed its divine origin and accepted contents, but they did not compile it, or decide on it. Perhaps Paul's comment to the Corinthians, in a slightly different context, is the best explanation of this supernatural gift we call the Bible. 'So neither he who plants nor he who waters is anything, but only God, who makes things grow' (1 Corinthians 3:7). Neither the author nor the interpreter is the secret of the Bible's composition, but the fact that God gave the living Word and he alone made it grow.

New Testament manuscripts

The process of that growth we can, however, explore. Let's begin with the documents. It is an obvious principle of documentary research that older documents taking us back as near in time to the original as possible are likely to provide a more authoritative text than later ones. Our oldest biblical documents, before the discovery of the Dead Sea Scrolls about fifty years ago, were actually New Testament passages, written in Greek, their original language. Dating from the first century of the Christian era, the New Testament books were likely to have been written on paper (papyrus) with ink (see 2 John 12). In the case of the largest books, a papyrus roll or scroll would have been used, while the shorter would have been accommodated on papyrus sheets. The life expectancy of papyrus is not great, so it was sensible, as well as providential, that the documents associated with apostolic authority should be often copied and widely circulated. There is evidence from the early church fathers, such as Clement of Rome writing in 95 AD, that already copies of the gospels and apostolic letters were available in the churches. Until the invention of the printing press in the fifteenth century that was how the Bible spread and was preserved. It has always been recognised that such copying of a detailed text, by hand, was bound to have the potential to produce errors in any particular manuscript. No copy, let alone translation, can carry the same implicit authority as the original autograph. Even the most careful and reverent copyist may miss a word or jump a line, so that it might be presumed that the original text has become changed and distorted down the centuries. But that is precisely why so much scholarly energy has been expended on the quest to produce the most accurate text possible. Some statements of belief recognise this when they speak of the authority of the Scriptures 'as originally given'. Far from being some sort of 'get out', this phrase quite properly recognises the need for detailed textual scholarship. We can be grateful that so much excellent work of this sort has been done that Professor Bruce can assert that no other body of ancient literature in the world has such a strong and reliable text as the New Testament.

There are good reasons for this. The sheer number of early Greek manuscripts which have survived, in whole or in part, constitute the primary evidence. Perhaps the oldest of all is a papyrus fragment of John 18, discovered in Egypt and dated about 120 AD, held by the John Rylands Library in Manchester. It represents a remarkably short time-gap between copy and original. It also indicates the wide circulation of John's gospel in the early second century, as strong evidence towards the confirmation of its apostolic authorship. In 1931, the discovery was announced of what have become known as the Chester Beatty papyri, dating from the first half of the third century, containing the four gospels and Acts, Paul's nine letters to the churches and the epistle to the Hebrews, and from the second half of that century a copy of the book of Revelation. But it is to the fourth century and the following two that we look for our fullest Greek New Testament texts.

Throughout the twentieth century the science of textual criticism developed and research multiplied. The number of early New Testament manuscripts, in whole or part, is estimated as about four thousand, so there is a vast resource of material by which to check potential scribal error and to explore the reasons for any textual changes or apparent discrepancies. Even considerably later manuscripts are not automatically of less significance, since they may be copies of much earlier versions. If it is argued that a larger number of manuscripts may produce a larger number of possible errors, it also provides a much surer safeguard by which to identify them. By contrast, it is often not realised how comparatively meagre is the manuscript evidence for the classical Greek and Latin authors of the equivalent historical period. There is a fascinating account of this in F. F. Bruce's popular treatment *Are the New Testament Documents*

Reliable? first published in 1943 and still in print today (Inter-Varsity Press). Surveying Caesar's *Gallic Wars*, the histories of Livy and Tacitus, Theucydides and Herodotus, Bruce points out that in almost every case our best manuscripts date only from the tenth century AD, but affirms that there is no question about their authenticity among classical scholars, even though 'the earliest manuscripts of their works which are of any use to us are over 1,300 years later than the originals'. Even the Old Testament texts are 'astonishingly well attested' when compared with these authors, in terms of manuscript evidence.

There are other factors we need to recognise, as well. The New Testament manuscripts multiplied due to demand. The gospel was spreading rapidly throughout the Mediterranean world. This meant also that translations of the text into other languages began to be made early in the life of the Church, and these too multiplied. The continuing existence of these early translations today means that scholars have been able to cross-check and compare texts and subsequently come to a clearer understanding of the underlying Greek, when manuscripts vary. A further source of information and authentication of the original biblical text occurs in the many quotations from the New Testament to be found in the writings of the early church fathers. In Greek, there is a direct relation back to the original, but many such documents occur in Latin, Syriac, Coptic and Armenian, so that the sort of cross-checking mentioned above is able to be carried out, but from a non-biblical source. All of this means that when Andy and Julia sit down to read the Bible in a contemporary English translation, they can have confidence that they are reading an accurate, scholarly rendering of a remarkably well-attested first-century text. Far from the Bible having been changed or distorted down the centuries, it has been amazingly preserved, and with all the textual scholarship of the past hundred or more years, our generation is in the favoured position of the easiest and most reliable access to the biblical text since its first readers. That doesn't make the Bible true, but it does mean that to read its text carefully and study its implications is to approach as nearly as possible to genuine, original Christian testimony and belief.

Old Testament documents

But what of the Old Testament, which is even older? What manuscript evidence do we have for its textual authenticity? When the Revised Version of the Bible was published in the late nineteenth century (it was a revision of the 1611 Authorised or King James Version) the translators commented that the earliest Old Testament manuscript which could be dated with certainty belonged to 916 AD. The reason for this relates to the extreme reverence in which the Scriptures were (and are) held by the orthodox Jewish rabbis. Rather than use old or threadbare copies of the Scriptures, these texts were withdrawn, stored away or even buried, so that new copies were continually needed. In order to guard the accuracy of these, Jewish scholars worked hard to establish and safeguard the purity of the text, becoming known as 'Masoretes', a title derived from the Hebrew word for 'tradition'. At the beginning of the tenth century AD a final authoritative version was produced, with vowel sounds added by 'pointing' since the Hebrew alphabet is composed only of consonants. However, we know that nine centuries earlier, a 'standard text' of the consonantal version had appeared and that great efforts were made to transmit this, with total accuracy, in the copying of the intervening centuries. All the evidence points to the success of this policy, since quotations from the Old Testament in other sources down the centuries, and not least Jerome's Latin translation of the Hebrew text, the Vulgate (about 400 AD), indicate little change or variation over the period. Other means of cross-checking include the Syriac Old Testament, translated from the Hebrew in the first century AD, the Samaritan Pentateuch (a text of the Bible's first five books preserved by transmission that is independent of the Masoretic tradition) dating from about 400 BC, and supremely the Greek translation of the Old Testament, known as the Septuagint.

The title of this important source is taken from the Latin word *septuaginta*, meaning seventy, often represented by the Roman numerals LXX. Under King Ptolemy of Egypt, a great library was founded at Alexandria, in the third century before Christ. Considerable numbers of Jews had been living in Egypt since the time of the Babylonian exile (587 BC), but it was in Alexandria, founded by Alexander the Great in 332 BC, that they exercised their greatest influence and lived in greatest numbers. It was, of course, a Greek-speaking city and the Jews were soon speaking the local language and needing a translation of their Hebrew Scriptures. Tradition has it that seventy translators did the work and presented the final version for Ptolemy's library. F. F. Bruce comments, 'The language suggests that the translators were Egyptian Jews, and quotations from the Septuagint text of Genesis and Exodus appear in Greek literature before 200 BC' (op. cit. p. 143). It seems well established that a standard Greek translation of at least the Pentateuch was available in the second century BC and that additions and revisions were probably being made over the next centuries, not least when the Christian gospel began to spread so widely and rapidly. Not surprisingly, many of the versions of the Septuagint which have survived seem to have been produced in Christian circles. Ultimately, Origen (the Christian scholar of the early third century), an Alexandrian himself, produced his own version of the Septuagint alongside the Hebrew text, and although only fragments of that have been preserved it became the basis of what soon became the standard Greek version of the Old Testament. Although scholarly opinion is that as a translation it is variable in quality, the Pentateuch being the most accurate, nevertheless the Septuagint takes us back a thousand years beyond the Masoretic text. It also had a profound influence on the Greek New Testament, providing a ready-made vocabulary by which to express predominantly Hebrew ideas and concepts, fulfilled by Christ in the gospel. It was the means by which the apostolic preachers were able to declare the Old Testament and what became the New as one book, by one divine author, bringing one story of the good news of God's rescue for all the world.

In the last fifty years, the 'hot' issue has been that of the Dead Sea Scrolls. The story of their discovery, in and around the Wadi Qumran on the northwestern shore of the Dead Sea in the spring of 1947, has often been told. The sound of breaking pottery as a result of a stone he had thrown into a cave attracted a young local shepherd and his friends to explore further. They discovered seven leather scrolls, the beginning of a massive find of some 500 documents, eventually gathered from eleven caves. Over one hundred of the scrolls are books of the Old Testament, in Hebrew, and every book is covered, with the exception of Esther. The oldest text, dated to 250 BC or even earlier, is a fragment of Exodus. The other scrolls are regarded as later, up to the middle of the first century AD. They were in effect the community library of a group of devout Jews, probably a branch of the Essenes, who withdrew to the Judean wilderness to study and practise God's law. They wanted to prepare themselves for God to bring in his new kingdom of righteousness to end the present darkness, and to be ready to be used as his agents of judgment on the ungodly. In fact, the Essene community was destroyed by the Romans in 68 AD as part of their brutal suppression of the First Jewish Revolt. A full scholarly account can be found in Professor F. M. Cross's essay in *Understanding the Dead Sea Scrolls* (ed. Hershel Shanks, 1993, Vintage Books, New York). But for our purposes, their great significance lies in the Hebrew texts now available, predating the Masoretic text by nearly a thousand years. Professor Edwin Yamauchi of Miami University explained the significance in this way: 'Thanks to Qumran we know that the Masoretic Text goes back to a Proto-Masoretic edition antedating the Christian Era, and we are assured that this recension was copied with remarkable accuracy. This means that the consonantal text of the Hebrew Bible must be treated with respect and not freely emended' (in *The Stones and the Scriptures*, 1973, Inter-Varsity Press, London). One of the earliest scrolls found in Cave 1 was a complete copy of a prophecy of Isaiah. There were differences from the Masoretic text in spelling and grammar, but no significantly major changes (only thirteen new readings in sixty-six chapters) in meaning or substance. We can best sum up the impact of the scrolls by quoting the considered judgment of another academic authority, Dr David W. Gooding, sometime Professor of Old Testament Greek at The Queen's University, Belfast.

> The great significance of these manuscripts is that they constitute an independent witness to the reliability of the transmission of our accepted text. There is no reason whatever to believe that the Qumran community would collaborate with the leaders in Jerusalem in adhering to any particular recension. They carry us back to an earlier point on the line of transmission, to the common ancestor of the great Temple scrolls and the unsophisticated scrolls from Qumran. (Quoted from 'Texts and Versions', article in *The Illustrated Bible Dictionary Part 3*, published by Inter-Varsity Press, 1980.)

How the Bible was put together

We must now turn to another of Andy's dilemmas. How did the Bible come together? Who decided what was to be included and on what criteria? This is the area of biblical study known as the canon of Scripture. The term originally meant a 'reed' or 'cane', from the Greek *kanon*. Derivative from this root came the idea of a reed or rod by which to measure, and so a standard, or rule. In that Scripture is to be the rule of our belief and practice as Christians, it is an appropriate quality to assign to the Bible. But it also meant an index or list of contents, perhaps derived from the marks on a measuring rod. Either way, the term is used to denote the agreed authorised contents of the rule or standard of God's self-revelation. But how did it happen?

It is important to realise that the books of the Bible were listed in this way not because some religious leaders decided that an anthology of inspired writing was needed and that sixty-six ingredients might be a good number to have. Each of the books was included in the canon because its divine authority had already been recognised. The practical logic of the situation is readily understandable. When Moses descended from Mount Sinai with the 'words' which God had spoken to him as his unchanging commands to his people, he presented what Exodus 24:7 calls 'the Book of the Covenant' to the Israelites. They, in turn, recognised its divine authority by responding, 'We will do everything the LORD has said; we will obey.' The existence and acceptance of such a 'book' indicates that what is contained in it is recognised as having an authority, which any other commands outside of it do not have. If other books are written and recognised, at later dates, as having the same divine origin and subsequent authority, together they constitute a 'canon', automatically excluding other claimants which are not recognised as authoritative.

With regard to the Old Testament canon, we need to remember that the process of revelation through its thirty-nine books stretches back over a long period of time, beyond a thousand years. The Pentateuch (law), the prophets and the psalms made up the three divisions of the Hebrew Scriptures to which Jesus referred in Luke 24:44. This was the usual method of sub-division and it was probably customary to refer to the 'writings' (the third section) as the 'psalms' because of the position of that book as the first and largest in the whole unit. As we have seen, Jesus regarded them as being 'written about me' and not only having divine authorship, but being 'canonical', since they had been gathered into a recognised collection, from which everything else was automatically excluded. There is another interesting insight into the status of the Hebrew canon in the time of Jesus, earlier on in Luke's gospel. In the midst of a series of 'woe' pronouncements to the Pharisees, Jesus affirms, 'Therefore this generation will be held responsible for the blood of all the prophets that has been shed since the beginning of the world, from the blood of

Abel to the blood of Zechariah, who was killed between the altar and the sanctuary' (11:50). Abel was clearly the first victim of such a murder (Genesis 4:8) and Zechariah is intended to stand as the last, probably because the books of Chronicles are the last books of the last section (the 'writings') in the Hebrew Scriptures, and Zechariah's story occurs in 2 Chronicles 24:17–22, almost at the end of that unit. So it is very likely that the three-fold division, itself defining and de-limiting the canon, was already well established in the first century AD. For the Christians, the dominical authority given to these Scriptures and continued by the apostles is decisive. Professor F. F. Bruce expresses it so well.

> The apostles, no doubt, found in their Master's attitude to these writings sufficient warrant for theirs, and He accepts them, not because their canonicity had been handed down by tradition, but because He recognized their divine quality. In many points He condemned the Jewish tradition, but not with respect to the canon-icity of Scripture. His complaint, indeed, was that by other tradi-tions they had invalidated in practice the word of God recorded in canonical Scripture. But in point of the canonicity of Scripture, He confirmed their tradition, not because it was tradition, but because He knew on independent grounds that it was right. And in this as in all else we are safe when we follow Him. (*The Books and The Parchments*, p. 102)

But can we go back further beyond the first century to determine with any clarity how the process of such recognition developed? There is a detailed and fascinating discussion in Dr David Dunbar's essay 'The Biblical Canon' in *Hermeneutics, Authority and Canon*, edited by D. A. Carson and J. D. Woodbridge, published in 1986 by Inter-Varsity Press. Yet his conclusions are that lack of evidence prevents us from dating the completion of the Old Testament with any certainty. Two important points must always be borne in mind. To quote Dunbar, 'With regard to Scriptural status, there is no historical evidence for the biblical books "acquiring" such a position. The earliest references to biblical books (or to portions of them) treat them as authoritative' (p. 314). The other is that at some point following the ministry of Malachi, the last of the post-exilic prophets, the Jewish religious leaders recognised that prophecy in its classical (biblical) form was now a thing of the past. This made the fixation of the Old Testament canon much more likely, scholarly estimates of the date varying from 300 to 100 BC. Discussion certainly continued about certain books, in Jewish rabbinical circles, well into the Christian era. Most famous among them are discussions held at Jamnia, in the years following the fall of Jerusalem in AD 70, which were ultimately recorded in writing. The debate centred on the canonical status of four books included in the 'writings' – Proverbs, Ecclesiastes, Song of Songs and Esther. Yet the outcome was to affirm each one and to reject other candidates, probably of a Jewish–Christian origin. No new books were admitted; no old ones rejected. By this date, at the very latest, the Old Testament canon was firmly established.

In turning to the New Testament, we find the same process in operation by which writings are first accepted as having divine authority and therefore included in later listings of such documents. The churches at the end of the first century had twenty-seven books of the New Testament in their possession, reading and valuing them as the authoritative teaching of Jesus and the apostles, but they were not yet a formal collection or canon. The need for such a development became clear in the second century but only came to its formal conclusion at the end of the fourth, when in 397 AD the Council of Carthage defined the twenty-seven books as canonical Scripture. This was the rule of faith, believed and taught throughout the orthodox churches and the touchstone of that orthodoxy, described in Jude verse 3 as 'the faith that was once for all entrusted to the saints'.

The criterion for accepting these writings as having divine authority was apostolic attestation, since it was through the apostles that the Master's own authority was delegated and exercised. This became an increasingly vital issue as alternative versions of Christianity began to appear and false teachers multiplied. One of the most famous challenges, from the second century, came from the new teaching introduced by Marcion to the church at Rome, which began to exercise considerable influence in the early decades of the century. Marcion was a dualist, based on his distinction between the merciful God and Father, revealed in Jesus Christ, and the just but cruel law-giver of the Old Testament. He therefore rejected the whole Old Testament Scriptures and accepted only one gospel (an edited version of Luke, whose author was a Gentile) and the letters of Paul, who was the only faithful follower of Jesus among the apostles, in his view. What

Marcion effectively introduced, as the basis of his challenge to Christian orthodoxy, was his own 'canon'. This related to what the churches had already accepted as their working 'canon', usually called the 'gospel' and the 'apostle', each gospel distinguished by its author and each letter distinguished by the sub-headings 'To the Romans', 'To the Corinthians' and so on. But it also forced the churches to begin to articulate more clearly a canon of orthodoxy.

The four gospels were never in doubt, since Mark was widely known to be Peter's interpreter, while Matthew and John had apostolic authorship, and Luke, although not an apostle, was a close associate of Paul, who had carried out his own detailed research. Luke's second volume, the Acts of the Apostles, contained a great deal of apostolic testimony, as did the thirteen letters of Paul and the first letters of Peter and John. It was the remaining seven books – Hebrews, James, 2 Peter, 2 and 3 John, Jude and Revelation, which were the disputed titles. Sometimes the disputes mirrored the geographical division in the early churches, as the eastern churches focused on Alexandria, while those in the west looked increasingly to Rome. Most often, the debate ranged around the apostolicity of the document concerned, since apostolic authorship was freely claimed for a variety of heretical productions, so that the mere ascription of a work to an apostle or the apostolic circle was not in itself proof of its authoritative origin.

The letter to the Hebrews is an interesting example. The authenticity of the letter's teaching was never questioned and there is evidence that it was known to Clement of Rome before the end of the first century. The question was over its authorship, not its orthodoxy. Could an anonymous letter be given 'biblical' authority? Vigorous claims were made for its Pauline authorship, but never with any generally persuasive conviction. What convinced successive generations of Christians of its inspiration and authority was its contents, what Donald Robinson has called 'the spiritual quality of the epistle as it spoke to their hearts' (in *Faith's Framework*, 1985, published by the Paternoster Press).

This important strand has been further developed by contemporary scholars, such as Herman Ridderbos and Oscar Cullmann, who stress that the criterion for authority must be related to the gospel, God's intervention in Christ's mighty works and revelatory words, and in their proclamation (both oral and written) by his appointed and authorised apostolic messengers. This is in keeping with the *purpose* for which the New Testament Scriptures were originally given and also explains why the canon is in principle closed. Having completed his great work of salvation in Christ, and spoken his last words in Christ, God has nothing more to reveal of his purposes and nothing more to say. Jesus *is*, in fact, God's final word to humankind (Hebrews 1:1–3). Just as it was the gospel which produced the Church, not the Church which created the gospel, so the work of Christ for the world's redemption (the fulfilment of salvation in history) proclaimed and explained became the canon or rule of the churches. This was not a subjective test by which authority would only be attributed to texts which 'resonated' with the readers. It was robustly objective, in that it was grounded in the historical facts of the gospel message, and in their direct experience as truth in the lives of every Christian believer. 'Faith comes from hearing the message, and the message is heard through the word of Christ' (Romans 10:17). That same understanding and acceptance of biblical authority is of course equally the experience of the contemporary reader. Many of us came to 'believe in the Bible', not primarily because of intellectual arguments regarding its inspiration, infallibility and authority, or about the composition of the canon. Rather, coming with a reasonably open mind, we found the Bible imposing its authority on our thinking, exposing our innermost thoughts, convicting us of our sin and leading us to put our faith in Jesus Christ. We began to read the Bible deciding what we were, or were not, willing to accept, and sitting in judgment on its contents, only to find the process being subtly reversed, and the Bible now imprinting its authority on us and sitting in judgment on our arrogant independence from God. We began by asking whether there was any way we could bring ourselves to accept the God whose self-revelation it claims to be, but soon began to ask whether there was any way that God could be brought to accept us, and found that, in Christ, indeed there is. David Dunbar's conclusion sums up this brief discussion of the New Testament canonicity.

> The church regarded apostolicity as the qualifying factor for canonical recognition; however, this apostolicity should be understood not strictly in terms of authorship but in terms of content and chronology. That which was canon must embody the apostolic tradition, and this tradition was to be discerned in the most primitive documents. (op. cit. p. 358)

But in all this, it is highly significant that the New Testament canon was never dictated or settled by any council or synod issuing an authoritative and binding decree. Such statements merely articulated the inner witness of the Holy Spirit and the objective evidence of gospel history, in both the individual Christian and in the believing community across the world, that the New Testament documents were indeed God's written Word. That conviction already existed; the canon formalised it.

The Word and the Spirit

Throughout our discussion of the issues surrounding the reliability and authority of the sixty-six books, which constitute the phenomenon we call 'the Bible', we have seen the interweaving of two equally important ingredients. We might identify them by a series of contrasts – the objective and the subjective, truth and experience, the human and the divine, the Word and the Spirit. Precision of language is particularly difficult when we attempt to describe what will always be something of a mystery to finite human beings – the mind and purposes of almighty God. Bible teachers often speak of the dual authorship of Scripture, by which they mean to draw attention to the essentially supernatural process which produced it. For the 'word of God written' was originally committed to papyrus or parchment by human hands, as the product of an intelligent human mind, written in a linguistic style and vocabulary peculiar to that author, and reflective of his own social and literary environment. Such a product very clearly requires a human author, but the claim of Scripture writers and readers is that the ideas, propositions, descriptions, speech, even the individual words of each chapter of every book were governed and over-ruled by God the Holy Spirit, so that in the words of the human writer we encounter the words of the living God. 'All Scripture is God-breathed', we read in 2 Timothy 3:16, but in what sense and how?

Here, the ministry of the Holy Spirit is of central importance. First, we need to recognise that the words translated 'spirit' in our English Bibles – *ruach* in Hebrew and *pneuma* in Greek – also carry the meaning of breath, or wind. As Dr Leon Morris once remarked, 'After all, what is wind but a lot of breath, in a hurry?' However, the analogy of breath with words may help us to delve a little deeper into the mystery of the Bible's origins. In Genesis 1:2–3, the Spirit (breath) of

God is pictured hovering over the waters of an empty, formless earth. Immediately, God speaks, 'Let there be light,' and light exists. The breath of God enables the articulation of God's will, in the word of his creative command. Reflecting on this in Psalm 33:6, the writer expresses the same truth in typical Hebrew poetic parallelism. 'By the *word* of the LORD were the heavens made, their starry host by the *breath* of his mouth' (italics mine). Just as 'heavens' parallel the 'starry host', so 'word' parallels 'breath'. The two are inseparable.

We are familiar with this as a fact of everyday experience. Take preaching, or any sort of public speaking, as an example. Thoughts are formed in the mind of the speaker, which he wants to communicate as accurately and effectively as possible to his hearers. Expressed in words, those unseen, and otherwise unknown, thoughts in the mind of the speaker are carried on his breath in the form of articulate sounds making up intelligible words. Without the breath there would be no communication. Without the communication, there could be no development of understanding, relationship or subsequent action. So the Spirit of God carried the otherwise unknown and unknowable thoughts of God into articulate verbal form in the minds of the inspired biblical writers, without error or distortion, but with individual particularity and focus. This is unashamedly supernatural in character. In this procedure we call 'inspiration', God the Holy Spirit initiates the process and so controls the human author throughout that he speaks or writes with a quality, insight, accuracy and consequent authority that is possible in no other form of human communication. In Peter's memorable and illuminating comment, 'men spoke from God as they were carried along by the Holy Spirit' (2 Peter 1:21).

While we can never, of course, fully understand the mystery of this divine process, any more than we shall ever be able fully to explain how the divine and human natures of the Lord Jesus Christ are united in the one person, nevertheless the Bible clearly indicates certain guidelines which help us to keep this concept of dual authorship in a proper balance. For example, God clearly chose a wide variety of different human personalities as the human authors of Scripture and these personal characteristics were neither superseded nor overridden. The lyricism of David's poetry, the logic of Paul's well-honed arguments, the meticulous investigations of Dr Luke are all indications of gifted and prepared individuals whose natural abilities and skills are being channelled and employed for the fulfilment of God's providential purposes. It seems very likely, then, that the varied backgrounds, temperaments, training, skills and life-experiences of the Bible writers are an integral part of God's plan, so that the authors might represent as diverse a range of individuals as the variety of circumstances experienced in God's world.

This same principle of variety led them to communicate in a wide diversity of literary styles or 'genres', each with its own conventions and methodologies, to which we shall need to give attention in later chapters. So there is nothing flat or depersonalised about the process of inspiration. Their writing was never mechanical. We must never think of the Bible writers as though they were merely word-processors into which God typed his messages. But neither should we imagine that they always saw the full implications of what they were expressing. There is a sense in which no writer can. Peter tells us, for example, that the prophets 'searched intently and with the greatest care, trying to find out the time and circumstances to which the Spirit of Christ in them was pointing when he predicted the sufferings of Christ and the glories that would follow'. He continues, 'It was revealed to them that they were not serving themselves but you' (1 Peter 1:10–12). So they were consciously writing God's inspired Word for their own and succeeding generations. But as they wrote, they used their own distinctive vocabularies and favourite stylistic devices, as every author must. So Paul is not like John, who is not like Peter or James. They also built on the past revelation that had already been given in earlier books and undoubtedly used such resources as source documents, oral testimony, extant genealogies and histories. Yet the divine control was such that God permitted no inaccuracy, misguided opinion or falsity to impair the truth and authority of his revelation.

To speak, then, of the whole Bible as the inspired Word of God is not to adopt a flattened, 'fundamentalist' reading of Scripture which irons out all metaphor or pictorial language. Sometimes I am 'pinned to the wall' by enquirers about the Christian faith who want to know, 'Do you believe the Bible literally?' To this my only possible reply is, 'Yes, I believe the Bible literally, when it is being literal. But I believe it metaphorically, when it is being metaphorical.' So when Isaiah 55:12 tells me, 'the mountains and hills will burst into song before you, and all the trees of the field will clap their hands', I am not committed to a view of the end of all things, in which 'the hills are alive with the sound of music'! But I do believe it is true that when God's kingdom comes in all its completeness, at the end of time, that the whole created order will be renewed and rejoice in the glorious freedom of the new world (see Romans 8:19–21). The truth of Isaiah 55 is no less truth because it is expressed metaphorically rather than literally.

In a similar vein, God has clearly caused the erroneous thoughts of misguided, fallible human beings to be recorded in Scripture. Job's 'comforters' spend many chapters in that book putting Job right, only to be contradicted by God himself and to see their arguments completely overthrown at the book's climax. Moreover, particular texts must be interpreted within their contexts, if we are not to fall into the critic's trap that the Bible can be made to mean anything. After all, the Bible actually says, in so many words, in black and white, 'There is no God.' It is in Psalm 14:1. But the context reads, 'The fool says in his heart, "There is no God"'! The Bible is not a book with which to play games. Each author described in his own language what he understood God's message to be, consciously applying his mind to its descriptions, propositions and applications. And the Holy Spirit, as the revealer and inspirer, provided adequate and accurate words and structures, for the expression of the mind of God.

By way of reflection here, it is important to note that the Spirit of God and the Word of God are therefore indissolubly united in the revelation of God in holy Scripture. There is no opposition between the Word and the Spirit. Christians today need to remember that and to draw the inference, 'What God has joined together let not man divide.' Sadly, the history of the last few decades in Western Christianity has all too often been soured by such divisions, caused by polarisations which the Bible writers would find it difficult to comprehend. The root of the divisions has often been over the ministry of the Holy Spirit and how that might be experienced today. 'Charismatic' Christians have stressed the ministry of the Spirit, with a strong emphasis on his fruit of love, producing a heart-centred, experiential faith. 'Conservative' Christians have sometimes defined themselves, or allowed themselves to be defined, in opposite terms, over against their charismatic brothers and sisters. Their stress has been on the ministry of the Word, with a strong emphasis on unchanging truth, on the mind being full-engaged in a doctrinally focused faith. Either side has become practised at drawing its caricatures of the other, as when 'cerebral' is pitched against 'emotional'. The net result has often seemed to be the separation of the Word and the Spirit, to the great disadvantage of both groups, and the bewilderment of many.

To assume that an individual, or a local church, might be governed by the Spirit without the Word, or the Word without the Spirit, is to betray a fundamental misunderstanding of basic Christianity. How do we know what the Christian faith, the gospel and its resultant life-style are? Only by the Word of God. As we have already argued, we are entirely dependent upon the Scriptures for the knowledge of God's truth. But those Scriptures would not exist had not the Holy Spirit inspired them, and we shall never be able rightly to understand and apply them if the same Spirit is not also our illuminator and teacher. Without the enabling power of the Spirit, we would not have faith in Christ or be able to live the Christian life for one moment. Without his new life and equipping power the Church would be powerless, impoverished and moribund. But the great ministry of the Spirit is to exalt Christ, to lead us to trust and obey him, to live consistent and godly lives as we love God and love our neighbours. And the only sure content as to what God requires of us, as well as the resources of his grace which are freely available to us, is found in the written Word. It is in the sixty-six books alone that the revelation of God is reliably, infallibly and sufficiently expounded, so that whatever I may think the Spirit may be saying to me must be tested against what God has already said in Scripture, and is therefore still saying. And whatever is not read in Scripture, or provable from it, cannot therefore have any binding authority on an individual or a church. The Word of Scripture will never be by-passed, much less contradicted, by the Holy Spirit. But its message cannot be received, believed and obeyed without the enabling ministry of the Holy Spirit. The two are inextricably bound together, for the Word of God is the expression of the mind of the Spirit. What a great step forward it will be when Christians on both sides of the divide realise this!

The Bible for today

As we conclude this chapter, it will be clear that the reliability of the Bible, understood and applied under the illumination of the Holy Spirit, is the indispensable requirement for all true Christian belief and practice. This is not just an optional extra, but the bed-rock foundation on which everything else is built. If it is true that God has spoken, and that what he has said is available in written form today, meticulously preserved and accurately translated, and if those words reveal the means by which I can be brought back into a right relationship with my creator, here in time, but with fulfilments on into eternity, then the reason for such a book being the world's best-seller of all time is not difficult to understand. The stakes are very high. Our happiness and fulfilment in the world, not to mention our hopes for the world to come, ride on this foundational claim. The reliability of the Bible is therefore of crucial importance.

If we know that the Bible is the source of heavenly wisdom, 'a lamp to my feet and a light for my path' (Psalm 119:105), then to study that resource, to understand and apply it rightly to our lives, becomes our greatest privilege and responsibility. When we think of the vast wealth of divine revelation contained in the Bible, the grace of God in inspiring its existence and preserving its integrity and the huge labours which human authors, scribes and translators have exerted to bring it to us today, we must surely take seriously the words of the British coronation service when the new sovereign is presented with the Bible and told that it is 'the most precious thing that this world affords'. Yet we can buy it in a variety of translations and bindings from any bookshop for just a few pounds. To give it an occasional cursory glance, or to ignore its wealth except for a few very familiar passages, or to keep it unopened, is surely a statement of ingratitude at best, and perhaps at worst, of practical atheism. If we knew that God would be speaking with us on the phone in an hour's time most of us would be ready to take the call. If he summoned us to an audience, we would probably make sure we were there. Yet both these possibilities – meeting personally the God who speaks in Scripture – are the daily opportunities given us by the Bible on our bookshelf at home, or in the hotel bedside cabinet, or the hospital room, or the school desk.

The problem is that it all seems so ordinary. 'Why doesn't God speak today?' people ask, unaware that he is speaking all the time. In the beauty and majesty of creation, 'his eternal power and divine nature have been clearly seen, being understood from what has been made' (Romans 1:20). In history, as he dealt with his people, Israel, he spoke of his righteousness and mercy, his covenant love and justice. Supremely he spoke through his Son, Jesus Christ, the living Word. And it is all in the pages of the Bible, waiting to be explored. But as with most worthwhile things in this life, the Bible demands time and application to understand it properly and live in the benefit of its instruction. Whether it is learning a practical skill, or an academic subject, or a sporting technique, or developing a friendship, it takes time and practice. The Bible is no exception. Some of its jewels lie on the surface, but much more lies buried, awaiting those who set aside time prayerfully to explore its highways and byways and who are prepared to give regular amounts of quality time to its study. If you have ever read that great English classic *The Pilgrim's Progress*, by John Bunyan, you will probably have been amazed at how much biblical quotation and allusion it contains. How did the Bedford tinker acquire such a knowledge of Scripture that it could be said of him that his blood was 'Bibline', that if you cut him the Bible would flow out of his veins? The answer is probably to be found in his long period of imprisonment in Bedford gaol, as a dissenter. Here he not only read the Bible but studied, memorised and meditated on it, until it became the dominant and controlling influence of all his thinking, speaking and writing.

That sort of understanding of God, through his Word, does not come 'on the back stroke', or in a few hastily reserved minutes of superficial reading from time to time. It depends upon a determination to make time for what matters most in time, with eternity in view, and that is to get to know God more deeply and intimately, so as to love him more worthily, obey him more completely and glorify him more passionately. That is what we can rely on the Bible to do for us, if we submit ourselves to the ministry of the Holy Spirit as our instructor and give time to study and live out its message. It's a personal choice we all make, because we all find time to do what we think is really important and what we really want to do. That is why it is worthwhile for Andy and Julia to persist through the unfamiliarity of the text, recognising that in their hands they have the chief means by which God has determined to reveal himself to men and women like them, and like us. It is time to consider now how that sort of serious commitment to Bible study might work out.

To remind you

- As we explore how the Bible has come down to us, the number and quality of the manuscripts of the New Testament are amazing (pp. 75–8).
- The stories of the Septuagint (Greek version) and the Dead Sea Scrolls

indicate the equivalent reliability of the text of the Old Testament (pp. 78–81).

- The canon of Scripture gradually emerged through the testimony of faithful readers and was never a committee decision (pp. 81–6).
- The ministry of the Holy Spirit generated the inspiration of Bible writers and illuminates the understanding of humble Bible readers (pp. 87–91).
- To hear God speak with certainty to us today we need to go to the Bible, and that requires reverence, attention and hard work (pp. 91–3).

Chapter 5

And What Does It Really Mean?

DAN AND RACHEL made themselves a cup of coffee and sat down to do a 'post-mortem' on the evening's Bible study session. They had to admit that it seemed as though a 'death' had actually occurred! The group had run into such problems in deciding what the Bible text actually meant that it had virtually ground to a halt. But worst of all, Matt had been there and all that had happened had only served to support his theories. He had held forth famously at the end. 'There you are; you've proved it!' he crowed. 'I always said you could make the Bible, or any other text come to that, mean exactly what you want it to mean, and that's what you've been doing all evening. You haven't been listening to yourselves, have you? How many times did I hear one or other of you say, "Well, to me, it seems as though what it's saying is this . . ." And within a minute or two somebody else is not wanting to be argumentative or offensive in any way, but, "Well, I take it another way and think something quite different."' Of course, Matt was right, but it all became rather embarrassing, especially when he said that no one could ever really work out the meaning of the Bible, because it didn't have one. 'Don't think I'm saying that what you're doing is a waste of time,' he had said. 'It's a perfectly valid activity to sit round in a group and share what a particular text is saying to each person. Isn't that what literature tutorials are all about? But why do you people have to insist that the words of the Bible have divine authority and then try to force other people to accept them as "gospel truth"? That's just not on! What right have you got to say what it should mean to me, or anybody else? What are you – a bunch of control freaks, or do you just enjoy trying to brainwash other people?'

The need for interpretation

When I was a sixth-former studying history, there was a question that seemed to crop up year after year, in different guises but in almost all of the exam papers. It was on the lines of 'Is it ever possible for the writing of history to be impartial?' or 'What objectivity can the historian reasonably hope to achieve?' Each of us, inevitably, sees the world through a pair of personal prescription spectacles. They are as unique to each of us as we are unique people. Genetic inheritance, upbringing, training, education, life-experience, all have a part to play in producing the framework of convictions and questions, prejudices and presuppositions with which we view the universe and our single, solitary lives in it. This is commonly referred to as our 'pre-under-standing' and we cannot entirely escape it. One of the aims of education is to remove ignorance and prejudice as far as is possible from our mind-sets. Nevertheless, when we open the Bible to read it, we inevitably bring our prior understanding with us. Take even a simple statement, such as John 3:16, 'God so loved the world that he gave his one and only Son', and it immediately becomes clear how much we automatically begin to interpret in order to understand. What content do we give to the word 'God'? How can he 'love' and in what way does 'giving his Son' relate to that? What is the 'world' – the planet, the people? How can God have a son? Some questions may have more obvious or clearer answers than others, but all of them will give rise to others, as we begin to think through the meaning and implications of even quite a straightforward sentence.

But for much of the time we are unaware that the process is happening. Good communication happens when a message is conveyed with such clarity and precision that its hearer or reader receives the meaning which the originator intended. But that has to happen via a medium, such as speech or print. We are not able to read one another's minds. All we can work with are the words which make up the written or spoken message. It is possible that the author may not have expressed his meaning clearly enough, or that the reader has not understood it fully, but there are realities hidden in their minds. They might meet each other and be able to discuss the issues concerned to come to a greater clarity, but whatever the author intended or the reader perceived, all we have to work with are the words on the page, and so our aim must always be to understand the meaning of that text. I imagine that is why you bought this book and (hopefully!) have persevered to this point in reading it. For my part there are things I want to say, convictions I want to share, enthusiasms I want to explain about the Bible. In writing the book, my endeavour is to be as clear, accurate and motivational as I can be, since my overall purpose is to encourage you to study the Bible for yourself, with enthusiasm and confidence. To that end I try to choose my words carefully and structure my sentences clearly, so as to make it as easy as possible to receive the message I am trying to communicate. If my style is cryptic and obscure, or vague and imprecise, the reader will find the experience unrewarding and give up. How many times have we walked away from a book (or sermon) with the comment, 'I really didn't see what he was trying to say'? But the unspoken agenda in writing and publishing a book is that it contains something worthwhile and informative to say and invites the reader to respond to the message which is perceived in the text. It is as though the author is saying 'This is so, isn't it?', to which the reader may reply 'Yes, indeed', or 'Yes, but . . .', or 'No, not at all.' The significance of the text will vary greatly from reader to reader, but we cannot begin to discuss it at that level until we have established its meaning. Let's see how it might work out.

Dan and Rachel's study group ran into the sands because they started asking the wrong sort of first questions. It's a common error. Faced with a complex passage, a heterogeneous group of readers and above all an awareness of the need to be 'relevant', Bible study leaders often plunge into the question which seems to pull them all together. 'So, Matt, what do you think this verse (paragraph) means to you?' It is the 'to you' bit that causes all our problems, because it fatally confuses the meaning of the passage for us all with its significance for an individual. In an article entitled 'What it means to me' (printed in *Christianity Today*, 26 October 1992), Dr Walt Russell, a Californian New Testament professor, tackles the issue with great insight and penetration. He asserts, 'The meaning of a text never changes. Our first goal is to discover this fixed thing. In contrast, the significance of that text to me and to others is very fluid and flexible.' In support of this view Dr Russell quotes the literary critic E. D. Hirsch Jr in his book *Validity in Interpretation* (1967, Yale University Press), distinguishing the two strands from each other. '*Meaning* is that which is represented by a text: it is what the author meant,' Hirsch writes. '*Significance*, on the other hand, names a relationship between that meaning and a person, or a conception, or a situation, or indeed anything imaginable.' If these two ingredients of biblical interpretation are fused or confused, all our reading of Scripture will be condemned to a relativism, which will never be able to establish or validate any interpretation as the real meaning of the text. That is why so many people give up reading the Bible. It all becomes too slippery, too difficult to pin down or have any degree of certainty about. If the author is located in a remote and very different culture from our own and if the meaning of the words on the page appears complex or ambiguous, then we shall turn to the only other available source of significance, which is ourselves, and consequently invest in the 'What it is saying to me' syndrome.

Such an approach has been the prevailing fashion in academic, literary and critical circles over the past two or three decades. It argues that the reader's response determines the only valid meaning that a text can be said to have. So the text does not exist as a repository of the author's intended meaning, since that meaning can never exist as predetermined or required. Rather, each reader brings his or her own prior understandings into reaction with the text and in that process a whole spectrum of possible meanings can be revealed. To speak of 'the' meaning would be to miss the point. So, it is possible to take a novel, say, and give it a feminist reading, or a Marxist reading, or an African reading. Each one will produce a different range of meanings, but each will be equally valid, because each is generated by interaction with the text. The focus of meaning has shifted through the text to the reader, so that any concept of a normative or given meaning is rejected. To deal with the Bible in this way is, of course, radically destructive of its authority. Instead of God speaking words of unchanging truth, which reveal his eternal nature and dependable purposes, we are left with a religious document, with which we may 'resonate' or 'react', but which has no ultimate authority to shape our thinking or judge our actions. To those wanting to escape from the searchlight of God's Word that may provide an attractive option, but it is true neither to the Bible's self-testimony, nor to the daily experience of millions of Bible readers, down the centuries and across the world.

Looking for the meaning

Our quest for the original, intended meaning of a biblical text is neither irrational nor forlorn. Later generations may have seen the fulfilment of biblical prophecies, for example, in much more detail and with greater understanding than the original authors themselves received, but that in no way changes the intended and foundational meaning to the original hearers, or readers, and that is what we must discover first. The textbook *Introduction to Biblical Interpretation* by W. W. Klein, C. L. Blomberg and R. L. Hubbard (1993, Word, USA) makes the point cogently.

> We assume that the writers or editors of the Bible intended to communicate to all people in the same way. Thus, for the most part, they intended their words to have only one sense. They may have encoded their message in metaphor, poetry, allegory or apocalypse, in addition to more straightforward techniques, but they selected appropriate ways to convey their intended meaning. The historical meaning of these texts remains the central objective of hermeneutics. (op. cit. p. 132)

But, of course, such an objective has to be pursued by fallible human beings, who bring their own pre-understandings to the text. That 'framework' of theological understanding inevitably colours what we see in the text, but if we do our best to let the Bible speak, we shall soon discover our own thinking being challenged, refined and even re-shaped by the authoritative text.

How then should we proceed? Let's go back to our example from John 3:16. The essential unit of communication in written prose is the sentence, which in its most basic and simple form consists of a subject and a verb, an actor and an action. Our text provides an example of a one-sentence verse: 'For God so loved the world that he gave his one and only Son, that whoever believes in him shall not perish but have eternal life.' Incidentally, the verse and chapter divisions of the English Bibles, while being very useful as reference points, must not be allowed to dictate our understanding, since they were not, of course, part of the original manuscripts. We are safer to work with the grammatical marker-points which are built into the text, in the form of sentences and subordinate clauses. Here we have a single sentence, in which the meaning or content of each word and its position and inter-relationship with each of the other words in the whole determines the message it conveys. This is a matter of simple vocabulary and grammar to which we have grown accustomed over many years of reading, and the principles of which we operate automatically whenever we read anything. But the sentence does not exist in a vacuum. Just as 'no man is an island, entire of itself', so is no sentence. It relates to what goes before and what follows. Usually, its own function is to relate as a bridge between the two, as it makes its own unique contribution to the advancement of the argument, the telling of the story, the development of the poem, or whatever the literary form may be. The text exists only in its context, and to ignore that would be to ignore one of the most important aids we have to help us understand its meaning.

> Just as Moses lifted up the snake in the desert, so the Son of Man must be lifted up, that everyone who believes in him may have eternal life. For God so loved the world that he gave his one and only Son, that whoever believes in him shall not perish but have eternal life. For God did not send his Son into the world to condemn the world, but to save the world through him. (John 3:14–17)

In our example, verses 14 and 15 have just related the Son who must be 'believed in', in order to receive 'eternal life', to an Old Testament story, from Numbers 21:4–9. Here the Israelites' sin in grumbling against God and being ungrateful for all his provision and protection brought upon them the judgment of a plague of venomous snakes, from which many of the people perished. However, God provided a rescue, so that they might not perish, but live. He commanded Moses to make a bronze snake, put it up on a pole, 'then when anyone was bitten by a snake and looked at the bronze snake, he lived'. The 'lifting up' of the Son of Man to provide a universal salvation is now explained in v. 16 as God 'giving' his Son, to rescue humankind, and the following verse 17 further explains Christ's mission (in Christ's own words here) as not to condemn but to save the world. It is this immediate context, then, which gives definitive meaning to God's love, the gift of his Son, the necessity for faith and the rescue from death (perishing) and condemnation to eternal life. All this is to be accomplished at the 'lifting up' of Jesus, which is the characteristic way in which John describes Christ's death on the cross.

But while the immediate context is very instructive and formative for our understanding, the verses we have examined are also part of a larger unit, John 3:1–21, where Jesus is in dialogue with Nicodemus, a Pharisee and a member of the Sanhedrin, the Jewish ruling council of seventy elders. Nicodemus has come at night, probably for secrecy, to meet Jesus personally and determine whether or not he is the Messiah, God's chosen and anointed one. He seems to have been genuine in his enquiries and the text relates the dialogue during which Jesus expounds who he is and what he has come to do, of which verse 16 is the famous climax. This is one of a number of such conversations in John's gospel, where individuals are confronted with both the claims of Jesus and the evidence that he is the Christ the Son of God. In the next chapter, he is in dialogue with the exact opposite of the highly respected, wealthy Jewish ruler. Now it is with a woman, a Samaritan not a Jew, and a woman whose moral notoriety has made her an outcast in her own community. All this is clearly part of John's big picture in his gospel, as he accumulates the evidence which should convince his readers that Jesus is the Christ. So the Nicodemus story sits in the broader context of the whole gospel, and though at this point we are not told of his reactions to Jesus after their interview, he later reappears twice. In chapter 7 verses 50–1, he is arguing in the Sanhedrin against the Jewish leaders' determination to do away with Jesus, asking 'Does our law condemn a man without first hearing him to find out what he is doing?' He is summarily dismissed for his pains. 'Look into it, and you will find that a prophet does not come out of Galilee.' Finally, when Jesus has been 'lifted up' on the cross, it is Joseph of Arimathea who secures Pilate's permission to bury the body in his garden-tomb 'accompanied by Nicodemus, the man who earlier had visited Jesus at night. [He] brought a mixture of myrrh and aloes, about seventy-five pounds' (John 19:39). This was a very large amount, equivalent to a very lavish expenditure, such as a royal burial might have demanded. Clearly, Nicodemus greatly revered Jesus and perhaps saw him by the end of the gospel, as Nathanael did at the beginning, as the Son of God and the King of Israel (cf. John 1:49).

The wider context also decides for us the meaning of the 'lifting up' by which God gave his Son for the world's rescue. For in 12:32–3 Jesus affirms, 'But I, when I am lifted up from the earth, will draw all men to myself' and John immediately comments, 'He said this to show the kind of death he was going to die.'

In these comments, we have been looking at two sorts of context without which we are unable properly to understand the meaning of the text under examination. Every text resides in its literary context. The sentence relates to other sentences on either side of it which constitute a paragraph. The paragraph is surrounded by other paragraphs which make up the narrative unit that is chapter 3 of John. Yet the chapter has its own context in the message of the whole book, and the book has its own unique truth contribution to the whole Bible. Just think how immeasurably poorer our understanding of Christ and the gospel would be if we did not have John's gospel! Then, as you think of its unique contribution (as, for example, in this story of Nicodemus) you begin to see how its main themes and distinctive teaching not only fit into, but also illuminate, the whole Bible. Every text also resides in its own distinctive historical, cultural context. This will relate not only to the internal ingredients of the text – the ruler of the Sanhedrin, the snake on the pole and so on – where historical information from elsewhere in the Bible informs our understanding, but also to the big picture of the book as a whole. This addresses the key question as to why the author wrote it and to whom. All the necessary evidence for these deductions is contained within the text, or other biblical texts, and it is by careful reading, meditation and re-reading that we begin to understand the author's predominant concerns and the applications of his message, so that we can better set a particular text within the controlling purposes of the book of which it is a part.

It is in the light of these two analyses of context, both literary and historical, that we can focus on the meaning of words and the structure of sentences. Of course, neither of these processes of understanding is watertight in itself. We cannot work at the contexts without examining the words, and vice versa. So each process is being worked through simultaneously, even though our particular focus will be on one particular aspect, at one particular time. In dealing with the words, we need to look for their normal meaning within the sentence, not the obscure or exceptional. It is important also to remember that the Oxford English Dictionary is not the final authority. The meaning of words is fluid over a period of time and a dictionary will always have to generalise. Remember, too, that we are dealing with a text in translation. This is where our reflection on the contexts can be really helpful. Seeing how a particular author uses the word in another, more straightforward context can often provide just the insight needed to make better sense of its use in a more difficult verse. It is a good test of whether or not we have really understood the meaning of the individual key words in a passage to try to express them in our own equivalents, not necessarily individual synonyms, but usually in phrases that explain their meaning.

The other important aid to understanding is to pay careful attention to the grammatical relationships between the different thought ingredients which make up the passage. Just as every sentence has a main verb and a subject, so every paragraph has a main idea, or point, usually expressed in a topic sentence, around which all the other ingredients are built. Each of these extra clauses, or phrases, is included in order to extend our understanding in some particular way and is connected to the main sentence by one of a whole series of linking words. When we come across them we need to stop and see what is being connected to what, and for what purpose. It is often said that when you come to a 'therefore' you should stop and see what it is there for. The same applies to a list of conjunctions and relative pronouns, too long to quote but containing many familiar friends such as 'and', 'but', 'although', 'so that', 'because', 'as if', 'since'. They are all ways of connecting ideas together, and they help us to analyse and examine the structure of a sentence or paragraph, so as better to appreciate its essential meaning.

Learning to listen

Expressed in these ways, it may appear that studying the Bible is a complex and demanding intellectual task. There is no doubt that it does involve hard work when we come to *study* Scripture in this way and that in our busy lives and the frantic rush of our culture, serious Bible study can appear to be a luxury available only to the professional or the retired. But I want to convince you that such thinking is misguided and potentially disastrous. I have little doubt that the weakness of the Christian cause today is largely due to the degree of biblical ignorance and illiteracy, both within the Church and outside it. At least some of our hesitations and reluctance to take studying the Bible seriously, as a central element of Christian discipleship, stem from our categorising it as an academic pursuit. It takes us back to the comprehension exercises we used to do in English classes at school, which for many will trigger memories of difficulty and boredom. I am not advocating that we come to the Bible in that frame of mind! We need, rather, to remind ourselves that instead of studying an impersonal text for information purposes, we are entering into a dialogue by which to deepen a relationship – with God himself. In fact, the same process of listening and understanding is going on, but it is in an interactive context, where response is required at a personal level.

That is why Christians always link their study of the Bible with prayer. It is our reactive side of the conversation. Of course, we need to bring our minds to the reading of Scripture, to be attentive, switched on and ready to think through what God says to us and its implications. But that is only the first, albeit vital, stage of the process. The aim of our study is not simply to be able to understand and express the meaning of a biblical text. That is only a means to a much more profound end, which is that we should respond appropriately in thought and action to what we have understood, in prayer, faith and obedience. Just as we are dependent on the illuminating power of the Holy Spirit to teach us the meaning of God's written Word, so we are dependent on his energy and power to put whatever we have learned into action in our lives, as faithfully and fully as possible. That is why all our study of the Bible and all our use of helpful methods and techniques to understand its message must be preceded by prayer, in which we consciously open our minds and hearts to the Holy Spirit's teaching, express our dependence on him for all spiritual understanding and ask for his enabling to put what we discover into practice.

The real test of any Bible study, then, is not an intellectual 'buzz' or a warm feeling inside, but a life of joyful discipleship, in which God's love is reciprocated by our personal devotion to him and shared in our care for others. This priority derives from our understanding of the uniqueness of the Bible as God's personal self-disclosure. Biblical revelation is not just a body of information to be understood and assimilated mentally, but an invitation (we might even call it a summons) from the living God to enter into a covenant relationship of loving obedience with him. In order to know biblical truth, we must live it. The Bible's knowledge of God is never merely theoretical, but experiential; never content with theological correctness alone, but rejoicing in personal relationship. In biblical terms, therefore, knowing

God's truth and doing it are mutually interdependent. You cannot have one without the other.

But their connectedness is often not appreciated. We study the Bible not to fill our minds with historical or theological information, as if we were swotting for a *Mastermind* interrogation or 'Bible trivia' contest. You may know the sort of thing – 'Who killed a lion in a pit on a snowy day?' – as though that was Bible knowledge. (See 2 Samuel 23:20, if you can't resist it!) Such a view does indeed 'trivialise' the Bible. No, we need the knowledge of God's truth in Scripture in order to act, in the recognition that it is only as we put it into practice that we are able to learn more. On our wedding day, my wife and I thought we had got to know each other pretty well over a period of three or more years, and we knew that we loved each other. That was why we got married. But thirty years on, we know each other so well and love each other so much more that the reality of that day seems but the faintest outline of the picture painted down the years. Putting our commitment to one another into practice, on a daily basis, through all the ups and downs of life, has meant that we know each other and love each other far more deeply than we could have imagined on our wedding day, though what we knew then was equally real. We have a factual, legal document to prove the historical reality of our wedding, but that is simply the foundation on which the practice of our vows and promises has been based. It is the living out of those verbal affirmations that has given substance and solidity to our marriage. The parallels between marriage and God's relationship with his people are developed by Paul in Ephesians 5:22–33, where the husband's love for his wife, modelled on Christ, and the wife's respect for her husband, modelled on the Church, highlight for us the relationship into which God has called all his believing people. That can only be entered into and developed by listening to God in his Word and putting it into action in our lives, as Jesus himself constantly emphasised.

> Not everyone who says to me, 'Lord, Lord,' will enter the kingdom of heaven, but only he who does the will of my Father who is in heaven. (Matthew 7:21)

> Therefore everyone who hears these words of mine and puts them into practice is like a wise man who built his house on the rock.

The rain came down, the streams rose, and the winds blew and beat against that house; yet it did not fall, because it had its foundations on the rock. (Matthew 7:24–5)

My mother and brothers are those who hear God's word and put it into practice. (Luke 8:21)

A woman in the crowd called out, 'Blessed is the mother who gave you birth and nursed you.' Jesus replied, 'Blessed rather are those who hear the word of God and obey it. (Luke 11:27–8)

If anyone chooses to do God's will, he will find out whether my teaching comes from God or whether I speak on my own. (John 7:17)

Plain for all to see

What we have been advocating as the basic template for interpreting the Bible is usually referred to as the 'grammatico-historical' method. Its aim is to discover the intended original meaning of the text by close attention to the meaning of words, to the grammatical structure of the writing, to the historical occasion that produced it and to the internal contents of the book providing the necessary clues as to its purpose. It may seem to us at our point in history to be the obvious way to approach the Bible, as indeed it did to the apostles of the early Church. But it was not always so, down the centuries of church history, nor indeed is it obviously so to all contemporary Bible readers. The principles of biblical interpretation, which we shall go on to explore in more detail in later chapters, were not invented at the time of the Protestant Reformation in sixteenth-century Europe, but they were re-discovered and powerfully articulated then, as a result of that movement of God's Spirit in spiritual re-awakening. If the Bible was to be the supreme authority over the Church in all matters of faith and conduct (*Sola Scriptura*), then it was vital to define very clearly the principles on which it was to be interpreted. The Reformers were especially conscious of this as they were battling against the obscurantist and sometimes bizarre uses, or abuses, of the Bible, which had become an entrenched feature of medieval religion. The scholars of the Middle Ages had become bogged down in apparently unchangeable traditions, more concerned about their own theological games than about nurturing spiritual devotion and faith. Significantly, the only irresistible force which could move the immovable object was the rediscovery of the Scriptures and their study in the original languages, in order to translate them into the languages of Europe. As the weaknesses of the Church's Latin text, the Vulgate, were exposed, so the quest for a more accurate Bible led to the desire for a more authentic interpretative method, generated by the Bible itself rather than arbitrarily imposed on it by the scholars from the outside.

There is an excellent detailed essay on the history of interpretation in Klein, Blomberg and Hubbard's *Introduction to Biblical Interpretation* (1993, Word, USA) to which I am indebted for the following summary. It was Martin Luther (1483–1546) who laid down the principle of *Sola Scriptura*, that only the Bible is divinely authoritative for Christian belief and practice, and with it the affirmation that the Bible is its own best interpreter. Rejecting the medieval allegorical interpretation as 'empty speculation', Luther 'affirmed that Scripture had one simple meaning, its historical sense. This is discerned, Luther said, by applying the ordinary rules of grammar in the light of Scripture's original historical context. At the same time, Luther read the Bible through Christocentric glasses, claiming that the whole Bible – including the Old Testament – taught about Christ' (op. cit. p. 41). John Calvin (1509–64) added to Luther's conviction his own view that the 'inner witness of the Holy Spirit' within the individual Christian served to confirm the correctness of a right and valid interpretation of Scripture.

> In brief, the Reformation represented a revolutionary break with the principles of Biblical interpretation formerly practiced. Whereas previous Bible scholarship had relied on church tradition and the interpretations of the church fathers, the Reformation leaned solely on the teachings of Scripture. If the past applied allegory to dig out Scripture's alleged many meanings, the Reformers opted for Scripture's plain, simple, literal sense. (op. cit. p. 41)

But why had the Church ever lost this essential biblical perspective? The roots of an allegorical approach to the Scriptures certainly go back as far as Philo (20 BC–54 AD), a Jewish scholar who lived and worked in Alexandria, where the Septuagint had been translated two centuries earlier. In that Greek context, Philo was impressed by Plato's philosophy that behind the 'forms' of reality perceived by the senses lay the 'ideas', which were the true reality. Applying this to the Old Testament, Philo began to look for a truer, deeper meaning than the plain, literal meaning of the text. Instead of drawing out from the text its clear significance, his method imposed on the text ideas which often owed more to Greek philosophy than to the Scriptures themselves. Culturally, this was an acceptable and popular method and it certainly influenced the leaders of the early Church, known as the apostolic fathers of the second century. As their influence grew, so their interpretations handed down gained the authority of apostolic tradition. A considerable school of biblical interpretation developed in Alexandria, committed to the allegorical approach, its main exponent being the famous scholar and apologist, Origen (185–254 AD). Eventually, a contrary school developed in Antioch, in which the literal sense of the text as a way to understanding its spiritual meaning was stressed. But in spite of attempts to reconcile the two views, it was the allegorical approach which dominated the Church, though not exclusively, through the Dark Ages. It was the influence of the thirteenth-century scholar Thomas Aquinas which started to pave the way for change, as he began to restore the insistence that the literal meaning of the text was the indispensable foundation for its understanding, at any level. The weakness of the allegorical method was its subjectivity, unsupportable from the biblical context, and once the tools of reason and logic were applied to it, large question marks appeared over its very validity. It was into that context that the Reformers' revolutionary approach exploded.

Among Bible-believing Christians, the basic principles of interpretation developed during the Reformation have been applied consistently over the past five hundred years. Foremost in their formulation was the dictum that Scripture must interpret Scripture: what has been called 'the analogy of faith'. This principle is a logical deduction from the recognition that the Bible alone constitutes God's self-revelation, and that the whole Bible is therefore an entity, having one author, the Holy Spirit, and a totally consistent revelation of Truth as a result. Because God is one and because the Bible is the product of the mind of God it demonstrates a consistency and coherence which guarantee that it cannot be contradictory. Since God's nature does not change, neither do his thoughts or purposes, and therefore what he once said in Scripture he is still saying. So no part of the Bible can be properly interpreted if it is held to be in conflict with what another part clearly teaches. It is a criterion which we would apply to any human thinker and author, and it should be applied so much more, with reverence and humility, to God's expression of his mind in Scripture.

In summary, then, we begin the process of understanding the biblical text by taking the natural meaning of the words in their relationship to one another, interpreting them according to the normal rules of grammar and syntax. We do this in the immediate context of the particular passage within its own book, but also in the wider context of the Bible as a whole, allowing the clearer parts of Scripture to illuminate the more obscure, with the recognition that the existence of coherence and consistency will validate our understanding. There is nothing of the 'magical mystery tour' in our interaction with the Bible. It is a unique book in its divine inspiration, but nouns are still nouns and verbs are still verbs. Sentences are still statements, questions or commands. Normal rules still apply. It may seem to be more exciting to work out the middle word of a long biblical sentence, chapter, or even book and say that its position indicates the kernel of the meaning, but it is a silly game of which we shall soon tire. It is equally foolish to treat the Bible as a lucky-dip, opening it at random, and, with closed eyes, putting a finger somewhere on the page, so as to determine what God is saying to us. There is an old story of the seeker who was 'given' by this method 'And Judas went out and hanged himself' (Matthew 27:5), only to follow up this unpropitious beginning with a second attempt, which yielded, 'Go and do thou likewise!' It's a healthy corrective to superstition and mysticism in our handling of God's Word.

But the 'hidden' meaning revealed only to the chosen élite, the *illuminati*, still exercises a powerful attraction to our human pride. Perhaps that is what lay behind the extraordinary best-seller of 1997, *The Bible Code* by Michael Drosnin. In that, and other subsequent books on the same theme, writers have claimed to discover predictions about events in world history, which occurred long after those books were written, including assassinations, scandals, bombings and the death of Princess Diana. All of these are said to be encoded in Bible texts and are only discovered by computer searches on the principle of the 'equidistant letter sequence'. In an article entitled 'A Cracked Code', published in *Christianity Today*, 12 July 1999, Professor Ben

Witherington of Asbury Theological Seminary had some telling criticisms to make of this approach. He noted that the 'researchers' read both right to left (Hebrew) and left to right to find the codes, that the 'universally accepted Hebrew text' they claimed to have used does not in fact exist, and that what Drosnin did use was a text with the added Hebrew vowels which would not have been in the original. For a while, however, in the media and the popular imagination, this novel way of discovering the Bible's 'secret messages' was the talk of the town. 'The reality,' Witherington comments, 'is that if you use the ELS method and apply it to any sufficiently long text, you can come up with names and messages of all sorts – you just need to keep trying different distances between letters and different directions until you get lucky.' There is nothing magical about the letters, sequence or form of words by which the Bible is constructed. Everything depends on what it actually says, and to that issue we must turn next.

To remind you

- Every form of human communication has to be interpreted, so it is vital to develop good practice based on sound principles. We need to distinguish between meaning and significance (pp. 96–8).
- We need to pursue the original, intended meaning of the writer, observing grammar, vocabulary and context (pp. 99–103).
- But this is not an arid, intellectual exercise. Through it we learn to listen to God and respond to him in a personal relationship of love and obedience, expressed in prayer and action (pp. 103–6).
- At the Reformation, Martin Luther re-affirmed the principle that the Bible is its own interpreter, challenging the allegorical interpretation of the past, which was essentially subjective (pp. 106–9).
- There is nothing magical about the Bible – its contents are plain for all to see (pp. 109–10).

Chapter 6

So How Do We Unpack the Old Testament?

CHRISTINE HAD TO admit it – against all the odds she was actually enjoying the weekly Bible study group with Alison at the church. She couldn't think why she had been so suspicious of it all at the beginning. 'I suppose I thought they'd try to brainwash me,' she explained to her husband, Dan, 'but it hasn't been like that at all. In fact, they really want you to ask questions and there's no pressure at all. It's all very relaxed! Oh, and by the way, they're having an evening in a couple of weeks' time when partners are invited to come too, so you will come, won't you? There will be a supper and . . .'

Dan grunted in a non-committal sort of way. He wasn't at all sure he approved of his wife getting so interested in 'religion'. You never knew what it might lead to. 'Hold on a minute!' he said. 'Do you mean to say you think you can really understand the Bible now? You don't want to believe all they tell you at the church, you know. Oh, I don't doubt that they're sincere enough in their way, but they can be sincerely wrong.'

Christine paused. She knew there was a lot she didn't understand at all yet, but then that didn't mean she had to doubt what she had begun to grasp. It all seemed to make so much sense. 'Well, of course, there's a huge amount I don't know anything about at all, but I love those stories in the Old Testament we're studying at present. The characters seem so real and normal, and I can identify so much with them,' she replied. 'Take Gideon, who we were reading about yesterday. He needed to be really sure that God was with him and was going to do what he had promised, because he was only a young farmer and God sent his angel to commission him to save Israel from her enemies.

So he asked God for a sign. One night he put a wool fleece out, and asked God to confirm his promises by dew being only on the fleece and all the ground around it being dry. And in the morning it was exactly so. The next night he asked for the opposite, the fleece dry and the ground covered with dew. And it happened again.'

'Yes,' Dan stirred, 'I think I do remember something about that from school, in the dim and distant. So what?'

'Well,' Alison said, 'we're just like Gideon and we can find out what God wants by "putting out a fleece". She told us about a young bloke at the church who had felt sure that God wanted him to be a missionary somewhere abroad, but he didn't know where. So, one day, he put out his "fleece" and said to God that the first place he brought to his notice that morning would be the place he should go to. Well, he went to buy his paper on the way to work, and there in the newsagent's was a big display of chocolate Brazils. So he knew where he had to go!'

Dan reflected, for only a second. 'Mmmm – just as well they weren't doing a promotion on Mars bars! Oh, come off it, Christine; you can't live your life like that! Just because it happened to some character in the Bible doesn't mean it's going to happen to you.'

Christine had to admit Dan had a point and she quietly stored the question away to ask next time round. How could you be sure that you'd really got the right message? How could the Bible's meaning be unpacked? She realised there was still a great deal to explore.

Our starting point is the realisation that the Bible is written in a wide variety of literary styles, or 'genres'. Among the different kinds of literary types within its covers are stories (narrative), poems, prophetic oracles, parables, allegories, logical argument, symbolism, proverbs, dramatic dialogue and letters. Each works in its own way, according to its own conventions, and if we want rightly to understand and interpret any part of the whole, we need to be aware of the broad principles which govern the composition of each of the major biblical genres.

Old Testament narratives

Let's start with the Old Testament and with 'narrative', or story-telling, since it has been calculated that this comprises over 40 per cent of the total. It also provides some of the most exciting and dramatically involving material, which has inspired generations of other story-tellers in music, the visual arts, drama and film. Many of us will recall the excitement of Bible stories from our childhood – Moses and Pharaoh, David and Goliath, Samson and Delilah. But do the stories exist at other levels for the adult reader of the Bible? When we have relished the unexpected turn in the plot, the shiver of excitement at the unpredicted outcome or the overturning of what seemed inevitable, what are we left with?

At this point, there are two favourite ways of dealing with the story, which suggest themselves readily enough and have a degree of plausibility, but which can actually hinder us from penetrating to its deeper meaning and grasping its full value. The first is moralising. This may owe something to the Victorian Sunday-school approach, devoted to regarding the Bible as a means of instilling social ethics into young people through force of example, good or bad. I'm sure that many Sunday schools did far more than that, but the tradition of learning improving moral lessons from Bible examples is still with us. 'Abraham did this and so should we' – but not in everything. Abraham is certainly the supreme example of faith in God's promises in the Old Testament. He is the man of faith *par excellence*, except when he isn't, which Genesis is honest enough to tell us was a considerable part of the time. 'We should be like David' – but not in every way. 'We must not be like Samson' – but does he have no redeeming features? The problem with a moralising approach is that it imposes an external framework on the passage in order to extract a 'meaning'. Of course, the actions of different Bible characters do provide us with examples of what obedience or disobedience to God looks like and its repercussions, but it is not always quite so easy to decide what is to be followed and what not, as Christine discovered in the matter of Gideon's fleece. The attraction of moralising is that it seems to bring us centre-stage in the story so that the matter of relevance is quickly established. Its danger is that its focus on us may actually destroy the primary (and therefore most significant) reason for the story's inclusion in the Bible at all.

The same is true of the other approach, which is psychologising. Here the interest focuses on the character(s) *per se* and on a psychological analysis of their actions, words and motivations. The attraction is that it brings the Bible within our contemporary cultural environment, shows us that Bible people were 'just like us' (as indeed they were), but then imposes the concerns of our world on to the text, in what usually has to be a highly speculative fashion. We know that we are losing the track when inferences are drawn, without any textual justification, about why a character acted in a particular way. For example, a whole strand of 'exposition' can be woven around the idea that David was the youngest son of his father Jesse. What that meant in terms of his brothers' attitude, his own psychology as he approached kingship, reasons for his later behaviour patterns towards his own children and so on: all this becomes the focus for 'understanding' the stories. But, again, its weakness is the importing of extra-biblical criteria, which are bound to be as arbitrary as the commentator's own judgments. They may resonate with our own psychologising culture, but that is no guarantee that we are listening to what God wants to say to us through the Bible. Rather, it may show how obsessed we are at listening to ourselves, and how skilled at screening out any voices that do not sound contemporary enough to us. The biblical narrative texts have considerable amounts of detailed information and description carefully integrated into the action of the story, and we must use all of it fully to understand their meaning.

However, 'reading between the lines' is always a dubious technique and its fruit will always be highly personalised and subjective. That may appeal to our 'reader response' contemporary values, but it will not help us to get to the timeless truths of God's self-revelation, which led the Holy Spirit to inspire these words through the original author. It is, in the end, a quick and easy approach, avoiding the 'given-ness' of the text, for a more attractive and superficially relevant agenda. Unfortunately, it doesn't bring the satisfaction of the deepening knowledge of God, which was the divine intention. Reading Old Testament narrative is designed to take the focus off me and my small concerns and to put it fairly and squarely on God, and on his majestic and universal purposes. Once I begin to get that right, I can return to my little world with much greater awareness of the resources of God's faithful mercy and providential care, with my vision clarified and my faith strengthened in a way that will not happen if the focus is always on me. In their excellent book *How to Read the Bible for All Its Worth* (1983, Scripture Union), two distinguished American scholars, Gordon Fee (New Testament) and Douglas Stuart (Old Testament), address the issue in their customary incisive way. 'No Bible narrative was written specifically about you,' they instruct us. 'You can always learn a great deal from these narratives, but you can never assume that God expects you to do exactly the same things that Bible characters did; or have the same things happen to you that happened to them' (p. 85). It is a healthy and much-needed corrective.

The first step towards a right reading of Old Testament narrative is to take seriously its historicity, because this is inseparably linked to its purpose. In Chapter 2 we argued that the whole Bible is the one story of God's loving plan to undo the effects of human rebellion against his rightful authority as creator and sustainer of his world. This he began through a man (Abraham), who became a family, which grew into a nation. That nation was entrusted with the commission of carrying God's light to all the nations of the earth, but its own sinfulness fatally flawed its character and mission. Eventually, in God's mercy, he came himself as the rescuer, focusing all his promises and their fulfilment in his own Son, who, having lived a perfect life, offered himself as the acceptable and atoning sacrifice for the sins of the whole world, through his death on the cross. In his resurrection, he proved the sufficiency of his sacrifice and his victory over all the hostile powers ranged against us, even death itself, and opened to all who trust him the privilege of a restored relationship with God the Creator, as a loving heavenly Father. This relationship begins here in this world through repentance and faith, receiving his forgiveness and submitting to his rule, and lasts for eternity. If this is the 'meta-narrative' of the Bible, then it will not be a surprise to recognise that all the constituent parts, the individual narratives, relate in some way to this big picture, and fit into their own specific place, along the chronological time-line of its development.

The historicity matters, because without it we have no guarantee that the contents have any more authority than wishful thinking. What I have written in the last paragraph would all be pious whimsy if the historical events on which it centres did not in fact occur in time and space. It might still be an interesting (more or less) way of explaining life and its meaning, a religious or philosophical viewpoint, but nothing more, for it would have no objectivity outside of the individual's mind. That is actually what most people assume Christian belief today to be. But the Bible's claims are far more radical than that. Old Testament narratives are not just stories about people and nations from the ancient Middle East; they are stories about God and how he acted in the ebb and flow of history, in and through, and even for, the lives of nations and individuals, to reveal himself authoritatively and without confusion or contradiction to all humanity. The history is essential; but the theological concerns which lie behind it control and dominate the narrative accounts. The historical and theological are therefore different but parallel approaches to the same revelatory events, each supplementing the other. Neither is dispensable and they are never contradictory. As Dr Francis Schaeffer stated in the early 1980s, 'It is essential for the truth of Christianity that the Bible relates truth about history and the cosmos, as well as about spiritual matters.' What we are concluding, then, is that the story itself, in the way it is told, together with its explanation, is the message, or meaning, for which we are looking.

God as the hero

If, as Fee and Stuart affirm, 'God is the hero of all Biblical narratives,' then his activity must be the key ingredient in every story-line. 'What does this story tell me about the character and purposes of God?' is an important foundation discovery to pursue in every narrative account, because that will provide both the clue to its central purpose and also the unifying principle around which its many different ingredients revolve. Of course, this information does not always sit on the surface of the story. The narrator may weave a tale of some subtlety, in which we have to be alert to follow the clues and draw the appropriate deductions. But those deductions must always be text-related and therefore capable of objective justification. However, as I observe the role of God in the story, I find it valuable to have in mind three separate 'levels' (or we might call them 'contexts') on which he is operating. They are closely inter-related, rather in the way that Russian dolls fit into one another. Largest and most significant is God working out his salvation-history plan for the whole human race, so I call that 'the big picture'. Next, because that plan focuses in the Old Testament on the nation of Israel, there will be a 'national level'. Israel is bound to God as her covenant lord, so in her community-life and relationship with him, much of God's character and purposes are revealed, as he makes and fulfils his promises. Third, within the covenant community there are individuals to whom God specifically relates, with whom he is particularly at work. I call this the individual, or personal, level of the story, dependent for its interpretation on understanding the first two levels properly. It is here that the temptation to put ourselves in the human figure's shoes is strongest, but we have to keep reminding ourselves that we are not Moses, for example, any more than we are Pharaoh. For which we may be thankful! We can learn from the observation of how the changeless character of God is revealed in relating with more or less sinful people, who are human like us, even though their uniqueness in circumstances or character does not directly apply to our very different context.

If these reflections help us to think about a story as a unit and to begin to explore its purpose in the scheme of the whole Bible, we need also to approach it as a literary construction and to give some thought to the ingredients of which it is made up. Story-telling is a universal art, and one in which the familiarity of technique does not make it at all threadbare. Children's stories are very instructive in this regard. What makes the three little pigs or Goldilocks and the three bears of huge delight to successive generations of children is the 'buzz' that comes when the third member of the trio bucks the trend and reverses what we have come to accept as the inevitable. It could be argued, surely legitimately, that the parables of the talents or the Good Samaritan work in exactly the same way. But every story has to build to a climax, frequently an unexpected turning-point, which is literally the reason for the story being told at all. This is especially true of story-telling in an oral, rather than written, form, which is how biblical narratives would have started their lives. Unlike modern written prose, which depends on a continuous and related flow of ideas, stated, explained, proved, by evidence, and always pressing on to its conclusion, biblical story-tellers have time to vary their pace, to give attention to relevant detail, to develop repeated phrases or ideas for emphasis, and so to lead up to the critical turning-point. Their approach is geared to the trained ear of the experienced listener, where every phrase or nuance is significant. Usually, at the heart of the story, though it may not be highlighted as such, there occurs a turning-point, or a central idea, around which, we come to recognise, the whole story revolves.

Turning points

That is what makes any story worth telling. Take a simple sentence – 'The book, which I really wanted, was on the top shelf.' The tension is built into this sentence, which might be the beginning of a story, in two ways – the need for the book is in conflict with its inaccessibility.

The story that follows will have to resolve that tension. The question that is sown in our minds is, 'How is the book to be obtained?' It might be resolved in a perfectly matter-of-fact, normal way. It could continue, '. . . so I moved the steps over to the shelves, climbed up and took it', or '. . . so I asked the librarian to fetch it for me, which she did'. That *is* a story, but hardly one worth the telling, because there is nothing unusual, dramatic, comic, or even tragic, about the resolution of the conflict. However, other alternatives will doubtless have come into your mind, which might include mounting an expedition of mountaineering proportions to scale the bookshelves and retreating with broken limbs, defeated. It may be only marginally more interesting, but at least it would be more of a story worth telling. The interest in story-telling and listening usually resides in how the conflict, or tension, at the narrative's heart comes to be resolved, and in biblical terms this is often the key to understanding the central meaning and ongoing significance of the story, to God's people, in every generation.

It may be helpful at this point to look at a specific example in order to see these principles working out. I have chosen a story which is very carefully and clearly constructed, and also one which is comparatively unknown, so that we do not bring too developed a prior understanding to it.

After Rehoboam's position as king was established and he had become strong, he and all Israel with him abandoned the law of the LORD. Because they had been unfaithful to the LORD, Shishak king of Egypt attacked Jerusalem in the fifth year of King Rehoboam. With twelve hundred chariots and sixty thousand horsemen and the innumerable troops of Libyans, Sukkites and Cushites that came with him from Egypt, he captured the fortified cities of Judah and came as far as Jerusalem. Then the prophet Shemaiah came to Rehoboam and to the leaders of Judah who had assembled in Jerusalem for fear of Shishak, and he said to them, 'This is what the LORD says: "You have abandoned me; therefore I now abandon you to Shishak."' The leaders of Israel and the king humbled themselves and said, 'The LORD is just.' When the LORD saw that they humbled themselves, this word of the LORD came to Shemaiah: 'Since they have humbled themselves, I will not destroy them but will soon give them deliverance. My wrath will not be poured out on Jerusalem through Shishak. They will, however, become subject to him, so that they may learn the difference between serving me and serving the kings of other lands.' When Shishak king of Egypt attacked Jerusalem, he carried off the treasures of the temple of the LORD and the treasures of the royal palace. He took everything, including the gold shields that Solomon had made. So King Rehoboam made bronze shields to replace them and assigned these to the commanders of the guard on duty at the entrance to the royal palace. Whenever the king went to the LORD's temple, the guards went with him, bearing the shields, and afterwards they returned them to the guard-room. Because Rehoboam humbled himself, the LORD's anger turned from him, and he was not totally destroyed. Indeed, there was some good in Judah. (2 Chronicles 12:1–12)

A contemporary reader might very well ask what meaning this historical narrative can possibly have for today. To answer the question we have to begin with an analysis of the way the story itself is constructed. It begins with an editorial, or narrator's comment, which explains the situation in Israel (Judah) at the time and provides the foundation on which the story is subsequently built. The tension is there from the outset. The king and all the people have 'abandoned the law of the LORD' (v. 1). What will happen? The answer lies in the attack of Shishak, king of Egypt. This is not accidental, or even coincidental, but is theologically attributed quite uncompromisingly to Israel's unfaithfulness (v. 2a). From verse 2b to verse 9 tells the story, in several scenes. An enormous Egyptian force, supplemented by his allies, led by Shishak, sweeps into Judah, mops up the fortified cities designed to block the aggressor's way to the capital, and presents itself at Jerusalem (v. 4). Surely the city must fall. That is how the tension of verse 1 will be resolved. But there is a sudden intervention, in the human form of the prophet, Shemaiah, although clearly its origin really lies with the Lord. He sends the prophet because he has given him the divine message, which seems one of hopeless judgment (v. 5) – 'I now abandon you to Shishak'. What looked as though it might provide a way out for Jerusalem, perhaps through a message of divine deliverance, has hit a brick wall. But then there is a second surprise reaction. Both the king and the leaders submit themselves to God's justice, humbling themselves before him (v. 6). This is quite unexpected (cf. v. 1), but it proves to be the turning point, the resolution, of the whole issue. Notice the causal connection in verse 7a, 'When the LORD saw that they humbled themselves . . .' Another prophetic message comes through Shemaiah (vv. 7–8) promising that Jerusalem will not be destroyed, but delivered. However, Judah will become Egypt's vassal, so that King Rehoboam and his people will 'learn the difference between serving me and serving the kings of other lands' (v. 8). That, of course, was the contention highlighted in verse 1. They did not want to have to serve the Lord. Shishak does attack; the temple is looted of all Solomon's gold treasures and Rehoboam is left to replace the royal shields with bronze, a constant reminder of his reduced state due to his rebellious disobedience. Matching the introduction of verse 1, verse 12 provides the narrator's summary conclusion, in which the theological significance of the narrative is driven home. 'Because Rehoboam humbled himself, the LORD's anger turned from him.'

The critical turning point is easy to identify. At the heart of the story lies the affirmation of previously rebellious people that the LORD (the covenant name – Yahweh) is just. They had previously abandoned his law because they did not find it 'just' or acceptable; they wanted to be free of the character of the God who had brought them into a covenant relationship with himself. But repentance (implied in their confession) and humble submission of themselves to God turned the tide of their circumstances. The seemingly inevitable destruction of the city did not occur, because the faithful covenant LORD delivered his people, when they cast themselves on his mercy. The key meaning of the story then, as Rehoboam doubtless recalled whenever he saw the bronze shields, is that God is just. He is faithful and dependable. He abandons those who abandon him, as he said he would, but he defends those who truly repent.

So, what of the three levels? On the 'big picture' time-line of God's salvation-history plan, we are at the beginning of the decline of the Davidic monarchy. The kingdom has already been divided and Rehoboam (Solomon's heir) is left with only Judah to rule over. Though for three years he walked in God's ways (2 Chronicles 11:17), yet, as verse 1 of the story shows, his comparatively established position quickly seduced him into an arrogant independence from God and his law. It is one of many reminders of the inadequacy of any human king to provide stability for the people of God, due to each individual's own inherent sinfulness. When Israel begged God for a king (1 Samuel 8) God revealed that at the root of their request was a rejection of him as their ruler, and we are being taught that only as they return to God's kingly rule can they be secure. In whole Bible terms, that kingly rule is fulfilled in Jesus Christ, and it is by submission to his authority that we enter into and enjoy all the benefits of the eternal kingdom of God. But the new covenant also contains its own requirements, and its grace never sanctions disobedience to God's instruction or development of our independence from him. These are issues of relevance to everyday life, for both the Church and the individual Christian. We have already slid into the national or covenant picture of the narrative. The lesson of attack and deprivation as a consequence of abandoning God, but that repentance secures God's mercy, is a constant biblical theme. Third, on the individual level, Rehoboam learns that though as king and representative of his people he has been made strong by God's goodness, if he is to continue to enjoy God's favour he must be obedient personally. The fact that he is the king does not exclude him from the responsibility of a personal life of devotion to, and dependence on, the LORD. The continuing message of the narrative is that we cannot play games with God. Heart-reality, demonstrated in faith and humble obedience, is his requirement for those who are in relationship with him. Our choices do determine the outcome of our lives, and perhaps in the emphasis on the bronze instead of gold, directly attributable to Rehoboam's rebellion, we are being given a warning that although God is gracious to forgive, we are not always spared the consequences of our foolish rebellion, so that we learn not to serve other masters.

This approach to Old Testament narrative accords with the emphases the Bible itself makes in its story-telling. One of its most extended and detailed is the story of Joseph, occupying most of chapters 37 to 50 of the book of Genesis. Undoubtedly, there is much that we can learn about God and the individual throughout the saga, but its aim is not primarily to encourage us to resist temptation, as Joseph did, or to bear adversity patiently, as Joseph did, or even to deal mercifully with those who have maltreated us, as Joseph did. For Joseph is not the hero of the story, but God is, and there are key verses which make that perspective abundantly clear. As Joseph reveals his identity as chief minister of Pharaoh to his bewildered, guilty brothers, he affirms, 'it was to save lives that God sent me ahead of you . . . to preserve for you a remnant on earth and to save your lives by a great deliverance. So then, it was not you who sent me here, but God' (Genesis 45:5–8). When those same brothers prostrate themselves before him as his slaves, he responds, 'Don't be afraid. Am I in the place of God? You intended to harm me, but God intended it for good to accomplish what is now being done, the saving of many lives' (Genesis 50:19–20). All the intricate details of Joseph's relations with his brothers are seen to be part of a greater salvation plan, mirrored in the preservation of the descendants of Abraham from starvation, through Joseph's wise work in Egypt, but coming to its fruition in their development as a great nation within that land and God's mighty exodus deliverance through his servant Moses, centuries later. The emphasis in Genesis is not that 'any dream will do' for a budding Joseph and that it will all come good in the end, but that God will work out his purposes in fulfilment of his promises and no force on earth will be able to hinder or divert him.

Such God-centredness matches the Christ-centredness of the New Testament's view of the Old, articulated by Jesus himself when he affirmed, 'These are the Scriptures that testify about me' (John 5:39). The same emphasis can be seen in the writer of the books of Samuel, reviewing the long biographical narratives of the life of King David, where the keys to understanding the significance of the narratives are all in God-centred terms. Following David's adultery with Bathsheba and the murder of her husband Uriah, a son is born, 'but the thing David had done displeased the LORD' (2 Samuel 11:27). The succeeding narrative of the almost total disintegration of David's family house is governed by God. Solomon is born and preserved as David's eventual heir because 'the LORD loved him' (2 Samuel 12:24–5). Although Absalom determines to overthrow his father and seize the throne, 'the LORD had determined to frustrate the good advice of Ahithophel in order to bring disaster on Absalom' (2 Samuel 17:14). So God is the chief player in the drama, and it is his will that is constantly being carried through. He is therefore the chief explainer of his actions, and when we are given such clear indications as to where the emphasis lies and what God's purposes are, we would be foolish to ignore them.

The power of poetry

From story-telling in narrative prose, we turn now to the second most common literary form in the Old Testament, which is poetry. 'Poetry' doubtless generates a wide variety of responses in our contemporary context. Much recent poetry written in the English language has a name for being opaque, intellectual, theoretical, deliberately confused and confusing. The lines seem to be of indeterminate length, rhyme no longer exists and the connections between ideas often seem inaccessible. That is certainly a widespread popular perception and it needs seriously to be taken into account, since many Bible readers are likely to import their negative presuppositions into their first encounters with the poetic text. Most readers do not come to poetry agog with expectation. Yet children love the intoxication of rhythm and rhyme, find it easy and delightful to memorise and enjoy revisiting the familiar favourites over and over again. The ability of verse, especially when coupled with music, to generate and give expression to the deepest human emotions is still a part of life, whether demonstrated in a love song or a football 'anthem', a pop concert or a choral symphony. If we can set aside any negative predisposition towards poetry and let the biblical material speak for itself, we shall find that it communicates at the deepest levels of our humanness still.

Hebrew poetry works in rhythm rather than rhyme. This is a help in translation, since if rhyme at the end of lines were the clinching factor it would be very difficult to translate. To most English ears, the rhyme at the end of a couplet completes and focuses the rhythmic pattern. Take, for example, the New International Version's translation of Psalm 19:9. It reads:

> The fear of the LORD is pure, enduring for ever,
> The ordinances of the LORD are sure and altogether righteous.

In this version we can detect something of the rhythmic structure of the two halves of the verse. Each begins with a statement in the same verbal pattern, 'The . . . of the LORD is . . .' and concludes with an explanatory phrase, indicating a further reason for the statement. But just a very small change to introduce a rhyme, to which English ears are attuned, helps us to pick up the rhythmic parallel much more clearly.

> The fear of the LORD is pure, enduring for ever,
> The ordinances of the LORD are sure and righteous altogether.

The rhyme binds the couplet together, to our ears, which is not the case in the first version. Of course, the translators have made their choice quite properly because the potential rhyme is an accident of English translation, not an intention of the Hebrew author, but the danger is that we miss the distinctive rhythmic effects of the original and drift into regarding the poetry as merely a slightly variant form of prose.

It is helpful, then, to note some of the key poetic devices of the biblical poets, of which parallelism is perhaps the chief characteristic. This is readily visible in our English Bibles where verse after verse is regularly printed in two sections, the second each time indented. The essence of parallelism is that there is a proposition first stated, which is then explained further, or perhaps contrasted, in the second half of the verse. The similarity in structure and form helps to drive home the point, but it is particularly to the differences that the focus of our attention is drawn. Parallelism is not mere repetition. Take, for example, Psalm 24:1.

> The earth is the LORD's, and everything in it,
> the world, and all who live in it

The second half of the verse deepens our understanding of the first proposition by focusing on ourselves as an integral part of the 'everything' that is owned by God. The implications are considerable, and the genius of the poetry is that it makes the point with a striking conciseness and penetration so that we are forced to take these implications on board and think them through as the poem develops. Two verses later, aware of the inevitable relationship with God which every human being has by virtue of our creation, we are asking with the psalmist, 'Who may ascend the hill of the LORD? Who may stand in his holy place?' – another powerful parallelism.

Although rhyme is not part of Hebrew poetry, assonance (a correspondence in sound) is. Points are often made by two words of similar sound, featuring in successive lines, in explanation of, or contrast with, one another. We are used to puns in English, which are points made by bringing together words which are alike or nearly alike in sound, but quite different in meaning. So Hebrew poetry will often make its point by juxtaposing two very similarly sounding words, but with very different meanings. A vivid example comes from Isaiah 5:7, where God compares his people, Israel, to a vineyard, planted, nourished and protected, but, instead of providing a crop of good grapes, yielding only bad fruit. His conclusion is expressed in the couplet:

> And he looked for justice, but saw bloodshed;
>   for righteousness, but heard cries of distress.

A transliteration of the Hebrew text reads

> And he looked for *mishpat* and behold *mispach*
>   for *tsedaqah* and behold *tse'aqah*.

Clearly the similarity of the sounds, coupled with the enormous contrast of meaning, combine poetically to make the point powerfully, and with much more penetration than our factual, but rather lame, English translations can achieve. It is difficult for us to pick up these nuances, though commentaries which work with reference to the Hebrew text are a great resource in helping us to get back into the position of the original hearers.

A poem exists as a single unit of expression, complete in itself. It may belong to a sequence of compositions, but it has its own life and structure, reflecting and conveying its own unique message. That separate unit, the poem, is also a totality and must be treated as such. Just as a prose paragraph of logical argument builds step by step to its conclusion, and none of those ingredients should be separated from its context or treated in isolation, so a poem is complete in itself, and none of its building blocks should be torn from the finished construction. To pick a verse out of a psalm, for example, and to deal with it on its own without relating it to the rest of the poem and understanding why it is there may make us guilty of taking the text out of its context to construct a pretext. Each poem is in itself its own context. This means that discovering the major purpose of its composition is an important exercise in coming to understand and appreciate its meaning today. For example, this treatment is often meted out to Psalm 46:10, 'Be still, and know that I am God.' Torn out of its context, it is used as a 'settling' verse in congregational worship. 'We have come from busy lives, lived in a frantic culture, into the presence of God, and now we just need to be still, to stop . . . listen to yourself breathe again, clear your mind of everything that clutters it, and in the emptiness and stillness know that God is God.' The verse has become part of the stock-in-trade of the 'worship' leader. Irrespective of the general truth or wisdom of the comments above, it is not what Psalm 46:10 means in its context. 'Be still' is not a gentle invitation but an imperious command. It means 'Stop fighting! Lay down your arms!' and the way you do that is by submitting to the Godness of God. The context is of a world in cataclysmic upheaval, both physically (earthquakes and tidal waves, vv. 2–3) and politically (nations in uproar, kingdoms falling, v. 6), yet through it all, in war, desolations (v. 8) and peace (v. 9), God is sovereign. He is God, exalted among the nations and in the earth. It is useless to fight against him, so lay down your arms, and submit, and in so doing you will find the Lord of hosts is your fortress and strength. It is the whole focus that provides us with the message, which, as always, is much deeper and stronger than our own little world of cosy comfort and self-indulgence, and which, rightly understood, nerves us to live with God, in the real world, with all its challenges, struggles and enigmas.

However, while it is true that the poem is a unit and must always be treated as such, the unit can be analysed and better understood as a whole by appreciating the individual ingredients and how they have been put together. In Psalm 46, which we have just looked at, the Hebrew word *selah* occurs on three occasions, in our English translations at the end of verses 3, 7 and 11. Clearly, it is a marker-post dividing up the thought-content of the poem. Its precise meaning is uncertain and its function may have been primarily musical, but it occurs over seventy times in the psalms and is one of the ways in which we can observe the poems' structures. The use of refrains, lines or phrases which recur, especially at the end of sections, is another way in which a poem can be divided up into segments or stanzas. For example, the question 'Why are you downcast, O my soul? Why so disturbed within me?' is asked in Psalms 42 and 43 on three occasions, and in the view of many scholars binds the two psalms together as originally one unit. Another poetic device (used in Psalms 9–10, 25, 34, 37, 111, 112, 119 and 145) is the acrostic, in which the first letters of each succeeding verse follow chronologically through the order of the Hebrew alphabet. In Psalm 119 (the longest of all the psalms) this is worked out section by section, and most English translations head the successive sections with the appropriate Hebrew letter. But perhaps the most common and effective device is what is known as the 'chiasm', where the point is made by contrast, through a reversed parallelism. A typical English example of this stylistic device could be, 'Do not live to eat, but eat to live.' Our attention is secured by the inversion of the order so that the emphasis falls on the second half. Psalm 33:6 provides a good example. The pattern of thought can be represented ab b, a,

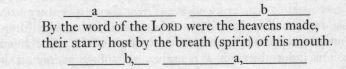

By the word of the LORD were the heavens made,
their starry host by the breath (spirit) of his mouth.

In a striking reference to the dawn of creation, the Word of God and the Spirit of God are identified as totally united in the command that made the heavens.

Using the psalms

Most Old Testament poetry is to be found in the prophetic oracles, which we shall consider as a genre in the next chapter, and in the psalms, to which we now need to turn our attention. They are, of course, very different from anything else in the Bible. Throughout this book, the concept that the Bible is the Word of God, spoken by him to people, has been central. We can see how that happens in propositional statements, narratives which reveal God's character and purposes, laws and commands, but the psalms are human words spoken (or sung) to God and to our fellow human beings. Fee and Stuart pose the challenge well when they ask, 'How do these words spoken *to* God function as a word *from* God to us?' (op. cit. p. 169). Their conclusion is that while the psalms' major purpose is to teach neither doctrine nor moral behaviour, they do provide an authoritative model both of reflection on God and his ways, and also of expression, by which we can learn how to relate the circumstances of our lives to God, in words. In similar vein, Eugene Peterson finds in the psalms the answer to his question, 'Where can we go to learn *our* language, as it develops into maturity, as it answers God?' (*Working the Angles*, 1993, Eerdmans). In the psalms and their divine inspiration, we have, then, God's authoritative model of the variety of ways in which we may rightly respond to him, corporately and individually, in praise and in prayer. The collection of 150 poems we call the Psalter, the book of Psalms, is rightly often referred to as the hymn book or the prayer book of Old Testament Israel, of Jesus and, through him, of the Church. As Athanasius is said to have expressed it, while most of Scripture speaks *to* us, the psalms also speak *for* us. They give us language by which we can answer God's initiating speech and enter into conversation, which deepens our relationship with him.

The types of response which individual psalms exemplify have led to a great deal of scholarly endeavour over the past century to categorise the different sorts of material, not according to author or general subject matter, but to the life situation which gave the poem birth. This is not an attempt to relate, say, each of the psalms of David to specific events recorded in the biblical histories of his life, but a recognition of dominant literary forms which were appropriate for response to God, in specific circumstances. So, there are psalms of individual and also national thanksgiving – for deliverance from sickness, enemies, antagonists, for victory in battle, for God's faithfulness to his covenant commitment. There are also general praise psalms, as for example the 'Hallelujah' sequence (145–150) with which the Psalter ends, the aim of which is to declare and celebrate the Lord's goodness, manifested both in the natural world and in the history of the covenant people. Private thanksgiving and communal praise unite together with a renewed invitation to the hearer to 'extol the LORD with all my heart' (Psalm 111:1). But there are also many psalms, categorised as 'laments', which provide words with which to come to God when the skies are black and life is threatening. A large number of these are individual, in which the psalmist turns to God in a situation of great need, or affliction. They are punctuated by urgent cries for help, specific prayers for deliverance, and contain the honest outpouring of the soul as the distressing circumstances are laid out before God. Sometimes the very description of distress is an implicit admission of guilt and preparation for penitence, as in Psalm 51, King David's prayer of repentance. But often the distress is that of unjust accusation, or undeserved suffering, where the problem is agonisingly dissected and explained, with resolution being found only in the dependable faithfulness of God, whatever the circumstances. Similarly, there are many national laments, prompted by defeat in war, plague, drought or other economic disasters, expressing repentance and calling on God for deliverance. Related to these are other psalms of confidence in which faith holds on to God's rescuing grace. The categorisation of psalms is a never-ending activity, but beyond the labels – royal psalms, messianic psalms, wisdom psalms, liturgical poems, canticles of Zion and many more – the right understanding and use of their content is what should govern our reading.

So how are we to go about things? First, we need to treat the particular poem as a literary unit, in its own right, and explore its content with the usual range of analytical questions. What is this psalm, or poetic oracle, about? What range of meaning exists in it, and where does the emphasis fall? It is often helpful to try to express the theme of the poem in a single sentence. Once we have grasped its main import or message, we can begin to benefit from its depth and subtlety by seeing how the details fit together. So we shall be asking how the points which flow together are related to each other and how they contribute to the main theme. This will prompt us to look at the pictures that are drawn, the metaphors that are employed, and how these work together, not just to produce an intellectual understanding of the subject-matter, but a personal and emotional involvement with it. For that is the genius of poetry. If we simply look at a psalm, abstract its cognitive content and express it in prose, we have destroyed the poetry. Our relationship with God is not simply one of cold doctrine, or of intellectual comprehension, but of personal interaction, of loving God with all our heart, soul, mind and strength, and the psalms provide us with a model for our affections and their expression. We must not destroy their warmth, their immediacy of relationship, their essential humanity, by putting them through a systematic theology mincing-machine and coming out with a depersonalised statement of propositional truth. God did not cause them to be written in that way.

Pointing to Jesus

There is one other important element to remember, so obvious, perhaps, that it appears to be frequently overlooked – namely, that the psalms belong to the era before Christ's coming. This means that they anticipate the fulfilment of God's purposes which the Messiah will bring, and that for us today, they must be interpreted in the light of the gospel. Indeed, Jesus applied the messianic predictions to himself and the apostles extended an ever wider range of references to Christ. There are three key psalms (2, 45 and 110) in which these concepts are focused and which can therefore serve as a summary for their significant interpretative insight. In Psalm 2, the rebellious world rulers are discovered plotting against God and 'his Anointed One' (v. 2) – the word is 'messiah'. The term refers to the separation by God of an individual to a holy status and resulting task. This is accompanied by a public act of anointing, indicating empowerment for the role, as in the case of a new king or high priest. So the anointed is also referred to by God as 'my King' (v. 6) and 'You are my Son; today I have become your Father' (v. 7). He is the one to whom rule over all the nations is given. There is a sense in which this was partially fulfilled by at least the godly kings in David's line, as they depended on God as Father and ruled invested with his authority, but their sinful, human nature meant that they could never adequately fulfil the image of the perfect Son, who would rule over all humanity. In Psalm 45, in the context of a royal wedding psalm, the king is addressed as 'God' ('Your throne, O God, will last for ever and ever' v. 6), though in the very next verse his subservience to God is also recognised ('Your God has set you above your companions by anointing you' v. 7). How can the two be reconciled? Finally, in Psalm 110, the king is seated at the LORD's right hand, as universal conqueror (v. 1) and further is invested with eternal priesthood, not in the line of Aaron and the Levites, but in the order of Melchizedek, the priest-king of Genesis 14:18ff, who blessed Abraham (v. 4). In these capacities the king will 'crush kings on the day of his wrath' and 'judge nations' (v. 5–6). Although these psalms use the language of earthly kingship in its Davidic, Jerusalem context, clearly no king of Israel began to fulfil these divine qualities, so that the psalms were increasingly attributed to the coming great King, great David's greater Son, the Messiah. It was in these terms that Jesus taught his disciples to see that he was spoken of. He is not only David's Son, but his Lord (Psalm 110 and Matthew 22:41–6). He is the one seated at God's right hand as ruler and judge of all, confirmed by his resurrection (Hebrews 1:3, 13). He is the firstborn who is worthy of worship even by the angels of heaven (Psalms 2, 45 and Hebrews 1:5, 8–9).

There are many other ways in which Jesus showed the fulfilment of everything that is written about him in the psalms (Luke 24:44), supremely in his crucifixion, where the details of his death foretold in Psalm 22 were amazingly fulfilled and where he identified himself as the rejected stone of Psalm 118:22–3 whom God has exalted to the position of capstone (Matthew 21:42ff). It is highly significant that Psalm 118 is itself the last of a sequence of psalms from 113 onward, known as the Egyptian Hallel, which celebrated the exodus and were sung at the end of the Passover feast. It was with these very words ringing in his ears that Jesus went out from the Upper Room to the Garden of Gethsemane, to his betrayal, passion and death, as the enactment of all that the psalmist had foreshadowed. That surely is Matthew's point when he tells us that following the inauguration of the new covenant in his blood, at the end of the last supper, with his disciples, 'When they had sung a hymn, they went out to the Mount of Olives' (Matthew 26:30). The psalms provide us with great resources for our Christian pilgrimage, in understanding God's faithful character and the majestic sweep of his eternal purposes more clearly, in seeing the glories of Christ, foreshadowed here, and shining from the pages of the gospels, in giving us perspective on the ups and downs of our human experience, 'the changing scenes of life', but especially in providing us with words with which to come to God ourselves, in all of life's circumstances. Calvin was right when he described them as 'an anatomy of all the parts of the soul'. God has given these words as authoritative patterns and examples for us, but it is as we take them into our hearts, making their praise the substance of our worship, their obedient submission the expression of our souls, their joyful acceptance of God's free grace and reliance on his faithful, steadfast love the fabric of our lives, that we know the happiness of the man who stands at the entrance to the Psalter, whose 'delight is in the law of the LORD [on which] he meditates day and night. He is like a tree planted by streams of water, which yields its fruit in season and whose leaf does not wither. Whatever he does prospers' (Psalm 1:2–3).

The wisdom literature

For life to prosper like that, in every area, is the goal of the wise man, which leads us to our third and last category of Old Testament literature in this chapter, which is usually designated 'wisdom'. This material is found in the 'writings' and particularly in the books of Job, Proverbs and Ecclesiastes. Of course, even in these three books there is a very wide range of literary styles, ranging from the dramatic dialogues of Job to the popular, pithy aphorisms of Proverbs and the extended reflective essay-form of Ecclesiastes. But wisdom material is also found in the historical sections of the Old Testament, as in the parables of Jotham (Judges 9:7–21) or Nathan (2 Samuel 12:1–12), in the prophets, as in the proverbial nature of passages like

Isaiah 28:23–9, and in the psalms, such as Psalm 49's reflection on the relative values of wealth and poverty in time and eternity, or Psalm 73's grappling with the riddle of the prosperity of the wicked. The genre of wisdom sayings and wise teachers is probably as old as writing itself. Certainly, it stretches back well into the second millennium BC in the cultures of Mesopotamia and Egypt. But the quality of biblical wisdom is very different in content, even though the material may be presented in a similar stylistic package. The difference, quite simply, is that of revelation. Hebrew wisdom writers are not groping after the good life; they are expounding it. 'For the LORD gives wisdom, and from his mouth come knowledge and understanding' (Proverbs 2:6).

At the heart of the wisdom literature, therefore, is the conviction that God has spoken to reveal his character and will, and that such knowledge is the foundation for life to be lived as a creature made in his image in the world he has created. 'The fear of the LORD is the beginning of knowledge, but fools despise wisdom and discipline' (Proverbs 1:7). So the world of human beings is divided into the wise and foolish, the righteous and the wicked. The former categories accept the world as God has made it, in all its 'givenness' and, with it, his self-revelation in the Torah. For them, this becomes the yard-stick of their values and life-style. The latter will not let God be God, either in their own lives or in the world. They spend their time fighting against the structures of reality, denying God's existence, ignoring their Maker's instructions and trying to construct their own independent pseudo-reality, barricaded against God. The distinctive of wisdom literature is that it applies the revelation of the Torah to the practical questions of everyday life in God's world, grappling with the seeming contradictions, and honestly facing the problems which living God's way can seem to generate. In short, wisdom consists in applying the Bible's teachings to every circumstance of daily life.

> I, wisdom, dwell together with prudence; I possess knowledge and discretion.
> To fear the LORD is to hate evil; I hate pride and arrogance, evil behaviour and perverse speech.
> Counsel and sound judgment are mine; I have understanding and power.

> By me kings reign and rulers make laws that are just; by me princes
> govern, and all nobles who rule on earth.
> I love those who love me, and those who seek me find me.
> With me are riches and honour, enduring wealth and prosperity.
> My fruit is better than fine gold; what I yield surpasses choice
> silver.
> I walk in the way of righteousness, along the paths of justice,
> bestowing wealth on those who love me and making their
> treasuries full. (Proverbs 8:12–21)

The great example of the wise king is Solomon, whose name is
inscribed at the entrance to the book of Proverbs. On his accession to
the throne, when invited by God to 'ask for whatever you want me to
give you', Solomon shows that he already has wisdom by asking for 'a
discerning heart to govern your people and to distinguish between
right and wrong' (1 Kings 3:4–14). God answers his request by
making him wiser than any other king, and from the outset of his
reign, the nation 'held the king in awe because they saw that he had
wisdom from God' (1 Kings 3:28). Solomon becomes the archetypal
'wise man', but the emphasis is constantly on this being God's gift,
not his natural ability. 'God gave Solomon wisdom and very great
insight, and a breadth of understanding as measureless as the sand on
the seashore' (1 Kings 4:29). This included three thousand proverbs
and a thousand and five songs, as well as extensive knowledge of plant
and animal life – a deep awareness and understanding of the whole
created order – as the next few verses show. But not only is covenant
Israel the beneficiary of such royal wisdom from God, his fame
spreads around the world and the Gentile nations begin to share in
these blessings to the children of Abraham. The classic example is the
visit of the Queen of Sheba, herself fabulously rich, to Solomon's
court to talk to him 'about all she had on her mind'. Her conclusion,
after all her questions have been answered by the king, is memorable.
'I did not believe these things until I came and saw with my own eyes.
Indeed, not even half was told me: in wisdom and wealth you have far
exceeded the report I heard' (1 Kings 10:1–9).

There is no doubt that this is to be seen as the highest point of the
monarchy in Israel. Solomon, 'in all his splendour', as Jesus described
him (Matthew 6:29), reigns over a united Israel, in great wealth, giving
his people rest from their enemies and receiving homage and

admiration from the kings of the earth. He recognises that all this is God's gracious gift and acknowledges, as the magnificent Jerusalem temple he has built is dedicated to the Lord, 'Not one word has failed of all the good promises [the LORD] gave through his servant Moses' (1 Kings 8:56). Things do not get any better for Old Testament Israel than this. Psalm 72, entitled 'Of Solomon', celebrates his reign as the climax of the second book of the Psalter. Intriguingly, it picks up the promise made by God to Abraham in Genesis 12:2–3 that 'all peoples on earth will be blessed through you', and affirms its fulfilment in King Solomon, concluding, 'All nations will be blessed through him, and they will call him blessed' (Psalm 72:17). But the sad reality is that not only was Solomon merely mortal, so he could never fulfil the eternal kingship role, but also he was sinful, and in spite of his enormous wisdom, the reign of splendour ended in tragedy. Having married many foreign wives, as Solomon grew old his heart was turned after their own pagan deities and a policy of syncretism began to creep into his religious practice. Although God had appeared to him twice, his heart turned away, and the greatness of the privilege he disregarded and even spurned required an equivalent severity of judgment to be pronounced:

> Since this is your attitude and you have not kept my covenant and my decrees, which I commanded you, I will most certainly tear the kingdom away from you and give it to one of your subordinates. Nevertheless, for the sake of David your father, I will not do it during your lifetime. I will tear it out of the hand of your son. (1 Kings 11:11–12)

The divided kingdom and the long, painful decline to the destruction of Israel and the exile of Judah is the agenda of the rest of the Old Testament.

What had happened that the 'wise king' erred so disastrously? The answer is that he was a fallen, sinful human being like anyone else. While he was totally dependent on God, he sailed the straight course of wisdom; but as soon as he began to rely on himself and to choose his own ways, perhaps through over-confidence, he drifted on to the rocks. Perhaps it is that very tragedy that gives the wisdom literature its urgency, for these issues are not just those facing a great king, they are the issues of life for every man and every woman. The monarchy, even at its peak, was no lasting solution for the problems of Israel's sinful heart, nor for the fallenness of the pagan nations, snared in the blindness of their idolatry. Something more was needed. It would require a king whose own character was perfectly obedient to God's revelation, flawless in righteousness, and so able to rule consistently in total wisdom. This king would be the seed of Abraham and a blessing to all the nations as he gathered a new international people of God, comprised of all who would receive his word and submit to his wisdom. And this fulfilment came when Jesus Christ declared, 'The Queen of the South will rise at the judgment with this generation and condemn it; for she came from the ends of the earth to listen to Solomon's wisdom, and now one greater than Solomon is here' (Matthew 12:42). It is wisdom to hear and obey him.

We can only sketch an outline of the three main wisdom books here, but, at the risk of over-simplification, it is perhaps helpful to think of them like this. The book of Proverbs is the basic wisdom text. It brings the whole of life into the presence of God and the Torah, to learn how to live according to his revealed will. Since this will be the way human beings function best, there is an unashamed appeal to the 'good life' emanating from wisdom. Obedience to God is always best. But this is not just a matter of social or personal expediency, it is because God is sovereign and because of his perfectly right character that living God's way (wisdom) works. However, it would be a mistake to absolutise the proverbs and turn them into promises which God is required to fulfil in every detail. Klein, Blomberg and Hubbard have a very helpful and pertinent paragraph, from which it is worth quoting.

> [The Proverbs] point out patterns of conduct that, if followed, give one the best chance of success. In other words, they offer general principles for successful living rather than a comprehensive 'legal code for life'. Further, Proverbs place a higher premium on etching themselves on one's memory than on theoretical accuracy. That is, their primary goal is to state an important, simple truth about life in easy-to-remember terms. Hence, they do not intend to cover every imaginable circumstance. (op. cit. p. 315)

Their assertions help us to choose to go God's way, to decide the path we are going to follow and to do that on the basis of divine revelation, not merely human observation. They remind us that since the whole of life is lived under God's judgment, 'the fear of the LORD is the beginning of wisdom, and knowledge of the Holy One is understanding' (Proverbs 9:10).

Proverbs, then, is the basic wisdom text, but what about when its precepts do not seem to be working out? This is the struggle dramatised for us in the book of Job, which of all biblical texts can be most misunderstood if we do not read it carefully in its own context. The book begins with the portrayal of Job as the archetypal 'wise man', described by God himself as 'blameless and upright, a man who fears God and shuns evil' (Job 1:8). He is the head of a large family, a wealthy household, 'the greatest man among all the people of the East' (Job 1:3), but he loses it all. His flocks (the source of his wealth) are destroyed, his children are killed and he himself is afflicted 'with painful sores from the soles of his feet to the top of his head' (Job 2:7). Is this what wisdom brings? Is this the pay-off for godliness? That is the debate which stretches out through the book. It is conducted between Job and his three 'friends' or 'comforters' who come to share in his sufferings. In a sense, they take up a classic wisdom position. Actions lead to consequences, which is what it means to live in an ordered world. God is constantly meting out his judgment through the events of life. So for Job to be suffering so horrifically there must be some hidden cause, some heinous sin lurking beneath the outward persona of godliness he presents. The thesis is that what happens is a direct result of whether or not you have pleased God, so, in some way, Job deserves what he is getting. The idea was still current in Jesus' day, when, encountering a man blind from birth, the disciples immediately took this position. 'Rabbi,' they asked Jesus, 'who sinned, this man or his parents, that he was born blind?' Jesus' reply is direct and uncompromising and also provides a key to the book of Job. 'Neither this man nor his parents sinned, but this happened so that the work of God might be displayed in his life.' And Jesus gives the man his sight (John 9:1–7). The same thinking still lurks in our hearts whenever we find ourselves facing trouble and exclaiming, 'What have I done to deserve this?'

Throughout the book, Job protests his innocence. He is horrified at his suffering and its inexplicability. His argument that it is all grossly unfair is blasphemous to his pious friends. Eventually a fourth counsellor appears who adopts something of a mediating position, defending God's superior wisdom in ordering human affairs. Clearly, the start of the book shows us that God has given permission to the Satan to act in this way. He is neither powerless nor disinterested. Eventually, God himself answers Job, affirming his total sovereignty in the creation of the universe and its sustenance, 'Would you discredit my justice? Would you condemn me to justify yourself?' (40:8). Job is vindicated by God against his counsellors and their accusations, with their misrepresentations of God (42:7–9), and all that he had lost is doubly restored (42:10–15). The resolution of the book rests in a recognition that greater purposes of good, displaying the work of God, may lie behind human suffering. Life is not fair in a fallen world, but God is sovereign, righteous and just and his ways are higher than ours. It was that confidence which built, and, in spite of everything, sustained Job's wisdom.

Ecclesiastes also grapples with too mechanistic a view of life in God's moral world. The 'Teacher' (*Qoheleth*), who presents himself as its author, also challenges the over-simplified view of life that righteousness leads to wealth and wickedness to poverty. From simple observation, in which exceptions to the rule can easily be cited, he concludes that the seeming randomness of life and the inescapable finality of death combine to render life 'under the sun' as ultimately 'meaningless'. This view is expressed frequently, with great plausibility and passion, and it resonates more profoundly with our contemporary philosophies and world views than almost any other part of the Old Testament. 'Build your castle in life, but know that it is on the edge of the abyss and there is nothing beyond' is not an exclusively contemporary position. Ecclesiastes was there over two millennia ago.

But is that the real position of the book? And if so, what is it doing in the Bible? There is great debate as to whether the book's view is ultimately pessimistic or optimistic. For many commentators, its pessimism is realistic, when life is looked at simply from what Derek Kidner calls 'ground level'. Finite man can only be given meaning if there is an infinite reference point. Existentialism recognises that reality but then denies the existence of God as the reference point. Ecclesiastes recognises its realism but affirms the reality of God, and in that perspective finds a resolution of the tensions: 'Fear God and keep his commandments, for this is the whole duty of man' (12:13b). Moreover, there is existence beyond Sheol (death), 'for God will bring every deed into judgment, including every hidden thing, whether it is good or evil' (12:14). Those categories of moral values do apply, beyond this world as well as in it. There may not be a traceable action-to-consequence pattern in the circumstances of this life, but there is certainly a character-to-consequence pattern built into eternity. The 'righteous' and the 'wicked' will find their life-style materially affecting the circumstances of life in this world and, more importantly, determining their eternal destiny. Life at 'ground level' is too bad to be true. It drives us to look for meaning elsewhere. Such wisdom can only be found in God himself, as we submit to his rule and seek to obey his commandments. The wise man always lives in this world in the light of the world to come. 'Remember your Creator in the days of your youth before . . . the dust returns to the ground it came from, and the spirit returns to God who gave it' (12:1–7). That is wisdom.

To remind you

- The Bible is written in a variety of styles, of which story-telling is especially a feature of the Old Testament. We must neither moralise nor psychologise the stories, but recognise that the history contains the meaning (pp. 112–16).
- Taking God as the hero we see him work with his people Israel and with individuals, carrying out his great salvation-plan (pp. 116–17).
- Often Old Testament narratives focus on a turning point at the heart of the story (pp. 117–22).
- The power of poetry in the Old Testament lies in its rhythm and its characteristic parallelism where words and ideas are compared and contrasted (pp. 122–7).
- The Psalms provide us with words which speak for us to God, in all the changing circumstances of life (pp. 127–9).
- Many of them point forward to Christ and help us to see the fulfilment of the soul's longings in him alone (pp. 129–31).
- The wisdom literature seeks to apply propositional truth to all the practical areas of life in God's world. Proverbs, Job, and Ecclesiastes explore the enigma of life from God's revealed perspective (pp. 131–8).

Chapter 7

But How Does the Old Relate to the New?

'IT DOESN'T GET any easier, this understanding the Bible, does it?' Andy had crashed out on the sofa and was idly thumbing his way through the Bible he and Julia had bought last weekend and promised themselves they would try to read. 'I mean, listen to this, Jule. "Know and understand this: From the issuing of the decree to restore and rebuild Jerusalem until the Anointed One, the ruler, comes, there will be seven 'sevens' and sixty-two 'sevens' . . . He will confirm a covenant with many for one 'seven'. In the middle of the 'seven' he will put an end to sacrifice and offering. And on a wing of the temple he will set up an abomination that causes desolation . . ." That's from Daniel, chapter 9. I'm never going to be able to make head nor tail of this sort of thing. It all seems so remote, so unreal. Makes you wonder what's the point, really!'

'Well,' Julia took a deep breath, 'according to that bloke at the church, the point is that it all points forward to Jesus, and that if you use him as a sort of key to unlock it all, everything becomes clear . . . well, eventually. He had a really good story about a jig-saw puzzle.'

'Oh, *did* he?' Andy tried not to express too clearly the cynicism that was beginning to build in him.

Julia continued, apparently unperturbed. 'Yes . . . let's see, what was it? Oh yes, I know. It was about a double-sided jig-saw. On one side was a very complicated map of the world and on the other a picture of a man. If you tried to do the world side first it would take ages, but if you did the man first, it would be really simple. And he said that the Bible was like that – big and complex and hard to put together, but once you get Jesus, the man, right, you find the other side has all fallen into shape too. Oh, and he said that you have to remember that the Old Testament is always pointing forward to the New. It was telling what was going to happen hundreds of years before Jesus came and the New Testament picks up lots of clues about the meaning of the Old, that we otherwise wouldn't be able to see. So it shows us how it all comes together in Christ and Christianity. I guess Daniel must be part of that.'

'I guess so,' Andy mused. 'I wish there wasn't this great gap between the two halves of the Bible. It's a pity somebody couldn't sort of build a bridge to help people travel between the two parts, so that we could make them fit together and see both sides of the story. Yes, a bridge is what we need, or maybe a Channel tunnel, or even a ferry . . . !'

Let's see what can be done! Our starting point will need to be another major genre of the Old Testament, which stands in a direct relationship to the New – prophecy. Klein, Blomberg and Hubbard in their *Introduction to Biblical Interpretation* (1993, Word) have the following encouragement for us. Quoting Martin Luther, the great leader of the Reformation, about the prophets, 'They have a queer way of talking, like people who, instead of proceeding in an orderly manner, ramble off from one thing to the next, so that you cannot make head or tail of them or see what they are getting at', their contemporary comment is, 'Probably no part of Scripture mystifies and frustrates readers more than the prophets. Indeed, Old Testament prophecy presents a veritable snake pit of interpretative problems' (op. cit. p. 302). Stay close!

The maze of prophecy

But why should prophecy be so daunting? One reason must be the extraordinarily bizarre interpretations put on some prophetic writing, reducing them more to the level of cosmic horoscopes, or the generalised doom-and-gloom predictions of an *Old Moore's Almanac*, or Nostradamus. Can this really be the Word of the living God? The answer is 'yes', but rightly understood and interpreted. So how should we go about it? If most people were asked to define 'prophecy', they would probably concentrate on its predictive content, the foretelling of the future, or as one Bible commentator summarised it, 'history, written in advance'. This is an unfortunate focus, because it generates a speculative interest about the unknown future, which does not reflect the original purposes of the prophetic writers. We are not dealing with impossibly secret messages which have to be decoded, not even in the symbolism of a book like Daniel. As in the rest of the Bible, we need to concentrate on the plain meaning of the text, and not import into it our own fanciful parallels from the contemporary world political situation. Our first level of understanding must always be that of the original hearers, and they were not specialists in the movements of the American fleet in the Persian Gulf or the 'no-fly' zones of Iraq! Nor should we seek to discover a mathematical symbolism, buried in the writings of the prophets, by which the date of the second coming of Christ and the end of the world can be predicted. Jesus himself warned us against such folly. 'No-one knows about that day or hour, not even the angels in heaven, nor the Son, but only the Father' (Mark 13:32). In fact, we should not be carried away by thinking that the predictive ingredient is predominant in the prophets. Fee and Stuart correct this false perception when they state that 'less than 2 per cent of Old Testament prophecy is Messianic. Less than 5 per cent specifically describes the New Covenant age. Less than 1 per cent concerns events yet to come, that is following the completion of the New Testament period' (op. cit. p. 158). So what is the purpose of the predictive content of biblical prophecy?

One of the most helpful explanations I have heard comes in the form of an illustration, though sadly I cannot remember its source. Supposing a large congregation is pouring out of a city-centre church on a Sunday morning, spilling out on to the pavements. As groups of friends are talking, individuals begin to edge off the pavement into the gutter and further into the road. If someone is standing too far into the road and his companion sees a car coming at speed, he may find that he is talking to a prophet. Certainly a warning would be in place and it may be phrased in predictive terms. 'Look out,' his friend alerts him. 'There's a car coming: you'll be run over!' That is a prophetic utterance, but of course its purpose is to correct behaviour in the present so that the prophesied future is actually avoided. If the person listens and moves back on to the pavement, the words have fulfilled their purpose. The car came, but he was not run over because he had taken action, while there was still time. The so-called 'prophet' will not be rejected as a liar and stoned (the penalty for false prophets in the Old Testament) because what he said would happen did not literally do so! But supposing no action was taken, and the unthinkable accident occurred so that the words were literally fulfilled, it would give the 'prophet' no satisfaction whatsoever, only the consolation that he had been right to warn his friend.

This illustrates the basic dynamic which operates in biblical prophecy. The prophets came to stir up lazy and complacent people, to disturb the comfortable, to warn of what the future outcome of their present behaviour will inevitably be. Their predictive message reminds the hearers that God is in control of his world and their lives, that he is working out his purposes through history, and he is moving everything towards its final goal in the return of Christ, the last judgment of everyone and the eternal states of heaven and hell. The prophets' work is to stimulate their hearers in the present to think rightly about the future, and so to live rightly here and now. So the prediction element reveals what will develop out of current events, or attitudes, if there is no amendment of life, no return to God, no change. The connection is temporal, but it is more importantly moral and spiritual.

The short Old Testament book of Jonah, the minor prophet, is an instructive example. It is a famous story of the disobedient prophet, told to go to Nineveh, the capital city of the ruthless world-wide Assyrian empire of his day, to prophesy God's judgment against it. Jonah's subsequent flight to Tarshish in the west, his shipwreck and the great fish which swallowed him are the details most often recalled. But that is only the first half of the book. Jonah is re-commissioned to go to proclaim God's message to Nineveh, which is, 'Forty more days and Nineveh will be overturned' (Jonah 3:4). It is a predictive message, which is designed to have a present effect, and it does. From the king downwards, a time of national repentance is proclaimed and enacted, in the hope that God's fierce anger will be averted, which is exactly what happens. 'When God saw what they did and how they turned from their evil ways, he had compassion and did not bring upon them the destruction he had threatened' (Jonah 3:10). Jonah's resulting anger is legendary. The last chapter reveals that he fled to Tarshish not because he was afraid to confront the heart of the mighty Assyrian war machine, but because he knew that God's nature was to be gracious and compassionate, and Jonah wanted pagan Nineveh to be destroyed. Instead, he has lost face because what he said would happen has not, and the pagans have got off the hook yet again. But God's response, with which the book ends, is a haunting question which takes us to the very heart of prophecy and of God. 'But Nineveh has more than a hundred and twenty thousand people who cannot tell their right hand from their left . . . Should I not be concerned about that great city?' (Jonah 4:11). In fact, Jonah is the most successful of prophets in this part of his ministry, for the message of judgment produced the desired effect and God showed his mercy. Ultimately, then, even the predictive elements in prophecy are a declaration of the character and purposes of God.

Preachers of covenant law

So, the prophets are preachers of the character of God in terms of their primary ministry, rather than foretellers of an already irrevocably decreed future. Fee and Stuart have a memorably helpful description, when they refer to the prophets as 'Covenant Enforcement Mediators' (op. cit. p. 151). Such a title reminds us that the ministry of the prophets was dependent on the Torah (law) already given and explained within the Pentateuch. They came to their generation, on the basis of what God had already said in the first five books, to remind, proclaim and apply that word into the current situation. In fact, the prophetic word and office themselves go right back to the time of Moses and his ministry. As the book of Deuteronomy draws to its end, along with Moses' life, the nation of Israel, about to enter the land of God's promise, is reminded of the stark choices they will have to make in Canaan. If they fully obey the Lord they will be blessed in every aspect of their lives, but disobedience will bring equivalent curses, 'confusion and rebuke in everything you put your hand to, until you are destroyed and come to sudden ruin' (Deuteronomy 28:20). The details of the two ways are spelt out and returned to many times later in the Old Testament, by the prophets, confirming God's faithfulness to what he said and spelling out the reasons for the consequences that are being suffered. In that sense, Moses is the first of the prophets, and all the later prophet-preachers follow in his footsteps. A little earlier in Deuteronomy the pattern had already been laid down.

The nations you will dispossess listen to those who practise sorcery or divination. But as for you, the LORD your God has not permitted you to do so. The LORD your God will raise up for you a prophet like me from among your own brothers. You must listen to him. For this is what you asked of the LORD your God at Horeb on the day of the assembly when you said, 'Let us not hear the voice of the LORD our God nor see this great fire any more, or we will die.' The LORD said to me: 'What they say is good. I will raise up for them a prophet like you from among their brothers; I will put my words in his mouth, and he will tell them everything I command him. If anyone does not listen to my words that the prophet speaks in my name, I myself will call him to account. But a prophet who presumes to speak in my name anything I have not commanded him to say, or a prophet who speaks in the name of other gods, must be put to death.' You may say to yourselves, 'How can we know when a message has not been spoken by the LORD?' If what a prophet proclaims in the name of the LORD does not take place or come true, that is a message the LORD has not spoken. That prophet has spoken presumptuously. Do not be afraid of him. (Deuteronomy 18:14–22)

Clearly, the provision of prophetic ministry is, in part, an antidote to sorcery. Ever since the law had been given at Sinai, Moses had fulfilled that function. He has been the means by which the Israelites have heard the word of God, particularly about their future in the land. Now, as Moses is nearing death, God is providing for the continuation of that process. Verses 18 and following indicate that this was fulfilled every time a prophet spoke in the Lord's name, which explains why the claim so to speak was so serious, and why the practical proof of the false prophet is that what he says does not take place. His words are not true; therefore he cannot be speaking on behalf of the God of Truth. But Moses was also a unique figure, superior to any of the other prophets, either at the time or afterwards. Numbers 12:6–8 explains it, in the Lord's own words. 'When a prophet of the LORD is among you, I reveal myself to him in visions, I speak to him in dreams. But this is not true of my servant Moses; he is faithful in all my house. With him I speak face to face, clearly and not in riddles; he sees the form of the LORD.' It therefore came to be believed that one day a prophet as great as Moses would be raised up. Possibly he would be the Messiah. Certainly the connection is made to Jesus in Acts 3:20 where the apostles, quoting Deuteronomy 18, see its fulfilment in 'the Christ who has been appointed for you – even Jesus'. Stephen, the first Christian martyr, quotes the same verse in Acts 7:37 and links Israel's refusal to obey Moses with his accusers' rejection of the

Righteous One (v. 52), 'You have betrayed and murdered him.'

Prophecy was the means by which God chose to visit and instruct his rebellious people down the centuries. Sometimes the prophets' ministry was directed to an individual, as when Samuel first anointed Saul as king and later challenged and rebuked his disobedience. Indeed, the withdrawal of communication from God to Saul was both the punishment of his rebellion and the cause of his future downfall. 'Saul died because he was unfaithful to the LORD; he did not keep the word of the LORD and even consulted a medium for guidance, and did not enquire of the LORD' (1 Chronicles 10:13–14). In the same way God sent the prophet Nathan to David to convict him of his guilt and bring him to repentance (2 Samuel 12; Psalm 51). It was treason and apostasy in the king of Israel for him to seek any other source of enlightenment or wisdom than the word of the Lord, as Ahaziah discovered when Elijah intercepted his courtiers as they went to consult Baal-Zebub, the god of Ekron, about Ahaziah's future (2 Kings 1:2–4). But as the Davidic monarchy descended into greater rebellion and chaos, the later prophets were sent directly to the people, to call them back to repentance and humility before God. This was to obviate the inevitable, predicted outcome of their apostasy, if it continued, which was their expulsion from the land, in national exile.

For this reason, the writing prophets of the Old Testament are located within a comparatively narrow time-band of three hundred years or so, approximately 760–460 BC. Beginning in the decades leading to the destruction of Samaria and the fall of the northern kingdom to the Assyrians, they move on through the century or more before the Babylonians similarly overthrew Jerusalem and Judah, and cover the period of the resulting exile, culminating in the return to the land and the decades of re-settlement. On a world scale, these were centuries of great upheaval, caused by the emergence of successive world empires – the Assyrians, Babylonians and Persians. National boundaries were overrun and even obliterated. There were great movements of people groups and shifts in population make-up. Israel and Judah felt the brunt of this politically and militarily, and therefore economically and socially, but, apart from a handful of notable exceptions, the response of both kings and people was to turn their backs on their covenant Lord, Yahweh, and to capitulate to the gods of the nations, in various forms of idolatry.

However, they were not dealing with wood or metal when they

related so faithlessly to the God who had created them as a nation and formed them to be his people. The ministry of the prophets reminds his recalcitrant people that Yahweh is the only living and true God, unlike the idols they have embraced in what amounted in reality to the worship of themselves. The Hebrew term for 'prophet' comes from the verb 'to call', reminding his people that it is God's grace which lays hold of a messenger, calls him, instructs him and gives him the word of the living God to speak. The message was frequently one which a rebellious nation did not want to hear and chose to reject, but God was being faithful to his covenant commitment. So the prophets came as God's mouthpieces, mediators of the covenant, sent by God to call his people back to repentance and a restored relationship with him. The edge to their message is the predictive element of warning and of promise, in which the hearers are challenged to make right decisions in their present in view of God's revealed plans about their future. This is what tears away the masks of self-deception and play-acting to reveal the corruption and rebellion which are gradually extinguishing the very life of the nation.

Applying the prophets today

But what does it all mean to us, in our very different circumstances, and how can we unpack its continuing significance for today? One of the advantages of studying the prophets is that their message to their own generation is almost as clear to us as it was to them. There may be place names we do not recognise and some allusions we find it hard to place, but the mainstream of their messages is strong and clear. Nor is it difficult for us to identify with their hearers' shortcomings, for their sins are our sins, too. It is not only God who is unchanging. Our sinful human nature shares that characteristic. So when we hear Amos, arraigning the leaders of Israel, declare, 'You hate the one who reproves in court and despise him who tells the truth. You trample on the poor and force him to give you grain . . . You oppress the righteous and take bribes and you deprive the poor of justice . . . Let justice roll on like a river, righteousness like a never-failing stream!' (Amos 5:10–11, 12, 24), we know that we live in the same world, guilty of the same sins. It is all too easy for the contemporary Christian, then, to apply these catalogues of sin to the secular society in which we live, and with them, the list of predicted judgments to which they inevitably lead. But that is to miss one very important consideration. It may be very comforting for cosy Christians to sit safe in their pews and listen to their preachers thunder 'prophetically' against the evils of this 'godless society' in which we find ourselves – comforting in the short run, but suicidal in the end. For who made up the prophets' target audience?

Of the three major and twelve minor prophets, only two focus on the pagan world around Israel. Jonah is sent to Nineveh, capital of Assyria, while Obadiah's single chapter is directed at Edom, one of Judah's neighbours. Certainly, Amos begins with a series of short oracles proclaiming imminent judgment on Israel's neighbours – Syria, Philistia, Tyre, Edom, Ammon, Moab, even Judah (1:3 – 2:5), but all the rest is directed to Israel. Similarly, Isaiah has a succession of chapters, 13–23, against Judah's neighbouring states and especially the super-powers, Assyria, Egypt and Babylon. But five-sixths of his total of sixty-six chapters are focused on Judah. God's prophetic words of warning and judgment are overwhelmingly directed to the people who are in covenant relationship with him. Of course, there is much that is true, and therefore urgently relevant, to all sinners, at all times and in all cultures, but we are not at liberty to draw a straight line from the theocratic covenant community of the Old Testament, whether Israel or Judah, across to a contemporary secular nation-state today, even if its name is Israel. For the people with whom God is in covenant relationship in the twenty-first century are those from every nation who have become rightly related to him through faith in the atoning death of his Son, Jesus Christ, on the cross, the shedding of whose blood has inaugurated the new covenant (Matthew 26:28) and rendered the old obsolete (Hebrews 8:13).

The primary impact of the Old Testament prophets must therefore be on the contemporary Church, and their warnings come to rouse us from our complacency and play-acting. It was Martin Luther who said that you may take the monk out of the world, but you cannot take the world out of the monk. The same is true of any Christian believer. We are involved in a daily struggle against the world, the flesh (or sinful nature) and the devil, and it is all too easy for us to opt for the easiest, most comfortable compromises, concentrating on outward conformity and ignoring the issues of the heart. That is why we need the message of the prophets in the Church. The same is true of our reading of the gospels, and especially the many detailed encounters and debates Jesus – the greatest prophet – had with the Pharisees.

They were the guardians of the covenant, in theory. Certainly, their doctrine of the authority of the Scriptures was impeccable and very highly developed. They were the biblical 'conservatives' of their day, but they had settled for an externalism, which preserved a veneer of respectable righteousness but concealed a heart of hypocrisy and bitterness. It is fatally easy for us to caricature them as the 'baddies' and to assure ourselves we would never do such things, while the supreme irony is that those very seeds of self-righteousness are growing in our hearts. Only when I realise that I have a Pharisee's heart do I begin to get the prophetic value of those gospel dialogue passages, and see how much I need to be corrected by God's Word. Else, I shall be like the Sunday-school teacher who had taught her children Jesus' parable of the Pharisee and the tax-collector in the temple at prayer (Luke 18:9–14). The Pharisee paraded his self-righteousness to God, while the tax collector could only beg God for mercy on him, as a self-confessed sinner. It was he who was made right with God. 'Well, children,' said the teacher, 'before we go home, let's just say a little prayer and thank God that we're not like the Pharisee'!

There is one other very important principle to bear in mind when dealing with Old Testament prophecy, which is that it all preceded the coming of Jesus, by about four hundred years at the least, and that through his coming everything has changed. We can only see and appreciate the light from the prophets as it is refracted through the prism that is Jesus. I find it helpful to keep this in mind by using an analogy from hill walking. Setting out on a walk, one may see three hill peaks which all seem comparatively close together. The distant view telescopes them together. But the reality of the walk reveals that the distances between them are considerably larger than one imagined and that there is a good deal of tramping down and up again before the final peak is reached. We can think of the three peaks as three points of reference or significance for the Old Testament prophecies. The first is what the prophecy meant in the prophet's own context to his own generation of original hearers or readers. We have to climb that peak first, since that is the plain, literal meaning of the text, and whatever significance it may have for us today, it will not be dissonant with that original purpose. The second peak is the fulfilment that is associated with the first coming of Christ in his life and ministry, death, resurrection and ascension. So much of the future blessing, promised by the prophets to those who repent, finds its fulfilment in the gospel of our Lord Jesus Christ. But there is a third and more distant peak, to which we are still climbing, and that is the second coming of Jesus, when he will come to judge the living and the dead and to inaugurate his eternal reign of glory in the new heavens and new earth. This will bring the ultimate fulfilment and completion of all God's promises.

This is not an imposition on the Old Testament's interpretation but the fruit of taking seriously that the two testaments are one Bible. 'The new is in the old contained; the old is by the new explained.' The pattern of the New Testament is overwhelmingly to interpret the fulfilment of prophecy, through the person and work of Christ, and in that way to demonstrate that he is the centre and theme of all that the prophets foretold. But while the kingdom of God has already broken into this present age and transformed it, in the coming of the King, the New Testament is also clear that there is a 'not yet' degree of total fulfilment, beyond the 'now' of present Christian experience. That awaits the 'third peak', when Christ returns, 'and every eye will see him' (Revelation 1:7), 'every knee should bow... and every tongue confess that Jesus Christ is Lord' (Philippians 2:10–11).

Let's end this section by taking an example from perhaps the greatest of all the writing prophets, Isaiah. The prophet has just predicted the exile of Judah from the land and the destruction of the city of Jerusalem at the hands of the Babylonians. It will look like the end of the line of David and the people of God (Isaiah 39:5–7). But immediately the exile has been announced, our attention is drawn to God's plans beyond that event, plans for a new exodus and a new covenant people, a great ruler and a universal kingdom. Chapter 40 is the overture to the second half of Isaiah's book.

Comfort, comfort my people, says your God. Speak tenderly to Jerusalem, and proclaim to her that her hard service has been completed, that her sin has been paid for, that she has received from the Lord's hand double for all her sins.

A voice of one calling: 'In the desert prepare the way for the Lord; make straight in the wilderness a highway for our God. Every valley shall be raised up, every mountain and hill made low; the rough ground shall become level, the rugged places a plain. And the glory of the LORD will be revealed, and all mankind together will see it. For the mouth of the LORD has spoken.'

A voice says, 'Cry out.' And I said, 'What shall I cry?' 'All men are like grass, and all their glory is like the flowers of the field. The grass withers and the flowers fall, because the breath of the LORD blows on them. Surely the people are grass. The grass withers and the flowers fall, but the word of our God stands for ever.'

You who bring good tidings to Zion, go up on a high mountain. You who bring good tidings to Jerusalem, lift up your voice with a shout, lift it up, do not be afraid; say to the towns of Judah, 'Here is your God!' See, the Sovereign LORD comes with power, and his arm rules for him. See, his reward is with him, and his recompense accompanies him. He tends his flock like a shepherd: He gathers the lambs in his arms and carries them close to his heart; he gently leads those that have young. (Isaiah 40:1–11)

When we think of the first peak (what did it mean to Isaiah's original hearers?) the answer is not hard to determine. Although the exile they have been warned about is clearly future (not during the reign of their present king, Hezekiah – see 39:8), they are now being told of a future restoration beyond the exile. A day of new beginnings will dawn for Jerusalem, when the price for her sinful rebellion has been fully paid (vv. 1–2). The remaining verses draw an exciting picture of God leading his people back from Babylon to the promised land, storming across the desert, or wilderness, with no physical features impeding his progress for one moment (vv. 3–4). He is sighted by watchmen, who relay the inspiring news of the LORD's return from hill-top to ruined city, until Jerusalem herself is presented with her king – 'Here is your God!' (v. 9). He comes as sovereign-shepherd, to rule his people and to care for his flock (vv. 10–11). At this level, the verses are full of promise for those of Isaiah's day who were prepared to listen to, and receive, God's word. They and the generations that followed, both before and during the exile, would have been strength-ened in the knowledge that Babylon did not have the final word, that the great plan of salvation-history was not stalled, that a day of great restoration was coming. Historically, that was so when Babylon fell to the Medo-Persian ruler, Cyrus, and one of his earliest decrees permitted and encouraged the re-settlement in their own land of the captive peoples.

And yet . . . ! The degree of disappointingly inadequate fulfilment, which followed the return from exile, is the substance of the last section of the Old Testament. The difficulties of rebuilding the temple are described in the book of Ezra, and of completing the city walls and re-ordering the community in the book of Nehemiah, while the prophecies of Haggai, Zechariah and Malachi are all designed to challenge and motivate an increasingly demoralised, downcast people. Where was the glory Isaiah had predicted? Why did the Sovereign Lord not rule for his people, with his mighty arm? By way of answer, we have to journey to the second peak and the greater fulfilment of the prophecy in the coming of Jesus. When *did* the exile end? In Isaiah's understanding, when the 'voice of one calling' in the desert was heard, preparing the way for the LORD (v. 3). So it is this verse which Matthew quotes in his gospel (3:3), when, following the infancy and childhood narratives of Christ, he introduces John the Baptist as the forerunner of Jesus the shepherd, who is the king. In the beginning of Christ's ministry, the exile is ending and the new kingdom is breaking in, because the king has arrived. In the opening chapter of his gospel, John echoes the same note, picking up Isaiah's promise (v. 5) of God's glory revealed to all the world, when he affirms, 'The Word became flesh and made his dwelling among us. We have seen his glory, the glory of the One and Only, who came from the Father, full of grace and truth' (John 1:14). Constantly, in the gospel accounts, the Old Testament fulfilment motif stands out. The ministry of Jesus is primarily a declaration of the 'word of our God', which 'stands for ever' (Isaiah 40:8). As his words reveal his divine nature, so he declares, 'Heaven and earth will pass away, but my words will never pass away' (Mark 13:31). He comes to Jerusalem and to Zion, the temple mountain, to declare 'Here is your God.' His powerful arm is demonstrated in his sovereign authority over all kinds of sickness and evil, ruling over men and nature. His divine rule is witnessed also in his cleansing of the temple, overthrowing the tables of the money-changers and evicting the traders, who had turned his 'house of prayer for all nations' into 'a den of robbers' (Mark 11:15–18). At the same time his shepherd care is constantly exercised towards his flock, gathering the outcasts, caring for the weak and disadvantaged, protecting from the wolf, feeding with the truth of his Word and ultimately, as the good shepherd, 'laying down his life for the sheep' (John 10:15).

And yet . . . ! Wonderful as these fulfilments are in the first coming of Jesus, there is a third and further level, a last peak, to climb. For we do not yet see 'all mankind' humbled before the manifestation of God's glory, in Christ. We do not yet experience his sovereign arm ruling in unchallenged power, distributing his rewards and recompensing human beings for their actions, good and evil. That fulfilment awaits the last day of Christ's judgment, when the restoration will be completed and he will reign for ever. This realisation places Isaiah's oracle in a context of which we are all a part. To us, as its readers, it presents an obligation to adjust our lives to those coming realities. Our understanding of Isaiah's prophecy is totally transformed in the light of Christ's comings, both past and future. All our reading of Old Testament prophecy necessarily involves us in a journey between the three peaks, and to keep these focal points firmly in our sights will help us not to lose our way.

There is so much to be gained from this frequently ignored biblical genre of prophecy. We must not allow it to become the preserve of the bizarre and the eccentric. As the contemporary Church of Jesus Christ, we need the instruction it contains concerning God's faithfulness to his promises, his righteousness and judgment, as well as his mercy and grace. The world still needs to hear that it is on a journey to the throne of God's judgment, at the end of human history, that the passage of time and the pattern of history are linear, not circular, and that we are finite beings in a finite world. The message of the prophets, with its warnings now and its appeal to take remedial action in the light of God's stated future plans, needs to be recovered in our 'laid-back' generation. The prophetic books provide us with just such vital ingredients of a full-blooded, vital Christian faith. Because they are composed of collections of oracles, or addresses (we might call them sermons), they were not designed to be read through at a sitting, but to be listened to and assimilated as individual units. Often those with similar themes are grouped together in sections. It is also important to go for the major ideas and key points in each oracle and not to be side-tracked into excessive concentration on details. If we keep asking, '*Why* was this written?', its value to us as contemporary hearers will become much clearer. We shall then be able to appropriate its unchanging message, whether of encouragement or rebuke, warning or promise, to our changing lives in God's changing world.

Apocalyptic writing

Earlier in this chapter, we shared some of Andy's difficulties in trying to come to terms with the obscure meanings of symbols in the book of Daniel. This sort of writing represents a particular and rather specialised form of prophetic writing called 'apocalyptic', of which passages in Ezekiel (38–9), Joel (2–3), Zechariah (9–14) and especially Daniel (7–12) are the outstanding Old Testament examples. The most famous example in the New is the last book, Revelation, whose title is a translation of the Greek word *apokalypsis*. What marks out apocalyptic writing from mainstream prophecy is that it reveals or unveils the hidden realities of the spiritual world and future events in world history, usually associated with dramatic interventions of God in human affairs, especially focused on the end-times. The purpose of the unveiling is not to satisfy curiosity about the future, but to strengthen the people of God in the midst of hostile and difficult circumstances, such as the exile or national apostasy. Apocalyptic writing pulls back the curtain to reveal God at work behind the scenes, working out his ultimate purposes of justice and grace. These glimpses of the future are designed to give courage and confidence to God's people in their beleaguered present. The language is often symbolic, representing future realities by significant images – curious beasts with multiple horns, numbers which have symbolic meanings, mysterious terminology. Often the medium of revelation to the writer is that of dreams or visions, in which these strange realities appear.

Because space-fiction and video games tend to be our nearest cultural equivalent, there is a danger that we relegate apocalyptic writing to a fictional, mythological category in our thinking. 'Weird and wonderful' might be an appropriate label! But that would be a foolish and serious mistake. We must not be diverted or bemused by the detailed symbolism. As with all other genres of biblical literature, the basic interpretative questions and methods apply. What is the major message of a particular vision or dream? The passage in Daniel 9, which Andy found so daunting, clearly teaches that God will bring history to an end, which will result in the vindication and deliverance of his people. In fact, it is a central theme of the second part of Daniel that if God's people persevere through their present opposition and difficulties, with a firm trust that God's sovereign rule is the eternal reality, they will most certainly share in his everlasting kingdom. When it comes to the detail, images of beasts with horns indicate great energy focused at a single point. A charging rhinoceros with all its poundage concentrated in its horn is an apt picture of a powerful tyrant heading up a seemingly invincible national war-machine. The imagery is significant in terms of political realities. The numbers also have a conventional symbolic meaning, as, for example, 'seven' being the number of completeness or perfection, connected with the seventh day of creation when God rested from all his labours and found them 'very good'. This genre is difficult to interpret with certainty, but its central message is loud and clear. God will bring history to his conclusion, demonstrating his sovereign rule and overthrowing all the forces of evil. There will be a certain judgment, when those who are God's people and those who are his enemies will be infallibly revealed. All this is most clearly understood in the light of Christ's coming and expounded further in the book of Revelation. And we need to keep in mind that faithful perseverance rather than fanciful speculation is the purpose of its existence.

New Testament controls

In these ways, prophecy and apocalyptic help to build the bridge between the two testaments, because they prepare the way for the coming of Jesus Christ and provide a framework of reference in which to locate the gospel. If God's character is unchanging, then the principles on which he deals with human beings must also be un-changing, so that there will be a fundamental congruence between the two parts of the Bible, or, to change the metaphor, a balance of which Christ is the fulcrum. Once we see that the unity of the Bible is guaranteed by the oneness of the God who is its author and subject, it becomes obvious not only that we must interpret Scripture on its own terms, in its own context, but that we must also allow the later revelation (chronologically) to interpret and illuminate the earlier. It is a fact of history that God chose to reveal himself progressively over a long period of time, with the inevitable result that those at the end of the revelatory process are in a position to view, understand and connect the whole together in a way which those at earlier stages could not. This is not in any way to assert that the earlier revelation is at all inferior, primitive or deficient. The principle of unity leads us not to expect the later to contradict or correct the earlier texts. All truth is God's truth and it is all equally truthful. There is nothing lacking at any period in what God chose to reveal for that time. However, when

Jesus, for example, said about Abraham that he rejoiced to see Christ's day and was glad (John 8:56), he did not mean that Abraham saw, as in a futuristic vision, all the details of Christ's life and ministry which we now have recorded in the gospels. Rather, he was pointing to himself as the fulfilment of the promise to Abraham, that through his seed one would come who would bless all the nations of the world, by rescuing the human race and crushing the serpent's head (Genesis 12:1–3, 3:15). The point is finally clinched by the apostle Paul in Galatians 3:16, when he affirms, 'The promises were spoken to Abraham and to his seed. The Scripture does not say "and to seeds", meaning many people, but "and to your seed", meaning one person, who is Christ' (see Genesis 12:7, 13:15, 24:7). All this confirms that the New Testament must be allowed to interpret the Old, that the bridge-building starts on the New Testament side of the divide and leads us back, through Christ, to a proper (and Christian) understanding of all that came before.

Our best method, then, is to see what the New Testament has to say about the Old, in the avalanche of quotations and allusions which stream through its pages. Here is Paul, comparing Adam with Jesus Christ in his letter to the Romans. He sees both as federal heads of a race of people. Their actions affect all who are in contact with them. Adam's sin brought death to the whole human race, while Christ's obedience to death brings righteousness and life to all who trust him. The process is explained like this. 'Nevertheless, death reigned from the time of Adam to the time of Moses, even over those who did not sin by breaking a command, as did Adam, who was a *pattern* of the one to come' (Romans 5:14). The Greek word *typos* is translated 'type' rather than 'pattern' by the Revised Standard Version. What is being observed is a characteristic of Adam, which is shared by Christ ('the one to come'), namely that their representative actions have a profound effect on the destiny of humankind. It is this practice of comparison, which is called 'typology', which lies at the heart of the New Testament's interpretation of the Old.

There are other ways in which this interpretative bridge is described elsewhere in the New Testament. For example, in Galatians 4:24 Paul uses the Genesis story of Abraham's two sons, Isaac and Ishmael, borne respectively by his wife Sarah and his slave girl, Hagar, as an allegory, or, as the New International Version translates it, 'figuratively'. The parallel he discerns is between children of the slave woman and those who are in slavery to the law as a means by which to make themselves acceptable to God, contrasted with the children of the free woman, representing those who have found freedom through Christ, in the gospel. The observance of the pattern of similarity leads up to the conclusion, 'Get rid of the slave woman and her son' (v. 30) which is exactly the message Paul has for those who want to follow the Judaisers in the Galatian church and go back to the law.

But it is the letter to the Hebrews which provides the richest range of comparative models. The Old Testament tabernacle, or temple, with its repetitive system of sacrifices and offerings, is only a 'copy' or 'shadow' of the heavenly realities (8:5), simply an 'illustration' or symbol of what Christ has accomplished in the sacrifice of himself on the cross (9:9). The law is simply 'a shadow of the good things that are coming' (10:1). It is therefore second nature to New Testament authors to interpret the gospel in Old Testament terms and pictures. The exodus from the bondage of Egypt through the death of the passover lamb (Exodus 12) is paralleled in the death of Christ and our subsequent deliverance from sin (John 1:29; 1 Corinthians 5:7). The manna from heaven which provided the Israelites' daily diet and the water which flowed from the rock (Exodus 16 and 17) are paralleled by the sustenance given to his people by Jesus, on their pilgrimage from earth to heaven (Egypt to Canaan). So Jesus is the bread (John 6:33, 35) and the rock from whom the water flows (1 Corinthians 10:4; John 7:38). All the covenant promises to Abraham and David are fulfilled in Christ, whose son he is (Matthew 1:1). He is the new temple, the place where God and man can meet in fellowship (John 2:19–22) and his blood inaugurates the new agreement, or covenant, between them (Matthew 26:26–8).

The question naturally arises, however, as to how we assess whether or not such parallels are biblically intentional or arbitrarily imposed by the ingenuity of later readers. I am indebted to Dr John Goldingay for the substance of what follows as guidelines concerning the interpretative tool of 'typology' and how its validity can be determined. The material is found in his book *Approaches to Old Testament Interpretation* (1990, IVP, Apollos). Starting from the point that what can be said about Israel's relationship to God under the old covenant can be said about the Church ('the Israel of God' – Galatians 6:16) under the new, Goldingay stresses that the point of correspondence is in the saving acts of God, because of the consistency of his unchanging character. But the analogy is also combined with a degree of contrast, in that the New Testament parallels are always greater than the Old Testament originals. The language of fulfilment is always appropriate in this area, because we are never dealing merely with equivalents or repetitions of Old Testament events. There is always an element of intensification, or to use the characteristic terminology of the letter to the Hebrews, the new covenant is in every way 'better' than its predecessor. Added to this, there is a greater degree of clarity. 'The heightening is a matter of the New Testament making clearer or more explicit what was allusive or implicit in the Old Testament' (Goldingay, op. cit. p. 101). Further, we must recognise that metaphor and symbolism are built into some Old Testament foreshadowings which will have a more concrete, though spiritual, fulfilment in the gospel. The prophecy of Amos, for example, after eight chapters announcing God's judgment on Israel at the hands of the Assyrians, ends with a vision of ultimate restoration, in which 'David's fallen tent' is restored and the Gentile nations seek the Lord and bear his name (see Amos 9:11–12). Does this refer to the restoration of the state of Israel and the Gentile nations being converted to Old Testament Judaism? Not according to James, the leader of the Jerusalem church, who in Acts 15:14–18 relates the quote directly to the conversion of Gentiles to Christ, through the preaching of the gospel, as for example in the case of the Roman centurion Cornelius and his household in Caesarea, to whom Peter was sent (see Acts 10:9–48). That is what Amos was referring to in characteristically Old Testament language and symbols, and so that becomes the paradigm for interpreting other prophecies about the restoration of the kingdom and the blessings God will pour on his covenant people. As Paul expresses it in Ephesians 1:3, 'The God and Father of our Lord Jesus Christ . . . has blessed us in the heavenly realms with every spiritual blessing in Christ.'

How then can we separate typology from allegory? The one is expository and the other imposed. A typological interpretation still works with the plain, natural meaning of the text in its historical context, whereas allegory attributes from the outside a meaning which the original writer or readers could not possibly have been aware of. 'Typology studies events, while allegory is a method of interpreting words' (Goldingay, op. cit. p. 107). Typology is not therefore a systematic principle for Old Testament interpretation, but it can help us to a deeper and truly Christian understanding. We realise how much more wonderful in their fulfilment in Christ and the gospel are the prophecies of Israel's restoration after the exile, than the partial historical fulfilments in the fifth century BC. But that was always God's intention, stretching his people forward to the far horizon, increasing their expectations and hope, because the glories of his eternal kingdom far exceed anything that might be known in this world. And while it is true that in Christ and the gospel we have entered into that reality, in a measure, for the kingdom of God is among us, yet we too have great expectations of an eternal future of fulfilment beyond all that we might ask, or even imagine. In Goldingay's memorable summary, 'Old Testament prophecy calls people to look at the future, in the light of the past, so as to see how to live in the present' (op. cit. p. 122). Typology does just that for the New Testament Christian, on the certain basis of the perfect fulfilment of God's promises, in Christ.

In all of these ways, Andy's 'bridge' between the Old and the New is constructed by the Bible authors. It is time now for us to examine its solid foundations on the New Testament side and to see how the genres of gospel and epistle there clarify, interpret and focus the whole testimony of God's self-revelation.

To remind you

- Old Testament prophecy is not a secret code-book to reveal the hidden future. It is designed to change behaviour in the present, in the light of the future (pp. 140–3).
- The prophets recall the people of God to faith and obedience, in the light of the covenant, with its blessings and curses (pp. 143–6).
- Because their message is primarily to covenant people, the prophets' application is first to the Church, rather than the world. But their message must be viewed through the reality of Christ's coming and the gospel (pp. 146–9).
- We need to interpret Old Testament prophecy in the light of its eventual completion at his second coming, in God's everlasting kingdom (pp. 149–52).
- Apocalyptic prophecy reveals God at work behind the scenes of human history, bringing his universal and eternal plans to fruition (pp. 153–4).
- The New Testament provides the controls for our Christian understanding of the Old. Patterns of understanding begun in the Old are filled out and completed in the New (pp. 154–8).

Chapter 8

So How Do We Unpack the New Testament?

MATT COULD HARDLY believe it had happened. He'd completely blown it. He should never have been there in the first place. What was he doing at one of those Christian meetings? They were designed to convert people – he knew that. But he'd gone anyway. The visiting speaker had rather surprised him. Matt had expected a ranting tele-evangelist type, who would have been such an easy put-down, but this guy seemed very normal and he presented his 'sales pitch' very reasonably, pretty persuasively actually, he had to admit. 'And I should have left it there,' he exclaimed to himself as he flopped on to his bed. 'But no, I had to go and ask some clever, clever question and engage him in conversation, didn't I?' He went through it again in his mind, the speaker asking him whether he'd ever really examined the evidence of Jesus Christ, at first hand, in one of the gospels of the New Testament. He'd blurted out something about he never thought it was that important and then this guy was offering him that little book; it was still in his pocket – the gospel according to John. 'Come on,' he'd said, 'you've got nothing to lose but your prejudice.' Matt saw himself back away and then he heard that incredibly stupid thing he'd said; he could still hardly believe it. 'No thanks,' he'd said, 'because I know that if I read it, I'll be convinced.' The bloke had laughed, put it into his hand anyway and he'd dashed off at top speed. And now here he was in his own room, with this little book, which was supposed to be able to change his life. But how could it? It was only black dots on white paper, only words. It didn't have any sort of mystical powers, did it? Matt grinned to himself. 'Just matter: that's all it is and all I am,' he assured himself. 'So it can't do anything to you, can it? It can't change you, but it can't harm you.' Drawing it out of his pocket, he turned to the first page.

The message of the gospels

What was Matt about to experience as he opened the pages of that little book and encountered a text nearly two thousand years old, in a literary form like nothing we are familiar with today? Coming from their context in the first-century Græco-Roman world, the four 'gospels' of the New Testament have elements that are very much part of that culture, but also much that is innovatory and unique. Our nearest contemporary equivalent might seem to be the biography, but we must be careful not to import our standards of detailed accuracy, chronological order and independent documentation back into that first-century world. It will not do to reject the gospels because they do not read like a modern scholarly work. Chronology was less important than the moral lessons that might be learned from a great man. Details of events and circumstances mattered less than the exposition of character. We must also remember that central to the purpose of the four evangelists lay their theological perspective, which governed the content of their work. They selected, as every writer must, from a collection of material which might have been used, but the criteria they used were theological and evangelistic. 'Jesus did many other miraculous signs in the presence of his disciples, which are not recorded in this book. But these are written that you may believe that Jesus is the Christ, the Son of God, and that by believing you may have life in his name' (John 20:30–1). Far from that pointing to a biased presentation, based on pious fiction, it stresses the factuality of John's account and the reasonableness of his method. Here is evidence, pointing, in the end, to only one possible conclusion. The truth of the evidence is the driving-force of the argument. The evangelists, therefore, declare the gospel, without reservation or demur. Their material is ordered and carefully shaped, yet each one is distinctive in style and emphasis, so that together the four evangelists provide a portrait of Jesus of such depth and breadth as would have been impossible for a single author to produce.

The first three gospels are usually grouped together, since they contain a considerable body of common material. It has been calculated that 92 per cent of Mark is reproduced in Matthew. For this reason among others, Mark is usually considered to have been written first, probably from Rome in the early 60s AD, with Peter as its apostolic source. Matthew is much larger, and consequently includes a good deal of extra material, some of which is used also in Luke, though Luke also has a considerable amount that is unique to that gospel. John is usually thought to have been written after the synoptics, to provide different material and particularly a Jerusalem, rather than a Galilee, focus for the ministry of Jesus, so that much of its contents are unique to the fourth gospel. The comparison of the gospel accounts is an important exercise, not for the discovery of so-called discrepancies, which are anyway few in number and resolvable, but so that we can tune our ears to the distinctive emphasis of the gospel writer, in the portrait of Jesus which is being drawn. In *How to Read the Bible for All Its Worth* (1982, Scripture Union), Gordon Fee and Douglas Stuart describe this process as reading 'horizontally' across the pages of the New Testament, comparing gospel with gospel. This will alert us to the distinctiveness of each account. But then, in recognition that the Holy Spirit inspired four separate gospels and not one massive harmonisation, we must also read and think 'vertically', interpreting each unit as part of the larger structure of that particular gospel, understanding its contribution to the overall theological and evangelistic purposes of the author. Indeed, that should be our priority (op. cit. p. 110ff). With that in mind, we will briefly survey the major distinctives of the four accounts.

Mark

Mark, the shortest of the gospels, is a work of great vividness and movement. I like to think of it as the news-reel gospel, with the camera zooming in and out, the focus always shifting, the sound-bite assessment predominating. There are passages of more prolonged teaching and reflection, but Mark is action-packed. The first verse sets the agenda. 'The beginning of the gospel about Jesus Christ, the Son of God' (Mark 1:1). But the agenda is pursued in a gradual, revelatory way. Although it is all there 'up front' at the start – it's good news; it centres on a man who is both rescuer (Jesus) and Messiah (Christ); it's going to demonstrate to us that the very life of God is within him – nevertheless, the structure of the gospel is to build the evidence gradually to its climax on the lips of a Gentile centurion, 'Surely this man was the Son of God' (Mark 15:39). This is the conclusion to which the disciples have come in chapter 8, Peter's confession that Jesus is the Christ (8:29), providing something of a watershed in the gospel as a whole. The first half of the gospel explores the question, 'Who is this Jesus?', leading to the confession, 'He is the Messiah/Christ.' Immediately, the focus shifts and the question becomes 'What sort of Messiah is he?' or 'How will the Messiah carry out God's work?', leading to the recognition of the path of suffering leading to the cross, and only then on to the glory of the resurrection, a path which those who follow him are required to walk too. Each half of the gospel is introduced with a summary statement, in which the later ingredients are contained, waiting, as it were, to be unpacked.

'After John was put in prison, Jesus went into Galilee, proclaiming the good news of God. "The time has come," he said. "The kingdom of God is near. Repent and believe the good news!" ' (Mark 1:14–15). At a particular point in time and at a particular place on the face of the planet, the kingly rule of God breaks into human history. The 'good news', of which the whole book is the developed account (1:1), is a message that has a past. Already Mark has alerted us to the fulfilment of Isaiah's prophecy in the ministry of John the Baptist (1:2–8). The same prophet predicted Galilee as the focus of the Messiah's ministry (Isaiah 9:2) and summarised the message God had called him to deliver as 'Your God reigns' (Isaiah 40:10–11, 52:7). At last, the time of fulfilment has come. God's rule is presented in the person of God's ruler, Jesus, and his royal summons is to turn from sin and self to believe that Jesus is God's king and rescuer, to submit oneself to his authority and so to enter the kingdom of God. For where the king rules in people's lives, there is the kingdom of God on earth. Mark's continuing agenda until chapter 8 is to pile up the evidence of Jesus' kingly authority, and as he does so to keep nudging us with the question, 'Who is this man?' The early chapters are full of examples of his power and authority, which can only be accounted for in terms of the divine. He has authority over the forces of evil (1:25–8), over every sort of sickness and disease (1:29–34). He has the ability to forgive sins, a divine prerogative (2:1–12). He is lord of the Sabbath, a divine provision (2:23–8). He is master of the storm (4:35–41) and even the conqueror of death (5:35–43). And so a great debate develops concerning his identity (see 1:27, 4:41, 5:42, 6:56) to which various solutions are proposed. To the religious leaders, staggered by his claims, he is 'a blasphemer' (2:7), 'possessed by Beelzebub, the prince of demons' (3:22). To the people he is 'the carpenter . . . Mary's son'

(6:3), or perhaps 'John the Baptist . . . raised from the dead' (6:14), or Elijah (6:15), or 'a prophet, like one of the prophets of long ago' (6:15). Only twice is the right answer given, and on both occasions by evil spirits. 'I know who you are – the Holy One of God' (1:24). 'What do you want with me, Jesus, Son of the Most High God?' (5:7). For the disciples it is a long, slow road to understanding, but eventually they see enough to be able to confess that Jesus is the Christ (8:29).

'He then began to teach them that the Son of Man must suffer many things and be rejected by the elders, chief priests and teachers of the law, and that he must be killed and after three days rise again. He spoke plainly about this . . . "If anyone would come after me, he must deny himself and take up his cross and follow me" ' (8:31–4). Here is Mark's agenda for part two of his gospel, and it is equally startling. How will the Messiah accomplish God's great plan to rescue the human race? 'He *must* suffer.' What does it mean to be his disciple? 'He *must* deny himself and take up his cross.' Again, the disciples cannot understand it (9:32). They have been raised on the idea of Messiah as a triumphant king, ruling over the nations. How could a crucified Jesus fit with that picture? They were more interested in sitting with him in his glory, not drinking the cup of his suffering (10:35–40). Yet the shadow of the cross falls more deeply and with increasing inevitability over the pages of the gospel, with a persistent call to follow in his footsteps. 'All men will hate you because of me, but he who stands firm to the end will be saved' (13:13). That is how God's mighty plan is fulfilled and that is, effectively, how Mark's good news comes to its climax. At the death of Jesus, the temple curtain, which kept everyone out of the holiest place of all because of their sinfulness was torn down from top to bottom by the hand of God, as a demonstration that the way into relationship with a holy God is open to all the world, for those who repent and believe the good news. And in the very next verse, it is a Roman soldier, a pagan, who makes the first confession, 'Surely this man was the Son of God!' (15:37–9).

Matthew

By contrast, Matthew's focus is more distinctly Jewish. The beginning of his gospel establishes the genealogy of Jesus back through David to Abraham and sees him as the long-awaited fulfilment of God's covenant promises to those two great men (1:1). The wise men come to worship him, but as the one who is born 'king of the Jews' (2:2).

Incidentally, the appearance of Gentiles at the beginning of the gospel worshipping Jesus (2:11) and the commission of the risen Christ at the end of the gospel to 'make disciples of all nations' (28:19), together with many other references concerning Gentile inclusion in God's kingdom throughout the gospel, should prevent us from seeing too narrow or exclusive a Jewish focus in Matthew as a whole. This note of kingship strongly pervades Matthew's work. It is seen in his frequently used titles of Jesus as 'Son of God' and 'Son of David'. The former links with the kingly figure of the messianic psalms and the latter with the promised descendant of King David, whose throne will be eternal and whose kingdom will know no end. Through the crucifixion narrative, the phrase 'King of the Jews' runs like a motif.

Also derived from Matthew's Old Testament roots is the other dominant characteristic of Jesus as the Teacher, which features throughout the gospel. Isaiah had envisaged the Messianic age as a time when the Gentile nations would stream to Jerusalem to worship the LORD and be instructed by him. Those 'without the law' would now be brought within the sphere of this covenant blessing. 'He will teach us his ways, so that we may walk in his paths,' the Gentile nations say. 'The law will go out from Zion, the word of the LORD from Jerusalem' (Isaiah 2:3). Most commentators are agreed that Matthew has organised his gospel around five major blocks of teaching, which may be intended to be equivalent to the five pillars of the law in the books of the Old Testament Pentateuch. The units (chapters 5–7, 10, 13, 18 and 24–5) are each marked out with similar phraseology at the end, and clearly the first, which we call the Sermon on the Mount, is intended by its introduction to direct us back to God speaking to his people from the mountain at Sinai (5:1–2). In this teaching Jesus is summarising, defining and instructing a new covenant people, just as in his ministry he confronts the hypocrisy of the old religious order and gathers to himself a new 'remnant', who will become the building-blocks of the new Israel, including both Jews and Gentiles, who acknowledge Christ as king. I have dealt with this in detail in my survey of Matthew's gospel, *Taking Jesus Seriously* (1994, Christian Focus Publications). This also explains why Matthew contains so many references to the fulfilment of Old Testament Scriptures, in Christ. As suffering servant, as well as exalted king and conqueror, Jesus demonstrates himself to be the one who was to come. By his death he inaugurates a new covenant relationship and in effect institutes a new

Israel. It is Matthew's concern to provide Christ's teaching for the further expansion and development of that new covenant community.

Luke

Luke is himself a Gentile, a travelling companion of Paul and a medical doctor. His skilled observation and habits of detailed analysis are clearly evident in his two volumes, the gospel and the Acts of the Apostles. Of the three synoptics, Luke has the largest amount of material unique to him, and much of it indicates his essential interests. For Luke, Jesus is supremely the rescuer, or Saviour, the only hope of the lost world. Those of us who are Gentiles can especially appreciate that emphasis. As Paul reminds us in Ephesians 2:12, we were 'separate from Christ, excluded from citizenship in Israel and foreigners to the covenants of the promise, without hope and without God in the world'. But Jesus has rescued pagans, who under the old covenant had no possible claim upon the grace and mercy of God, bringing us into his kingdom and adopting us into his family. It is not surprising, therefore, that Dr Luke is particularly interested in those from the outside who are brought into relationship with God, through Christ and the gospel. The note is sounded repeatedly from the opening chapter onwards (1:31, 47, 69, 71, 77) and finds its formal announcement in the message of the angel to the Bethlehem shepherds, 'I bring you good news of great joy that will be for all the people. Today in the town of David a Saviour has been born to you; he is Christ the Lord' (2:10–11). When Jesus begins his ministry in Luke 4:16–21, in the synagogue at Nazareth, he sets it firmly in the context of Isaiah's prophecy of rescue – good news for the poor, freedom for the prisoners, sight for the blind, release for the oppressed, the Lord's grace and favour (see Isaiah 61:1–2). 'Today,' says Jesus, 'this scripture is fulfilled in your hearing.' And just before his arrival at Jerusalem, with the inevitability of the cross ahead of him, at his last port of call, Jericho, it surfaces again as Jesus transforms the life of Zacchaeus, the tax-collector. 'Today salvation has come to this house, because this man, too, is a son of Abraham [i.e. an inheritor of the promise]. For the Son of Man came to seek and to save what was lost' (19:9–10).

Luke's focus is constantly on the lost whom Jesus is seeking and saving. What we discover is that they came from all the categories of life-style and strata of society which the pious religious Jews rejected. The clue is given as early as Mary's song (the Magnificat) in reflecting on the angel Gabriel's message that she is to be the mother of the Messiah. In celebrating the great things the Mighty One has done (and will do), she lists the upside-down nature of the kingdom which her baby will eventually inaugurate. 'He has scattered those who are proud in their inmost thoughts. He has brought down rulers from their thrones but has lifted up the humble. He has filled the hungry with good things but has sent the rich away empty' (1:51–3). In some ways, the gospel of Luke is a procession of fulfilment of that song. The shepherds are the first to receive the good news. Social rejects are found worshipping the king of heaven, but at a manger. Everything is being turned upside down. Many of Luke's notes and stories centre on the care and ministry of Jesus towards women, whom no rabbi would bother to teach. Mary herself, and later Anna, the prophetess, realise Christ's true identity at the very beginning (2:36–8). A sinful woman is forgiven and sent away in peace, as she shows her love for the rescuer by anointing his feet with perfume (7:36–50). At the home of the Bethany sisters, Mary sits at Jesus' feet listening to his word, while Martha is rebuked for not giving her attention to this one necessary thing (10:38–42). A crippled woman is healed on the Sabbath (13:10–13). Luke even lists the women who, with 'many others', played a supporting role financially in the ministry of Jesus and the apostles 'out of their own means' (8:1–3).

In 7:1–10, it is a Gentile centurion in Capernaum who is commended by Jesus, who is himself amazed at the man's faith. 'I tell you, I have not found such great faith even in Israel.' The outsiders are coming in; even Samaritans, the hated half-breed relics of the northern kingdom with whom the pure-bred Jews would have nothing to do. But it is Luke who records the parable of the Good Samaritan (10:25–37), who shows Jesus travelling through Samaria and rebuking his disciples' desire to call down fire from heaven to destroy them (9:51–6), and who tells the story of the healing of ten lepers, of whom only one returns to give thanks – 'and he was a Samaritan' (17:11–19). But perhaps the clearest focus of the theme is in Luke's fifteenth chapter with its famous three parables of the lost sheep, the lost coin and the lost son. The stories are told in response to a specific situation where Jesus is under fierce criticism from the Jewish religious leaders because as the tax-collectors and 'sinners' gathered round eager to hear his teaching, he not only welcomed them but actually ate with them (15:1–2). As the lost are sought and found, so those who think they are on the inside, because of their religious heritage or personal pedigree, are actually excluding themselves, by rejecting God's rescuer.

One other major theme of Luke is the power of the Word of God to do the work of God. At the start of the gospel, he describes Christians as 'servants of the word' (1:2), and at the end, Jesus commissions his disciples to be word-witnesses of all that they have seen and learned (24:48–9). But all the way through, it is the Word of God that accomplishes the will of God. Perhaps this emphasis was especially precious to Luke as it stressed the availability of the Word of God to those who had hitherto been without it. For him, the seed to be sown is always and only 'the word of God' (8:11) and it is only that seed, heard, retained and persevered in, with a noble and good heart, that can produce a crop, the harvest of eternal salvation (8:15, 21).

John

There is so much in John's gospel which is different from, and yet wonderfully complementary to, the portrait of Jesus painted for us by the synoptics. With a stronger background in Greek philosophy, yet combined with a profound understanding of the Old Testament, the apostle John presents us with a unique picture of the Lord Jesus. His famous prologue (1:1–14) in which Jesus is revealed as the *logos* made flesh, God's Word in human form, the incarnation of the mind and principle behind the whole universe, establishes from the beginning his deity and the fundamental unity between himself and the unseen 'Father'. John wants everyone to 'believe' (used over fifty times) and so 'see' this truth of who Jesus is, for he is the way to the Father, the key to knowing God and eternal life (John 14:6, 17:3). It is not seeing that leads to believing, for the post-apostolic disciple, but believing that leads to seeing. 'Blessed are those who have not seen and yet have believed,' Jesus tells Thomas (20:29), who should have believed the resurrection because of his fellow disciples' testimony, 'We have seen the Lord.'

As 'the Word made flesh', Jesus is naturally the subject of his own teaching. In a series of dialogues, first with individuals such as Nicodemus and the Samaritan woman, and then with the Jewish crowds and especially the religious leaders, Jesus constantly focuses attention on himself. This is centred on the seven 'I am' declarations and the seven signs of divine power with which they are interwoven.

Such revelation is always presented, however, in a context of challenge. Choices are to be made by every person, between faith and unbelief, and so between light and darkness, life and death. Again and again, the evidence is presented that Jesus is the revelation of the glory of God, the outshining in incarnated human life of the hidden inner nature and being of God. 'We have seen his glory,' John exclaims (1:14). Each of the miraculous signs demonstrates it. 'He thus revealed his glory, and the disciples put their faith in him' (2:11). His claims, using the Old Testament name of God ('I am') are all only explicable in terms of his deity. 'Anyone who has seen me has seen the Father' (14:9), he assures Philip. With the approach of the cross, the theme of God's glory revealed intensifies, and finds its locus in the 'lifting up' of Jesus to die. John's partiality for double meanings finds its full rein here as, in a number of references to the coming of 'the hour', we are led to understand that the glory of God will be seen in all its totality in the love of Christ's self-sacrifice, in the provision of atonement and mercy that flow from his broken body and poured-out blood. If, like Mark, we can divide John's gospel into two sections, we might express their content in this way. Chapters 1–12 concentrate on the revelation of the Word to the world, while 13–21 focus on his lifting-up (both as exalted king and as suffering servant) on the cross for the world. He is both the sacrificial lamb of God who bears away the world's sin (1:29) and the Good Shepherd-king whose love for his flock is seen in his voluntary laying down of his life for the sheep (10:11, 15, 17–18).

Jesus, the king

It will be clear that there are common, central themes running through all four gospels, in spite of their noted and valuable distinctives. Each of them places Christ at the centre of God's fulfilment of his long-promised blessings to all the world, through Abraham's seed. It was always true that the God of Israel was the universal sovereign, but now with the breaking in of the kingdom that is about to be fully demonstrated. The throne of David is occupied by the 'Son of Man' to whom is given authority, glory and sovereign power, over all people and nations, eternally and irrevocably. Jesus of Nazareth is that king. The old models of a renewed national Israel conquering the Gentiles are no longer valid. This king enters his city, not on a war-horse, but on a donkey, 'righteous and having salvation, gentle' and proclaiming peace to the nations, as Zechariah predicted (9:9–10), and as all the gospel writers record. For this kingdom is neither a geographical nor a political entity. Rather, it is a dynamic relationship, a covenant community, where each individual, submitting to the active rule of the king in mind and heart, finds forgiveness and peace through his atoning sacrifice, and newness of life in his resurrection. The kingdom, then, is present, here and now, but secretly. It is not recognised by many in this world, but wherever the king is ruling in an individual human life, there is the kingdom, 'within you' (Luke 17:21). And the kingdom is spreading, 'soul by soul and silently', as the good news is proclaimed through all the world and new believers are brought to see who Jesus is and to trust him. But the kingdom is 'not yet' experienced in the fulness which will be revealed, when the king personally returns to his world, in power and with great glory, to take this throne and set up his everlasting kingdom. That will be a day when the choices made, for or against him, will be finally revealed, a day of rejoicing like a great wedding banquet, but a day of judgment and exclusion too. It is the urgent, 'prophetic' appeal of the gospel writers to get ready for that day now, by repenting and believing the good news, and to enter into the present enjoyment of life with the king, even in this world.

Jesus, the teacher

We have investigated the great subject themes of the gospels, but we also need to give some thought to their literary styles and composition. In part, these are determined by the methods of Jesus' own ministry, which all the evangelists tell us was a blend of his wonderful words and his mighty acts. The teaching of Jesus took many different forms. Often he responded to questions or criticisms, enunciating key principles. He pronounced blessings and woes. Sometimes he taught by means of an extended dialogue, with either his disciples or his opponents. Frequently he used parables, especially with the crowds. The parables are among the most famous and popular of Jesus' teachings, because they are good stories, vividly recounted. Over the centuries, different interpretative methods have been applied to them. For a long time, they were seen as detailed allegories in which every ingredient had a hidden, symbolic meaning. The problem with that, as with all allegorical interpretation, is that ingenuity overcomes sense and meaning, until each exposition has a different gloss to put upon the story. In reaction, most modern interpreters have insisted that the story has one plain meaning and none of the details has symbolic significance. I remember being taught at school that a parable is 'an earthly story with a heavenly meaning'. That is probably sound advice in seeking to follow the main line through the story, but we should not ignore the vivid details which many parables contain, even though we do not deal with them allegorically. There are frequently nuances of understanding tucked into the details which reward careful investigation. Kenneth Bailey's works *Poet and Peasant* and *Through Peasant Eyes* (1983, Eerdman's) draw upon a lifetime of experience of living in Palestinian villages and are full of helpful allusions to deepen our understanding of the riches in the stories. While these things would have been obvious to Jesus' hearers, they are not to us in our culture, so that any help which enriches our understanding is to be valued. What we must not do is lose the vitality, colour and bite of the original story by reducing its 'lesson' to a piece of bland moralising or an abstract theological proposition. Parables are meant to surprise us, to stir us up to think, to challenge our preconceptions, and perhaps one of the most effective ways to make sure they are doing their work on us is to seek to re-express them in the cultural setting and dress of our own society.

Another key way in which Jesus taught was by what are sometimes called pronouncement stories, or what we might describe (less technically) as 'punch-lines'. An event occurs (such as a miracle) or a conversation is held in response to a question or criticism, or Jesus is in direct conflict with the religious authorities, but in each case the unit ends with a pay-off line, in which a key principle or important truth is expressed by Christ. This is usually related to the challenge his ministry brought to the complacency of traditional religion in his day. Further, it is important to realise that the miracle stories are used by the gospel writers as teaching tools. Their historicity is taken for granted, but their significance is the hard evidence they supply of Christ's divine power and nature, of which his own resurrection and ascension are the greatest example. However, they also reveal the quality of what he has come to achieve in his spiritual kingdom by demonstrating in the physical realm his sovereign authority and his compassionate grace. This does not mean that we are to 'spiritualise' the miracles in order to understand them. But we are to take encouragement, for example, from the fact that the Christ, who was able to open the eyes of a man born blind, is well able to give spiritual sight even to the most blind Pharisee, if only they were willing to admit their need (see John 9). Again, the punch-line makes the point. 'For judgment I have come into this world, so that the blind will see and those who see will become blind' (John 9:39).

Let us try to put these principles into practice by following a short sequence of events recorded in Luke, chapter 8.

'No-one lights a lamp and hides it in a jar or puts it under a bed. Instead, he puts it on a stand, so that those who come in can see the light. For there is nothing hidden that will not be disclosed, and nothing concealed that will not be known or brought out into the open. Therefore consider carefully how you listen. Whoever has will be given more; whoever does not have, even what he thinks he has will be taken from him.'

Now Jesus' mother and brothers came to see him, but they were not able to get near him because of the crowd. Someone told him, 'Your mother and brothers are standing outside, wanting to see you.' He replied, 'My mother and brothers are those who hear God's word and put it into practice.'

One day Jesus said to his disciples, 'Let's go over to the other side of the lake.' So they got into a boat and set out. As they sailed, he fell asleep. A squall came down on the lake, so that the boat was being swamped, and they were in great danger. The disciples went and woke him, saying, 'Master, Master, we're going to drown!' He got up and rebuked the wind and the raging waters; the storm subsided, and all was calm. 'Where is your faith?' he asked his disciples. In fear and amazement they asked one another, 'Who is this? He commands even the winds and the water, and they obey him.' (Luke 8:16–25)

The context (8:1–15) is that Jesus has just told what is usually called the parable of the sower, but might more accurately be the parable of the soils. He has explained its meaning to his disciples as indicating the various results of sowing the seed of God's Word. This parable comes at the end of a succession of events, in each of which the power of the simple word of Christ has been illustrated. At Jesus' word, Peter and his fishing companions let down their nets, after a fruitless night's work, and are so successful in the volume of fish they find that their nets begin to break and their boats start to sink (5:1–11). By a word, 'Be clean!' Jesus heals a leper (5:12–16). With a word, he forgives the sins of a paralysed man and then heals his body (5:17–26). By a word, 'Follow me!' Levi the tax-collector's life is transformed into discipleship (5:27–31). With a word a man's shrivelled hand is completely restored (6:10–11). A Roman centurion's servant is saved from death because of his master's faith in the power of Jesus' word. He did not even expect Jesus to come under his roof, but sent messengers to ask for the healing. 'Say the word and my servant will be healed,' and he was (7:1–10). With a word, Jesus can even raise the dead son of a widow woman in Nain, 'Young man, I say to you, get up!' (7:11–17). With such a growing confidence in the power of the word of God, it may well be that the disciples began to think nothing was beyond them, but Jesus wants them to be realists. On the one hand, he wants them to know that there is nothing deficient in the seed they are to sow. It can produce a yield a hundred times more than what was sown, far in excess of any yield a farmer might anticipate. But the seed will often be sown in hostile soils – hardened and compacted, rocky or infested with weeds. While some listen for a brief moment only, others believe for a while, and then fall away. Still others become diverted from Christ and the gospel by life's worries, riches and pleasures. The disciples are not to imagine that there is something wrong with the seed and start to look for an alternative message. It will always be that way. The challenge is to be good soil in oneself, and to keep sowing the good seed as widely as possible.

Our verses begin with the responsibility for disciples of diligent listening to Christ's word. 'Consider carefully *how* you listen' is the thrust of the first paragraph (vv. 16–18). Just as the purpose of a lamp is to give light to all, so the secret of the kingdom will not always be hidden; indeed, the disciples will be required to bring it out into the open and proclaim it far and wide. But the danger is that they themselves will not have received it as good soil. The implicit challenge to them is whether or not they are hearing, retaining and so producing a crop, or whether they are in fact losing that word, so that what they think they have turns out to have disappeared. One thinks of Judas Iscariot, who must have heard these words.

The next paragraph is concerned with a similar point (vv. 19–21). One might expect family loyalties to have first claim on Jesus' time and attention. His mother and brothers have made a special visit to see him, but instead of breaking off to talk with them, Jesus redefines what membership of his family actually involves. Those who are closest to him are those whose attitude to the heavenly Father is the same as his own. They are the ones who share with him the badge of membership of God's family, the only one that matters in eternity, and that is to 'hear God's word and put it into practice'. One can imagine that the disciples might well have been encouraged to see themselves in precisely that role. Had they not left everything to become his followers? But the danger is that unless that word is being retained and practised with perseverance, it will be lost, and so the third and last paragraph links it all together (vv. 22–5).

Jesus decides to show the disciples what sort of soil characterises their hearts by taking them out on the lake. Here we have a miracle story which is designed to strengthen the disciples' faith in the power of Christ's word. It is Jesus who initiates the trip and he seems to be the only one to fall asleep as they are crossing Lake Galilee. The sudden storm, not uncharacteristic of that lake, must have been of unusual ferocity for the experienced fishermen among the disciples to be afraid they were about to drown. Once awoken, Jesus first rebuked the wind and the waters. The immediacy of the total calm is testimony to the divine power of the creator at work, ruling over the natural forces of his world. But how does he do it? The answer is by his word. Shouldn't they have known it? This seems to be the point of his penetrating question, 'Where is your faith?' Do you have any? What are you putting it in? Here is a demonstration *in extremis* of the power of Christ's word to bring rescue from all the hostile forces beyond any sort of human control or even influence, totally and instantly. It is not a guarantee that his people will be 'air-lifted' out of all their difficulties, nor do we have to turn it into a glib spiritualised lesson, like the old song of my youth, 'With Christ in the vessel we can smile at the storm as we go sailing home!' The disciples did not smile at the storm. They thought they were about to drown. But they learned two lessons that day. First, that their hearts were not quite the unadulterated 'good soil' they seem to have taken them to be; but second, and much more important, that to put one's faith in the Word of God is to trust the most reliable and powerful authority in the cosmos. That is what it means to be 'good soil' and that is how they (and we) learn to put it into practice. As with the disciples, it is sometimes only in the most difficult and demanding circumstances of life that we really learn to believe in the Bible.

Acts and Revelation

Of the remaining twenty-three books of the Bible, twenty-one are letters and on these we must now focus, as the last of the biblical genres for us to examine. But first we must consider the two exceptions. The Acts of the Apostles is really the second volume of Dr Luke's gospel, and as such, much of what has been said about the gospel genre applies there as well. Although the apostolic ministry provides its contents, Luke is keen for his readers to understand what he describes as the continuation of 'all that Jesus began to do and to teach' (Acts 1:1). The spread of the gospel is the work of the risen Lord, carried out through his apostles. Luke's interest focuses, therefore, on the content of their message, with several of the early sermons carried in considerable detail, and then the impact of their mission, with the record of the founding of many churches in Asia Minor and Greece. Beginning in Jerusalem, the Church testifies to Jesus as Lord and Christ, spreading throughout Judea and Samaria, and on to the ends of the earth (Acts 1:8), so that at the conclusion of the book Paul is preaching the kingdom and teaching about the Lord Jesus Christ 'boldly and without hindrance', at the heart of the empire, in Rome (Acts 28:31).

The book of 'the revelation of Jesus Christ', with which the Bible ends, belongs to the genre of apocalyptic, which was discussed in Chapter 7. Its use of symbolism (the beasts with multiple heads and so on) would not seem as strange and unfamiliar to its original readers as it does to us. The opening paragraph spells out for us that it is also a 'testimony' or witness of Jesus Christ, a 'prophecy' interpreting God's sovereign rule of his world, in both the writer's present and throughout the future until the end of all things, and a 'letter' reminding us of its pastoral purpose which relates it to the historical setting of its recipients (1:2–4). The seven congregations specifically addressed, in chapters 2 and 3, were clearly undergoing many trials and suffering persecution for their testimony to Jesus as Lord. The interpretation of the book has produced shelves of volumes suggesting, at the two extremes, that it was exclusively a tract for that period of history (the end of the first century) or that its meaning will only be known by the generation on earth at the end of all things. Many commentators agree, however, that Revelation is built on a base of seven sevens, as follows: seven churches (1–3), seven seals (4:1 – 8:2), seven trumpets (8:3 – 11:18), seven visions (11:19 – 15:1), seven bowls

(15:2 – 18:24), seven last things (19:1 – 21:8) and the seventh day rest of the eternal sabbath (21:9–22). Some would see these sections as typical of successive stages of church history, though there is a considerable degree of subjectivity in such an approach. What is certain is that Revelation summarises the content of the Bible, as a whole. In a sense, it is an equal and opposite balance to the teaching of Genesis 1–11.

Throughout the book, the world continues its rebellion against God's rightful authority as creator and ruler. The heinousness of humanity's crimes against God and themselves inevitably generates God's righteous wrath and judgment of evil. But, in the midst of this maelstrom of human history, the book's 'revelation' is that heaven rules and that the throne of the universe is occupied by the lamb who was slain, now alive for evermore, that is Jesus Christ. It is to him that the future belongs, throughout time, and beyond, into eternity. His victory over all the hostile powers that may range themselves against him is total. What is revealed, then, is Jesus Christ reigning in unchallenged supremacy, a king of all kings and lord of all lords, with complete authority over all earthly rulers, power blocs, tyrants and ideologies, over the whole process of human history, and over the devil and all his agents. All of this reality, hidden at present, will be revealed in its totality when Jesus comes again, until which climactic conclusion of history, God's people must remain faithful and patient. They are to be committed to doing his will in every aspect of their lives, on a daily basis, as they wait for his purposes to be completed. The promises made to Abraham are now fulfilled in the numberless international community found around the throne of God, rejoicing in the salvation secured for them through the atoning sacrifice of Jesus, the lamb (see 5:9–12). As the book (and the Bible) ends, the people of God are found in the presence of God, under the rule of God, enjoying the restored relationship, which was lost in Eden, of unhindered fellowship and joy with their creator, who is now their redeemer. Is it any wonder that the Bible ends with a prayer, 'Come, Lord Jesus', and a promise, of his grace with his people until that great and glorious day (22:20–1)?

In the meantime, the great challenge to the churches, as to the individual believer, is to remain faithful in belief and behaviour, with the priorities Christ has taught us governing our lives in this world. 'Watch your life and doctrine closely,' Paul instructed his young colleague, Timothy (1 Timothy 4:16), and that crisp challenge could well provide an overall heading or summary of the purpose and contents of the New Testament epistles, or letters. Remarkably, thirteen of the twenty-one letters were written by the apostle Paul. Nine of these were to churches, and take their titles from their destination, the other four to individuals (Timothy twice, Titus and Philemon). Of the remaining eight letters, three are credited to John, two to Peter, one to James, one to Jude and the letter to the Hebrews is anonymous. The most obvious fact about the letters is that they arose to deal with questions, problems and potentially divisive issues in the churches to which they are addressed. They are not 'holiday postcard' communications, where the main reason for writing is to keep in touch, or reaffirm friendship. Although there is a personal ingredient in most of the letters, and in some a whole list of names of individuals who are to be 'greeted', much more serious purposes drive the author to put pen to paper. In interpreting these first-century letters for today, we need to keep this in mind and to do all we can to understand from within the letters themselves what was going on in the situation which provided the 'occasion' for the letter to be written. Here, as always in the Bible, a text which is not related to its context may degenerate into a pretext.

The letters of Paul

It is clear that this body of New Testament correspondence began during Paul's missionary journeys, in the earliest years of the 50s AD. A helpful way of dealing with the nine church-addressed letters is to see them in three groups of three, written over a period of a dozen or more years. The precise order is a matter of some dispute, but the three phases are fairly self-evident. The earliest letters are the two directed to the Thessalonians and the letter to the Galatians. These were churches founded by Paul's missionary endeavours, but already the target of false teachers. In Thessalonica, deceivers were claiming to have Paul's authority for saying 'that the day of the Lord has already come' (2 Thessalonians 2:2), while in Galatia the danger was of 'turning to a different gospel – which is really no gospel at all' (Galatians 1:6–7). As the letter develops it becomes clear that the infiltrators were Judaisers, who wanted to add the Jewish distinctives of circumcision and the ceremonial law to the gospel of salvation through faith in Christ alone. The letter expounds the nature of true

Christian freedom, received through faith in the crucified Christ and experienced through the powerful presence of the Holy Spirit in every individual believer. This raises an important interpretation point, which affects much of our understanding of the message of the epistles in our contemporary context. How do we move from the particularity of the problems addressed in the first-century world to bring the essential message of the teaching into our different cultural environment? After all, very few (if any) Christians are today under pressure from Jewish sources to be circumcised or to observe Jewish food laws or the ritual of the sacrifices and offerings.

Does that mean Galatians is irrelevant to the contemporary Church? Of course not. The precise clothing in which the problem appears will differ according to time and place, but the issue underneath remains a challenge to Christians in every generation, because it is based not in historical circumstances but in our sinful human nature. If we had to sum up the problem in Galatia, we might describe it as 'legalism', or 'the gospel plus . . .' The issue is that justification by God's grace alone, through faith in Christ's atoning sacrifice alone, is not sufficient ground for our acceptance with God, according to the legalist. Something else has to be added – extra beliefs, particular patterns of behaviour, unusual experiences – these are the things that will ensure you are really in the right with God. They will also ensure that you become a member of an élite club, more spiritual or more acceptable to God than the ordinary run-of-the-mill Christian, which Paul and the apostolic gospel seem to produce. The club may be marked by wealth and prosperity, super-spiritual experiences, keeping the letter of the law in the traditions of the elders or a whole range of additional ingredients to the New Testament gospel. They may sound extremely plausible and look very attractive. They will always prove very popular. But none of these are the criteria by which they should be assessed. That role belongs to the apostolic gospel alone. Anything which adds to Christ actually subtracts from him. He is no longer the fully sufficient rescuer and Lord. But not only is Christ dethroned by adherence to additional man-made rules and practices, the Christian who pays the club subscription is strait-jacketed by that commitment and ends up serving the new guru, rather than the risen Lord. That, of course, was precisely the reason the false teacher set up shop in the first place! So, far from being irrelevant, Galatians provides us with an indispensable tool by which to counteract legalism (a many-headed beast if ever there was one!) in all its attacks on the gospel of God's grace, without falling into the opposite error of libertarianism, or licence, on the other side of the narrow gospel pathway.

The middle group of letters, 1 and 2 Corinthians and Romans, come from the next phase of Paul's ministry. The church at Corinth, founded by his ministry, is facing a wide range of divisive issues. As a newly established church, in a city which was a by-word for its immorality and paganism, the Corinthian Christians were extremely vulnerable to teachers whose style and message presented a less radical challenge to their cultural habits than Paul's did. They wanted impressive speakers and leaders, inescapable demonstrations of spiritual power to 'out-glitz' the culture of their pagan city, for Christ. Paul's response is to regard them as 'mere infants in Christ', 'not yet ready for solid food' (1 Corinthians 3:1–2), their immaturity being evidenced by their obsession with the visibly impressive. As the correspondence proceeds, it becomes clear, especially in 2 Corinthians, that they have come under the spell of new teachers, pseudo or 'super-apostles', as Paul dubs them (2 Corinthians 12:11). But Paul wants to 'answer those who take pride in what is seen rather than what is in the heart' (2 Corinthians 5:12). His concern is with the heart, because that is the only guarantee that the gospel really is changing people's lives. Yet when he looks at the heart of the Corinthian church he finds gross immorality being tolerated (1 Corinthians 5), lawsuits between Christians (1 Corinthians 6), irregularities in marriage (1 Corinthians 7), improper behaviour in their meetings, divisions, excessive self-indulgence by some and deprivation of others (1 Corinthians 11). The most basic and essential of all Christian distinctives seems to be almost totally lacking from their corporate life – and that is love (1 Corinthians 13). And all this has happened because they are deserting the gospel of 'Jesus Christ and him crucified' (1 Corinthians 2:2) and his apostle, who demonstrates, in both his message and methods, the power of God made perfect in weakness (2 Corinthians 12:9).

That gospel becomes the great subject and theme of Paul's magisterial letter to the Romans, a church he had neither planted nor visited at the time. This is the nearest equivalent to a theological treatise in the whole of the body of Paul's letters and has been used by the Holy Spirit down the centuries to bring countless thousands to faith in Christ, and an assured discipleship. From its magnificent opening, the letter's one theme is the 'gospel of God . . . regarding his Son . . . Jesus Christ our Lord' (1:1–4). It is that message alone, promised in the Old Testament Scriptures, which now summons the Gentile nations, and so the whole world, to 'the obedience that comes from faith' which is the only way to 'belong to Jesus Christ' (1:5–6). Almost identical words are used at the very end of the letter, so that we are left in no doubt as to its contents and purpose. Paul ascribes glory to 'him who is able to establish you by my gospel, and the proclamation of Jesus Christ . . . now revealed and made known through the prophetic writings by the command of the eternal God, so that all nations might believe and obey him' (16:25–6).

Through the first eight chapters, Paul traces the story and development of God's great rescue-mission to the human race. In a masterly *tour de force*, he presents the whole human race, Gentiles and Jews, before God as guilty rebels, universally sinful and deserving nothing but his wrath and punishment (1:18 – 3:20). But into this scene of hopeless despair steps God himself to provide a 'righteousness from God . . . through faith in Jesus Christ to all who believe' (3:22). Paul explains how it can be possible for God to restore guilty sinners into a right relationship with their creator, through the work of the Lord Jesus (3:21 – 5:20). Chapters 6 to 8 deal with the realities of living as Christians with sinful natures in a fallen world, but rejoice in the provision to live differently in the present (although imperfectly) through the gift of the Holy Spirit and the expectation of transformation to perfection in the eternal kingdom, with its certain and complete salvation. Chapters 9 to 11 explore the relationship of the Jewish people to this gospel of their Messiah and to the Gentile churches it has produced. The remaining chapters (12 to 16) deal with the practical outworking of these gospel realities, in the offering of our whole selves 'as living sacrifices, holy and pleasing to God' (12:1) and in the loving and supportive relationships by which Christians authenticate the truth of the gospel's claims in the world and in the Church.

The final trio of Paul's church letters, Ephesians and Colossians (which are parallel letters in subject matter) together with Philippians, are usually dated to the early 60s AD and called the prison epistles. Each letter contains reference to Paul's imprisonment, for Christ and the gospel, yet his overall purpose is to keep the churches focused on the gospel and on their responsibility to live it and proclaim it faithfully. The Ephesian letter, which was probably circulated to several other churches in that city's hinterland, concentrates on the eternal plan of God 'to bring all things in heaven and on earth together under one head, even Christ' (1:10) and shows how the Church already is the prototype of that reality, in this world. Only the gospel could break down 'the dividing wall of hostility' between Jews and Gentiles, making a new unity out of the two, by reconciling both to God through the cross of Christ (2:14–16). For Christians living in Ephesus, in which all kinds of occult and magic practices thrived, it was of vital importance to know that no other power, however threatening, could have any authority over Christian believers who 'put on the full armour of God' in order to stand their ground (6:10–18). In the same way, Christians in Colosse need to continue to be rooted in Christ and not allow the alternative agenda of either legalism or licence to tempt them with a spurious claim of 'fulness', which they already genuinely had in Christ and in the faith they were taught (Colossians 2:6–10). For the Philippians, the challenge is to keep on 'holding on to the word of life' by 'holding it out' to others in a joyful, outgoing evangelism (Philippians 2:16). By this time the fires of persecution are beginning to be stoked, probably by Emperor Nero, and Paul is aware that he and his readers need not to retreat but to press on to know Christ better, with their eyes on the heavenly horizon, for only then will they be prepared to share in his sufferings (3:10–11). Similar themes surface in Paul's pastoral letters to Timothy (a pastor in Ephesus) and Titus (in Crete) as he urges them not to compromise the gospel or their faithful life-style of service to Christ whatever the cost may be.

Indeed, these concerns permeate the shorter and generally later letters at the end of the New Testament. Peter's focus is on the suffering congregations of Turkey, whose faith is being refined in the fires and who need neither to give up, nor to go low-profile, but to 'live such good lives among the pagans that . . . they may see your good deeds and glorify God' (1 Peter 2:12). John deals with churches from which there has been widespread apostasy, where the attacks of antichrist forces are already being experienced, and where the gospel values of light (truth) and love will be the only means by which they will be able to preserve themselves from idolatry. There is an urgency to these later letters, short though they are. As the generation of the apostles began to die, and the return of Christ had not yet occurred, it became clear that a church without the apostles was a coming reality.

That was why the written Scriptures had to be produced as an authoritative guide to apostolic teaching and practice, as derived from the Master himself. It also explains why the later letters are so full of urgent exhortation and application. The apostles' great twin concerns are to keep the churches faithful to the gospel (the truth, the whole truth and nothing but the truth) and active in propagating the gospel. The only way to hold on to the gospel is to give it away. Evangelism is always the way to a spiritually healthy church, but what is given away must be the pure gospel, and not a distortion by addition or subtraction, or any other corruption.

Finding the theme tune

In this brief survey, I have tried to indicate that the most important key to unlocking the huge relevance of the epistles for ourselves and our churches today is to find the theme tune, or what Dick Lucas has often called the 'melodic line' of each book. If we can travel back in time, through a really careful reading of the text, picking up the clues which it gives as to what was going on in the original situation, we shall begin to see how that same melody plays in our context. To quote Klein, Blomberg and Hubbard, 'Interpreters must reconstruct those original "occasions" and purposes as precisely as possible in order to separate timeless principles from situation-specific applications' (op. cit. p. 352). It is clear that the letters were largely written to churches and that their applications are often corporate. Paul expected the whole church to hear what he had written. 'I charge you before the Lord to have this letter read to all the brothers' (1 Thessalonians 5:27). The second person pronouns ('you', in English) are nearly always plural. Now, of course, it is true that the plural reality of a congregation is dependent on the individual Christians who comprise it and they all have individual responsibility for their choices, words and actions, just as they have an individual personal relationship with God to cultivate. But in our excessively individualised culture in the West, we can very easily lose, and then ignore, the corporate element of teaching and application which is built into the letters. When we read them, it is more like listening to a sermon, which will address both individuals and the congregation as a whole. It is the nearest we can come to sitting at the apostles' feet and hearing the teaching of Christ directly from them. It is worth remembering that the letters (like a sermon) were being prepared for the ear rather than the eye, and that the literary devices which are used are designed to aid the understanding and the memory. Repetition of phrases, patterns of words, specialist terminology, balanced sentence structures, debating with imaginary objectors, 'marker points' or 'book-ends' at the beginning and end of a specially important section using similar phraseology – all of these play their part in focusing the attention and driving home the point.

At one level, then, the New Testament epistles are much like any other letters of the Græco-Roman first-century world. They follow the commonly accepted structures, beginning with the author's name, the destination of the letter and a greeting. This often led on to an expression of good wishes for the well-being of the reader, which the apostles transform into a prayer and/or a thanksgiving for their readers' spiritual life and health. When this is absent (as in Galatians) it is highly significant, since it is a mark of Paul's urgency, expressing his distress and even anger at the current state of affairs. Where it is doubled (as in 1 Thessalonians) it is equally significant, though, of course, for the opposite reason. There then follows the main 'business' of the letter, laying out the arguments, together with evidences and proofs for the author's standpoint, and appealing with the reader to agree, to be convinced and to act accordingly. After this exhortation, there is often a closing summary of the main thrust before the farewell, which will frequently include greetings to other people known to both author and reader, and a closing wish, expressed as a prayer. But there are major differences in that the New Testament letters have a didactic authority implicit in their inspiration, which means that their teaching comprises a theology – a 'pattern of sound teaching' (2 Timothy 1:13), 'the faith that was once for all entrusted to the saints' (Jude v. 3). Therefore, our understanding will be greatly deepened by comparing Scripture with Scripture, by gathering together the major ideas and propositions, under a number of subject headings doctrinally, and by relating them to one another, identifying and describing a coherent theological position, which is systematic and biblical. This is why the epistles have become the major teaching materials of the Church and why so many theological issues turn on their exposition.

Now let's look at an example, to draw these principles together and work them out in practice.

It was necessary, then, for the copies of the heavenly things to be purified with these sacrifices, but the heavenly things themselves with better sacrifices than these. For Christ did not enter a man-made sanctuary that was only a copy of the true one; he entered heaven itself, now to appear for us in God's presence. Nor did he enter heaven to offer himself again and again, the way the high priest enters the Most Holy Place every year with blood that is not his own. Then Christ would have had to suffer many times since the creation of the world. But now he has appeared once for all at the end of the ages to do away with sin by the sacrifice of himself. Just as man is destined to die once, and after that to face judgment, so Christ was sacrificed once to take away the sins of many people; and he will appear a second time, not to bear sin, but to bring salvation to those who are waiting for him. (Hebrews 9:23–8)

First, we need to set this very rich paragraph within the historical context of the whole letter to the Hebrews. Its author is unknown, but as its title and contents make clear, it has Jewish Christians particularly in view, throughout what the writer describes, at the end, as 'my word of exhortation' . . . only a short letter' (13:22)! The letter is punctuated with a series of increasingly solemn warnings about the danger of 'drifting away' and ignoring 'such a great salvation' (2:1–3), hardening the heart through sin's deceitfulness and so falling short of God's promise of rest (3:7 – 4:11), 'falling away' and so 'crucifying the Son of God all over again' (6:4–12), 'trampling the Son of God underfoot', 'throwing away your confidence' and shrinking back to destruction (10:26–39). The 'occasion' is clear. These Hebrew Christians are being tempted to turn back to Judaism, probably because their Christian profession is exposing them to persecution. At first, the Roman empire was happy to regard Christianity as a variant of Judaism, a new sect within an established ethnic religion, such as was tolerated provided it was not politically subversive. But when the Jews became increasingly hostile towards the Christians, not least as a result of the mission to the Gentiles, the Roman authorities were alerted to the fact that this new belief did not sit comfortably under the umbrella of Judaism. It was in fact an illicit religion, and its creed 'Jesus is Lord' was exclusive, rather than pluralist. Its adherents would not declare 'Caesar is Lord' and so the wrath of the Roman machine was turned against the followers of the Way.

How tempting it would have been for Hebrew Christians quietly to

drift back to their Judaism and to avoid all this trouble! Doubtless
their families and friends were not slow to persuade them. They had
already experienced public exposure to insult, persecution, prison
and the confiscation of property (10:33–4). Why undergo any more?
The letter sets out to answer that pressing question. In a nutshell, its
argument is that such a retreat would be apostasy and that it would
represent a movement from reality to shadow-land, from light to
darkness. This is the argument which is coming to its climax in our
passage. While the Jewish people claimed that they had received God's
law spoken by angels (2:2), Christians know that God has spoken to
us by his Son (1:2ff). While Judaism rightly took pride in the heroic
grandeur of Moses and the priestly dignity of Aaron, they were but
servants in God's house. Christ is the Son over the household (3:6)
and the great high priest, not subject to an earthly temple and a mortal
succession of priests, but eternally alive and active in the heavens
(4:14), appointed by God as his eternal agent (5:10). While the temple
with its sacrifices and the entrance of the high priest into the holy
place, once a year, to atone for the sins of the people were marvellous
pictures of God's grace, Christ has completed all they stood for and
brought the reality of heaven to his people. 'This is an illustration for
the present time, indicating that the gifts and sacrifices being offered
were not able to clear the conscience of the worshipper. They are only
a matter of food and drink and various ceremonial washings – external
regulations applying until the time of the new order' (9:9–10). The
new order, or covenant, is now explained, so that the readers see its
amazing superiority to all that preceded it. This background is
obviously essential for a proper understanding of the passage itself.

It is also essential to work at how the argument of the passage itself
holds together. Verse 23 contains a contrast between the Old Testament
sacrifices which served to purify the copies on earth of the heavenly
realities and the heavenly things themselves. The blood of animals
would serve for purification of the earthly copies in the tabernacle
and temple, but they would be totally inapplicable to the sanctuary of
heaven in which the divine majesty is enthroned. How could an earthly
animal's blood possibly have any heavenly, eternal efficacy? The
contrast continues in verse 24. The 'better' sacrifice can only be that
of the Son of God, but it is so acceptable to God that Jesus, as the real
and perfect high priest, has access into the very presence of God in
heaven. Verses 25 and 26 present a further development of contrast,

based on what we have just understood. This is between the high priest having to make atonement for the nation's sin year after year and Christ dealing with sins 'once for all at the end of the ages' (i.e. it is God's last major act in history before the end of everything). Furthermore, the high priest had to offer an animal's blood, but Christ sacrificed himself. In these two ways, his offering is immeasurably 'better'; in fact, the two bear no comparison. Verses 27 and 28 then present the final contrasts between man's one death leading to judgment and Christ's one death leading to salvation for those whose sins have been forgiven.

The method of contrast shows us then four ways in which Christ's sacrificial death, as both priest and offering, is immeasurably superior to ('better' than, in Hebrews vocabulary) all that went before in Jewish Old Testament belief and practice. Each of these constitutes another reason why it is impossible for any true Christian believer to countenance a return to Judaism, however personally demanding being a disciple of Christ may prove to be. To get the point of the passage it will be a help to list the points.

1 Christ has entered heaven itself to gain us access, not a shadow-land earthly tabernacle or temple.
2 Christ's sacrifice is sufficient and complete. Once for all, it never needs to be repeated, unlike the annual ritual of the Day of Atonement.
3 Christ offered his own blood, in his self-sacrificial death, not the blood of an animal, and so a full atonement is made.
4 Our death will lead to judgment, but Christ's death leads to salvation for those who belong to him.

There is, in addition, one last thread running through the passage, in the form of a verb, which occurs on three different occasions but binds the whole unit together. Each appearance is in a different tense, which enables us to see the spread of what is being taught, across past, present and future. The verb is 'to appear', and in each case Christ is the subject. In verse 26 'he has appeared' in the decisive once-for-all act of atonement on the cross, which was the very purpose of the incarnation. Having dealt with our sin by his sacrificial death, the risen Christ is able to be our trail-blazer into God's presence where he 'now appears' for us, as our intercessor and advocate (v. 24). Our acceptance with God depends on the certainty of sins forgiven through the finished work of Christ and his present session at the Father's right hand, where like the Israelite high priest he carries the names of his people on his hands and on his heart. That is what guarantees our future experience of this great salvation in its fulness. 'He will appear', not to deal with sin, which was the purpose of his first coming, culminating in the cross, but 'to bring salvation to those who are waiting for him' (v. 28). The qualification for receiving that full and final deliverance is that we live now, trusting in Christ's finished work on the cross and eagerly expecting the full experience of salvation, throughout eternity, in his presence. In the light of such realities, how could any true believer ever contemplate drifting away from such a great salvation? What could a return to the old system possibly offer?

The epistles of the New Testament provide an enormous reservoir of truth concerning Christ and his work for his people. They require careful reading, with attention to vocabulary and the way specialist terms are used within a particular letter, as well as an appreciation of how logical arguments build and the importance of connecting words, which relate ideas together, in parallel or contrast. It is always a good test to see whether we really understand the text's meaning by trying to express its ideas in vocabulary, images and metaphors of our own and relevant to our culture. The most important thing, as always, is to let the text speak, to encounter it with all its surprises and shocks, its questions and issues, and not to try to squeeze it into some preconceived theological grid, but to let it challenge and perhaps change our frameworks as we listen to God speak. It is to the question of the application of the Bible to our contemporary context that we must now turn in more detail.

To remind you

- The four gospels of the New Testament provide a rounded account not only of the life, death and resurrection of Jesus, but also of the reason why he came. They show us God's rescue-mission for humanity in action, each with its distinctive emphasis on particular aspects of the good news (pp. 160–8).
- Common to all the gospels is the conviction that Jesus is the long-awaited King, who will reign for ever, over everything (pp. 168–9).
- The teaching of Jesus explains the purpose and the meaning of his ministry. By a variety of approaches, he calls on his disciples to be

responsive and obedient hearers of his words, by putting them into practice (pp. 169–74).

- Of the rest of the New Testament, only two books are not letters. Acts tells the story of the spreading gospel, while Revelation generates faith in God's sovereign rule throughout history (pp. 174–6).
- Paul's letters represent the fullest theological understanding of the person and work of Christ and the impact of God's great salvation plan on the Church and the world (pp. 176–81).
- Interpreting the letters for today involves travelling back to the original purpose for their composition, and identifying the theme tunes which govern their contents (pp. 181–6).

Chapter 9

How Can I Hear God Speaking in the Bible?

As CHRISTINE SAT down to reflect on the past few months, she was amazed at the changes that had happened in her life. She smiled ruefully as she remembered how she'd bitten Alison's head off when she had come up to her, really politely (and incredibly nervously, as Christine now realised) and asked her to come to a mums' Bible study. It had seemed such a weird thing to do. She stirred her coffee, reflectively. And now, tonight, she and Dan were off to another couple's home to do just that together, in a group that had been really welcoming and non-judgmental. But it wasn't really the people – she had lots of good friends – it was that Book that had done it. She smiled again. The God behind the Book and in its pages might be a better way of explaining it. Through the Bible, God was changing their lives, and so much for the better. Of course, there was still a huge amount she didn't understand, but she'd come so far so quickly. It was such a relief to know that you didn't have to switch off your mind to be a Christian – quite the opposite, in fact. All that stuff she had trotted out about science disproving the Bible seemed so trivial now that she was understanding what the Bible actually said. And yet she had been so confident in what amounted to ignorance. She might never have opened a Bible, never have known about Jesus, never have found his forgiveness, peace and joy, never have seen how God intended marriages to work and how to bring the kids up positively in such a negative world, if Alison hadn't approached her at the school gate that afternoon. She glanced at the clock, swallowed her coffee and headed off to meet the kids. As she rushed out of the door, a thought crossed her mind. 'I wonder if Sarah down the road might be interested in a group to study the Bible . . .'

Matt couldn't believe where he was. The arch-atheist of his set, Mr Cool personified, he who could destroy a Christian at ten paces just by the curl of his lip, he, Matt, was standing at the front, in a students' Christian meeting, about to tell a roomful of fellow students how he had met God. But it was true, and he was so pleased about it! He told them about the guy who had 'forced' the John's gospel on him and told him that all he had to lose was his prejudice. That had really struck home to him. It was uncomfortably true. He really was totally prejudiced, not only against Christianity, but against anything else that didn't fit into his tidy little world, where he was king and everybody else was expected to bow down and worship. But it was that little book, John's gospel, which had got underneath his radar and exploded his cosy defence-systems. Actually, it was the person he had met in the book, who strode through its pages with such incredible authority yet blended with humility. His teaching was so obviously right and true. It was like a searchlight trained on to his life, exposing all his grubby compromise and petty self-seeking, penetrating even to the rats in the cellar, which he could still hardly bring himself to recognise were there. And yet he wasn't condemning or judgmental; there was such love and compassion in the way he dealt with people and put their fragmented lives back together again. He gave it to you straight, up-front, no nonsense. Heaven was a reality, so was hell. God is there; he is real and we're all going to meet him one day, but he's come in Jesus to meet us first, to offer us forgiveness and real freedom. Our part is to believe him, receive his rescue and follow his rule. Mind you, that wasn't an easy step. Matt had tried to find a way out for several days, but he knew that Jesus had 'cornered' him, with his truth and love, and he had to come home to God.

Andy and Julia had to admit that things were becoming clearer. When their relationship started to crack up, the last place they would have looked for help was the Bible. They knew nothing about it and they weren't religious types, anyway. But Julia's friend had given them one of those modern versions of the Bible which was surprisingly easy to read, and some help on which bits to look at to get started. What had surprised them was how much material there was about making relationships work. It was all in the context of marriage, of course, and that had made them think. Perhaps what was wrong was that they were really frightened of that sort of commitment. When they looked at the pattern of marriage and family life laid out in the Bible, it seemed to make a good deal of sense and, far from presenting them with a list of unwanted restrictions, it was quite liberating to see that what it advised actually matched in with their own deepest needs. But that was when they had hit the brick wall. How could anybody live that way? They had really tried, on and off anyway, but they just couldn't hack it. This unselfish love, putting your partner's needs above your own, building one another up – great when you're on the receiving end, but how would you ever be able to keep it going? Or want to?

Perhaps that was what Julia's friend had meant when she talked about the need for a 'heart transplant'. It sounded like one of those really weird phrases Christians use, but Andy and Julia were slowly coming to realise that some sort of change deep inside each of them was what was needed. If ever their relationship was going to be built on giving rather than getting, then somebody had to change. And they were rather beginning to suspect that only God could deal with something that big . . .

Getting to know God

In each of these scenarios, what is happening is a basic ingredient of every Christian's experience – people are coming to know God through his word, the Bible. The difference is between knowing about God and knowing him in a personal, relational way. Both sorts of knowing depend on the Bible. The first might be the substance of the religious studies syllabus at school. Different religions can be studied, their sacred texts, practices and rituals analysed and documented, what 'they believe' explained, without this content impacting the personal life of the student any more than a knowledge of the geography of Israel would. This is knowing about the world's religions and their 'gods', but in a clinical, detached and academic way. It can take you all the way to a research degree in theology. But knowing the God of the Bible as one's heavenly Father, living one's life in daily contact with him, experiencing his love and power, understanding his plans and purposes – that is knowledge of a different order altogether. Yet it is equally dependent on reading the Bible. As we noted in an earlier chapter, it is by the Word of God that the Spirit of God produces the people, or children, of God.

Everybody wants to know whether God has anything to say to us today. If he were to be advertised as giving a TV broadcast in the place of the nightly news, it is a fair guess that current record viewing figures would be shattered around the world. Even 'unbelievers' are curious. But very few people realise what is available through that familiar book, on sale in any bookstore, whenever it is opened and read seriously. The Bible is God speaking; what Scripture says, God says, and what he has said, he is still saying. Our problem is often with his method (a book that needs to be read, or listened to) or its content. But that does not invalidate the word God speaks, it simply deprives us of its benefits. Supposing a friend were to contact me about an urgent matter by leaving a message on my telephone answering machine, which I then choose not to listen to, because I say I haven't time. Does that invalidate my friend's communication? Of course not. I may ring him and berate him for not speaking to me, while all the time he has already spoken, but I have chosen to ignore it. That is not his fault, but mine. Yet that is precisely what so many of us do today, when we demand that if God exists he should address us personally, while all the time ignoring what he has already said in the Bible.

This is what is meant when Christians speak of the 'sufficiency' of Scripture. It does not imply that the answer to every question we might ask about life and the decisions we have to make is sitting there, waiting to be unearthed, in the pages of the Bible. It will not tell me whether to change my job this year, or next, or not at all. What it will tell me is how to do my work in a way that glorifies God and benefits others, and the sort of person I need to be whatever workplace I happen to be in. Similarly, it will not tell me whether to buy this house or that one, or to go on renting my present flat. What it will tell me is how Christians should use the material resources God has entrusted to them, as stewards in his world. It will warn me of the dangers of self-indulgent luxury and encourage me to use my home as a centre of God's love for my family, my neighbourhood and further afield. The reason the Bible works this way is that it has an agenda for personal change, deep in our characters and at the level of our motivation. That is where the real issues of life are and where we need to do business with God. But our agenda is usually for God to be changing our circumstances, not us. We tend to come to these issues with the presupposition that if our job was different, or if we lived in a different home or neighbourhood, we would be such excellent Christians. If only God would just arrange our circumstances the way we really want them, then we'd live for him, be fully committed to loving God and our neighbour. So wouldn't it be in God's interest just to tell us to do what we want to do, to legitimise that decision and take the weight of its responsibility for us?

It is not difficult to see why he doesn't play our games our way. We would remain hopelessly immature. The God who created us in his own image, to think and choose and love, is not going to short-cut the process by which we learn to think in line with his thoughts, which reflect his character, as revealed in his Word. He is not going to deprive us of the human dignity of making decisions, which use that knowledge and link it with the moral courage of doing what we believe to be right, as we choose how to live. When we submit to his authority, he doesn't turn us into zombies, programmed externally to carry out his plans, as though he was some bizarre inventor of robots. He puts his Word in our mind and heart (the biblical term means the control centre of the personality, where we make our decisions) and calls us to understand, trust and obey him. That is what the personal relationship at the centre of Christian experience means. God calls us to a life of faith and the object of that faith is himself, as he is infallibly revealed in the words that he has spoken. Our faith is that God is not deluding us, or playing games with us, when we give him our trust and try to obey him. It is a faith confirmed daily in the school of experience. It means that we do not have to read between the lines, or imagine that God may be giving us additional personal messages, without which we could not function as Christians. The Bible is God's sufficient Word, to bring us safely from earth to heaven, to guide every footstep of our life in this world and to tell us all that we need to know to enable us to trust him and obey him.

> His divine power has given us everything we need for life and godliness through our knowledge of him who called us by his own glory and goodness. Through these he has given us his very great and precious promises, so that through them you may participate in the divine nature and escape the corruption in the world caused by evil desires. (2 Peter 1:3–4)

Peter is convinced that in the 'divine power' and in the 'very great and precious promises' we have the total resources needed to know God, to live godly lives and to grow in holiness of character. The word translated 'power' is often used to describe the Holy Spirit, who is both the author and illuminator of Scripture, where the promises are to be found on every page. So in God's Word and through his Spirit, God has provided us with sufficient resources to be sufficient Christians in this world. There are many things we might like to know, but cannot. 'The secret things belong to the LORD our God, but the things revealed belong to us and to our children for ever, that we may follow all the words of this law' (Deuteronomy 29:29). The content God has revealed is totally sufficient to accomplish his purpose in our lives. Of course, God may use other secondary means to bring us into line with his will revealed in Scripture. He may 'speak' to us through a preacher, or a book, or a telephone call, or a group of friends who have been praying for us, or an unexpected contact, or an unlooked-for providence, or a sudden inspirational idea, or a subconscious memory. The list would be endless, if we tried to put one together, to adequately describe the variety of ways by which the living Spirit of God prompts and directs, checks and channels, rebukes and encourages God's children. But none of these means of God's grace needs to be written down and bound into the covers of the Bible, and all of them need to be checked and weighed against what is already written within those covers. All other communications, outside us or within, are necessarily subjective and fallible, but the sufficiency of Scripture is an expression of its unique authority and entire trustworthiness.

> All Scripture is God-breathed and is useful for teaching, rebuking, correcting and training in righteousness, so that the man of God may be thoroughly equipped for every good work. (2 Tim 3:16–17)

Our next step is to realise that such sufficiency is only experienced by those who put into practice, in their lives, what they have understood from the biblical text. The proof of the pudding really is in the eating. The Bible itself is especially clear about this. Its purpose is always to promote action, never simply to provide knowledge. To know God is to love and obey him. This keynote is sounded loud and clear, as the people of Israel are about to enter the promised land. Summarising God's requirements, in the law, Moses concludes, 'Now what I am commanding you today is not too difficult for you or beyond your reach . . . No, the word is very near you; it is in your mouth and in your heart so that you may obey it' (Deuteronomy 30:11–14). Practical application is its purpose. At the other end of Israel's Old Testament pilgrimage, after they have returned from the Babylonian exile and completed the rebuilding of the temple and the walls of Jerusalem, the community itself was reconstructed by the reading of the law to all the people and its explanation by the Levites. 'They read from the Book of the Law of God, making it clear and giving the meaning so that the people could understand what was being read' (Nehemiah 8:8). As a result the whole community celebrated the Feast of Tabernacles, in obedience to what they heard, and re-dedicated themselves to God and to the covenant. Similarly, Jesus links the application of his word to the reality of a personal relationship with God. 'If anyone loves me, he will obey my teaching. My Father will love him, and we will come to him and make our home with him. He who does not love me will not obey my teaching. These words you hear are not my own; they belong to the Father who sent me' (John 14:23–4). By contrast, the greatest danger any Bible-hearer or Bible-reader can fall into is the hardening of the heart which comes by not acting on what has been understood. 'Today, if you hear his voice, do not harden your hearts', we are exhorted (Psalm 95:7–8). The reference is to Israel in the desert who saw God's deeds, such as providing water from the rock, and heard his words through Moses; but instead of trusting him, they tested and tried him. Their hearing was not combined with faith and so, through unbelief, they were unable to enter God's rest (see Hebrews 3:7 – 4:2).

Relating the Bible to our lives

Application, then, is all-important, but it depends upon a right understanding of the text first, and then the drawing of legitimate and appropriate lines from that context to our own. We have argued earlier that a biblical text has a fixed, intended meaning. Calling it a 'single' meaning can be misleading if it applies a reductionist approach to the limitless riches of God's word. But the text is not plastic; it cannot mean contradictory things. However, it may also have a wide variety of applications, built on that base. That is to say, the unchanging truth will have different significances to different readers. Sometimes these are cultural. Applying a particular text to life in a village in Papua New Guinea may produce a different significance from life in a Western mega-metropolis. Sometimes the differences are personal, to do with an individual's life situation, temperament or opportunities. The same meaning is applied in different ways. It is important to underline that this is not a charter for saying that the Bible means different things to different people. The text has one meaning, but the ways in which that meaning is worked out, in dependence on the illumination and enabling of the Holy Spirit, will be many and various.

What we need to discover are principles which can be used to keep us from making inappropriate or invalid applications. Otherwise, we may actually distort the meaning, which we originally rightly understood. This process properly begins with the general methods of interpreting the text we have already discussed and illustrated. As we set the text in its context, particularly the book of which it is a part, and see how its particular contents match with the book's theme tune, we begin to understand the purpose which the author had as its primary application. One of the key ways of hearing God speak through the Bible is to do our reading of Scripture with our antennae up, looking for the surprises, being prepared to ask questions. 'Why does he use *this* word? Why does he say it *that* way, and why at *this* point in the argument, or story?' It's especially helpful when we are stopped in our tracks and find ourselves recognising that we wouldn't have said it like that at all. All these investigative questions will find their answers within the larger textual context, including the overall purpose for it being written. Once we begin to see *why* the writer says what he says, in the way that he does, we shall begin to realise how the message gets under our twenty-first-century skin, as well. The more carefully we interpret the text in its context, the more likely we are to relate to its original applications, and the more likely we shall be able to recognise the common factors between the people being addressed and ourselves.

Let's take a short example from the teaching of Jesus on prayer in the Sermon on the Mount.

And when you pray, do not be like the hypocrites, for they love to pray standing in the synagogues and on the street corners to be seen by men. I tell you the truth, they have received their reward in full. But when you pray, go into your room, close the door and pray to your Father, who is unseen. Then your Father, who sees what is done in secret, will reward you. And when you pray, do not keep on babbling like pagans, for they think they will be heard because of their many words. (Matthew 6:5–7).

How does this apply to us? Obviously, the need for us to pray and to do so in a way that is acceptable to God is a common factor between the original hearers and ourselves. So it would be easy to see this simply as a straightforward teaching passage, which it clearly is, saying that the secrecy and sincerity of prayer are what matters most to God. That is fine, but it's not the whole story. After a while, simply to read the Bible 'on the flat' in that way will make it all rather predictable and even boring. Ask the bigger questions before you apply it. To whom does Jesus say this, and why? The sermon is directed to disciples (5:1–2), though doubtless many in the crowds listened in, too. But as we saw in our survey of Matthew, Jesus is gathering a new Israel, a new community of covenant people, and this is the manifesto of his kingdom, the statement of its citizens' life-style. Its cutting edge shows how following Jesus turns upside-down conventional ideas of religiosity, the exponents of which Jesus calls 'hypocrites' (6:5) and 'pagans' (6:7). This is not just information. The disciples would be perfectly familiar with the ostentatious prayers of the religious leaders and the mindless mantras of pagan religion. The one they might have admired; the other they would scorn. But they would not want to be called by either title. However, the direct instruction of verse 6 implies that they (and we) might very easily fall into either category. As soon as our confidence is removed from a child-like dependence on our heavenly Father, prayer will become either a point-scoring exercise of hypocrisy or a psychologically engineered exercise in self-persuasion. When we see that our hearts are by nature hypocritical and pagan, we begin to realise that the external form and practice of prayer means nothing unless it is accompanied by a right relationship with God, and that is the purpose of Jesus' sermon. The motivation to change comes from hearing Jesus describe my self-regarding religious formalism as hypocritical and pagan. That is a salutary shock to the system.

In the example we have just looked at, the transfer from the text's context to our own is not very difficult to make. We may not attend synagogues, and street-corner prayer is hardly in fashion, but prayer in public where our concern is more on the evaluation of its verbal quality by others than its honesty before God is a constant threat to our Christian meetings. Nor is it difficult to see that the strongest line of application will always be found by asking the question, 'What is God teaching us about God in this text?' As we have underlined already, that is why the Bible does not have to be made relevant.

Nothing matters more than that we should read, mark, learn and inwardly digest all that God is willing to reveal of his unchanging nature and his eternal purposes, in every part of Scripture. Nothing can be more relevant to every part of our human experience.

Diagnostic questions

But there are also other general questions which help us to draw valid lines of application from the Bible to ourselves. For example, 'What aspects of unchanging human nature do we find explained or illustrated by this passage?' Because God's rescue plan through Christ is clearly demonstrated in the Bible to be his last word to humankind before the end of all things, it can be reasonably assumed that we shall not see the effects of the fall reversed in human nature, this side of heaven. The gospel is going to be needed throughout human history, in each generation, and there is no alternative. If we take away the particular cultural clothing in which the individuals appear in their biblical context, what are the common human factors beneath, which we share with them? It is easy for us to sit in judgment on the Pharisees, in the gospels, for example, since we know they are the villains of the piece, but that would not have been at all evident in Jesus' day, when they were widely respected for their outward piety and their reverence for the Torah. It is only when I stop detaching myself from them and begin to identify the Pharisaical characteristics lurking in my own heart that the application of the gospel passages really start to bite and challenge, as they should.

Another application question would be, 'What can we learn from this passage about covenant people in their relationship with God?' This is one of the great values of the stories of Old Testament heroes. Chapter 1 of the book of Daniel tells the story of the Babylonians' siege of Jerusalem (597 BC) and the exile of the young Jewish élite to Babylon, of whom Daniel was one. Given Babylonian names and trained in the royal palace (equivalent to a top university education), Daniel and his friends are expected to assimilate to Babylonian culture and religion. This they refuse to do; yet at the end of the training period, they come out top of this intake. One of their 'rebellious' acts was to refuse the royal food and wine, and to request only vegetables to eat and water to drink. So is this a text to teach the values of vegetarianism and abstinence from alcohol? It might well be argued so and devotees of both today might well provide corroborative medical evidence, but there is no hint of that in the text. Daniel and his friends are not successful because of their diet. Their diet is an expression of their faith in their God. Three young men are in covenant relationship with the true and living God, and they want to prove to the pagan court that his power and ability are vastly superior to anything the wealth of Babylon, or its false idols, can be said to produce. The passage is not about diet but about God, and it all revolves around three statements about God and his covenant faithfulness, which leads us to its application. 'The Lord delivered Jehoiakim king of Judah into [Nebuchadnezzar's] hand' (Daniel 1:2) – the circumstances are entirely God's doing. 'Now God had caused the official to show favour and sympathy to Daniel' (v. 9) – he rules in the lives of those who do not even acknowledge him. 'To these four young men God gave knowledge and understanding of all kinds' (v. 17) – he honours covenant people who commit themselves to his faithful sovereignty. These are applications which we can immediately relate to our life in a world which is still opposed to God's rule, puts its confidence in its own idols and often wants to squeeze God's people into its mould. This process is what the American scholar, Walter Kaiser, calls 'principlization' in his stimulating book *Towards An Exegetical Theology* (1981, Baker Books, pp. 206ff). It can be expressed in terms of the question, 'What timeless principles does the author intend to stress?'

The most difficult parts of the Bible to apply tend to be the moral or spiritual exhortations of the New Testament, where it may be difficult to separate out the timeless truth from the specific cultural example. I well remember as a young minister having to deal with a middle-aged single gentleman who, a week or two after he arrived at our church, placed himself at the entrance door and planted a kiss on the cheek of any unaccompanied ladies of his own age or (particularly!) younger. This, we were told, was obedience to 1 Thessalonians 5:26, 'Greet all the brothers with a holy kiss.' Though one might have pointed out that the 'brothers' were conspicuously *not* those he was greeting, the wind was taken out of his sails when he protested that he meant nothing by doing it. The obvious retort was, 'Well, then, don't do it!' One modern British paraphrase renders the verse, 'A hearty handshake all round,' which is certainly safer and a more appropriate application of the principle, in a different cultural setting, even if it is somewhat redolent of the 'stiff upper lip' approach to life. As a rule, and it covers the great majority of New Testament cases, where the life situation or cultural context is directly parallel, or equally understandable, to our own culture, then the principle taught by the passage transcends the historical differences and needs to be translated straight across to our context. In debatable situations, we need to work from the foundation truths of the gospel outward to their ethical application and to consider whether other New Testament passages or similar issues help us to distinguish between the absolute principle and the culturally related application. There will always be applications about which equally sincere and biblically centred Christians disagree, and these can vary from generation to generation. Slavery was once such an issue, as were (and often still are) alcohol consumption, Sunday observance and tithing, to name but a few. In such situations, Christians should humbly understand and listen to one another's convictions and their biblical underpinning, recognising that after all is said and done they may need to 'agree to differ' on the application of these texts. There are larger issues at stake than everyone dotting their 'i's and crossing their 't's identically, where cultural factors are at work in application.

That is the burden of Romans 14, where Paul discusses two controversial issues of application in the early Church – should a person be a meat-eater or a vegetarian? (v. 2), and is one day more sacred than another, or is every day alike? (v. 5). Differences like this may be characterised as weaknesses and immaturity, but Paul's teaching is not to judge one's fellow Christian or look down on him because of such issues (v. 10). God is the only qualified judge (v. 11). Our responsibility is not to put any stumbling-block in a brother's pathway (v. 13), not to distress one another, but to act in love (v. 15). 'For the kingdom of God is not a matter of eating and drinking, but of righteousness, peace and joy in the Holy Spirit . . . Let us therefore make every effort to do what leads to peace and to mutual edification' (vv. 17, 19). The old motto, 'In all things charity', is one that needs to be followed when Christians disagree about their application of the Bible, and it can be, without any diminution of conviction. Remembering Jesus' warning that it is easier to concentrate on the speck of sawdust in one's brother's eye and miss the plank in one's own (Matthew 7:3–5), it is a wise position to be less dogmatic about disputed matters, and to cultivate a predisposition to question more vigorously one's own position when others disagree. That is especially the case when one's own reading blends in rather too readily with the prevailing cultural climate of one's own times. The Bible will always be at variance with the cultural norms of any generation, and we need to be especially vigilant not to nullify its counter-culturism by adapting its teaching to contemporary 'correctness', whether political, ethical or social. As soon as we start to argue that the Church had got this wrong until our generation appeared, all the warning lights should start to flash. It is highly unlikely that views which have been uniformly held as biblical and therefore binding on Christians down the centuries will now suddenly be revealed to be grounded in false exegesis or an unreliable text. It is much more likely that we find the application of Scripture too challenging for our own comfort and decide to soft-pedal, or even deny it, in the foolishly mistaken idea that it will somehow make the gospel more acceptable in the current climate. In over a century of such capitulation, it has never worked and it never will. The more the Bible challenges the ethical and cultural norms of a rebellious world, the more likely it is that we are encountering God's timeless truth, which demands not fashionable 'fudging', or cultural 'kow-towing', but radical obedience.

This is arguably the greatest challenge which the Christian Church faces as we enter the third millennium. Just as when the apostolic generation was dying out, the issue was whether it would be authentic, apostolic Christianity which their successors would hold on to and propagate, or a more dilute synthesis with the prevailing culture, so the challenge is for us to bring the Bible back to the churches and the churches back to the Bible. 'Do not conform any longer to the pattern of this world, but be transformed by the renewing of your mind', Paul exhorted his Roman readers (Romans 12:2a). The pressure of the culture around us will always squeeze us into its way of thinking, unless there is a daily counter-cultural pressure, illuminating and directing our thinking and behaviour. That power, or ability, is provided for the Christian by the Holy Spirit living within us, the life of God planted in the personalities of ordinary men and women, such as we are. But the channel which the Spirit has chosen and by which our minds are renewed is the Bible. If as individual Christians, and as churches, the Word of God is not constantly renewing our thinking, in a culture like ours, where the voices of the media, of commerce and of consumerism are so insistent and pervasive, we shall not stand the slightest chance of resisting being sucked into their vortex. Our 'Christianity' will become a thin veneer covering an idolatrous society, where the price of acceptance will be compromise to the prevailing norms, a 'dumbing down' of all that is biblically distinctive. That is why I so passionately 'believe in the Bible'. The practical issue is how we can ensure that our thinking is responsive to biblical teaching, on a daily basis and at every level of our lives. 'Then you will be able to test and approve what God's will is – his good, pleasing and perfect will' (Romans 12:2b).

Methods of Bible study

There are at least four ways in which most of us can ensure an increasing intake of healthy biblical truth in our everyday lives. They are a personal Bible study programme, reading the Bible with one other person, group Bible studies and listening to expository biblical preaching. First of all, it is helpful to settle on one translation of the Bible and to get to know it well, since the memorisation of key Bible verses is a very helpful practice and it is difficult to achieve across different translations. Probably the most widely used English translation today is the New International Version, which is published in a variety of editions, many with study guides and helps. Other popular translations are the New Revised Standard Version, the Good News Bible (with a simple vocabulary) and the King James (Authorised) Version of 1611, also available in an updated form. Each translation will have its pros and cons, since it is a translation, but accuracy and accessibility of language are criteria of great importance. In English, we have so many translations available that the choice can be bewildering. It is helpful to know that the spectrum of translations ranges from the literal, where sentence structures are as close to the original as possible and the translation is largely word for word, to the paraphrase, where contemporary language and thought forms are used to convey as accurately as possible the biblical ideas. At the literal end is the King James or Authorised Version and its Revised Version of the 1880s (especially valuable for a literal translation of Old Testament narrative and poetry), together with the New American Standard Bible. Moving across from the New Revised Standard Version, through the New International Version, to the New English Bible and the Jerusalem Bible (both about the middle point), the Good News Bible is the bridge towards the more free paraphrase approach, exemplified by J. B. Philips, the recently published *The Message* by Eugene Peterson, and the Living Bible. Every individual reader will have his or her own favourite version, and it is certainly worthwhile having more than one translation available for comparison and clarification. But for serious study purposes it is important to work with the more literal end of the spectrum so that we can be as close to the original as is possible in a translation.

Personal daily Bible reading is an essential ingredient of the healthy Christian life. Before the invention of printing and the widespread and comparatively cheap availability of books, this was impossible. But even then the rabbis (scribes and teachers of the law) would hold daily teaching sessions, and the office of the oral teacher was always of key significance in the Church, too. It has always been recognised that hearing God speak through his Word, to understand, learn and obey, is essential for a Christian's well-being. The irony is that in our generation, when we have more readily available Bible study aids, printed and visual, than at any other time in history, the practice of daily Bible reading is declining among Christian people. For many decades organisations such as Scripture Union, the Bible Reading Fellowship and the Crusade for World Revival have published daily notes, expounding and applying passages of the Bible, working through whole books consecutively, and systematically covering the whole Bible over a period of years. While it is possible to accept the pre-digested thoughts of others about the Bible and to end up reading the notes rather than the Scriptures, these programmes nevertheless have enormous value and ought to be more widely used. There used to be a popular phrase among Christians – 'No Bible, no breakfast'. But as I see all the advertisements for nutritious chewy bars to provide us with breakfast 'on the hoof', I realise that the demise of the British breakfast and the daily morning Bible reading have the same root cause. Life is too pressurised; we are too busy. It can't be fitted in.

There are two remedies for this. The first is to recognise that we all do, in fact, make time for the things we consider to be most important and the things we most enjoy. We are driven by the twin priorities of profit and pleasure. If we are convinced of the necessity of listening to God on a daily basis, then other things need to be fitted in around that. We shall need to plan the time into our routines, on a daily basis. While there is clearly great value in starting the day with God, for many another period of time is more productive, say in the middle of the day, or immediately after work. But the more one's appetite for the Bible grows, the less satisfying the 'quick snack' approach becomes. It needs therefore to be augmented with a longer period of personal Bible study, probably in a weekly schedule.

Our second remedy, then, is to make quality time for the luxury of some in-depth Bible study, understanding, applying and meditating on a book of the Bible. Set aside an hour a week, perhaps at the weekend, to soak yourself in God's Word, and see what a difference it will make. Persuade your spouse to take over the children, the phone, the dog or whatever for a whole hour, and give yourself in that time to listening to God. I would recommend that you choose a book of the Bible to work on over a period of weeks. Don't be too ambitious to start with. It is probably best to start with one of the shorter New Testament letters, such as Philippians, or 1 Peter, or 1 John. Perhaps the best Bible study aid you can acquire is a notebook in which to record your observations, what you have learned and how you are going to apply it to your life. Begin by reading the whole book through, carefully and attentively, two or three times, perhaps using a couple of translations. Try to get the big picture clear in your mind. What is it all about? What messages does the writer want most persistently and urgently to get across? What words or themes recur? What issues does he address? Then take the book, section by section, and work out what the heart of each paragraph is. What is being taught? Why does it matter? What are the surprises? Jot down your thoughts. Then take some time to reflect on its impact on your own life – personally, in the family or with friends, in the work place, in the church, in society at large. How ought your thinking to change, as a result? What actions do you need to take? How are you going to pursue with God the project of working what you have discovered into the fabric of your living this week? Write it down and pray it in. It is especially important to move from theory to practice, from knowledge to experience, so don't be afraid to be very practical in your resolves and in your prayer, for, as Jesus said, 'Apart from me you can do nothing' (John 15:5). The following little rhyme, which I learned as a child, has been a great stand-by all my adult life in studying the Bible, especially when I have felt spiritually dry and lethargic, as we all do from time to time. It can be applied to any passage of the Bible, and you will discover an answer to at least one of its questions, to get you started.

What have I learned about Jesus and God?
What have I learned to cause shame?

What have I learned about following good?
Is there a promise to claim?

Try it and see!

Another helpful method of Bible study is to read regularly with one other person. For many people newly starting out on the Christian life, this is the most helpful and positive way to get into the Bible, but every Christian can benefit from it, throughout life. There has to be commitment on both sides, since regularity is a key ingredient to its success. A more experienced Bible student may help a newcomer to the benefit of both, since the understanding and application of the text is the purpose of the exercise. A couple may do it together, or two colleagues at work. Sometimes a threesome can work well. The aim is to follow the sort of pattern I have outlined above, but with the added advantage of input from someone else. This will help to prevent an individual from being blinkered, or becoming 'rutted' in their study. It also provides accountability, not only for the study time itself, but also for the practical outworking of what has been learned and resolved, and fellowship and prayer to see it accomplished. It is probably best to commit to this style of Bible study on a fixed-term informal 'contract'. Agree to meet weekly for a month or two, or to complete the study of a particular book. Many people have found such arrangements developing into years and many different biblical books, which can be very valuable, but variety is also important, and no one should see such an arrangement as a life-sentence!

House groups

Studying the Bible in a group is an extension of the principle, which has become extremely popular in the last thirty years or so as many churches have inaugurated house groups or other types of small group ministry. In this type of study, everything depends upon competent leadership, which facilitates the growth in understanding of every group member. The yields can be very high in such a group, but it has to be admitted that for many the disappointments can be equivalently great. For, in this context, we are simply not dealing with the Bible but with the social phenomenon of group dynamics. Groups can be hijacked to the personal agendas of the most dominant member. They can develop a negative spirit of corrosive criticism. They can wallow in the quicksands of relativism, so that the Bible becomes a slippery, indeterminate collection of religious ideas, rather than the Word of God. The answer to all these, and the other problems which frequently beset house groups, is to have a clear, agreed agenda of the group's (united) purposes, combined with leadership which is well prepared and firm in moving the group to achieve its goals. Exegeting a Bible passage in a group where no one is adequately prepared is always a nightmare. So golden rule number one is, 'Don't let it happen!' Those who come to the group should agree that they will at least read through and consider the Bible passage before they attend the meeting. That means there needs to be a syllabus for the sequence of studies so that everybody knows which verses will be under consideration.

Groups should also contract together that they will use only one translation for their discussion. Many become bogged down in a meaningless comparison of English translations – meaningless because no one is competent enough in the original languages to be able to make a judgment, and so eventually agreement is reached (or not!) on 'what I like to think', or 'what appeals most to me'. In such a situation, 'I' have just usurped the Bible's authority. Nor should the group become a preaching session for the leader, or an opportunity for the display of biblical knowledge by the most experienced, or vocal, members. The aim of the group is to help one another to the intended meaning of the biblical text, and then to its varied applications in the particular contexts represented by the lives of the group members. Experience has shown that the most productive route to achieving these ends is the question method leading to open discussion and consolidation in agreement. In this, the leader's role is critical, and it has to be carried out in two different parts. The first is personal preparation, in which the leader works hard to understand the text so as to be able to facilitate the group's discovery of its meaning for themselves. The second is when the group meets and the fruit of this study guides the discussion, under the leader's chairmanship. A profitable Bible study occurs when these two ingredients come together and the group leaves understanding the passage and motivated to put it into action.

For the leader's preparation there are many aids. Various publishers produce outline materials suitable for group study and often with suggested questions to move the discussion to the heart of the matter. Outstanding among these is the growing collection from an Australian publisher, St Matthias Press. But no aid can be a substitute for time spent by the leader in careful, prayerful study of the Bible passage. A worthwhile group study cannot be prepared, on the back stroke, in a quarter of an hour snatched between supper and the members' arrival, by 'mugging up' somebody else's questions from a pre-packed outline. All such 'leadership' achieves is a progressive devaluation of the currency, with people drifting away often disillusioned with the Bible (they imagine) when their disillusionment is actually with the leader. Asking lots of good questions is the key to successful preparation. What does this passage say? Why was it written? Why does it occur here – in the book and in the Bible? Why are these particular words used? These 'what' and 'why' questions are an essential discipline for proper Bible study, at every level. The leader will be tempted to rush on to the application stage, as will the group when it meets, but thorough understanding is the only sure guard against misleading application. Only when the meaning is clear and can be expressed in the leader's own words should the application be considered, paying attention first to how the passage applies itself, and, second, considering how its principles relate to us today.

At this point, the leader is half-prepared. The meaning of the passage and some of its applications have become clear so that the overall content of the group's study is decided. This is not, of course, an arbitrary decision of the leader which is being imposed upon the group. It springs from the contents of the text and a right understanding of its meaning and significance. The leader is not deciding what to have the discussion about. The text has already decided that. But the leader is responsible for guiding the group towards the goal, and so careful thought must be given to the questions which will be most helpful in achieving that. It is best to divide the passage into sections and to prepare questions on each. Usually, these will be factual to begin with, simply encouraging the group members to take the text in and to recognise its contents. They need to be interestingly phrased and not to invite wooden answers, which are either monosyllabic or just involve reading the text back to the leader. From this basic comprehension, in which difficult vocabulary or technical terms will need to be explained, the group can be moved on to the meat of the study, discovering the meaning of the passage. This is where the 'how' and 'why' questions come into their own. They need not to be too complex, but to mirror the step-by-step process through which the leader came to understand the meaning, so that the group can share that experience. Of course, the leader needs to be creative enough not to insist that everyone follows along in his footsteps, and expansive enough to take a whole variety of suggested answers, value and sift them, but only to follow those which keep the group on the main road to understanding. Lastly, with the meaning established, the 'so what about us?' questions of application can be asked. They may be rather general at first, but as the group get to know one another better the discussion will become more personal and the degree of support and empathy among them will deepen. The leader also needs to think hard about the questions the group may want to ask, and be as ready as possible to field them. All the time, in the questions that are planned and throughout the discussion, the movement must be into the Bible text and what it is actually saying, not away from it, either into other passages which may be easier to understand, or into mere speculation.

The spin-off benefits of well-run groups are numerous. They become a focus for fellowship, support and mutual prayer. They can develop particular evangelistic and service projects within the community and perhaps support work further afield in international missions and relief schemes. But it is the quality of the Bible input which will largely determine the effectiveness of the group's existence. It is especially in the area of application that such groups are strong, because of the life-experience of their members. When I was minister of a city-centre congregation, which had over forty groups meeting regularly all over the city, I remember that some of the most effective study series we ran linked the mid-week group meeting with the Sunday preaching/teaching programme. It was my custom to preach my way through whole books of the Bible on a systematic, consecutive, expository basis, but in a single sermon and with a large congregation representing a wide cross-section of the city's population, as well as all age groups, it was always difficult to do more than sketch in the outlines of how we might apply the text to our lives. From time to time, however, we synchronised house groups with the teaching programme and invited members to reconsider the passage which had been preached the previous Sunday, especially with a view to more detailed discussion of the application. Another way to ensure maximum benefit in the group can be for a ten-minute taped introduction to be produced, by the minister or one of the Bible teachers in the congregation, copied and circulated to each leader so as to give an introduction common to all the groups, before the discussion. The tape can deal with more difficult or contentious points of exegesis and so free the way for the discussion to be profitable in areas of mutual need and experience.

The importance of biblical teaching

This leads me to the last great provision by which the Bible can consistently change our thinking and impact our behaviour, and that is the regular preaching and teaching ministry of the local church. One of the most devastating blows to the vitality of the churches, over the past half century, has been the gradual decline and virtual disappearance of a regular biblical preaching ministry in many local congregations. This is not the place to argue the case for biblical preaching to be restored to its rightful place at the very heart of the life of the local church. I have done that, in company with others, in the volume entitled *When God's Voice Is Heard* (edited by Christopher Green and the present author, and published in 1995 by Inter-Varsity Press). But if you are serious about believing in the Bible, do all that you can to persuade the leader of your local church that what must be central to the meetings of the congregation is the clear, authoritative and applied preaching of the whole counsel of God to the whole people of God. Whatever else may happen, if the seed which is the Word of God is not being regularly sown, there can be no lasting harvest. There is no alternative product.

One of the books I have most profited from reading in recent years is John Piper's work, *The Supremacy of God in Preaching* (1990, Baker Books). In the course of its stirring call to biblical preaching, the author quotes the words of Cotton Mather, one of the New England Puritan preachers of three hundred years ago. 'The great design and intention of the office of a Christian preacher,' he declared, 'is to restore the throne and dominion of God in the souls of men.' Piper points out that the quotation is taken from a sermon Mather preached on Romans 10:14–15, one of the great New Testament texts on preaching.

How, then, can they call on the one they have not believed in? And how can they believe in the one of whom they have not heard? And how can they hear without someone preaching to them? And how can they preach unless they are sent? As it is written, 'How beautiful are the feet of those who bring good news!'

The word translated 'preaching' at the end of verse 14 means to herald, to make a public proclamation. This work is to be done by those who are sent (v. 15a). The word is the same root as gives us our word 'apostles'. The content of the commissioned herald's proclamation is 'good news' (v. 15b), the gospel. And the detail of the message is contained in the original context of the quotation from Isaiah 52:7 with which verse 15 ends. It is that 'your God reigns'. That is why God sends out preachers of the Bible, to restore his throne and dominion through the gospel. It follows, then, that if that work is ignored and if God's own methodology is spurned, it will not be done by any other alternative method. It will not happen. And all around us we see the proof of that, in the Church and in the world.

The problem is that so many have given up on preaching, but for all the wrong reasons. As John Stott has commented, for many congregations the only sort of preaching they have ever known consists of three types of sermon: 'the dull, the duller and the inconceivably dull'. Yet the answer to bad preaching is not less preaching, but better preaching. For Jesus Christ, this was the focus of his whole earthly ministry. As the crowds wanted to detain him in Capernaum, pressing in on him and demanding more and more healing miracles, it is striking how he responded. 'I must preach the good news of the kingdom of God to the other towns also, because that is why I was sent.' And Luke adds, 'And he kept on preaching in the synagogues of Judea' (Luke 4:43–4). Clearly the same priority lay at the heart of the ministry of the apostles, too. The Great Commission instructed them to make disciples of all nations, 'teaching them to obey everything I have commanded you' (Matthew 28:19–20). Two passages from the writings of Paul show how his preaching of the Word of God was absolutely central to his apostolic ministry. Indeed, it would not be an exaggeration to say that the key ministry the New Testament recognises and wants to develop for the future well-being of the Church is the ministry of the Word.

I have become its [the Church's] servant by the commission God gave me to present to you the word of God in its fulness – the mystery that has been kept hidden for ages and generations, but is now disclosed to the saints. To them God has chosen to make known among the Gentiles the glorious riches of this mystery, which is Christ in you, the hope of glory. We proclaim him, admonishing and teaching everyone with all wisdom, so that we may present everyone perfect in Christ. To this end I labour, struggling with all his energy, which so powerfully works in me. (Colossians 1:25–9)

In the presence of God and of Christ Jesus, who will judge the living and the dead, and in view of his appearing and his kingdom, I give you this charge: Preach the Word; be prepared in season and out of season; correct, rebuke and encourage – with great patience and careful instruction. For the time will come when men will not put up with sound doctrine. Instead, to suit their own desires, they will gather around them a great number of teachers to say what their itching ears want to hear. They will turn their ears away from the truth and turn aside to myths. But you, keep your head in all situations, endure hardship, do the work of an evangelist, discharge all the duties of your ministry. (2 Timothy 4:1–5)

The apostles knew that the regular declaration and exposition of the Word of God was the only way to counter false teaching and to promote authentic discipleship. The pastoral letters are full of such references (1 Timothy 1:3, 2:7, 3:2, 4:1, 6, 13, 5:17; 2 Timothy 1:13–14, 2:2, 4–6, 14–15, 24–6, 3:14–17, 4:1–5; Titus 1:9–11, 2:1, 7–8, 15, 3:8) as are the later, more general epistles (e.g. 2 Peter 1:12–15, 2:1–2; 2 John 9–10; Jude 3, 20). There is a body of divinely revealed truth to be conveyed and believed, from one generation to the next, and it is central to God's purpose that this should be done by teaching.

I am sometimes asked whether a distinction should be made between teaching and preaching. I would not wish to push the point too far, but I think it is true to say that all good preaching is teaching (at least as a major part of its composition), while not all teaching is preaching. It would be possible to give a teaching lecture on a biblical theme or text, in which information was relayed truthfully and accurately but without any appeal to the hearers to act upon it, simply to acknowledge or learn its content. But preaching cannot remain at that level. What may be appropriate to the lecture room is inadequate for either the pulpit or the market-place. Biblical preaching teaches God's truth with a view to life-change, with a summons to action. It is therefore never merely cerebral. It begins by engaging the mind with the truth God has revealed, but then proceeds to apply this to the heart, the seat of the affections and the locus of our decision-making, in order to activate the will. 'Do not merely listen to the word, and so deceive yourselves. Do what it says . . . The man who looks intently into the perfect law that gives freedom, and continues to do this, not forgetting what he has heard, but doing it – he will be blessed in what he does' (James 1:22–5).

Bad preaching, which is sadly so prevalent, is bad not because of incompetence of technique or style, but because of its paucity of biblical content (and therefore of true spiritual authority) and its absence of heart-felt passion for change. If all I got for going to church was a ten-minute reverie on what has been happening in the news this past week and what we think of it in the vicarage, or a kebab-stick of half-cooked, disconnected moral platitudes, or a parading of intellectual doubts about the basic doctrines or the moral absolutes of the faith, of course I wouldn't bother to go back next week – if ever! That is what has emptied churches for the last hundred years or more and is still doing so. But what produces joyful, confident, yet humble, and gracious, godly people is the hearing and receiving of the living and enduring Word of God, Sunday by Sunday, year in, year out. Last year, I preached at a guest service in a parish where a friend of mine had recently become the rector. Over coffee afterwards, I got talking to a middle-aged lecturer at the local university, who had regularly attended church for many years, since his youth in fact, but who, in his words, had never really understood what the Bible was all about. 'But do you know what our new rector is doing?' he asked me. 'Well, when he goes into the pulpit each Sunday, he just opens the Bible and starts to explain it, so that we can all understand what it means. And,' he added, 'what's more, it's changing my life!' Biblical preaching always does.

Those of us who really do believe in the Bible must therefore do all we can to encourage our ministers and lay preachers to preach the Word and to make it their priority. Good preaching takes time in preparation and prayer, but it yields great dividends. In a church which is regularly taught the Bible, a great deal of preventive pastoral care is accomplished through the preaching. It is good to establish a consecutive programme, expounding either whole books or sections of them over a series of sermons. If a team of preachers is involved, this brings consistency to the teaching and ensures that all the exponents are seen to be under the same divine authority. It also means that the balance of biblical truth dictates the subject matter, rather than the bees that are currently buzzing in the preacher's bonnet. Over a period of years, a theme or doctrine which is frequently treated in the Bible will have to be covered with corresponding frequency in the preaching, whereas one may have to wait a while for something rarely mentioned to be preached on, however dear it may be to the preacher's heart. It also ensures that the hard passages are not 'dodged' and that the favourite pastures are not worn out by too-frequent trampling. Best of all, the Bible sets the agenda, rather than the preachers. The same effect can be obtained partially by preaching through a lectionary, but continuity is often a problem and the range is more restricted. If we take seriously the way God has given us the Bible, book by book, then our preaching programmes should reflect our submission to his wisdom, in recognition that he knows better than we do what will help us most. So do encourage your preachers by expressing your appreciation when you are taught the Bible. It can be a lonely and discouraging business, and very easy to decide that other higher-profile activities are more significant than time spent in study and in prayer, preparing to feed the flock with a good, nourishing biblical diet. Yet the absence of that diet is perhaps the greatest single cause of the Church's present anaemia.

Some years ago, a cartoon was published in *Leadership* magazine. It showed a harassed, exhausted minister sitting at his desk with an in tray either side of him, piled high with paper. His wife, or secretary, is coming in with yet another huge pile, and as she enters she is saying, 'Cheer up! God loves you – and everybody else has a wonderful plan for your life!' It is not only ministers who know that feeling, of course, but it is fatally easy, in a self-employed work situation, where there is no direct supervision or accountability and where one's own choice determines where one's energy is spent, to be diverted into a hundred and one useful things but to miss out on what is the most important of all – 'Preach the Word' (2 Timothy 4:2). I do not think many ministers are lazy; most work enormously long hours, for very little earthly remuneration, dealing with complex and resistant human problems. The likelihood is not that they will not work hard, but that they may not work 'smart', and so they may find little lasting success for their labours. The 'smart' way to do ministry is God's way and the Bible is clearly the pattern book for anyone who is willing to search it out and put it into practice.

If you cannot find a church with a biblical teaching programme, one of the great blessings of the modern age is the existence of audio-tapes and videos of excellent Bible exposition from large conventions and conferences, and from a number of biblical preachers and pulpits. Certainly, I know of a number of Christians who keep their minds fed with God's truth by listening regularly to teaching tapes on their car journeys to and from work, even though where they live seems to be a land of famine. There are also many printed commentaries and studies on Biblical books and themes readily obtainable from Christian bookstores, as well as reference and background books which will greatly enrich one's biblical understanding. The best list I know of such excellent resources is an annotated bibliography at the end of *Introduction to Biblical Interpretation* by Klein, Blomberg and Hubbard (op. cit. pp. 459–91). This is as valuable as it is detailed and provides much information for further study. The Scriptures are an inexhaust-ible treasure-house, by which God continues to speak to his twenty-first-century people with as much truth, clarity, relevance and urgency as he has always done. 'He who has ears to hear, let him hear' (Matthew 13:9).

To remind you

- The Bible is the primary means of getting to understand and know God, because all of its contents communicate his mind and constitute his Word (pp. 190–4).
- In relating the Bible to our own lives, understanding the purpose of the original writing will help us to see the application (pp. 194–7).
- Other diagnostic questions need to be asked about the character of God, the picture of human nature and the relationship between the two. The cultural setting may be very different today, but the timeless truths and principles need to be carried over into our world and applied (pp. 197–201).
- Bible study needs to be a priority in the Christian's programme, whether this is individual, with one other person, in a group or by being taught through preaching. There are skills to be developed in each of these areas (pp. 201–4).
- House groups have great potential but need skilled leadership. Good questions that lead group members into the biblical text need to be carefully prepared (pp. 204–8).
- Clear and careful explanation of the Bible, through preaching which is related and applied to life, is one of the greatest needs of the con-

temporary Church. The heart of all ministry in the New Testament is ministry of the Word, and ministers need to make this their priority (pp. 208–13).

Chapter 10

Is There Anybody Out There Listening?

IN THE AUTUMN of 1995, a letter was circulated to all Anglican clergy in the English diocese of Chelmsford, proposing 'an alternative Bible'. It was written by one of their number, a parish vicar, who suggested, 'Having now an Alternative Prayer Book in the Church of England, it is possible to contemplate an Alternative Bible to stand alongside it.' This new publication would remove considerable parts of the Old Testament on the grounds of the material being 'unclear', 'virtually obsolete' or 'repetitive'. It would include 'inspired' writings from the centuries since the canon of Scripture was completed, and especially 'adequate guidance and teaching on many of today's moral problems: e.g. capital punishment, euthanasia, birth control, homosexuality, divorce and re-marriage'. Contemporary writers 'of recognised spiritual authority' would be commissioned to compose works for inclusion, 'in prayer and obedience to the will of God'. Publication was scheduled for the year 2000, but there is no word as to its progress at the time of writing.

The proposal is a fascinating document, not least for the presuppositions which it uncovers about God, about the Bible and about 'us'. It all sounds so eminently reasonable and contemporary; indeed, it is unmistakably positioned in the culture of the 1990s. The Bible is an artefact, the product of human workmanship, described in the proposal as 'an extremely valuable collection of sacred writings'. To such thinking, its origin is human, its contents are dispensable, its authority entirely dependent on our authorisation. What it may say to us is only relevant in so far as it is 'helpful' to us. It is a book over which 'we' (the Church, or presumably the individual) have ultimate control, and if we decide that it isn't up to the job we want it to do, we can substitute it with a better, more up-to-date alternative. We have almost all grown up in a culture where that attitude to the Bible is taken for granted, in our schools and universities, in the media, in the public forum of debate and in the market-square of commerce. It is a little unnerving, however, to see how deeply this presuppositional virus has penetrated even the Church's bloodstream.

The challenge ahead

I use this example because it seems to me to express so well the challenge all those of us who want to affirm that we 'believe in the Bible' face, in this new century. The Bible goes on being translated, published and sold in vast quantities around the world, but is there anybody out there listening? Sometimes it seems, at least in the 'post-Christian' West, as though there are very few prepared to let the Bible speak for itself, or to listen with any sort of serious attention. What is the future of the Bible, as we enter the twenty-first century? Christian believers will immediately (and rightly) want to affirm the words of our Lord Jesus Christ, 'Heaven and earth will pass away, but my words will never pass away' (Mark 13:31). Yet the same Lord also asked that poignantly haunting question, 'When the Son of Man comes, will he find faith on the earth?' (Luke 18:8). Again, we can affirm with confidence that there will always be a Church on earth in every generation, not least the last (see Matthew 16:18, 24:30–1), but its existence is not guaranteed in any specific location, or within any nation, at any point in history. The challenge for Bible-believing Christians in the West is to let the Bible loose, to let it be our mouthpiece in all the cultural debates in which we engage, to make it the substance of our proclamation and teaching, to build our own lives on its truth, in faith and obedience.

In the course of this book, we have examined the evidence and arguments for accepting the inspiration and authority of the whole Bible, as the living Word of the living God. There is a vast literature supportive of this position, of course, dealing with many of the issues raised in much more detail, linguistically, philosophically and technically. In addition, we have sought to take the Bible seriously in its description of itself and its internal methods of interpretation and use, so as to develop handling-skills of coherence and integrity for those who want to derive true value from the text. But in this final chapter, I want to think through some of the challenges which Bible believers currently face, and endeavour to sketch an outline strategy by which we might work together for a fresh recognition of the Bible's truth and power, and therefore a fresh encounter with the God who is still speaking, in a way that will impact our time. If we believe in the Bible, we can be content to work and pray for nothing less.

First, it will be helpful to draw a map of where we are with regard to our culture's perception of the Bible. I have found great help in this area from an extended essay entitled *Scripture and Authority Today* written by Professor Richard Bauckham of St Andrew's University and published in Cambridge in 1999, in the Grove Biblical Booklets Series, No. 12. Professor Bauckham's thesis is that the traditional concept of the Bible's authority is a combination of both 'extrinsic' and 'intrinsic' elements. The first was attacked by the Enlightenment thinking known as 'modernity', and the second by the contemporary movement we call 'post-modernity'. The 'extrinsic' claim is that the Bible is the Word of God and has divine authority, because God has authority to say it and has done so. It is therefore both to be believed and obeyed. To this, modernity replied, in the famous quotation of Immanuel Kant, 'Have the courage to use your own intelligence.' Elevating the principle of autonomous reason, one should accept only what can be demonstrated from first principles in a universally accessible way. This broadside led theologians to construct a 'modernist' theology, based on what seemed reasonable because it was independently verifiable, but evacuating the Bible of much of its supernatural content and consequent authority. The 'intrinsic' claim is that the same Holy Spirit who inspired Bible authors to write inspires Bible readers to understand and accept it as God's Word. Nor is this simply an intellectual perception, for as we put into practice what the Bible says, we find it works. Biblical truth is realised, in our experience, and so proves to be self-authenticating. To this, post-modernity replies, 'I must be free to believe my own truth.' Any claim to a universal truth is simply a power ploy, an attempt to dominate me by the so-called knowledge of a particular élite. Christianity is, of course, a prime 'offender' here; but once all truth claims are shown to be simply the expression of personal preference, its hold is broken and we are set free to live in an unrestricted pluralism. As with modernism, so with its successor: the danger will be that Christian thinkers will accommodate the faith to the premises of post-modernism and capitulate to a privatised form of religion. That is an area in which the range of acceptability tolerated by the prevailing culture is constantly shrinking.

These are real and powerful challenges at a variety of levels. While it may be argued that the philosophical issues of deconstructionism are the interests of the academic world, their trickle-down effect in society as a whole is already plain to see. When a public leader, on oath, declares that he has not lied, he does not mean by that that he has spoken the truth. For what is 'the truth'? It is many-sided and no one can perceive its entirety, so what he has said represents what he believes to be his personal perception of what happened. In such a world you cannot lie, since truth no longer exists. When a businessman reneges on a deal on which he gave his word, all that word implied was a readiness to act in accordance with the terms of the contract as he interprets them now or at any time in the future. And if that should be tried in a court of law, the aim will not be to establish the truth, because such a thing does not exist, but to convince the arbiters of the validity of his own 'reading'. At the popular level, this translates into a pluralistic culture where the only position that will not be tolerated is intolerance. We are already seeing the disintegration of many of the structures which have given our society its cohesion and stability, not least the family unit, and with it the inevitable isolation of the individual. A generation free to believe its own truth is also a generation desperate for deep and lasting relationships. But they require 'commitment', and in a world without ultimate values, other than myself, such a commodity is in short supply. These challenges are real and pervasive, but they also represent great opportunities and potential openness to a voice from outside. Whether that 'voice' will be another round of totalitarian tyrants (which will always be attractive to a disintegrating society) or that of the living God may depend, in human terms at least, on how committed to the Bible's message his people are.

In facing the intellectual challenge of the contemporary situation, Professor Brian D. Ingraffia of Biola University, California, has produced a volume entitled *Postmodern Theory and Biblical Theology* (1995, Cambridge University Press) which is full of good things. First, it is helpful to realise that there is 'nothing new under the sun' and that these issues have confronted Christians in many different contexts. The apostle Paul himself faced them, in Athens, Corinth and when writing to the church at Colosse. For the common denominator in both first- and twenty-first-century attacks on the Bible's authority is that they all start with human philosophising and proceed from there to the deconstruction of the Bible. But all that is actually rejected, or deconstructed, is what Ingraffia calls 'theology based upon human imaginings about God' (op. cit. p. 241), for which the current technical term is 'onto-theology'.

This was precisely the problem Paul encountered in Athens when he delivered his famous speech at the meeting of the Areopagus.

Men of Athens! I see that in every way you are very religious. For as I walked around and looked carefully at your objects of worship, I even found an altar with this inscription: TO AN UNKNOWN GOD. Now what you worship as something unknown I am going to proclaim to you. The God who made the world and everything in it is the Lord of heaven and earth and does not live in temples built by hands. And he is not served by human hands, as if he needed anything, because he himself gives all men life and breath and everything else. From one man he made every nation of men, that they should inhabit the whole earth; and he determined the times set for them and the exact places where they should live. God did this so that men would seek him and perhaps reach out for him and find him, though he is not far from each one of us. For in him we live and move and have our being. As some of your own poets have said, 'We are his offspring.' Therefore since we are God's offspring, we should not think that the divine being is like gold or silver or stone – an image made by man's design and skill. In the past God overlooked such ignorance, but now he commands all people everywhere to repent. For he has set a day when he will judge the world with justice by the man he has appointed. He has given proof of this to all men by raising him from the dead. (Acts 17:22b–31)

The very description 'To An Unknown God' illustrates both how dependent on revelation human beings inevitably are, for no real god could be 'known' in any other way, and how fundamentally insecure such ignorance makes us feel. We ought to put up an altar so as not to offend, to cover off all possible options. If we are starting from a human base that will always be the problem. So Paul 'reveals' the nature of the Creator God, 'Lord of heaven and earth' (v. 24) in terms of three negatives which expose the emptiness and folly of all human-based religious constructions. The real God 'does *not* live in temples built by hands' (v. 24), 'is *not* served by human hands' (v. 25) and 'is *not* far from each one of us' (v. 27). Far from needing humans to construct a shrine for him to live in, the living God made the earth for them to live in. Far from needing humans to serve him, by bringing food offerings or looking after his shrine and image, the living God served them by giving them life itself and all that is needed to sustain it. Far from being static in one place and needing to be visited for worship, the living God is everywhere, constantly available to anyone who will reach out to find him.

So what is the categorical mistake which human beings will always make whenever they start with themselves as the basis of their understanding about God? Verse 29 is the crunch verse. 'We are God's offspring'; he is not the projection of our desires, or the construct of our finite minds. Therefore, 'we should not think that the divine being is like gold or silver or stone – an image made by man's design and skill'. But that is precisely what we humans always do think, whenever our imaginings become the ground of our belief-systems. Paul calls it 'ignorance', not knowing. Agnosticism is a more polite synonym, but it lacks the bite, because not knowing is no longer excusable. The reason is that God has revealed himself, in Jesus Christ, raised from the dead, the coming judge of all, and on that basis he 'commands all people everywhere to repent' (vv. 30–1). Whenever we try to formulate a human understanding of God rather than receiving the divine revelation of God in Jesus Christ, crucified and risen, mediated to us through the Scriptures, we shall produce a 'god' who is merely a figment of the human imagination and inevitably a distortion of the divine reality, which can only be known by revelation. In the same way, atheism is equally onto-theological, since it affirms from its own base that we are able to know, of ourselves, that the idea of God is an illusion. It is this false base which Paul attacked in Athens, and which is still there in post-modernist critics of the Christian faith. As Ingraffia expresses it, 'We *should*, therefore, vanquish god's shadow (a phrase of Nietzsche's), the shadow god created by human reason's imagination, that we might seek the revelation of the living God in the cross of Christ' (op. cit. p. 241).

It is the cross which becomes the focus in the similar argument which Paul conducts with the Corinthians at the opening of his first letter to them. In a pagan city, surrounded by idol temples and immoral practices, the Christians were tempted to compromise the message of the gospel with a much more culturally acceptable presentation of rhetorical wisdom and miraculous powers. Paul is by no means anti-intellectual. He himself had a first-class mind, as his writings show. But he is not prepared to allow a philosophy built from human origins with human wisdom, which is in the end mere speculation, to overthrow the revelation of God's unique historical intervention in his world, in the cross and resurrection of his Son, Jesus Christ. The following argument makes the point with great clarity.

> Where is the wise man? Where is the scholar? Where is the philosopher of this age? Has not God made foolish the wisdom of the world? For since in the wisdom of God the world through its wisdom did not know him, God was pleased through the foolishness of what was preached to save those who believe. Jews demand miraculous signs and Greeks look for wisdom, but we preach Christ crucified: a stumbling-block to Jews and foolishness to Gentiles, but to those whom God has called, both Jews and Greeks, Christ the power of God and the wisdom of God. For the foolishness of God is wiser than man's wisdom, and the weakness of God is stronger than man's strength. (1 Corinthians 1:20–5)

The next chapter goes on to point out that there is a 'message of wisdom' which Paul does preach, but it is the otherwise hidden wisdom of God's rescue plan for humanity accomplished through the self-emptying of Jesus, crucified for the world, and revealed only by the Holy Spirit (see 1 Corinthians 2:6–10). Again, the point is made that Christianity is not a ladder by which to climb up to God. That may be a feature of all other religious beliefs, with their systems and disciplines, self-denials and offerings by which to make one acceptable to God. Each of them provides a ladder to climb, but it is not the God of the Bible who is at the top, but rather a product of our own imaginations. For the God of the Bible comes down the ladder to us, to rescue us when we are helpless and hopeless, and the way in which he conquers evil is to surrender himself to the death of the cross. 'The theology of the cross pronounces an either/or: either biblical revelation or philosophical speculation. The same either/or must be proclaimed to the present age: either biblical theology or post-modern theory. Only as a theology of the cross will Christianity recover its prophetic voice' (op. cit. p. 241).

Two other New Testament examples underline the point still further. The churches in Colosse and Philippi were in danger from false teachers, whose message reflected the amalgamation of Jewish and Greek thinking which characterised much first-century religion. Greek thought was always dualistic, separating body and spirit, earth and heaven, the material and the spiritual. Sometimes this showed itself in asceticism, where the body was denied, even denigrated, and sometimes in libertinism, where the pure spirit was thought to be so superior to the flesh that any behaviour could be indulged in the body with impunity. There are signs of the first in Colosse and the second at Philippi. In Colosse, some want to bring the young Christians under ascetic rules ('Do not handle! Do not taste! Do not touch!' 2:21), but Paul says 'such regulations indeed have an appearance of wisdom, with their . . . harsh treatment of the body, but they lack any value in restraining sensual indulgence' (2:23). The answer is in the cross, realising that there 'you died with Christ to the basic principles of this world' (2:20). The Colossian mistake is that they are working from the ground up, 'taking the earthly situations as their starting point from which by their own efforts and techniques they will ascend into the heavenlies. Paul moves in the reverse direction, since he sees the starting point and source of the believer's life in the resurrected Christ in heaven, from where it works itself out, into earthly life (3:5ff)' (Andrew T. Lincoln in *Paradise Now and Not Yet*, 1991, Baker Books, quoted by B. D. Ingraffia, op. cit. p. 75).

In Philippi, the stress is on liberty, not just from legalistic rules but from most moral constraints, it seems. Earthly life was being devalued as meaningless, because only the life of the soul in the world beyond really mattered. Again, Paul turns to the theology of the cross to refute this error. Our citizenship is in heaven (3:20), but the Christ who once came to earth, emptying himself even to death on a cross (2:5–8) will come again to earth to redeem and transform our physical bodies (3:21). This is what gives meaning and significance to life on earth. Again, the movement is from heaven to earth, in divine revelation and redemption, not from earth to heaven, in human speculation and imagination. This is where we need the Bible's own emphasis on revelation to engage in the debate with post-modernism. Its theories may well have deconstructed the gods of human imagination, whoever their builders may have been, but they are human constructs, not the God of the Bible. We need to be set free from these false gods, because they have so frequently been a reflection of current ideologies, masquerading as the God of the Bible. In Brian Ingraffia's words, 'Christian thought must not let postmodern theory guide its critique: it should be guided by a hermeneutic of faith, which in turn must be guided by biblical revelation' (op. cit. p. 238).

Living the Bible's story

The rise of post-modern thinking and attitudes, therefore, presents Christians with a moment of great opportunity. If 'I must be free to believe my own truth', then the Bible must be free to tell me its truth, to present to me its story. Or, more significant still, I, as a Christian, am free to tell you 'my' truth, 'my' story, which happens to be the Bible's. For while the essence of being *post*-modern is that the old over-arching stories or 'narratives', as ways of explaining reality, are no longer legitimate, so that any so-called 'meta-narrative' is rejected automatically, nevertheless what might be called local, or personal, narratives continue to thrive. We all sense the need to own models or paradigms which describe our identity and give definition to our existence. Again, this is not new. A large percentage of confessing Christians today who were converted to their faith, rather than growing up in it, would bear testimony to the fact that the biggest single factor in their conversion was seeing the gospel work out in the life-story of someone they knew well. I recently heard of a middle-aged Christian woman who came to faith in Christ while holding a senior management position in a city firm. What was it that got her thinking about Christianity in her mid-thirties? The change in behaviour of a man in her office was the key. He was a well-known womaniser, always sailing close to the wind in terms of sexual innuendo and offensive behaviour, and suddenly it all stopped. He announced that he had become a follower of Jesus Christ, and he was instantly different and gradually transformed. It was when she heard his 'local' narrative that she began to be interested in the 'meta-narrative' which lay behind it. Eventually, she too became Christ's disciple.

Of course, we do have to get to the 'meta-narrative', for that is the heart of God's revelation, the gospel, which constantly needs to be proclaimed. It will not do just to share our story, since it may strike very few chords with those who listen, particularly if their age, background or other characteristics are different from our own. The reaction will frequently be, 'Well, I'm very pleased for you, but I'm a very different person, so please don't ask me to accept your outlook and please don't try to force your religion down my throat!' Personal testimony alone will always be working from a merely human base, and if it remains at the level of 'I found this works. Why don't you give it a try?', people will come to regard the gospel as just another remedy on the shelves of the ideological supermarket, for which they have neither need nor interest. But the quality of life Christians live, and especially the expression of genuine Christian love, can open doors for the gospel which would otherwise remain firmly shut. It is important to remind ourselves that though the Bible is a book containing timeless truths and moral principles, it is not presented in that format. As we saw at the start, it is a story, stretching from creation to the new creation and embracing the meaning of all reality within its compass. As Richard Bauckham sees it, becoming a Christian is making the Bible's story (or meta-narrative) our own. He writes,

> To accept the authority of the story is to enter it and inhabit it. It is to live in the world as the world is portrayed in this story. It is to let this story define our identity and our relationship to God and to others. It is to read the narratives of our own lives and of the societies in which we live as narratives which take their meaning from this meta-narrative that overarches them all. (op. cit. p. 10)

The fascinating fact is that when the Bible's story of God's self-revelation is actually heard, it subscribes to none of the stereotypical categories by which post-modernist thinking would seek to dismiss it. Far from it being the tool of a knowledgeable élite who would use it to exercise power over others, the gospel is the greatest agent of personal liberation the world has ever witnessed. 'If the Son sets you free, you will be free indeed' (John 8:36). For the gospel's central motif is not one of demand from a remote and autocratic deity. That is the product of onto-theology, as we have seen. The revelation of Scripture is of a God of grace, who demonstrates his incredible love and mercy through Jesus and the cross, and invites from me a free response of love, expressed in faith and repentance. The movement is from heaven to earth. As Bill Hybels has often said, 'Religion may be spelt "Do" but Christianity is spelt "Done".' Or, in the apostle Paul's memorable words, 'God demonstrates his own love for us in this: while we were still sinners, Christ died for us' (Romans 5:8). All the way through the biblical meta-narrative, the pattern is the same. God chooses to take the initiative, to bring rebellious human beings back into a right relationship with himself, but there is always the necessity for personal response, the call to faith. The gift of God's grace is constantly presented first, preceding all requirement of response. Indeed, it is only because of this unmerited favour and compassionate mercy of God that we ever could respond to him, or be brought into relationship with him. So Abraham was given great and gracious promises by the Lord at the very beginning of salvation history, promises of a great name and a great nation, a great land and a great blessing, but there was a response of faith required. He had to leave his country and go. 'So Abram left, as the LORD had told him' (Genesis 12:4). Yet as he travelled on with God he found, not a set of arbitrary rules and impossible demands, but a relationship of covenanted faithfulness in which God's generous gifts of grace were lavished on him and his wonderful promises increasingly fulfilled. No wonder he was the man who believed God.

Faith like that is the use of the freedom God's grace brings to obey God freely from the heart. The Bible's story is full of examples by which the love of God reaches out to transform human lives. At the heart of its self-revelation lies the understanding of God as a trinity in unity, three persons in one divine being, co-equal in nature and status, yet different in function and role. One of the clearest and deepest statements in the whole Bible about the nature of this triune God is that made twice by John in his first letter, 'God is love' (1 John 4:8, 16). It is not just that God loves, but that he is, by nature, love. Relating this to the concept of the trinity, we can see that at the heart of God, the very essence of his divine being, there exists a dynamic interaction of constant love between the three persons. The Father loves the Son, the Son loves the Father, the Spirit loves the Son, and so on, in constant, eternal activity. And humankind are made in the image of God, to love God and our neighbour. 'There is no commandment greater than these' (Mark 12:31). But love must be a free response, an act of the will. The one thing it cannot be is coerced, or it ceases to be love. How, then, will God freely win the response of love from sinful human beings who continue to rebel against him? John has the answer.

> This is how God showed his love among us: He sent his one and only Son into the world that we might live through him. This is love: not that we loved God, but that he loved us and sent his Son as an atoning sacrifice for our sins. Dear friends, since God so loved us, we also ought to love one another . . . And we have seen and testify that the Father has sent his Son to be the Saviour of the world. If anyone acknowledges that Jesus is the Son of God, God lives in him and he in God. And so we know and rely on the love God has for us. God is love. Whoever lives in love lives in God, and God in him. (1 John 4:9–11, 14–16)

The Bible's story is validated by the transformation which occurs in the life of the Christian, in gratitude for such amazing grace. That is how it impacts the world still, irrespective of whatever philosophies may come into, or go out of, fashion. There is no argument against a life transformed, from the inside out, by God's grace, turned around from serving self to loving God and loving people. The Bible's story of God's transforming love and power, through Christ crucified and risen, is the only dynamic by which alienated people can be reconciled and a broken world restored. It is not true because it works; but it works because it is true.

The bigger picture

However, the Bible's impact must be wider than our personal acts of love, essential though they are to God's great plan. Our individual part in the 'big story' is infinitesimally small alongside the massive scope of the story itself, so we must never be content with the small canvas of our individual lives alone. The 'meta-narrative', which is the Bible's story-line, encompasses time and eternity, the universe and everything within it. This is not separate from our local, personal stories: they are an integral part of it, but its scope is immeasurably vast. We noted the pattern in the opening chapters of Genesis and its three distinctive movements, or stages in creation, fall and rescue, or redemption, as the rest of the Bible calls it. In the beginning, God brings into being, by his sovereign will executed through his word, a created order of perfection. At its apex is a creature made in his own image, with God-like abilities to know him, love him and relate to him in trust and dependence. But the creation of a being with potential for such free response inevitably implies the possibility of wrong choices, of using this autonomy to usurp the creator's rightful place. This was realised in the fall. 'Your eyes will be opened, and you will be like God, knowing good and evil' (Genesis 3:5). This act of rebellion fractures the perfection of God's creation and alienates humankind from the creator. The Bible shows us that this is not some localised event, with significance only for Adam and Eve, but one with cosmic consequences. As a result of human sin, the ground is cursed (Genesis 3:17) and the whole creation is 'in bondage to decay' (Romans 8:21). This does not mean that God has rejected his creation. Its structure remains and God is committed to its sustenance and continuance. 'For everything God created is good, and nothing is to be rejected if it is received with thanksgiving' (1 Timothy 4:4). But the direction of the whole created order is one of distortion and perversion because of the arrival of evil, in the fall of humankind. A. M. Wolters makes the point cogently:

> Anything in creation can be directed either toward or away from God – that is, directed either in obedience or disobedience to his law. This double direction applies not only to individual human beings but also to such cultural phenomena as technology, art, and scholarship, to such societal institutions as labor unions, schools, and corporations, and to such human functions as emotionality, sexuality, and rationality. To the degree that these realities fail to live up to God's creational design for them, they are misdirected, abnormal, distorted. To the degree that they still conform to God's design, they are in the grip of a countervailing force that curbs or counteracts the distortion. (*Creation Regained*, 1986, Inter-Varsity Press, p. 49)

Into this situation God steps, in his intervening grace. We see it in his rescuing mercy to Noah and his family, brought through the judgment of the flood to the new world beyond, by the provision of the ark. But bound up with Noah and his family in the floating zoo are 'two of all living creatures' (Genesis 6:19). The animal creation shares both in the judgment that falls on humanity's sin, but also in the rescue that comes through God's grace. So the covenant which God makes, following the flood, in which he promises, 'Never again will all life be cut off by the waters of a flood; never again will there be a flood to destroy the earth' (Genesis 9:11), is directed not only to humanity, but to 'every living creature'. The redemption and restoration which God brings extend as widely as the effects of the fall, to all the created order. This is supremely the case in the greatest rescue mission of all, the atoning death of Jesus Christ, for the sins of the world, on the cross. Paul reminds us that God's purpose was fulfilled through Christ, 'to reconcile to himself all things, whether things on earth or things in heaven, by making peace through his blood, shed on the cross' (Colossians 1:20). As the cause of all evil is dealt with at that cross, the possibility of restoration exists in every area infected by mankind's fall. But that will be part of the progression towards the eternal city, not a return to a primitivism, in a forlorn attempt to recover Eden. Christians are not Luddites or antiquarians, wanting to put the clock back to an age that is past. Much of the development of the creation mandate has been good and valuable, although inevitably always tainted by sin and distorted in many ways. To talk of restoration is not to look backwards to a day before antibiotics or computers and to yearn to return to a 'golden age', which actually never existed. Rather, it is to look forward to the restoration of everything in the new heavens and the new earth where righteousness will dwell, to the heavenly Jerusalem where Christ's kingly rule in righteousness will be unchallenged and unending, and where at last his people will be, as he intended, in unbroken relationship with him. Christians are not looking to 'build Jerusalem, in England's green and pleasant land', or anywhere else for that matter, as though some earthly Utopia was the goal of the gospel. We know that perfection can only be in heaven, and that the only way we 'build Jerusalem', the eternal city, is by spreading the gospel throughout the world, so that, through faith in Christ, multitudes may become members of that community.

So what is our present role? On the basis of what we have seen of the totality of the pattern of creation, fall and restoration, all cosmic in their scope, we put our energies and skills, our time and talents into fighting the spiritual battle for the kingdom of our God and of his Christ, here in this world, as citizens of the heavenly Jerusalem. 'For our struggle is not against flesh and blood, but against the rulers, against the authorities, against the powers of this dark world and against the spiritual forces of evil in the heavenly realms' (Ephesians

6:12). To accomplish that battle, God has given us the armour of the gospel 'and the sword of the Spirit, which is the word of God' (Ephesians 6:13–17).

Every Christian is aware of this at the personal level, within our own minds and hearts. We are not yet sinlessly perfect, not yet what one day, by God's grace, we will be. To imagine we are is to delude ourselves, and usually depends on moving God's goal posts. We rejoice in the power of the Holy Spirit, living within us, to enable us to resist temptation and to produce the fruits of his character within us, as we depend upon him. But we know, from bitter experience, what a daily battle that will be, and that, in spite of the words of the Victorian hymn, the option is not open for us 'to float to heaven, on flowery beds of ease'! Rather, we are involved in spiritual warfare against the world, the flesh (our sinful nature) and behind them the devil, who uses both to pursue his destructive ends. The battle will have different dimensions and contours in each individual life. Temperament, background, genetic inheritance, early life experience – these and many other factors combine to make us the people we are, who are called to become progressively what God intended us to be, through God's great restoration plan. For God's grace restores nature, and the new directions we receive through the gospel redeem the whole person, as God made us. The image of God, marred but not totally destroyed through sin, is being restored, as we grow into the likeness of Christ, in the process we call sanctification. Of course, all that is a gift of God in the gospel.

Our progress in godly living is entirely dependent on God's grace to us, through Christ's sacrifice, mediated to us by the Holy Spirit within. On the one hand, we know the sharpness of the battle, identifying with the apostle Paul when he writes, 'So I find this law at work: When I want to do good, evil is right there with me . . . So then, I myself in my mind am a slave to God's law, but in the sinful nature a slave to the law of sin' (Romans 7:21–5). We know, as Romans 8 tells us, that the power of the Spirit is given to keep us fighting in the battle all our life long, not to air-lift us out of the conflict into a super-spiritual state of near perfection. We know that it is only in heaven that we shall experience the full redemption and restoration Christ has accomplished, when our mortal bodies are redeemed and we share in his glory. That is future. 'For in this hope we were saved. But hope that is seen is no hope at all. Who hopes for what he already has? But if we hope for what we do not yet have, we wait for it patiently' (Romans 8:24–5). Yet, on the other hand, we have wonderful experiences of God's transforming grace, here and now, through the work of his Spirit within us. The more we respond to his Word, the more we depend on him in prayer and the clearer our focus on Christ is, the more we shall experience the freedom of liberation from our old sinful agendas, with their destructive self-centredness, and the inflow of God's strength and ability to live differently, a redeemed and restored life. For 'we, who with unveiled faces all reflect [or contemplate] the Lord's glory, are being transformed into his likeness with ever-increasing glory, which comes from the Lord, who is the Spirit' (2 Corinthians 3:18).

It is a critical and central ingredient of our Christian living to fight the good fight of the faith and take hold of the eternal life to which we are called (1 Timothy 6:12). The Bible is the great resource God has provided to enable us to know how to live, and the Spirit is the great energiser within, to motivate our will and empower our actions. There is no part of a Christian's human experience which is outside of these influences. Our thinking, our feelings, our sexuality, our relationships, our work, our leisure, our material resources – all of these are elements of our life in God's world as God's created beings. 'The directional battle does not take place on a spiritual plane above creaturely reality but rather occurs *in* and *for* the concrete reality of the earthly creation' (A. M. Wolters, op. cit. p. 73). Realisation of this will have a profound effect upon our thinking. It means that our lives are whole entities in God's sight, and that there can be no division between the sacred and the secular. We do not take parts of our lives (church, prayer, Bible study, evangelism, works of mercy, etc.) and pack them off to a separate upstairs level, labelled 'spiritual', leaving work, home, family, leisure, etc., downstairs, labelled 'secular', or, still worse, 'the real world'. This is an error of devastating proportions and consequences. It will lead us to restrict God's interest, and therefore ours if we are to follow him, to the spiritual realm alone, and everything else will matter far less to God, and so to us. That in turn commits us to a 'privatised' religion, in which no word of God is ever spoken in the public forum or the market-place. The result is a very damaging sort of spiritual schizophrenia. It leads one to suppose that only 'spiritual' work matters to God – activities such as mission, evangelism, Bible study – so that spending one's time in a so-called 'secular' occupation is always and inevitably to be second-best. This in turn distorts the Bible's view of priorities, putting emphasis on what I do rather than on who I am, and so defining myself in terms of my activity, rather than my relationship with God. Such a view must in the end produce ghettoised Christians, in a marginalised Church, which is seen as clinging to a life-negating message by an increasingly alienated society.

Impacting our culture

The remedy lies in a more radically biblical approach to our involvement in every area of life. It has been said that what the gospel needs as we enter the new century is not so much more salesmen, but more free samples. The climate is such that intellectual theorising may cut very little ice, but a life which embodies and exemplifies its belief and value systems is always going to have a magnetic attraction. Wasn't it Nietzsche who said that if ever he was to become a Christian, the Christians would have to look a lot more like Jesus Christ than they did? So one of the greatest contributions any of us can make to the spread of biblical understanding and gospel credibility is our personal godliness. That begins with our marriages and family lives, where the Bible's values need not simply to be accepted, but to become the building-blocks of how we relate to one another. Our practice and our proclamation need to go hand-in-hand here, if either is to be credible to a sceptical culture. Marriage is not merely a human construct, a dispensable social structure, the Bible tells us. Marriage is God's idea (Genesis 2:24), both as the context for our sexuality and also as the foundation blocks of a stable society. But it will not do to preach the virtues of marriage, if Christian marriages do not demonstrate the fragrance of Christ. The critical issue is whether we allow our direction of the structure to be shaped by Scripture or by culture. If it is the latter, then we should expect to see a drift away from both faithfulness within marriage and celibacy outside it. In fact, of course, we are aware of a landslide in this area which threatens to engulf our social structures in the culture at large. The danger is that the more Christians accommodate to that trend, the greater will be its penetration in the Church, until in this key area of human life the one is indistinguishable from the other. The only counter-force is the Bible's clear teaching. God's design is for a man and woman to live together in monogamous marriage until death parts them. Adultery is always wrong. Sex outside of marriages is always contrary to God's will.

Such sentiments will never be popular with *Newsnight* or the icons of popular culture, but that is nothing new. What is new is the capitulation of so many churchmen and Christians to the spirit of the age. That must stem from a deep lack of confidence in the Bible's truth and lead to a version of Christianity bereft of any real moral authority. In this area of life, the Bible has a great deal to say, but unless Christians demonstrate marriages that are dependent upon God's grace and living testimony to the power of his Spirit, in spite of all their human fallibility and weakness, it will not be heard.

Extending beyond the circles of the nuclear family and friends, we need also to consider the impact of the Bible in the life of God's wider family, the Church, at both the local and national levels. Archbishop William Temple was not being cynical when he commented that the biggest hindrance to the spread of the Christian Church is the Christian Church. For unless the people who claim the authority of Scripture demonstrate its credibility in their corporate life, what reality does it actually have? Throughout this book we have recognised the primacy of Scripture over the Church. It is not that the Bible was 'invented' by the Church, but that the Church exists because of the Bible. The Reformers were always keen to underline that the mark of the reformed Church is that it is constantly being reformed, by the word of truth in the gospel. However, our current danger is that the Church, of any and every association or denomination, is seen as an autonomous corporation and run in rather the same way. The local minister is seen as a jack-of-all-trades, with the inevitable consequence. His training is often a mish-mash of various theological influences, coupled with add-ons from sociology, business management, media studies, and so on. Because there is little understanding of the (biblical) priorities of his role, the practice tends to be unfocused and often unsatisfactory. If, however, we believe that we stand in the apostolic tradition of Christ and the gospel, from which all truly Christian ministry must derive, ought we not radically to review by those criteria what is happening in our churches? The direction a local church takes will largely depend on its leadership, and if there is confusion over its aims and goals, even sometimes its *raison d'être*, there will certainly be no clarity over its priorities and subsequent programmes.

But local churches are made up of individual Christians, however confused or confusing the context may be, and they constitute the greatest resources at the Church's disposal. This is where the cutting edge of the gospel is experienced, and it is enormously encouraging to see so many congregations keen to move out with the good news into their community. Once again, the Bible is the spearhead. What a joy and privilege it would be to belong to a church where new believers in Christ were being added on a daily basis. That was the situation in Jerusalem described in Acts 2:47, after the Day of Pentecost. But before Luke tells us that, he paints a pen-picture of what that congregation looked like.

> They devoted themselves to the apostles' teaching and to the fellowship, to the breaking of bread and to prayer. Everyone was filled with awe, and many wonders and miraculous signs were done by the apostles. All the believers were together and had everything in common. Selling their possessions and goods, they gave to anyone as he had need. Every day they continued to meet together in the temple courts. They broke bread in their homes and ate together with glad and sincere hearts, praising God and enjoying the favour of all the people. And the Lord added to their number daily those who were being saved. (Acts 2:42–7)

We cannot put the clock back, and any attempt to re-live the times of the early Church is doomed to failure. We are not in their situation, for which we may be grateful when we think of the lions in the arena! But we are surely right to see in Luke's account strong pointers to the sort of church God delights to honour, and it would be a useful exercise, at least, to measure our own contemporary experience of church against theirs. Where do we need to be more biblical in our life together as God's covenant people?

We should make a start in the area of greater unity among those Christians who really do 'believe in the Bible'. I am not pleading for a revival of the wilting structures of ecumenism. Such a plan contained two fatal weaknesses. It would have to be imposed hierarchically, working from the top down in the already existing denominational structures, rather than from the grass roots out. Also, it was institutional and organisational, rather than vibrant and confessional. It was always going to falter on the rocks of divergences over the basic content of the gospel, reflecting the fundamentally different value placed on Scripture by different groups and individuals. Bible

Christians will always anathematise those who preach a gospel other than that of the apostles, contained in the pages of the New Testament, as the apostles Paul (Galatians 1:8–9) and John (2 John 9–11) did. However, a truly radical biblicism should want to take our present denominational and local church structures back to Scripture as their judge, and to be submissive to its teaching. Let me exemplify this from both ends of the denominational spectrum. If the ancient system of parish boundaries means that some areas of the country are actually prevented from hearing the gospel message and seeing it lived out in community, because the local church building is closed or has lost its congregation, ought not that system to be reformed, so as to allow gospel work to be re-planted in those locations? If an independent, nonconformist church allows its independency to degenerate into isolationism from other Christians in the same location who clearly believe and preach the same biblical gospel, so that it only ploughs its lone furrow, ought not that system to be reformed to embrace the biblical priority of gospel unity, in practice as well as theory? God is not just interested in 'you in your small corner and I in his', as the cynic put it! Jesus was passionate about the unity of all who believe in him through his message, which he saw as powerfully evangelistic (John 17:20–1).

This is where Bible Christians can have a real impact in our culture. When we can begin to demonstrate that we are prepared to give up our secondary differences in order to unite around the greater and vastly more important truth of the gospel and getting it out into the world, perhaps more people will be interested in listening. One of the persistent warnings of the New Testament letters is against that club mentality that so easily develops and takes over when we start to add something else to Jesus Christ, crucified and risen. It can be a particular system of church government (episcopal, presbyterian or congregational), a particular view of baptism or holy communion, views on prophecy or eschatology, spiritual experiences and charismatic gifts, or a myriad other issues, but not one of them is as important as the gospel. Why, then, do we drive the gospel down the agenda by elevating these issues as the required ground of our fellowship and unity, and failing to work together for what matters most of all? Local churches are not fast-food franchises working a neighbourhood in cut-throat competition. We are 'all one in Christ Jesus' (Galatians 3:28), and we need to demonstrate that reality to the watching world.

Lastly, there is a vast agenda of need in seeking to bring the Bible back into our public life and the decision-making centres of our culture. We can be thankful that there are several excellent Christian agencies which are dedicated to doing exactly that and are very active in bringing biblical perspectives and principles to bear on current social and political issues. They need more support by prayer, finance and personal involvement. Committed biblical Christians in high-profile national positions have a unique opportunity to bring the Bible to bear on matters of public debate. They need the support and encouragement of their fellow-Christians in their demanding and sometimes vulnerable positions. But while only a few may be capable and called to such national responsibilities, all of us can have a biblical influence in the communities in which we live. It is not our role to provide glib and easy 'proof text' answers to what are often complex and almost intractable problems. What we can do is to present God's values, as revealed in Scripture, and seek to apply them not only to the problem and its solution, but also to the process and the people involved in it. To take seriously the pattern of creation, fall and restoration, and to seek to relate these to the structures of which we are a part and the directions in which they are moving, is to fulfil, at least in part, Christ's intended role for us as 'the salt of the earth' (Matthew 5:13). It provides a 'narrative' by which the confusing cross-currents of modern life can be mapped and understood. It does not short-circuit the hard work of careful observation and analysis, but it does provide a coherent foundation on which moral decisions can be made and a consistent world view by which alternatives can be evaluated. Those who 'believe in the Bible' are always needed as active participants across the spheres of influence that make up our culture, and their presence will be more important, not less, in the coming decades. Thankfully, many are already there, but they need courage to speak up and perseverance to keep going, and many others to come and share the load. So whether it is in the classroom or the board room, the operating theatre or the department store, on the factory floor or at the office desk, there are great opportunities for God's Word to be heard and exemplified, through articulate, humble and gracious Christians who are prepared to stand up for their convictions. Wherever there is human life and activity, there the Word of God needs to be known and heard.

This is the immensely challenging and exciting agenda that

presents itself to those who believe in the Bible at the dawn of the twenty-first century. I am deeply thankful to be among them, as we give gratitude to God for the Word he has spoken, for the privilege of unrestricted access to it and for freedom to believe and proclaim it. The Bible is God's gift to us. It will be so, as long as the world endures, far beyond our time and on into eternity. There is nothing more precious we can give our children, or they can give their children, than the opportunity of hearing the living and enduring Word of God, which is 'able to make you wise for salvation through faith in Christ Jesus' (2 Timothy 3:15). But that is God's gift, too. Our responsibility is to be good stewards of what he has given us, so that we shall not need to be ashamed at his appearing. What better way to affirm 'I believe in the Bible' than by letting it loose to speak its own truth?

'For my thoughts are not your thoughts, neither are your ways my ways,' declares the LORD. 'As the heavens are higher than the earth, so are my ways higher than your ways and my thoughts than your thoughts. As the rain and the snow come down from heaven, and do not return to it without watering the earth and making it bud and flourish, so that it yields seed for the sower and bread for the eater, so is my word that goes out from my mouth: It will not return to me empty, but will accomplish what I desire and achieve the purpose for which I sent it.' (Isaiah 55:8–11)

Now that you have purified yourselves by obeying the truth so that you have sincere love for your brothers, love one another deeply, from the heart. For you have been born again, not of perishable seed, but of imperishable, through the living and enduring word of God. For, 'All men are like grass, and all their glory is like the flowers of the field; the grass withers and the flowers fall, but the word of the Lord stands for ever.' (1 Peter 1:22–5)

Your word, O LORD, is eternal; it stands firm in the heavens. Your faithfulness continues through all generations; you established the earth, and it endures. Your laws endure to this day, for all things serve you. (Psalm 119:89–91)

Oh, how I love your law! I meditate on it all day long. Your commands make me wiser than my enemies, for they are ever with me. (vv. 97–8)

How sweet are your words to my taste, sweeter than honey to my mouth! I gain understanding from your precepts; therefore I hate every wrong path. Your word is a lamp to my feet and a light for my path. (vv. 103–5)

'Let the prophet who has a dream tell his dream, but let the one who has my word speak it faithfully. For what has straw to do with grain?' declares the LORD. 'Is not my word like fire,' declares the LORD, 'and like a hammer that breaks a rock in pieces?' (Jeremiah 23:28–9)

Heaven and earth will pass away, but my words will never pass away. (Mark 13:31)

To remind you

- The contemporary believer in the Bible faces many challenges ahead from the culture – relativism, pluralism and post-modernism (pp. 215–18).
- However, much of the New Testament was written in a precisely similar context. Letters to Corinth, to the Colossians and Philippians, all deal with cultural challenges which threatened to distort or obscure the good news (pp. 218–23).
- In a post-modern society, living the Bible's story of love for God, issuing in obedience to his will because of his great love for us, is a powerful dynamic for change (pp. 223–6).
- Every individual life matters because we all affect the bigger picture in which society is moving either nearer to God, in obedience to Scripture, or further away from him (pp. 226–31).
- We need a more radical biblical approach to our involvement in everyday life – in the family, Church and nation. In each of these contexts, Scripture's priorities need to be recognised, believed and practised (pp. 231–5).
- The way to affirm our belief in the Bible is to let it loose in our own lives, and through them in the world at large, to declare and demonstrate its eternal truth (pp. 235–7).

Bibliography for further reading and study

The Bible's 'Big Picture'

Clowney, Edmund P.   *The Unfolding Mystery – Discovering Christ in the Old Testament*. Colorado Springs: Nav Press, 1988.

Gibson, R. J. (ed.)   *Interpreting God's Plan*. Carlisle: Paternoster, 1997.

Goldsworthy, Graeme   *Gospel and Kingdom – a Christian interpretation of the Old Testament*. Exeter: Paternoster, 1981.

Strom, Mark   *Days are Coming*. Sydney: Hodder & Stoughton, 1989.

Old Testament Books and Themes

Dumbrell, William J.   *The Faith of Israel – Its Expression in the Books of the Old Testament*. Leicester: Inter-Varsity Press, 1989.

Martens, Elmer A.   *God's Design – A Focus on Old Testament Theology*. Leicester: Inter-Varsity Press, 1994.

Motyer, J. Alec   *A Scenic Route Through the Old Testament*. Leicester: Inter-Varsity Press, 1994.

Motyer, J. Alec   *Look to the Rock – An Old Testament Background to our Understanding of Christ*. Leicester: Inter-Varsity Press, 1996.

New Testament Books and Themes

Barnett, Paul — *Bethlehem to Patmos – The New Testament Story*. Sydney: Hodder & Stoughton, 1989.

Gundry, Robert H. — *A Survey of the New Testament*, third edition. Carlisle: Paternoster, 1994.

Holwerda, David E. — *Jesus and Israel – One Covenant or Two?* Leicester: Inter-Varsity Press, 1995.

Ladd, George Eldon — *A Theology of the New Testament*. Guildford: Lutterworth Press, 1975.

Interpreting the Bible

Fee, Gordon D. and Stuart, Douglas — *How to Read the Bible for All Its Worth*. London: Scripture Union, 1993.

Klein, William W., Blomberg, Craig L. and Hubbard, Robert L. Jr — *Introduction to Biblical Interpretation*. Dallas: Word, 1994.

McCartney, Dan and Clayton, Charles — *Let the Reader Understand – A Guide to Interpreting and Applying the Bible*. Wheaton: Victor Books, 1994.

Reid, Andrew — *Postcard from Palestine – A Hands-on Guide to Reading and Using the Bible*. Kingsford: St Matthias Press, 1989.

The Bible's Reliability

Bruce, F. F. — *The New Testament Documents – Are They Reliable?* fifth edition. London: Inter-Varsity Press, 1960.

Carson, D. A. and Woodbridge, John. D. (ed.) — *Scripture and Truth*. Leicester: Inter-Varsity Press, 1983.

Packer, J. I. — *God Has Spoken*. London: Hodder & Stoughton, 1965.

Stott, John R. W.   *The Bible: Book for Today*. Leicester: Inter-Varsity Press, 1983.

The Bible's Message

Boice, J. Montgomery   *Foundations of the Christian Faith*. Leicester: Inter-Varsity Press, 1986.

Guthrie, D. and   *The New Bible Commentary – 21st Century*
Motyer, J. A. (ed.)   *Edition*. Leicester: Inter-Varsity Press, 1998.

Jensen, Peter   *At the Heart of the Universe – What Christians Believe*. Leicester: Inter-Varsity Press, 1991.

Milne, Bruce   *Know the Truth – A Handbook of Christian Belief*, second edition. Leicester: Inter-Varsity Press, 1998.

About the Authors

Dana Facaros and Michael Pauls are professional travel writers. Over the past ten years they have lived in several countries, concentrating mainly on the Mediterranean area. In Turkey they were, in their own words, 'fortunate to have had experiences as diverse as participating in a dervish ceremony and being invited in for tea by Cappadocian troglodytes squatting in the remains of a 2000-year-old underground city'. In addition to this guide, their travel books include over twenty highly successful guides to the Greek Islands, Italy, Spain and France.

Acknowledgements

Dana and Michael would like to thank Hasan Kocatürk, Assistant General Director of Information and Promotion of the Ministry of Culture and Tourism; Kamil Muren, Director of their National Tourist Office in New York, and Köksal Başaran of the Tourist Ministry for their kind assistance and insights into 'the whole bird'. We also owe a considerable debt of gratitude to the many provincial and local tourist offices throughout Turkey. Special thanks too to Wolfgang Feldmann and his photographic talents, to the Turkish Tourism Office in London for their kind assistance at the last minute and to Mrs Emine Türkece Connor for kindly checking our Turkish spelling.

In addition, in our most recent trip to Turkey we are grateful for the assistance of Döne Çay of the Turkish Tourist Office in London, Cemil Bayraktar, Tourism Director of Bodrum, Fehmi Ceyhan of Merhaba Tourism in Bodrum, Kemal Tuncer of Bursa (and special thanks also to Merih, the 'Blind Well of Bursa'), Talat Cengiz in Izmir, Cemal Gül in Marmaris and Ferhat Malcan in Kaş, as well as a thousand or so bus conductors, hotel keepers, talkative waiters, laughing children and everyone else who reminded us that once in a while, one can indeed recapture that first peerless rapture. And special thanks to the ever-patient and ever-tolerant Dominique.

The publishers would like to thank Animage for the design, Stewart Wild for proofreading, Isobel McLean for indexing, Suzan Kentli for the illustrations and Map Creation for the maps.

Contents

Introduction   vii   Guide to the Guide   viii

Travel   1–14

Getting There	2	Getting Around	7
By Air	2	By Air	7
By Sea	3	By Sea	8
By Rail	4	By Rail	9
By Bus	4	By Bus	9
By Car	5	By Car	10
Entry Formalities	5	By Taxi	13
		By Dolmuş or Minibus	13
Main Tour Operators and		Orientation	14
Special-interest Holidays	6		

Practical A–Z   15–42

Antiquities	16	Photography	28
Climate	16	Police	29
Disabled Travellers	16	Post Offices	29
Drugs	17	Public and Religious Holidays	29
Embassies and Consulates	17	Shopping	30
Festivals	17	Sports and Activities	34
Food and Drink	19	Telephones	36
Geography	23	Terrorists	37
Health	24	Time	37
Maps, Media	25	Toilets	37
Money	26	Tourist Offices Abroad	38
Museums	27	The Turkish People	38
Packing	28	Where to Stay	39

History   43–58

Ancient History to 546 BC	45	1454–1700: The Height of the	
546–334 BC: Greeks and Persians	47	Ottoman State	52
334–150 BC: Alexander the Great	48	1700–1910: The Empire Crumbles	53
150 BC–AD 300: Roman Rule	49	1911–19: The War Years	53
AD 300–1071: Byzantine Empire	49	1919: The Turkish Revolution	54
1071–1243: The Selcuks	50	1922–60: The Westernization of	
1300–1453: The Ottomans	51	Turkey	55
1453: Capture of Constantinople	52	1960 to the Present	55

CADOGAN
guides

Dana Facaros and Michael Pauls

WESTERN
TURKEY

Introduction and Guide to the Guide	vii
Travel	1
Practical A–Z	15
History	43
Topics	59
Istanbul	73
Thrace, the Marmara and Bursa	149
The North Aegean Coast	179
The South Aegean Coast	21?
The Southern Coast	261
Inland Anatolia	307
Architectural Terms	350
Chronology	351
Language	355
Further Reading	367
Index	369

Cadogan Books plc
London House, Parkgate Road, London SW11 4NQ, UK

Distributed in North America by
The Globe Pequot Press
6 Business Park Road, PO Box 833, Old Saybrook,
Connecticut 06475–0833

Copyright © Dana Facaros and Michael Pauls 1995
Illustrations © Suzan Kentli 1995

Expanded and updated from *Turkey* © Dana Facaros and
Michael Pauls 1986, 1988, 1993

Book and cover design by Animage
Cover illustrations by Povl Webb
Maps © Cadogan Guides, drawn by Map Creation Ltd

Series Editors: Rachel Fielding and Vicki Ingle

Editor: Dominique Shead
Proofreading: Stewart Wild
Indexing: Isobel McLean
Production: Rupert Wheeler Book Production Services

A catalogue record for this book is available from the British Library
ISBN 0–86–0110–05–3

Printed and bound in Great Britain by Redwood Books.

The author and publishers have made every effort to ensure the accuracy of the information in the book at the time of going to press. However, they cannot accept any responsibility for any loss, injury or inconvenience resulting from the use of information contained in this guide.

Please Help Us Keep This Guide Up to Date

Every effort has been made to ensure the accuracy of the information in this book at the time of going to press. However, practical details such as opening hours, travel information, standards in hotels and restaurants and, in particular, prices are liable to change.

Prices in Turkey can be a very confusing subject. The country suffers from a chronically high rate of inflation (as much as 40%), but, on the other hand, the Turkish lira is devalued against Western currencies. As a result, hotel prices and large purchases are often quoted in US dollars or Deutschmarks and the actual costs of your trip remain about the same—though the numbers are always changing. Food prices and transportation remain wonderfully inexpensive.

We would be delighted to receive any comments concerning existing entries or omissions. Significant contributions will be acknowledged in the next edition, and authors of the best letters will receive a copy of the Cadogan Guide of their choice.

Topics 59–72

Atatürk	60	The Green Man	65
East and West	61	Music	66
The Evil Eye	61	Perusing the *Polis*	67
Eleven Days at the Pera Palace	62	Religion	69
The Fatal Glass of Beer	63	The Sultan of Scholars	71
Futbol	64		

Istanbul 73–148

History	75	Istanbul in Asia	129
Getting There	78	The Bosphorus	131
Getting Around	79	Shopping	135
Tourist Information	81	Where to Stay	137
Orientation	83	Eating Out	142
Old Istanbul (Stamboul)	87	Entertainment and Nightlife	147

Thrace, the Marmara and Bursa 149–78

Edirne	151	Bursa	165
The Northern Marmara Coast	157	Uludağ	172
The Gelibolu Peninsula	159	North and East of Bursa	175
The Southern Marmara Coast	162	Iznik	176

The North Aegean Coast: Troy to Izmir 179–216

Troy and Çanakkale	181	Bergama to Izmir	201
The Troad	187	Izmir	203
Assos/Behramkale	188	Inland from Izmir	210
Ayvalik	191	Sart/Sardis	211
Aeolia	194	Çeşme Peninsula	213
Bergama/Pergamon	195	Çeşme	214

The South Aegean Coast 217–60

Kuşadasi Bay	218	Didyma	236
Selçuk	220	Aphrodisias	240
Ephesus	222	Pamukkale	242
Kuşadasi	228	Caria	244
Priene	231	Bodrum	248
Miletus	234	Marmaris	256

The Southern Coast · 261–306

The Lycian Coast: Marmaris to Antalya	262	Aspendos	287
Around Lake Köyceğiz	263	Side	288
Fethiye	265	Cilicia	293
Kaş to Antalya	271	Alanya	294
The Pamphylian Coast	277	Alanya to Silifke	298
Antalya	278	Silifke	300
East from Antalya	284	Uzuncaburç	302
Perge	285	Kizkalesi	303

Inland Anatolia · 307–48

Ancient Phrygia	310	Gordion	315
Eskişehir	310	The Lake District	319
Kütahya	311	Eğirdir	319
Afyon: City of Opium	313	Konya	325
The Phrygian Heartland	313	Cappadocia	333
Midas City	314	South and West of Göreme	344

Architectural Terms, Chronology, Language, Further Reading · 350–68

Index · 369–76

Maps

The Best of Turkey	inside cover	Ephesus	223
Ancient Western Turkey	44	Priene	232
Central Istanbul	84–5	Aphrodisias	241
Covered Bazaar	108	Bodrum and Marmaris	251
Istanbul: Outlying Sights	116–7	The Mediterranean Coast	262
Thrace and the Marmara	150	Antalya	279
Bursa	165	Perge	285
The North Aegean Coast	180	Side	289
Troy	183	Inland Anatolia	308–9
Pergamon	197	Konya	327
Izmir	205	Cappadocia	341
The South Aegean Coast	218		

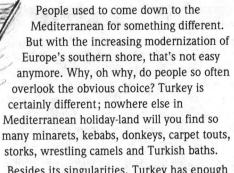

People used to come down to the Mediterranean for something different. But with the increasing modernization of Europe's southern shore, that's not easy anymore. Why, oh why, do people so often overlook the obvious choice? Turkey is certainly different; nowhere else in Mediterranean holiday-land will you find so many minarets, kebabs, donkeys, carpet touts, storks, wrestling camels and Turkish baths.

Besides its singularities, Turkey has enough positive attractions to make anywhere else's tourism directors green with jealousy. The

Introduction

most delicious coastline on the entire Mediterranean, for starters—over a thousand miles of it. Along with that come more classical ruins that Greece itself can offer, the magnificent, endlessly fascinating and endlessly surprising city of Istanbul, near-perfect weather most of the year, and some of the best food anywhere. Currently, the big story is prices. Thanks to the monetary shenanigans of the government, the currency has practically collapsed, making Turkey for now the greatest travel bargain going.

It may be that Turkey seems a bit too different, for those who have never visited. Today as much as ever, it turns an enigmatic face towards the world. Since independence in 1921, Turkey has grown up to be a curiously introverted, nearly self-sufficient country. It grows its own tea, tobacco and bananas, and makes its own cars and televisions. Stuck in its strategic position between two continents, it does not know whether to look west, towards Europe, or east, towards Islam and the emerging Turkophone world of central Asia. Its economy and political affairs are a god-awful mess, as they always are. The country simply can't seem to stay out of the headlines, and the news is usually bad.

None of that, however, need have anything to do with you or your holiday. On the contrary, whatever is happening, you are assured of spending your time among some of the most charming and hospitable people you'll ever meet. The Turks, with their grave courtesies and sympathy and glasses of tea, are their country's best advertisement. After the first shock of difference wears off, they will see to it that you feel at home, wherever and however you're travelling.

The book covers the western part of the country, including the Aegean and southern coasts, and the interior as far as Cappadocia—all the most popular parts of the country. For starters, there's incomparable **Istanbul**, the main attraction for most visitors. If you haven't seen the city for a while, new developments and improvements have transformed it completely, and mostly for the better. After that comes a brief foray into **Thrace**, the 3 per cent of Turkey on the European continent that includes Edirne and the battlefields of Gallipoli; in this chapter we have included the southern **Marmara shore**, with the delightful if overcrowded city of Bursa, the original Ottoman capital.

Turkey's coasts, separated from the interior by difficult mountains, are a world unto themselves, and we have grouped them together, beginning with the **Aegean coast**, with its famous resorts and Greek ruins. The northern half, the quieter stretch of the Aegean, includes a number of agreeable small resorts as well as ancient Troy and Pergamon, and modern Izmir. In the southern Aegean, brash and noisy resorts leap out at you: Bodrum, Marmaris and Kaş. The coastline crumbles into a jagged maze of peninsulas and bays, ideal for sailing and beachcombing. Here too are dozens of archaeological sites, from places such as Ephesus, where everyone goes, to Ionian and Carian cities lost in the woods that few have heard of.

The **southern coast** divides neatly into three distinct regions: lovely Lycia, with its spectacular coastline; the flat Pamphylian coast, jam-packed with more ancient ruined cities; and the pine-scented, largely undiscovered Cilician coast. **Inland Anatolia** gets a chapter to itself, a catch-all including the heartland of the ancient Phrygians around the modern city of Kütahya, famous for ceramics, the beautiful, seldom-visited lake district in the southeast, Konya, city of the whirling dervishes, and the natural wonderland of Cappadocia.

Getting There 2
  By Air 2
  By Sea 3
  By Rail 4
  By Bus 4
  By Car 5

Entry Formalities 5

Main Tour Operators and
  Special-interest Holidays 6

Getting Around 7
  By Air 7
  By Sea 8

Travel

  By Rail 9
  By Bus 9
  By Car 10
  By Taxi 13
  By Dolmuş or Minibus 13
  Orientation 14

By Air

From the UK

British Airways, 156 Regent Street, London W1R 5TA, ℗ 0345 222111, and Turkish Airlines, *Türk Hava Yollari* (THY), 11 Hanover St, London W1R 9HF, ℗ (0171) 499 9249, both have daily, scheduled flights to Istanbul from London Heathrow. The lowest official fares start at £245 return and can spiral to almost double that in high season, July and August. THY's discounts are usually inconveniently tied to to a fixed period of stay in Turkey (four or five weeks). Discounted tickets are available from bucket shops for scheduled flights on BA and THY: Sunquest, ℗ (0181) 800 8030, consistently offers low fares (currently a £163 Gatwick–Istanbul flight, off season Wednesdays and Sundays).

Other airlines serving Istanbul include Akdeniz Airlines, 46 Newington Green, London N16 9PX, ℗ (0171) 359 9214, with flights from London Stansted from £177; and Istanbul Airlines, 542 Kingsland Road, London E8 4AH, ℗ (0171) 249 4002, with flights from Heathrow, Gatwick and Manchester, and in summer, Stansted too; fares from £173 to £217, including tax. Onur Air, 23 Princes Street, London W1R 7RG, ℗ (0171) 499 9991, serves Istanbul year round with flights from Gatwick from £173 to £217.

One welcome improvement over recent years—you don't have to go via Istanbul if your destination is on the coast. THY has two weekly flights non-stop to Izmir on Mondays and Saturdays; even better is Cyprus Turkish Airlines, 41 Pall Mall, London SW1Y 5JG, ℗ (0171) 930 4851, offering the lowest regular fares varying from £198 to £243 (including tax) according to season, with flights from Heathrow on Mondays and Saturdays and from Stansted on Wednesdays. Cyprus Turkish Airlines also serves Antalya from Stansted on Sundays, with fares from £218 to £258, including tax.

In summer only, Istanbul Airlines has weekly flights from Gatwick to Izmir, Dalaman and Antalya, and from Stansted and Manchester to Antalya on Mondays. Fares to all three destinations range from £177 including tax. Onur Air offers Izmir from Gatwick, Birmingham and Newcastle, and Dalaman from these three airports plus Stansted and Manchester; fares from £161 to £197, including tax.

There is not much advantage in charter flights either in price or convenience, but it's worth perusing the travel pages of the Saturday and Sunday papers, or trawling through Teletext in search of a bargain. Thomson Holidays, ℗ (0181) 200 8733, offers good-value flights from late April to October to Dalaman, Antalya and Izmir from Gatwick, Manchester and a variety of regional airports. Fares range from £199 to £254. Much cheaper fares are available, but be careful from whom you buy your ticket. It's not worth taking a cheap charter flight to Greece for the purpose of visiting Turkey. Greek border officials zealously scrutinize passports on departure and even if only a single night's stay in Turkey is revealed (day trips are OK), the price of the return flight can be increased to that of the scheduled flight.

From the USA and Canada

THY, 437 Madison Avenue, New York, NY 10022, ℗ (212) 339 9650, flies non-stop daily from New York (Newark Airport) to Istanbul. There are no other direct flights but several European airlines, for example British Airways, American, Delta, TWA and KLM, have daily flights from the States with onward connections to Istanbul. It is less expensive to fly to London on Virgin, and take a cheap flight to Turkey from there. As yet, there are no direct flights between Canada and Turkey. A connecting flight is the only option, with an airline such as KLM (from Toronto and Vancouver) or Swissair (from Montreal).

From Europe

Istanbul is linked daily with most European capitals via THY and the relevant national carrier. Flights from Germany are the most frequent due to the high concentration of Turks working there; daily services operate from Munich, Frankfurt and Berlin. Some smaller carriers also operate from Germany with bargain fares, as from London. From southern Europe, Olympic Airways and THY connect Athens with Istanbul at a cost of around £110.

Airline Offices in Istanbul

THY: Atatürk Airport, Yeşilköy, ✆ (212) 663 6363; Aksaray, ✆ (212) 635 2287; Mustafa Kemal Paşa Caddesi 27, ✆ (212) 586 7514
THT: Airport, ✆ (212) 574 7240
British Airways: Cumhuriyet Caddesi 10, Taksim, ✆ (212) 234 1300
Cyprus Turkish Airlines (KTHY): Elmadağ, ✆ (212) 267 0973
Istanbul Airlines: Firazköy Yolu 26, Avcilar, ✆ (212) 509 2121
KLM: Abdi Ipekçi Caddesi 8, Nişantaşi, ✆ (212) 230 0311
Lufthansa: Esentepe, ✆ (212) 288 1050
Olympic Airways: Cumhuriyet Caddesi 171, Elmadağ, ✆ (212) 246 5081

THY's city terminal for Istanbul's Yeşilköy airport is at the Meşrutiyet Caddesi office in Şişhane (Beyoğlu). Departure times of buses to the airport can vary (see **Istanbul**, p.78, for getting in and out of the city).

By Sea

Between late March and December, Turkish Maritime Lines runs a weekly car ferry from Venice to Çeşme and Izmir (direct in summer, otherwise via Piraeus, Greece), leaving Venice every Saturday at 9pm to arrive in Izmir the following Tuesday at noon. Prices range from £140 for a Pullman seat to £350 for a luxury cabin; £165 extra for a car. TML also runs a weekly, summer-only service from Venice to Marmaris and Antalya, similarly priced. If you're going by car, these ferries cut a considerable amount of driving off the trip. Students get a 10% discount on TML fares. Minoan Line will take you from Ancona (3 hours from Rome by train on the Adriatic) to Kuşadasi, via Patras: a weekly trip in season only. Rates are slightly higher, for a shorter distance. Other lines also follow this run: Horizon Sea Lines, every Saturday afternoon in summer, to Çeşme via Patras. Another summer service is the Stern Line, Saturdays from Bari, on the southern tip of Italy, to Çeşme.

Car ferries also operate from Haifa, Alexandria, Cyprus and Odessa, and, year round, between the Greek islands and their nearest Turkish port. Crossings are daily in summer but can drop to only one or two a week in winter; boats cross between Rhodes and Marmaris, Mytilini (Lesbos) and Ayvalik, Kos and Bodrum, Samos and Kuşadasi and Chios and Çeşme (the last two have some room for cars). Both Greeks and Turks levy capricious 'port taxes' on these short runs, which are all very overpriced as it is.

The London agent for Turkish Maritime Lines is Sunquest Holidays Ltd, 9 Grand Parade, Green

Lanes, London N4 1JX, ℗ (0181) 800 8030. In Istanbul, the TML office is on Rihtim Caddesi, Karaköy, ℗ (212) 249 9222, and in Izmir it is at the harbour in Alsancak, ℗ (232) 421 0094.

By Rail

From the UK and Northern Europe

Until recently there were two direct rail routes from London to Istanbul, leaving London daily from Victoria Station in summer, less regularly in winter, and both taking three days—one via Belgium (Ostend–Aachen–Munich–Salzburg–Zagreb and Sofia), and a less expensive one via France (Paris–Vallorbe–Simplon–Iselle–Venice–Ljubljana–Zagreb and Sofia), costing £298. Both services are suspended at the time of writing, because of the fighting in former Yugoslavia. It is still possible to travel from London to Istanbul by train, via Hungary, Romania and Bulgaria, although this involves changing trains at Vienna and Budapest—a three day trip, and about £100 more expensive than the cheapest air fares. For more information on available routes, and for reservations, contact the **British Rail International Travel Centre**, Victoria Station, ℗ (0171) 834 2345 (if you're lucky someone may actually answer the phone). A transit visa will probably be needed to cross Romania, ℗ (0171) 937 9667, and Bulgaria, ℗ (0171) 584 9400: check at the time of travel.

Even with the discounts that are on offer to pensioners, children and those under 26, going by rail is still more expensive than flying. Yet travelling this way has its advantages. Both the one-way and return tickets are valid for two months and you can break the journey and restart it at any or several points within that time; the train offers a good opportunity to see a little of Europe while en route to Asia.

From Greece

A train leaves Athens daily for Istanbul via Thessaloniki. The journey time will be an excruciating 36 hours taking into account the likely long delays at the border. There are no first-class seats. Fly, sail or take the bus instead.

InterRail and EurRail

Anyone travelling **InterRail** (£270 full price, discounts available for those under 26), which offers unlimited travel on all European railways for one month, can use his ticket to travel to and within Turkey. However, since rail travel in Turkey is so slow and so cheap, it's far better to use up the month's travel on the more expensive lines in northern Europe before heading south. The InterRail ticket is available to all EU citizens who have been resident for six months in the country in which they purchase their ticket. It can be bought from any British Rail main line station or from some travel agents. North Americans can travel to and within Turkey on a **EurRail** ticket, but like InterRail, it is not really cost- or time-effective.

By Bus

This is no longer the cheapest way to get to Turkey, as it was in the 1970s and '80s, and there is no longer any direct service from London. Still, with some effort and planning true masochists may enjoy the pleasure of bumping across Europe's highways on the three-day slog to Istanbul, with changes in Paris, Munich, or Budapest and perhaps elsewhere. The fighting in Yugoslavia, and the need for transit visas in some countries have further complicated the situation. For further information and for reservations, contact **Eurolines**, ℗ (0171) 730 8235, or any National Express booking agent.

A bus runs daily between Athens and Istanbul, taking about 24 hours and costing around £25. It won't be pleasant but it will be better than doing the same journey by rail. Travel agents in the Plaka and Omonia Square areas of Athens sell tickets. Occasionally the Greeks are wont to hassle people at the border stop, but recent travellers report no problems.

By Car

From London, it's a good four-day 1900-mile (3000km) drive to Istanbul. The quickest route—through Ostend, Munich, Salzburg, Ljubljana, Belgrade, and Sofia—cannot be managed, because of the fighting in former Yugoslavia. Possible alternatives are to detour to the east, via Hungary, Romania and Bulgaria, or to drive to Venice and take the ferry (*see* above). A transit visa may be needed to cross Hungary, ✆ (0171) 235 2664, Romania, ✆ (0171) 937 9667, or Bulgaria, ✆ (0171) 499 6988: check at the time of travel.

Motorists have a choice of four points of entry from Europe: Ipsala and Kastanea–Pazarkule on the Greek border, or Kapikule and Aziziye on the Bulgarian frontier.

To bring your car into Turkey you'll need an **international driver's licence** and **insurance** that covers both European and Asian Turkey; the AA Five-Star policy is specifically designed for motorists abroad and can be adapted to cover this. Otherwise, a Turkish policy may be purchased at the border. The vehicle is noted on your passport and must be taken with you when you leave, or else be placed in the care of customs until you return to Turkey. A *Carnet de Passage* is required for a stay of longer than three months. Motorists must carry a fire extinguisher, a first-aid kit and two warning triangles. The driver's best friend in Turkey is the **Turkish Automobile Club** (*Türk Turing ve Otomobil Kulübü*) which gives information on all aspects of driving in Turkey, as well as a repair service (free if you belong to your home auto club) and excellent maps; for TTOK addresses in Turkey, *see* below.

Entry Formalities

Visas

British citizens require a visa for Turkey. They are no trouble to obtain and can be purchased upon entry for £5 (it's a good idea to have a £5 note handy). Nationals of Austria, Ireland, Hungary, Poland and Italy are also required to buy visas in the same manner. Citizens of most other countries, including the USA, Australia and New Zealand, do not require a visa.

Those intending to travel on to either Armenia or Georgia from Turkey should contact the relevant embassy in their home country before leaving, as border formalities concerning these fledgeling states are still in a state of flux. If there is no embassy, speak to the Russians. Iranian visas must be purchased before leaving home, a very lengthy process that can take up to 3 months. They are impossible to obtain at the border.

You can't get a visa at the Syrian border either, although you can get one quite quickly at home. You may—just may—be able to purchase a visa at the Syrian Embassy in Ankara. Whether you can or not depends on your nationality (less chance if you're British or American) and on the mood of the official at the time. Remember that for the Syrians, as with so many people of the Middle East, 'no' may mean 'not unless you can convince me otherwise'. The border with Iraq is, at present, closed.

Turkish customs officials generally don't look in the luggage of tourists entering the country. You are allowed to bring in 400 cigarettes, 5 litres of wine or spirits and 1.5kg of coffee, something you may want to consider if you can't live without it. Most places don't have coffee that isn't Turkish (thick, black and served in Lilliputian cups). Customs controls are very tight on leaving the country. You should keep receipts of any large purchases in case they get you.

currency

Limitless amounts of foreign currency may be brought into Turkey but no more than $5000-worth of Turkish lira (TL) may cross the border, going in or coming out. Up to $5000-worth of foreign currency may be bought from Turkish banks. **Currency exchange receipts** should always be retained: they help prove to customs the cost of large purchases, and are also needed to reconvert any extra Turkish lira into foreign currency before you leave. On your last few days in Turkey, keep close track of the amount of Turkish currency you have; it's expensive to convert it back to any other currency, and you'll find it's almost impossible to get rid of back home.

Main Tour Operators and Special-interest Holidays

There are more than 100 companies offering holidays and travel to Turkey; for financial safety make sure the one you choose has an ATOL licence and/or is a member of ABTA or AITO. The Turkish Tourist Office (in London, 1st Floor, 170–73 Piccadilly, ✆ (0171) 734 8681, ✆ 491 0773) can send you a useful list of companies and destinations offered.

Mainstream operators with large programmes, and flights from a variety of UK regional airports, include Inspirations, ✆ (01293) 822244; Intra Travel, ✆ (0171) 383 7701; Metak Holidays, ✆ (0171) 935 6961; Mosaic Holidays, ✆ (0181) 532 9050; President Holidays, ✆ (0171) 249 4002; Sunquest, ✆ (0171) 499 9992; Suntours, ✆ (0171) 434 3636; Sunworld, ✆ (0181) 290 1111; Thomson Holidays, ✆ (0181) 200 8733; and Turkey & Beyond, ✆ (0171) 486 3338.

Tour operators are becoming quite sophisticated concerning holidays in Turkey. Seven days yachting, seven days *terra firma* holidays are growing in popularity, as is fly-drive, unheard of in Turkey only a few years ago. Also, together with the standard, attractively priced two-week-plus beach package, several alternative, more off-beat options are available.

Alternatif Turizm (cycling tours around the Lycian coast and elsewhere), Caroline Williams, Samnu Iş Merkezi, Kiziloprak 81031, Istanbul, ✆ (216) 345 6650

Before Sunset Travels (culture tours of Istanbul, trekking tours), Zambak Sokak, Beyoğlu, ✆ (212) 293 0438

Crestar Yacht Charters (luxury yachts), Colette Court, 125 Sloane St, London SW1X 9AU, ✆ (0171) 730 9962

Dive and Sail (scuba diving, yachting), Nastfield Cottage, The Green, Frampton on Severn, Glos GL2 7DY, ✆ (01452) 740 919

Exodus Expeditions (adventure, trekking), 9 Weir Rd, London SW12 0LT, ✆ (0181) 675 5550

Explore Worldwide Ltd (adventure, trekking), 1 Frederick St, Aldershot, Hants, GU11 1LQ, ✆ (01252) 319 448

Fotograf Evi (nature tours all over Turkey for photography enthusiasts), Zambak Sokak, Beyoğlu, Istanbul, ✆ (212) 251 0566

Holt's Battlefield Tours (Gallipoli peninsula), 15 Market St, Sandwich, Kent CT13 9DA, ✆ (01304) 612248

Inter-Church Travel (steps of St Paul), Middleburg Square, Folkestone, Kent CT20 1AZ, ✆ (01303) 711535

McCulloch Yacht Charter (luxury yachts), Number 5, 32 Fairfield Road, London E3 2QB, ✆ (0181) 983 1487

Mosaic Holidays (educational), Patman House, George Lane, London E18 2LS, ✆ (0181) 532 9050

Moorings Marinair (yachting, flotilla sailing), 188 Northdown Road, Cliftonville, Kent CT9 2QN, ✆ (01843) 227 140

Naturetrek (birds and flowers of eastern Anatolia), Chautara, Bighton, Nr Alresford, Hants, SO24 9RB, ✆ (01962) 733 051

Prospect Music and Art (art and archaeology), 454 Chiswick High Road, London W4 5TT, ✆ (0181) 995 2151

Sherpa Expeditions (trekking and mountaineering), 131 Heston Rd, Hounslow, Middx TW5 0RD, ✆ (0181) 577 2717

Simply Turkey (trekking, flowers, yachting, painting, cuisine), Chiswick Gate, 598–608 Chiswick High Road, London W4 5RT, ✆ (0181) 747 1011

Sunsail Clubs (water sports, yachting), The Port House, Port Solent, Portsmouth, Hants PO6 4TH, ✆ (01705) 210 345

Swan Hellenic (Ionian and Lycian Turkey tours), 77 New Oxford St, London WC1A 1PP, ✆ (0171) 831 1616

Temple World Tours (archaeology, wild flowers), 13 The Avenue, Kew, Surrey TW9 2AL, ✆ (0181) 940 4114

Trek Travel (four-wheel-drive expeditions, trekking), 8 The Grange, Elmdon Park, Solihull, B92 9EL, ✆ (0121) 742 5420

UK Express (coach tours), 41 Whitehall, London SW1A 2BY, ✆ (0171) 839 3303

Worldwide Christian (Seven Churches of Asia), 50 Coldharbour Road, Bristol, BS6 7NA, ✆ (0117) 973 1840

Getting Around

By Air

For the vast areas of western Turkey, the air network is relatively undeveloped. You may find a flight handy to get from Istanbul to Izmir, Antalya, or Ankara. Besides these, there are less frequent services from Istanbul to Dalaman Airport (between Fethiye and Marmaris), and Adana (the nearest airport to the eastern Cilician coast), and in summer to Denizli and Bodrum. Most connections will be by the old standby THY, the national airline, or its subsidiary THT (at Istanbul's domestic airport, Yeşilköy, for information ring ✆ (212) 663

4600). But deregulation in recent years has opened the airlines to a number of smaller lines: Istanbul Airlines, besides its flights to Britain (*see* above), makes connections from Istanbul to Izmir, Antalya and Dalaman, and Sönmez Airlines is a small line that runs a shuttle service from Istanbul to Bursa (Atatürk Airport, ✆ (212) 573 9323).

We can't give more detailed information on schedules or prices, because all of these lines change them radically from season to season and year to year, trying to use their limited resources to best meet the demand. In general, though, the longest internal flights cost between £45–£55/$67–$83 for a single ticket, without discount. Fares are generally slightly higher on THY and THT than their competitors. On both, discounts for students, families, and frequent fliers are available. Children between 2 and 12 get a 50% discount on THY flights, and infants of 2 years and under, 90%.

Flights to Dalaman are strictly tourism-orientated, and dry up almost completely in winter. Istanbul–Izmir flights run daily at least, and there will be several a week from Istanbul to Antalya even in winter. THT runs a weekly service to Konya. No matter what flight, it is best to book your ticket a few days in advance as seats can be in great demand. And on any flight, make sure you're at the airport **two hours in advance**. Security at Turkish airports is admirably tight, or annoyingly tight, depending on your point of view. Passengers are frisked and their baggage X-rayed when they enter the airport terminal and—remember this—you will subsequently asked to identify your luggage on the tarmac before it is loaded; watch out for this while you're getting on the plane. All unidentified luggage is destroyed.

Istanbul's domestic terminal is about half a mile from the international terminal; a bus service connects the two. Some domestic flights, however, do leave from the international terminal. For details on Istanbul's airports, and getting in and out of the others, see the 'Getting Around' sections for each town.

By Sea

Turkish Maritime Lines, which not so long ago operated a substantial schedule of long-distance ferries and cruises around the Aegean, is now sadly reduced to an Istanbul–Izmir run (another goes to Trabzon via other main towns on the Black Sea). The Izmir line runs twice weekly in summer, on Mondays and Wednesdays, weekly the rest of the year. Between May and October, every two or three weeks, a ferry leaves Istanbul for a 10-day cruise stopping at Izmir, Kuşadasi, Bodrum, Marmaris, Kaş and Antalya. Unfortunately, dates and times are not specified until a couple of weeks before sailing. These large, slightly dilapidated floating hotels are very popular, and you should make reservations, especially for a cabin, in advance. Their main address is in Istanbul, Rihtim Caddesi, Karaköy, (by the Galata Bridge) ✆ (212) 245 5366, and in London, Sunquest Holidays, 9 Grand Parade, Green Lanes, N4 1JX, ✆ (0181) 800 5455.

Beyond these, Turkish Maritime Lines has frequent car ferries over the Dardenelles and Bosphorus, as well as the metropolitan ferries around Istanbul (*see* **Istanbul**, p.80), and ferries to the Marmara Islands and their nearest port, Bandirma, and to Gökçeada and Bozcaada in the Aegean. They also run the ferries to the Turkish Republic of Northern Cyprus, from Taşucu to Girne (Kyrenia) with hydrofoils and car ferries several times weekly, and less regularly from Mersin to Gazimağusa (Famagusta); in summer there are also services from Alanya to Girne (information ✆ (324) 233 9858). Note that if your passport carries the stamp of the Turkish Republic of Northern Cyprus, you will be barred from entering Greece (but officials at the border will stamp the visa on a separate sheet of paper for you).

By Rail

Turkish State railways (TCDD) has a rail network 5127 miles long. However, for the most part the trains are old and slow, and there's no reason you would ever need them; buses are much faster, much more convenient, and almost always cost less. Lack of speed is definitely the big drawback. Turkey built its railway network a century ago on the cheap; there are few bridges and tunnels, and tracks meander all over the countryside instead of taking the most direct route. You're sure to see parts of Turkey out of your window that no tourist ever visits. If you have the time and money, however, it's fun to take the train, especially on overnight journeys, where you can get an inexpensive *küşet* (couchette). And for a change from riding buses, a comfortable, air-conditioned first-class seat can be nice; compared to anything in the world besides a Turkish bus, the fare is still a great bargain. A reduction of up to a third is available on return tickets; students get 10% off in addition.

In Istanbul, the starting point for all routes to Europe and the west is Sirkeci Station (© (212) 527 0051); all trains to Anatolia depart from Haydarpaşa Station in Asia, © (216) 336 0475. Some of the more popular trains are night express trains between Ankara and Istanbul (the *Yatakli Ekspres* and the *Fatih Ekspres*) and the Ankara–Izmir express, all with sleeping cars. The country's 'old faithful', however, is the *Doğu Ekspresi*, which leaves Haydarpaşa daily at 8.30am to wheeze its way for nearly two days across Anatolia to Kars, calling in at Izmit, Bilecik, Eskişehir, Ankara, Kayseri, Sivas, Erzincan and Erzurum. Note that there are no trains at all on the southern coast: the mountains foiled the engineers completely, and they never got further than Aydin. You can get to little Eğirdir on the lakes by train, but not to the major city of Antalya. In the provinces the train always seems to come in the dead of night—and even if it's the only train in 24 hours, there may well be eight timetables posted, all utterly incomprehensible. The TCDD publishes an annual schedule, the *Yolu Rehberi*, which is more helpful than anything you'll see in the stations. The nation's rail network is also marked on the Tourist Map of Turkey, available from any Turkish Tourism Office.

By Bus

Forget the trains; you are most likely going to spend a fair piece of your holiday on the humble but praiseworthy Turkish bus. You'll be keeping company with white-shirted businessmen and penniless army recruits, housewives and laughing children, students and scholars. The Turkish bus is a great democratic institution, and also one of the most pleasant ways of getting around ever invented, an essential part of the Turkish experience.

Unlike the trains, the coach companies in Turkey are all privately owned and extremely competitive. Taking advantage of Turkey's ever improving highway system, they are wonderfully efficient and incredibly cheap. Fares are usually proportionate to time; as a rough guideline, each hour spent on the bus costs around £1/$1.50. All the buses are made by Mercedes-Benz and are quite comfortable, although some companies keep them in better shape than others.

It is always possible to purchase tickets in advance, from bus company offices in the city centres, but between cities this is really hardly ever necessary. All you do is show up, and before you know it, a bus agent will have you on a vehicle to your destination; one out of ten times, you'll have to wait an hour or two, but five out of ten times someone will find you and put you on a bus to your destination within fifteen minutes. There's a carnival atmosphere in the average *otogar*, or bus garage, nowhere more so than in Istanbul, where a hundred or so line employees scour the new, ultramodern terminal for potential passengers, shouting out the names of their destinations and hauling away passive Danish backpackers who never suspected they were on their way to Erzurum.

It's worth your while to do a little shopping around the station ticket hall; another company may have an earlier, faster or more direct bus; it is permissable to look for it while the first agent to have found you is already carrying your bag. Although prices are supposedly controlled, you may find that some companies offer a slightly better deal than others (in any case prices are too cheap to worry much). Since almost all of the *otogars* are on the outskirts of towns, some of the bigger companies have shuttle buses (*servis araci*) to take you in and out of the centre; always remember to ask if you buy your ticket in advance. Usually, you'll have to take a city bus, taxi or dolmuş to and from the *otogar*, which is no problem. Some are close enough to walk to from the centre with a bag or two; details for each town in the 'Getting Around' sections.

There is a difference between companies. Some of them are growing quite large and monopolistic in their areas, which may reflect itself in better service, swank double-decker buses, tea and biscuits and old Burt Lancaster westerns on the bus TV; *Istanbul Seyahat*, *Varan*, Bursa's *Uludağ*, and *Edirne Birlik* are all dependable lines. Others, especially the ubiquitous *Pamukkale*, have a habit of treating their passengers like cattle; this one should always be avoided if you have another convenient choice. Further east, the smaller *Kent* and *Akdeniz* always give a good ride. Almost every bus station (and train station) has an *emanet*, a left-luggage facility. These are very convenient, but always remember to find out when they close.

One problem on the buses is that the windows don't open. On hot days, try to get a seat directly behind a roof vent; also, look at the map while you're waiting, to see which side will be away from the sun. A few small companies, as a point of honour, seat foreigners in the front. On steep mountainous routes, this is a dubious privilege: one can only do as the signs over the driver's seat advise, and 'Trust in Allah'. Stops for tea and snacks are frequent, usually lasting about 20 minutes, and on long journeys there will be a stop for lunch or dinner in a roadside inn, where meals will inevitably be simple and very cheap. Most buses carry cold bottled water, free on request from the conductor. And buses have another of the sweet courtesies that always surprise first-time visitors to Turkey: every hour or so, the conductor will appear with a bottle of lemon cologne to splash some into your cupped hands. The idea is that if you rub the cologne over your face, neck and arms, it will both refresh you and mitigate the more malodorous effects of a crowded bus on a roasting day with 52 sweaty passengers; it works.

By Car

Apart from Istanbul, where traffic is a law unto itself, driving can be the best way to see the country, especially its many archaeological sites. Many of these cannot be reached by any public transportation. And there are always unspoiled beauty spots along the coast or up in the mountains only a half-hour away from you—if only there were a way to get to them.

Most of the main routes along the coasts have been finished, improved and widened, and traffic is still usually light. Almost all signs have been converted to conform with the international highway code, and towns are clearly signposted (blue), as are most archaeological sites (yellow). Petrol is cheaper than in most of Europe, and the Tourist Office's free map is very helpful, updated regularly to show all new stretches of asphalt.

Be careful: Turkey's accident rate is disproportionately high. Night driving is best avoided, simply because you can't see many of the hazards, such as sharp winding roads, cattle and sheep crossings, drag-racing tractors, slow buses or oil trucks careering to petrol stations that all close at 10pm. According to the highway code, passing is on the left, but in practice, in city or country, you will be overtaken on either side (or both at the same time). The busiest stretches of highway are on the E5 between Edirne and Istanbul, and from Istanbul to Ankara. Auto club repair trucks are available to those in need. The speed limit, unless otherwise marked, is 90kph in the country and 50kph in villages and towns.

Law enforcement on the roads is in the shaky hands of the **Trafik Polis**, a force nearly indistinguishable from the regular police except for special markings on their black-and-white cars. They either clear up traffic jams or create them in the cities, and molest bus and truck drivers at rural intersections to make sure papers are in order and the weight limits observed. They may stop you too, and give your car the once-over, looking for mechanical faults. They do not seem to be much of a nuisance to tourists. Some of their behaviour can be alarming, though— they may zoom up behind you in heavy *trafik* and screech something incomprehensible over their loudspeakers, which may mean *pull over*, but is actually more likely to mean *hurry up!* It's your guess. Occasionally, in Istanbul, they will block a busy street and send everyone up the side streets, or even dead-end alleys; apparently the plan is to prevent big blockages down the road by breaking them up into smaller ones everywhere else.

Getting involved in an accident can be a major problem even if you aren't hurt. You must find someone to call the *Trafik Polis*, and wait at the scene to make a police report (no matter how long it takes). Do not move the vehicles. You may be taken for a breath test, and if it's a serious accident there will be a court hearing to determine the cause; this can happen the same day.

In the cities, especially Istanbul, parking can be a real headache (*Park Yapilmaz* means 'No Parking'). If Turks are parking on the pavements, they probably have special permits to do so. If your car has foreign plates, you may park anywhere as the police won't ticket you. They may, however, haul your beast away, something that is becoming increasingly common in cities and even in some resorts, such as Bodrum, where parking problems are as bad as the cities. Fines are not high, but the inconvenience can be considerable. The *Trafik Polis* often do drivers the courtesy of announcing a sweep, cruising down the avenue with a siren that sounds like an eagle with haemorrhoids, bellowing the tag numbers of illegally parked cars over a loudspeaker, a warning before they haul them away. If you hear any such noise (outside of electoral campaign periods, when sound trucks are everywhere) go out and check.

Traffic lights are scarce even in Istanbul and are rarely heeded; street signs anywhere are also rare. The basic principle of driving, as in most other Mediterranean countries, is that wherever a car *can* go, sooner or later it will; Turkish Fiats seem to be specially adapted for driving up and down stairways, and creating third and fourth lanes on two-lane roads.

If you have a breakdown or need a repair, every town has a street or quarter on the outskirts called the *oto sanayi*, given over to mechanics, each specializing in a certain type of repair. In Istanbul, the closest to the centre is in the Dolapdere neighbourhood in the centre of Beyoğlu; in other cities, there are little car-repair compounds that hardly ever close on the outskirts. Spare parts are likely to be your chief problem (though not for most Renault or Fiat cars, which have Turkish-made counterparts), especially outside the big cities. Bring a kit with you if you can. Turkish mechanics, on the other hand, are very experienced: if they can't fix the problem, they can probably get your car going so that you can get to the next big city.

Most of the filling stations are along the main highways: you'll find BP, Mobil and Shell and the Turkish company, *Petrol Ofisi*, at the sign of the wolf, and *Türkpetrol* at the sign of the tipped cap. Outside the major tourist areas, there is only super petrol at the pumps. The price varies from one place to another, depending on how far the fuel has to be transported. Unleaded fuel is available at most stations.

car hire

Credit cards can be used for car rental in the major centres. Plastic money has yet to reach the outlying provinces, and in general the further east you go, the more decrepit your Renault or Fiat-Murat will be. If you hire from one of the large international firms on the coast, there is usually no charge for dropping the car off at another point. Unfortunately, for whatever reason hiring a car is the only prohibitively expensive thing you can do in Turkey; rates are currently as high as any European country.

It's best to arrange your car rental in advance, either through your travel agent, or direct with companies like Avis, ☎ (0181) 848 7433; Hertz, ☎ 0345 555888; or Holiday Autos, ☎ (0171) 491 1111. Your valid UK or EU driver's licence is acceptable.

common road signs

Signs conform to the international standard, and there are only a few cases where you're likely to be confused:

DUR	(Stop)	YAVAŞ	(Slow)
DIKKAT	(Caution)	TEHLIKE	(Danger)
GIRILMEZ	(No Entry)	TEK ISTIKAMET	(One Way)
ŞEHIR MERKEZI	(city centre)		

YASAK BÖLGE, ASKERI BÖLGE (Forbidden Area, Military Area, i.e. no photographs)

The Türk Turing ve Otomobil Kulübü

The TTOK is certainly one of the nation's remarkable institutions. They do the normal things an Auto Club is supposed to do: help with breakdowns, insurance and such, but even if you aren't driving you will cross their path many times. Under its longtime director Çelik Gülersoy, a legend in his own time, the TTOK became the country's major force in promoting tourism, and also in historical preservation. Especially in Istanbul, you will be enjoying the lovely parks and drinking in the cafés they have refurbished. They have even started hotels in some of the wooden Ottoman houses they restored, around the Aya Sofia and Kariye especially. Most of the park benches and street signs you'll see are their work too.

The TTOK has mobile repair units along many of the main highways. They have reciprocal agreements with the British AA and RAC (whom you should contact before you go if you're a member and mean to drive), though not the American AAA. They have offices in the following places:

Antalya: Milli Egemenlik Caddesi, Dallar Yildiz Çarşisi 9, ☎ (242) 247 0699
Istanbul: Şişli Meydani 364, ☎ (212) 231 4631
Izmir: Atatürk Bulv 370A, Alsancak, ☎ (232) 422 2621
Taşucu: Abel Ipekci Caddesi 27B, ☎ (324) 741 1463
Mersin: Mücahitler Caddesi 10, ☎ (324) 232 0492

and at the following border posts: Kapikule (Bulgarian, ☎ (284) 238 2034), and Ipsala (Greek, ☎ (284) 616 1574) .

By Taxi

The Turkish driver can coax movement out of a car that would remain dead to any other driver. He can also drive a car containing singularly few of the more generally accepted essentials, such as windscreen, mudguards, brakes. As long as the engine can turn over, a Turkish driver will somehow manage to take his car across open country and to the tops of mountains.

H. V. Morton, *In the Steps of St Paul*

Morton wrote this back in 1936, but some day, out in the wilds looking for an obscure ruin, you may find it's still true. It must be said, though, that the motor trade in all aspects is modernizing even faster than the rest of the country. Taxis are fairly ubiquitous, hold together under most circumstances, and by European standards they are very cheap. Almost everywhere, they are equipped with meters, and within towns there's no nonsense about them—no bargaining, no surprise, and only rarely a surcharge (for airport runs, night driving, etc). Turkish taxi drivers are usually honest, but don't be surprised if it costs more to ride in a vintage '55 Chevy, where such things still exist, than a new car; this is allowed because the former consume more petrol. Almost always (except in Istanbul and Izmir, where folks have taken on big-city manners) taxis provide another object lesson in the amiable differences of Turkish life. If you care to, sit in front—you aren't a pasha being chauffeured, but a companion, at least for the duration of the trip. Often, the driver will offer you a cigarette (if you don't offer him one first). And —wonderful to relate—when you reach your destination this gentleman may well *refuse* a tip. Of course, if you're on your way to the bus station, he may offer to drive you to whatever town you're bound for instead. He'll bargain the rate ferociously even if he knows you have no intention of taking a taxi to Erzurum; it passes the time.

If you haven't a car, taxis are the only alternative for seeing many of the outlying archaeological sites; in many places, the drivers do it regularly and have set prices, for a half or a whole day or for individual excursions. To cut costs, you can often share the taxi fare with other travellers. In many places the tourist office will arrange a trip for you.

By Dolmuş or Minibus

Dolmuş taxis (from the Turkish for 'stuffed') run certain routes in and between cities and towns. These are very inexpensive and can be distinguished by the little sign in the corner of the windscreen stating the destination. You just wait for a suitable one, and pile in. You can get off wherever you like along the route. Two decades ago the car would probably have been a shiny old American bathtub with tons of chrome, left behind in their thousands by the US military in the '50s. There are still a few of these around, especially in the old parts of Istanbul. Today, the dolmuş is more likely to be a purpose-built minibus (*dolmuş* and *minibus* are used interchangeably in this book, as they commonly are by the Turks). Your fellow passengers—a woman with a giant potted geranium, a man with a chicken on his lap—will welcome you aboard in the grand old spirit of dolmuş conviviality. Using them is an excellent way of meeting the locals.

In cities: Regular city buses are gradually replacing dolmuş lines, but there are still plenty around and you will often find them helpful. The red dolmuş stop signs are rare, but anywhere on the main streets of a town you can wait and flag one down; usually though, it is more convenient to go to one of the dolmuş terminals (in the centre of most cities; Istanbul has many), and find one that goes close to your destination. They're very cheap, and the driver will make change for you while he's waiting for a stoplight; no need to hurry to pay as you go in. (Few Americans would believe it now, but dolmuşes just like Turkey's were very popular in US cities eighty years ago. They were called *jitneys* then, from a Yiddish slang word for a nickel, the usual fare; bus lines used their influence with city governments to force them out of business after 1920). City buses are very very cheap, but you almost always need a ticket before you board. These are sold at the main stops, at little stands.

Between towns: On long-distance routes, you get a proper Mercedes bus; for towns close together, or between a provincial capital and outlying villages, there'll be a dolmuş/minibus. In some places, they leave from a central minibus *otogar*; in others, they will start from the main *otogar*, or at least make a stop there. In some small towns there's no terminus at all, but only a stop along the main street (see the 'Getting Around' sections in the text). In practice these work just like the city dolmuşes; all you have to do is find one for your destination and you're gone. They usually run very frequently, and you'll be using them all the time to get around.

Orientation
Turkish cities

Most Turkish cities are compact and easy to explore on foot. Many larger cities, such as Bursa, have grown up on a linear plan, with all the main points of interest spread out along one or two main routes, served by dolmuş. You'll know you're in the centre of town if you can see the Atatürk Monument. One major problem in towns of all sizes is the lack of street signs, but almost every local tourist office can provide you with a map, sometimes hand drawn, of the vicinity, which does help. Tourist offices almost always provide an acceptable map of cities; those for Istanbul and Izmir are as good as any you could pay money for. For maps of the country as a whole, do not expect to find anything with the detail available in maps of western European countries, and nothing like the Ordnance Survey or US Geodetic Survey is on offer. The familiar 'Tourist Map' of all Turkey, given out by any tourist office, is surprisingly accurate and helpful within its limits. Commercial maps are no improvement; their road networks particularly will usually be far out of date.

Addresses can be a minor nightmare in any Turkish town. Izmir is the worst, with its bizarre habit of numbering streets randomly, up to four digits—imagine trying to ask someone the way to the corner of 1348 and 655 Streets in Turkish. Antalya and other cities do this too. Often an address includes the city district, or *mahalle* (abbreviated *mah.*), with the street name after it. And often too, instead of or in addition to a district name there will be the name of a main street; so if your hotel is at Gazi Mah. Atatürk Cad. Zeytin Sokak, you're looking for a side street called Zeytin, just off Atatürk Caddesi, in the Gazi neighbourhood. *Caddesi* means avenue; *Sokak*, street, *Bulvar*, boulevard, *Meydan*, square. In smaller towns, you'll find yourself looking up addresses like *Hasan Postaci Evi*—'by the house of Hasan the postman'.

historical sites

Most sites are near villages, and can be visited without recourse to a taxi, by taking a minibus from your base to the village and walking (a place that was convenient for a town in 500 BC is often just as convenient in the 1990s—they're rarely more than a mile or two apart). However, **be sure you have transport back**. If it's a very small village, the minibus that brought you often returns at noon the next day, and in the village itself there may not be anything remotely resembling food or lodging. If you do get stuck somewhere, hitching a ride back is your best bet (and a good way of seeing the country if you're footloose and carefree). Buses will almost always stop for you anywhere along the road, if there's room.

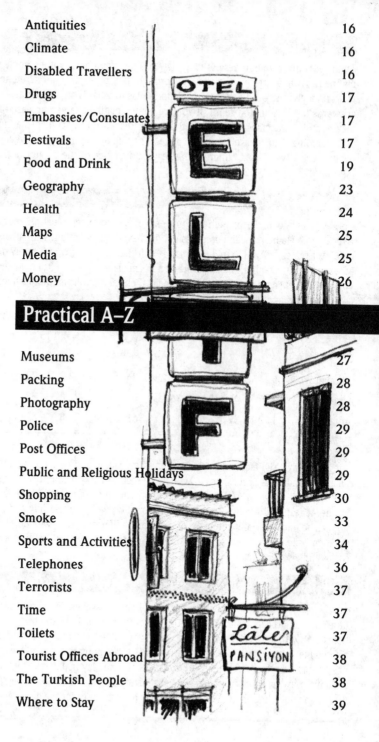

Antiquities 16

Climate 16

Disabled Travellers 16

Drugs 17

Embassies/Consulates 17

Festivals 17

Food and Drink 19

Geography 23

Health 24

Maps 25

Media 25

Money 26

Practical A–Z

Museums 27

Packing 28

Photography 28

Police 29

Post Offices 29

Public and Religious Holidays 29

Shopping 30

Smoke 33

Sports and Activities 34

Telephones 36

Terrorists 37

Time 37

Toilets 37

Tourist Offices Abroad 38

The Turkish People 38

Where to Stay 39

Antiquities

Trying to smuggle antiquities out of Turkey could result in your getting home much later than planned, with a stripey tan gained through the bars of some wretched Turkish jail. Unfortunately, there is no clear legal definition as to what is an antique and what is not. The answer is to use common sense. If you are contemplating a large purchase that you consider may be antique, such as a carpet, ask the dealer to draw up a document stating that the item is not, including in its text the purchase price. If he will not do this, you have a problem and it is best to seek advice, from either the nearest tourist office or the curator of the local museum (*see also* 'Shopping', p.30).

Climate

Turkey is large enough for each region to have its own meteorological tendencies. The south Aegean and Mediterranean coastlines get the best of the weather, with a bathing season that extends from early April to mid-October. It rains here in winter but is rarely desperately miserable—unlike in Istanbul, the Marmara region and Thrace, where from November to February you can expect snow and long, gloomy spells. Central Anatolia and Cappadocia can be bitingly cold in winter, and roasting in summer.

average daily temperatures

	Jan 15		Apr 15		Jul 15		Oct 15	
	°C	°F	°C	°F	°C °	F	°C °	F
Istanbul	5	41	12.2	54	22.8	73	16.1	61
Izmir	8.9	48	16.1	61	27.8	82	16.1	61
Antalya	11.1	52	16.1	61	27.8	82	20	68

When to Go

For a few days' sightseeing in Istanbul, any time is a good time, although you should take a thick coat and waterproof shoes in winter. To see the Turkish countryside at its most colourful and flower filled, go in April or May. Those intent on close perusal of the archaeological sites on the Aegean and Mediterranean shores would do well to avoid July and August, when the sun can be uncomfortably intense. For a guarantee of near-perfect weather, however, these are the months in which to go. In May, June and September it will still be deliciously warm on the coasts and also less crowded.

Disabled Travellers

Turkey is not the easiest of countries for the disabled traveller. There's no easy way onto a bus, or around an archaeological site, and pavements are usually in an atrocious condition, full of holes and with kerbs knee-high in places (Istanbul, especially, has bottomless abysses in its pavements, with no rails). Worse, the Turkish tourist industry seems to have no concept of the needs of the disabled. Yet this is not to say that a holiday in Turkey is impossible. Turks are waking up to this poor state of affairs and recently the tourist office has begun to publish hotel lists that include information on which hotels have facilities for the disabled. It's not much but at least it's a start. They do not publish lists of tour operators that provide facilities for the disabled in their holiday packages; however, local and national organizations for the disabled should be able to help out here.

Drugs

You may have thought *Midnight Express* a fine film, or you may have dismissed it as racist trash, but its basic message was spot on: don't do drugs in Turkey. Even a conviction for possession will almost certainly result in a prison sentence. How long depends on the amount in question; for a few grammes, expect at least 6 months, for anything over 2kg, 15 years and upwards. If you are offered drugs—unlikely but possible, especially if you're young, scruffy and long-haired—don't even think about accepting.

Embassies and Consulates

Adana

US Consulate: Atatürk Caddesi, Vali Yolu, ✆ (322) 234 2145

Antalya

British Consulate: Kazim Özalp Caddesi 149, ✆ (242) 247 7000

Istanbul

Australian Consulate: Tepecik Yolu Üzeri 58, Etiler, ✆ (212) 257 7050
British Consulate: Tepebaşi, Meşrutiyet Caddesi 34, ✆ (212) 252 6436
Canadian Consulate: Büyükdere Caddesi 107, Gayrettepe, ✆ (212) 272 5174
Irish Consul (honorary): Cumhuriyet Caddesi 26, ✆ (212) 246 6025
US Consulate: Meşrutiyet Caddesi 104, ✆ (212) 251 3602

Izmir

British Consulate: Mahmut Bozkert Caddesi 49, Alsancak, ✆ (232) 463 5151
US Consulate: Atatürk Caddesi 386, Alsancak, ✆ (232) 483 1369

Festivals

The two major national festivals in Turkey follow Ramazan (*see* 'Religion', p.69), and thus the time changes from year to year. The first, **Şeker Bayrami** or Ramazan feast, lasts for 3½ days and comes directly after the month-long fast. Shops are stocked with sweets for the children; the general mood is light and carefree. More important is the 4½-day **Kurban Bayrami** or Feast of the Holy Sacrifice, about a month after Ramazan. It is a time of visiting, giving gifts to children, and feasting. Traditionally, a sheep or lamb is bought and sacrificed on the day the festivities culminate, in imitation of Abraham's sacrifice of Ishmael, who takes the place of Isaac in the Mohammedan version. Both are bad times to travel; buses, trains, and aeroplanes are crowded with people going to visit relatives.

Other annual festivities are listed below. If you're in the vicinity, it would be a shame to miss one; the Turks will probably go out of their way to treat you as a special guest. Indeed, the summer festivals in the major tourist centres along the coast are put on to entertain visitors with displays of folklore, music, and dancing.

January

	Sarayköy camel fights, Denizli, Aydin, and Selçuk

March

15 March	Anniversary of the 1915 Sea Victory, Çanakkale
Last 2 weeks	International Film Festival, Istanbul

April

Mid-month	Historical and Traditional Mesir Festival, Manisa
Last weekend	Sultan Hisar Nyssa Festival, Aydin
Last week (to first week May)	Tulip Festival, Istanbul

May

First week	International Ephesus Festival, Selçuk; Spring festivities, Iznik and Bursa; Kirkağaç Pine festivities, Manisa; Yunus Emre Culture and Arts Week, Eskişehir
Mid-month	Regatta, Marmaris; Silifke Music and Folklore Festival
Last week	Marmaris Festival; Pergamum Festival, Bergama; Mesir Festival, Manisa
Last Sunday	Rose Festival, Konya

June

First week	International Mediterranean Festival, Izmir; Tekirdağ Cherry Festival; Isparta Cherry Festival; International Bandirma Bird Paradise Festival, Balikesir
Second week	Kirkpinar Festival and Greased Wrestling, Edirne; Enez Fish Festival (Thrace)
Third week	Bursa Keles Kocayayla Festivities
Last week	Nasrettin Hoca Festivities, Eskişehir
Mid-month (to mid-July)	International Istanbul Music and Arts Festival

July

First week	Şarköy Wine Festival, near Tekirdağ; Zeybeks Day, Kütahya; Yarimca Sports and Folklore Festival, near Izmit; Uluborlu Greased Wrestling; Sea Festival and International Song Contest, Çeşme; Ihlara Tourism and Culture Festival, Aksaray
Weekends	Javelin Competitions and Rahvan Horse races, Konya
Mid-month	Traditional Circumcision Feast, Kütahya; Şarkikaraağaç Halvah Festivities, Isparta; International Bursa Festival
Last week	Datça Knidos Festival; Dereçine Black Cherry Festival, near Afyon; Sultandaği Black Cherry Festival, near Afyon; Avanos Handicrafts and Tourism Festival; Babaeski Agriculture Festival, near Kirklareli

August

First week	Veli Baba Memorial Day, Isparta

Mid-month	Çanakkale Troya Festival; Haci Bektaş Remembrance Day and Ceremonies, Nevşehir
August 15	Assumption of the Virgin, Selçuk
End August–mid September	Burdur and Insuyu Festival; Izmir International Fair

September

First week	Bodrum Festival; Çal Wine Harvest Festival, near Denizli; Kirşehir Ahi Evran Crafts and Folklore Festival; Çankiri Honey Festival; Kuşadasi Tourism Festival; Elmali Yeşilyayla Wrestling Matches, near Antalya; Insuyu Festival, Burdur
Mid-month	Iznik Grape Festival; Cappadocia Wine Harvest Festival, in Ürgüp and Göreme; Ayvalik Tourism Festival; Aydin Arts Festival
Last week	Konya Culinary Contest; 'Golden Orange' Film Competition, Antalya; Cirit Games, Konya; Mersin Textile and Fashion Fair; Pigeon Competition, Konya
Weekends	Kizilcahamam Soğuksu Festival; Mahmudiye Horse Races

October

First week	Seben Apple Festival; Antalya Film Festival; Ürgüp Wine Festival
Mid-month	Şuhut Karadilli Wrestling Festival, near Afyon; Turkish Troubadour Week, Konya
Last week	Bağkonak Sugözü Festivities, near Isparta

November

| First week | Yacht Races, Marmaris |

December

All month	Camel Wrestling, Aydin province
First week	St Nicholas festival, Demre, near Antalya
December 14–17	Mevlâna Remembrance Day and Ceremonies, Konya

Food and Drink

People unfamiliar with Turkey are always pleasantly surprised when they discover Turkish cooking. The Turks themselves are fond of saying that there are three great cuisines in the world—Chinese, French, and Turkish. Whether or not you agree, eating is one of the main pleasures of visiting Turkey; there is a wide variety of dishes, the freshest ingredients are common, and, on the whole, the diet of the Turk is a healthy one, based on fresh fruits and vegetables, grilled fish and meat, with many kinds of salad and yoghurt dishes.

Have a close look at any Turkish market. Without too many of the chemical tricks used in Western countries, the Turks manage to grow fruits and vegetables that not only taste better than you get at home, but are much more colourful: tomatoes redder and more luscious than anywhere, and aubergines perfect in form and of a heartbreaking shade of violet (not to mention some exotica like the little purplish carrots of a type that originated in Afghanistan, the ancestors of all the carrots in the world). Western Anatolia has the perfect climate, and some of the most fertile land in the world. Give credit also to the Anatolian farmer, one of the most careful and loving tillers of the soil you'll ever see. Wherever nature permits, he turns his difficult land into little gardens, planted in meticulously straight patterns with never a weed in sight.

Turkey is one of the few nations to be self-sufficient in agriculture. From tea along the Black Sea coast to bananas along the Mediterranean, everything a Turk could desire grows well somewhere in the country; everything except coffee, and they've been diligently working on that for years (so far without success). Fruit is abundant and wonderful, especially the cherries, strawberries and peaches from around Bursa. The Turks have been exporting fruit for centuries, and even today in Egypt a lemon is called *adaliya*, after Antalya on the southern coast.

Turks are especially fond of hot or cold hors d'oeuvres (mezes), of which they often eat several instead of a main course. The bread is delicious and plentiful. While we look at bread as an accompaniment to meals, they look at their meals as something to go with their bread. The most popular dishes are based on lamb, aubergine (eggplant) and beans, found in the simplest *lokantas*, or tavernas. By Western European or American standards, prices are very low; if you're on a limited budget, you can eat well for a dollar or so a night.

Although Turkish establishments call themselves either *lokanta* or *restoran*, the difference isn't clear cut (like that between an Italian *trattoria* and *ristorante*): some fancy places affect the name *lokanta*, while some very simple places proudly call themselves *restoran*. In practice, there are two different types of eating place in Turkey. The more expensive type has glass cases full of mezes, with fish and various meat dishes cooked to order, wine and beer available, and probably at least one English- or German-speaking member of staff; here the price of a dinner will be from £4/$6 up. A typical menu will offer antipasti (*mezeler*) and soups (*çorbalar*) for starters. Turks think about soup all the time, and argue constantly about different ways of making it. There are innumerable varieties, but you aren't likely to find them in restaurants. Here the most common is *mercimek çorbası*, red lentil soup served with a squeeze of lemon—nothing could be simpler or more satisfying. Instead of, or in addition to soup, you are offered cold and hot mezes (*soğuk mezeler* and *sıcak mezeler*). The former will commonly include stuffed vine leaves, 'Russian salad' in mayonnaise, various kinds of beans in sauces, mushrooms, and cooked aubergine salad. The hot meze you'll see most often is *börekler*, stuffed with cheese or meat, but here is the chance for a good cook to be creative (and these can really run up the bill if you aren't careful). Seafood restaurants often have prawns or other shellfish. Almost always, you can pick out what looks good from the cooler or have the waiter bring you a mixed plate with a little of everything, which is the best way to do it.

For the main course, there'll be the ubiquitous kebabs (*see* below) or a mixed grill of various kinds of kebab served on *pide*, along with steaks (*bonfile* or a cheaper *biftek*), barbecued chicken, grilled meatballs (*köfte*), roast lamb or grilled lamb chops (*pirzole*). Another popular dish is *saç kavurma*, a stir-fry of lamb and vegetables, often done at your table. If it's seafood, some consultation with the waiter is in order. You should get a chance to pick out your fish; always ask the price beforehand, since fish is the only really expensive food in Turkey. Wine, at a healthy markup, can be had, as well as beer and booze. Along with the main course comes bread or *pide* or both, maybe chips or pilaf if you want, and almost always a typical Turkish salad of tomatoes, cucumber, onion, peppers (often these will be hot peppers) and parsley, occasionally with olives, lettuce, rocket and other ingredients. After this comes dessert, though this is hardly ever as elaborate as what you can get in the pastry shops, and a coffee or glass of tea. The bill is a *hesap*.

Some tips on restaurants: every tourist resort has lots of them, usually around the harbour. Most of these are open summer only, and scrape by with temporary staff. You'll do better trying to find one that stays open year-round. Hotel restaurants—as in most countries—are also usually better left alone. Asking a local where to dine is a good idea, but not so much taxi drivers or hotel staff, who all have cousins with a restaurant around the corner. If you're in a provincial, non-touristy town and can't find a decent restaurant, head for the town park; if there's only one place in town, that's where it will be.

At the less-expensive type, usually called a *lokanta*, already-cooked dishes are displayed on a steam table, and you point at what looks good: there will usually be a nice choice of stewed chicken and lamb dishes, plenty of beans and *patlican* (aubergine) cooked in various ways, stuffed peppers or tomatoes, rice pilaf and *bulgur* (cracked wheat, a favourite out in the east). Portions are usually small, so don't be shy about choosing several. Many of these places do kebabs too, as well as salads and sometimes barbecued chicken. Such places, where working Turks dine, are breathtakingly cheap, especially those with self-service (*kafeterias*), but they almost never offer wine or beer. Places serving *ocakbaşı*—a kind of Eastern barbecue, where you sit around a charcoal grill and the chef cooks the food of your choice—are also very good value.

Turn to the language section (p.355) for menus and their pronunciation. As well as *lokantas* and *restorans*, there are several types of restaurants that specialize in particular dishes.

Kebab salons: *kebap* can really mean almost any kind of grilled, roasted or barbecued meat in small pieces, from favourites like *şiş kebap* and *döner kebap* (a herbed lamb roll that cooks slowly as it rotates, served in slivers with sauce, often as a sandwich on pita bread) to specialities like *kağit kebap* (lamb and vegetables cooked in foil), *taş kebap*, stewed lamb, sometimes with vegetables, *çöp kebap* (literally rubbish kebab, small pieces of lamb or beef on wooden spits cooked over charcoal), *firin kebap*, a roast lamb dish popular in Konya and on the southern coast, or *İskender kebap*, a mixed platter with a tomato-based sauce and drenched in melted butter. This is the speciality of Bursa; a good one can be divine, while a bad one will lurch about in your stomach for hours. *Piliç kebap* is a new fad, chicken white meat done up in a roll and shaved off like a lamb döner (it's a little dry without the right sauce). Keep a look out for places that advertize 'Gaziantep style' or have names like 'Kahramanmaraş' or 'Şanliurfa'—these three cities out in the southeast are all famous for their kebabs, and cooks out there have spread out all over Turkey. Adana has a reputation too, and *Adana kebap* is a special treat for anyone who likes it hot.

Pide salons are the Turkish approximation of pizza parlours; *pide* is a delicious flat bread, served with various toppings. *Lahmacun pide* has ground meat, tomatoes and onions, the delight of the Anatolian peasants. *Ramazan pide*, eaten during the holy month of fasting in lieu of bread, is plain with sesame seeds. Perhaps the best is the Black Sea variety (*Karadeniz peynirlisi*) with cheese, sausage, and so on. **İşkembeci** have only tripe, sweetbreads, brains, etc. The Turks claim tripe soup is the best cure for a hangover, which in part accounts for the popularity of the *İşkembeci*. **Börekci** specialize in *börek*, a flaky pastry filled with cheese and herbs, or meat. **Muhallebici** concentrate on milk puddings, yoghurts, sweets, and chicken soup. Many **meyhaneler** (bars) also do food, either just simple snacks, or chips, or they will grill some kebabs in the evening.

On the coasts, near highways and around beaches, look out for small outdoor seafood restaurants, usually a house with a few tables and no sign. Here the owner goes out with his boat before dawn, and what he catches will be in the refrigerator for you to choose. Another kind of 'informal' restaurant (they don't really exist, you see, and consequently pay no taxes) can be found at picnic spots or any other place in the country where people from towns come for an outing. Someone comes and sets up a grill and tables, and there you are—instant restaurant. Some of these can be amazingly elaborate, with mezes, salads, chips and desserts. Both these kinds of places are fun and very inexpensive, and the food can be a real treat, but you'll only find them by accident, or by asking around.

Pastry shops and some restaurants specialize in sweets, some with evocative names like *Hanim Göbeği* (Lady's Navel) and *Dilber Dudaği* (Lips of the Beloved), both served in syrup as is the better-known *baklava* and shredded *kadayif*. Turkish pastry chefs produce a number of excellent cakes (often with chestnuts and hazelnuts), a large variety of *helva* (halva), good ice cream (*dondurma*) and of course Turkish delight (*lokum*), jellied squares flavoured with rose or mastic, coated with powdered sugar. Pistachios, almonds, chestnuts, and hazelnuts are often used, plain or in a number of exotic dishes; dried fruits and jams are excellent and plentiful, and fresh fruits in season are second to none. In many restaurants you can top off your meal with a fruit platter of plums, medlars, cherries, strawberries, and every Turk's favourite, *karpuz* (watermelon). **Cheeses** are also very good, made from the milk of cows, sheep, or goats. Popular varieties found throughout Turkey include *tulum* (made in a skin), *beyaz* (soft, white, salted), *mihaliç* (rich, unsalted, made from sheep's milk) and *kaşar* (hard).

Wherever you eat, the service will be somewhere between very good and wonderful. Service is almost always included in the bill, but it's good form to leave a tip, 10% or so, on the table.

Street food, no matter where you go, will be as varied and pleasing as the restaurants. Every streetcorner seems to have its *büfe*, a small stand that makes sandwiches or plates of döner, köfte, or other kebabs; many have a few tables in the shade for you to sit down. Vendors on the street sell sandwiches, *lahmacun pide*, *böreks*, mussels and other things (watch out for the carts where something that looks like a very long roast is being barbecued—it's really wound-up *kokoreç*, or sheep's gut; it can come as a real surprise but in fact it's not too bad). Any of these will do you for a light lunch (or breakfast), and any time of day you will also have your choice of a dizzying array of snacks. Vendors sell *simits* (bread rings covered with sesame seeds), peeled cucumbers, fruit in season, fruit juice (sometimes sold from elaborate, jingling brass dispensers borne on the back), pumpkin seeds, chick peas, dried fruit and nuts.

Kahramanmaraş, out east, is an inferno in summer but every Turk knows it as the capital of ice cream (*dondurma*). So when you see a fellow out on the street dressed in a sort of Hollywood-Arabian Nights costume, manipulating what seems to be a gigantic wad of bubble gum with two sticks, he's making Kahramanmaraş-style home made ice cream (which is pretty much the way your grandma probably made it, only with more exotic flavours). And for another summer treat, look for kiosks with coolers of *vişne*— fresh black cherry juice, which is tart and utterly delicious and makes being out in the sun worthwhile (at least when it hasn't been sitting in the cooler too long)

Drink

Turkish **wine** is quite good and inexpensive (except in restaurants). It is produced all over the country, especially in Thrace, Cappadocia and scattered parts of western Anatolia. Two good varieties are *Buzbağ*, a red (*kirmizi*) from out east around Elaziğ, and *Turasan*, a Cappadocian white (*beyaz*). The most popular labels in restaurants are Kavaklidere and Villa Doluca, which come in both red and white. Two decades ago, Turkey was the world's sixth-largest wine producer, but wine has been in steady retreat with competition from beer, the most popular drink in Turkey. Everywhere, you'll find *Efes Pilsen*, made by the state alcohol and tobacco monopoly TEKEL, under licence from Pilsener Urquell. It isn't bad, but you may prefer a good imported beer; most likely this will be Tuborg.

Raki, the favourite strong drink (50% proof), is distilled from raisins and flavoured with aniseed; it's the same as Greek *ouzo*, really, and always cut with water. You'll often see a group of Turkish men in a cafe or restaurant with a few bottles on the table, arguing for hours—the secret to doing this properly, as every Turk knows, is a long drawn-out meal or a constant supply of snacks to go with it. The *raki* you'll see most often is the corrosive *Yeni Raki*. Ask the man in the TEKEL stand if he has any *Külüp*, which is much smoother (Turkish folklore says the two tipplers on the label are Atatürk and Ismet Inönü), or *Altinbaş*, the best of all. All three are made by the state monopoly, as is most of the gin, vodka and brandy on offer; imports are much more expensive. In most places, bottles of all alcoholic beverages can be purchased only at TEKEL outlets; one can be found in the centre of any town.

Soft drinks are mediocre, though in the generally beerless *lokantas* and kebab stands you're going to see a lot of Coca Cola and a decent orange soda called *Yedigün*. The fizzy bottled mineral water (ask for 'soda' or *gazli su*) is readily available, and good for you, as the red crescent on the label testifies. Fresh or bottled fruit juices may be found at snack stands (*büfes*) in all but the smallest villages. The white, milk-like drink you see everywhere is *ayran*, yoghurt and water whipped together. Turkish **coffee**—very sweet (*şekerli*), with a little sugar (*az şekerli*) or without sugar (*şekersiz*)—is good and thick, and sold in restaurants and city cafés.

Tea, however, is far more common. It is grown on the Black Sea coast and sold by the State Monopoly, and all Turks can afford it. As a guest, you will constantly be offered tea (or even apple tea)—as soon as you arrive almost anywhere, someone will appear with a tray and several glasses. Ubiquitous as tea is, however, the old-fashioned tea houses are increasingly hard to find, with their beautiful gleaming samovars and *narghile*. But in towns you will never be more than a short walk away from a *çay bahçesi* (tea garden). Every park and square has one or several, and in the town centres there will usually be a whole collection of them, packed in the evening when the Turks make their promenade.

Geography

Turkey is more or less a rectangle, 400 miles wide (north to south) and almost 1000 miles long (east to west), at once in Europe and Asia and the Middle East. The variety of its topography tends to surprising and dramatic extremes; Turkey is a country of verdant forests and of vast, empty plains, of rivers and lakes and scorched desert wastes.

Wherever you go, you are never far from mountains; 89 have peaks that climb to 10,000ft and above, and both the Mediterranean and Black Sea coasts are bordered by tall ranges. The great Anatolian plateau is an extension of the Himalaya-Alpine range that rises gradually as you head east to culminate at majestic Mount Ararat (Agri Dağ), 16,786ft high. The Taurus mountains stretching along the southern coast are the largest chain in the country, sweeping upwards in an arch towards Malatya where they become the Anti-Taurus mountains, the roof of Turkey.

With so many heights, Turkey cannot help but be a land of lakes; the most famous is soapy Lake Van, far out in the east, but there is an entire district of big lakes around Isparta in the southwest, an interesting corner of Turkey not yet much bothered with tourism. There are rivers too, many flowing down from the Anti-Taurus mountains; the Tigris (*Dicle*), the Euphrates (*Firat*), the Halys (*Kizilirmak*) and the Yeşilirmak. Another river famous in antiquity, the Maeander (*Menderes*), flows from the Taurus mountains to the Aegean, its annual floods creating the country's most fertile valley.

Geography has a lot to teach us about Anatolia's history. The west has big rivers that flow all year, the Menderes, Gediz, Sakarya and Göksu, among others, but none of them are big enough to be navigable. The coasts are also ringed with mountains. Because of these two factors, Anatolia's coasts have always had different destinies than the interior—as in ancient times, when the coast was populated by Greeks, facing an interior under Persian rule; the two had little to do with each other. Greeks continued to populate much of the coasts until 1923. Until the modern Turkish republic, there has never been a state with an inland capital that also controlled the coasts; even the Hittites couldn't manage it.

Health

No inoculations are required for Turkey. However, a tetanus booster and a typhoid jab are wise precautions for travellers heading east of Ankara. If you plan to visit the Cilician plains east of Mersin, or any place in southeastern Turkey for any length of time, you should take malaria tablets. A gamma globulin vaccination will protect against hepatitus A and is advisable if you intend to travel in eastern Turkey, which is less developed than the rest of the country.

Rabies does exist in Turkey, as in most countries, although cases are extremely rare. Nevertheless, you should avoid any contact with any animal. If this worries you (and it should no more than if you were going to, say, France or Germany), ask your doctor about immunization shots. If camping rough, particularly amongst rocks, be aware that Turkey has several species of poisonous snakes and scorpions.

Tap water is not always safe to drink; in Istanbul it can be very dangerous in summer (*see* p.113). Bottled water, however, is inexpensive, and you may want to stick to it rather than have the discomfort of new bacteria in your system.

Most towns have at least one doctor that speaks English; in the tourist areas they advertise their bilingual proficiency on the doors of their surgeries. The quality of care is usually good, although as a rule it is better in private hospitals than the state-run hospitals and clinics. Amongst some doctors there is a worrying, ill-informed paranoia about AIDS. For minor problems—if you can make yourself understood—consult a chemist (a hospital is a *hastane*, a pharmacy, an *eczane*). Every town has a night pharmacy, or *nöbetci*, open by turns; most pharmacies have the schedule posted in their window. The Turks themselves are quite fond of herbal remedies, and in the towns you will see special shops for these.

In **emergencies**, call ✆ 112 for an ambulance, and ✆ 110 for the fire service.

Medical Insurance

Turkey has no reciprocal health agreement with any Western country and you must pay for all treatment received. Costs are lower than in Europe and the United States but even so can still be expensive. The best medical insurance policy is one that will fly you home in an emergency. Any tour operator or travel agent will be able to suggest one suitable for your needs. Be sure to read the small print concerning 'activities' before you sign (scuba diving, for example, may be viewed as a 'dangerous activity' by some companies and thus exclude you from protection). Some policies require you to pay on the spot and then to reclaim the cost (in which case you must keep all bills and documentation), while others simply require that the doctor or hospital concerned send the bill directly to the insurance company. The latter is preferable. Policy premiums begin at around £20 a week and usually include cover against theft and loss as well as health problems.

Tummy Bugs

'And how was your stomach?', people will ask on your return from Turkey. Chances are you'll be able to say it was fine. Problems with food poisoning in Turkey are vastly exaggerated and in many restaurants, particularly in the west of the country, standards of hygiene in food preparation are the same as you would expect in Europe. If you are worried though, the things to watch out for are raw, unpeeled fruits and vegetables, restaurants with steam tables where things have been sitting around, the tap water, and certain kinds of street foods (mussels, for one obvious example) in hot weather.

If afflicted with diarrhoea or food poisoning, rest yourself and your digestive system for a day or so, sticking to water and dry bread. It's better to let your body fight the infection first, strengthening your own immunity, before taking codeine or anti-diarrhoea tablets. If you do resort to tablets and the symptons persist after 36–48 hours, see a doctor. Diarrhoea dehydrates the body very fast and can leave you feverish; if suffering, it is important to drink lots of (bottled) water, even if that doesn't seem like a very good idea at the time.

And while we are on the subject of bugs, we can't help mentioning the **mosquitoes.** Especially on the Aegean and southern coasts, these are lusty, magnificent beasts; they take long drinks. Mosquito coils, available anywhere, are a sound investment; nothing else seems to work.

Foreign Hospitals

Istanbul

Pasteur Hospital (French), Taşkişla Caddesi, ✆ (212) 248 4756
Italian Hospital, Tophane Defterdar Yokuşu 37, ✆ (212) 249 9751
German Hospital, Siraselviler Caddesi 119, Taksim, ✆ (212) 251 7100
International Hospital, Istanbul Caddesi 28, Yeşilköy, ✆ (212) 574 7802
Admiral Bristol Hospital (American), Güzelbahçe Sokak, Nişantaşi, ✆ (212) 231 4050
The American and German Hospitals have emergency services.

Izmir

American Hospital, 1375 Sokak

Maps

The free map distributed by the Turkish Tourism Office is quite good and up to date; for minor roads, the Auto Club's map is good. Beware the Turkish habit of putting all provincial capitals in large type; sometimes these have only a few thousand inhabitants (like Bilecik), while an insignificant-looking dot may have a population of 100,000 (like Tarsus). Maps sold in your home country are often out of date or inaccurate; none of the ones we have seen is really worth buying.

Media

Turks love reading newspapers, and they are big business, with most of the large dailies being distributed nationally. As in Britain, the press has two levels. *Cumhuriyet*, a highbrow daily with a small readership, is the most respected paper. *Hurriyet, Milliyet* and *Sabah* are three more of the respectable dailies; they bring politics out into the open and scramble for circulation as best they can. Below these comes a vast array of colour-printed mass-circulation rags such as *Tan* and *Bulvar*, focusing on scandal, football and pin-ups; not tabloids though, but full size. For the tourist, there's the *Turkish Daily News*, in English, printed in Ankara, an invaluable source of education on Turkish life and politics—though the lessons are often unintentional, from the cryptic, roundabout and very Turkish way this paper goes about discussing difficult subjects. There's nothing cryptic about its belligerent attitude towards the State Security Courts, the repressive body, constitutionally beyond political control, that has been locking up journalists and intellectuals in growing numbers. This attitude is naturally shared by all the responsible press. Right now there is a war being waged over freedom of the press in Turkey, one that is of the utmost importance for the future of the nation.

The *Turkish Daily News* is available in the big cities and resorts and occasionally turns up elsewhere. Foreign papers and magazines will only be found in Istanbul and the popular resorts, and they may be several days old. Usually you'll be able to find one or two British dailies and the *Herald Tribune*.

If you have a **radio**, the Third Programme of the state-run *TRT* (Turkish Radio and Television) gives very limited news in English, French and German at 9 and 12, and 2, 5, 7 and 10pm, in various places on the FM band. Turkish radio can be entertaining, with a mixture of Turkish and Western classical music, good home-grown jazz, and wild music-hall entertainments that are funny, even if you can't make out a word. In all, there is more good music on Turkish radio than most of its European counterparts, though Western ear candy and Turkish pop are making increasing inroads.

Television, until recently limited to the state-run channels of the TRT, is currently undergoing a revolution. Private channels began broadcasting from over the borders via satellite dish in the late 1980s and are now operating in Turkey itself; though technically illegal, they have the blessing of the current government. Mostly, they show garish, Italian-style variety spectaculars, obscure old Turkish and western films, game shows, football and such, though tune in late and you may hear a concert of Turkish classical music. More important, though, is the role their news programmes are assuming in discussing political affairs, even those previously taboo, such as the Kurdish question. The new stations are all run by newspapers, or by the biggest Turkish holding companies, and they may not always be entirely professional or well-intentioned, but simply by being there they are bringing about a new openness to a society that is long overdue for it.

Money

Ten years ago, it was 2000 liras to the pound, and tourists joked about using 10 lira notes as toilet paper in bus station bogs. Three years ago, your pound got you 10,000 liras, and 100 lira notes were in jeopardy. At writing, it's a vertiginous 50,000 lira, or 35,000 to the dollar, and Allah only knows what the going rate will be when you read this. Before you go you had better learn to count at least up to 18,000 in Turkish, because that's how much a *döner* sandwich costs. Your cheap hotel room will be at least 150,000. The numbers are in the language section on p.359; study this well, because you're going to need it a dozen times a day. Many Turks have given up trying to make sense of their chronically evaporating currency, and it has become quite common everywhere to hear prices quoted in dollars or Deutschmarks.

At present, currency ranges from the impressive blue 500,000 lira note to the rapidly disappearing 1000 lira coin. The Turks do not like coins, and you'll find yourself carrying huge wads of small notes for change. They don't like bills of large denominations either, because they are a struggle to change. Learn the colour and design of the current banknotes as soon as you can; there are over a dozen varieties of obsolete ones, now legally worthless, and in places frequented by tourists somebody might try to fob one off on you.

Changing money will be a major source of entertainment. We remember a laughing bank teller, showing us the current rate on a telex, and then showing us the time printed in the corner—it was changing every hour, like Germany in the 1920s. When the telexes from the Central Bank break down, which is often, no money can be exchanged at all. Rates and commissions differ from bank to bank, and from day to day. Most banks will have rates posted outside; often the little numbers have fallen off the boards since they were last changed, several years ago—but this is less important than the rate of commission, which you should always find out before handing over any money. We have noticed that Akbank and T. C. Ziraat Bankasi will usually give you a fair shake. Some banks put out cash exchange machines, or bank card machines, in places where tourism is big business. These often actually work, but don't count on finding one when you need it. More helpfully, many bank offices will give you some cash against a major card; as anywhere, though, fees can be high and this is best left as a last resort. Banks also run exchanges at airports and many border crossings, and you'll get as good a rate there as in their main offices.

Major international credit cards are still only honoured in major towns and tourist centres, but bring them along anyhow, as they can be very handy for getting cash in a pinch, for airline flights and for car rentals.

Cash, Traveller's cheques and Eurocheques are easily cashed in any bank, and sometimes in main post offices too. If you're carrying cash, though—fat wads of dollars like every Turkish businessman does—you'll want to change it in a *döviz*, private exchanges that only recently have been made legal. These invariably have up-to-the-minute rates displayed on illuminated, computer-controlled screens, and these rates will always be slightly better than any bank. Most of these accept any convertible currency, but very few of them, unfortunately, take travellers' cheques or any other kind of funny paper. Ask at any *döviz* in a large town and they can probably send you to one that does.

Having money sent from abroad to a bank can be very complicated, and it's wise to start the process at least two weeks or so before you need the money. It's a good idea to bring as much Western currency into the country as you can; dollars or Deutschmarks are best, although sterling is easily changed too. You can use it in most cases to pay for your hotel, or for any large purchase; the Turks prefer it, though they won't give you much of a discount for it (*see also* 'Entry Formalities', p.5). Banking hours in Turkey are 8.30–12 and 1.30–5, Monday–Friday.

Museums

Most museums in Turkey date from the early years of the Republic. To Atatürk, recreating an interest and pride in Turkey's great civilizations of the past was an important part of nation-building, and his government fostered the creation of archaeological collections and the restoration of old buildings throughout the country.

Today, besides the great museums of Istanbul and Ankara, almost every town of any size has its own. Don't assume they aren't worth visiting; even the most obscure often have surprises even for the jaded culture tourist.

Almost all are government owned. Hours vary slightly, but most are closed for an hour or so at noon, and almost all are closed on Mondays. Note that almost all the ruins and castles of Turkey, in fact all the outdoor sites of any archaeological or antiquarian interest, are maintained by the government as 'open-air museums' to which the same closing times apply. There may or may not be an admission charge, and the person on duty or caretaker may or may not feel like collecting it. In any case, very few of the smaller sites are enclosed in any way, so if you can reach them (most of the ruined ancient cities are far from public transport; those that are will be noted in the text), don't worry about 'opening hours'. Someone may be around to sell a ticket or give a guided tour, but you'll be pretty much on your own. If there's a gate, there will also be an easy way around it.

Packing

Those who intend to visit Turkey in the height of summer should pack a few items to guard against the sun's more malevolent effects: a **hat**, for example, which should always be worn. A large (at least 1-litre) **water bottle** is essential, particularly if you plan to do some hiking. **Sun tan lotion** should be at least factor 15 and preferably factor 24.

A **torch** can be useful for exploring dark nooks and crannies (and for when your cheap hotel suffers a power cut), and a **sink plug** is also worth packing. **Fast film** can be difficult to get hold of (although you can buy ASA100 almost anywhere), as can **pipe tobacco**. **Toilet paper** is not supplied in cheap hotels or public lavatories, so unless you're prepared to use your left hand, bring some. Women may want to pack a **headscarf** and a **long skirt** for visiting mosques and for travelling in Turkey's more conservative regions. **Hard cash** (sterling, dollars or Deutschmarks) can be easily changed at hotels or with shopkeepers, and it's handy to have a few notes in your pocket to cater for any emergencies that occur when the banks are closed.

Electricity is 220 volts. Some outlets have two prongs, some three, so if you must be plugged in, come with **adapters** and **converters**.

Finally, if you're travelling alone, a small **transistor radio** can make for an amiable companion; take one along or get a locally made one in a Turkish radio shop for next to nothing (including licence fee!). The BBC World Service, the Voice of America and English-language programmes from Greece, Egypt and Cyprus can all be picked up on the medium wave band; Turkish radio plays lots of excellent music, from *sanay muziği* to jazz; other programmes border on the insane, and can be good fun even if you can't make out a word. Down in the southern reaches of Turkey, all sorts of weird and wonderful programmes come crackling through, from 'Gardeners Question Time' beamed to Iraq, to lovely traditional Irish music, broadcast to entertain the Irish soldiers in the UN force on Cyprus, to the 'Voice of Peace', Israel's pirate radio station, 'coming to you from somewhere in the Mediterranean ...'

Photography

Turkey is wonderland for photographers, with some reservations. Look out for military or prohibited zones; the government can be touchy about them and they aren't always obvious. All the land around the ancient Phrygian site of Gordion is one, for example, and all harbours. At some important sites, such as Aphrodisias, and many museums, cameras are prohibited at the request of the archaeologists. These busy scientists will make you wait until their monographs are in print before you may take photographs. Finally, don't make a nuisance of yourself by waving your camera at picturesque country people in traditional clothes; most Turks don't mind at all, but you may find some good Muslims who find the depicting of the human form offensive.

Police

Turkey is certainly a well-policed country, and cops come in all shapes and sizes. First the regular police, in their new blue uniforms with golf caps, designed to make them look less threatening. It hasn't really worked, but foreigners will usually find them courteous and helpful. Related to these is the *Trafik Polisi* (*see* p.11) who are assigned traffic duties. In towns, there is a special branch of the police that oversees trade and business matters, the *zabita*. They control weights and measures in the markets, watch over the bus and dolmuş services, and investigate complaints from consumers about all sorts of things. Istanbul and Bursa have their own *tourist police*, which may be very useful if you have trouble; they always have someone around who speaks English or some other Western language.

In remote country districts (mostly out in the east), the peace is kept by the *jandarmas*, part of the armed forces, much like the famous Mexican *federales*; dressed in green fatigues and sometimes carrying rifles. Finally, there are the *military police*, in full army gear with a red stripe on the helmet with the letters AS.IZ. They were much in evidence during the troubles of the 1970s, but now their only job is to stand around post offices waiting for AWOL soldiers.

Crime in Turkey is still rare, except perhaps for pickpocketing in the larger cities—especially in the marketplaces; there are almost no robberies.

Post Offices

These are easy to find by their yellow PTT signs. Larger ones have telephones (*see* below) and *poste restante* (general delivery) services. To make sure letters reach the central post office, have them addressed care of Poste Restante/*Merkez Postanesi*, followed by the name of the town. For telephones *only*, large central post offices in the major cities are sometimes open 24 hours a day, or as late as 11.30pm. For postal business, most close at 5 or 6pm.

The Turkish Post does work, though it can be slow. Don't count on getting anything to or from Britain in less than a week, air mail (two weeks, sometimes). There isn't any real express post, and the only way to do it faster is the *acele* service; there is a special window for this at most post offices, but it is fantastically expensive (about £20/$30 for a mere letter), and even here speed is not guaranteed. Sending packages can be time-consuming, since there are plenty of regulations and red tape. Postal rates are not much cheaper than in Europe or the US, and you might as well carry the thing home with you if there's room in your bag.

Public and Religious Holidays

Banks and post offices are closed during the festival of *Kurban Bayrami* (*see* 'Festivals') and on the following official holidays:

1 January: New Year's Day

23 April: National Independence and Children's Day

19 May: Atatürk Commemoration and Youth and Sports Day

30 August: Victory Day (victory over the Greeks, that is, in 1922)

29 October: Republic Day (anniversary of the declaration of the Republic)

There are plenty of other holidays, but the only ones likely to interfere with your travelling or shopping are the two important religious holidays, *Şeker Bayrami* ('sugar festival') a three day period at the end of Ramazan, and *Kurban Bayrami*, in commemoration of Abraham's sacrifice. Trains, buses and resort hotels (in resorts frequented by Turks) will be crowded, and banks and shops mostly closed. Both of these holidays are determined by the Islamic lunar calendar, so their dates slide backwards about 11 days each year. *Kurban Bayrami* in 1996 begins 29 April, and last four days; *Şeker Bayrami* will be 20–22 February. Ramazan in 1996 begins with the new moon in January—the best time for it, in winter when the days are short.

Whenever it falls, though, Ramazan should cause the non-Muslim traveller in Turkey little inconvenience. In resorts and big cities, you might not even notice it, and elsewhere, you'll be able to find restaurants open for lunch (though they may put curtains over the windows in conservative areas; in these places, such as Konya, you should be discreet about eating or smoking in public). By Islamic tradition, travellers are exempt from fasting anyhow. You might also consider keeping the holiday; it is a peculiar sensation, a kind of sense of community, knowing that almost everyone around you is doing the same. You'll find yourself sitting in the restaurant in the evening with a big crowd of hungry Turks, waiting for the cannon to boom from the local castle to mark sunset—or more likely, watching the television to see their town's name appear at the bottom of the screen. Dinner appears in an instant, and always tastes wonderfully good.

Shopping

Customs men in most countries are on to this. 'And what did *you* buy in Turkey?', they ask. There are so many pretty things, and prices are so low, that everyone goes home with something, aided in their choice by a merchant whose spiel will equal that of even the most high-powered time-share sales executive. The real masters of patter are to be found in the Covered Bazaar, Istanbul, where, after a few hours' strolling, you could be forgiven for wondering if the city's name is merely a derivation of 'instant bull'. Almost all purchases in Turkey incur a steep value-added tax (KDV). Find out first if it's included in the price (*KDV dahildir*) if you're doing any bargaining.

Carpets

Turkish carpets are famous the world over and Turkish carpet merchants think you're only there to see them. They'll entice you into their shop, bring lots of tea and unfurl with a flourish dozens of wonderful creations, from carpets hand-woven in silk to machine-made *kilims*, thin, colourful cotton rugs that serve the Turks as coverings for floors, walls, beds or furniture. Remember, however, that a carpet is not a cheap buy—prices start at around £90. If you've a notion to purchase one, it's worth talking to your local rug dealer before you go, or scouring the libraries, to get some idea of what to look out for. Turks know a great deal about carpets (it's a degree course in many Turkish universities), but for the very basics, read on.

Turkish carpets can be either hand- or machine-made. Those that are hand-made are better. Not only will they last much longer (for several generations, if cared for), but they have a greater nostalgic value; knowing that your carpet was hand-woven in an outlying Anatolian village is infinitely more pleasurable than knowing it came off a factory production line in downtown Istanbul. The difficulty, of course, is telling the difference between the two. Look at the knots: if they are irregularly spaced (and thus better binding), the carpet is probably handmade; if the knots are neat, even and tidy, the chances are it came off a machine. The carpet must be of either silk or wool; anything else, such as cotton, will not last beyond a few years. To discover whether the wool used in the carpet was hand- or machine-spun, ask the dealer to snip a length off one of the tassles and burn it: hand-spun wool will flare and exude a strong odour, machine-spun wool will not. In actuality, how the wool was spun makes little difference to the quality of the carpet, but following this ritual may fool the dealer into thinking that you know a little more than you do.

The quality of the dye used to colour the yarn should also be ascertained. Most carpets these days are chemically dyed, and while most are OK, inferior dyes will run and smudge when wet. To check, rub a damp white cloth over the carpet; if colour comes off onto the cloth, imagine the effect of a pot of tea spilt onto it. Investigate the carpet's origins: which outlying village of which town it is from, what the design signifies, whether that design is exclusive to that village, and so on. If the dealer can't tell you, there's something fishy about him. Besides, it's nice to know.

Although the traders there will do their best to convince you otherwise, Istanbul is not the place to buy a carpet, and neither are the main coastal resorts. The quality of the carpets will still be good, but prices will almost certainly be higher. This is not because the dealer is trying to rip you off (not necessarily, anyhow), but because he will have had to buy in his carpets from wholesalers in the carpet-making regions, around towns such as Ayvacik, Kayseri and Konya. If you can, buy your carpet in a 'carpet town' and cut out the middle man.

Always insist on, and keep, an official receipt—customs men sometimes like to see proof of purchase—and never, but never, purchase an antique carpet unless you have no intention of taking it out of the country. If you are caught trying to smuggle an antique carpet out of Turkey (*see* 'Antiquities'), you will almost certainly be jailed.

If you are unsure of the age of a particular carpet, consult the curator of the local museum. If he or she then declares it not to be antique (60 years or less should be OK), ask for an official letter confirming this before handing over your money.

Jewellery

Jewellers are everywhere, particularly in Istanbul's Covered Bazaar where whole streets and *bedestens* are devoted to their wares. The gold is normally of fair quality but be careful about buying silver, unless you know what you're doing. Fakes abound. In general, Turkish jewellery tends towards the heavy and showy, but in recent years the jewellers have learned to adapt a little to the tastes of visitors.

Leather

After carpets, leather is the next big buy and here again, time spent shopping around is time well spent. Jackets, in particular, can be of very variable quality. Have a look at the stitching, especially on the inner lining, and at the buttons: if buttons are shoddily sewn on, it doesn't say much for how the rest of the jacket was put together. Leather jackets are cheaper in Turkey than elsewhere in Europe, although not substantially so; for anything of decent quality, expect to pay at least £60. Handbags, holdalls and briefcases are also popular buys (check the stitching; it's a good sign if the flaps have been turned twice and double-stitched).

Ceramic plates and **tiles** range from tourist trinkets to works of a very high quality; many are beautifully hand-painted in traditional designs from the 17th and 18th centuries. In Istanbul prices range from £4–£400, but you can do much better, and have a much wider choice, in their town of origin, Kütahya, the ceramic centre of Turkey, where almost every street is lined with workshops and showrooms. Similar work, though not as good, is done in Iznik, the town that was once synonymous with fine ceramics.

On a more practical basis, **clothes** are very good and very cheap; a trip to Turkey may be your opportunity to outfit your children for the next ten years. It isn't just cheap stuff anymore, though. In Istanbul's modern districts and malls, you will be introduced to the world of Turkish haute couture—sharp designer fashions at very attractive prices (*see* the shopping section under **Istanbul**, p.135). Many well-known Western European and American concerns, such as Levi's and Benetton, have much of their clothing made in Turkey, and it is available here for much less than you'll see it at home. The speciality of Bursa is **linens and embroideries,** on display everywhere in that city's Covered Bazaar. These are one of Turkey's real shopping surprises, everything from simple towels and cloths to spectacular embroidered silk bed linens. The backstreets of Anatolian bazaars are full of surprises. Ask a tailor to make you up a pair of *şalvar*, the traditional baggy trousers for men or women: he'll do it in an afternoon for about £5, and you'll be a fashion sensation back home.

Copper is also a popular purchase; the best and the cheapest is found out east, in places like the bazaar of Urfa, where you can buy direct from the manufacturer, in a street full of old men and their much put-upon apprentices who beat out designs on trays and plates with careful precision. They've been there for centuries. In the west you'll see them occasionally at big markets. Antique **metalwork** of all kinds is popular, as in the flea markets of Istanbul; just make sure that what you're buying is not a genuine antique that may not be taken out of the country. Traditional **musical instruments**, from a simple *ney* to a hand-made, medieval-style lute, can be tremendous bargains; *see* the shopping section in Istanbul.

Pipe-smokers may want to invest in a **meerschaum** pipe. They can be found across the country but all originate in Eskişehir; the best are beautifully carved with a wealth of intricate detail. Water pipes, daggers, belly-dance costumes, mother-of-pearl inlaid hamam slippers, Karagöz puppets and other such oriental paraphernalia can be bought in all major towns, and in plenty of smaller villages near the tourist centres.

Shopping Protocol

Bargaining (*pazarlik*) is an accepted form of doing business for large purchases and is, except in Western-style shops, entirely expected. 'Tell me what you will pay,' shopkeepers urge. Bargaining is not a game, however, and merchants will be extremely displeased if you waste their time haggling over an item of small price, or one you have no intention of buying. It's a good idea not to disclose immediately the item you're interested in, but enquire about it last when the merchant is giving up hope of making a sale. As a bargaining guideline, offer a price of about two-thirds of what the dealer asks, and go on from there (if you're knowledgeable at all about the wares, offer two-thirds of what you think it's worth). You cannot drop your price to below that of your first offer. If you plan to buy a number of items, get your best price for just one first, and then ask if there might possibly be a discount for buying in quantity.

If you allow yourself to be guided into a shop by a friendly chap who has a 'brother/cousin/friend who sells carpets/jewellery/leather', and then buy something from that shop, you will have paid over the odds. Charming though that chap may be, he will expect a cut of the profit that the shopkeeper makes on your purchase. The shopkeeper will add the cost of the commission to the 'best price' he will offer you.

Don't be intimidated by *pazarlik*. Our Western, fixed-price way of doing things is a triumph of banality over humanity, from the Turkish point of view, an aberration that could only have been invented in a society where people basically dislike and mistrust each other. You may look at the glass of tea you are offered as a trick, something that makes you feel obliged to buy. Or you may see it as an elementary courtesy, which it is. You may consider bargaining as a grim battle of wits, in which someone is going to get handled, while the other party is making a sinful extra penny he doesn't really deserve. But how is it any different from the sort of deals Western businessmen make with each other every day? The point of bargaining, strangely enough, is to produce satisfaction, to allow two people to come to an agreement that both will be happy with. Buying something in the bazaar of a big tourist colony such as Bodrum, though, you may find the procedure somewhat lacking in grace. Sadly, it often is. Many merchants have become a bit jaded by too many tourists that are either easy marks, or at the opposite extreme are full of suspicions and none too polite. It is also true that the situation encourages some merchants (and their commission minions) to be so persistent that they make nuisances of themselves. To these, just say goodbye.

As shopkeepers are quick to remind you, 'looking is free'. And if just looking is what you intend, say so clearly at the beginning; most shopkeepers, if they have the time, won't mind showing off their wares and teaching you a little something about them. A promise to consider, and perhaps return later on is something no honest merchant could object to. Never, ever, buy something you don't want, or for a price you aren't happy with. Why should you? And don't be put off if whatever you happen to say, about the weather or whatever, he seems to be constantly steering the conversation back to those carpets. In most cases, he isn't really being pushy. Many merchants, if they know English at all, have a deceptively good commercial vocabulary in it but are hard pressed to say much on any other subject. It isn't an easy part of their job—they may have to do the same in German, French and Arabic too, and some of the more enterprising ones are polishing up their Japanese.

Bargaining can be pleasant enough if you know what you want, know what you care to spend for it, and go about in a cool and courteous manner (and it's usually over in a minute, unless you're as good a talker as the shopkeeper, and mean to be really hard). Use Turkey as a chance to match wits with the experts; it'll be good practice for the next time you buy a car.

Smoke

> *Sublime tobacco! which from east to west*
> *Cheers the tar's labour or the Turkman's rest*

> Byron, *The Island.*

More than almost anything, Turks love to smoke, and they do so at all times of the day and night, on buses, in hospitals, in gas works, anywhere you can think of. Where smoking is forbidden, the ban is generally adhered to—on some local buses and in ferry lounges; shocking though it may seem, the TCDD and a few of the bigger inter-city bus lines have even introduced non-smoking sections. Otherwise, expect to be shrouded in a grey fog almost everywhere you go. There is very little you can do about this, particularly on the long-distance buses where the situation is worsened by the Turks' dread of draughts, which makes them close all fresh air vents on anything but the hottest of days; the smoke will be less dense at the front of the bus.

If you want to smoke like a Turk, the proper way to do it is with a *nargile*, or hookah, the glass contraption that the English in their quaint way used to call a 'hubble-bubble'. They seem to be making a comeback, and you'll find plenty of humble *kiraathaneler* (old-fashioned working-mens' coffee houses) and boulevard cafés where you can have one brought over, along with a sinister-looking wad of rough-cut *tömbeki* tobacco that smells like a camel's bum even before it's lit. You'll catch Turkey's only legal buzz, and watching you try to keep it going will entertain the locals royally. In between cafés, you'll have to settle for cigarettes. Western imports are prohibitively taxed, but Turkish smokes are better anyhow, with excellent tobacco from the lovely green valley of the Yeşilirmak, near the Black Sea. *Samsun*, as the name implies, are strongest and best, deliciously aromatic like the finest cigars; then *Tokat*, somewhat milder, and finally *Maltepe*, which are closest to Western tastes.

Sports and Activities

Water Sports

Water sports are the rage in Turkey and can be indulged in to the full in the resorts along the south Aegean and Mediterranean coasts. **Yachting** (*see* below) is extremely popular and opportunities for **windsurfing** and **snorkelling** abound. For **scuba divers**, there are schools in Çeşme, Kuşadasi, Bodrum and several of the other more obvious resorts; rates are comparatively cheap when compared to, say, Greece. Sea pollution will only be a problem near the main shipping harbours, around Istanbul, Izmir, Mersin, Iskenderun and several of the ports on the Black Sea coast. In July and August the Aegean coast is often plagued by the *meltemi* wind, making rough seas.

Yachting

Chartering a yacht or sailing your own along the Turkish coast is becoming more popular every year. Prices for the former are still quite reasonable when compared to other Mediterranean countries: the Tourist Office has lists of agents and charterers with whom you can reserve a boat (bare or with crew) in advance; outside July and August you can usually get a boat on the spot in the major resorts—Antalya, Marmaris, Bodrum or Kuşadasi. One of the most memorable ways of spending a holiday in Turkey is to float along the delightful pine-forested coast, in and out of a hundred picturesque coves dotted with the remains of ancient cities, dining every evening off the day's catch.

Sailing along the southwest coast between Kuşadasi and Antalya is known as a **Blue Cruise**. Once on board, where you go is entirely up to you, but opting for the full cruise will take you to the following: Kuşadasi, Didyma, Güllük, Bodrum, Gökova Bay, Cnidus, Datça, Turunç, Marmaris, Dalyan, Fethiye, Kalkan, Kaş, Üçağiz, Demre, Finike, Phaselis and Antalya. You may want to stop off at a few of the Greek Aegean islands en route; nearest to this length of coastline are Samos, Patmos, Lipsi, Kalymnos, Kos, Nissiros, Symi, Rhodes and Kastellorizo. Basic information on these is supplied in the text; for more, refer to Cadogan's *Greek Islands* guide.

Since a full Blue Cruise would take at least one month, most prospective sailors have to opt for a shorter voyage that can be fitted within the given length of their charter. As a guideline, in one week you could travel from Kuşadasi to Bodrum, from Bodrum around Gökova Bay and back again, or from Bodrum to Marmaris. Two weeks could take you from Kuşadasi to Marmaris (via a few Greek islands), or from Marmaris to Antalya.

For companions, you can either get your own group together (between 7 and 12 persons) or take a 'cabin charter', whereby specific berths are set aside for individual passengers. The boats themselves are likely to be *gulets*, pine-built with a rounded aft and a pointed fore, with double berths (bunk beds) measuring 2 metres long by 2 metres wide. Luxury yachts can also be chartered, from a company such as Crestar Yacht Charters Ltd, Colette Court, 125 Sloane Street, London SW1X 9AU, ✆ (0171) 730 9962.

The cost will be between £35 and £55 per day, per person, not including food, depending upon the season, the size of the boat and the facilities on offer. April, May, September and October are the cheaper months. The tourist office publishes an annual list of tour operators offering yachting holidays; alternatively, you can talk to owners of the boats that crowd every resort harbour and probably make a better deal if the time is right.

If you have your own yacht, official **ports of entry** are Çanakkale, Bandirma, Istanbul, Akçay, Ayvalik, Dikili, Izmir, Çeşme, Kuşadasi, Güllük, Bodrum, Datça, Marmaris, Fethiye, Kaş, Finike, Kemer, Antalya, Alanya, Anamur, Taşucu, Mersin, Iskenderun, Samsun, Silifke, Trabzon, Adana, Didyma, Derince, Tekirdağ, Zonguldak and Ordu. On arriving in Turkey the captain must fill out a transit log. If you leave Turkish waters for seven days or less, you can leave the transit log with port authorities and reuse it on your return. Foreign yachts may remain in Turkey for up to two years for maintenance and winter berthing.

Mountains, Rafts and Caves

Mountain climbing is another fair-weather sport; due to the dangers involved, it is strictly controlled. Foreign mountaineering groups need special permission before setting off; apply to the Ministry of Foreign Affairs in Ankara. Those wishing to climb the steepest peaks—those only for experienced mountaineers—should contact the tourist office who will supply names of travel agencies who will arrange all documentation, guides, provisions and so on.

Several other activities, well developed elsewhere, are just being discovered in Turkey. **White-water rafting** enthusiasts have sent out rave reviews about the River Goksu on the southern coast. The tourist office can help out with information on excursions to Turkey's numerous and often dazzling **caves**. The greatest collection of these is found in the mountains north of Antalya.

Skiing

Skiing, cheaper than elsewhere in Europe, is growing in popularity in Turkey. The best-known and most developed resort is **Uludağ**, located in a national park near Bursa with 25 runs of varying difficulty and a view of the Sea of Marmara. The season here lasts from November to March, although those not enamoured by the patter of tiny skis should avoid Uludağ in late January/early February when the pistes become packed with Turkish schoolchildren. At other times the slopes should be blissfully uncluttered. Agents for Uludağ are Ski Turkey, ✆ in UK (0181) 461 5701 (UK office manned April–December only). Otherwise try President Holidays, ✆ (0171) 249 4002.

There are **other resorts**, though the best snow and most challenging runs are in eastern Turkey. Just north of Antalya, in the Beydaği mountains at Saklikent, you can, during March and April, ski in the morning and swim in the Mediterranean in the afternoon. Ski Turkey can arrange a tailor-made holiday here.

Fishing and Hunting

Fishing for sport requires no licence; **hunters**, however, can only go out in organized groups sponsored by a travel agent. Wild boar hunts in the autumn are organized in Muğla province (Marmaris), in the Taurus mountains and on Mt Ida, near Akçay. Write to the Union of Travel Agencies, Atatürk Bulv 107/71, Ankara, for a list of sponsors.

National Sports and Recreation

If you're in the right place at the right time (*see* 'Festivals'), you may be able to see three of the Turks' home-grown sports. Although football (*see* p.64) has more of a following, **wrestling** is still considered the national sport, and contests take place throughout the summer. Edirne is the greased wrestling capital of Turkey and hosts the most famous tournament. **Camel wrestling** (*Deve Güreşi*) pits camel against camel in a slow, clumsy-elegant ritual in which one beast eventually establishes dominance; they are separated before doing each other any harm. This is most common along the Aegean coast in December and January, especially in Selçuk. To see **Cirit** ('javelins'), a rather dangerous but exhilarating sport featuring galloping horsemen hurling blunted wooden javelins at each other, you'll usually have to head out east to Erzurum where it's still popular. There are exhibitions in Konya in September.

Less strenuous activities include lounging around a **spa** (there are famous ones in Bursa, Yalova and Gönen, all easily accessible by sea from Istanbul; also at Ilica near Çeşme, Pamukkale and Hüdayi, in Afyon province), playing *tavla* (backgammon) in the coffee houses and, of course, taking a **Turkish bath** or hamam.

Almost every town has a hamam, either with separate facilities for men and women, or open to men and women on alternate days. The Turkish bath is a direct descendant of the Roman bath, adopted by the Byzantines and then the Ottomans; it is a wonderfully sensuous ritual, especially if you have a chance to luxuriate in one of the historic hamams in Istanbul: the 18th-century Çağaloğlu Hamamı, on Hilali Ahmer Caddesi 34, near the Blue Mosque; the 16th-century Galatasaray Hamamı, at Suterazi Sokak 24 in Beyoğlu; or the 19th-century Pangalti Hamamı, on Dolapdere Caddesi 224 in Pangalti; or, in Edirne, the beautiful 16th-century Sokullu Mehmet Paşa Hamamı.

The *halvet* is the hot room where you perspire; the *göbektaşi* is the hot stone slab on which the bath attendant rubs you down. This they tend to do with great enthusiasm, either with a glove that removes dead skin or even by walking across your back; if it hurts, you can always call out '*yavaş, yavaş*' ('slowly, slowly'). Be sure to tip the bath attendant when you leave.

Telephones

Turkey's telephone service is modernizing rapidly. The entire system is in the process of being rebuilt, and nearly every area has changed over to uniform, three-digit area codes and seven-digit numbers—any old numbers you have won't be good. Finding the new ones can be a problem; most of the directories in the post offices date back to 1991 or earlier. **Phone cards** are becoming very common in the west of Turkey and are particularly useful for short long-distance and international calls, saving you the trouble of constantly nourishing the phone with handfuls of *jetons* (tokens). The cards come in units of 30, 60 and 100. A 100-unit card will give you an international call of around 3 minutes' duration—at least enough to have somebody at home ring you back at the phone box. You'll still see many phones operated by *jetons*, but these are gradually being phased out. You can buy both cards and tokens at any post office.

Making long-distance calls from your hotel is as bad an idea as in any other country; hotels always take a substantial mark-up. The other practical way to do it is from any town's central post office, where there is usually a separate room for telephone services. Give the man your number and sit down and wait. Some offices have metered booths, though at others, they'll simply hand you a telephone over the counter when your call goes through, and you can talk to your sweetie back home from the middle of a crowd of amused Turks. You cannot tell the price of the call from the meter, but expect it to be nearly as much as long-distance rates anywhere in Europe (and some postal employees are not above adding a bit on if you're a foreigner). For a long-distance call within Turkey, dial 0, then the provincial area code, and the number. For international calls, dial 00, then the country code (Britain 44, US and Canada 1, Ireland 353, Australia 63), then the area code (omitting any 0s before British city codes) and the number.

Useful Telephone Numbers

Police:	155	Ambulance:	112
Fire Service:	110	Directory Enquiries:	118

Terrorists

In 1993, the Kurdish terrorist group PKK decided to expand its efforts to a bombing campaign in the western resorts, designed to frighten away tourists and so hurt the Turkish economy. The results so far have not been too impressive: three small bombs in 1994, in Fethiye, Bodrum and Marmaris, injuring a few foreign visitors, some severely. It remains to be seen whether the PKK has the resources to keep up the threat. Local tourism officials are rather sanguine about the situation. They note that many of the timid Germans, French and Dutch have been frightened away, though the number of people visiting from Britain (on the southern coast especially) has been steadily rising. 'They have plenty of bombs at home,' we were told; 'they aren't as easy to scare as the Germans.'

The PKK's campaign has had some effect, and nowhere more than in Cappadocia. People think that because this lovely region is 'out east' it must be full of troubles. On the contrary, Cappadocia is very far from the Kurdish area and still utterly peaceful. But right now it is full of hotel owners wondering where their clientele has gone. Take advantage of the situation while it lasts; the discounts are wonderful and everyone will be glad to see you.

Time

Throughout most of the year Turkey is 2 hours ahead of Greenwich Mean Time and 7 hours ahead of Eastern Standard Time (New York), 10 ahead of California. At times this may vary by an hour either way, depending on when daylight saving hours are introduced.

Toilets

Conveniences in varying states of decomposition will be found in petrol stations, bus depots, etc.—just ask for the *tuvalet* or WC (pronounced 'veh-veh-jeh'); attendants collect a nominal fee. French-style holes in the floor await you in many of the cheaper hotels—but never in the government-listed establishments. The use of toilet paper is not a universally accepted custom (that's what the little taps are for); seasoned travellers carry their own. Turkish loos that flush with enthusiasm are rare. Please put toilet paper in the little bins provided; if no bin is provided, it is more hygienic to start a small pile of paper in a corner than to cause a blockage in the plumbing!

Tourist Offices Abroad

UK

First Floor, 170–173 Piccadilly, London W1V 9DD, ✆ (0171) 734 8681, 📠 (0171) 491 0773

USA

821 United Nations Plaza, New York, NY 10017, ✆ (212) 687 2194, 📠 (212) 599 7568

1714 Massachusetts Ave NW, Washington DC, 20036, ✆ (202) 429 9844, 📠 (202) 429 5649

The Turkish People

Othello didn't like the Turks very much:

> In Aleppo once
> Where a malignant and a turbaned Turk
> Beat a Venetian and traduced the state
> I took by the throat the circumcised dog
> And smote him thus.

History has been unkind to the Turkish people, especially history written from a European point of view. To writers and commentators of the past they were slothful, lazy, dirty, backward, and devious, yet to be fair to those bigoted scribes, most Ottoman sultans did run their country in a manner that did little to dispel such prejudices. Of course, all of the adjectives above are utter nonsense; in fact, it's hard to meet a people nicer than the Turks.

The word for guest in Turkish is *misafir*, and to the Turks it is almost sacred. Wherever you go, you'll be offered a glass of tea; for many people, Turkish hospitality is almost overwhelming. Yet one never has the feeling that it derives from a sense of religious obligation, rather from a warm and spontaneous friendliness and concern for their fellow man. Coupled with this, especially in the small villages, is a keen curiosity about the foreigner. In eastern Anatolia the good farmer may just stop and stare at you; it's a bit unnerving but he means no harm. Anyone who knows a few phrases of English, especially the school children, will want to try them out on you ('Is Turkey beautiful? Yes?'). The country women are shyer. If they're in a group (you'll see them coming and going from the fields in large trailers pulled by jaunty tractors), they may smile. Otherwise, they probably won't address you, unless you're a woman on your own. Then they open up and are even more friendly than the men. Turks dote on children and if you take them with you, they'll spoil them horribly. '*Maşallah, maşallah!*' they'll say, patting them on the head and giving them more sweets and fruit than they could eat in a year. '*Maşallah*' means 'God willing'; children are too precious to receive any direct compliments that might incur divine jealousy.

As well as warmth and hospitality, the other central characteristic of the Turks is their intense nationalism and pride. This is the heritage of the Great Atatürk. When Turkey was still referred to as 'The Sick Man of Europe', he boosted his countrymen's morale with slogans that you still see everywhere, even inscribed on hillsides in giant white letters: '*NE MUTLU TÜRKÜM DIYENE* ('How lucky for a man to call himself a Turk!') and '*BIZ BIZE BENZERIZ* ('We resemble ourselves'). Speak disparagingly of Turkey at your own risk; although you'll find plenty of sympathy on many subjects, from telephones to traffic conditions in Istanbul, Atatürk himself is the one really taboo subject, unless you want to pay his memory a compliment. It's also bad form to say 'Constantinople' instead of Istanbul, or to imply that Turkey is not a member of the Western community. Turks are easily insulted. They are also quite modest and conservative socially; wearing your bikini in the village and becoming noisy and drunk are provocative.

While travelling with children in Turkey poses no special problem (except that disposable nappies and baby foods are hard to come by in many places, and many children dislike the milk served in the cafés), a woman travelling on her own, or with a girlfriend, may have to contend with stares, personal questions and some typical Mediterranean male annoyances. The Turks, especially off the well-travelled tourist routes, are simply not used to seeing women on their own. Don't be afraid to use the word '*Ayi!*' ('shame') loudly if harassment reaches uncomfortable levels; this may elicit the help of passers-by. Face-slapping is stupid and potentially very dangerous. But don't be afraid to go. It is rare for a man to try to force you into something you don't want. Turks may make the women sit in the back of the mosque, but they have a respect for their rights and dignity that could be an example to many men elsewhere.

Where to Stay

1994 was the year of the great tourism bust in Turkey: the crest of a speculative wave of hotel-building arrived at the same time as a drop-off of visitors from continental Europe, frightened off by a pitiful few PKK bombing attacks, heavily reported in the news. As a result, both pansiyons and hotels were often running at a third capacity in the height of the season, and harried desk clerks and small proprietors were sending all their relations out on the pavement looking for somebody, anybody, to fill their rooms at any price. This situation will naturally correct itself over the next few years, but for the time being accommodation in Turkey will continue to be a tremendous bargain, and usually easy to find.

Hotels and Pansiyons

Four and five-star hotels will supply all that their counterparts do elsewhere in the world. The staff will speak excellent English, and there will be restaurants and bars, usually a disco and often a hamam. Expect a pool (except in city centres) and equipment for water sports on offer. Rooms should have a balcony, and usually satellite TV and air-conditioning; minibars are also common, though with the usual criminal mark-up for drinks. Some of the luxury and expensive hotels are housed within converted Ottoman mansions or caravanserais (nearly all of these are in this book), though most are very modern—and surprisingly sharp-looking, well-designed and well-equipped; the best are as good as those of anywhere in Europe. If you can afford to splurge, these can be great bargains just now, especially out of the high season. Rates are often negotiable (try a little *pazarlik* over the phone). You will often be able to enjoy the comfort and facilities of a top-flight resort hotel for £40–£50/$60–$75, and, at the right time, maybe as low as £30/$45.

Three- and two-star hotels will also be what you would expect, although in the tourist areas they can be hastily flung together and consequently very functional and soulless, the kind of places built specifically for package tours. In the one-star category, you may struggle to find a member of staff who speaks English, and although the rooms will be very clean and often have private showers, you may have to share the toilet that will be down the hall.

The **staff** in Turkish hotels, like the Turks in general, are extremely friendly and helpful. They may not shine shoes (this being the exclusive province of the *boyaci*, shoeshine boys or men, who may be found almost everywhere with their artistically embellished brass boxes), but are willing to handle almost any other difficulty that may arise: giving directions, finding taxis, making reservations and handling laundry (*çamaşir*). If you get a room that is dirty, or the lock or lights don't work, don't hesitate to complain or demand another one.

Breakfast, on offer in all hotels with stars and many of the *pansiyons*, is usually a simple Mediterranean affair with rolls and jam or honey, cheese, olives, and tea or coffee, though in fancier establishments it will often be an elaborate buffet. Before you check into one of the two-to-four-star places in resorts that mainly cater to package tours, remember that most of them require at least half-board. Hotel restaurants, even in Turkey, the land of wonderful cuisine, are, in general, overpriced and dull, although we've found several exceptions.

Turkey's *pansiyons* and unclassified hotels are a mixed bag: some have en suite rooms and telephones and would not disgrace a two-star hotel; others are miserable flea-pits, especially in the outlying regions, where you should check the sheets which the staff are sometimes prone to straighten rather than change.

The sort of *pansiyon* you are most likely to encounter in the coastal resorts will usually be quite pleasant: a modern concrete building which your hosts may have all to themselves, or share with other apartments. The rooms are generally bright and airy, and there may be a roof terrace for breakfast (part of the deal in some, but not all establishments; you'll almost always have a choice whether you want it or not). Most of them also have heating; you'll notice a lack of blankets, though if you ask for some they will be supplied. Unless the hotel has 'continuous hot water', take your shower early in the morning or in the evening when the hot water's turned on. In smaller hotels and *pansiyons* you may have to ask for it to be turned on at the desk.

A double room in a simple *pansiyon* can go from £5/$8 to £14/$21. Some areas are a bit more expensive than others, such as Bodrum and Marmaris, but you will find a choice at both extremes of the price range wherever you go. The highest prices in all hotel categories are in Istanbul, and there do not expect always to get what you pay for.

There may well be a younger member of the family in your *pansiyon* who speaks some English—but you will already have met him, at the bus station. Of course, you don't have to work to find a *pansiyon* in any Turkish town where tourists come; they'll find you. When you're getting off the bus, or even walking down the street carrying a bag, someone will probably materialize from a doorway and start on about the lovely place run by his mom or brother or cousin, where the hot water is ever so dependable. Surprisingly, if you can't find a room in one of the places mentioned in this book, you'll find that just giving in and following him gives you the same odds as hunting up a place yourself. Times are hard and competition is fierce, and if a hotel has to go out looking for trade, it does not necessarily mean their establishment is a dive. It's just as likely that the family that runs the *pansiyon* is working hard to succeed, and will give you the same attention during your stay.

Some tips for playing this game. (1) Most importantly, find out whether the tout is a family member or just someone paid on commission; a little casual conversation will usually tell you a lot about the person you're dealing with. (2) Ask the price straight off; don't wait until you get to the place; then, if you care to, tell them you're looking for some place a third cheaper. (3) Get clear answers about the place's location, facilities, etc. (4) If there are lots of touts around, look helpless and talk to them all, then enjoy watching them bid the price down amongst themselves.

Rock Bottom Accommodation

Even today, it is possible to find a room in non-touristy areas of western Turkey for as little as £1–£3/$1.50–$5 if you look hard. Hotels and *pansiyons* at the very bottom of the scale provide little more than a bed and plastic slippers; you have to supply your own towel, soap, and toilet paper. Like almost all of the *pansiyons*, these unclassified hotels are regulated, not by the Tourism Ministry, but by the municipal authorities (*belediye*), who fix their prices and will listen to any complaints; the chances of being ripped off are very slight. Some are grungy and depressing, others quite tolerable; many proprietors of cheap hotels in outlandish places go to great lengths to provide pleasant accommodation. These places see mostly Turks—migrant workers, TIR drivers and such—who turn in early and snore loudly. Usually, you will find them in provincial towns and villages, inland where few tourists go.

Holiday Villages, Hotel Chains and Ski Resorts

At the opposite end of the scale are the four Club Méditerranée holiday villages (at Kuşadasi, Yeni Foça, Kaş, and Kemer) and big international chain hotels in Istanbul, Izmir and Antalya (Hilton, Sheraton, Ramada, etc.). There are several Turkish chains, almost all along the west coast and Antalya region: Turban (which also operates several yacht marinas and camp sites—get their latest booklet from the Tourism Office), Tusan (mainly motels on the outskirts of the most popular towns), and Etap (in Ankara and Istanbul—usually expensive). Chain hotels are never good bargains—they get too many businessmen on expense accounts—and there will always be comparable places nearby with much more character. It must be said though, that in Turkish cities the chain hotels are *the* social centres for the city's elite, with the most lavish (and by far the most expensive) restaurants, gyms and sports facilites (usually open to the public), night clubs and casinos.

Mainly on the coasts, there are several Turkish holiday villages (*tatil köyü*) that are quite nice and very good for families; in listings they are rated TK 1 or TK 2—but you'll probably always get a better price on these as part of a package deal arranged at home. In Turkey's rapidly growing winter sport centres, there are a number of alpine-style chalets classified as *Oberj* (*auberge*).

Prices

We wish we could tell you! Unfortunately, it is utterly impossible to give more than a rough estimate of prices for any establishment. The main reason for this, of course, is Turkey's chronic inflation, and the regular currency devaluations that go with it. But beyond that, in the true homeland of *pazarlik* (bargaining), there is simply no such thing as a fixed price. We ask hotelkeepers their prices, and we know perfectly well that some of them are quoting them too high, hoping that they might get it from our readers, while others give a price too low, hoping to attract some business. All hotels are supposed to post their prices near the desk; a few actually do. It's standard procedure to walk in, scrutinize the price list, and then ask the man at the desk the price of a room. At the time of writing, places in all categories are often happy to get less than half of their officially listed price, especially in the off-season. All this can be confusing for people who like things just so, but it helps make Turkey the best bargain in the Mediterranean today. As people realize this, they'll be coming in increasing numbers—and the prices will start going up. Note that at some establishments, usually in the higher categories, there is an additional service charge and tax, up to 18% of the total bill.

Note also that **all the prices for individual hotels in this book are for double rooms**. And these will be the highest price you can expect to pay, except perhaps in July or August in a place that's really crowded. Listed below are the average high season prices for double rooms in each category

★★★★★	£45–£50/$68–$75	
★★★★	£40/$60	
★★★	£25–£32/$37–$48	
★★	£20/$30	
★	£15/$23	
unlisted hotels and *pansiyons* (**P**)	£6–£12/$9–$19	

Note that there are other ratings: **S** means a special licence, often a historic building (or at least an old one) that has been remodelled, as in Istanbul's Sultanahmet or Antalya's old town; prices for these can be the same as a one or three-star hotel. A motel, **M**, is usually on a highway, and charges the same as the higher-class *pansiyons*. Holiday villages are **HV1** and **HV2**, roughly corresponding to three and two-star hotels (though some can be a lot more). And **O** is an *oberj* (auberge, or inn). All categories, as you see, cover a wide range. Of the extremes, the higher are usually in Istanbul, the lower in the eastern provincial cities. You may take the middle of these ranges as typical of prices.

Youth Hostels

Youth hostels are rare. In Istanbul there are several unofficial ones along with the official ones, for which you need either an International Youth Hostel Federation Card or an International Student Travel Conference (ISTC) card. All are likely to be open only in season. With budget accommodation as cheap as it is in Turkey, they are not worth going out of your way to find, especially as some are a good way out of town.

Camping

As with the hotels, there has been a boom in the opening of campsites in recent years, and if you're travelling this way there will be no problem finding one around any of the coastal resort towns. There are even campsites in Istanbul, near the airport. Don't think of camping here as a way to save money. Prices are complex: separate charges for each person, tent, trailer, and so on, but at the average site the total ends up pretty much the same as staying in a *pansiyon*.

A detailed brochure (*Turkey: Camping*), listing over a hundred of the larger, better-equipped places in western Turkey is available at any local tourist office. These often have tent rentals, as well as electric hook-ups and running water. Most of the bigger campgrounds have restaurants, or snack bars, and some cooking facilities, which is fortunate since camping gas bottles and refills are very hard to find. Some of them even have swimming pools. Beyond these, unofficial camp sites are everywhere, although their quality can be very erratic; some are easily as good as the official sites, others offer you little more than a square of grass. Many *pansiyons* outside the towns have set up rudimentary campsites.

Ancient History to 2500 BC 45

2500 BC–1180 BC: The Bronze Age 45

1180 BC–546 BC: New Nations in Anatolia 45

546 BC–334 BC: Greeks and Persians 47

334–150 BC: Alexander and the Hellenistic World 48

150 BC–AD 300: Under Roman Rule 49

AD 300–1071: The Byzantine Empire 49

1071–1243: The Selcuks Lead the Turkish Invasion 50

1300–1453: The Coming of the Ottomans 51

1453: The Capture of Constantinople 52

1454–1700: The Height of the Ottoman State 52

1700–1910: The Empire Crumbles 53

History

1911–19: The War Years 53

1919: The Turkish Revolution 54

1922–60: The Westernization of Turkey 55

1960 to the Present: Three Coups, Three Constitutions 55

Turkey Today 56

The Turks, in their tourist literature and in the archaeological exhibitions they send round to the world's museums, like to bill their country as the 'Land of Civilizations'. Unlike other nations of the Mediterranean, such as Italy or Greece, Turkey's present inhabitants are relative latecomers, and the 7000 years of history before their arrival witnessed an incredible pageant of peoples and cultures. If we learned in school that early history belonged almost entirely to Egypt and the Fertile Crescent, it is only because chance led the archaeologists there first. The mountains and plains of Anatolia, which in recent decades have seen more digging and theorizing than perhaps any corner of the globe, can now also stake their claim as one of the birthplaces of civilization.

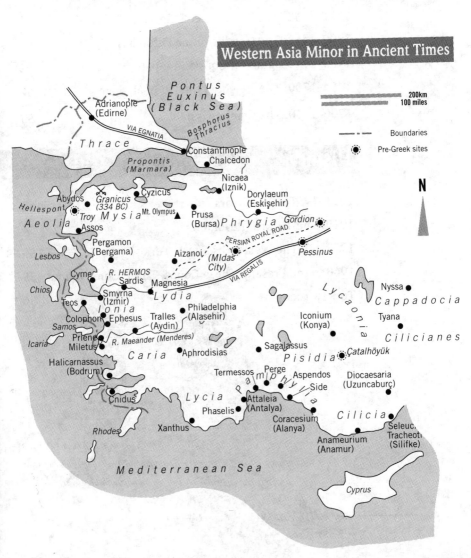

Western Asia Minor in Ancient Times

Ancient History to 2500 BC

Discoveries in the Karain Cave and other sites around Antalya have taken Turkey's history back as far as Neanderthal man, but the really exciting event has been the recent excavation of an accomplished and artistic culture, 9000 years old, at **Çatal Höyük** near Konya, a peaceful, matriarchal town that lived on agriculture and the obsidian trade. It eventually grew into a city of some 32 acres, the oldest truly urban culture ever discovered. Its chubby goddesses and bull-horn shrines, along with the rest of its remarkable artworks, can be seen at the Ankara Museum. The latest levels of the excavations begin to show evidence of fire and strife, and we can take Çatal Höyük's end, in about 5500 BC, as the beginning of the first dark age. The Neolithic cultures that replaced it, as at **Mersin** and **Hacilar**, near Burdur, were not nearly as sophisticated.

2500 BC–1180 BC: The Bronze Age

After its great beginnings Anatolian civilization entered a period of little interest, falling behind Egypt and Mesopotamia. Revival came with the **Hattian culture**, another recent discovery, about which little is yet known. The Hatti people flourished in central Anatolia c. 2500–2000 BC, caused their neighbours little trouble, and created some of the finest works of art of their age. At this time, a separate Bronze Age culture began to develop around **Troy**, more closely related to the peoples of the Aegean than to those of Anatolia.

Around 2000 BC, a new nation arrived from Thrace, the **Hittites**, a warrior aristocracy (as the later Turks were to be) who imposed themselves on the Hatti and founded a great capital at Hattusas, east of Ankara. They introduced writing to Asia Minor by learning the Assyrian cuneiform and later developing their own hieroglyphics to fit their Indo-European tongue. They also gave Anatolia its first empire, a Bronze Age superpower that contended with Egypt for the mastery of the Middle East after King Mursilis I captured Aleppo and Babylon c. 1590 BC. Throughout this era, Hittite control over the coastal areas was tenuous at best. Their records show constant problems with the peoples of the Kingdom of Arzawa, in the southwest of the peninsula, the 'Lukka Lands' (Lycia) and a people called the **Ahhiyawa**—probably the Mycenaean Greeks, the *Achaeans* of Homer. Besides Greece proper, the Ahhiyawans ruled a bit of the Anatolian coast, with a capital there called Millewanda, probably Miletus.

About 1180, just as the Hittites had reached the peak of their political and artistic accomplishment, their empire came to a sudden end at the hands of unknown invaders from the west (possibly the Phrygians). The slender evidence available suggests a period of warfare, migrations and famines all through the 12th century. A mixed multitude, called the **'Sea Peoples'** in Egyptian records, seems to have ranged over Anatolia and the Levant, briefly threatening even Egypt; one of the nations listed among them is the Achaeans (the other tribes later spread across the Mediterranean, including the Sicels of Sicily, the Sards, the Etruscans, the Phrygia' and the Philistines). This period of catastrophes, which also witnessed the fall of Troy, s Asia Minor into another dark age.

1180–546 BC: New Nations in Anatolia

Political and cultural unity in Anatolia died with the fall of the Hittites, and for c' come the region was divided among a number of new peoples, many of whom into the region only after the Hittite collapse.

Urartians

During the Hittite empire, a confederation of two peoples, forming the 'Hurri–Mitanni state', survived precariously as a buffer between the Hittites and Assyria. As successor to the Hurrians, a related people, the Urartians, appeared in the region around Lake Van in the 12th century BC. They called themselves the Biainili, but as the Urartians (as they are known in the Assyrian chronicles) they gave their name to Mount Ararat. It is likely that they are the ancestors of the modern Armenians. An Urartian state gradually coalesced, reaching its greatest extent under King Sarduri II, *c.* 750 BC, extending from the Black Sea to the Caspian. The Assyrian King Tiglath-Pileser III soon cut them down to size, however, and the Scythians finished them off in 609 BC. Urartian stone reliefs and metalwork, recently recovered in a number of sites around Lake Van, at its best equals anything produced in that age.

Late Hittite Kingdoms

These survived all over southeastern Anatolia, usually as Assyrian dependencies such as Malatya, Kahramanmaraş, and Carchemish. Kizzuwadna, roughly all of what would later be called Cilicia, was throughout the period ruled by relatives of the Hittite Kings. Though politically powerless, they carried on the traditions of Hittite art, in the occasionally grand but often peculiar sculpture that takes the pride of place in so many museums in Anatolia.

Phrygians

This people, talented in music and art, took the place of the Hittites in much of west-central Anatolia; their real name was the *Mushki*, or Moschians. A little empire, ruled by kings alternately named 'Midas' and 'Gordius', flourished until about 695 BC, when it was wrecked by an invasion of nomadic Cimmerians. The Lydians picked up the pieces in 650, and replaced Phrygia as the dominant power. The Phrygian capital was Gordium, west of Ankara. After the conquest, a Phrygian state lived on in the hills south of Eskişehir, leaving many monuments. A pastoral people, the Phrygians exported wool to the Greeks and diverted themselves with their orgiastic cult of Cybele and their music. They claimed to have invented the panpipes; Marsyas, the mythological flautist who had the bad judgement to enter a contest against Apollo, was a Phrygian.

Greeks

Recent finds around Izmir suggest that Greeks began expanding into Anatolia's coasts as early as the 11th century. The colonization was not a single, unified movement, but undertaken individually by Greek cities, and colonies long retained the tribal characters of their founders: the **Aeolians**, who probably came first, in the north, around Troy and Assos; **Ionians** in the centre, and the latecomers, the **Dorians**, in the south. **Pamphylia**, the 'land of all tribes' on the southern coast, may also have been colonized early.

As in Greece itself, the cities of Asia Minor never worried much about political unity. The self-sufficient city state remained the model, and the greatest of these was **Miletus**, which by the 8th century was probably the leading commercial and sea power of the Aegean. After *c.* 700 BC, the Greek city-states found themselves blocked by the power of Lydia, and unable to expand their territories further inland. To compensate, they moved into sparsely-populated coastal areas further north. Miletus took the lead, founding Abydus (Çanakkale) and other towns on the Marmara and Black Sea, while the Megarans founded a number of colonies including Byzantium.

Lydians

The wealthy and commercially minded Lydians lived to the east of Izmir, but in their heyday in the 6th century BC they controlled an empire that included a vast area of western Anatolia. Under kings like the famous Croesus, the Lydians were a contented, blissfully decadent people who exported perfumes and other luxury goods around the Mediterranean. Ancient writers credit them with the invention of money. Before 546 BC, when the Persians under Cyrus put a brutally sudden end to Lydia as an independent power, its kings held sway over all the Greek coastal cities, though they were content collecting tribute from them.

Carians

One of the more obscure nations, the Carians, or Lelegians were related to the Lydians and originally occupied the area from Miletus to Lake Köyceğiz; they are mentioned in Homer as allies of the Trojans. Though the Carians may once have been an important sea power, the Greeks pushed them from the coast at an early date. The interior (roughly between modern Aydin and Muğla) remained Carian throughout antiquity, though subject to ever-increasing Greek cultural influence. Their modest, backwoods cities formed a confederacy on the Greek model.

Lycians

On the southwest coast of Anatolia, the Lycians, like the Phrygians and Lydians, were a native people speaking an Indo-European language who were later Hellenized by the Greeks. Their origins are lost in time, though opinion in antiquity had them coming from Minoan Crete, and that they founded Miletus before migrating to the southern coast. Although mentioned by Homer, their relative inacessibility and reputation for fierceness kept them out of the mainstream of history; their most remarkable accomplishments were the lovely rock tombs they carved into cliffs all over Turkey's southwestern coasts.

None of these states was destined to last long. The aggressive and brutal Assyrian Empire (860–612 BC) kept Anatolia in constant turmoil. Even worse, tribes of mounted warriors from across the Caucasian mountains were constantly marauding through Anatolia. The **Cimmerians** learned cavalry tactics from the Scythians; in the 7th century BC, they occupied most of the eastern half of Anatolia. The **Medes** (c. 620–549 BC), who founded the first great Persian empire, destroyed the Assyrians and the Cimmerians, and succeeded to both their domains.

546 BC–334 BC: Greeks and Persians

The Achaemenid kings of Persia, who replaced the Medes in 549 BC, created a world empire for themselves within two generations. After Cyrus' conquest of Lydia had given them undisputed control of the whole of Anatolia, the Persians sent their general Harpagus on a campaign through Ionia to enforce the submission of the Greek cities. Satraps, or governors, were appointed over the various provinces, and although Persian rule was on the whole just, unoppressive and enlightened, the Greeks, accustomed to governing themselves, found it hard to take. An **Ionian revolt** in 499, supported by Athens, was brutally crushed by the Persians, and resulted in the burning of Miletus. Persian military power was now embroiled with Greece at the height of its classical age, and a confrontation was inevitable.

Under King Xerxes, the Persians invaded Greece in 490 and were defeated at Marathon. The second attempt, ten years later, again resulted in defeats at the battles of Salamis and Plataea. In the aftermath, the Greek cities liberated themselves and joined the Athenian-led alliance called the Delian Confederacy. Athenian ambition and arrogance, however, led to this league of equals gradually becoming more of an Athenian empire—the cause of the long and bloody **Peloponnesian War**, in which Athens and her allies were finally defeated by the Spartans (404). Even though the Asian cities had generally managed to avoid the fighting, their fate was no longer theirs to decide. The exhausted Spartans could not maintain control, and by the King's Peace of 387 they reverted to Persian rule.

From the beginning, these cities were more than mere colonies. An integral part of the Greek world, they contributed perhaps more than their share to the culture of Greece's golden age, despite usually being under foreign rule. Homer, who lived in the 8th or early 7th century, was probably born at Smyrna. In the 6th century, the Ionian cities, notably Miletus, produced the first Western philosophers: Thales, Anaximander, Xenophanes and Heraclitus. Art and architecture also flourished. The first temples were only built in the 8th century, but by the 6th century Ephesus and Samos were contending with the equally wealthy Greek cities of Sicily to build the biggest temples in the world.

334–150 BC: Alexander and the Hellenistic World

The Persian army, meanwhile, had not been keeping up with contemporary battle tactics. The Greek hoplite, or armoured infantryman, was the ultimate weapon of the day, and it was only necessary for one Greek state to afford enough of them to really make a splash. Thanks to a chance discovery of gold, that state was Macedonia, and as Philip of Macedon recruited his forces it was with the announced purpose of a crusade against the Persians. After his assassination, the job was left to his son **Alexander the Great**. With some 40,000 men, he crossed the Hellespont in the spring of 334 BC, and almost immediately defeated a large Persian army. Within a year's time, Alexander had conquered all Anatolia, opening up the way to turning the Persian Empire into Alexander's.

Soon after Alexander's untimely death in 323, his generals carved up the newly-created empire for themselves. Anatolia fell to Antigonus, but his attempts at reunifying the empire led the others to combine against him, and his cause died at the Battle of Ipsus in 301. Another general, named Lysimachus, seized Anatolia, and he in turn was beaten by Selucus in 280; the **Seleucid Kingdom** he founded stretched from the Aegean to India, and was to last over a century; meanwhile, Cappadocia had become a virtually independent kingdom on its own, and another former general, Philetarus, who had grabbed Alexander's treasure after his death, used the booty to found the city state of **Pergamon**, which grew in power and influence for another century and came to control much of western Anatolia by *c.* 150.

While all this was happening, Anatolia was becoming thoroughly Hellenized. Trade and commerce boomed; vast and wealthy new cities appeared, such as Pergamon and Antioch, while older ones, particularly Smyrna and Ephesus, grew to metropolitan size. Greece proper was beginning its long economic decline, partly thanks to the emigration to Asia sponsored by the Seleucids and other rulers, and Anatolia's new wealth and power gradually made it the centre of the Greek world. Most of the ruins you will see in Turkey date from this time, if not from the centuries of Roman rule; Anatolia still had another 800 years of calm and prosperity ahead of it.

One unusual event of the time was the invasion in 275 BC of the **Galatians**, Celts really, who installed themselves right in the centre of the peninsula. Though eventually defeated by the Pergamenes, the Celts stayed, and their red-haired and freckled descendants can still be seen on the streets of Ankara and in many other Turkish towns today.

150 BC–300 AD: Under Roman Rule

Roman control came gradually and irresistibly, a province at a time. With Pergamon and Rhodes for close allies, the Romans carefully watched their influence grow through the 3rd century, while they were busy with their death struggle against Carthage. An ambitious Seleucid king, Antiochus III (223—187) conquered Syria and Palestine and forged an alliance with Macedon against Rome. The legions marched in and bloodied them both. By 146, Greece proper was under direct Roman rule, and the Seleucid kingdom a mere fragment. In 133 the last king of Pergamon saw the writing on the wall and willed his entire kingdom to Rome.

Outside their Pergamene windfall, the Romans never ruled much of Anatolia directly; there were client kings, as in Armenia and Cappadocia, and many of the Greek cities maintained control over their internal affairs, and the right to mint their own coins. The Romans were happy to soak the wealthy cities with taxes that were as high as the cities could bear, plus the occasional pillaging of art treasures. A trip east with the legions, with its promise of loot and fame, was the perfect stepping-stone to power in Rome. Sulla used his victory over the last independent Anatolian state, the Pontic Kingdom of Mithradates, to become dictator of Rome in 82, and a decade later, Pompey's successful campaign against the Cilician pirates allowed him to become Sulla's successor. After that, Anatolia was disturbed only by the civil wars after Julius Caesar's assassination in 44. Brutus passed through, grabbing all the men and money he could, and sacking cities that resisted. After him came Antony, demanding ten years' taxes in one, and dallying with Cleopatra at Alanya and Tarsus.

After all this, Anatolia deserved a rest, and the new Empire founded by Augustus laid the foundations for over two centuries of peace and prosperity, in which the region reached its fullest measure of wealth and ease. The height, perhaps, came in the reign of Hadrian (117—38 AD), a Grecophile and great benefactor of the cities. Commerce and the arts flourished, and cities like Ephesus, Smyrna (Izmir) and Antioch (Antakya) each counted over 500,000 inhabitants. Throughout this time, the opulence of life and loss of independence and responsibility was working a slow change on the Greeks. It can be seen in the art of the Imperial centuries, wilder, more emotional and intense, and above all in the growing obsession with religion and the 'salvation of the soul'. The old mystery cults of the Anatolian goddesses, especially Cybele, attained new popularity, while newcomers like Mithraism, a Persian import, gained many adepts. In the cities were large and prosperous Jewish communities after the diaspora, and their religion too found many converts. More importantly though, these communities provided the basis for the surprisingly rapid spread of Christianity. St Paul began his travels around Anatolia, as recorded in the *Acts of the Apostles*, in 43 AD.

AD 300–1071: The Byzantine Empire

The **founding of Constantinople** in the 4th century AD, and the division of the empire into halves seemed to confirm Asia Minor in its central role. While the West receded into anarchy, successful Eastern emperors like Theodosius the Great (379–95), Justinian (527–65) and Heraclius (610–41) effected the successful transition of the state into the theocratically Christian, Greek-speaking Byzantine Empire, while keeping Avars, Alans, Persians, and Slavs at bay.

Unfortunately, the diseases that had sapped the strength of the old Empire were built into the new one from its birth: a gigantic bureaucratic state, with crushing taxes to support itself along with the army and the bloated Imperial court. Christianity, while providing a new basis of unity, wiped out what remained of free thought and learning. And an already great gap between rich and poor continued to increase. For most of Anatolia, this period witnessed a gradual but irreversible decline, as Byzantine misgovernment slowly strangled the economies of the cities and the great landowners pushed the majority of the country people into serfdom. Remember what you learned in school about the Dark Ages, and then consider that most parts of western Europe managed better under barbarian rule and constant war than Asia Minor did under the successors of the Roman Empire. Beginning in the 7th century, mutually destructive warfare with the Persians and a new menace, the armies of the Muslim Arabs, added the finishing touches. Trade died, and the coastal cities withered and disappeared; the once-fertile farmlands around them reverted to empty malarial plains. After a millennium and a half of sophisticated civilized life, Asia Minor had been destroyed.

Throughout the 8th century, the Byzantines had been preoccupied with the Iconoclastic struggles, in which disputes over the desirability of painted icons demonstrated a tremendous confusion of religious, economic, and political conflicts (the example of rising Islam made the Greeks' love of divine images seem pure idolatry to many minds, but behind that stood a deeper discontent with the power of the monks and the Church hierarchy). The prohibition of icons began with a Church council of 754, and lasted until 843. Attacks from the surrounding Arabs, Avars, Serbs, Bulgarians, and Petchinegs brought the Byzantines to their senses, and under emperors Basil I (867–86), Basil II, 'the Bulgar-slayer' (976–1025), and Nicephorus Phocas, the 'Pale Death of the Saracen' (963–9), Byzantium achieved a cultural revival and a level of political stability. This was a little relief to devastated Anatolia; such culture as survived existed only in Constantinople.

1071–1243: The Selcuks Lead the Turkish Invasion

In the emptiest of Asia's empty spaces, north of Manchuria, the Chinese chroniclers note a 'hill shaped like a helmet' that is the ancestral home of the 'Tu-kueh'—the Turks; they first appear in history c. 500 BC, making trouble for the Chinese emperors. In about AD 800, a confederation of tribes called the Oğuz was gradually heading towards Europe. By AD 900, many of the tribes had become Muslim, mounted warrior clans that helped the central Asian states as they infiltrated, just as the various 'barbarians' had done in Rome. Though not the first Turks to find their way into the desolated cockpit of Asia Minor, the Selcuks, under their chief Alp Arslan, were the first to do it in style, gobbling up the hapless Armenians and ending Byzantine rule over much of Anatolia once and for all with a resounding victory at Manzikert, north of Lake Van, in 1071. They called their state, centred at Konya, the Sultanate of Rum— to the peoples of distant Asia, Rome was still a magic name. As soon as they settled down, the Selcuks transformed themselves with amazing speed into gifted rulers and patrons of the arts. At the height of their power, under the early 13th-century Sultan Alâeddin Keykubad, they were the strongest and most civilized state of the eastern Mediterranean, one considerably influenced by the culture of Persia, then under the rule of a separate Selcuk clan; Selcuk architecture, seen in the schools and mosques of Konya and so many other Anatolian cities, marks not only the beginning of Turkish art but one of its greatest achievements.

The Selcuks, unfortunately for them, were only the first wave of a huge migration from central Asia. As well as the many other Turkish tribes who set up petty emirates across the Middle East, the **Mongols** came, putting an end to the Sultanate of Rum at the Battle of Kösedağ in 1243 and once more returning Turkey—for now we may call it that—to anarchy. The most important result of their invasion was to push other Turkish tribes further westwards, into the wastelands still nominally ruled by Constantinople. The first Turks to settle the Aegean coast, the Menteşe, founded a little emirate around Milas and Bodrum in the 1260s. By 1300 the situation had stabilized somewhat, with the powerful Karamanli emirate ruling central Anatolia, the 'six emirates', including the Menteşe, the Hamitoğullari and the Germaniyids, in the southwest, and a number of tribes in the northeast.

Even before 1243, the Selcuks had been beset on all sides, not only by Turks, but also by the **Crusader States** founded by the Franks in the 12th century. The greatest of these in Anatolia, the County of Edessa (Urfa), survived for over a century, and orders such as the Knights of St John controlled much of the southern coast throughout the Middle Ages. The Crusaders soon learned to leave the Selcuks alone, and not wishing to tackle the other Muslim nations either, decided to go after the heretics in Constantinople. A new Crusade in 1204, serving the ends of Venice and the Pope, took advantage of the absent Byzantine army to storm and sack the city for the first time, humbling its pride, violating most of the women, and carrying off nearly every bit of its 900 years of accumulated treasure.

The Byzantine empire ends here. Although a government in exile was set up at Iznik (Nicaea), from which Emperor Michael Paleologos chased out the Italians and reclaimed the city in 1261, it was an impoverished, enfeebled Constantinople that survived until 1453 behind its impregnable walls. In 1359, Emperor John Paleologos gave in and became a tribute-paying vassal to his son-in-law, Sultan Orhan, leader of a new and growing Turkish tribe, the Osmanli, or **Ottomans**.

1300–1453: The Coming of the Ottomans

According to legend, these Turks were riding across Anatolia when they chanced upon a battle being fought on the plain beneath them. Under their chief, Ertuğrul, they chivalrously decided to join the losing side, and soon turned their defeat into victory. The victors turned out to be the Selcuks, who rewarded their new allies with lands in western Anatolia. About 1300, Sultan **Osman** laid the foundations of the state and dynasty that was to bear his name. Equally talented in war and government and virtuous to an extreme, Osman made his little state a power in the region. All his successors were girded with his sword in place of a coronation, and the cry that went up was not 'Long live the Sultan' but 'May he be as good as Osman!'

Orhan (1324–59), his son, conquered Bursa in 1326 and made it his capital. His marriage to a Byzantine princess was not a rare case; by the 14th century Greeks and Turks had come to know each other very well. Anatolia's gradual process of 'turning Turk' had begun with the Selcuks. Gradually, many of the Greeks had converted to Islam, often entire towns at a time; most of the rest, considering their alternatives, saw the tolerant Turkish Muslims as a lesser evil than the schismatics of Europe and their hated pope. (The average Turk of today probably has far more Greek and native Anatolian blood in him than Turkish.) Orhan, an able and liberal ruler, increased the Ottomans' prestige as he widened their boundaries. Early in his reign, a group of adventurers called the Catalan Grand Company, paid to defend Constantinople, had ferried Orhan's army across the Bosphorus to help. The Ottomans took one look at Europe and decided they wanted to keep it; Orhan conquered Thrace, and his son Murat I (1359–89) added Serbia, Bulgaria, and Macedonia.

The Turks, in transition from their days as nomadic warriors to an imperial aristocracy, still suffered from a shortage of women, and consequently, a shortage of Turks for so small a state with such big ambitions. They solved this problem ingeniously with the *devşirme*, a harvest of

5 per cent of the infant boys from captured Christian provinces (first-born sons were excluded). All were educated and brought up as Muslims; the best became the sultan's generals and *vezirs* (ministers), while the rougher were enrolled in the Janissaries (*yeniceri*, or 'new troops'), a corps of highly trained soldiers that were to become the terror of Europe. The Janissaries were kept under the control of the Bektaşi dervishes, from whom they inherited an unusual tradition of rituals and titles based on the eating of soup. To show their displeasure with a sultan, for example, they would turn their large kettle upside down and refuse to eat. In later years, as the Janissaries became a law unto themselves, they did this whenever they felt like deposing a sultan. As long as discipline was maintained, though, they were the finest fighting force in the world.

For Beyazit I, 'Thunderbolt' (1389–1403), they destroyed the flower of French chivalry at Nicopolis in 1396, finally damping the crusading urge. Beyazit, a young hothead, addicted to battle even more than to wine, met his destiny in the person of Tamerlane in 1403. The invincible Mongol destroyed the Ottoman force at Ankara and took Beyazit prisoner, and then mysteriously turned around and went back east. Mehmet I (1413–21) and Murat II (1421–51) picked up the pieces and carefully rebuilt, finding time in 1444 to win undisputed control of the Balkans at the Battle of Varna, after which the head of King Ladislas of Poland and Hungary ended up on the top of a pike in Bursa.

1453: The Capture of Constantinople

Almost from the beginning, this had been the Ottoman goal. Several earlier attempts against the city had failed, and it was left to **Mehmet II** (1451–81) to win the prize. Mehmet, perhaps the most remarkable of the sultans, was a poet and scholar who had mastered six languages and, unthinkable for a Muslim, had his portrait painted, by Gentile Bellini. He saw himself as a man of destiny, sent to fulfil Mohammed's prophecy about the capture of the city, and went about the task methodically. By 1453, he was ready with an enormous army, the biggest cannons in the world and a fleet. Inside the city, whose population had dwindled from over a million to under fifty thousand, an Italian *condottiere* named Giustiniani led 8000 Greeks and mercenaries for the defence. In spite of the odds, they held out for two months. The tide turned with Mehmet's brilliant trick of dragging his ships over land, around the famous Byzantine chain across the Golden Horn, to the exposed side of the city. On 23 May, Giustiniani died and the disheartened mercenaries fled. The few Greeks remaining beat back a furious attack, but in their excitement left open a postern gate; some Turks found it, and the empire breathed its last. Mehmet ordered that the usual three days' pillage should spare all the buildings; he walked in awe through the Aya Sofia and the long abandoned palaces, and remembered a bit of Persian poetry:

> The spider weaves the curtain in the Palace of the Caesars,
> The night-owl keeps the watch in the Tower of Afrasiyab.

To the Turks, Mehmet is *Fatih*, the Conqueror. He knew what the city meant, and rebuilt it as fast as resources allowed. In 1461 he added the Empire of Trebizond to his conquests, the last free Greek state, founded by refugee noblemen after the sack of 1204.

1454–1700: The Height of the Ottoman State

Mehmet's son, Beyazit II, 'the Mystic' (1481–1512), seldom disrupted his reading for further conquests, but Selim I (1512–20) made up for him by swallowing up Egypt (thus gaining the Caliphate) and much of Mesopotamia. *Yavuz* Selim, as the Turks call him, is really an honorific meaning 'the Formidable', but historians like to call him Selim the Grim for his frequent massacres of Shiite heretics (he was the first Ottoman to trouble himself about religious orthodoxy), and his habit of beheading his grand vezirs at an average of one a year. His son, **Süleyman the Magnificent** (1520–66), presided over the glorious noonday of the Ottoman state; under him the empire reached its greatest extent with the conquest of Hungary and North Africa. His title comes courtesy of his close allies, the French; to his own people he was 'the Lawgiver' for his thorough reforms of the legal code and commercial regulations.

Unfortunately, he also began the empire's slow decline. The trading concessions he granted to Francis I were the first step in the Ottomans' loss of control of their own economy. From his weakness for his scheming harem-favourite Roxelana, he brought the harem into the palace itself and inaugurated the period of palace intrigue that was eventually to ruin the state. The sultans that followed show clearly how far the decay had already penetrated. Selim the Sot (1566–74), and Ibrahim the Mad (1640–8) lead the parade of wastrels, drunkards, sex perverts, and imbeciles that decorated the latter-day Ottoman throne. Directly upon Süleyman's death the real power had passed to the Janissaries, the eunuchs and the ladies in the endlessly changing factions in the harem. Osman II (1618–22), who wanted reform, was murdered; his successors until 1832 were virtual prisoners of the Janissary guard.

In the *Divan* (cabinet), meanwhile, a remarkable dynasty of grand vezirs of Albanian descent, the Köprülü family, did their best to hold the leaderless state together throughout the 17th century. By the 18th, decadence had progressed so far that the European powers had to keep the Ottoman corpse propped on its throne to keep the Russians from occupying the straits.

1700–1910: The Empire Crumbles

For three centuries, the Russians kept the pressure on with 43 declared wars while, in the 19th century, some of the empire's captive nations, the Greeks, Serbians, Bulgarians and Egyptians, successfully gained their independence. Attempts to reform were too few and too late. Under Mahmut II (1808–39), the Janissaries were massacred in what the Turks call the 'Auspicious Event' but the empire was too far behind the Europeans militarily and technologically for it to make much difference. Mahmut's successors, Abdülmecit I (1839–61) and Abdülaziz (1861–76), proved too stupid and indifferent to keep his reforms going, and the paranoid Abdülhamid (1876–1909) sold his nation to European economic interests while ruthlessly stamping out any progressive thinking at home.

Despite his efforts, underground efforts to bring Turkey out of its political nightmare continued, especially among circles in the army. In Salonika, now Greek Thessaloniki, a group of discontented army officers formed the Committee for Union and Progress, known in the west as the **Young Turks**, led by Enver Paşa. Their manouverings within the upper echelons of the Ottomans led in 1909 to the fall of the hated Abdülhamid and the creation that same year of a constitutional monarchy, governed by an elected parliament.

1911–19: The War Years

During this period, the 'Sick Man of Europe' finally expired. It was the Italians who started the final collapse. In 1911 they invaded the Turkish colony of Tripoli (Libya) and took it with ease. Encouraged by this, Montenegro, Serbia, Bulgaria and Greece joined forces to drive the Ottomans out of Europe in the First Balkan War (1913). A truce had been negotiated by Istanbul before too much territory was lost, but Enver Paşa and the Young Turks seized power in a *coup d'état* and restarted the war. More defeats followed. Crete was lost; so too were the Dodecanese, and by 1913 Turkish domains in Europe consisted of just Istanbul and half of Thrace, the latter only because Bulgaria and Greece could not agree who should have it.

All of this should have put Enver Paşa off wars for good. Unfortunately, it did not. When the Great War exploded in 1914, the Ottomans threw their fez in with the Germans, whom the Paşa hoped would help him realize his pan-Turkish dream of an empire extending to the shores of the Caspian Sea. Immediately, the Turks found themselves fighting on two fronts, at Gelibolu (Gallipoli) in the west and against the Russians in the east, and their empire gradually fell apart, country by country. Sultan Mehmet V announced a *jihad* against the Triple Entente, hoping that all Islam would rise in his support, but the Ottomans had done the Arabs no favours when ruling them and now all blithely turned a deaf ear. By autumn 1918 Enver Paşa and others of the Young Turk *junta* had fled the country in disgrace, smuggled out on a German destroyer. By November of that year, British warships were at anchor in Istanbul.

In May 1920 the Triple Entente handed down their judgement on the old Ottomans, in the form of the Treaty of Sèvres. Effectively it decreed that the country be carved up: Istanbul and a few surrounding areas were to be retained, but Izmir fell to Greek jurisdiction, an independent Armenia and an autonomous Kurdistan were to be set up in the east and any remaining areas of Anatolia handed out to France and Italy as spheres of economic influence. The Greeks, delighted by the turn of events, saw their opportunity to put their long-dreamed-of *Megallo Idee* ('Great Idea') into practice—the recapture of Constantinople and the recreation of the Byzantine Empire. Encouraged by the British, the Greek army advanced east from Izmir into Anatolia. Old, silly Mehmet VI, the last of the sultans, sat in his palace and wondered what would happen next.

1919: The Turkish Revolution

What did happen was astounding. Throughout the Ottoman Empire, as under the Byzantines, Anatolia had been a surprisingly neglected backwater of the empire, which saw its heartland more as Thrace and the Balkans. Even more surprising is the fact that to be called a 'Turk' was something of an insult among the aristocratic Ottomans; the patient Turkish peasants and townsmen of Anatolia had to put up with as much scorn and as little help as any minority of the empire. Now, for the first time, Anatolia was to make a stand. Opposition to the Sèvres treaty centred around a brilliant, difficult general, **Mustafa Kemal**, with a military reputation earned at Gallipoli and a head full of nationalist ideas. He escaped from the intrigues of Istanbul on 19 May 1919, and landed at Samsun with the force of a Napoleon returning from Elba. Nationalist congresses were soon held at Sivas and Erzurum, and a provisional government set up for the deliverance of the nation.

Somehow a new army was created. Under Kemal's leadership the Turks chased out the French and Russians and decisively defeated the Greeks at the two battles of Inönü in January–March 1921. Retreating before the nationalists, the Greeks burnt and pillaged their way to the coast; by September 1922, the country was clear of all foreign troops. A republic was declared one year later, with Mustafa Kemal as its first president and Ankara, right in the middle of Anatolia, as its capital. A new treaty was negotiated at Lausanne to replace the redundant Treaty of Sèvres, and it included the ghoulish 'Exchange of Populations', by which some two million Greeks were forced out of Anatolia, where Greeks had lived for nearly 3000 years, in return for pushing a few hundred thousand Turks out of Greece. In retrospect, it seems a historical turning point. Neither Mustafa Kemal nor the Greeks probably had any idea of the evil they were loosing on the world. It was the beginning of the tribal politics and 'ethnic cleansing' we know today, the insistence that people must not be allowed to get on together if politicians and propagandists find it inconvenient. In all our bloody 20th century, few greater crimes have been committed—yet at the time, the whole world believed they were doing the right thing.

1922–60: The Westernization of Turkey

Few nations have ever had the will or unity to effect as many reforms as the Turks did in the 1920s and '30s, trying desperately to make up for so many centuries of lost time. Mustafa Kemal's republic was to be thoroughly secular, and to accomplish this, the Caliphate was abolished, education and marriage secularized, the wearing of the fez banned. Turkey adopted the Christian calendar and made Sunday the day of rest. The language was also reformed. Arabic and Persian words were rooted out, and the Roman alphabet replaced the Arabic.

As the simplest way of Westernizing its laws, Turkey simply adopted the entire Swiss Legal Code, almost word for word. Women acquired equal rights. International time and measures were adopted, and the government worked with its meagre resources to improve industry and communications. To crown it, the President decreed that every Turk should have a Western-style surname. Mustafa Kemal's was chosen for him by the nation—Atatürk, 'Father of the Turks'.

It was only his moral authority as the nation's hero that enabled the changes to be accepted with so much enthusiasm and so little resistance. In politics, Atatürk began what has become a modern Turkish tradition by establishing a dictatorship to make reforms, while constantly and sincerely telling his people that their first aspiration must be democracy. After his death in 1938, his right-hand man from the War of Independence, Gen. Ismet Inönü, took over with a pledge to bring democracy. World War II, in which the Turks remained neutral, postponed the experiment, but free elections in 1949 resulted in the victory of the new opposition Democratic Party and its charismatic leader Adnan Menderes. For the coastal areas, the most important event in over a millennium was something that few histories even bother to mention—the anti-malaria campaign of 1948, made possible by the invention of DDT and American aid. DDT may be murder on birds (that's why it's outlawed in most countries now), but by cutting down drastically the number of anopheles mosquitoes, it made possible the resettlement of places that had been wastelands since Byzantine times. Without it, Turkey's coasts would still be empty today.

The Democrats' corruption, mishandling of the economy and their attempt to create a one-party dictatorship resulted in an army coup in 1960, after which Menderes was executed. The memory of this complex character is still alive in his political stronghold, the farming lands of western Anatolia. In the last decade nearly every town has named a street after him, something that earlier would have been unthinkable. Every Turkish populist party in the decades since has been more or less the Democrats under a different name.

1960 to the Present: Three Coups, Three Constitutions

Democracy was restored the following year, under an extremely liberal constitution proposed by the coup's leader, General Cemal Gürsel, and a new coalition government bumbled along under the watchful eye of the army. In 1965 the Justice Party (the old Democrats), led by Süleyman Demirel, achieved a working majority but his government was beset throughout its term by the Cyprus crisis; domestic issues, including a rapidly worsening economy, took second place. By 1970 the mild civil unrest that marked the preceding years had exploded into bloody riots and once again the army stepped in.

It was not until 1973 that a new civilian government took office, led by Bülent Ecevit of the Democratic Left Party, but it was to fare no better than its predecessor, the war in Cyprus and the OPEC oil-price hike dominating its attention. Amidst the economic troubles, political violence between left and right threatened to turn into civil war. In 1980, after a year that saw over 3000 politically inspired murders, the army stepped in once more, with a coup orchestrated by a real martinet, General Kenan Evren.

All opposition to the new regime was stamped on, firmly. Political leaders from both sides, including Demirel and Ecevit, were jailed, sharing their cells with dissident journalists, student leaders and trade unionists. In 1982, Evren proposed a new constitution, providing for a strong presidency. A referendum was passed—with the support of the vast majority of the country—which included an election for the new office of president with only one candidate, Evren himself. It was a post he was to hold until 1988.

Parliamentary elections the next year were won by the new Motherland Party (ANAP), led by Turgut Özal, an economist from Malatya. A typically Turkish paradox, Özal was a modern, Western-trained technocrat, a believer in democracy and a devout Muslim—the first prime minister of the republic to have made the pilgrimage to Mecca. His skill in mastering the moribund Turkish economy and his diplomatic treatment of the army started Turkey on the longest period of freely-elected government it has yet enjoyed—13 years, so far. In 1988 he stepped into Evren's presidential shoes and lasted until his death in 1993, popular abroad for his ready support of the United Nations during the Gulf War and popular at home among those who can remember the condition their country was in before he achieved office. Support for Özal, however, was not transferred to the Motherland Party in the 1991 elections, when that old stager Süleyman Demirel gained a working Parliamentary majority for his centre-right True Path Party (DYP), in coalition with the mildly leftist SHP. After Özal's death Demirel became president.

Turkey Today

Modern Turkey stands between the developed and developing countries. Any statistics relating to economic development are affected by millions of Anatolian farmers, only just now working their way out of primeval poverty; some stay on the land, others migrate to Istanbul, Ankara, or the cities of Western Europe (they joke that Berlin has become the 68th Turkish province). Their fertility is startling: the 50 million Turks today have one of the highest rates of population growth in the world. Despite this and other drawbacks—high inflation and a creaky and bureaucratic government among them, the Turks are determined to push their way into the developed world; although they have tacitly agreed to suspend temporarily their request for EU membership, negotiations for a customs union are currently underway (the main issue is how much they will have to bribe the Greeks not to veto it).

Or at least that is the case at present. Opinions and priorities may soon change. For as an EU member Turkey might once more be the sick man of Europe, bossed around and buoyed up by grants, and this realization is fast sinking in among many Turkish politicians. Already, some are urging the government to look to the east, to the new states of Azerbaijan, Uzbekistan, Turkmenia and Kazakhstan, all Turkic-speaking, all with predominantly Muslim populations, who see Turkey as an economically successful, capitalist, modern Muslim role model to follow.

Let us form a Near-East Community, say these politicians. Far better to be king of your own castle than doorkeeper to another's in the West.

Internal problems are much more pressing. Rapid industrialization and modernization have brought huge waves of migrants to the big cities, and a host of social problems. Unemployment is high, and the Brazilian-style inflation, while helping along the export boom of the 80s, is increasingly becoming a liability. A more immediate problem is the Kurdish minority in the southeast of the country. Some 20 per cent of the country's population are Kurds, a proud people with their own distinct language, culture and history who have never, ever had their own state (though Saladin, who turfed the Crusaders out of the Holy Land, was Kurdish). Most Kurds are scornful of the Atatürkian creed that a Turk is a Turk and nothing but. Denied their own homeland by the 1923 Treaty of Lausanne that negated the Treaty of Sèvres, the Kurds have always seen themselves as second-class citizens of Turkey and with some justification. For decades their aspirations to autonomy and their culture were suppressed, sometimes with horrible violence, as in the rebellions of 1925 and 1939; it was only in 1991 that speaking Kurdish was decriminalized.

There was little the Kurds could do about this while Turkey was under military or semi-military rule, but now, as the nation emerges into democracy, they are making their voice heard, most sinisterly in the form of the terrorist Kurdish Workers Party, the PKK. Created, financed and trained by a rogues' gallery of Turkey's enemies—Syrians, the then Soviets and the Palestinians—the PKK now lives by extortion and racketeering, and kills everyone it can who disagrees with it, occasionally entire villages at a time. Much of the southeast has been under martial law for decades, and the desultory skirmishes the army used to have with the PKK turned into full-scale warfare in the late '80s. The government's response, sadly, has been witless and nearly as destructive as the guerrillas: hundreds of villages in unsafe zones have been forcibly evacuated, and Turkey's already hard-pressed cities are filling up with Kurdish refugees. Half the people who work in Turkish hotels and restaurants are Kurds; ask them about it and you'll get an earful. Ten years ago they would have been reticent about saying anything, but the one ray of hope in a continuing tragedy is an increasing openness in talking about the situation. Both Özal and the current Prime Minister, Tansu Çiller, have made at least some baby steps towards addressing the problem, and the scores of new private television and radio stations are telling people things they never heard over the old state networks.

The military may or may not win the war against the PKK, but whether or not Turkey can find a peaceful solution to the Kurdish crisis depends above all on the nation's ability to change the more authoritarian aspects of the army-designed 1980 constitution. At the time of writing, the State Security Courts are sending journalists, writers, and even members of parliament off to prison wholesale on the flimsiest of charges. These courts, run by grim hard-liners who work closely with the nastier spooks in the security services and the army, are accountable to no one, and few politicians have the courage to speak up against them. Among their most frequent victims are members of the new pro-Kurdish DEP (Democracy Party). Its supporters, often local Kurdish businessmen, have been turning up floating in rivers in alarming numbers. The government claims they are only a PKK front, and even that they are linked to the drug trade.

Behind all the political troubles is an economic situation bordering on total anarchy. Prime Minister Çiller, an economist and a friend of Margaret Thatcher, took office in 1993 and has sought to bring similar policies to Turkey. Mrs Çiller, the 'lovely blond lady who won't go away', as one newspaper calls her, has not had an easy time. Her currency manipulations contributed much to Turkey's recent runaway inflation, while causing a debt crisis in an overheated economy. Businesses can't pay their obligations, leading to a bizarre situation at the time of writing that sees big business and labour temporarily allied against the banks and the government. Turkey has everything it takes to make the final leap into the ranks of the developed nations; whether this deeply troubled society can organize itself to make the effort is another story.

Fifteen years of market economics have also greatly widened the gap between Turkey's rich and poor; the resulting discontent has done much to put votes in the column of the newly-prominent fundamentalist Refah Party (usually mistranslated as 'Welfare Party' in the press, but *refah* really means luxury, affluence—they tell the peasants they'll make them all rich). With a big Saudi Arabian bankroll, Refah has made spectacular gains, even winning the mayoral elections in Istanbul and Ankara in 1994, though only with a small percentage of the vote, courtesy of Turkey's peculiar election rules. Refah gets its votes from the old Democratic supporters in rural districts, and the vast numbers that have moved to the cities to seek their fortune. Surprisingly, they also draw much support from the generally non-fundamentalist Kurds—it's the only possibility they have for a protest vote. Much of the rest of their support may be protest also: disgust with the outrageous corruption of the political cliques, and with squabbling parties that all look much the same, is at an all-time high.

Refah is growing, and many Turks worry that in a future election they will be able to form a government, or at least take part in a coalition. Fundamentalism of all kinds is growing too, and has been since the days Turgut Özal was quietly encouraging it. Proselytizers and preachers run as thick as in North Carolina, ugly new mosques with nickel-plated domes are going up everywhere, and more and more women are compelled to wear the baggy coats that mark them as male property. For now, the fundamentalists turn their most moderate face to the world, claiming that all they want is a little morality, and to help the down-trodden poor. For some light on Refah's true nature, consider that its candidates once ran on a common ticket with the overtly fascist and quite dangerous nationalist party, the 'Grey Wolves' of the MHP.

But there is a deep and responsible side to the strange currents that have been flowing through Turkey lately. Having got a noseful of Western market madness from the policies of Özal and Çiller, many educated, modern Turks are convinced they do not want to see their country travel down the same road, even if it means mosque on Fridays and fewer electronic gadgets. A sense of community, and a sense of continuity and tradition, are two things very important to all Turks. In conversation, you will hear many of them express the hope that there might be some 'middle way' that would give them the best of Western prosperity and democracy, while keeping their country a place where they can feel at home. May they find it.

Atatürk	60
East and West	61
The Evil Eye	61
Eleven Days at the Pera Palace	62
The Fatal Glass of Beer	63
Futbol	64
The Green Man	65
Music	66
Perusing the *Polis*	67
Religion	69
The Sultan of Scholars	71

Topics

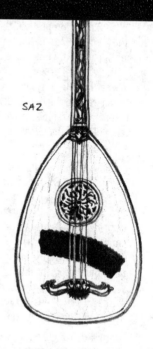

SAZ

Atatürk

People in the west who are unacquainted with Turkish history have probably never heard of him, but in Turkey his face is everywhere: in statues, in the portraits that adorn all public places and most businesses, on coins and banknotes, on banners and even in neon lights. The best ones try to emphasize his sharp features to make him into a kind of mythological hero; instead he comes out looking like the Wizard of Oz.

At first he was just Mustafa, a sullen, red-haired, blue-eyed boy from Salonika (no doubt with a lot of Celtic blood, like so many Turks). His house there still stands, next to the Turkish consulate, and woe to the Greeks if they ever knock it down, as they threaten to whenever they feel the urge for Turk-baiting. A teacher who recognized his abilities gave him the name Kemal, meaning 'perfection'; by the time he and his crack 57th Division were helping whip the British at Gallipoli, he had become General Mustafa Kemal Paşa, a leader with a reputation for putting himself in the thick of the battle—a habit that got him wounded at Gallipoli.

Emerging from the disastrous war as the only general with a record of victory, Mustafa Kemal was the man of the hour, at a time when the Ottoman Empire had collapsed and the Turkish lands found themselves descending into total anarchy. The Allies, particularly Lloyd George, had decided on a cynical rape of Anatolia, meaning to parcel it out among themselves and the Greeks. No novice to political affairs—he had led one of the units that occupied Istanbul in the Young Turk coup of 1909—the general found himself in the same position as de Gaulle in 1940, and he made the most of it. Even more than de Gaulle, Mustafa Kemal was able personally to lead his hastily-rebuilt army to victory against the Greeks, defy the will of the Allied powers, and force the British, French and Italians to leave the country.

With that accomplished, there was still the task of dragging a proud but woefully backward and disorganized nation into the twentieth century. Make no mistake, without him not a tenth part of it would have been accomplished as quickly or as successfully. All the important initiatives of Turkey's unique cultural revolution came from Mustafa Kemal: a republic, a Westernized legal system, women's rights, language reforms, economic modernization, educational reforms and the divorce of religion from politics. Nowhere in history is there a comparable example of such rapid, radical change in a nation's life and institutions—only the reign of Peter the Great in Russia comes remotely close.

Atatürk, or 'Father of the Turks', was the surname he assumed by general acclaim during his campaign to westernize Turkish names in the 1930s. Cults of personality were all too common in those days, and we might easily dismiss Atatürk as just another strongman. On the contrary, he has earned a place among the very few great statesmen this century has produced. One of the famous photos of Atatürk shows him in European formal attire, demonstrating Roman letters to a crowd of his earnest but probably bewildered countrymen. It wasn't just what a modern politician would call a 'photo opportunity'; he did it many times all over Turkey. He took his job seriously, and after so many centuries of decay, the job couldn't have been done any other way.

ATATÜRK

Atatürk thoroughly deserves all the statues and tributes, but they are more than just a memorial to a leader. They stand as a symbol of the revolution he began, and of the modern, secular nation that is still the aspiration of most Turks today. Though he died in 1938, Atatürk in a way is still the bulwark against fundamentalists, terrorists, and all the other bogeys that threaten the peace of Turkey today.

East and West

William Butler Yeats, in his murky meditation, *A Vision*, wrote of east and west eternally contending. He saw them as alternately fertilizing each other with new cultures in successive ages. However you choose to interpret this aspect of the world's secret history, it undoubtedly exists, and Turkey is its battleground. The Aegean coast, in fact, has usually been the front line ever since the rise of the ancient Greeks. It may go back even further, to Mycenaean times, when early Greek people occupied the Aegean islands and part of the coasts. The Greeks do get credit for inventing Western civilization, of course, and looking back beyond them means looking into a glass that is very dark indeed. But remembering that both the Hittites and the Phrygians probably invaded Anatolia from Europe, it just might be possible that this old quarrel goes back even earlier.

As far as we know however, it begins with the Trojan War (of which there is still no reliable historical record—but sometimes legend can be more significant than mere fact). The next round, some 700 years later, was what the Greeks knew as the Persian Wars, an attempt by the greatest empire of its day to squash a minor but troublesome nuisance on its far western border. It was the Greeks' finest hour, and in victory they began to grow conscious of their strength. A century and a half after that, Alexander the Great carried Greek culture and philosophy triumphantly eastwards through Anatolia, and pushed the boundaries of the west as far as India—for a short time. His successors brought back roses, astrology, and among a hundred other things the Persian concept of the divine ruler, without which the cult of the deified Roman emperors could not have been.

Christianity began its drive westwards in Asia Minor, in a score of towns and churches mentioned in the New Testament; from the Sufi poets, the Crusaders adopted the cult of chivalry; the troubadours, alchemy and many themes found in medieval literature owe their beginnings to Islamic culture. Today, the Republic of Atatürk heads the incursion of our secular, mercantile culture into the Middle East.

Somehow, Homer's epic had the power of summing up all this to-and-fro, and evocations of Homer fill the pages of Turkey's history. Like Alexander, Mehmet the Conqueror took time to visit Troy. In 1453, he declared that by taking Constantinople he had avenged the 'peoples of Asia' on the arrogant Greeks. On his entry into the city after the conquest, Mehmet, according to tradition, knocked off with his sword one of the serpent heads of the old bronze column that stood in the Hippodrome. This monument had been brought to the city by Constantine the Great, who had looted it from Delphi. There is probably no way Mehmet could have known that it commemorated the victory of the Greeks over the Persians at Plataea in 479 BC—almost 2000 years before.

The Evil Eye

You'll notice them everywhere; hanging from necklaces, on babies' cradles, dangling from the rear-view mirror of a dolmuş, over the front door of a home, wherever there is anything of value and importance. The *boncuk* ('bead', sometimes called a *göz boncuk*, or 'eye bead') is easily recognizable; sometimes big, sometimes small but always a circle or oval of blue, centred with two other circles to represent an eye. They are worn to guard against that unseen, most nefarious of forces, the evil eye.

Folklore dictates that some people, either knowingly or otherwise, have in their eyes an evil spirit that can do untold harm. The blue 'eye' medallion reflects this wicked spirit back to the originator, so that he or she who displays one has nothing to fear. The medallion can be made from any substance—usually glass, but sometimes stone, bone, shell, even silver and gold—the important thing is that it's there. One newspaper prints a *boncuk* in colour in the top corner of the front page, perhaps to protect readers against all the malevolent influences emanating from the news. Most of Turkey's evil-eye medallions are manufactured near Izmir, at the villages of Karabağler, Kaşiyaki and Kadifekale. This is perhaps suprising, for this region is one of the most prosperous and developed in the country. But it is also a region that was Greek, not so long ago, and the *boncuk* is really Greek in origin.

In ancient times, the Greeks feared the mysterious influence of the eye, particularly the eyes of serpents or snakes, which they believed had the power of hypnotizing their prey. They called this power Βασκανια, a word that passed through Latin into modern languages as *fascination*. Some people have it too; you'll know you do, if you go to Greece, and old women cross the street when they see you coming. Something very similar to the snake's eye, surprisingly, is flattery. Any unsuspecting person can be the bearer of the evil eye in this manner. Compliments of any sort induce pride, and so invite Nemesis—especially where children are concerned.

Not only in folk customs, but in music, cuisine and nearly everything else, much of what you see in Turkey comes from the Greeks. Why shouldn't it? The average inhabitant of western Anatolia has as much Greek blood in him as Turkish. The influence works both ways, of course; you'll still hear old men in Greece greet each other with *selâm aleyküm—aleyküm selâm* (peace be with you—with you be peace), like any good Muslim would. The two peoples lived together so long, and have so much that is similar—from worry-beads to coffee—it is often hard to disentangle them and puzzle out who influenced whom the most. In fact, the more time you spend in this part of the world, the more you'll think that Greeks and Turks are really the same people, divided only by language and religion. Maybe that is why they love each other so dearly. It's fortunate at least that both have their blue beads. With politicians on both sides constantly making the evil eye at each other, both peoples need them.

Eleven Days at the Pera Palace

Even if only to sip tea with pinky extended in its splendiferous lounge, try to visit the grand old Pera Palace Hotel. Walking in, you may feel time-warped, rushed back to the days when Europe's elite carved up the crumbling Ottoman Empire on paper and stroked their moustaches as a grand piano tinkled gently in the background. The Pera Palace was founded in 1892, to provide travellers on the Orient Express with suitable accommodation in Istanbul after their trying journey, and the original fittings are still here: the chandeliers dripping wealth, the antique carpets, the elaborate electric-powered elevator, the piano. It may be a five-star no longer—there is no swimming pool—but few hotels are richer in charm and elegance.

Atatürk stayed here often. The guest list also includes Edward VIII, the last Shah of Iran, Mata Hari, Greta Garbo, Tito and Jackie Onassis. Agatha Christie wrote *Murder on the Orient Express* here. In fact, there is an unusual tale concerning Agatha Christie and the Pera Palace.

Agatha Christie 'lost' eleven days in her life. Neither she, nor anyone else, could account for her whereabouts during this time. In their film of her life, Warner Brothers had to account for the missing days as best they could. Their best wasn't good enough for most and the film was savaged by the critics. Affronted, Warner Brothers took the rather bizarre step of consulting a medium, Miss Tamara Rand, requesting her to call up the soul of Agatha Christie and solve the 'missing days' puzzle once and for all.

Which is what happened—well, almost. Agatha Christie told Miss Rand that the key to the mystery could be found in room 411 of the Pera Palace Hotel, Istanbul.

On 7 March 1979, with the world's press gawking on, a search of room 411 was made, aided by a telephone connection to Miss Rand in the States who gave the searchers long-distance directions after consulting Agatha Christie. Eventually, they found the key—literally. Under a wooden panel near the door was a large, rusty key. Warner Brother's representatives were ecstatic; they grabbed telephones to babble the good news to their bosses Stateside. As they did so, Hasan Süzer, chairman of the Pera Palace, quietly pocketed the key. Later, at a press conference, Süzer announced that he would give the key to Warner Brothers in return for $2,000,000, to be spent on sorely needed refurbishments to the hotel.

Warner Brothers decided to go back to Miss Rand who called up Agatha Christie and told her their woes. She told Miss Rand that if the medium were to hold that key in her hand, she would be told the location of the long missing and long sought-after diary of Agatha Christie, in which would be the secret of the missing days. Warner Brothers hot-footed it back to Istanbul and begged the loan of the key. Negotiations were held. Eventually it was agreed that Tamara Rand would come to the Pera Palace on 20 August 1979, to hold the key and to reveal the site of the diary.

Unfortunately, on 30 June that year, staff at the Pera Palace began a year-long strike and the visit had to be postponed. During that year further negotiations collapsed and the two sides decided that they disliked each other enough not to care about unlocking the past. So it is that the key to the eleven missing days in the life of Agatha Christie now lies in a safety deposit box in a bank in Istanbul.

The Fatal Glass of Beer

After another hot day tracking down Phrygian ruins or Selcuk medreses in a small Turkish town far from the tourist trails, you might think a glass of beer would be a good idea. Depending on the town, you may unfortunately expire before you find one. These days, the Islamic equivalents of the bluenoses and prohibitionists that often plague America are having it all their own way. As in some rural county in Kentucky or Tennessee, there will be plenty of alcohol all around you, but you may have to ask a man with a red nose if you want to find any. Bars tend to be tucked away behind curtained windows, or upstairs, or in hotels; look for the blue and yellow *Efes Pilsen* sign. Most small towns also have at least one outdoor beer garden on an obscure side street. In any case, the availability of beer will always provide a convenient index of the mood and morals of the place you're in. The fundamentalists may wish to get rid of bars altogether, but in the secular Turkish Republic they must be content trying to keep them out of sight, so that innocent lads who never yet tasted beer need not suffer constant temptation.

Ever since Plato recommended mixing wine with three parts water, alcohol has been an issue in this part of the world. Ironically though, this recurring monster of Temperance exists in a land that has developed a great drinking culture. In the cities' cafés and restaurants, you'll see parties of men at their *raki* sessions, with a bottle of the 'lion's milk' in the centre of the table. It goes down very slowly, interspersed with plates of mezes or snacks and plenty of lively conversation. Such an evening is a Turkish ritual, an art, and getting too drunk would be very bad form. The best place to do it is in an old-fashioned *meyhane*, or tavern, a smoky den that stays open late; you'll know you've found the right joint if someone produces a lute or other instrument and begins some impromptu music.

It is entirely possible that great ages of creative drinking go hand in hand with great periods of art. Certainly the Ottoman Empire was at its best during the 'Tulip Period' of the early 1600s. Encouraged by the example of the decadent sultans, Istanbul at that time was quite a swinging place. The famous Turkish traveller and writer Evliya Çelebi wrote of the hundreds of *meyhaneler* in the cosmopolitan quarter of Pera with amazement. Though these were largely patronized by infidels, notably sailors, Turks began to catch on. They had, after all, just introduced coffee to Europe, and the Europeans were returning the favour with beer and gin. There was already plenty of wine and *raki*. The Greeks never stopped making it, and they ran most of the bars.

All things considered, the current rise of prohibitionism, or closed-curtainism, should only be taken as one more example of the tenacious continuity of history. All through the Ottoman centuries, it seems that periods of serious public tippling alternated with waves of reaction. Whenever a serious-minded sultan, prodded on by the imams, decided to clean up the Empire, the curtains would appear for a while, or the *meyhaneler* would be driven upstairs. The Turkish Republic so far has been a golden age for drinkers. Partially inspired by the example of Atatürk himself, who died of cirrhosis of the liver, drinking was respectable—also Western, and therefore a sign of modernity (not to mention the fact that the state monopoly was bringing in bushels of lire from its alcoholic products, in a country where more direct sorts of taxation have always proved problematical). There's a story that Atatürk once heard that one of his provincial governors went out drinking every night with his cronies, behind curtains in a hotel. 'Pull them down!' he ordered. 'With curtains up they'll think you have girls dancing on the tables too!'

Futbol

Not really a topic, more of an obsession. Turks are football fanatics, pure and simple, and if there's a game scheduled on TV, they'll cancel all else to watch it. They are very good at watching and are always keen to point out solemnly the deficiencies of a team, a manager, or an individual player. They're not so good at playing it, however, and the national team regularly gets trounced by all comers. The Turks are nothing if not good losers, and when reminded of their national team's woeful shortcomings, they just smile ruefully, tilt their heads back and raise eyes and palms imploringly upwards to Allah. Besides 1453, the capture of Istanbul, or the various battles of the War of Independence, there's one historical date every Turk knows by heart. Ask any man when Turkey was last in the World Cup, and he will look down at the ground and mumble '1958'.

Of the Turkish teams, Galatasaray are currently the best. The most consistent winner, though, and by far the coolest, is Beşiktaş, in Juventus-style black and white stripes. They are coached by Gordon Milne, one-time manager of Manchester United and a man who has achieved such hero-status in Turkey that one suspects Atatürk may soon have to share space with him in the country's town squares. Beşiktaş is an Istanbul team, as is the third perennial contender, Fenerbahçe. A good provincial team is Trabzon, from the Black Sea coast. Football matches are played from September to April on Saturday and Sunday afternoons; even if you are not especially interested in the sport, going along can make for an enjoyable excursion.

Despite their love of the game, the Turks still have a lot to learn about football, as exemplified by the reply of one young hotel porter when asked his opinion of the great English striker, Gary Lineker: 'Gary Lineker? Well, yes, he's alright. But all he can do is score goals!' But no one would deny the Turks have the proper sporting spirit. We caught a bit of the last World Cup from a hotel balcony in a small Turkish town; in the evening, the owner of an electronics shop across the street pulled one of his new colour sets out onto the pavement, and brought out some chairs for his friends and anyone else who chanced to be passing by. Now and again someone would whistle for the boy from the bar down the street to bring tea. Greece was playing that night, and whenever the woebegone Greeks did something right, which wasn't often, the crowd that had gathered broke out into cheers—it wasn't the home side, but at least the next-door neighbours, so everybody wished them well against those foreigners from far-off Colombia. Try and imagine Greeks doing the same thing, if cruel destiny should ever be moved to let Turkey in the Cup again.

The Green Man

The vast spaces of the Anatolian interior pull at the heartstrings. Almost all of it is wonderfully lonely and wonderfully beautiful, with a hint of paradise and a hint of the Waste Land, sometimes side by side. So much time and history: the Turks often seem innocents to it, relative newcomers who've been in the neighbourhood a mere 800 years.

Somewhere, dozing off by a bus window while riding through these endless landscapes, you may catch a fleeting glimpse of a man in green, riding a grey horse. *Khidr* (the 'green one') is clearly a character of pre-Islamic mythology, though his origins remain unknown. There seems to be a mention of him in the story of Utnapishtim in the Sumerian *Book of Gilgamesh*, the world's oldest written epic. As Khizr, he is mentioned in the Koran as the 'unknown'; some old legends say he was a vizir to a Persian king in the 6th century BC, who was blessed by God with eternal youth. Muslim Sufi mystics mention him often; his sudden and unpredictable appearances are a symbol for the sudden inspiration or enlightenment that comes without warning. In a way, Khidr is a kind of patron saint for the Sufis, and he made his way into Europe with so many other tales and legends in the early Middle Ages, the time of the Crusades and the troubadours, when the influence of the more civilized Muslim world was extremely strong, much stronger than you will ever read in conventional Eurocentric histories.

Christian stories taken from Islamic sources sometimes transform him (God knows why) into the prophet Elijah, or St George. Reminders of this mysterious character turn up in unexpected places, in the 'Green George' of Gypsy and Slavic spring festivals and, some scholars contend, the 'Green Man' of so many English pub signs. We might see Khidr also in that greatest of medieval allegorical poems, *Sir Gawain and the Green Knight*, a profoundly mystical work whose meanings have never been completely explored. And there is little in

Professor Tolkien's *Lord of the Rings* that doesn't strike an echo from somebody's mythology; we shouldn't be surprised to find the Green Man turn up here too, in the person of Tom Bombadil. Khidr has been with the Turks since they first rode off the far Asian steppe into Anatolia. He is mentioned in the *Legends of Dede Korkut*, the collection of epic tales from the Oğuz Turks' nomadic days that was first written down in the 1400s. In the *Tale of Boğaç Khan*, he appears out of nowhere to save the life of the wounded hero; miraculous cures, often involving the 'water of life' are often attributed to him.

The Turks of today, besides being wonderfully meticulous farmers and gardeners, must also be among the most manic tree planters on the globe. The first thing you'll notice in Istanbul, if you haven't been there for a while, is the trees—a few hundred thousand of them, in a belt of brand-new parks that line the Marmara shore and the Golden Horn. Someone comes out to water the younger ones nearly every day, and they all look green and thriving despite the city's notoriously bad air. In many parts of the interior, the *Orman Genel Müdürlüğü*, the national forestry service, has done wonders with scant resources in preserving forests and reclaiming land wasted by millennia of deforestation and neglect. We have an entirely unconfirmable suspicion that Khidr spends a lot of his time in Anatolia. Travelling west from Beyşehir to Konya, through some of the bleakest and emptiest spaces Turkey has to offer, your eyes will fall on a vision: tiny young pines planted over the hillsides for miles and miles, stretching belief as they stretch on and on. This is the Atatürk Centennial Forest, a wonderfully Quixotic and uneconomic attempt at creating a huge forest on what was previously barren land. In all there must be several million trees already planted. Look closely; you might catch sight of him there.

Music

Music is an important part of the Turks' cultural heritage and still one of the things they do best. Western travellers unsympathetic to it have given Turkish music a bad name, calling it monotonous; even if you don't go out of your way to find it, you'll hear enough of it on radios and in buses to get accustomed to it and make up your own mind. What you hear most of, unfortunately, is something called *şarki* ('oriental') or *arabesk*, a noxious Arab-influenced pop style. Irritating as it is, the vocal strength and feeling of the performers, especially the women, makes Western popular music sound like a nursery school pageant.

Western classical music came into fashion with Atatürk, although the last sultans had cultivated opera and kept large dance orchestras. Today it is quite popular, and several Turkish singers and musicians have made names for themselves abroad. The Turks have their own classical tradition, however, and you hear what they call *sanat müziği*, 'art music', anywhere, even in night clubs. At first, this was heavily influenced by the Mevlevi dervishes; its main instrument is the lute (our word comes from the Arabic *al ud*). The lutes hanging in Turkish music shop windows differ in no respect from those in medieval tapestries and illuminations; the Crusaders brought them back from Anatolia. To this the Mevlevis in their own music add the *ney*, a ghostly, reedy flute. Both types of music are governed by modes (*makams*), like ancient Greek music. Their subtleties will require all your attention and good will.

The real treat, however, is Turkish folk music, which Béla Bartók said was the richest he had ever experienced. The *aşiks*, rural troubadours who improvise to a stringed instrument called the *saz*, similar to the lute, can still be found (there may be one seated next to you on a bus) and folk music and dancing are still practised widely (the Black Sea and Aegean coasts, Konya, Kars, and Silifke are especially known for them). Wild dances for men like the Aegean *zeybek* and the *horon* of the northeast are its most spectacular manifestation, along with popular, mainly improvised dances like the *çiftetelli*, traditionally performed at weddings. Besides the *saz* and lute, other instruments are the clarinet and accordion, a two-headed drum called the *davul*, the *kanun* (a 78-stringed dulcimer related to the Hungarian cimbalom), the *kaval* (shepherd's pipes), the *kemençe* (a tiny violin played like a cello) and the *cura* (a sort of zither that has been traced back to the Hittites).

Finally, there's the inimitable *Mehter* music played by the Janissaries under the walls of Vienna and a thousand other towns to dishearten the defenders. With the aid of enormous drums carted around in their own wagons, the 66-piece Mehter bands made grand and gloriously noisy music (you can hear a Mehter concert any afternoon at three, at the Soldiers' Museum in Istanbul). Though its art and melodiousness were probably lost on the besieged garrisons, Mehter is the ancestor of all our military music and marching bands; it has also found its way into western classical music through the Turkish bagatelles of Mozart, Beethoven, and Weber.

Perusing the *Polis*

There are certainly plenty of other things to do on Turkey's coasts, but as far as sightseeing goes one item stands out above all—ruins. No place around the Mediterranean, possibly no place in the world has so many once-thriving cities that simply became abandoned and disappeared. Thanks to the earthquakes that regularly shake down all the products of human vanity in this part of the world, not too much of these cities is left standing. To get anything at all from your visit requires a little imagination, and a little knowledge. Here is a very brief primer on Greek cities, so you'll know your way around when you visit one.

A Greek city was more than just a convenient place for people to live and work. It was the sacred *polis*, from which we get words like politics and politeness (the Romans carried on the idea in their *civitas*; to be 'civilized' was to live in a city). The Greek *polis* was a noble creation, unlike anything the world had ever known. These little walled towns, self-governing and self-sufficient communities of free citizens, were the seeds from which our Western culture grew. And as its living heart, each one had its *agora*, much more than just a central square. At first only an open stretch of ground at the centre, with a platform for speakers at the citizens' assemblies, the agora also served as a marketplace, and there were also religious shrines or images, and many statues of civic benefactors, victorious soldiers and athletes (and later, the reigning Roman emperor; often they'd just knock off the head and stick on a new one when a new emperor was proclaimed). Greeks did not compartmentalize the various aspects of their public life the way we do: the political, the sacred, civic monuments and day-to-day business shared the same space, a symbol of how life in the *polis* was a seamless whole.

To define the agora, the Greeks came up with an invention perfectly suited to their climate and their way of life: the *stoa*, a long, colonnaded portico, usually closed by wings at the ends. The 'stoic' philosopers took their name from the stoa, because that is where they liked to gather—along with the rest of the population, it seems. At all hours of the day, the stoa gave citizens an attractive place to spend their idle time and talk about the weather or argue about politics. Greek stoas were infinitely adaptable; some excavated examples show stone tables for meat and fish stands. The same ones might have been used at other times by bankers and merchants, or by the city's courts to hear cases. You'll have to go to Athens to see the reconstruction of a stoa, but they were always mentioned as among a city's major architectural works, often with famous frescoes on the inner wall; Pergamon, always the flashiest of cities, had some that were two storeys tall.

The two important public buildings of the *polis* will also be found around the agora: the *bouleuterion*, or council house, usually in the form of a small, enclosed theatre; and the *prytaneion*, the city's 'common house'. Here a perpetual fire was kept on the sacred hearth, as a symbol of its communal life of the city; a separate room served as a a dining hall, in which the city could offer hospitality to distinguished visitors, ambassadors, or citizens who brought home victories from war or the games.

In Hellenistic times, planners began to think symmetrically, and when there was a chance for rebuilding they started making perfectly rectangular 'peristyle' agoras surrounded on all sides by stoas (there is a good example at Ephesus; the same idea was used in the Imperial Forums of Rome). But originally, stoas would also be built that closed off one side of the agora, and continued from there down one of the main streets—a pretty trick of town design to make a gradual transition from the private spaces of the residential districts to the public space of the agora. In the opulent conditions of the 1st and 2nd centuries AD, this idea grew into the *colonnaded street*, the main status embellishment of any town of the Roman Empire. These often extended as far as the town gates. Towns that had two or more of them, such as Side, Perge or Ephesus, were really doing well. Whenever you're exploring a ruined city in Turkey, it should be remembered that most of what you see dates from this period, when the economy of Asia Minor reached its height; it was then that the most impressive public buildings, the basilicas and the gymnasia were built. Only towns like Priene, that did not flourish in Roman times, give the full effect of what a classical Greek or Hellenistic city was like.

The greatest temples, however, were raised in the 5th–3rd centuries BC. Before Roman rule came, when the ethos of the Greek city-state was at its height, individual towns competed to build the most impressive temples, as the towns of medieval France vied to build the biggest cathedrals, or American cities the tallest skyscrapers. A Greek temple did not have to be in the centre of town, though. Its site was usually determined by ancient tradition, some place that had been holy for centuries or even millennia before. The temple itself was a relatively late idea, and never the centre of religious observance, the way a church or a mosque is. It housed a cult image (usually a statue), as well as the ex-votos and other gifts to the sanctuary, and architecturally it served as a kind of stage backdrop for the sacrifice and other rites. In the sophisticated, secular age of the Empire, temples were little more than glorified art museums.

The important business of Greek religion was the sacrifice, and this took place in the open air. The *temenos*, or sanctuary, dedicated to a god, is the holy ground where sacrifices were performed, and it could be in or near the agora, or anywhere else, even out alone in the countryside. The temenos would usually be walled off, and it would contain the altar for sacrifices, with the temple façade behind it to the east, as well as a home for the priests or priestesses, and often a sacred grove; important sanctuaries might be entered by a monumental gateway, a *propylaea* or *propylon*. Originally the altar itself was just a simple slab or even a heap of stones—every passer-by would add another to the pile. But by Hellenistic times these often grew into magnificent buildings, such as the Altar of Zeus at Pergamon.

Of the Greeks' homes, you will see almost nothing. It would be surprising how simply they provided for themselves, did we not know how all-important to them was their communal life. Neither were there sharply defined wealthy districts or slums. The Greeks never minded rubbing elbows with their fellow citizens, of whatever condition; their houses, in any case, differed little in outward appearance or in any other way besides size. Few details of Greek houses are well known, only that the fancier ones were built around courtyards. In Roman times these often developed into impressive peristyle courts, with a fountain or pool at the centre.

Where the outlines of streets survive, as at Priene, you'll notice they usually run straight as arrows. The first town planner whose name has survived is Hippodamus, an Ionian who redesigned the port city of Piraeus in a gridiron plan for the Athenians in the 5th century. Hippodamus did not invent this sort of plan, but brought it back from his home city of Miletus, which had recently been rebuilt on a grid plan after its sacking by the Persians. Rectilinear street plans came naturally to the geometrically-minded Greeks; in the colonies of Asia Minor, this form was the easiest way to lay streets, measure land accurately, and get a new town started, just as it was in 19th-century America.

The Greek ideal of *paideia*, intellectual and physical education, treated as one, is symbolized in the *gymnasion*, usually a large complex of buildings that included an enclosed *palaestra*, or exercise ground, but also classrooms and lecture halls (Plato's Academy was a gymnasion). If space permitted, there would also be plane trees for shade (any kind of greenery was very rare in a Greek city), a spring or fountain, and often a temple, perhaps dedicated to Hercules or Hermes. In Roman times the gymnasion grew much more luxurious; palestrae became monumental colonnaded courtyards, and often a bath complex was added on—Pergamon, as usual, gives the most lavish examples. Occasionally, where there was room for it, there would be a *stadion* too, a course for footraces so called from the measure of length (about 200 yards). Classical stadia were simple open spaces with an earthen bank on one side for spectators; real stadia, with marble seats, colonnades and elaborate entrance gates, did not arrive until Roman times.

The first Greek theatre was the agora itself; in archaic Greece the open space of an agora was often called the *orchestra* , a word that means a 'dancing place'; it is a reminder of how classical theatre grew up out of the rites and dances that attended the cult of Dionysos. To accommodate growing populations, cities began to build proper theatres wherever there was a natural slope, with a banked, semicircular area for spectators called the *theatron* (or *cavea*), sited wherever possible with a grand panoramic view for a background to the play. When the classical plays were first performed, the orchestra (unpaved, and generally circular or trapezoidal) was still the centre of the action. Only in later centuries was a *skene*, or stage, built; this logical and adaptable feature served much the same functions as the simple, two-level stages we usually use for productions of Shakespeare. Again, only in Roman times did impressive columned stage buildings appear, and they were never universally popular in Greek towns. Neither were the Romans' barbaric gladiatorial games, which explains the lack of amphitheatres in Greek cities—though in many places you can see the Greeks slipping, and building walls around an orchestra to protect spectators at such games. It's a sad sight: theatres meant for the works of Euripides and Aeschylus being transformed into arenas for butchery. Nothing could illustrate more clearly the decay at the heart of that opulent age.

Religion

In the *hadis*, the collection of traditions and stories from the days of Mohammed that serves as a commentary on the Koran, it is recorded that the angel Gabriel, disguised as a Bedouin, confronted the Prophet on the road one day and demanded to know the practices of the true belief. Mohammed's five answers satisfied the angel, and, as the 'five pillars of Islam', they continue to guide Muslims today, a solid foundation for the simplest of the world's great religions.

One of the pillars is the professing of the simple formula 'There is no god but Allah and Mohammed is his prophet.' This is painted or inscribed in elegant Arabic calligraphy over all the mosques of Turkey. Another pillar is the pilgrimage to Mecca, for all who are able. Giving alms to the poor is a third; however, begging is frowned upon and the mendicant dervishes and calenders have been outlawed since 1925, and so this duty is performed discreetly.

Muslims are also expected to keep a total fast during the daylight hours of Ramazan, the holy month of the Muslim calendar. In public, at least, the fast is well observed. During Ramazan a mood of peaceful contemplation occupies the faithful. Much of the time on radio and television is given over to religious programmes, and every evening at sunset in many towns a cannon booms out the signal that the fast has ended. Mosques are often gaily decorated with coloured lights, nowhere more so than in Istanbul where Koranic messages are spelled out in strings of lights between the minarets of the great imperial mosques.

The most conspicuous of the five pillars is the obligation of saying prayers five times a day, at hours proclaimed by the muezzins from the minaret balconies. It is permitted to perform these anywhere, and although Muslims usually go to the mosques for the midday Friday prayers, there is no Mass or ritual in the Christian sense. In the main, Islam avoids ritual and ceremony. The imam (priest) is present merely to lead the prayers, and the formulaic discourse he declaims afterwards is hardly a sermon.

The architecture of the mosques serves to illustrate the simplicity of Islam. Most are large halls furnished only with the mimber (a pulpit), and the mihrab (the niche in the wall facing Mecca) that concentrates the thoughts and prayers of the faithful like a lens. Unlike in other Muslim countries, you are allowed inside a Turkish mosque, except during prayer time. Don't forget to leave your shoes at the door, dress sensibly (no shorts, short skirts, or bared arms and shoulders) and don't make a nuisance of yourself, but by all means don't feel unwelcome, either. Muslims themselves enjoy coming to the mosque for meditation and quiet, and they are pleased to share them with you. To miss the interiors of the Ottoman mosques of Bursa and Istanbul and the Selcuk 'Great Mosques' of the cities of Anatolia would be to miss much of the finest in Turkish art and architecture.

One Islamic ceremony you may encounter, which accompanies the rite of circumcision, is a small parade with a bravely smiling nine-year-old in a costume, crown and cape. Most weddings in Turkey are civil and the ballyhoo and decorated cars differ little from those in other lands; the busy marriage chapel next to Istanbul's city hall is a good place to watch them.

Most Turkish Muslims are Sunnis, the majority, orthodox creed, but all around the country you'll find a substantial minority of Alawis (or Alevis), a fascinating sect who have no mosques. They do have a refreshingly relaxed and tolerant attitude about religious matters, combined with a practice of equality of the sexes and often radical political beliefs. Alawis include groups around the Black Sea, the Bektaşi dervishes (*see* p.337) and entire villages inhabited by the nonconformist *Tahtacis* in the southern mountains. They are also strong among Turkish intellectuals. In these times, Alawis are often the subject of violent attacks by radical fundamentalists (often with the police turning a blind eye). One dark event you will often hear mentioned is the 'Sivas massacre' of July 1993, in which a mob in that city, led by outside agitators, burned a hotel in which Alawis, including some writers and journalists, were staying for a conference, killing 37 of them. Big demonstrations in Ankara, Istanbul—and Frankfurt— commemorated the anniversary of the event in 1994; a similar demonstration in Sivas was harassed by the police.

According to the last census, 99.04 per cent of Turkey's population are Muslim, but there are no figures on how many actually practise their religion seriously. During the 1930s, when Turkey was hell-bent on reform and secularism, religion became unfashionable, at least in the cities. Today, Turkey, like many of its neighbours, is experiencing an Islamic revival. The late President Özal was a *haci* (the title for someone who has made the pilgrimage to Mecca), and in many towns, mosques that were once almost empty for Friday prayers are now almost full. Big money pouring in from Saudi Arabia and elsewhere finances not only the fundamentalist Refah Party, but scores of rabble-rousing preachers and tract publishing houses; you'll notice the stands they set up on weekends outside the main mosques.

Much like what is happening now in the United States, a strange and shadowy battle is currently underway in Turkey for the hearts and minds of the people. The fundamentalist forces, well organized and well financed, have so far been able to manipulate the masses, portraying any and all political issues as a struggle between good and evil. Those who support the secular republic of Atatürk seem confused and divided amongst themselves, and they have been yielding ground for years. No one knows how this struggle will end, but the spectre of the radical side of fundamentalism should not blind the visitor from the diversity—and beauty—of Islam in this country. Religion's moderate voices here have some interesting points to make, and they show a sincere concern for Turkey's future. More than in most Muslim countries, a gentler and more tolerant side of Islam has always flourished in Turkey, a long tradition best symbolized by the figure of Celâleddin Rumi, the Mevlâna.

The Sultan of Scholars

Islam has no saints, but Celâleddin Rumi, poet and Sufi mystic of Konya, approaches as nearly to that exalted state as is allowed. For Westerners who have never been able to take Islam seriously, he is the man to know. Born on 30 September 1207 in Balkh, Afghanistan, Celâleddin and his family—his father Bahaeddin Veled was a renowned scholar—fled before the Mongol invasions to Anatolia, where they took refuge in the Selcuk capital, then in its heyday under Sultan Alâeddin Keykubad. Here he remained as a teacher in the city's mosques, withdrawing more and more into his meditations and his poetry until his death on 17 December 1273. The Mevlevi order of dervishes—the 'whirling dervishes'—he founded was tremendously influential throughout the Middle East, and the hereditary line of its sheikhs, descended from the Mevlâna (literally 'our master'), even intermarried with the Ottoman dynasty during the reign of Beyazit I.

Few poets in the world have been more prolific. His greatest work, a subtly arranged medley of lyric poetry, mysticism and anecdotes called the *Mesnevi* (or *Mathnavi*), runs to some 25,000 couplets (longer than the *Faerie Queene*, the longest poem in English), and there are 44,000 more couplets in the anthology called the *Divan of Shems-i Tabriz*. The title of a third work, *Fihi-Ma-Fih*, 'in it what's in it', clearly expresses the Sufi informality and disdain of dogmas and church establishments. All were written in Persian, the language of court and culture in Selcuk times (good translations of selections exist, notably by Professors Nicholson and Arberry).

The Mevlâna's poetry has been described as an ocean; vast and boundless, encompassing all the systems and creeds of lesser men within it. In truth there is no readily discernible philosophy in his work that does not state the obvious; the Mevlâna wanted it to appeal to all men at all levels. The unity of God and of creation is a recurring theme, consistent with Islam and the teaching of the Sufis. It is the revelation of divine love that sets his work apart, and the spiritual allegory of the 'lover' and the 'beloved', the soul and its dissolution into the infinite, is the core of his thought. On this rarefied plane of understanding, the claims of the various religions seem mere games of language, and issues such as predestination or free will simply cease to be relevant.

As for the whirling dervishes, the Mevlâna and his followers believed as much in music and dance as forms of spiritual expression as they did in poetry. The *sema*, the ritual dance still performed annually in Konya on the anniversary of the Mevlâna's death, is his teaching of the abandonment of the self set into motion. The dervishes' tall hats represent their own grave-stones, the jackets, which they shed, their graves. As the dancers spin around the floor, symbolically reflecting at once the movements of the cosmos and the soul's search for God, the dancers themselves attain a controlled mystic communion. With one hand raised and the other extended towards the ground, they '... take from God and give to man, keeping nothing for themselves ...'

History 75

Getting There 78

Getting Around 79

Tourist Information 81

Orientation 83

Old Istanbul (Stamboul) 87

Istanbul in Asia 129

The Bosphorus 131

Shopping 135

Where to Stay 137

Eating Out 142

Entertainment and Nightlife 147

Istanbul

HAREM, TOPKAPI PALACE

Just to vex the Turks, the Greeks still insist on calling it Constantinople, and print it that way on all their maps. The Ottomans never really meant to change the name; they probably thought of themselves as the successors of the Romans, just as the Byzantines had, and they did their best to keep Constantine's column in good repair. But through centuries of trade and diplomacy with the Greeks, they had often heard this fabulous remnant of antiquity referred to as *Stin poli* or 'in the city'. Turkish has no prepositions, and to their ears it must have sounded like one word.

The name stuck, and what could be better for such a place than to be called, simply, The City. To the Turks, the Mongols, and other peoples of distant Asia, this was a kind of half-mythical land of dreams, known more through poets than historians or travellers, just as Cathay and the Indies were for medieval Europeans. All these Asian peoples migrated west to the 'Land of Rome' and its golden capital, and one day made it their own.

For sixteen centuries, Istanbul was the metropolis of the eastern Mediterranean. The Byzantines had a word for their legitimate heirs to the throne, those sons of emperors born in the famous Purple Chamber of the palace; it was *Porphyrogenitus*, or 'born to the purple'. This we can take as a title for the city itself, whose location astride both the land and sea routes between east and west guaranteed its long rule. There is a sinister aspect to this. Istanbul, both under the Byzantines and the Ottomans, was the most predatory city the world has ever known save Rome itself, sucking the economic lifeblood out of hundreds of provinces—even entire nations. For a long time, its matchless fortifications protected, even encouraged the kind of decadence that nature and history usually root out of societies. Only now is the city just waking up from the terrible Ottoman hangover; it can take its place as a modern commercial emporium, realizing what a blessing it is to have the burden of governing lifted from its shoulders.

Its new burden, and one it gladly accepts, is carrying the Turkish economy; one-third of the nation's factories are here, and more than two thirds of Istanbul's population of over 10 million are recent migrants from Anatolia come to try their luck in what may already be the largest city in Europe. The old diversity of peoples remains, even increases; added to the long-established Greeks, Armenians, and Jews, are vast numbers of new arrivals from Eastern Europe, the Middle East and Turkophone Central Asia.

Istanbul will not disappoint. It is inexhaustible, pleasant to walk around, full of surprises. You could take your old aunt here on holiday or have a Bohemian dream vacation, live like a tycoon or a tramp. For those who have already been to Istanbul, if your last visit was more than a few years ago it's time to have another look—you'll hardly know the place today. Istanbul is booming, perhaps blossoming, a mildly schizophrenic metropolis of skyscrapers and street vendors, where some women wear veils and others the latest in Italian designs. All the energies of the nation seem concentrated in it now, as the millennary City transforms itself, while doing its best to drag all Turkey with it into the 21st century.

History

Byzantion was already a sizeable town when the decision was made to transform it into an imperial capital. Set on the Bosphorus, bridging Europe and Asia, it was certainly the logical site for one, and it's surprising that no one took better advantage of its strategic position before Constantine the Great. The town's acropolis stood roughly where the Topkapi Palace is now, and archaeologists have uncovered fragments going back to Mycenaean times. The Greeks had a legend, though, that the city was founded by a certain Byzas of Megara, in the 7th century, the great age of Greek expansion and colonization.

By the 3rd century AD, decadent Rome had already been largely abandoned by the emperors. Concerned above all with maintaining the two key strategic fronts, the Danube and Euphrates, many of them kept their court at Milan, or at places like Sirmium and Serdica (Sofia) in the Balkans. The Balkans, in fact, was one of the most important regions of the late Empire. Most of the army and its generals came from there, and more than a few emperors, including Constantine himself. As soon as he had consolidated his hold on the empire, Constantine began work on his new capital, in 328.

Like Rome, the new city was said to have seven hills (*see* p.87). It was given its own lavish dole, a racetrack, a forum and its own Senate. The fleets of ships that had previously brought Egypt's bounty of grain to fatten Rome were now rerouted to Constantinople. Constantine meant the new capital not only as a base to defend the two hot edges of his realm, and as a monument to himself, but for a third purpose too: creating a specifically Christian city as capital for his new Christian Empire. No pagan temples were allowed to be built, but facing the new Forum, the Augusteion, rose one of Constantine's great basilicas, later rebuilt as the Aya Sofia. Constantinopolis' official birthday is 11 May 330, the day the city was consecrated by Christian priests.

With the rich imperial subsidies and building programmes, Constantinople rapidly grew into the metropolis of the eastern empire, drawing population and economic life from the older ciities of Greece and Asia Minor and beginning their fatal decline. A second wave of growth and embellishment of the city came with the reign of Justinian (527–65). As the booty rolled in from Byzantine conquests around the Mediterranean, Justinian found the money to rebuild the Aya Sofia, the imperial palace and much else. The beginning of his reign, however, saw the most serious outbreak of civil strife in the city's history: the Nike Riots of 532, really a full-fledged popular revolt against the emperor's oppressive rule, crushed by the army with tens of thousands of deaths.

After Justinian's bloody but glorious reign, Constantinople hung on for almost a thousand years as the capital of a venerable, declining, somehow unsinkable empire. For all that it has surprisingly little history of its own. By the 12th century, appearances were still kept up but both empire and capital were mere shadows of their former selves. The new quarter of Galata was growing up across the Golden Horn, largely inhabited by the Italian merchants—Genoese, Pisans, Amalfitani and above all Venetians—who had seized control of the empire's economy. So resented were the predatory Italians that in 1180 a Greek mob massacred those they could catch; the state exiled the rest soon after.

In 1203, the Venetian fleet ferried the largely French troops of the Third Crusade down to Constantinople on their way to the Holy Land. The Crusaders couldn't pay their passage, and so the Venetians arranged a clever intervention into the empire's affairs. Alexius, the rightful heir to the Byzantine throne whose father had been deposed in a coup, agreed to pay the bill if only the Crusaders would get him back his throne. That was easily done, but the empire was broke and Alexius could not come up with the money. Another coup drove Alexius out, and in February 1204 the Crusaders and Venetians decided to take the undermanned city. After a siege of two months, they smashed their way in, the first time anyone had done so in 900 years. The sack that followed may well have been the richest in all history. The Westerners took their time and methodically looted everything, nailed down or not, and the Venetians, who had masterminded the whole affair and completed the Italians' revenge for 1180, got the lion's share—including the famous bronze horses of St Mark's, which originally stood in the Hippodrome.

Constantinople would never be the same. For the next forty years, the city endured life as capital of a ludicrous French-run 'Empire of Romania', and when the Greeks retook the city in 1246 under Emperor Michael Paleologos, they had neither the cash nor the energy to restore it. Constantinople's last two centuries were a sad affair, with much of the city centre in ruins; even the court deserted the old palace for the newer Blachernae Palace out by the Theodosian walls. It was those incomparable walls, besieged so often by Bulgars, Avars, Arabs and Turks, that kept the dilapidated capital and the pathetic empire in business for another two centuries, while the Ottoman Turks were gradually grabbing all Anatolia and the Balkans and eventually even building castles on the Bosphorus.

The end finally came in 1453, with the determined Sultan Mehmet, along with his matchless army, modern fleet and the most advanced artillery in the world. Largely empty, and defended by a handful of Greeks and Venetians, Constantinople fell after a siege of two months. Getting the city back on its feet again proved to be a much greater task than capturing it, but Mehmet proved as capable a ruler as he was a Conqueror. The presence of the court itself helped in the economic revival, but Mehmet also moved quickly to re-establish the Covered Market, corner-stone of the economy, while pumping in lots of money for public works: fixing up the walls, streets and water supply, building the Topkapi Palace and scores of mosques. Incentives were given to get people to move back into the city and improve property. His successor, Beyazit II, resettled thousands of Jewish refugees from Spain after 1492, starting the city off on its new career as a polyglot, cosmopolitan city where Turks, Greeks, Armenians, Jews, Arabs, Slavs, Albanians and every other nationality lived side by side. Beginning with Mehmet, each Sultan in turn embellished the city with new mosques, pavilions and religious foundations. 'The City' was back in business.

From the 17th century to World War I, The City did not share fully in the Ottoman decay; rather, it monopolized whatever art and architecture, modernity and economic progress there was. Non-Turks, particularly the Greeks, dominated both business and culture, and the Greeks' Phanar (Fener) quarter grew into a city within the city. Istanbul really opened to the West after 1839, the year of the Tanzimat reforms. Foreign businessmen poured in to take advantage of the empire's weakness, and Beyoğlu, or 'Pera', transformed itself into a proper European city where French was more commonly heard in the streets than Turkish.

All this was a mixed blessing. The reign of Abdülhamid especially (1876–1909) was a disaster for Istanbul, as it was for the rest of the empire. With the state desperately in need of foreign investment and technology, the city was completely at the mercy of the foreign interests

Abdülhamid's vezirs invited in. The beautiful shore of the Golden Horn was degraded into an industrial nightmare, while the new railroad line to Sirkeci Station devastated the equally scenic Marmara side.

In 1919, British and French troops occupied Istanbul. The British government hoped to prop the gormless Mehmet V on the Ottoman throne as a puppet, while gaining de facto control of the straits for itself, plans that came to naught with the victory of Atatürk's nationalists. Much of the Greek population fled, though like Mehmet, Atatürk took pains to reassure those who stayed behind. Though no longer a capital, Istanbul remained the economic heart of Turkey and its window to the West. One of the saddest, and least remembered, events in Istanbul's recent history was the anti-Greek riots of 1955. The whole story has been pretty well buried by now, but from the evidence it seems that local elements of the Menderes government and Democratic party had plotted to whip up sentiment against foreigners to distract attention from the country's economic problems. For a week, mobs burned out churches and monasteries, and attacked businesses belonging to Greeks, Armenians, Jews and others. When it was over, a majority of Istanbul's already dwindling non-Turkish population quickly decided to move elsewhere.

Istanbul Today

Over the last two decades, the big story has been the tremendous surge of migration into the city. Mostly rural folk, some 400,000 of them a year from every corner of Turkey come to try their luck. Istanbul is where the jobs are; today the metropolitan area has over a third of all Turkey's industry and a population estimated at over 10 million. Istanbul will soon be the largest city in Europe, if it isn't already. The newcomers have been a tremendous burden on the city's resources; water and public health lead a long list of serious urban problems. Even so, the immigrants are contributing their hopes and hard work to a city that is changing faster than at any time since Mehmet the Conqueror—a city alive, exploding with energy.

You'll see the new Istanbul clearly if you arrive from the east; after the car passes over the Bosphorus Bridge you're on the ring motorway, the Çevre Yolu; for miles you'll look down on vast new neighbourhoods, full of attractive blocks of modern flats. Amidst these are shopping malls as modern as anything in California (one has crystal chandeliers), and over it all rises a new crown of skyscrapers. The two tallest are the headquarters of the Koç and Sakinci holding companies, the two giants that between them now run much of the Turkish economy.

There's a new metro, progressing slowly, two new tramways, a ring motorway, and a second suspension bridge over the Bosphorus. New suburbs have gobbled up almost all of the countryside along the Bosphorus, and for sixty miles down the Asian shore. In the '80s major infrastructure and slum clearance programmes were begun under Mayors Bedrettin Dalan and Nurettin Sözen. Much of the impetus to all this came from Istanbul's as-yet unsuccessful bids for the Olympics. Because of that, a large part of the effort has been devoted to cosmetics— most spectacularly, the ambitious plan to reclaim all of old Stamboul's waterfront. Already over half the Golden Horn and Marmara shores have been cleared and turned into parkland. It may not look too impressive for a few decades, until the tens of thousands of trees have grown up, but people then will be praising the Stamboullu for their foresightedness and care for their city.

One ironic effect of the massive peasant immigration has been the election in March 1994 of a fundamentalist Muslim mayor, Tayyip Erdoğan (see below, p.126). He has already wreaked some mischief with the city's cultural programmes, while tough city problems like water and housing have wreaked some mischief with him. It is encouraging to consider that, counting those who didn't bother to vote, some 85 per cent of Istanbul's adult population did not vote for the fundamentalist party, Refah. Ask them what they think of Erdoğan, and you will find opinion neatly divided between those who will tell you he's the Devil incarnate, and those who think he's just another corrupt, cynical politician like the rest. Erdoğan will have to work magic to get re-elected, but for now Islamic fundamentalists have a rare chance to show they can draw on their ideals to effectively run a booming, fantastically complex modern city.

Getting There

by air

They're building a metro line out to **Atatürk International Airport**, but no one has any idea when it will be finished. In the meantime, your options are a taxi ride, which should cost about £8/$12 from the centre, or the inexpensive **HAVAS bus** connection, from the THY Turkish Airlines terminal on Şişhane Square in Beyoğlu. This runs every half-hour, until 9pm, and less frequently at night. The bus also stops on Atatürk Boulevard in Aksaray—and if you ask the driver he'll probably let you get off anywhere else you like. This bus also serves as the only connecting link between the airport's foreign and domestic terminals, which are about a mile apart. If you need to change money when you arrive, the bank offices in the foreign terminal give as good a rate as anything you'll find in town.

Atatürk International Airport, ✆ 663 6400
THY Turkish Airlines, Airport, ✆ 663 6363
Atatürk domestic terminal (Yeşilköy), ✆ 573 2920

by train

The days of the Orient Express are long gone, but just in case you should be riding the Turkish rails, know that European destinations are served from **Sirkeci Station** (✆ (212) 527 0050) at the tip of Stamboul's peninsula; besides international arrivals the main event here is the daily train to and from Edirne. Trains for Ankara and everything else on the Asian side (also to Russia) begin at **Haydarpaşa Station**, in Kadiköy (✆ (216) 336 0475). The express runs to Ankara (the Fatih Ekspres and the overnight Yataklı Ekspres) have the most comfortable cars and best services in the country, and are the only train runs in Turkey that come close to competing with the buses in speed and price. The only way to get from one station to the other, besides a ludicrously long taxi ride over the Bosphorus Bridge, is to take the ferry from outside Haydarpaşa to Karaköy, by the Galata Bridge, and then walk or take a taxi to nearby Sirkeci.

by coach

Every traveller will agree that the new **main coach station** at Esinler, out in the far western suburbs—so new it doesn't even have a name yet— is one of the most gratifying of the city's many recent improvements. Instead of the old Topkapi Station, a vast, chaotic and sometimes dangerous mudflat outside the walls, there is a completely modern facility, a bizarre, space-age architectural apparition among the grim concrete *gecekondu* (overnight) suburbs. Every bus that comes to Istanbul uses it; if you're heading for any big town there will be no need for a reservation; just turn up and you'll probably be on a bus within ten minutes. Getting there is no problem. The new tram/metro from Aksaray Meydan pulls right into the middle of the station—about a half-hour trip, or else you can take a taxi for about £4/$6 from Sultanahmet.

Getting Around

Many travellers take one look at Istanbul's medieval street plan on a map and surrender to despair, a feeling that is confirmed after the first attempt at reaching a destination on foot ends in utter bewilderment.

It isn't really so bad; as in most old cities, remember that the streets are laid out to make sense to your eyes, more than to be read on a map. After walking a while through old Istanbul, you'll learn to orientate yourself to the major landmarks. Public transport in all forms is refreshingly inexpensive.

by bus

Istanbul's transit system, the IETT, doesn't publish a route map, so until you learn your way around the best thing is to walk over to the nearest main station; all lines begin and end at one of these: Beyazit Square; Eminönü, in front of the Spice Market by the Galata Bridge; Karaköy, on the Beyoğlu side of the Galata Bridge, Sirkeci Station; Taksim Square; Beşiktaş; and on the Asian side, Harem, near Haydarpaşa Station.You'll need tickets beforehand, and you can buy books of them at the unmarked orange kiosks at these stations; more conveniently, men in the street will sell tickets to you for a few pennies extra. Aypa publish a quite detailed city map which includes a bus map and a list of the Istanbul buses and their routes, though this can be hard to find. Buses are efficient and cheap, but they will usually be indecently crowded. Tickets, at time of writing, sell for TL 10,000 (about 20p). The word for bus stop is *durak*; signs are usually painted orange.

In distant parts of the city you'll also encounter *Halk Otobusleri*—'people's buses', a special service provided by suburban councils; these usually have a conductor to sell tickets.

by tram, metro and train

As part of Istanbul's unsuccessful Olympic bid, the city has built itself the beginnings of a modern rapid transit system. Don't expect an underground—imagine the difficulties of digging one here, with all the world's archaeologists looking over the workmen's shoulders. Instead, they've made the logical compromise of two inexpensive above-ground tram lines, which run underground where they can. One (the *Cağdas* line, or **Metro**) starts from Aksaray Meydan as an underground, eventually surfacing and heading out to the new coach station in the distant suburbs on the European side. This will eventually be part of a Metro network; work on a second line heading north from Taksim Square is well under way. The other line in operation, the **Hizli** ('speedy') is an above-ground tram all the way; it starts at Sirkeci Station, climbs up to Sultanahmet Square and then passes down the Divan Yolu, Stamboul's main street, ending up at the Topkapi Gate.

There's yet a third line, which runs along the main rail tracks from Sirkeci Station around the tip of the peninsula and along the Marmara shore, but it isn't much use to visitors. The tram/metro lines use different (equally inexpensive) tickets from the buses; at every stop there will be a booth that sells them—but they aren't always open so it's a good idea to carry a few around. Istanbul's most entertaining public transport is found on the Beyoğlu side. If you're traveling from Galata Bridge to Taksim, you'll meet first the **Tünel**, the world's shortest underground (and one of the oldest) with the world's smallest tokens, sold in booths at either end. The Tünel is really an inclined railway, and it's perfect for getting you from the Bridge up the steep hill to the bottom end of Istikâl Caddesi. From there, you can take the delightfully named **Nostaljik Tramvay** up Istiklâl to Taksim Square—real turn-of-the-century streetcars, carefully restored, with conductors in costumes to match.

by taxi

All the taxis are yellow, and all have meters now, and you'll have no trouble finding one on any major street. Don't be surprised if the drivers seem to be going a little out of the way; often they will stick resolutely to the main thoroughfares to avoid traffic jams. Taxis are quite inexpensive—less than £2/$3 for an average trip in the city—and invaluable when you get hopelessly lost. If you're staying in a small hotel or in an out-of-the-way street, be sure to write the name down, as well as any nearby main streets or landmarks, as the drivers often don't know the city as well as they might—especially when you try to pronounce your destination in Turkish. One strange custom here—if you cross over one of the Bosphorus bridges, you'll be expected to cough up the toll.

by dolmuş

The bad news for anyone who loves Istanbul is that dolmuşes seem to be on their way out. The other means of transport—minibuses, IETT buses and trams—work well enough that it is becoming hard for the individual dolmuş driver to make a living. Nevertheless there are still a few operating around the centre, some still running their ancient, magnificent American jalopies. If you want to know which American cars of the last 45 years were the best built, examine the dolmuş lines of Istanbul. At least two thirds will be '49 Chryslers, '55–'56 Chevys or '51–'57 Plymouths and Dodges. There are no Fords. The dolmuş is a communal taxi. Getting into one is easy; just wait near one of the red, white, and black dolmuş signs, or hail one from anywhere on the street, see if the destination sign on the roof of the car is anywhere near your own, and pile in. In some outlying parts of the town, they're simpler to use than the buses, and equally inexpensive.

by minibus

These work much like the dolmuş, and operate mostly from the city walls, going down the main streets of Istanbul; few penetrate further in than Beyazit Square. Above all they'll be helpful if you mean to do some exploring around the Theodosian walls and the outlying quarters of old Stamboul. Like the dolmuş they have destination signs. Don't mistake Topkapi Gate for Topkapi Palace.

by boat

Outside Venice, there's no city in Europe better for messing about in boats. For many of the Stamboullu, a ferry ride with some of the world's most remarkable cityscapes for background is just a part of the daily commute. Ferries for all points depart either from docks on either side of the Galata Bridge, or the Kabataş landing near Dolmabahçe Palace. Cruises up the **Bosphorus** depart from the Stamboul side of the bridge (pier 4, just to the right of the bridge), usually twice a day; you can get off where you please, or stop for lunch and catch the boat on the return trip, from any of its stops along the straits.

Ferry-boats to the Asian side depart every hour or so from Galata Bridge (the docks nearest Sirkeci Station; from pier 2 to **Üsküdar**, or pier 1 for **Kadiköy** and **Bostanci**), and from Kabataş for Üsküdar. Other boats for **Kadiköy–Haydarpaşa Station** leave from Karaköy landing, on the Beyoğlu side of the bridge (Kadiköy maritime station, ✆ (216) 244 4233).

For the **Princes' Islands**, several boats a day (more in the summer and at weekends) leave from both Galata (pier 5, behind Sirkeci station) and Kabataş landings. Some are express, getting to Büyükada in about an hour; others call at all four islands and several Asian ports as well. Note that you only pay for the trip to the islands—the return fare is included in the price. The shortest trip to the islands is from Bostanci landing on the Asian side. Another, less frequent boat from pier 5 goes to **Yalova**, across the Marmara; there are also boats from Kabataş to Yalova. From the pier to the left of the Galata Bridge on the Stamboul side (pier 6), a boat leaves every half-hour to go up the **Golden Horn** to Eyüp and beyond.

Other boats leave from the docks near Tophane Square for Marmara Island (5 hours) and Avşa Island (6 hours), in the Marmara, and for Mudanya, the port of Bursa. Ticket booths are never clearly marked; in some cases you cannot buy tickets in advance, but most lines run on tokens that can be used anytime. Don't expect to find time-tables posted, or any sort of system; the chaos of the Istanbul ferries is perfect and impenetrable. Just go and ask; with luck, someone behind a window will sell you some sort of ticket or token. Then, when you see a crowd gathering around a boat, try and push your way to the front.

car hire

If you're willing to risk the Istanbul traffic, and ridiculously high rates, the major car hire chains are here:

Avis: airport, ✆ 663 0646, Taksim Square, ✆ 241 78 96
Budget: airport, ✆ 663 0858, Taksim Square, ✆ 253 9200
Europcar: airport, ✆ 663 0746; Taksim Square, ✆ 254 7788

The tourist office has a long list of (often cheaper) local firms. At a pinch, try:

Er Rent, Topçu Caddesi, Taksim, ✆ 235 5990
Oscar, Mustafa Kemal Paşa Caddesi, ✆ 588 3057

For anyone driving in Istanbul, some explanation is in order. First of all traffic is nowhere near as insane as many would have it; from end to end of the town, it hardly ever moves fast enough to let the Turkish driver express himself. Parking is the real problem. Don't worry so much about parking tickets—but if you leave your beast in a really dumb place it could well be towed.

Tourist Information

Sultanahmet: facing the Aya Sofia; ✆ 518 1802
Beyoğlu: Meşrutiyet Caddesi 57, ✆ 243 2928

Taksim Square: in the Hilton Hotel lobby, ✆ 233 0592
Karaköy: at the cruise ship dock, ✆ 249 5776
Yeşilköy: Atatürk airport, ✆ 663 6363
Tourist Police: Yerebatan Caddesi 2, near the Aya Sofia: ✆ 527 4503
TTOK: Halaskargazi Caddesi 364, ✆ 231 4631

post offices

Branches are all over town, including one in the Covered Market and one in Istiklâl Caddesi, Galatasaray, but the big one is near Sirkeci Station, on Yeni Postane Caddesi. This is where you should have Poste Restante mail sent: *Post Restante, Büyük Postane, Yeni Postane Caddesi, Istanbul*. All big offices have telephone services, which usually stay open until 10pm or even midnight.

laundry

Behind the Aya Sofia on Caferiye Sokak is Hobby Laundry which, in addition to offering a fully automatic washing and drying service, will serve you tea and coffee while you wait. Open every day 9am–8pm.

maps and publications

All the usual rules for Turkish cities apply here: there are no street signs, streets are known by different names to different people, and many people know nothing of the city outside their own neighbourhood. Although the map handed out by the tourist office is perfectly adequate for most needs, if you plan to do any detailed sightseeing, you'll want a better one; of the several available, the best are published by the Turkish Automobile Club (available at their offices) and by Keskin Colour (from hotels, news stands, and shops in the tourist centres).

Currently, the indispensable reference for events in the city, culture, shopping, etc. is a monthly publication in English called *The Guide*, available from any of the bookshops listed below. *Hello Istanbul*, a free monthly guide to the city, is available from hotels. The best selection of books in English about Istanbul and Turkey will be found in the booksellers' stalls of the **Sahaflar Çarşisi**, on the Beyazit Square side of the Covered Market. Another good place is the bookshop in the lobby of the Sheraton Hotel on Taksim Square. Other shops offer somewhat less: most of these can be found along Istiklâl Caddesi, just north of the Tünel: *Haşet, Sander* and *ABC*. They also sell the previous day's editions of Europe's leading quality papers, plus *Time* and *Newsweek*. For the British tabloids, try the kiosk at the Yeni Cami end of the Spice Market.

money

Those needing a bank over the weekend will find one open, 9.30am–4pm, at the entrance to the Topkapi Saray. Istanbul also has two 24-hour post offices, one near Sirkeci railway station (the main PTT on Postane Caddesi), the other at Kadiköy in Asia. The Galatasaray office, on Istiklâl Caddesi, has fax facilities and is open until 8pm. Local post offices close at 6pm. Most people change money at the little *döviz* offices that have sprung up all over the city; you'll generally get a better rate, and with some asking around you'll find one that takes travellers' cheques.

Credit Card Hotlines

American Express: ✆ 230 4792
Mastercard/Eurocard: ✆ 250 6070
VISA: ✆ 266 0620
Diners Club: ✆ 275 0510

youth discount card

Good value for those under 26, this can be purchased from the front desk of the ·Interyouth Hostel on Caferiye Sokak behind the Aya Sofia. It grants free admission to most government-maintained museums, such as the Topkapi Saray and the Aya Sofia, and pays for itself after only two or three visits. Keep hold of the card; it's valid throughout Turkey.

Orientation

A brief orientation will help much in sorting out the complexities of the layout. Note that there are three parts. On the European side, the triangular peninsula south of the estuary of the Golden Horn is **Stamboul**, the old town—formerly Constantinople and Byzantium—which rises like Rome on seven hills, surrounded by the largely intact Byzantine walls; most of the sights—the Aya Sofia, Topkapi Palace, the Covered Market, Süleymaniye and the Blue Mosque—are concentrated within the square mile of its tip. We mention this only because you may not notice. Whether you're walking or in a cab, the impenetrable maze of meandering streets makes them all appear to be in different parts of the city. Take time to study the map before you set out.

Two bridges span the **Golden Horn**: the Atatürk and the famous, newly-rebuilt Galata, connecting old Istanbul with **Beyoğlu**, the 'European quarter' ever since Italian merchants colonized it in the latter days of Byzantium. Its outer fringes have been fashionable for two centuries now. Galata Bridge, and the Eminönü Square behind it in the old town, are the nearest thing Istanbul has to a centre; the busy comings and goings here were a feature of Istanbul life before there was a bridge, going back to the days of the Byzantines.

Ferryboats from Galata Bridge go to the districts of the Asian shore: **Kadiköy**, **Haydarpaşa** and others. The Bosphorus protects them, and has kept them quiet residential suburbs for centuries. Up the Bosphorus, Istanbul's metropolitan area has absorbed the picturesque villages on both sides, almost as far as the Black Sea.

The Streets of Istanbul

You may come to this city for the monuments and museums, to see the sultan's jewels or the gold of the Byzantine mosaics, or simply to watch the sunset over the skyline of minarets and domes. The fantasies you entertain may be out of the Arabian Nights or an Eric Ambler spy thriller of the 1930s. Whatever your particular purpose, take care that you keep your eyes and ears open to the life in the streets. This is the real Istanbul, for which the mosques and palaces are merely decoration, and the people of the city have had centuries to cultivate this life of Istanbul into an art form.

Especially in the small things, Istanbul has sacrificed little to modernity. If your hotel is in one of the older residential districts, like Aksaray or Sultanahmet, you are likely to be awakened to the

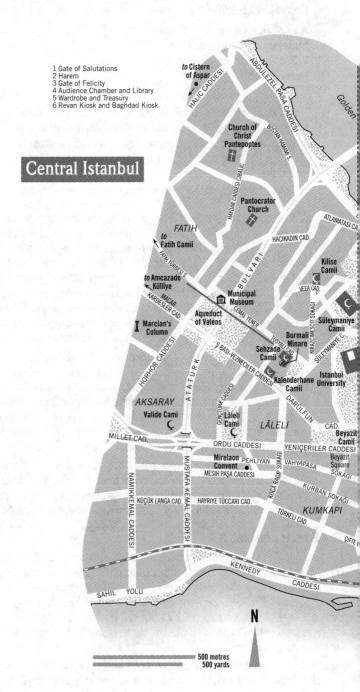

1 Gate of Salutations
2 Harem
3 Gate of Felicity
4 Audience Chamber and Library
5 Wardrobe and Treasury
6 Revan Kiosk and Baghdad Kiosk

Central Istanbul

to Cistern
of Aspar

HALIÇ CADDESI

ABDÜLEZEL PAŞA CADDESI

BOSTAN HAMAMI S.

Golden

Church of
Christ
Pantepoptes

Pantocrator
Church

ATLAMATAŞI CA.

HAYDAR CADDESI CIBALI

FATIH

HACIKADIN CAD.

to Fatih Camii

FATIH TÜRBESI S.

BULVARI

Kilise
Camii

to Amcazade
Külliye

VEFA CAD.

MACAR
KARDEŞLER CAD.

Municipal
Museum

CEMAL YENER

KIRAZLIMEŞCIT SOKAĞI

Süleymaniye
Camii

Aqueduct
of Valens

SÜLEYMANIYE C.

Marcian's
Column

Burmali
Minare

Istanbul
University

HORHOR CADDESI

Ş BAŞI-VEZNECILER CADDESI

TOSTALI CAD.

Şehzade
Camii

Kalenderhane
Camii

ATATÜRK

DARÜLFÜN

AKSARAY

GENÇTÜRK CADDESI

Lâleli
Cami

LÂLELI

CAD.

Valide Cami

Beyazit
Camii

MILLET CAD.

ORDU CADDESI

YENIÇERILER CADDESI

Mirelaon
Convent

PEHLIYAN

VAHYAPAŞA

Beyazit
Square

MESIH PAŞA CADDESI

KOCA RAGIP SOKAĞI

SOKAĞI

MUSTAFA KEMAL CADDESI

KURBAN SOKAĞI

NAMIKKEMAL CADDESI

KÜÇÜK LANGA CAD.

HAYRIYE TÜCCARI CAD.

KUMKAPI

TÜRKELI CAD.

ÇIFTE

KENNEDY

CADDESI

SAHIL YOLU

N

500 metres
500 yards

to
↑ Balikpazari

Şişhane
Square

Tünel

BEYOĞLU

Museum
of Divan
Literature

Tophane
Square

to Nüsretiye
Cami

St Benoit
Church

Kiliç Ali
Paşa Camii

YOLCUZADE CAD.

OKUMUSA CAD.

AIRZIYA PAŞA CAD.

GALIPPEDE CAD.

MÜKSEKKALDIRAM

KUMBARACI YOKUŞU

KEMERALTI CADDESI

Galata
Tower

Arap Cami

TERSANE CADDESI

VOYVODA CAD.

NECATIBEY CADDESI

GALATA MÜMHANE

Atatürk
Bridge

Horn

Tünel

Yeralti Cami

Karaköy
Square

To Üsküdar

Galata
Bridge

Bosphorus

UNKAPANI EMINÖNÜ

TAHTAKALE CADDESI

Rüstem Paşa
Camii

Eminönü
Square

EMINÖNÜ

Yeni
Camii

Ferry Docks

Seraglio Point

Atatürk
Monument

HASIRCILAR CAD.

SIYAVUŞŞA SOK.

HAMIDIYE CADDESI

Spice
Market

SIRKECI

KENNEDY   CADDESI

HESPÇESME CAD.

UZUN ÇARŞI CADDESI

FIRINCLAR

YENI POSTANE CAD.

YOKUŞU

CADDESI

Sirkeci
Station

Goths'
Column

Beyazit
Tower

FUATPAŞA CAD.

MAHMUT PAŞA

Main
Post Office

M. HUDAVENDIGAR

EBUSSUUT CAD.

HATUN CAD.

Archaeology Museum,
Museum of the
Ancient Orient,
Çinili Kiosk

6

4   5

2
3

Şahaflar
Çarsisi

Beyazit
Camii

Mehmet Paşa
Camii

BEZCILER SOK.

TÜRKOCAĞI CAD.

ANKARA

Vilâyet

Cağaloğlu
Baths

Sublime
Porte

Gülhane
Park

Aya Irene

Topkapi
Saray

Covered
Market

Çorlulu Ali
Paşa Medrese

Nuruosmaniye
Camii NURUOSMANIYE CAD.

CAGALOĞLU

Çemberlitaş

YEREBATAN C.

SULTANAHMET

Karamustafa
Medrese

Atik Ali
Paşa Camii

DIVAN

BABIALI CAD.

KLOT FARER

Kaiser Wilhelm
II Fountain

Yerabatan
Sarayi

AYEMDAR CAD.

SOĞUK-ÇESME
SOK.

Bab-i Humayun

PIYERLOTI
CAD.

YOLU

Firuz Ağa
Camii

MIMAR MEHMET AĞA

Fountain of
Ahmed III

TIYATRO CADDESI

TÜLCU SOK.

Museum of Turkish
and Islamic Arts

Sultanahmet
Sq.

Aya
Sofia

ŞAPRASCA CAD.

Mehmet Paşa
Camii

Binbirdirek
Cistern

TERZIHANE SOK.

Hipodrome

Blue
Mosque

Aya Sofia
Baths

KABASAKAL KUTLUGÜN SOK.

KADIRGA CADDESI

TAVUKHANE

Küçük
Aya Sofia

AYASOFYA CAD.

Mosaic
Museum

CANKURTARAN CAD.

S. KÜÇÜK

MUSTAFA-PAŞA S.

YOLU

Bucoleon
Palace

SAHIL

Sea   of

Marmara

85

cry, *Nefis ... simit, simit ...*—'exquisite *simits*'—and the
man who carries these sesame-encrusted circles of bread,
on a stick or in a glass box, may differ only in dress from
those in 16th-century prints. If you were a Stamboullu,
you might drop down a basket on a long rope for one. After
the *simit* man comes the tinker's rattling empty cart, and his long
unintelligible cries seem less a plea for trade than an eternal rambling
monologue on God's unfairness to tinkers.

Of course there are street markets: some of the old quarters are named
after the day of the week on which they would occur. In Istanbul,
though, in the Middle Eastern manner every street is an actual
or potential market. Some have permanent sites: by Galata
Bridge each morning, housewives and stray cats circle
around tired fishermen, angling for their share of the day's
catch, while, opposite, in the narrow maze of streets
climbing to the Covered Bazaar, the metal doors bang open
to reveal thousands of tiny shops, segregated into streets
according to their trade: an avenue of baby clothes, a street
of copper pots, a cul-de-sac of used Korans. More money
probably changes hands on the bridge itself than in a large
department store. On Galata Bridge, on any given day you
may spend a few lira on socks, wind-up monkeys, copies of
the Turkish Highway Code, contraband blue jeans, clothes
hangers, pastel knickers, aubergines, spanner sets (English
or metric), bicycle mirrors, hamsters, or portraits of Mehmet the Conqueror. Turkish street
vendors are nothing if not up-to-date. Recently we spotted a young man on the bridge selling
satellite dishes.

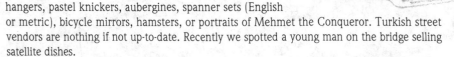

SIMIT-SELLER

To all these, add the shoeshine boys: young apprentices with cheap wooden boxes and old
paint tins to sit on, and dignified professionals with dozens of cut-glass bottles in gold-plated
cases, embellished with scenes of Mecca and autographed pictures of overripe chanteuses.
Sellers of sherbet, *ayran*, unidentifiable pastries, and even water, abound. The fellows with the
jingling sacks and packs of untaxed Marlboros are on the lowest rung of Turkish organized
crime; you choose a number, pick a numbered token from the sack, and if you click, the
Marlboros are yours. You can try your hand at shooting with the young men who have
invested their capital in an air rifle and target, or patronize the poorest of all, those whose business consists of a single rusted set of bathroom scales, waiting to weigh all-comers—perhaps
10 people a day, when business is good.

As background, add the beggars (more than in Paris, fewer than in Philadelphia), military
policemen, hosts of shabby-genteel cats and pigeons, farmers on donkeys, sleek 1949 Chrysler
dolmuş cabs—still with their original half-ton of chrome, tourists from Iran and Indiana, seven
hills, 1300 minarets, gypsies, ferryboats, Roman cisterns, and the strangest Art Nouveau buildings east of Palma de Mallorca.

The older neighbourhoods have no monopoly on all this; it is the everyday ambience the
Stamboullu takes for granted, varying in degree from the venerable precincts of Eminönü and
Sultanahmet to the newer streets around Taksim Square and those on the Asian side. Try not to

be too influenced by preconceptions. Istanbul is not especially dirty or dilapidated. The old town is the real surprise. Following Turkish rather than European ideas of town planning, there are lots of trees, and the houses are as spread out as land values permit. Many of the outlying districts are really suburbs within the Theodosian walls, or better, aggregations of villages.

The Seven Hills

Constantine very consciously meant to make his foundation the New Rome; that was its name, at first, until the emperor's vanity overcame him. Like the old Rome, it had a golden milestone, a senate house, and a forum; to govern it, Constantine divided it up into fourteen wards, just as Rome had been, and most importantly for imperial continuity, he declared that it had seven hills. Finding some of these requires an effort of the imagination.

Only these three reach any height: the **First Hill**, where the Topkapi Palace and Aya Sofia are; the **Fifth Hill** along the Golden Horn with the Fener and the Selimiye Mosque; and the **Third Hill**, crowned by the Süleymaniye. None of the others will strain your legs: the **Second Hill**, roughly north of the Burnt Column; the **Fourth Hill**, around the Fatih Mosque; the **Sixth Hill**, at the Topkapi Gate, the centre of the land walls; and the **Seventh Hill**, in the southwest corner of the city.

Old Istanbul (Stamboul)

Sultanahmet Square

Most visitors begin their tours of Istanbul in the old city in **Sultanahmet Square**, the lovely garden of fountains and flowers between Aya Sofia and the Blue Mosque. A pavilion housing a very helpful **Tourist Information Centre** is here, near the **Kaiser Wilhelm II Fountain**, a small gift from Sultan Abdülhamid's big brother in Berlin, in the days when Germany was the declining Ottoman Empire's greatest ally. The low buildings along the southern edge, the **Aya Sofia Baths**, are among the few that survived the modern reconstruction of the square, when acres of Ottoman buildings were cleared (*see* below, p.91).

If you could have stood here in Byzantine times, however, you would have been in the city's grand ceremonial square, the **Augusteion**. Just to the left of Aya Sofia, the main street of the city entered through the Bronze Gate. A tall column bearing a golden statue of Justinian stood in front of the church, and near it was the golden milestone from which all distances in the empire were measured. The baths of Zeuxippos, a domed structure probably not unlike the modern Turkish hamams, occupied the western edge of the square and next to this, the bulk of the Hippodrome could be seen behind the towers of St Stephen's. The south edge fronted the Senate House, where the last remnant of the Roman Republic survived as a rubber-stamp council almost until the end of Byzantium. In this square the emperors could be seen at their accessions, and on the feast days of the Church. After the sack of 1204, when the Crusaders looted the square of its gold and ornaments, the area drifted gradually into ruin. Already the emperors had moved to the Blachernae Palace in the suburbs, and the restored empire after 1261 lacked the resources even to keep up the Aya Sofia. One traveller of the 14th century wrote of finding the great church eerily empty, its doors lying on the ground.

You may feel the same, and may hear the ghostly echo of Justinian's 'Solomon, I have surpassed thee!', as you walk under the dome of the denuded church, once glowing with golden mosaics and chandeliers, a golden altar and iconostasis; now it is just chilly, dark and old.

The Aya Sofia

Since 1933, the Aya Sofia has been a museum, and lacks even the prayer rugs and mihrab to relieve the tremendous desolation. Even so, in its present state, the lack of ornamentation perhaps makes the beauty and audacity of the architecture easier to appreciate. Undoubtedly this is the greatest dome in Christendom, though St Peter's in Rome and St Paul's in London are larger. In the 6th century, nothing like the Aya Sofia had ever been built, or even imagined, and, even today, the impression it makes cannot be experienced anywhere else.

The original Aya Sofia, which the Byzantines called simply the Great Church, was built by Theodosius II in 415, on the site of an even earlier church built under Constantine the Great. Theodosius' Aya Sofia burned during the street battles of the Nike Revolt. To provide a symbol for his dreams of imperial grandeur, and to a certain extent to justify them, Justinian determined to rebuild as quickly and as large as possible. The cornerstone of his new church was laid exactly 40 days after the suppression of the revolt.

Building Aya Sofia

The two men chosen to design the church were not really architects. Not long before, the emperor had decreed an end to the Athenian Academy, the centre of learning of the classical world, and the last stronghold of philosophy untainted by the Gospels. In doing so, he put two of the greatest mathematicians of the age, Anthemius of Tralles (modern Aydin) and Isidore of Miletus, out of work. Between them, they accepted the job, and got it built in only five years. The imperial treasury had been strained to the limit, but the new Great Church was consecrated in solemn ceremony on 26 December 537, St Stephen's Day.

The difficulties in the construction were manifold; no architect alive had experience of a task of such magnitude. Improvisation was a daily necessity. The four massive piers on which the entire structure is hung have stones held together not with mortar, but with molten lead. The distinctive shape of Aya Sofia's capitals is no mere design conceit, such as those of the classical Greeks; it is absolutely necessary to the structure. The 'impost capital', as it is called, had already been invented to give proper support to arches and vaults, but here it was perfected. One of the problems was reconciling the strengths and weaknesses of so many different types of stone. Just as the emperor spared no expense in getting in the best architects and workmen, every variety of stone in the empire is represented here: green marble from the Peloponnese, yellow from Libya, rose from Phrygia and Lydia, great slabs of porphyry that were floated down the Nile from upper Egypt. Ancient buildings were looted for tall columns; of those in the galleries, the red are from the Temple of the Sun in Baalbek, the green probably from the Artemision of Ephesus.

In the Church

One enters just as a Byzantine commoner would, through side gates in the outer porch (the exonarthex). The centre gate was for the emperor alone, and it continues through a long thin hall to the narthex. Here, where the emperor passed into the church itself, one of the surviving gold mosaics portrays Emperor Leo IV kneeling before a seated Christ. Below, on the brass lintel, the Holy Spirit descends with a book, open to the words, 'The Lord said, "I am the door of the sheep: By me if any man enter in ... he shall find pasture."' An empty throne stands concealed behind.

One of the first things Atatürk did after converting Aya Sofia to a museum was to arrange for the restoration of the mosaics. The work was done over the next two decades by the Byzantine Institute, a private organization in Boston. Justinian's church had none. Mosaics were a later fashion, and those that remain—of the estimated 4 acres—date mostly from the 9th century or later, after the defeat of the Iconoclasts.

You, of course, may usurp the emperor's privilege and walk right in. The central gate opens at the rear of the great nave. As you pass through, stop, turn and look up at the best-preserved mosaic of the Aya Sofia. It shows the Virgin Mary cradling the infant Jesus. To her right, Constantine offers her the city of Constantinople; to her left, Justinian proffers the Aya Sofia. More mosaics, mostly geometric and floral patterns, cover the rest of the narthex roof. Though these have not yet been restored, they will give you some idea of how the decoration of the church's interior must have looked.

As you approach the centre of the church, you realize the particular architectural problem Anthemius and Isidore faced, and their brilliant solution. From preference, and for reasons of grace and symmetry, with a little bit of geometric mysticism mixed in as well, the emperor desired a central plan, symmetrical on two axes. The forms of Byzantine ritual, however, required a basilica-plan church with a long nave. To accomplish this, Anthemius flanked his dome with two semi-domes along the axis of the nave and enclosed the space under the lateral arches with solid walls full of windows. Underneath these, the mass is distributed down to the ground through a network of smaller semi-domes (exedrae), vaults and columns, thus opening to the light a space six times the area of the dome. This conquest of gravity is the magic of Aya Sofia. Sixth-century chroniclers tell of visitors and citizens afraid to enter lest all collapse, or becoming dizzy trying to look at the top of the dome, 181ft above the floor. The Byzantines always spoke of this dome as being suspended from heaven by a golden chain.

Artistic details in the interior are few; little survived the Iconoclasts, the Crusaders, and the Muslims. The bronze doors of the narthex are original, and the monograms of Justinian and Theodora can be seen on many of the capitals. The largest mosaic, on the apse above the place where the altar stood, is a portrait of the *Virgin Mary with the infant Jesus*; below it, figures of the Archangels Michael and Gabriel can be made out. In place of the altar and iconostasis, only the Muslim mihrab and mimber fill the void, along with the raised loge built for the prayers of the sultans, with Iznik tiles and fine carved wood details. The four huge medallions on the columns, painted calligraphically with the names of Allah, Mohammed and the early caliphs, were removed by Atatürk but have recently been replaced as a gesture to the Muslim fundamentalists (also, recently they have started broadcasting the call to prayer from Aya Sofia's minarets). Above the medallions, four sinister-looking Byzantine seraphs stare down from the pendentives.

The Muslims, like the Greeks, segregated their women, putting them upstairs in the spacious galleries around the nave, making them climb about 50ft of ramps to get there. It's worth the walk, for the view and for the best of the remaining mosaics. In the centre of the galleries, at the far end of the church, two green columns from Ephesus mark the place where the empresses worshipped. The ladies, in fact, had only the **North Gallery**; the **South Gallery** was reserved for the rest of the imperial family; the Turks gave the lovely screen that partitioned it off the fanciful title of 'Gates of Heaven and Hell'. A celebrated series of the 13th-century mosaics, one of the last improvements to the church under the Byzantines, can be seen around the gallery: *Emperor John Comnenus* and his family, *Empress Zoe* and her third husband (his face painted over that of number two) and Jesus with Mary, and John the Baptist. On the floor near this last one is a slab inscribed with the name Henrico Dandolo, the aged, bitter Duke of Venice who led the Sack of 1204. Surprisingly, the Greeks never disinterred him when they recaptured the city; the Turks did, within weeks of Mehmet's conquest. This south gallery often served for the transaction of church business; two General Church Councils, the second and the sixth, were held in it. High on a wall of the adjacent gallery is a faded mosaic of the *Emperor Alexander* who ruled only from 912 to 913. The inscription above his diademed head reads: 'Lord help thy servant, the orthodox and faithful Emperor Alexander.' Lord help him indeed. He was an habitual drunkard who died of apoplexy after a particularly heavy session.

You may be disconcerted to see that very few of the columns of the galleries are actually in plumb. Some list at alarming angles, many are cracked and bound with iron rings, and the impression of a house of cards is inescapable. Even before Atatürk, the Turks kept a constant vigil over this fabulous patient, on and off the critical list for 14 centuries. Anthemius and Isidore, for all their skill, could not make their church perfect. The dome, shallow enough now, was originally 20ft lower, and had to be reconstructed when a 40-day series of earthquakes toppled it in 558. In the 10th century, the next thorough restoration kept the church closed for 10 years. Again in the 14th century, a collapse seemed imminent; the emperors scraped the bottom of the treasury to construct the four colossal buttresses that so mar the exterior. No more money could be found to complete the repairs, and by the time of the Conquest, the church was no longer in use. Mehmet added more buttresses and the first minaret, and Mimar Sinan himself tore down much of the ruined old imperial quarter to get stone for further strengthening. Seven thorough restorations since have accomplished the preservation of the mosaics and the reinforcement of the dome with steel; specialists are still on guard for any further signs of weakness. The galleries, they say, are in no danger now— though yet another extensive (and expensive) restoration programme is now under way; expect the interior to be graced with plenty of scaffolding for years to come.

The theology of the Muslims would, on the whole, have seemed almost acceptable to a man like Justinian, and, as fate would have it, the Muslims were to be the vehicle for preserving his symbol and his dream over the centuries. Justinian must surely have thought the building of his church would mark the advent of a new world age. His choice of men from the Academy to put it up was as much symbolic as practical. Here, the entire harvest of classical science and philosophy was to serve the ends of the Christian God. The Muslims, who already had taken their own deep draughts of Greek thought, felt entirely at home after 1453. More than any other place in the Christian or Islamic worlds, this is the great house of monotheism, the place where human understanding and accomplishment were recognized as the Divine Wisdom, the *Hagia Sofia* both faiths believed it to be.

Around Aya Sofia

Just outside the main entrance, recent excavations have uncovered the foundations of the portico of Theodosius's church; an architect's reconstruction posted by the door shows an elegant classical building, architecturally a bit old-fashioned. Some bits of the columns and the cornice have survived, with reliefs of the Lamb of God.

The Muslims had more of a sense of humour than the Christians. In the **mausoleums** they built around Aya Sofia's garden were interred nearly all the worst of the worst Ottoman sultans: Mustafa I, an imbecile and tool of the Janissaries, Ibrahim the Mad, the ultimate libertine who picked off his subjects from the Topkapi walls for target practice, and Selim the Sot, whose honorific tells us all we need to know. His mausoleum, decorated with fine Iznik tiles, is a work of Mimar Sinan. Facing the row of mausoleums is the pretty, covered **Fountain of Mehmet II**, and a primary school built by the same Sultan in 1742.

Behind the Aya Sofia, adjoining the walls of the Topkapi Saray, the indefatigable restorationists of the Turkish Automobile Club have rebuilt an entire street of characteristic Ottoman wooden houses, **Soğukçeşme Sokak** ('Cool Fountain Street'), many of which are now in use as guest houses. This is only one part of their plan for beautifying the centre of old Stamboul. South of the Blue Mosque, they have a complex including shops in a restored medrese and the lovely wooden **Yeşil Ev Hotel**, one of the best-restored examples of Ottoman vernacular architecture in Istanbul.

Also behind the church, a famous monument of the Tulip Period can be seen as introduction to another aspect of Turkish architecture. The **Fountain of Ahmed III**, built in 1729, really a small pavilion, is covered with a wealth of green and blue tiles painted in floral motifs, and with verses of the emperor who built it. Currently under restoration, its tiles and gilt trim will soon shine with their original splendour, highlighting one of the finest works of the Ottoman 18th century, one that captures perfectly the super-refined and delicate sensibility of the 'Tulip Period'. There is much more of this behind the walls of Topkapi; the outer gate, the **Bab-i-Humayun**, stands only a few yards away.

Between the Aya Sofia and the Blue Mosque, the Aya Sofia baths have become the **Turkish Handwoven Carpet Sales Centre**. Don't let the name fool you. Once Sultanahmet's most elegant, most regal hamam, this was built by Sinan in 1556 on the orders of Süleyman the Magnificent to honour his favourite wife, the cunning and perfidious Roxelana. The first room is domed, and adorned with 16 lovely arched stained-glass windows. The baths lead on through three rooms into the central steam room, with numerous cubicles secreted away around it for more personal bathing, and continue onwards for its full length. This was a double hamam, men bathing at one end, women at the other. Ignore the carpets draped everywhere and picture the place as it once was, a haven of refreshment for the empire's most illustrious. Or if you're crazy for carpets, compare what is on offer here with the fine antique works in the **Museum of Turkish Carpets and Kilims**, just around the corner on Mimar Mehmet Ağa Caddesi (*open daily exc Sun and Mon, 9–4; adm*).

The Blue Mosque (Sultanahmet Camii)

Across the square from Aya Sofia, Sultan Ahmet in 1619 constructed the Sultanahmet, or the Blue Mosque, like a matching bookend—not so much to compete with the old church, but because all the other available sites already had big mosques on them. Even then, he had to knock down the palaces of several of his ministers in order to make space. None of the city's other monuments has occasioned more argument; some critics claim it is the finest work of architecture in the city, while others say it is overdone and uninspired. Certainly there are no new departures in the plan; just another copy of the Aya Sofia, only more rigidly symmetrical than the others. Like Mimar Sinan's mosques, the plan is an almost perfect square.

The main attraction here is the 21,043 blue Iznik tiles inside, predominantly painted with the blue arabesques that give the mosque its familiar name. Each one of these tiles set Ahmet back 18 *akçes*—twice the daily wage of a teacher in the palace school. The great dome, 70ft across, stands on four semi-domes, each of these on three exedrae and each of the exedrae on two arches; it doesn't hang, magically suspended, like the dome of the Aya Sofia and if you've seen the Byzantine church first, this may well disappoint. Also, the columns tend to crowd out all else, an effect worsened in season by the press of fellow visitors. At any time, two-thirds of the mosque will be given over to Muslims at prayer and a rail zealously watched by a mosque official separates the faithful from the flummoxed. The imperial loge is a lattice of pure marble, and the window shutters are of exquisite design, inlaid with ivory, mother-of-pearl and tortoiseshell. The windows, all 260 of them, are not original and could be better. At the same time the Ottoman Empire was collapsing, so were the windows of the Blue Mosque, and their replacements do little to complement the marvellous tiles.

Ahmet was sure he was building for the ages, and with an arrogance possible only to a Commander of the Faithful, he had his architect, Mehmet Ağa, build six minarets instead of the two or four customary in Ottoman imperial mosques. Previously, only the shrine of the Ka'aba in Mecca had been allowed six, and after a shrill chorus of protests from the divines of Islam, Ahmet was forced to send Mehmet Ağa down to Mecca to build a seventh. Don't forget this; knowing that the Blue Mosque is the one with six minarets may come in handy sometime when you're good and lost in old Stamboul. Also unusual in this mosque are the rows of great doors around the lovely courtyard—36 of them, all leading nowhere.

Ahmet died young at 27 and was buried near his creation; his *türbe* stands in the square between the mosque and the Aya Sofia. Buried with him are his wife and his sons, two of whom, Osman II and Murat IV, went on to the sultanate themselves. As in the great mosque, the tiles on the walls are from Iznik.

Topkapi Saray

Buildings and museums open daily 9.30–5; closed Tues in winter; adm. There is a separate admission to the Harem buildings, with guided tours offered hourly 10–4 in various languages—check ahead for times of tours in English.

Immediately after the Conquest, Mehmet Fatih built his first palace on the hill north of Beyazit Square. In 1468, he began a summer palace on the beautiful and largely unoccupied hill at the tip of the peninsula, where the Golden Horn joins the Bosphorus. Later sultans favoured the site, and Süleyman the Magnificent was the first to move here permanently. Most of the present buildings are from the 18th century; by then the sultans had made themselves captives in this lovely soap-bubble of a world. Some of them spent more of their revenues here than in all the rest of the empire. Even though much of the Topkapi's treasures were sold off in the 19th century, when the Empire was constantly facing bankruptcy, the hoard that survives is incredible, including the richest collections of porcelain and emeralds in the world. There's hardly enough space to display all the trinkets the Sultans squirreled away here—the curators say they can only show about 3 per cent of it at a time.

The hill had been the acropolis of ancient Byzantium, with two theatres on its slopes over-looking the Bosphorus, several temples, a stadium, and an arsenal and drill field called the *Strategion*. Just inside the Bab-i Humayun stood the little city's main square, the *Tetrastoon*. Not a trace of any of this remains, and we know surprisingly little of the use the quarter was put to after Constantine.

Tulips

The Great Tulip Speculation of the 17th century is one of the oddities of European history. In Germany, France, and Holland, these flowers briefly became an obsession pursued with the kind of fervour we now devote only to gold bullion and commodity futures. The bulbs of some exotic vari-eties actually brought more than their weight in gold; great financial houses and canny opportunists rose and fell with the fortunes of their favourite blooms, and tulip quotes filled coffee-house conversation as stock market closings do today. The Turks can take all the credit. Tulips, like cherries, pizza, parchment, and angora wool, are among Anatolia's contributions to civilization.

A century later, it was the Turks' turn to get silly over tulips. What Ottoman historians call the 'Tulip Period' is generally associated with the reign of Ahmet III (1703–20). Here the sultans and their court reached their most Chinese extreme of abstraction and contrived refinement, while their empire careered into decay. With their wedding cake turbans, layers of silk and brocades, and turned-up slippers, the bizarrely decorous Ottomans made a picture that fascinated contemporary Europe. Night garden parties among the tulips were the rage, illuminated by candles on the backs of wandering turtles.

Tulip art—for the sultan interested himself in little else—can best be seen in the lovely tiled chambers of the Topkapi harem. If you want to see what started all the hubbub, there are wild tulips in the national parks around Ankara and Yozgat.

First Courtyard

The **Bab-i Humayun**, a simple stone gate, looks to have been more for defence than decora-tion, and it was. The many revolts and skirmishes of the empire's decadent years put it to the test. Mahmud II hid here from his bloodthirsty Janissaries. Whatever the outcome, the gate would usually be adorned with the heads of the losers. Through it, one enters the **First Courtyard**, a large park. Two centuries ago, it was full of the palace outbuildings: the imperial mint, and, most importantly, the barracks of the Janissaries. From this spot this praetorian guard was able to keep a constant watch on its sultans, standing between them and any hope of aid from the outside world. Mahmud demolished their buildings soon after their demise in the Auspicious Event.

In the same year Aya Sofia was completed, Justinian and Theodora dedicated a smaller church, the **Aya Irene**, just behind it. The two churches shared a common sanctuary, but were cut off from each other when the Turks enclosed Aya Irene in the First Courtyard. The site may have originally been occupied by a temple of Aphrodite; like the Aya Sofia, the church you see now replaced a work of Theodosius burned down in the Nike Riots. Aya Irene, the Divine Peace, was never used as a mosque: its keys were given to the Janissaries who, following the precepts of the Bektaşi order of dervishes, were never allowed to enter a mosque. Instead, they used it as their arsenal, and kept it in surprisingly good shape over the centuries. The church is a basilica in form, but with a small dome and transepts, a very unusual plan for a Byzantine work. On the apse where the altar stood, a simple black and gold mosaic of a cross is believed to be original. For a while under the republic, Aya Irene was kept open as a military museum making use of the curiosities accumulated over the years by the Janissaries. The church is now closed to the public, although occasionally used for concerts during the Istanbul festival.

Gate of Salutations

At the end of the First Courtyard stands another wall and the **Gate of Salutations**, the entrance to the official part of the Saray for which permission was required to enter; now it's where you buy the ticket. The medieval air of this gate, with its conical spires, is no accident. Süleyman was so taken with the castles and churches of Hungary when he campaigned there that he brought back Hungarian architects to build it for him. One of the customs of this gate was that no one except the sultan and his mother might pass through it on horseback. The head gardener of the Saray had his office here; this is a good example of the Turkish fancy for euphemism, for the 'gardeners' were really armed guards who shared fully in the palace intrigues, and the 'head gardener' was none other than the sultan's chief executioner. The block, and the fountain in which he washed his blade, can be seen near this gate, along with the 'warning stone' on which severed heads would be displayed *pour encourager les autres*.

Second Courtyard: Court of the Divan and Harem

The next courtyard, the **Court of the Divan**, was divided between the highest council chamber of government and the palace kitchens; this arrangement would never seem silly to an Ottoman, for whom all real government was embodied in the person of the sultan. For *Divan*, understand the sultan's cabinet; the vezirs met once a week in the Divan hall, under its tower on the left-hand side of the courtyard. The earlier sultans would have been present at these meetings, where the affairs of the government were discussed. Süleyman introduced the screen to keep his vezirs honest; they could never know if he were behind it listening or not. His successors hardly went to the Divan at all.

Unfortunately, most of the Divan chambers are usually closed, but they may let you in to see the lovely, thoroughly restored 16th-century council chamber. Other rooms house a collection of arms and armour, including the swords of many of the sultans. From a distance, the landmark of the entire palace complex is the Divan's **tower**, built in 1825 by Mahmut II as a watchtower, and strangely reminiscent of a New England church steeple.

The Divan is attached to the **Harem**, a group of buildings and courtyards that cover one-sixth of the total area of the Saray. Süleyman began its construction when his favourite wife Roxelana convinced him he could not live without her; as power devolved upon the ladies and their eunuchs, later sultans expanded it into the labyrinthine complex we see today. After Abdülmecit moved to the Dolmabahçe Palace in 1853, the surviving favourites of his predecessors lived on here, lonely and forgotten, some well into the 20th century.

Birds in a Gilded Cage

Harems are good business, as the Turkish Culture Ministry well knows; not only do they make a fair amount of the money needed for the palace's upkeep from Harem tours, but nearly every summer, as part of the Istanbul Festival, they put on a production of Mozart's *Entführung aus dem Serail* in the Harem courtyard. Tickets sell out fast. *Harem* is really an

MÜDÜRLÜĞÜ
ELEDİYESİ

ÖRENYERİ

0870

Arabic word; the Turks called this place the *Darissade* (and, as you may have guessed, *seraglio* is a corruption of the Turkish *saray*, or palace). It isn't a barbarous oriental innovation; Turks and Arabs both learned the joys of confining women from the Greeks, who from their beginnings right up to the end of Byzantium were possibly the champion male chauvinists of all time.

Ottoman sultans led normal private lives up to the time of Yildirim Beyazit. When he and his family were captured by Tamerlane, the sultan's wife was forced to serve dinner naked to the conqueror and his generals. After this ultimate humiliation, no sultan ever legally married again—save only Süleyman the Magnificent, besotted with his Roxelana. The others had their collections of concubines, though they were only shut up in a harem after the conquest of Constantinople. When Roxelana brought the Harem inside the palace, she intended only a means of getting closer to Süleyman and increasing her influence over affairs of state, but over the next two centuries the Harem stayed, gradually building up its famous institutions and peculiarities. The cast of characters included the girls, or 'odalisques', as many as 800 of them, who lived in drab dormitories; apparently status was the only reason for having so many. The 'Favourites', including the 'First Four Women' (the first to give birth to sons) rated luxurious apartments. To watch over the girls, and more often after themselves, there were the Black Eunuchs. These ugly creatures (the sultan's slavemaster picked out the ugliest, to avoid any chance of arousing the girls) were usually given names like 'Hyacinth' or 'Daisy'. With the silver tubes that assisted them in trips to the WC perched nattily in their tall turbans, the Black Eunuchs became, in the latter days, a power unto themselves. Their chief, the *Kizlar Ağasi*, or 'Lord of the Girls', was after the Ağa of the Janissaries the most useful ally any scheming lady could have. The only other men allowed in the Harem were the 'Tressed Halberdiers', whose job was to bring in the firewood. They had to wear their long hair in coils, hanging over their faces so they would be less likely to catch a glimpse of the women.

Sultans prefer blondes. Many of the women were slender, fair Circassians, Slavs, Armenians or Georgians. All of them, of course, were slaves, and despite the little courtesies of Harem life it is not likely that many of them ever had any illusions about their true status. The vast majority of them led wretchedly dull lives here, chaste as any nuns except for the few who managed to catch a sultan's fancy. Even these were left only with a thank-you, a small present, and the fervent hope that they might conceive a male child. It is pretty certain they did not get up to much highjinks; the eunuchs installed old women to sleep next to their beds, to keep an eye on them at night, and, as an astonished Venetian ambassador once noted in his memoirs, care was taken even to ensure that all cucumbers were sliced before being brought in.

If you wish to visit the Harem—after the big jewels, it's the most popular attraction in the palace—make sure you stop beforehand at the booth by the Harem gate to buy a ticket and check the times for English-language tours. Just inside the gate are the apartments of the eunuchs, including the **Court of the Black Eunuch**, all rebuilt after a fire in the 1660s. From here the *Altin Yol*, the 'Golden Road', the corridor down which the Harem women would walk to meet their rendezvous with destiny when a sultan called, leads to the rest of the harem, beginning with the **Courtyard of the Sultan Valide** (the Sultan's mother), adjacent to the eunuchs' quarter. Considering the bizarre issues of Harem politics—the steering of the right girls into the sultan's bed, the manipulation and sometimes murder of prospective heirs—it becomes clear how only the greatest schemers of all could attain the glorious position of Sultan Valide. Their suite was usually the vortex of all palace intrigues. The next courtyard to the west housed the women servants, again mostly blacks, and beyond them lay the damp, chilly, unadorned quarters of the beauties themselves.

Perhaps the greatest attraction of the Harem quarters, now that you're thoroughly disillusioned, will be the rooms of the northern half of the Harem, the chambers where the sultans came for their pleasures. Several of these, the **Bedroom of Murat III**, and the **Library of Ahmet I**, for example, are adorned with some of the most beautiful painted tiles to be found anywhere in Turkey. The **Dining Room of Ahmet II**, the most famous room of the whole Topkapi palace, is lined with wood panelling painted with colourful flowers and fruits the apotheosis of the gentle art of the Tulip Period. The designs may have violated Muslim taboos against images, but then few imams or members of the Ulema, the Muslim hierarchy, were ever invited in to see them. From here, the tour guides may take you to see the swimming pool put in by Murat III, and the chambers of the Favourites, on a pretty terrace. Some of the rooms on the upper floors are thought to have been the location of the notorious *Kafes*, or 'cage', the most thoroughly perverse of all the perverse customs of the Ottoman throne.

Beyazit II, a scholarly, peaceful sultan, had his reign plagued by his younger brother Prince Cem, a romantic adventurer who caused plenty of trouble trying to seize the throne for himself. When Beyazit caught him, he sent him off to exile in Italy, where it seems he was eventually poisoned by his keeper, the Borgia Pope Alexander VI. After that, sultans began murdering their brothers as soon as they were able. Eventually, the 'cage' was decided upon as a more humane solution. Younger brothers were simply locked up, with a few Harem girls for company and a few deaf mute slaves for servants. They stayed there the rest of their lives unless the chance death of their reigning brother should make them a sultan (and if any of their concubines got pregnant, they would be bundled up in a silk bag with some stone weights and dropped into the sea). A few of these unfortunates actually did make it out of the cage and onto the throne. All of them turned out to be both insane and dangerous; the most notable of these was Ibrahim the Mad, who had spent 22 years in the *Kafes*. In his short reign it is estimated that he ordered the death of over 4000 of his friends, relatives and servants.

Carriage Room and Palace Kitchens

After the Harem there are two more sections of the museum you may wish to visit before passing through to the third courtyard. The **Carriage Room**, once the sultan's stables, is full of the various conveyances of the 19th-century rulers, who apparently were as fond of fancy phaetons and landaus as modern autocrats are of shiny new cars. The **Palace Kitchens** across the courtyard, partly designed by Sinan, were ready, at the sultan's command, to whip up almost anything for a party of from one to five thousand. In the 17th century some 1200 people worked here, and the archives record as many as 22,000 sheep being turned into kebabs every week. The kitchens contain some of the largest soup pots ever constructed on this planet, and a tedious infinity of silver and china from the 19th century. The sultans accumulated these as presents from foreign rulers, in greater numbers than even a dinner for five thousand could require. The collection of **Chinese porcelain** is world-famous and priceless; note especially the celadon ware, a favourite of potentates everywhere, since it was reputed to change colour in the presence of poison.

The Third Courtyard

This is a wonderful park of plane trees and poplars. Visitors are often surprised to see how open and airy old Turkish palaces are. A love of nature, the necessity of having more than a bit of green around, was something the Ottomans never lost, even in their years of decay. They copied the form of the Saray—three successive courtyards of increasingly greater isolation— from the Byzantine imperial palace that once stood nearby (curiously the Hittite palace at Boğazköy also had the same plan). However, where the Byzantines probably had small, paved squares in the classical mode, the Turks built gardens like this, squeezing their buildings into thin quadrangles between them and the forested slopes of the Topkapi hill, for a view of trees on both sides.

To match this setting, the Turks evolved an architectural style very different from the grey mathematics of their mosques; this style was a unique 18th-century concoction of distinctive, very oriental shapes and forms, limited perhaps to the Topkapi and the now-vanished gardens and palaces that once lined the Golden Horn and the Marmara shores. One of the finest examples is in this courtyard: the **Gate of Felicity**, the entrance to the *Selamlik*, the sultan's quarters. Very few outsiders were ever allowed the privilege of using this gate. On ceremonial occasions, such as an accession to the throne, the Bayram festival, or the commissioning of a new general, the sultan would meet the assemblage seated directly under it, on the same portable bejewelled throne that went with him on campaigns. The chief white eunuch had his rooms here in the buildings around the gate, from which he and his fellow castrati oversaw the smooth operation of the *Selamlik*.

The **Audience Chamber**, a pretty parlour just inside the gate, served for the sultan's meetings with his grand vezir and foreign ambassadors. Its ambience is thoroughly Turkish; perhaps for the sultans it recalled the tents of their nomadic ancestors. The fountain in this chamber wasn't just for decoration; its running water made it difficult for anyone to overhear the Sultan's conversations. The coloured tiles and lovely hearth were added to Mehmet Fatih's original building by Ahmet III, but the Baroque ceiling came much later. Ahmet also built the **Library** next door, a marvellous small pavilion with lots of glass and window seats, to be envied by all serious readers. Before the 17th-century fire that damaged much of the *Selamlik*, this space was occupied by the Great Hall, a building that housed the *Enderun*, the school for pages where the Christian children collected in the *devşirme* round-up were converted into the ministers and generals of the empire. Before the decline, it had a reputation as the finest school in Europe, counting all the great Turkish poets and scholars among its instructors. The Enderun was the special preserve of the Chief White Eunuch, and any of these who were fortunate enough to serve under a sultan who liked boys better than girls would find themselves, and not the Chief Black Eunuch, top dog around the palace.

Treasures of the Sultans

Most of the fabulous treasures of the sultans, the gold and jewels and the holy relics, are exhibited in the halls around the third courtyard. The spirit of the Topkapi was never to throw anything away, and one result is that costumes of every sultan after Mehmet Fatih can be seen in the **Wardrobe**, from the gaily coloured flower-printed robes of Mehmet to the dreary European monkey-suit of Abdülhamid. Osman II, most tragic of the sultans, is represented by the blood-splattered caftan in which he was murdered.

It may prove difficult to get excited over the riches of the **Treasury** next door, simply because it's hard to convince oneself that they're all real. The four rooms of bejewelled vessels and weapons, coffee sets and cabinets, as well as famous gems like the 86-carat Spoon Diamond, make up the richest hoard in the world, particularly if you include the additional warehouseful they haven't room to display. Other stars of the collection include the Emerald Dagger, made famous by the film *Topkapi*, and a golden casket supposedly containing the head of John the Baptist.

At the far end of the courtyard, the collection of **Miniatures** displays examples of another very Turkish art form; it seems the first portraitists of Islam felt guilty about breaking Mohammed's law, and so made their paintings very, very small. One two-volume set of these, the *Hünername*, or *Book of Talents* ranks among the greatest works of Turkish painting and calligraphy. The celebrated **clock collection** occupies the next room. Byzantine historians often wrote of their emperors' love of mechanical contraptions, like the famous golden tree full of singing birds, and like them, the Ottoman sultans were always pleased by gifts of clocks and music boxes. Again, those on display are only a small part of the whole collection.

When Selim I conquered Egypt, whose ruler at the time was the Caliph—the head of all Islam, that title fell to him and his successors. The later emperors' oriental inapproachability had not a little to do with the fact that now they were Commander of the Faithful and the Shadow of God on Earth. In token of this great office, the Sherif of Mecca sent Selim the keys to the Ka'aba, and here at Topkapi they remain in the **Hirka-i Saadet**, the hall of holy relics to which Muslims make pilgrimages, located near the clock collection.

Under a great silver dome added by Murat IV are Mohammed's sword, bow, and standard, and the famous cloak he once bestowed on a poet who converted to Islam. Other relics include the Prophet's seal, a broken tooth, a cast of his footprint, hairs from his beard, and a letter he sent with an embassy to the Copts of Egypt—a bullying letter, full of threats. The sword of Osman, symbol of the Ottoman state, is also kept here.

Sultan's Residence

Next to this chamber, a fourth and final gate connects with the residence of the sultan, this a group of individual pavilions around a courtyard, all with the best views of the Bosphorus and the Golden Horn. Two of these, the **Revan Kiosk** and the **Baghdad Kiosk**, must be accounted among the very greatest works of Turkish architecture for the simple magnificence of their form and decoration. Murat IV built them both, to commemorate his conquests of Baghdad and Erevan (now capital of Armenia), and here he drank himself to death in the increasing revels of the last years of his reign. Among the marble terraces and roses of the Revan Kiosk is a marble fountain of three basins that approaches perfection more nearly than any other work of art in all the halls of the Saray.

To leave Topkapi, you must retrace your steps to the First Courtyard; from here instead of returning through the Bab-i Humayun, you can take the other route, around Aya Irene and down a shady cobbled lane towards the Gülhane Park and the imperial museums.

Hats

On the whole, Turks are sharp dressers, and always have been. What is unusual, however, is the way in which matters of dress manage so frequently to insinuate themselves into matters of state: hats, for example.

Most of us have heard of Atatürk's famous Hat Law of 1925, outlawing the wearing of the fez, the conical felt hat with a tassel that Egyptians call a *tarboosh*. Here, what the Father of the Turks had in mind was to do away with one conspicuous symbol of pious reaction; in public, he always wore a fedora or smart cloth cap to set an example. Ironically, the fez itself had been introduced during the 19th-century *Tanzimat* reforms for the same purpose: to replace the then disreputable old Turkish turban.

Hats in politics go back much further. As far back as the 1460s, Mehmet the Conqueror was enacting a hat law, governing the colours of turbans that could be worn at court: green for vezirs, red for chamberlains, white for muftis, red, yellow or black for everyone else except infidels, who weren't allowed a turban at all. Mehmet followed this up with a shoe ordinance: black for Greeks, blue for Jews, violet for Armenians, and so on.

The Hat Law of 1925 accomplished its purpose in a roundabout way. Today most Turks have given up and don't wear any hat at all, except for the Kurds with their inevitable flat grey caps. Meanwhile, street hawkers go on selling fezes to tourists in front of the Aya Sofia every day.

The Imperial Museums

All three museums open daily exc Mon, 9.30–5, adm.

Hamdi Bey, by the standards of the late 19th century, was one very unusual Turk. A painter by trade, his knowledge of the ancient Greeks got him a job under Sultan Abdülhamid looking after the empire's antiquities. So well did he perform his duties, and with such panache, that he revolutionized the affairs of archaeology and museum-keeping, not only in Turkey but in the rest of Europe. Personally responsible for the first law anywhere governing the export of antiquities, he also made patriots of all the nations under Ottoman control work hard to keep their own archaeological discoveries from being shanghaied to the new **Archaeology Museum** that he had talked Abdülhamid into building. More often than not, they didn't succeed. Among the many excavations he oversaw was the one that uncovered the famous Alexander sarcophagus in Sidon. During the lengthy process of transporting this block of several tons to Istanbul, Hamdi Bey literally bound himself to it to impress upon the sailors that they had better take good care of it. On one later occasion, the sultan proposed presenting the sarcophagus to the visiting Kaiser Wilhelm II. Hamdi Bey had the effrontery to inform the sultan that this would only be accomplished by dragging it over his dead body, and the Kaiser went home empty-handed.

Archaeology Museum

The collection he and his successors piled up in this tasteful eclectic building—the very image of what his generation thought a museum should look like—is one of the greatest in Europe. Sarcophagi were Hamdi Bey's speciality, and there's not enough room for them all; many more line the square in front of the museum. The *Alexander sarcophagus*, not *of* Alexander, but decorated with scenes from his conquests, is perhaps more bombast than art, but it's considered one of the finest examples of late Roman sculpture. Two other sarcophagi, one Hamdi Bey called '*des Pleureuses*', and the other a barn-roofed Lycian model, are in the same room, along with a famous bust of Alexander.

The museum's other attractions include bronze pedestals that once supported statues in the Hippodrome, carved with scenes from the games; coats of arms of various states and knightly orders from the old walls of Galata; Egyptian works; Greek and Roman bronzes; the famous statue of a young man called the Ephebos of Tralles; a mosaic of Orpheus and the wild animals; and a remarkable 12-foot statue of the Phoenician god, Bes—the Greeks know him as the 'Cypriot Hercules'—toying with a lion.

Museum of the Ancient Orient

Across from the Archaeology Museum, the government has more recently created the **Museum of the Ancient Orient**, an equally impressive cache of pre-classical finds from Turkey and the Middle East. Some of its best works are from Babylon; the city's Ishtar Gate is largely reconstructed here with its glazed reliefs. In the Assyrian Room are reliefs from the palace of Assurbanipal; nearby, two 3600-year-old copulating Kassites (from Northern Mesopotamia) may well be the world's oldest erotic art.

Also in the Assyrian room the museum has assembled a collection of 'interesting documents' from ancient civilizations, with translations: love poems and tables of astronomical events in Assyrian cuneiform, laws and penalties for various crimes ('2/3 mina of silver for cutting off someone's nose with a copper knife'), and the King of Lagash describing his struggles against his own government bureaucracy. The Treaty of Kadesh is here, an agreement of 1269 BC between the Pharaoh and the Hittite King Hattusilis, found in the state archives at Boğazköy, the oldest treaty ever discovered.

Museum of Turkish Ceramics (Çinili Kiosk)

The third building in the square is the **Çinili Kiosk**, an exquisite small palace built by Mehmet Fatih in 1472 as part of the original Topkapi Saray. Its painted tiles show the lingering influence of the Selcuks in their design. Fittingly, the kiosk now houses a museum of Turkish ceramics from Selcuk times up to the present.

Sublime Porte and Gülhane Park

Continuing down towards Gülhane Park from the kiosk will take you to the north gate of the Saray, none other than the **Sublime Porte** that became a figure of speech representing the Ottoman government during the 19th century. Built into the Topkapi walls here is the **Alay Kiosk**, the Saray's window on the outside world where the sultan would review his troops and be seen by the people—on very rare occasions. **Gülhane Park**, a part of the Saray, was converted to a public garden in 1913. This lovely oasis, with a pond and woebegone zoo, stretches all the way to Sarayburnu, Seraglio Point. Here, Istanbul keeps its **Atatürk Monument**, perhaps the only one in Turkey not on a main square. Across the road just under the walls of the sultan's quarters of the Saray, you can see the stump of a granite column that is the oldest monument in the city: the **Goths' Column**, commemorating the victory of the Romans over the invading Goths in AD 269.

Yerebatan Sarayi

Returning to Sultanahmet Square down Alemdar Caddesi, just across the street from the Aya Sofia stands the unprepossessing entrance to the **Yerebatan Sarayi**. No one has yet proposed old Constantinople's water supply for associate membership in the Wonders of the Ancient World, but this perhaps is only because this network of underground cisterns is so little known. The 'Underground Palace', as the Turks call it, is a great hall 230 by 460ft, supported by ranks of columns and vaults. Though the largest, it's only one of several in the city. Two more have recently been discovered near the Aya Irene, and it is possible that some others remain unknown. By the 16th century, although the old aqueducts were still in use, these reservoirs had been quite forgotten. A French antiquarian named Petrus Gyllius spent weeks looking for this one in 1545, until he had the good fortune to find a resident of the quarter who had a trap door in his house. Down in the cistern, this gentleman kept a boat and used it daily to catch fish, which he sold to his puzzled neighbours. No one suspected the cistern existed, even though the wells of their houses led directly into it.

Each of the 40ft columns—there are over 300 of them—has a capital to bear the arches, and some of these are carved as if they had been part of a church, instead of a reservoir. Justinian, who was responsible for most of these works, was forced to demolish an old basilica that stood above the cistern, and simply reused the capitals. Two of the columns are supported by massive carved heads which have clearly been reused: one is upside down, the other on its side.

The Hippodrome

In Byzantine times, the site of the Blue Mosque held the Golden Hall, the outermost building of Justinian's palace where the throne was kept and the affairs of government transacted. A private corridor connected this part of the palace with the *Kathisma*, or imperial box of the **Hippodrome**, which once stood just to the west. No stadium, ancient or modern, was ever so famous in its time, or played such an important role in its city's public life. Much more went on here than just chariot races and athletic events. Emperors celebrated their victories here, and executed their enemies. Even the games should not be taken as simple entertainment; during the Roman period, they had evolved into a strange sort of mystic communion between the emperor, who of course picked up the bill, and his people. Everything about the games became a symbol, reflecting some aspect of the politics of the day.

Blues and Greens

Construction of the Hippodrome began in 203, the same year Septimus Severus was building the Circus Maximus in Rome, but it remained unfinished until the reign of Constantine. Subsequent emperors improved and enlarged it, and by the time of Justinian it was nearly a third of a mile long, with seats for 100,000. Much has been made of the Hippodrome factions, the Blues and Greens, that caused so much trouble in the 6th century. It would be giving the Byzantines more credit for decadence than even they deserved to suppose that the course of the empire was governed by militant sports fans. Originally, there were four factions, the Reds and Whites later merging into the others. They were nothing less than the organized *demes*, or tribes, traditional in any Greek city. (Rome had the same four colours and factions, though it is likely that the Romans adapted the idea from the Greeks or the Etruscans). They had both military and civilian functions; it was they who built the city walls, and their leaders received salaries as officers of the state. Gradually they came to identify with socio-economic divisions within the city (exactly how the historians can't tell, though it seems the Greens were somewhat more proletarian and politically radical), but when the Blues and Greens joined forces in the Nike Revolt, they were fighting for the city's liberty, and their own, against imperial absolutism and all its aggression abroad, its cops and spies, and its unbearable taxes.

Nike means Victory, the battle cry of the rebels; the revolt began in 532, five years after Justinian's accession to the throne. The rebels soon gained control of the city; chroniclers paint a picture of the young emperor staring helplessly from the palace balcony, too amazed to act; the story goes that Theodora, the dancing girl that had so captivated Justinian that he made her an empress, finally snapped him out of it and put a little steel in her man's soul. The rebels were defeated when the great General Belisarius, at the head of an army of Goths and Alans—the Greeks could not be trusted— surrounded the rebels in the Hippodrome and massacred them all—60,000 of them if contemporary sources are to be believed.

The Crusaders in 1204 thoroughly wasted the Hippodrome, and as the restored empire had little spare money to spend on games, the great stadium gradually fell into ruin. Under the Turks, most of its stones found their way into new building projects, but the sultans always left the surviving monuments alone, and kept the ground clear for practising their game of *cirit*, a form of polo. From this, the square where the Hippodrome once stood came to be known as the *At Meydan*, Horse Square, and this name is still sometimes heard. In the late 1960s, the square became something of a hippie encampment, until Turkish patience finally ran out.

The Monuments of the Hippodrome

The present square, though it follows the contours of the Hippodrome's field, is less than half as big. Its centre line can be traced through the three surviving columns. This line was the *spina*; the Byzantines liked to call it the 'Axis of the Empire'. Originally its two ends were marked by golden columns representing the sun and the moon—the symbolism of the games was astronomical as well as political. These were the pylons around which the charioteers raced, and, between the two columns, the *spina* had an almost unbroken line of monuments; the Crusaders carried away or wrecked most of these, most famously the bronze horses of Lysippus that now adorn St Mark's in Venice. The three that remain were too heavy to move.

In the case of the first, the **Column of Constantine Porphyrogenitus**, the Crusaders had to settle for melting down the bronze plates that covered it. The second monument, the **Serpentine Column**, a twisted stump of bronze, retains little of beauty or interest to remind us of its fascinating history; from faint inscriptions on its base, it has been determined that this column was the monument dedicated by the united Greek cities to celebrate their victory over the Persians at Plataea in 479 BC. After transporting the column in joyous ceremonies through all the towns that shared in the victory, it was erected at the Temple of Apollo at Delphi, where it stood until Constantine the Great stole it to embellish his capital. Before it toppled, sometime around 1700, the column had the form of three intertwined serpents, their heads supporting the legs of a great golden tripod dedicated to Apollo.

The third monument, the **Obelisk of Theodosius**, was acquired by that emperor in 390 especially for the Hippodrome; an obelisk was something no stadium could be without. This one came from Heliopolis, and the hieroglyphic inscriptions on its sides record the victories of the mighty Pharaoh Thutmose III. Like most of the Egyptian obelisks that have found their way to the world's capitals, this one is in surprisingly good shape for its 3400 years; all the hieroglyphs still stand out clearly.

The marble base on which the obelisk was raised has been called one of the finest works of 4th-century sculpture; its reliefs portray Theodosius and his family in the *Kathisma*, viewing the games, the emperor with a wreath in his hand ready to crown the victor. Another relief shows the transporting of the obelisk, and the inscriptions on the sides, in both Greek and Latin verse, recall the difficulties of erecting the heavy stone and the praise due to Proclus the prefect for accomplishing it. The wells in which these three monuments are sunk will give you an idea how much the level of the land has risen since the Hippodrome was last in use. A group of British officers on leave excavated the bases of the three monuments during the Crimean War.

North of the Hippodrome, back near Kaiser Wilhelm's Fountain, stands a small mosque that is one of the oldest in Istanbul. The **Firuz Ağa Camii**, built in 1491, has nothing of the grandeur of later imperial mosques, but its architecture definitely points towards them, in a transition from the old, plain Ottoman style, the masterpieces of which you can see in Bursa. Five times a day, a real müezzin climbs up the short minaret to give the call to prayer. The big mosques usually have only loudspeakers, but with the renaissance of Muslim piety in Turkey, many mosques have gone back to the old-fashioned way. The unexcavated ruins near this mosque belonged to a nobleman's palace, converted in the 7th century to the **Martyrium of St Euphemia**.

West of the Hippodrome

Just across the street from the monuments of the Hippodrome, the palace of Ibrahim Paşa, a grand vezir first favoured, then executed by Süleyman the Magnificent, has recently been restored to house the **Museum of Turkish and Islamic Arts** , with a well-arranged collection of ceramic and brass works, carpets and carved lecterns, some dating from the first centuries of Islam (*open daily exc Mon, 10–5; adm*).

Over the last decade this museum has grown into one of the best planned and presented in Turkey, as well as one of the most comprehensive collections of its kind anywhere. Objects on display go back to the earliest times: peculiar mosaics from the Abbasid Caliphate, along with acanthus-leaf capitals that show a Greek influence. There are some fine Selcuk ceramics, with figurative representations of people and animals (and one relief carved with warriors and griffons in a way that suggests the sculptor had been looking closely at the monuments of the ancient Assyrians). Beyond these there are Persian miniatures, lovely geometrically carved doors and window shutters, and early Korans. Ottoman works, not surprisingly, make up the best parts of the collection: 16th- and 17th-century silver and brass work, Iznik tiles, Tulip art, inlaid wood chests and Koran stands. There is a 'magic shirt' that belonged to Beyazit I (it didn't help him against Tamerlane) and a number of *mülkname*, state decrees in exquisite calligraphy, adorned with the Sultan's personal *tuğra*. On many old Ottoman buildings, such as the Sublime Porte in Istanbul, you will have noticed this unusual symbol, made of Arabic characters in a scroll of concentric loops. The *tuğra* was the mark of the Ottoman Empire from the early days. It originated with Murat I, who like his predecessors was illiterate and signed documents with his thumbprint.

It's easy to overlook the the museum's basement, entered by a small door off the courtyard. This section is devoted to traditional Turkish life, and the star exhibit is a complete *toprak ev*, or *yurt*, the sort of tent used by the Turks' nomadic ancestors, along with some fascinating dsiplays on the natural dyes and other crafts that went into making it. There is also a 'black tent' of goat hair (the *yöruklar*, nomads of eastern Turkey, still use these today), and tableaux of an Anatolian village house and 19th-century homes, complete with authentic costumes and furnishings.

All of the area west of the Hippodrome is built over another of Justinian's underground cisterns, though the entrance is difficult to find. From Divan Yolu, the main street of the city, head three blocks south on Klodfarer Caddesi to a playground where bits of a large retaining wall are visible. Here you'll find the entrance to the **Binbirdirek Cistern**—the 'thousand and one columns', the name a familiar Turkish hyperbole. This one, though smaller than the Yerebatan Saray, is dry, and you can explore its entire extent. In Byzantine records it was known as the Cistern of Philoxenes.

Sultanahmet District

In Istanbul, the Blue Mosque is more commonly referred to as the Sultan Ahmet Camii, after its builder, and in this form, the mosque has given its name to the quarter west and south of it, one of the most interesting old residential neighbourhoods of the city. Some parts of the Sultanahmet near the Marmara shore, with street after street of characteristic Ottoman wooden houses, do not even have a modern water supply, and the women of the district can be seen gossiping around the corner *çeşme* (fountain), just as they are pictured in engravings of centuries ago—although the plastic jerricans make the scene somewhat less picturesque. The lower parts of Sultanahmet are charmingly schizophrenic these days, with half the Ottoman houses restored as hotels in pretty pastel colours, and the other half falling to pieces; poor children playing football share the narrow streets with bewildered-looking young tourists.

The plumbing was probably better when this part of the town was the **Palace of the Byzantine Emperors**. Since no excavations have ever been made, it's impossible to tell much about the layout. The palace began to decay already in the 12th century, when Alexius Comnenus abandoned it for Blachernae out by the city walls. From contemporary accounts we can expect there were plenty of golden domes and towers, and that its three divisions, the Chalce, the Daphne and the 'Sacred Palace', covered an area not much smaller than the Topkapi Saray. The **Arasta Bazaar**, a restored shopping arcade opened in 1985, is southeast of the Blue Mosque. It was built by Sultan Ahmet to provide revenues for his mosque and lies on top of remains of the Byzantine palace. Among the shops can be found the new **Mosaic Museum**, opened in 1987, housing 6th-century floor mosaics from the large peristyle court of the palace (*open daily exc Tues, 9.30–5; adm*). These mosaics are largely *in situ* and the museum winds subterraneanly several yards beneath the shops of the Arasta Bazaar. Much still remains to be excavated. Otherwise, all that is left of the palace is a small court, believed to have been part of the stables, that housed another Mosaic Museum before its removal to the Aya Irene, and a section of the sea walls to the west where Justinian built his Bucoleon, the seaside pavilion. The area between the Blue Mosque and the Marmara, apparently, was devoted to the imperial polo grounds. Throughout the history of the empire, polo was the top snob sport, and most of the emperors, if not too debilitated by their lifestyles, indulged in it.

To the east of the Arasta Bazaar is what has to be the prettiest prison in the world. It is painted yellow ochre and is decorated with turquoise and cobalt-blue floral-patterned Kütahya porcelain tiles. It is now deserted, but there are plans to turn the building into a luxury hotel or a cultural centre for the 67 provinces of Turkey.

Küçük Aya Sofia

If you follow the twisting sidestreets south of the Hippodrome, where you can see the stone walls that supported the closed end of the stadium above the slope, with luck you will find the **Küçük** ('little') **Aya Sofia**, the name the Turks give to the 6th-century church of St Sergius and St Bacchus. Emperor Justinian's first major building project in his capital, modelled after the famous church of S. Vitale in Ravenna, begun the year before, can be seen as an experiment on the way to the big Aya Sofia, with its semi-domes, exedrae, and two levels of arcades around the central space (on the map, you can see how the Aya Irene, the Aya Sofia, Hippodrome, Palace and Little

Aya Sofia are laid out in a line—the main axis of old Constantinople's plan). This church, like S. Vitale, is square with an octagon of piers and columns inside it, supporting a dome just small enough to avoid the need for pendentives. Many of the capitals are finely carved, and like those of Aya Sofia they bear the monograms of Justinian and Theodora. Some vine motifs can be seen in playful allusion to Bacchus, who with his comrade Sergius was the first Christian soldier in the Roman legions to suffer martyrdom. Sergius and Bacchus were the patrons of soldiers, and especially meaningful to Justinian, preoccupied in the early years of his reign with one war after another. As an adjunct of the imperial palace, Küçük Aya Sofia was given the role of occasional Catholic church, where embassies from the pope were allowed to say Mass according to their own usages. Pope Gregory the Great, before his election, was long the papal legate to Byzantium, and he must have prayed here often.

The Divan Yolu and Cağaloğlu

On your way back to the Divan Yolu, try to find Kadirga Sokak and the **Mehmet Paşa Camii** built in 1571 for one of the Sokollu grand vezirs. This small mosque, along with its courtyard, porticoes and school complex, is one of the most beautiful of all the works of Sinan, though few people trouble to see it in its out-of-the-way location.

The **Divan Yolu** was and is the main street of Istanbul. Though today it changes its name every few blocks—to Yeniçeriler Caddesi, and then to Vezneciler Caddesi after Beyazit Square—in Byzantine days, the whole stretch as far as the Adrianople Gate was known as the *Mese* (the Middle), lined with arcades on one side, and on both where it passed through the choicer districts.

Cağaloğlu, the area north of Divan Yolu, takes its name from the **Cağaloğlu Baths** on Hilal-i Ahmer Caddesi, built in the 18th century and still popular. This is one of the prettier parts of old Stamboul, where mostly 19th-century buildings are interspersed with fine mosques and institutions endowed by the sultans and their courtiers. It is also the home of most of the national newspapers and book publishers—in the years of political troubles its streets were often a battleground (the *Başan Muziği*, or Press Museum, is on the Divan Yolu here).

Çemberlitaş

Çemberlitaş, the 'bound monument' further up Divan Yolu, commemorates the very beginnings of the Byzantine Empire. The Column of Constantine, as it was called, was the first monument erected by that emperor on his refounding of the city; with the modesty for which his house was so renowned, Constantine had a golden statue of himself bolted on top. The Forum of Constantine, of which the small square you see today is the only remnant, was the business centre of the city, and the monument served as the site for many public festivals, including the annual ceremony on the anniversary of the foundation. A storm in the 11th century brought the old emperor down to earth, and the golden cross with which Manuel Comnenus replaced it did not survive long under the Turks. The sultans left the column standing, however, contributing the bronze bands that have held it together since a fire in the 18th century; from these, the scorched monument took on its other popular name, the 'Burnt Column'.

Immediately before the Burnt Column, on the same side of the road, is the **Türbe of Sultan Mahmud II**, a dull and ugly building set behind high steel railings within an Ottoman cemetery. Beneath the outrageous glass chandelier rests Mahmud II, with his son, Sultan Abdülaziz and his grandson, Sultan Abdülhamid, plus family members of each and their favoured ministers. Across the road is the **Köprülü Kütüphenasi Library**, built in 1661 by members of the distinguished Köprülü family of Albania, which contributed five grand vezirs in the 17th century. There is little of interest inside apart from a few dusty tomes and it may soon be closed. Next to the Burnt Column itself is the 17th-century **Çemberlitaş Hamam**, commissioned by the wife of Selim II and still open for bathers.

Just past the Burnt Column, still on Divan Yolu, is the **Atik Ali Paşa Camii**, built for that gentleman in 1497 by Beyazit II in honour of services rendered as grand vezir. It is a peaceful mosque, plain and simple, set in a lovely garden with lots of Christmas-tree firs. The larger mosque behind it, the **Nuruosmaniye Cami**, the 'light of Osman', is one of the better examples of Turkish Baroque. By the 18th century, the religious architecture of the Ottomans had lost all the momentum built up in its earlier inspirations. The result, an attempt to maintain the form, while prettifying it in a bastard half-Italian, half-Persian style, seems sensible enough here, but the greatest horrors were still to come. The main entrance to the Covered Bazaar leads through the tout-patrolled courtyard of the Nuruosmaniye. Near the Nuruosmaniye, the **Mehmet Paşa Camii** is the oldest in Istanbul, built just 10 years after the Ottoman conquest. **Nuruosmaniye Caddesi**, leading from here back towards Aya Sofia, has recently been given a complete facelift; lined with graceful plane trees, it is the fashionable shopping street of old Stamboul.

Back on the Divan Yolu, the **Külliye of Koça Sinan Paşa**, grand vezir under Murat III and Mahmud III, stands just beyond the Atik Ali Paşa Cami. The complex was erected by Davut Ağa, who had the unenviable task of succeeding Sinan as chief architect to the sultan. Nearby is the **Çorlulu Ali Paşa Medrese**, built in 1711. Across the road to the left, the **Karamustafa of Merzifon Medrese** was built in 1690 in honour of the Grand Vezir Karamustafa by Mehmet IV. It has an octagonal plan, unusual in a mosque. Now it is a research institute named for the 20th-century Turkish writer, Yahya Kemal. Here the Divan Yolu becomes Yeniceriler Caddesi, lined with buildings from the 1960s breezeblock and cement school. Signs point the way to McDonalds.

Sirkeci and Eminönü

Crossing Nuruosmaniye Caddesi, one of the main thoroughfares of Cağaloğlu is Babiali Caddesi; if you follow it north to where it becomes Ankara Caddesi, passing the most conspicuous of Istanbul's consulates—the Iranian—and the provincial government house, the **Vilâyet**, you'll end up in the **Sirkeci** quarter, a scrofulous twilight zone of cheap hotels and auto parts shops around the ornate Victorian **Sirkeci Station** (1885). Foreign companies built the first railway into Istanbul, and they and Sultan Abdülhamid are responsible for the greatest act of municipal vandalism in the city since the Sack of 1204: for the tracks, they destroyed the entire Marmara shore and many of the gardens and woods of the Topkapi hill.

Eminönü, the area just west of Sirkeci along the Golden Horn, was in the last century the business district of old Stamboul, as opposed to the

'FISH + BREAD' VENDOR

European-dominated Beyoğlu across the Golden Horn. Its streets are still lively, its property values the highest in the city, and if you must pass through to visit the monumental **Main Post Office**, take time to admire this and the many other outlandish works of *c.* 1910, eclectic architecture. Two of the best Art Nouveau works, grimy fantasies with cast-iron flowers on their balconies and pseudo-Ottoman painted tiles, are the small business block on the square opposite the Post Office and the **Büyük Vakif Han**, an enormous landmark just two blocks away, in the direction of **Eminönü Square**, old Stamboul's window on the Golden Horn. From the square, the famous Galata Bridge crosses over to Beyoğlu, carrying the life of the city back and forth.

The Galata Bridge

Just after the Conquest, Mehmet's army engineers built the first bridge here, of boats lashed together and covered with planks. One of the succeeding sultans, the Turks say, invited Leonardo da Vinci to design a permanent structure, but he declined, and none was constructed until 1845. The present, like its companion Atatürk Bridge further up the Golden Horn, is a floating metal drawbridge. Caissons could only have been planted into the mud bottom with great difficulty, and so this unusual method was adopted. German engineers built it in 1912 but the Turks had to reconstruct it almost from scratch after a fire in 1992. Both bridges are opened only in the early morning hours, when long lines of ships pass in and out. In the days of the sultans, they were also opened at the least sign of trouble in the city, to prevent insurrection from spreading. The 1992 fire began in one of the little fish restaurants housed on the bridge's lower level. For the rebuilding, there was much talk of making a proper modern bridge, instead of the incredible floating café and jumble sale the old one always was. In the end, fortunately, custom and sentiment won out—the new bridge looks exactly like the old one, with plenty of room on the pavements for hawkers to sell their wind-up turtles and polyester negligées, and of course spaces underneath for the restaurants.

The docks on either side, from which you can catch ferry boats to Asia, the Bosphorus, or the Princes' Islands, once were the busiest part of the commercial waterfront. Old travellers always remarked how close the city's life was to the life of the sea; any trip through town was likely to involve elbowing your way past deck hands and stevedores, and staring into the cannons of the ships-of-the-line. Today, besides the creaky ferries, the maritime experience is limited to the informal fish market on the Beyoğlu side, and the cafés on the lower deck of the bridge, where you can sit and sample the notorious aromas of the Golden Horn. All this lies in the shadow of one of the great imperial mosques, the **Yeni Cami**.

Yeni Cami and Spice Market

This mosque, a landmark more for its location than for any special virtue of its architecture, was begun by a Sultan Valide (mother) named Safiye, a wife of Murat III, in 1597. Three different architects had a hand in the work, only finished in 1663. Of the original *külliye* of foundations, only two fountains and the Sultan Valide's *türbe* remain, along with the **Spice Market**, whose rents still go to the upkeep of the mosque. Most of the locals call this market the *Misir Çarşisi*, the 'Egyptian market', since most of the herbs and concoctions traditionally sold here came from the banks of the Nile. Today, in the long, L-shaped hall, a smaller version of the Covered Bazaar, you may purchase anything from jewellery to electric tin-openers to caviar, but at a few of the old stands it's still fun to guess just what the hundreds of items displayed in barrels, bags, and jars could possibly be. 'Spices' to the Turks, as to the rest of

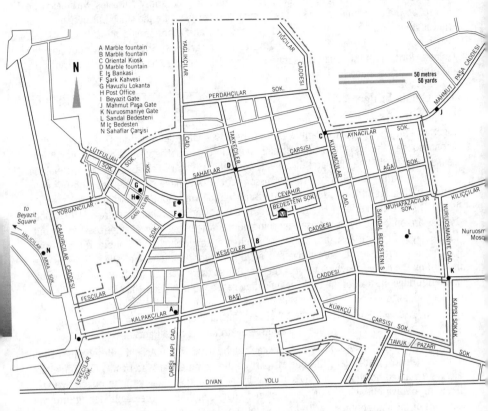

A Marble fountain
B Marble fountain
C Oriental Kiosk
D Marble fountain
E İş Bankası
F Şark Kahvesi
G Havuzlu Lokanta
H Post Office
I Beyazit Gate
J Mahmut Paşa Gate
K Nuruosmaniye Gate
L Sandal Bedesteni
M İç Bedesten
N Sahaflar Çarşisi

Europe, once meant not simply herbs for cooking, but drugs, dyes, preservatives, cosmetics and any other useful substance that grows. One of the biggest sellers today is *kina*, or henna, for ladies' hair.

The Eminönü Market, a green and crowded yard between the Spice Market and the Yeni Cami where caged birds, seeds, bulbs, and garden tools are sold, was also the traditional home of the city's scribes, the placid gentlemen with typewriters on little stands, who composed letters for the unlettered and filled in government forms for the bewildered. Perhaps it is a sign of progress—on our most recent visit we didn't see a single one.

Rüstem Paşa Camii

As seen from the bridge or from Beyoğlu, the Yeni Cami stands in the shadow of the great Süleymaniye, on the heights to the southwest. Between the two, the little mosque called **Rüstem Paşa Camii** is hardly even noticed. A closer look will reveal one of Sinan's most elegant works, built in 1550 for Süleyman's grand vezir. The real surprise, though, is within;

the mosque is almost entirely covered with the very best Iznik tiles, in a spectacular variety of colours and patterns. For all these Ottoman creations, it will never do to ask where the funds came from. Rüstem Paşa was a son-in-law of Süleyman the Magnificent and Roxelana, and the sultan's favourite, in her endless intrigues, determined to make him grand vezir. To accomplish this, all she had to do was to convince Süleyman to have his old friend, the Vezir Ibrahim, murdered. She had little trouble; Ibrahim was soon strangled by the palace mutes, and Rüstem distinguished himself by inaugurating the practice of putting government offices up for sale, an Ottoman tradition ever after.

The Covered Bazaar

Open every day except Sunday, 8am–7pm.

It seems likely that Constantinople had some kind of market on this spot; over one of the arches of this vast and rambling structure, a Byzantine eagle can be made out clearly. Long before the days of shopping malls, covered markets like this were an Eastern tradition, not only for convenience but to discourage burglars. No one disputes Istanbul's claim that theirs is the largest in the world. Since Mehmet Fatih built the two *bedestens*, or stronghouses, in the 1460s, street after street of shops, covered with simple barrel vaults and skylights, have grown up around them, always well maintained and promptly rebuilt after such disasters as the earthquake of 1896 or the fire of 1954. Today, the *Kapalı Çarşı*, as it is called, is a city unto itself, with several thousand shops, a mosque, a school, even its own post office and police station.

It isn't just for tourists—far from it. Though you'll see plenty of trinkets and little signs proclaiming the owner's proficiency in English or German, the Covered Bazaar has its more prosaic side, as the purveyor of all manner of goods to the Stamboullu, from diamonds to dust pans; note that Mehmet built it before embarking on either his mosque or his Topkapi palace. The market was the key to bringing the half-abandoned city back to life. Even today, despite the advent of industrialism and high finance in Turkey, what goes on here, and in the seemingly endless maze of wholesalers, warehouses, and workshops to the north of it, still carries some weight in the nation's economy.

This mighty citadel of the independent businessman also stands ready to give any perceptive visitor some advanced lessons in a free market economy. The location of shops, for example, will tell you all about everyone's profit margins; the jewellers will be found in the centre and around the entrances, of course, while the dealers in raw leather or children's mittens are tucked away in low-rent alleys where you'll never find them.

Most of the street names tell what trades were followed long ago—for example, the Fezmakers' Street or the Avenue of the Slippers—though the locations gradually changed with the years. Atatürk put the fezmakers out of business long ago, and now their street sells mostly blue jeans. Other names are more colourful, like the Louse Bazaar. You may wander its broad avenues and dim cul-de-sacs, recently renovated and cleared of their ugly thicket of electric signs, and look for bargains to your heart's content. Don't miss the **Iç Bedesten** at the centre, devoted to copper and rare antiques; they glitter in Mehmet's dim hall like the treasure in the Cave of the Forty Thieves.

Stamboul's market district really stretches as far as the Golden Horn, and the Kapali Çarşi is only its glamorous retail end. Many of the surrounding streets, like those inside, have a particular function. One of the most interesting is the **Sahaflar Çarşisi**, the old Booksellers' Market, just outside the Beyazit Square entrance to the Covered Market. This lovely courtyard full of tiny shops, with its fountain and large population of cats, is believed to have been around in one form or another since Byzantine times—it's the best place in Istanbul for books and souvenirs. North of the Covered Market, around Uzunçarşi Caddesi, are a number of old *hans*, no longer performing their old functions as merchant hotels, but still buzzing with porters and handcarts, the whirr of old machinery, and decorous transactions made over tea.

Beyazit Square and Beyazit Camii

An old story relates how when Beyazit II was building the mosque that bears his name, the oldest of the Ottoman imperial mosques still standing, a pious old woman offered a pair of pigeons—Turks are fond of pigeons—for the courtyard and gardens. Their descendants rule **Beyazit Square** today, and you'll earn some credit in Allah's bank of grace for spending a few liras on them; someone will always be there to sell you a plate of seeds. The square, entirely redone several years ago by some berserk minimalist architect, has become an outstanding piece of urban design with few admirers apart from the pigeons, who seem happier than ever even if there are fewer trees. This is what the critics would call an architectural square, a vast expanse of grey granite blocks on different levels; it is a veritable symphony in grey, between the pavement, the pigeons, and the subtle variety of grey tones in the **Beyazit Camii**, the grand and beautiful mosque the square was designed to show off.

Whether or not this was the mosque that set the pattern for later imperial foundations we cannot tell. The mosque of Beyazit's father Mehmet, the original Fatih Camii, was destroyed in an earthquake. Its architect was a Greek named Christodoulos, and the Beyazit Camii, completed in 1504, is the work of his sons. They built their mosque after the plan of the Aya Sofia, only without the upper gallery, and endowed it with a particularly fine courtyard and fountain.

Also on the square is what is claimed to be the world's only **Museum of Calligraphy**, concentrating on the art in the Ottoman era (*open daily exc Sun and Mon, 9–4; adm*).

Istanbul University

Across the square, the monumental gateway in some sort of Persian Rococo is the entrance to **Istanbul University**. The date over the arch, the Roman numerals 1453, is a sorry deception. That was the year of the Conquest, but the university was not founded until 1845, as part of the reforms of Abdülmecit. Since Atatürk, the university has expanded greatly, taking over the buildings of the old *Seraskeriat*, the War Ministry, in the large park behind the gate. If you want to meet the students, the wonderful, tree-shaded open-air **café** behind the Beyazit Camii, at the entrance to the Sahaflar Çarşişi, is full of them.

Mehmet II built the 200-foot **Beyazit Tower** on the campus in 1823 as a watchtower for fires (or insurrections); it is the tallest structure in old Stamboul. Along Yeniceriler Caddesi, on the south side of the square, the recently excavated ruins lying about belong to the Forum of Theodosius—Beyazit Square's ancestor on this site.

Süleymaniye Cami

Mimar Sinan, in the last years of his life, is supposed to have said that the Selimiye in Edirne was his favourite among all his scores of mosques; the great architect chose to live, however, near his Süleymaniye (1557), and nearby also is his tomb.

If you have the chance to visit only one of the imperial mosques, your time would be best spent here. No features of the construction are unique or original; the same elements of the classic design will be found in the same places. The building's only excuse for existing is perfection. Just as a mathematician can sometimes look at a complex equation and understand it by what seems to be intuition, so, when we look at the Süleymaniye we have no need of measurement or analysis to know that each proportion and line is nothing either more or less than right. The outstanding features are subtle: the excellent stone porticoes on either side, the courtyard and the smooth plain hierarchy of domes, to which we could add the surviving stained glass, the work of a legendary artist called Ibrahim the Drunkard.

No mosque in Istanbul, and certainly not the Aya Sofia, has such a feeling of openness within. For a moment, it's easy to forget the reality of columns, arches, and vaults and imagine the Süleymaniye as a great stone tent, hung on the four square solid piers at the corners of the dome. Just as Süleyman's reign marked the high noon of the Ottoman state, so does this mosque that Sinan built for him declare the zenith of his nation's art. Time would show that neither had much more to give.

Almost alone among the imperial mosques, the Süleymaniye retains almost all of its *külliye* (complex of religious and educational institutions). This is the grandest *külliye* ever built by the Ottomans, an integral part of Sinan's perfect composition, and no one has dared to tamper. The eight low buildings, with over 200 domes between them, have all recently been restored, and several are creatively reused, one as a library, and another as a clinic to benefit the people of the neighbourhood, just as their builders intended. In the courtyard of the mosque, you can see the separate *türbes* of Süleyman and Roxelana, both done in fine Iznik tiles. A smaller tomb, at the narrow angle of a street in the northernmost corner of the complex, is that of Sinan himself.

Mimar Sinan

Not all Christian boys pressed into the Janissary corps ended up as soldiers. One young Greek, born about 1489, worked his way up through the military engineering branch to become the head architect of the Ottoman state. At the age of 59, Sinan built his first mosque, the Şehzade in Istanbul, for Sultan Süleyman the Magnificent. It was the beginning of a brilliant collaboration that created scores of mosques, schools, bridges and fortifications—the launching of the Ottoman imperial style, as well as its greatest achievements. For the Turks, his profession became a title; they call him *Mimar* Sinan—Sinan the Architect.

It would have been impossible for one man to have accomplished the tremendous output with which Sinan is credited, several hundred buildings in all. Like the Renaissance artists who attached their names to everything that came out of the workshop, even if all the details had been handled by students, Sinan must really be thought of as head of a huge public works collective. All these works (most are in Istanbul) are distinctive and gracefully proportioned, but those that most clearly bear the stamp of the master are the Selimiye in Edirne, the little Sokollu Mehmet Paşa Mosque, and the Süleymaniye.

Just west of the Süleymaniye, in a small courtyard off Kirazli Mescit Sokak, stands the small Kilise Camii, formerly the **church of St Theodorus**; although much was rebuilt in the 12th century, the foundation and much of the structure are from the 5th, making this the oldest religious structure in Istanbul.

Returning to Beyazit Square, and continuing west along Vezneciler Caddesi, still following the route of the old *Mese*, we pass reminders of the Ottoman or Byzantine eras on almost every block. The **Kalenderhane Cami**, at the corner of the Büyük Reşit Paşa Caddesi, where six streets meet, was originally the church of the Akataleptos Monastery; 13th-century frescoes have recently been discovered inside, but they have been removed and cannot be seen. A *kalender* is a kind of dervish, and it appears that the function of this and many other monasteries changed little after the Conquest.

Şehzade Camii

Many consider the **Şehzade Camii** (1548), two blocks further east, to be one of the finest of the Ottoman mosques, but its lofty dome conceals a great crime—also, perhaps, the secret of the decline of the Ottoman Empire. Süleyman the Magnificent had a son named Mustafa by one of his concubines, an intelligent and virtuous young man who gave every promise of being an excellent soldier and ruler. All that stood between him and a brilliant reign was the unfortunate matter of his mother's name not being Roxelana. The sultan's favourite had sons of her own, younger than Mustafa, and she was determined to do anything to see them on the throne. She had already driven Süleyman to murder once, in the case of the Grand Vezir Ibrahim, and now, on the evidence of forged letters that suggested that Mustafa was planning to stage a revolt, she persuaded the sultan to do him in.

Mustafa, called back from the province he was governing, went unsuspectingly to his doom; it is said Süleyman watched from behind a curtain while the mutes and the bowstring went to work—spilling royal blood was an unthinkable crime, and a garrotting with a bowstring was the custom for such necessities. Roxelana, ironically, never lived to enjoy the power of a Sultan Valide, but her son Selim II, called the Sot, was to reign for eight years, as the first dissolute Ottoman, before succumbing to cirrhosis. It is said Süleyman built the Şehzade Camii, the 'Prince's Mosque', out of remorse. Sinan used the opportunity to experiment, bestowing upon his mosque one of the most unusual exteriors to be seen in Istanbul, with plenty of Persian and Moorish-inspired detail on the minarets, domes, and windows. Later Turkish architects were to draw on these, especially during the Baroque era, but Sinan himself returned to his accustomed austerity just in time to design the Süleymaniye.

Just behind the Şehzade, a small mosque called the **Burmali Minare** was built by an Egyptian *paşa* two years after its larger neighbour. The name refers to the 'twisted' minaret, unique in the city. All this area around the intersection of the *Mese*—called Şehzadebaşi along this stretch—and Atatürk Boulevard was developed into a park as part of Istanbul's first ambitious planning scheme in the 1940s. Across the street, the steel and glass City Hall was its centrepiece, and broad **Atatürk Bulvari**, designed for cars, its major improvement. Amazingly, this is the first street ever laid out in 1600 years to form a direct connection between the Marmara and the Golden Horn.

Aqueduct of Valens

The park was opened up partly to expose the **Aqueduct of Valens**, supported by an arcade over a half-mile in length between the Third and Fourth Hills, and nearly 60ft tall where it passes over Atatürk Bulvari. The 4th-century Emperor Valens really only expanded and repaired an older aqueduct, but the popular name credits it to him even though most of what you see was constructed by, of course, Mimar Sinan, who rebuilt the city's water supply for Sultan Süleyman. The aqueduct was in use well into the 20th century; today you can follow its crumbled end into a street of car mechanics in the Fatih district. In its shadow, next to the boulevard, the early 17th-century Gazanfer Ağa Medrese was restored in the 1940s as Istanbul's **Municipal Museum** (*currently closed for restoration*). The humble and dusty collection includes maps and views of the city, expropriated relics from the dervish orders, imperial firmans directed to the city, portraits, Karagöz puppets, and other bric-à-brac.

And By The Way, Istanbul's Tap Water Will Give You Typhoid and Dysentery

We hoped that might catch your attention. It's no exaggeration. In the summer of 1994, hundreds of people were checked into city hospitals for those diseases, and health officials feared for a full-scale epidemic—while the political authorities denied there was any problem at all. Water has been Istanbul's biggest problem since the time of the Byzantines; fortunately for them they had a long heritage of Roman know-how in building aqueducts, such as the Aqueduct of Valens, part of a complex system that extended for miles into the countryside. Water was stored for dry periods in the underground cisterns that are still one of the marvels of Istanbul today. Rebuilding the system was a first priority of Mehmet the Conqueror after 1453, and all through the worst centuries of Ottoman rule the Turks managed to keep it in good nick.

For a population of over ten million, however, it just isn't enough. It would take over half a billion dollars just to get a good start on the problem. The city simply doesn't have it, and the government in Ankara hasn't been much help. New pipelines and reservoirs have been built, but much of the money leaked away in political graft, and in one reservoir, the soil contaminated the water with ammoniac minerals, making it unusable. To make matters worse, both former Mayor Sözen, a Social Democrat, and current Refah Party Mayor Erdoğan won office on a platform that promised nearly-free water to the city's poor.

Water rationing is traditional in Istanbul, and it has been especially bad after the droughts of the last few years. And that is the cause of the problem. In summer, typically, the tap comes on for 18 hours, then goes off for 30. Stagnant water sits in the warm pipes, and the germs multiply. Fortunately, almost all the hotels have their own cisterns, with safe water brought in by tank truck—but if you're in a cheap dive it won't hurt to ask. If you are staying anywhere with city water, the Istanbul Chamber of Medicine recommends that you not drink the water, not brush your teeth, wash food, or even bathe in it unless it has been boiled.

Church of the Pantocrator

A walk a few blocks north along Atatürk Bulvari will take you past the Zevrek Kilise Camii, once the **church of the Pantocrator**, built in 1124, its history intertwined with that of the empire in its last centuries. John Comnenus, 'Good John', who presided over the last spell of peace and prosperity for Byzantium, built it, and he was buried here along with his Hungarian wife Irene, a great patroness of the arts. During the occupation of the Crusaders it became a Catholic church, the seat of the Venetian Bishop Morosini; ironically, later it was to be the church of Gennadius, the prelate who worked so fervently in the 1440s to avert the proposed union of the churches, Constantinople's last hope for aid from the west against the Ottomans.

Mehmet rewarded Gennadius after the Conquest by making him the first patriarch under the new dispensation. The monastery of which this church was a part has completely disappeared; the retaining walls of the huge cistern that served it and the neighbourhood are all that is left.

After passing Atatürk Bulvari, the old *Mese* changes its name one last time, to Fevzi Paşa Caddesi. The *külliye* here, a fine example of Turkish architecture, is the 1698 **Amcazade**, built by one of the grand vezirs of the Köprülü family. Two blocks south of Fevzi Paşa, the most complete surviving Roman monument in Istanbul stands on a quiet street of apartment blocks; the **Column of Marcian**, built *c.* AD 450. The tall granite shaft, surmounted by a Corinthian column and a much-effaced winged symbol, once bore a gold statue of this vain emperor, an intriguer with no real successes to commemorate. Traces of the reliefs on the base can be made out.

Lâleli District and Aksaray

East of Marcian's column, the quarter around Atatürk Bulvari south of the *Mese* is called ·Lâleli, named after the **Lâleli** (tulip) **Cami**, on busy Ordu Caddesi, a famous work of the Turkish Baroque, built under Mustafa III in 1760. The high stone platform on which the mosque stands now contains a little bazaar of shops added in the 1950s. Long ago, before the mosque was even built, it was the central hashish and opium den of Istanbul, a distinction it seems also to have had under the Byzantines. Murat IV, a tremendous drunkard, closed it down for the good of the nation.

Across Ordu Caddesi, **Aksaray** is a bustling, thoroughly modern district packed with hotels and foreigners. A decade ago there was a large Arab and Persian influence; now in a transition that native Stamboullu find amazing and amusing, the quarter has become home to thousands of Russians, Poles and other East Europeans. Many of them are in the textile and fashion trades, and their boutiques can be seen along every street. Aksaray and Lâleli have become the most most frenetic corner of the city, a raucous street scene, day and night, that includes wall-to-wall street vendors, *hamals* (porters) struggling under enormous burdens, Slavic prostitutes (Turks call them 'natashas') and suspicious-looking folk from all over the world. It explodes into total confusion several times a day when lorries packed with cloth pull in from the docks, or from Adana, centre of the cotton country of the southeast. Brokers and shopkeepers descend on them like locusts, and impromptu auctions start in the middle of the street. Here too, tucked away on Mesihpaşa Caddesi, is the Bodrum Cami, originally the church of the **Mirelaon Convent**, rebuilt and renovated so often since the 6th century that no one knows to whom to credit it.

The Lâleli Cami may be the place where Turkish Baroque went over the edge, but the indescribable **Valide Cami**, on Aksaray Square, must be the supreme example of the preciosity of a decadent nation carried to its wildest extreme. The Turks were as eclectic as anyone in 1870, and the idea here was to invent Turkish neo-Gothic.

Fatih District

North of Lâleli, **Fatih**, the enormous quarter named after Mehmet the Conqueror and the great complex of religious buildings he erected at its centre, is home to over 100,000 of Stamboul's working people; plain and honest, it has survived both urban decay and creeping modernity. At present, it has a reputation as the stronghold of the fundamentalists in the city—though the Refah Party candidate for sub-mayor recently lost out to a socialist. When Mehmet built his **Fatih Cami** here in 1463, this Fourth Hill was one of the choicer districts of the city. Here stood the church of the Holy Apostles, the church second in size and importance only to Aya

Sofia. Mehmet demolished it, one of the few instances of wanton destruction of Christian build-ings on the part of the Turks. Eighteen of its columns can be seen in the mosque's courtyard. It should not be too hard to imagine how the Holy Apostles looked; St Mark's in Venice was modelled on it. The church is also said to have had a unique conical dome; underneath it for a time lay the remains of the city's founder and 'thirteenth apostle', Constantine.

Mehmet's mosque, which we know had two equal domes in the fashion of the earlier Ottoman mosques of Bursa, was shaken down by an earthquake in 1766. The reigning Sultan Mustafa III had it rebuilt even bigger in the classical style, but the result is just another unin-spired copy from the same mould. The *külliye*, an enormous complex elevated on a platform that turns a vast blank face towards Fevzi Paşa Caddesi, is even larger than that of the Süleymaniye; its institutions and foundations still provide important services for the people of the Fatih. Yet another small, inconspicuous Byzantine building can be seen a few blocks to the north on Küçük Mektep Sokak, the 12th-century **church of Christ Pantepoptes** built by Alexis I Comnenus. Now it's the Eski Imaret Cami, though much of its attractive exterior survives, decorated with patterns of tiles and bricks.

Outlying Areas to the West: the *Exokionion*

On the map (*see* pp.116–17), you can follow a line of avenues—Haliç Caddesi, Akdeniz Caddesi and Kizil Elma Caddesi among others—starting at the Golden Horn and winding an irregular course behind the Fatih complex and across the peninsula. These generally follow the line of the original long-vanished walls of Constantinople, paced off by Constantine himself after a vision showed him how best to defend the city. Even after the Theodosian walls were built further west, this area beyond the older line had the legal status of an extramural district, and during the various conflicts over church dogma, heretics were allowed to hold religious services here. The Greeks called this wide swathe of land between Constantine's and Theodosius' Walls the *Exokionion*. Today it is home to hundreds of thousands of Stamboul's poorer residents, in a disorganized conglomeration of villages and market gardens, with some dense concentrations of flats, all up and down the Fifth, Sixth, and Seventh Hills.

With the help of the dolmuş and minibus, those with a real interest in tracking down the wealth of Ottoman and Byzantine monuments here can start their expeditions. Doing it prop-erly will require some walking, and some climbing—around the Fifth Hill in particular, the only one of the seven that truly deserves the name. Your troubles will be rewarded by an endless supply of curiosities past and present, as well as insights into the working life of the more prosaic corners of the fantastical city.

The neighbourhood directly north of the Fatih, along Darüşşafaka Caddesi, gets the travelling market on Wednesday (*Çarşamba* in Turkish), which has given the quarter its name. From here Yavuz Selim Caddesi ascends the Fifth Hill to the **Sultan Selim Camii** or Selimiye, begun by the conqueror of Egypt but not completed until 1522, in the reign of his son Süleyman. Behind this austere and beautiful mosque, Selim built his *türbe* in its garden. From here, you can look out over the rooftops of one of Stamboul's oddest neighbourhoods, a pretty sunken village built around crags of antique masonry at the bottom of the **Cistern of Aspar**, a 5th-century addition to Constantinople's water supply.

Fener Quarter

Progressing any further will require a stout heart and shoes, for the streets that introduce you to the quarter of the Fener are the steepest and roughest in all Istanbul. The old ladies storm

Istanbul: Outlying Sights

Stamboul
A Greek Orthodox Patriarchate
B St. Mary Mouchliotissa
C Fethiye Cami (Pammakaristos Church)
D Kariye Cami (St. Saviour in Chora)
E Dungeon of Anemas
F Palace of Constantine Porphyrogenitus
G Mihrimah Camii
H Koca Mustafa Paşa Camii (St. Andrea in Crisal)
I Altimermer Cistern
J Cerrahpaşa Camii
Beyoglu
K Soldiers' Museum
L Naval Museum
M Çirağan Palace
In Asia
N Selimiye Barracks
O Mihrimah Camii
P Yeni Valide Camii
Q Şemşi Paşa Camii
Bosphorus
R Ortaköy Camii
S Beylerbey Palace
Inset map
T Kücukşü Palace
U Anadolu Hisar
V Rumeli Hisar
W Emirgân Park
X Genoese Castle

1km
½ mile

– – – Metro Line
▪ ▪ ▪ Tram Line

N

cemeteries

Eyüp Cami

EYÜP

cemetery

KURTULUŞ CAD.

Kurtuluş

FATIH KOPRUSU

E
F
AYVANSARAY

TEPEBAŞI

BAHRIYE CAD.

TARABI

Edirne Gate

D

FENER

Golden Horn

ŞİŞHANE

ISTIKLAL

To Edirne

G

DRA MAN CAD.

C

A
B

Selimiye Camii

GALA

KARAGÜMRÜK

FEVZIPAŞA CADDESI

YAVUZ SELIM CAD.

HALIÇ CAD.

Çarşamba

Atatürk Bridge

ADNAN MENDERES BULVARI

Topkapi Gate

FATIH

Fatih Camii

Galata Bridge

6   4   3
     5   2 1

MILLET CADDESI

AKDENIZ CAD.

Süleymaniye Camii

Yeni Cami

Rail St
(Sick

Mevlâna Gate

City Hall

aqueduct

EMINÖNÜ

Covered Market

CAĞALOĞLU

I

KIZILELMA CADDESI

ORDU CAD.

L Beyazit Square

DIVAN YOLU

ALTIMERMER

HASEKI CADDESI

YENI CERILER CAD.

Aya Sofi

Siliviri Gate

SILIVRIKAPI CAD,

J

Column of Arcadius

AKSARAY

KUMKAPI

SULTANAHM

YENIKAPI

H

KOCA MUSTAFA PAŞA CAD.

Belgrad Gate

SAMATYA

Sea of Marmara

To Marmara Island
To Avsa Island
To Bostanci

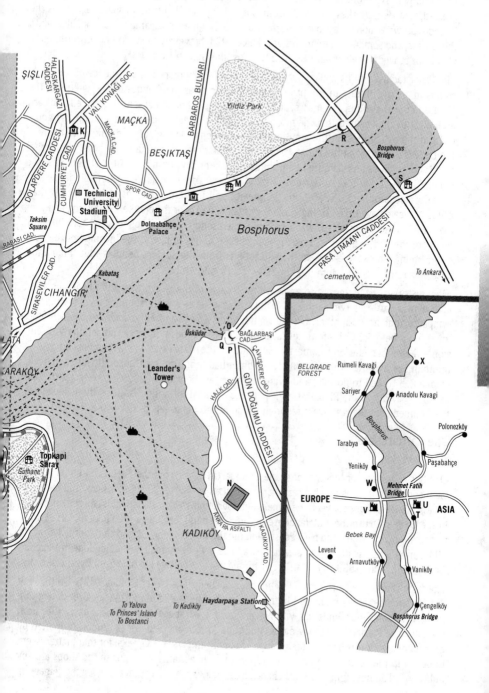

up and down like mountain goats, and the children play vertical tag, but you may be hard pressed. The Fener takes its name from the old Phanar (lighthouse) Gate, a part of the Theodosian walls along the Golden Horn. After the Conquest it became the district allotted to the Greeks, and some live here to this day. Since 1923, however, most have either returned to Greece or moved to newer parts of the city across the Golden Horn.

The Fener today, with its melancholy, half-empty streets, wrapped in the silence of the tomb, stands in sharp contrast to the past centuries. Even after the Conquest, the talents of the Greeks in the arts and in commerce, and the natural disinclination of the Ottoman elite to earn an honest living, ensured that the more accomplished of the infidels would find many doors open to them. Throughout the empire, the Greeks controlled shipping, finance and many of the trades, and provided the sultans with most of their officials and tax collectors. The capital of this conspicious and favoured community was here, and on many of the streets near the Golden Horn you will see the ruins of great houses, and even some fashionable late 19th-century blocks of flats, to testify to the wealth and influence the Phanar—as it was then called—once enjoyed. The stranglehold they maintained over the empire's economy, and thus over the sultans themselves, was notorious; the monopolies they effectively held in many fields contributed as much to the economic decline of the empire as the incompetence of the government, and so great were their exactions from the subject peoples that 'Phanariot' became a term of opprobrium used by Slavs, Turks, and Arabs alike.

Most historians have chosen to present the struggle of the Byzantines and Ottomans as an apocalyptic battle of two faiths, both incapable of either understanding or showing any sympathy at all for each other. On the contrary, the Greeks and Turks had known each other for so long before 1453—four centuries of alliances, intermarriages, and scholarly discussion—that when the end came for Byzantium, the transition was accomplished with a minimum of hysteria. After the pillage Mehmet had promised his troops, life for the Greeks gradually returned to normal, and even improved, as the sultan's efforts to re-establish trade began to pay off. In the Phanar, the heirs of the imperial Byzantine families, the Paleologues, the Comneni and the rest, were reported still to be around as late as the 1900s.

The Patriarchate

[NB: Letters in [ ] refer to map of Istanbul on pp.116–17].

One of the first acts of Mehmet after the Conquest was to co-opt the Greek church by naming Gennadius patriarch, as much a servant of the sultan as was the Sheikh ul-Islam, and meant to act as an intermediary between the Greeks and the Ottoman state. Gennadius' successors live on in the **Greek Orthodox Patriarchate** [A] on a steep hill just above the Golden Horn. Old St George's Church, where the patriarchs sat on the throne of St John Chrysostom, burned down in 1941, and the centre of the complex is now a huge tower—incredibly enough done in Victorian Gothic, built in the 1880s. The Patriarchs' throne inside is believed to date from Byzantine times.

The main gate of the Patriarchate has not been opened since Easter Sunday 1821. On that day the Patriarch Gregory, implicated in the Hetairist conspiracy of the Phanariot Greeks working for their nation's independence, was hanged from it. All those with business here enter from the side. The Patriarchate today has a lonely and forlorn air. The Greek school, supported by the republic, as it was by the sultans, appears almost empty. Few Greeks, for that matter, seem to be left in the neighbourhood, if the faces of the inhabitants and signs in the shops are any indication. The tiny, unpretentious chapel, a block away, has great meaning for the remaining

Greeks: **St Mary Mouchliotissa** [B], from the 13th century, is the only surviving pre-Conquest church never to have been converted to a mosque. Its benefactress, 'Saint Mary of the Mongols', was a Byzantine princess married off for political reasons to a Khan of the Ilhanli Mongols in 1282. After his death she returned to the city and built this church as part of the great monastic complex in which, long before, the Empress Theodora had spent her last days.

Just a few blocks away, overlooking the Golden Horn, have a look at the strangest church in Istanbul, **St Stephen of the Bulgars**. When Bulgaria gained its independence from the Ottoman Empire in 1871, the Turks weren't sore losers. They allowed the Bulgarians of Istanbul to build this church in celebration of the event. A church that defies all attempts at architectural classification, St Stephen's is made entirely of cast iron. A foundry in Vienna cast it, then shipped it down the Danube and Black Sea on barges to Istanbul, where the pieces were assembled. Each Orthodox New Year's Day, an ancient ceremony is held here in which the priest tosses a cross into the frigid waters of the Golden Horn, while the young men of the congregation (there can't be many these days) leap in and try to retrieve it.

With luck, you'll be able to pick your way through the tortuous lanes towards the walls to see two other important Byzantine monuments. The 11th-century **Pammakaristos Church** [C], quite near the Patriarchate, has one of the most unusual and most elaborate exteriors of any church in the city, in patterns reminiscent of those on the apse of the famous Greek–Norman cathedral of Monreale in Sicily, built at the same time. One distinctive feature is the delicately carved window mullions, unique to this church. Inside, a fine 13th-century mosaic scene of the baptism of Christ has recently been restored, along with a large number of mosaic figures of saints. The Pammakaristos ('most blessed') was the seat of the Patriarchate from 1456 to 1586. If you ask for directions, try using its old name of Fethiye Cami even though it's been a museum for some years. Unfortunately, it is now closed, but if you really want to see the mosaics ask at the museum office of the Aya Sofia, which has charge of it.

Church of St Saviour in Chora (Kariye)

From here, Fethiye Caddesi, changing its name to Draman Caddesi, will bring you to the **church of St Saviour in Chora** [D], or *Kariye*. This is nothing less than the finest collection of Byzantine mosaics and mural painting in Turkey. You'll find the trip worth the trouble, especially since Çelik Gülersoy and his Automobile Club have transformed the surroundings—in the middle of a very shabby neighbourhood—into a small oasis with a garden café and a number of restored Ottoman houses. The art inside, like that of the Aya Sofia, was restored by the Byzantine Institute.

Originally built by Justinian, and completely rebuilt by the Comneni in the 11th century, it is always associated with the name of Theodore the Logothete, a high official in the late 14th century who fell victim to political intrigue and ended his days as a poor monk in the church he had restored and beautified. In the latter days of the empire, when the Aya Sofia was falling into decay and the emperors had moved to the Blachernae Palace nearby, the Chora became the city's fashionable church, where the imperial family usually attended services. An icon of the Virgin kept here, one of those supposedly painted by St Luke, was credited with saving Constantinople from the siege of Murat II in 1428; the Turk's final attack failed shortly after the icon was carried solemnly around the walls.

Architecturally, little in the Chora is outstanding; the major attraction is its wealth of frescoes. Byzantine painting has always been undervalued by the critics, their eyes dazzled by the gold of the less expressive, less articulate mosaics. The restoration of the frescoes in the **Paraecclesion**, or mortuary chapel of the Chora, as well as those in other late Byzantine churches like the Aya Sofia in Trabzon, has already gone a long way towards correcting this. In these paintings, it is easy to see the influence and the inspiration without which the Italian Renaissance would not have been possible.

Of these, the greatest perhaps is the spectacular version of the **Last Judgement**, in which Jesus raises the dead over a shower of broken locks and keys; Adam and Eve are shown redeemed, along with the unbaptized kings and prophets of the Old Testament. The remainder portray various biblical scenes, the Burning Bush and Jacob wrestling with the angel, as well as a whole catalogue of Orthodox saints and some unusual *trompe l'oeil* borders. Theodore the Logothete himself appears in one of the mosaics, presenting his rebuilt church to Christ. A figure of the Christ Pantocrator and other mosaics with scenes from his life and portraits of apostles and saints cover the outer and inner narthexes; unfortunately few have survived in the nave of the church.

Theodosian Walls

The **Theodosian Walls** can be seen just a few blocks west of the Chora. In their own right, they are among the greatest monuments of Istanbul. No city has ever had better; without them, the Byzantine capital could easily have succumbed on scores of occasions to Huns, Avars, Bulgarians, Russians, Arabs, Goths or Turks; with them, even in its darkest and most decadent moments, the empire was able to maintain itself as the bulwark of Christendom and the heir of Rome.

Fully 17 miles in length, the walls stand almost intact between the Golden Horn and the Marmara, but in fragments along the shores. The inland walls, the easiest to attack, are the most impressive. Anthemius, Theodosius's prefect, made them invulnerable by doubling them, with a raised inner wall looking down over and protecting the outer, and a deep ditch in front of that. For most of their length, you can walk between them or even on them. A word of caution is in order, though; some of the areas around the walls, particularly in the Topkapi Gate area, have a reputation as being a bit dangerous (also, a lot of Turkey's drug manufacturing business is said to go on here).

Where the wall meets the Golden Horn, two towers stand as remnants of the **Dungeon of Anemas** [E] where the Byzantines kept unsuccessful schemers and political prisoners. These walls are actually not part of the original work, but a long loop added around the **Palace of Blachernae**, the huge suburban garden palace of the late emperors. Very little of it remains; the palace encompassed all of what is now the green district called **Ayvansaray**, its houses and gardens betraying occasional traces of an old wall or a bit of carved stone. The **Palace of Constantine Porphyrogenitus** [F] adjacent to the Blachernae still stands, a stony pile, literally a shell of what it once was, without roof, floors, or even its marble façade.

Edirne Gate

Just inside the **Edirne Kapi**, the old Adrianople Gate, is another fine mosque built by Sinan for Süleyman the Magnificent, the **Mihrimah Camii** [G] (1562), named after the sultan's favourite daughter. The section of the walls to the south, in the dangerous spot depressed by the valley of the Lycus stream, saw much of the heaviest fighting during the Siege of 1453. Here Mehmet's cannons pounded away relentlessly for days. Giustiniani, the Venetian commander, was wounded then, and although the wall was not breached, his loss greatly disheartened the defenders and contributed much to the fall. The postern gate of Charisius, the one accidentally left open that caused the defeat, is just north of the Mihrimah. The tallest of the towers is at the old Roman Gate, now the **Topkapi** ('cannon gate'), the major entrance to the city by road.

On the Marmara shore, the **Marble Tower** at the end of the inland walls was a famous Byzantine landmark. Just to the north, all the emperors, on their accessions or their triumphs, entered at the **Golden Gate**. Most of its legendary embellishments are long gone, including the famous golden doors, but the Crusaders could not remove the marble triumphal arch at the centre of the gate, built to commemorate Theodosius' victory over the pretender Maximus in 391. To its four towers, the Turks of Mehmet II added three more and an inner wall, creating the **Yedikule** (seven towers) **Castle**, recently restored and now open to visitors (*open daily exc Mon, 9–5; adm*). Here Osman II was murdered by the Janissaries. Later sultans used it for incarcerating foreign ambassadors when the mood struck them; many of these, along with other prisoners, have left interesting inscriptions on the walls.

Southwestern Istanbul

This part of the city has little to offer. Byzantine churches like those of the monastic complex at Studion, and the Peribleptos Monastery have long ago been battered out of recognition by earthquakes and subsequent rebuildings. Under the Byzantines, the Studion was the centre of learning of the Greek world, the prototype of the university. All that is left of it today is one of its churches, **St John in Studion**, now the Imrahor Camii on Imrahor Ilyas Bey Caddesi. Even this has little to show from its past: a few capitals and a 12th-century patterned pavement. Another church, that of **St Andreas in Crisal** [H], is still substantially intact, just to the north at the western end of Koca Mustafa Paşa Caddesi; now it is the Koca Mustafa Paşa Camii. Many Armenians live in this area, and their mostly 19th-century churches are still in use, including the Armenian Patriarchate in Sarapnel Sokak near the Marmara end of the Atatürk Bulvari. The largest of all open cisterns, the **Altimermer** [I], may be seen in the quarter of the same name, and the 1593 **Cerrahpaşa Camii** [J] is the most interesting of the area's mosques.

Rather than visiting these, take yourself to Adnan Menderes Bulvari, one of the broad empty boulevards driven through Stamboul in the 1940s, and see the ancient metropolis from the top of the Ferris wheel in the little amusement park there. Not long ago this street was called Vatan Caddesi; they had to change it because this was the lowest-rent street in the Turkish version of Monopoly; the highest, by the way, is Barbaros Bulvari in Beşiktaş.

Eyüp

Once upon a time, the Golden Horn was the most beloved of all the embellishments of Istanbul. From Eminönü Square all the way up the estuary, both banks were lined with *yalis*, the wooden mansions of the paşas, set among gardens and groves of plane trees and cypresses. Marble quays brightened the shores, and the only boats to be seen were pleasure craft and water taxis. Then, in the 19th century, Abdül the Damned—Abdülhamid II, the sultan not even the Turks will speak kindly of—let in the foreign syndicates and industrialists and, in no time at all, the Horn became a seamy polluted waterfront, the black sewer of Istanbul.

Just beyond the inland walls at Ayvansaray, the little village of **Eyüp** was, before Abdülhamid, a rare jewel of the waterway. Set on a height, enjoying the best view of the domes and minarets of the city, Eyüp was a garden suburb of lovely modest houses, favoured by the most influential artists and public men of the Ottoman Empire. Also, it was a holy place, a traditional spot for pilgrims to stop on the way to Mecca. Today, surrounded by factories and *gecekondu*, Eyüp has become a poor district and somewhat bedraggled, but still tries its best to keep its head above the miasma.

Although it is believed the spot has been holy ground since ancient times, Eyüp acquired its sanctity for Muslims during the Siege of 1453, when Mehmet or one of his vezirs had a dream directing him to the unmarked grave of Eba-Eyüp el-Ensari, the standard bearer of the Prophet Mohammed, who had died here during the first Arab attack on Constantinople in the 7th century. Eyüp—the name is the Arabic form of Job—was found just where the dream had promised. Mehmet built a *türbe* and mosque, and when an earthquake knocked it down in 1800, Sultan Selim III replaced it with the **Eyüp Cami** you see today. It was here that the sultans, upon their accessions, were girded with the sword of Osman, which served them in place of a crown as the symbol of sovereignty.

All around, between the blocks of small shops selling Korans and a strange assortment of Islamic trinkets, the living village shares the space with acres of beautiful cemeteries, their marble headstones laid out in walled gardens with names like the Pavilion of Idris and the Valley of the Nightingale.

Beyoğlu

In Byzantine times, there was no bridge over the Golden Horn—there was no reason to cross it. The little settlement on the opposite shore called Sycae never played much of a role in the life of the city. Galata, the port of Beyoğlu on the tip of the Golden Horn, began as a Genoese trading colony in the 9th century. As the Italian control of trade routes strengthened, Constantinople's economic power declined, and by the 14th century, Galata was a large and prosperous town; such trade as passed through the Bosphorus landed here, not at the impoverished capital.

Italians had long played a role in the city, not only the Genoese, but Pisans, Venetians, and Amalfitani. At one point in the 12th century, some 60,000 of them were reported to be living within the walls. Their commercial arrogance, not to mention their heretical Christianity, infuriated the Greeks, and in 1180, a mob—among whom we may guess were many of the Italians' debtors—massacred thousands. Diverting the Fourth Crusade to sack Constantinople was the Italians' way of returning the favour.

When the Greek emperors returned in 1261, Galata began to build walls against the possibility of another such debt moratorium. The restored empire, weak as it was, became entirely dependent on the Genoese. The Genoese nonchalantly declared their neutrality during the Siege of 1453, and kept some of their privileges under the Turks for as long as Genoa remained a maritime power. Under Ottoman rule, Galata maintained its role as a foreign compound; the Genoese were gradually replaced by the French and others, who were granted their first commercial privileges, or 'capitulations', by Süleyman the Magnificent in 1525.

Life in Stamboul was perhaps too unsettling for the ambassadors of the European powers, and they soon began to construct large embassy compounds on the lovely hills of **Pera** (Beyoğlu) above Galata. Fashion and influence followed, and enough money flowed into the capitulations to build Galata and Pera into the real centre of the city. As the Turks and their government became increasingly impotent and irrelevant, eventually even the sultan joined the migration, building a new palace, the Dolmabahçe, on the Bosphorus in the 1850s. Most of the recent growth of the city has occurred on the Beyoğlu side of the Golden Horn. While in many places you can still look out over open countryside from the Theodosian walls of

Stamboul, new districts have spread for miles northwards from Pera; today even the villages along the Bosphorus are considered part of the metropolitan area.

These streets were once legendary throughout the world for their scenes of ostentatious wealth mixed with age-old grime and squalor, their Levantine mix of a hundred nationalities and languages, their excesses and their intrigues. The departure of the embassies, after Atatürk moved the government to Ankara, simply let all the air of out of them, and now they display a kind of decayed grandeur that only cities like Naples and Palermo or certain parts of New York can approach. Nothing urban is as romantic as the capital of a vanished empire—think of Vienna, or Venice—and in its decay this quarter really blossomed, the natural habitat of Joel Cairo and Casper Gutman from the *Maltese Falcon*, and every other sort of spy and adventurer, real and fictional.

About a decade ago, this neighbourhood had hit rock bottom. Istiklâl Caddesi, its main thoroughfare, was a grimy, degraded shadow of its former self, lined with sordid night spots and porno theatres; few of its buildings were occupied above the ground floor. Since then the change has been dramatic. Istiklâl has been scrubbed up and polished and closed to traffic, embellished instead with the charming (and also totally practical and efficient) Nostaljik Tramvay, to carry people between the Tünel and Taksim Square. Businesses are moving back in, and the renewal is starting to spread to the side streets.

Karaköy

Coming across the Galata Bridge, you meet first the grey mess of warehouses, workshops and office blocks of **Karaköy**, or 'black village', the modern name for Galata. If the gritty surroundings suit you, walk around; Istanbul's oldest Catholic church and other peculiar relics of Galata's past are tucked away in corners where it will take you some effort to find them.

Just a block east of the bridge, the **Yeralti Cami**, or 'underground mosque', originally occupied the cellar of a defence tower believed to have been built by the Romans. The more conventional mosque building over it was added in the 1750s. To the west, off Tersane Caddesi, the **Arap Cami** started as a Byzantine church, and was rebuilt as a Dominican chapel in the early 14th century; in 1492 Beyazit II converted it into a mosque for Arab refugees expelled from Spain.

Voyvoda Caddesi takes its name from the redoubtable 15th-century Voyvode of Transylvania, Vlad Dracul, stalwart enemy of the Turk and inventor of a hundred novel ways of disposing of captives and indiscreet ambassadors. His metamorphosis into the blood-sucking Count Dracula at the hands of novelist Bram Stoker is well known. The Turks say they caught him and stuck his head on a pike; somewhere along this street it is supposed to be buried. The Romanians, and most of the historians, maintain Vlad was never defeated. Come around some night and look.

The **Galata Tower**, the most conspicuous symbol of the quarter and the centre of its skyline as seen from the

GALATA TOWER

Stamboul side, was built in 1350 as part of the Genoese fortifications. Under the Ottomans, it was put into service as a fire tower. Recently restored, it has a restaurant on the top floor with a fine view of the city. The streets surrounding the Galata Tower are an enticing tangle of steep and crumbling steps and narrow walkways, flanked by old, looming apartment blocks. Workmen's hammers clang from within dark and musty workshops and cars hoot ceaselessly as they try to squeeze their way through. This area houses a small section of Istanbul's Jewish population and a plain and modest synagogue can be found 100 yards down from the tower towards the sea on Büyük Hendek Caddesi. Called the **Neve Shalom**, it is identifiable only by the row of Stars of David above the glass doorway. It was here that Palestinian terrorists massacred 21 worshippers one terrible *Shabbat* in 1986.

Nearby, on Galip Dede Caddesi, the **Museum of Divan Literature** (*open daily exc Mon, 9.30–4.30*) is really the subtle Turkish republican way of preserving Istanbul's Mevlevi House, the tekke of the whirling dervishes, after the order's dissolution in 1925. While the *tekke* began here as early as the 1490s, most of what you see now are the contributions of the 19th-century sultans, traditionally the friends of the Mevlevis. There are exhibits of musical instruments and other dervish paraphernalia, a smaller version of the Mevlana Museum in Konya. This is also part of a working monastery; performances of the dervishes' dances are given on 17 December and other dates.

Kemeralti Caddesi

As a perfect counterpoint to the dervish house, Istanbul has long kept its **red-light district** in a compound of shabby blocks off Kemeralti Caddesi, guarded by a policeman at the front gate to keep out unlicensed females and anyone with a camera. This is a highly organized, officially sanctioned operation. Kemeralti continues westwards, past the 15th-century **St Benoit Church**, tucked awkwardly between two warehouses. Long the church of Pera's French community, St Benoit holds the remains of Ferenc Rakoczy, the 18th-century Hungarian patriot who fought not the Turks, but the Hapsburgs of Austria, and ended his life in exile in Turkey after the defeat of his revolutionary army.

Kemeralti ends at **Tophane Square**; the name commemorates the first Turkish cannon foundry built here in the early 19th century by Sultan Selim III. The **Kiliç Ali Paşa Camii** here is a noteworthy late work of Sinan; the larger mosque to the east, the 1826 **Nüsretiye Cami**, was completed just as Mehmut II won his death struggle with the Janissaries, hence its name 'Victory Mosque'.

The Tünel

No trip to Istanbul would be complete without a ride on the world's shortest underground, the **Tünel**, which will take you from the environs of Galata Bridge some 600 yards up the modest slope to Istiklâl Caddesi. The motives for building this little inclined railway in 1877 are unclear; some say its original purpose was to move livestock through to Istanbul avoiding the crowded streets of Pera. Affectionately known as the 'Mouse Hole', it was built by the Frenchman Henri Gavand in 1873 and if it takes longer than 90 seconds to hurtle through the 2034 feet of its length, then it's travelling slowly. From Tünel Square, where it ends, you may start up Istiklâl or go back to **Şişhane Square**, one of the few real tragedies of Istanbul's recent redevelopment. Once a frilly, cobbled Italianate piazza with its radiating avenues and overdressed buildings, and the site of the city hall, it has been almost totally obliterated to make more room for cars. Turkish Airlines' city terminal is here, and Şişhane may be your introduction to Istanbul. Walking up the hill from the square, along Meşrutiyet Caddesi, you will come to one of the city's great institutions, the **Pera Palace Hotel** (*see* **Topics**, p.62).

Istiklâl Caddesi

Istiklâl Caddesi was once known as the *Grande Rue de Pera*, where the ambassadors rubbed elbows with the city's commercial élite. In the 19th century it became heavily built up with European-style apartment and business blocks. Many of these are glorious Art Nouveau works from the turn of the century, their balconies dripping cast-iron vines and flowers over the street; one of the best is at no. 479 (more good ones are on Kemeralti Caddesi and other streets in Pera). Another feature of the street is the old embassies, now reduced to the status of the world's fanciest consulates. Many of the embassy compounds included churches; today you'll need to peek behind the shops into their quiet courtyards to find them: two especially fine ones, both Italian, are the church of S. Maria Draperis (1783) and S. Antonio di Padua (1725) at nos. 431 and 331 respectively.

The antique trams run every 10 minutes up Istiklâl Caddesi to Taksim Square but it is more interesting to walk, taking care that the trams—stealthy, quietly whirring contraptions—do not flatten you along the way. Starting from the Tünel entrance, the first noteworthy consulate is the Swedish, on the right hidden behind big gates. Two hundred years old, it exudes a lofty elegance. Just beyond it is the Russian consulate, splendidly overblown, all neo-Grecian columns and carved cornices, painted a purple that is, oddly enough, quite fetching. Designed by the Fossati brothers, the Italian architects of Czar Nicolas I, it was completed in 1837. A short way up, still on the right, is the church of S. Maria Draperis.

If the Dutch consulate, very white and very pretty, looks familiar it's because you've seen its big brother only minutes before; this too is the work of the illustrious and prolific Fossati brothers. Just before the consulate a narrow street declines sharply to a Dutch chapel which today is the base of the Union Church of Istanbul, a Protestant congregation which embraces all nationalities. Sunday services are held in English. Back on Istiklâl Caddesi, the last church in this sector is the S. Antonio di Padua, imposingly Gothic. A daily Mass is held here at 6pm.

Istiklâl is full of arcades (*pasaji*, in Turkish), dim covered alleys or grand follies like the Avrupa Pasaji, serving a wide variety of purposes. Most famous is the one devoted to beer, the narrow **Çiçek Pasaji**. Despite all the good things that have happened to this neighbourhood in recent years, we can still shed a tear for the 'flower arcade'. Not long ago this was the most beloved and atmospheric watering hole in Turkey, four feet wide and lined with crowded cafés and stand-up joints with sawdust on the floor. You would get a beer in a huge glass called an 'Argentine', and the barman would dump a depth charge of vodka in it if you looked like you needed it. A dancing bear might come in to entertain. All that's gone now. Well-painted and cheerful, the arcade shelters a few colourless new cafés and fish restaurants. The building in which the Çiçek Pasaji is located is itself part of the Istiklâl scenery, a florid, incredible pile with iron letters proclaiming CITY OF PERA on the cornice. Now beautifully restored, for decades it was a burned-out, empty shell. Across the street, the school behind the big gates is the **Galatasaray Lisesi**, once the most prestigious in the empire, where instruction was carried on, naturally, in French. At the end of a side street near the school is the **Galatasaray Hamam**, built by Beyazit II in 1481 and still the city's most opulent.

Language Quiz!

You may well know more Turkish than you think. Try and puzzle out these common words:

şoför	küaför	şantöz	komplo	şofben	Lozan Otel
org	otogar	fayton	şanjman	pardesu	

Partly thanks to the Lise (*lycée*) of Galatasaray, where the late Ottoman Empire's elite was trained, French cultural influence has always been strong here, and hundreds of French words insinuated themselves into the language, mostly for modern inventions and innovations. After Atatürk's revolution all of these were spelled out phonetically in Turkish, so they may not look familiar at first glance. The answers: *chauffeur, coiffeur, chanteuse, complot* (a conspiracy), *chauffe-bain* (a water heater), *Lausanne Hotel, orgue* (organ), *autogare* (the bus station), *phaeton* (the horse-drawn carriages they still use on the Princes' Islands), *changement* (gearshift), *par-dessus* (those ugly overcoats pious Muslim women have to wear).

Behind the Çiçek Pasaji, Istanbul's liveliest market, the **Balikpazari** (fish market) covers a maze of streets; most of the *meyhaneler* (bars) chased out of the Çiçek Pasaji by restauration have taken refuge here, on Nevizade Sokak and other streets. Immediately to the right of the entrance to the market is the Armenian church of **Surp Yerrortutyun**, its doors adorned with two distinctive Armenian *katchkars*, raised crosses, in wooden relief. Inside, the church is long and arched and graceful; incense hangs in the air. The street to the left of the market leads down to Meşrutiyet Caddesi and the **British Consulate**, built by Sir Charles Barry, architect of the Houses of Parliament. If you keep straight on past the consulate, you reach a large iron gate on the left. Through the gate is a courtyard, centred on a tree twisted around an old Victorian lamppost; to the right, a short flight of steps leads up to the Greek Orthodox church of **Panaya Isodion**. The church will be locked but the narthex will be open; it is hung with silver icons and gloomy paintings, the best of which is a serene Madonna set high inside the central dome. From the church, retrace your steps to the Balikpazari and turn left. A few strides away is the small **Avrupa Pasaji**, the European Arcade, now serving as a second-hand book bazaar. The books are mostly in Turkish but some shops sell old newspapers and colourful prints from the Ottoman era and you may pick up a curio or two.

Continuing down Istiklâl Caddesi, you pass on the left the **Ağa Cami**, a small and peaceful mosque constructed during the reign of Mahmut II. At the low, elegant French consulate, marked by a gargantuan tricolour, a narrow street opposite leads to another Greek Orthodox church, the **Aya Triada** or Holy Trinity. Built in neo-Gothic style, it is set in a well-kept garden and the narthex contains a gentle mosaic of the Virgin cradling the baby Jesus.

The Battle of Nevizade Sokak

When the Refah Party's Tayyip Erdoğan began his campaign for mayor of Istanbul in 1994, his biggest and most-repeated promises had nothing to do with crucial issues like water or housing. Erdoğan told the voters he would clean up Beyoğlu's crime and wide-open night life, and build a mosque among the godless cosmopolitans of Taksim Square. The mosque hasn't started yet—it's hard to get big trinkets financed when you're 38 thousand billion liras (about a billion dollars) in debt, even when your party is financed by Saudi Arabia. But the clean-up, at least, is well under way.

Refah won not only the metropolitan government (*Istanbul Büyükşehir Belediyesi*) in the last elections, but also the local mayoralty in Beyoğlu, and the job is in the hands of the new mayor there, Nusret Bayraktar. His idea of cleaning up, however, went a little further than the election promises. There are indeed more police in evidence around Istiklâl Caddesi, and the ragged child beggars/thieves have been carted off to wherever the Turks put such people; a few of the most offensive sort of 'night clubs' have been closed down—the sort the back streets off Istiklâl used to be famous for, where tourists are enticed in, and then forced to empty out their pockets slowly, buying overpriced champagne for whores.

But as it has turned out, Bayraktar's campaign against vice also extends to bars and even restaurants. One of the new mayor's first acts was to order the restaurants on Nevizade Sokak, the famous street behind the fishmarket and the Çiçek Pasaji, to get rid of their outside tables. He told them to put up curtains on their windows too. Respectable people walking by them must of course be spared the sight of reprobates drinking beer, but Bayraktar also claimed concern for poor people who can't afford to eat in restaurants, being forced to watch the more fortunate doing it. Turks of a cynical turn of mind, in other words most of them, will tell you that the new administration just wanted to shake down the restaurateurs for a little money before allowing them to put the tables back.

What followed was something rare in Turkey. Restaurateurs, neighbourhood people and Istanbul celebrities organized to form a group called the Beyoğlu Platform. Their demonstrations—often involving crowds conspicuously enjoying themselves out on the street—attracted wide press coverage. Refah was starting to look silly, and the mayor had to climb down; to celebrate, the bar and restaurant owners and Beyoğlu Platform threw a weekend-long party on Nevizade Sokak. The tables are back. The fish is frying and the beer is flowing, and Beyoğlu is getting back to normal.

But Erdoğan and Bayraktar aren't through cleaning up yet. Lately they have taken on that notorious haven for vice, the Atatürk Cultural Centre on Taksim Square. They're very concerned about what the ballerinas are wearing. And to get yet a little more decency into culture, they are insisting that the city-supported theatre company split up into male and female troupes.

Taksim Square

When Istiklâl finally gives out, it leaves you stranded in **Taksim Square**, the centre of Beyoğlu, a dull place full of cars where the dilapidation of Pera fades into the well-painted concrete of the newer areas. The *taksim* itself, a squat building with a pointed roof, is at the very end of Istiklâl Caddesi. Istanbul's fresh water was once piped here direct from the Belgrade Forest, and distributed throughout the city from the *taksim* via a smaller, more intricate piping network. The **Atatürk Cultural Centre**, a bland block of glass and stone, was completed in 1962 as the home for the Opera and a showpiece of the city's cultural life. Grand opera has had a home in Istanbul since Donizetti Paşa, brother of the famous composer, conducted the Palace Symphony in the 1840s. There is also a small Municipal Art Gallery on the square itself, with exhibits of mostly contemporary Turkish artists. On the northern fringes of Taksim, really more a large park than a square, are the two oldest of the city's fancy chain hotels, a Hilton and Sheraton, looming above the trees. Both are isolated, self-contained compounds, seemingly the last survivals of the days of capitulations and trading colonies.

Soldiers' Museum

The modern neighbourhoods beyond, Harbiye, Şişli, and Maçka, are bright and busy, but there is little to see. If you're anywhere near, though, stop in at the **Soldiers' Museum** [K] (*Askeri Müzesi*), housed in an old barracks in the hillside park a half-mile north of Taksim (*open daily exc Mon and Tues, 9–5; adm*). The Janissaries, like the sultans, never threw anything away, and the vast hoard of souvenirs and curiosities they piled up on their tours of Europe and Asia, and saved in the Aya Irene church armoury, made this natural museum collection: crusaders' swords, Byzantine battle flags, Tamerlane's coat of mail, flags of the '16 historical Turkish Empires' (including Tamerlane's and Attila the Hun's), the famous chain the Byzantines used to close off the Golden Horn, a whole hall of wax dummies of the sultans and Janissaries—the whole crazy hierarchy from the Ağas, the Makers of Soup and Water Carriers, down to the dwarfs, the *soytari* who as their card explains 'do funny things for sultan'—and a table-and-chair set made entirely out of rifles, a gift of Kaiser Wilhelm. If you come at 3pm, you'll be treated to one of the best shows in Istanbul, a performance of the **Mehter Band** in all its glorious cacophony. The early Ottoman armies marched to this music, the precursor of all band music in Europe.

Dolmabahçe Palace

At the end of the park, where it descends towards the Bosphorus, your view of the water will be blocked by the **Dolmabahçe Palace** (1852). No better monument to the spirit of the later Ottomans could be imagined. Abdülmecit, the reforming sultan of the Crimean War, was acutely aware of, and sensitive to, the growing backwardness of his nation, compared to the rest of Europe. To restore Turkey to its place in the sun, he emptied his treasury—literally putting the Ottoman Empire into receivership—not on armies, or railroads, or factories, but on this preposterous Versailles, all marble and only about half a block shorter than the Tünel. Ahmet Fethi Paşa, the Ottoman ambassador to France, scoured the luxury workshops of Europe to furnish the place, and persuaded the stage designer of the Paris Opera to come to Istanbul and put it all together. Here Abdülmecit could receive ambassadors in a proper frock coat, hold grand balls, even indulging in a waltz or two himself, or treat his guests to a private performance of Donizetti Paşa's orchestra. The empire was now officially up to date.

The real tragedy is that to make room for this pile, Abdülmecit tore down a lovely expanse of gardens and pavilions that probably included some of the finest works of Tulip Period architecture, wood and tile pavilions like those at Topkapi and Yildiz Park. Eighteenth-century Sultans such as Ahmet II and Mahmut III spent much of their time here. Anyhow, take the tour; you'll never have seen anything like it before. More bad taste is concentrated in this one building than in Napoleon's Tomb, the Great Hall of the Soviets and the Vittorio Emanuele Memorial all combined, with still enough left over to balance all the funeral homes in Los Angeles. All the gold and silk and crystal are real, of course; there is plenty of Czech and Baccarat crystal, Venetian glass, Sèvres vases, Belgian carpets (not Turkish!). No particular style predominates; probably early on it occurred to the architects and decorators that the sultan only desired that they lay it on thick. Czar Nicholas sent polar-bear rugs, and a present of elephant tusks came from the governor of the Hejaz. The British, though, knew what the Ottomans really liked; Queen Victoria sent him the biggest chandelier in the world.

The Dolmabahçe has lots of clocks, and they've all been stopped at 9.05am, the hour that Atatürk died here on 10 November 1938. To his credit, the Turkish leader occupied only a small room on his visits here; he converted the rest into a conference centre and exhibition hall. Today, the city uses it to put up whatever kings, sheikhs, and presidents happen to visit.

Beşiktaş and Yildiz Park

Beşiktaş, the neighbourhood directly east of the palace, further up the Bosphorus, begins the fashionable quarters of the modern city. Where its main street, Barbaros Bulvari, meets the Bosphorus, Turkey's **Naval Museum** [L] (*open daily exc Mon and Tues, 9.30–5; adm*) contains not only ship models, elaborately carved figureheads and other relics, but entire ships: pretty things like the 1876 gilded barge used by Abdülaziz's harem for outings, and a 144-oar naval galley from the 18th century. The point is to remind you that the Ottoman state was, in the early 16th century, the leading sea power of Europe. The **Tomb of Barbarossa**, just outside, honours the brutal Greek-born corsair who, in the service of Süleyman the Magnificent, made that pre-eminence possible.

Eleven years after Abdülmecit built Dolmabahçe, in 1863 his successor Abdülaziz grew tired of it and built a new one half a mile up the Bosphorus. **Çirağan Palace** [M] is only a third as large; presumably that was all the great powers and their Ottoman Debt Commission would allow. A fire in 1910 left only the four enormous exterior walls standing, and Çirağan was for years a ghostly shell before being converted into a luxury hotel.

In another 13 years, Abdülaziz was gone—deposed for his reckless extravagance—and his successor Abdülhamid, finding the treasury even emptier, could only build the small pavilions in **Yildiz Park**. These were left to rot after the deposition of the sultans, but recently the Automobile Club has restored both the buildings and the grounds to their original appearance, adding open-air cafés and terraces with a view over the Bosphorus. Altogether the park is one of the most beautiful in Turkey, and the restoration of the **Malta Kiosk** has won an architectural award. Another pavilion, the **Şale Kiosk**, was a residence for guests of the sultans, and is now open for visits (*open daily, 9–6*).

Istanbul in Asia

In truth, the Asian side is older. The Delphic oracle had told Byzas the navigator to settle 'opposite the land of the blind'; when his Argive expedition arrived at the Golden Horn, they found a colony of Megarans already established near what is today the suburbs of Kadiköy. Byzas knew who the blind were; the advantages of the European side for building a city were plain. In the Roman and Byzantine eras, Kadiköy was the sizeable town of Chalcedon, the site of many councils of the early Church. The emperors never favoured Chalcedon; on the contrary, they sealed its fate when they took most of the stone from its walls to rebuild their own aqueducts after various sieges. Chalcedon dwindled to nothing in the last days of the empire, and the Turks took the rest of its stones for their own projects; columns from its famous Church of St Euphemia can be seen in the courtyard of the Süleymaniye.

On the ferry from Eminönü or Karaköy, you pass **Leander's Tower**, a landmark in the Bosphorus since Byzantine times, with its lighthouse and customs house. You can also see the two main landmarks of Asian Istanbul, the Haydarpaşa Railway Station and the Selimiye Barracks.

Kadiköy and Üsküdar

The Stamboullu claim that the Asian side of the city is far different to the European side. It's calmer, they say; so much more relaxed. They're right, and you'll notice the change the minute you alight from the ferry, probably at **Kadiköy** (the destination of most boats from Europe), to set foot in another continent. It's the space that does it; ahead is a wide, uncluttered square with only a statue of a benevolent Atatürk stretching out his hand to Turkish youth. The extravagant blue building across the square (Buckingham Palace meets the Blue Mosque) is another 19th-century disaster of Ottoman architecture, now housing the local government offices. The mosque near the dock is the 1761 **Sultan Mustafa III Cami**, simple and appealing. In the streets around Kadiköy there are snazzy clothes shops, while at the port at least a dozen boot-blacks line up in a row, semi-pornographic pictures pasted to their elaborate gold-painted foot rests.

A 5-minute walk along the dock leads to the most elegant railway station in Turkey, the **Haydarpaşa**. Sirkeçi is nice but this is quite remarkable. Built in 1908 by Sultan Abdülhamid's friends, the Germans, it is named after an old general of Selim III. The ceiling is vertiginously high and twistingly ornate, the windows colourfully stained and the waiting room a revelation; wood-panelled, with chandeliers and a huge rubber plant. There is a police station, a restaurant of considerable repute, a barber shop and a post office; you can catch a train as well. A plaque outside gives more information on the station's history, in a head-scratching sort of way: 'Since putting into service the station building has the large (gross) restoration up to date (now)'.

Further along, up a gentle hill on the road to Üsküdar, are the **Selimiye Barracks** [N]. Built as part of the military reforms of Selim III, this was the home of the new model army the reformers hoped would replace the Janissaries—until the Janissaries ordered it to be disbanded. During the Crimean War (1854–6), when Britain was allied with Turkey against Russia, it served as a hospital and it was here that Florence Nightingale made her name. Her work room and personal quarters have been converted into a small and simple **museum** by the Turkish Nursing Association (she is as big a heroine in Turkey as she is in the UK). A selection of the books she wrote and published are on display, their titles holding clues as to her formidable personality: *Notes on Nursing: What It Is and What It Is Not.* Tours of the museum are conducted by a courteous young officer.

The Selimiye Barracks are now the headquarters of the Turkish First Army, charged with the defence of Thrace and the Dardanelles. At their entrance is the **Selimiye Cami**, built by Selim III for the spiritual health of his ill-fated army and set in a charming garden. At the top of the street, over the road, is the immense, haunting **Karaca Ahmet**, the largest cemetery in Istanbul, prettified with shady cypress trees.

From here **Üsküdar** is a 5-minute dolmuş ride away. Like Kadiköy, it is a bustling yet relaxing place. To the Byzantines it was Chrysopolis, 'city of gold'; today it is more a 'suburb of food' with a lively fish, fruit and vegetable market held daily and lots of good, inexpensive restaurants where the menus are in Turkish, not English. No one takes much notice of tourists here and you can stroll amongst the noisy shoppers and traders enjoying an anonymity impossible to achieve in, say, Sultanahmet.

Two large and beautiful mosques decorate the open space around Üsküdar landing. Sinan was responsible for the **Mihrimah Camii** [O] (1547), which, like the other Mihrimah, was built in honour of Süleyman's favourite daughter. Standing opposite it is the 18th-century **Yeni Valide Camii** [P], built by Ahmet III. Up the hill from the dock is another work of Sinan, the Şemsi Paşa Cami [Q].

BOSPHORUS YALIS

The Bosphorus

Even if you have only a little time in Istanbul, you will probably want to invest some of it on a trip up this lovely waterway. Roads follow both the European (*Rumeli*) and Asian (*Anadolu*) sides, but the best way to see the Bosphorus is by boat. Regular ferries from Galata Bridge traverse its length, most taking a zigzag course up and down the straits and giving you the chance of a fine fish dinner in one of the villages before your return. Unfortunately, in the last decade almost all of the Bosphorus shore has been swallowed up by the relentless growth of the city. On both sides of the straits, as far as Rumeli Kavaği and Anadolu Kavaği, villas and blocks of flats have been built on every square inch wherever the slope isn't too steep.

The Bosphorus Bridge

Just as you leave the built-up areas of the city, you will pass the **Bosphorus Bridge**, a new symbol of Istanbul often seen on souvenirs and brochures these days. It's the fifth-largest suspension bridge in the world, the longest in Europe and the only one to link two continents. It was completed in time for the fiftieth anniversary of the republic, and the Turks like to think of it as an emblem of the great progress they have made. The tolls on this bridge have already paid for the construction of another, the **Mehmet Fatih Bridge**, positioned further up the Bosphorus at the point where the waterway was first spanned, in 512 BC by King Darius of the Persians, using a bridge of boats. The Mehmet Fatih Bridge was opened in 1988, exactly 2500 years after Darius first made the connection.

Two symbols of the bad old days are underneath the Bosphorus bridge: the 1854 **Ortaköy Cami** [R], on the European side, a mosque with Corinthian columns, looks even more like a '20s American movie-palace than the others of its ilk; on the Asian side Sultan Abdülaziz found the money for yet another marble pile, the **Beylerbey Palace** [S] (*open daily exc Mon and Thurs, 9–12.30 and 1.30–7; adm*).

Napoleon III's wife, the Empress Eugénie, spent a few weeks here in the 1860s, and she must have felt right at home. The Beylerbey's other famous occupant was Sultan Abdülhamid, who was allowed to stay on at the palace by the Young Turks after they deposed him. Abdül the Damned lived out his life here in a simple room with simple furniture; he brought none of his wives or servants with him—just his cat, the only creature he trusted. On the hills above Beylerbey, Turkey's tallest structure, the TRT television tower, stands atop **Çamlica Hill**, a popular resort in the old days, with a wonderful prospect of the city and the straits. There are cafés and carriage rides, part of the recent rehabilitation and relandscaping of the hill by the Automobile Club.

Arnavutköy and the Rumeli Hísar

Back on the European side, **Arnavutköy**, the 'Albanian village', was once the prettiest town along the Bosphorus, with tall, elegant 19th-century houses built right up to the water's edge. A few of these are still left, but Arnavutköy has suffered more than any of the villages from creeping urbanization. A little further on, the straits open up into **Bebek** ('baby') **Bay**. The little palace across the way, a cupcake compared to the over-frosted wedding cakes down the straits, is the **Küçüksu Palace** [T] built by Abdülmecit (*open daily exc Mon and Thurs, 9.30–4; adm*). This is often called the Palace of the Sweet Waters of Asia, for the lovely stream that flows down from Çamlica. In Ottoman times, the rivers that led into the Golden Horn were called the 'Sweet Waters of Europe'.

Just after Bebek Bay, the straits close to their narrowest point, guarded by two Turkish castles that antedate the Conquest. Sultan Beyazit I built the **Anadolu Hisar** [U] in 1393 to choke off Constantinople's Black Sea trade. Across the straits, Mehmet tightened the grip with the **Rumeli Hisar** [V] in 1452. It's difficult to believe the latter could have had any military purpose; draped languidly over the slopes, with its neat crenellations and perfect round towers, the Rumeli Hisar is the most picturesque castle imaginable. Once it had wooden towers inside, but these have been cleared out and, instead of old cannons and dust, the castle is filled with flowers and trees; it also has an open-air theatre where plays and concerts are presented in the summer.

From Emirgân to the Kavaği

Emirgân [W], on the European side, was a garden-palace compound the sultans used for captured or exiled potentates in their care. The grounds and pavilions have been restored (by the Automobile Club, of course), most notably the lovely **Yellow Pavilion**, an outstanding example of the Turkish talent for fairy-tale architecture. An annual Tulip Festival is held here in May. All the land west of this section of the Bosphorus is Istanbul's famous and beautiful suburban park, **Belgrade Forest**, originally a hunting preserve of the Ottomans. The name comes from the Serbian prisoners of war that the sultans settled here; they and their descendants formed a tight little community charged with the responsibility of keeping up Istanbul's aqueducts and reservoirs, until the paranoid Abdülhamid had them expelled for fear they would poison the water supply. Much of the city's water still comes from here, transported via a graceful **aqueduct** built by Mimar Sinan.

The oldest surviving wooden *yali* can be seen at **Kanlica** on the Asian side, hanging gracefully out over the water. A few miles north, in the hills above Çubuklu, you can see a very different kind of house, the **Hidiv Kasri**, an Art Nouveau palace of an exiled Khedive of Egypt, now restored with a restaurant and tea salon. From nearby Paşabahçe, you can get to **Polonezköy**, some 5 miles (8km) to the east. This weekend resort, famous for food and scenery, has been, as its name implies, a thoroughly Polish village since 1842, when refugees from the freedom struggles against Russia settled here. The land was a present from the sultan, in return for the Poles' services in the Crimean War. (Having a common enemy in the 18th and 19th centuries, the Poles and the Turks were quite close, and devotees of Polish culture will be interested in the **Adam Mickiewicz Museum** on Tatlibadem Sokak in Beyoğlu, the home in exile of Poland's greatest poet.)

More towns on the European shore are **Yeniköy**, where a small Greek church overlooks the waterfront, **Tarabya**, a quite ritzy corner of the Bosphorus with a yacht harbour, and **Sariyer**, where cafés and fishing boats crowd each other along the tree-lined waterfront. South of Sariyer at Büyükdere, the **Sadberk Hanim Museum** contains a small but beautifully displayed collection of ancient Anatolian arts and Turkish handcrafts (*open daily exc Wed, 10–6; adm*). The last two towns the ferry visits are **Rumeli Kavaği** and **Anadolu Kavaği**, a pair of perfect bookends on either side of the Bosphorus, both relatively quiet and pleasant. Beyond these, much of the land is given over to the military; it's very discreet and you'll never see them, but these straits are well guarded now, just as they always have been, as several ruined fortifications testify, including the **Genoese Castle** [X] north of Anadolu Kavaği: a half-hour's climb up from the port, to a castle with medieval inscriptions and great views over the Bosphorus.

At the end of the straits, where the Symplegades, the clashing rocks of Greek mythology, were defeated by Jason and the Argonauts, all is quiet and still; two old lighthouses, the Anadolu Fener and the Rumeli Fener, wait to guide ships into the channel.

It's Only a Shanty in Old Shantytown...

Under Turkish law, the authorities may remove no squatter's shack if the roof can be raised in one night. As country people flocked to Istanbul and Ankara in the last 30 years, in search of modern life and good jobs, the outskirts of these and other cities filled with *gecekondu* (overnight) neighbourhoods. They are the outward manifestation of Turkey's continuing social revolution. Most of them, as you will see if you travel out into the vast suburbs beyond the Theodosian Walls or on the Asian side, by now have grown into real neighbourhoods with real houses, as their hard-working inhabitants gradually make their way into urban society. Turkish planners once looked upon them as their greatest problem, and their populations are still a tremendous strain on the city's budget; but by the curious and immutable laws of urban economics, it seems their resourceful, upwardly mobile people may be one of the nation's great resources. Big cities in western Europe and America went through stages like this in the 19th century, and it was just as rough for them.

In Istanbul, though, the poor aren't the only ones who can enjoy the delights of the *gecekondu*. Largely because of the ludicrous bureaucracy involved in getting a building permit, some 70 per cent of *all* construction in the city is now illegal, a figure probably much higher than even Naples. About 300 new buildings get started every night, and some Turkish genius has invented a concrete that sets in half an hour to help them along. Istanbul's boom involves not only penniless migrants, but an exploding class of *nouveaux riches*; they need houses too. More money is flowing around Istanbul these days than at any time since the days of Süleyman the Magnificent, and a sizeable proportion of it is being invested in real estate. The ultimate status symbol in Istanbul today is a villa with a balcony overlooking the straits. Nearly all of them are *gecekondu*—even if they're worth a million dollars or more.

Nothing—not the best efforts of the few, underpaid city building inspectors, nor the outcries of Turkey's small environmental preservation groups—has been able to stop the tidal wave of villas and flats that has irrevocably ruined the Bosphorus shores. There is simply too much money at stake. A new class of building speculators has rapidly become the richest and most powerful interest in the city. Often tied to organized crime, it has its ways of corrupting local governments and muscling common people off desirable plots of land they own. Sariyer (*see* above) is at the storm centre of the building boom these days. About forty of those illegally-built villas you see sprouting around you belong to one of the biggest of all the speculators—Prime Minister Tansu Çiller. Former Mayor Sözen, who came from a different party, took her and the Sariyer sub-municipality to court about them and won, but as always seems to happen in Turkey, the villas got built just the same.

The Princes' Islands (Ada Günleri)

There are nine of these in the Sea of Marmara, and ferries from the Galata Bridge, Kabataş or Bostanci call at the four largest, inhabited islands—Kinali, Burgaz, Heybeli and Büyükada. The first two are inhabited mainly by Armenians who commute to jobs in Istanbul, while the last two, especially Büyükada ('Big Island'), have long been favoured as summer retreats from the city, with their lovely pine groves, often dramatic cliffs dropping into a clean azure sea, colourful flower gardens, and lanes plied by horse-drawn carriages called *faytons* instead of cars. All the islands are car-free, and despite moves to 'modernize' and bring in traffic, the friends of the islands have so far been able to keep the beasts at bay.

Their name seems to derive not from any son of the sultan, but from the fact that from the earliest days of Byzantium up until the 15th century, they were a place of royal exile, as well as a popular spot for monasteries and, occasionally, pirates' nests. A few ruined churches and monastic buildings remain, but far more impressive, especially on Büyükada, are the grand old wooden summer houses, in all their pastel, 'gingerbread' Victorian-Gothic splendour. Another advantage of taking a trip out to the islands is the twilit return, 'sailing to Byzantium', when the great domes and minarets of the imperial mosques glow in the rosy dusk, creating one of the most rarefied and poetic cityscapes in the world.

Büyükada, *Prinkipo* in Byzantine times, is as its name implies the largest and most populous of the islands. Sights include the Anatolia Club, originally built by British residents as a yacht club a century ago, and a number of Greek relics, churches and monasteries, on the hill above the town. Carriage-taxis offer tours up to these, or you may walk or rent a bike and have a picnic; like the other islands Büyükada is largely covered with pines, planted a century ago. The most interesting, but the hardest to reach, is the **monastery of St George** on the southernmost hill, dating in part back to Byzantine times. There are small beaches at Yörük Ali and Dil Uzantisi.

The next-largest island, **Heybeliada**, lies just a mile or so to the west of Büyükada. The Turkish Naval Academy is here; on their grounds is the last church of the Byzantine Empire, the last one to be built before 1453, the **Kamariotissa** (you'll need to get permission from the naval authorities to visit). Overlooking the village from the top of the island is the **Aya Triada Monastery**, now closed but once the most important orthodox school of theology. As on Büyükada, you can easily find a *fayton* to take you around the island, and there are some decent beaches, the biggest of them at Değirmen, and others on the undeveloped western half of the island.

Two more islands are served by the ferries: **Kinaliada**, small and rather barren, is the closest to Istanbul, and largely inhabited by Armenians. **Burgazada** is steeper and greener, with ruins of another old monastery at its summit.

Shopping

You can get anything you want in Istanbul, from a 20p *boncuk* (anti-evil eye charm) to a full-size 20ft granite replica of a Hittite relief. For those born to shop, it's the best and the worst of all possible worlds. All the treasures of the Orient at your feet—but at a much higher price than out in the provinces. Those Kütahya plates seem a bargain at £6/$9; a few hours' bus ride away in Kütahya, they can be one third the price. The finest antique Ottoman-era jewellery is on display in the *bedestenler* of the Covered Market—but you might not be able to take it out of the country with you.

Metropolis Istanbul has another trump: *haute couture*, Turkish style, the logical development of a very talented nation with a very large textile industry. A few of the newer districts have concentrations of shops where you can find not only Turkish surprises but well-known designer labels at prices lower than you'll see them at home (Benetton and Levi's for example; almost everything they sell here is actually made in Turkey). Such fashion strips include **Rumeli Caddesi** and surrounding streets in Nişantaşi, **Bağdat Caddesi** in Erenköy on the Asian side, the **Galleria** mall in Ataköy, and the incredible **Akmerkez Shopping Mall** on Ulus Caddesi in Etiler: a totally colour-coordinated experience on four levels, with glass elevators, Wendy's, Dairy Queen and Buffalo wings, and all the Italian designer clothing chain stores; you might as well stay at home.

Istiklâl Caddesi in Beyoğlu, since its recent facelift, is once again becoming a fashionable shopping street; plenty of new addresses have joined old established clothing stores like **Beymen** and **Vakko**. The latter, with many other branches around town, is currently tops in Turkish fashion for both men and women, with clothes in beautiful fabrics often employing colourful, traditional Turkish motifs. Beymen tends to be more traditional, with an emphasis on simple elegance and fine materials in clothing, shoes and accessories; they also have a big department store in Akmerkez. Some other style leaders include **Mudo**, for men and women, at Akmerkez, Rumeli Caddesi and 162 Istiklâl Caddesi, **Vekem**, for women's clothing, on Kuyulu Bostan Sokak in Nişantaşi, and **Gazellini**, on Gazi Ipekci Caddesi in Nişantaşi. **Zeki Triko,** 64 Rumeli Caddesi and sold in many other shops, is internationally famous for swimwear. The **Silk & Cashmere** shop in Akmerkez has unusual things in those materials at bargain prices—it all comes from Mongolia and central Asia. For leather, a Turkish speciality, the latest can be seen at **Derishow** in Nişantaşi and on Bağdat Caddesi, **Modello**, on NIspetye Caddesi in Etiler, and **Desa** on Istiklâl by the Beyoğlu Cinema. For shoes, Beymen is good; there are also many shops in Nişantaşi, especially **Hotiç**, on Teşvikiye Caddesi, and **Demirel**, on Akkavak Sokak.

For jewellery, the obvious choice is the Covered Market, where tons of it are on display, but there are other fine shops around the city: **V–22**, on Teşvikiye Caddesi; **Artisan** and **Ayşe**, both on Iskele Caddesi in Ortaköy; **Bazaar 54** and **Lapis**, both on **Nuruosmaniye Caddesi** in Cağaloğlu. This tree-lined street, running from Yerebatan to the Covered Market, has recently been refurbished; rapidly becoming old Stamboul's only fashionable shopping strip, it has jewellery, clothing and other speciality shops.

Antiques, as you may imagine, are big business, and there will be exotic trinkets to take home in all sizes and price ranges—just keep in mind Turkey's tough laws about exporting things of genuine value (*see* p.16). Istanbul doesn't exactly have flea markets. It has *bit pazarlari*, literally 'louse markets'—not much difference. The word came from a street in the Covered Market called the Bit Pazar that now serves other purposes. Today, the biggest and most popular one sprawls around **Çukurcuma Caddesi** (east of Istiklâl, behind the Galatasaray Lisesi), a great place for every kind of Ottoman-era trinket and off-beat souvenir. Another big louse market takes place on the Asian side in **Üsküdar**, indoors in a rambling old building at 30 Büyükhamam Sokak; mostly furniture. The same description goes for the **Kuledibi Bit Pazari**, an alley devoted to antiques near the Galata Tower, and the **Horhor Bit Pazari**, a big indoor market on Kirik Tulumba Sokak in Aksaray.

Still, the address for the real treasures is still the **Covered Bazaar**, particularly in the enclosed Iç Bedesten and Sandal Bedesten: the choicest in antique jewellery, silver and gold work, even Byzantine icons and medieval astrolabes. As for **carpets**, their buying and selling is the national pastime, and Istanbul is not necessarily the best place to do it if you are concerned about price. Carpet shops around the Aya Sofia in Sultanahmet come as thick as flies, and some of the country's finest productions are brought to them. If you're experienced in the carpet game you may get a correct price there; otherwise, the carpet avenues of the Covered Bazaar or on the side streets off Istiklâl may be a better bet.

Depending on the room in your suitcase, you might take advantage of Turkey's peculiar economy and rotten exchange rates to pick up some familiar items at prices much less than at home: Turkish-made jeans and other Western duds, eyeglasses, lace and curtains, children's clothing (or anyone's clothing, really)—or spend a Sunday touring one of the dozens of suburban fields where people come to sell cars. For a small admission, you get a look at '49 Cadillacs, '50 Mercurys, '55–'59 Chevys and Chryslers, all with no rust and for a pittance; all you have to do is work them through the government bureaucracy, and then figure out how to drive them home.

As in the quarters around the Covered Market, some of the older streets in Beyoğlu are devoted to particular trades and kinds of shops. **Galip Dede Caddesi**, right at the top of the Tünel, is lined with **music** shops where you can find lutes, *neys* and other traditional Turkish instruments, along with books on how to play them, records and cassettes. For the best selection in recorded music though, look in the myriad little shops around the Stamboul side of the Atatürk Bridge. For **books** in English, and books in general about Turkey, the booksellers in the **Sahaflar Çarşisi**, between the Covered Market and Beyazit Square, have by far the best selection (*see also* p.109). They are also probably the best place to pick up inexpensive **souvenirs**: old prints and watercolours of the city, hand painted boxes and other trinkets. There is a **flower market** on the side streets off Taksim Square.

If you're cooking for yourself or planning a picnic, **food** will prove no problem at all. The **Balikpazari** in Beyoğlu isn't just a fish market, you can get just about anything there, and in the delicatessens and speciality shops in surrounding streets. Polish-run **Sütte**, on Duduodalar Sokak, is one of the few places where you can get ham and other pork products. For health foods, there is **Zencefil** on Kurabiye Sokak. Most of the better delicatessens are out in the newer districts, such as **Abant Çiftliği**, on Valikonaği Sokak in Nişantaşi. The Spice Market has plenty of food stands, with fruits and vegetables outside, and there are weekly markets in all of the city's neighbourhood high streets. An especially big and popular one takes place in **Kadiköy**, Tuesdays and Fridays; also **Cihangir** (downhill from Galatasaray) on Tuesdays, and the big daily market in **Beşiktaş**.

Sports and Activities

One thing you couldn't do in Istanbul ten years ago is shoot a round of **golf**. Now there are two nine-hole courses open to the public: the Istanbul Golf Club in suburban Ayazağa, ✆ 264 0742, and the new Kemer Golf and Country Club, a serious development in the beautiful Belgrade Forest (how'd they get permission to build there?). With views of Mimar Sinan's aqueducts, you can golf, ride a horse, etc. Call ✆ 239 7913 for information about opening hours for non-members. Some of the luxury hotels are pretty liberal about letting folks in to use their **tennis**, handball and racketball courts, gyms, etc; try the Hilton on Taksim, ✆ 231 4646, or the Swissotel, ✆ 259 0101, first. The Merit Hotel on Ordu Caddesi, ✆ 513 9300, has one of the few **swimming pools** in Stamboul; again, most of the big hotels around Taksim and the Bosphorus let the public use their pools. There's even a place to ice-skate: the Galleria Shopping Mall in Ataköy, open daily until 10pm.

Most of Turkey's top **football** clubs call Istanbul home, and you can watch them get battered regularly by foreign competition at: Beşiktaş (Inönü Stadium in Beşiktaş); Fenerbahçe (in Kiziltoprak), and Galatasaray (in Mecideyeköy).

Hamams

Altogether, this is a wonderful town to take a bath. All of the luxury hotels and a number of the less pretentious establishments (*see* under 'Where to Stay') have their own hamams. Wherever you stay, there will be one nearby. Some of them are historic landmarks; perhaps the poshest and most well-known is the **Çağaloğlu Hamam**, on Kazim Gürkan Caddesi, a palatial, 18th-century hamam which even has its own bar; open for men and women 8am–8pm. They are accustomed to tourists, and though expensive, this may be a good place for first-timers to take the plunge. Nearby, and slightly less expensive is the 17th-century **Çemberlitaş Hamam**, on Vezirhan Caddesi.

One of the nicest is the **Çinili Hamam**, in a very out-of-the-way location on Itfaiye Caddesi, just off Atatürk Bulvari north of the Aqueduct of Valens. This 'tiled' hamam was built in the 1600s for the pirate admiral Barbarossa, and it retains some of its original decor, with baths for both men and women. Because of its location it has avoided becoming touristy.

Where to Stay

The subject is inexhaustible; besides the ones you'll find listed in the official tourist literature, there are literally hundreds of unclassified establishments—so you shouldn't have trouble finding a place even in summer. Prices naturally tend to be a bit higher on the average than elsewhere—but there is plenty of room for bargaining in all categories. The first thing is to decide where you want to stay. For seeing the sights, the most logical location by far is the **Sultanahmet** and **Çağaloğlu** districts around the Aya Sofia and Blue Mosque. In addition to the older hotels, plenty of new places, many of them in restored, pastel-painted Ottoman houses, have opened in the last ten years. Walk around here with a bag or a backpack and someone who has a brother who runs a hotel will find you before long (and that's the best time to bargain).

Another large concentration of hotels, mostly in the moderate range, can be found in **Aksaray/Lâleli**, a noisy, modern district about a kilometre to the west, but still convenient to most of the sights. And there are still plenty of inexpensive hotels in the Sirkeci area around the rail station, though this thoroughly dismal quarter will not make your holiday any happier.

For businessmen and travelling paşas, most of the luxury hotels are on the Beyoğlu side, on or near the **Bosphorus coast** south of the bridge, and around **Taksim Square**. Some of the older ones, along with less expensive choices, can be found on and around **Meşrutiyet Caddesi**, a street that runs parallel to Istiklâl Caddesi through Beyoğlu.

Phone codes for the European side are 212; for the Asian side 216.

luxury

Istanbul probably has as many really posh hotels as anywhere in Europe, Paris included; quite a few have opened up in the last few years. Counting up all the royal and presidential suites, this city could accommodate about 85 kings and presidents at once.

Near the Dolmabahçe Palace at Beşiktaş, the ★★★★★**Çirağan Saray**, Çirağan Caddesi, ✆ 258 3377, 🖷 259 8677, is perhaps the city's most sumptuous, a one-time palace built by Sultan Abdülaziz. Everything you may possibly require from a hotel is here: rooms overlooking the Bosphorus, sauna and hamam, a casino and deluxe suites in the sultans' apartments (all the furnishings are modern; the palace was gutted by fire long ago).

For those who like their hotels modern, spotless, comfortable and international, there's the ★★★★★**Marmara Oteli**, ✆ 251 4696, 🖷 244 0509, on Taksim Square, once the tallest building in Istanbul, with a swimming pool, as well as television, air conditioning, refrigerators in every room, and a baby-sitting service. Of similar ilk, a totally self-enclosed compound built in the '60s, back when most foreign businessmen were too timid ever to venture out much in such an exotic city, the ★★★★★**Sheraton**, a block north of Taksim Square on the edge of Taksim Park, ✆ 231 2121, 🖷 231 2180; pool and casino.

The ★★★★★**Hilton Oteli** on Cumhuriyet Caddesi, ✆ 231 4650, 🖷 240 4165, has the same facilities, as well as tennis courts, a hamam, sauna, squash, tennis and, if you need it, a chopper pad. Among the newer competitors, there is the ★★★★★**Swissotel Bosphorus**, ✆ 259 0101, 🖷 259 0105, a striking modern building across from the Dolmabahçe Palace. Many rooms have a view of the straits. There is a wide choice of bars and restaurants on the premises, including a roof garden, a hamam, two pools and tennis courts. And for some outrageously flash architecture straight from Dallas or L.A, there's the 27-storey ★★★★★**Holiday Inn Crowne Plaza**, Sahilyolu, Ataköy, ✆ 560 8100, 🖷 560 8155; 'fitness centre' and gargatuan pool; satellite TV and trouser press built into every room.

Far more convenient for the sights, and affording a lavish view over the Golden Horn, is the magnificent ★★★★**Pera Palace** at Meşrutiyet Caddesi 98/100, Harbiye, ✆ 251 4560, 🖷 251 4089 (see **Topics**, p.62). The Pera Palace is the city's most famous hotel, a great Edwardian pile built by the Wagons-Lits Company for their passengers on the Orient Express. It has changed little over the years, and has provided the setting for several novels about the city. Its bar is legendary, its restaurant excellent; you can ask for a free tour of the suite, now a museum, that Atatürk used when staying here. There is no swimming pool (and we've had complaints about the service here). In Lâleli, the ★★★★★**Merit Antique**, Ordu Caddesi 226, ✆ 519 9300, ✉ 512 6390, is the only luxury hotel near the sights, with rooms more like small apartments than anything else; all the amenities but can be a bit noisy.

On the Asian side, the pick of the bunch is the ★★★★★**Hidiv Kasri** (Summer Palace of the Khedive), in the village of Çubuklu on the Bosphorus, ✆ (216) 331 2651, ✉ 322 3434, built at the turn of the century by the King of Egypt as a holiday home, and restored by the Automobile Club. It's lovely, set in its own peaceful park with immaculate gardens; there's a restaurant.

expensive

In Sultanahmet, the ★★★★**Yeşil Ev,** Kabasakal Sok 5, ✆ 517 6785, ✉ 517 6780, is a wonderful establishment, another 19th-century mansion once the home of an Ottoman paşa—and another restoration project of the Auto Club (it was one of their very first). It's a blissful bolt-hole of tranquillity between the Blue Mosque and the Aya Sofia, with a back garden; all rooms have period decor. Reservations are essential. Very similar in price, quality and style is the ★★★★**Hotel Sokullu Paşa**, in an 18th-century house at Şehit Mehmetpaşa Sokak, ✆ 518 1790, ✉ 518 1793, south of the Hippodrome. In the same spirit, but somewhat cheaper, are the old Ottoman houses called the ★★★**Aya Sofia Pansionlari** on Soğukçeşme Sokak behind the Aya Sofia, ✆ 513 3660, ✉ 513 3639; a couple of the rooms have their own private hamam. For an alternative to restored clapboard mansions, try the stylishly decorated ★★★**Kybele**, ✆ 511 7766, a small, welcoming establishment that has recently opened at 35 Yerebatan Caddesi, with a lovely restaurant, or else the ★★★★**Kalyon**, ✆ 517 4400, ✉ 638 1111. This is a smart, motel-style place on the coastal Sahil Yolu, just a short walk from the Blue Mosque. Rooms have air conditioning and minibar, and most look out over the Marmara.

Another tremendous renovation job, again by the Auto Club, has been carried out on another Ottoman mansion across the street from St Saviour in Chora, the ★★★**Kariye Oteli,** at Kariye Camii Sokak, Edirnekapi ✆ 534 8414, ✉ 521 6631—a nice place, though the neighbourhood is an unlikely location for such a hotel.

Across the Golden Horn, the only hotel on Istiklâl Caddesi is the ★★★★**Richmond**, at no. 445, ✆ 252 5460, ✉ 252 9707. It is a thoroughly modern establishment; there are fine rooms with air conditioning and other amenities, but nostalgia is still the selling point here—no traffic to keep you awake, just an occasional antique tram rattling by. On Meşrutiyet, the second choice to the Pera Palace in the old days was the ★★★**Büyük Londra**, ✆ 293 1619, ✉ 245 067. Now it's a similar faded beauty, completely unrestored, worthwhile if you can get one of the front rooms with a balcony and a view over the Golden Horn. There are any number of hotels in the middle range around Taksim Square, and a few in Lâleli/Aksaray, but most of these are purely for businessmen, and not distinguished in any way.

One serendipitous alternative to city hotels, for anyone who doesn't mind a ferry ride commute for sightseeing, is to stay at Büyükada, largest of the Princes' Islands. The domed ★★★**Splendid Palas**, 23 Nisan Caddesi, ✆ (216) 382 6950, ✉ 382 6775, has pretty, old-fashioned rooms with balconies, and a small pool; built in 1908, it's nice though a bit faded. On Heybeliada, the ★★★**Halki Palas**, ✆ 351 8543, used to belong to the Orthodox seminary; now it is a pretty, restored hotel with lovely rooms and a pool.

moderate

In one of the nicer parts of Sultanahmet, south of the Aya Sofia, quite a few reasonably priced places have opened up in restored old houses. Two of these are next to each other on Amiral Tafdil Sokak off Mihmar Mehmetağa Caddesi, called the ★★★**Obelisk**, ✆ 517 7173, ✉ 517 6861, and the ★★**Sümengen**, ✆ 517 6869, ✉ 516 8282. Both are converted Ottoman houses. The Sümengen is especially nice, with spacious, attractive rooms—with the trademark Ottoman-era sash windows with latticed screens—a terrace with a sea view, and its own marble-lined hamam. Two more pleasant, very similar places stand opposite one another on Utangaç Sokak, just behind the Blue Mosque, one painted pink and one painted green. The green one is the ★★**Side Pansiyon**, ✆ 512 8175, the pink the ★★**Hotel Uyan**, ✆ 516 4892, ✉ 517 1582; simple rooms and a breakfast terrace on the roof.

For comforts equal to these, though a bit less character, you can try the more conventional hotels on and around Yerebatan Caddesi, north of the Aya Sofia; in any of these, ask for a room on the upper floors and you may well get a memorable view. The ★★**Pamphylia**, an older hotel on Yerebatan at Alayköskü Caddesi, ✆ 526 8935, may be all painted in cheerless greys, but it's quiet, friendly and the rooms are comfortable; prices near the inexpensive range. At about the same rate, you can do just as well around the corner at the ★★**Ema**, ✆ 511 7166: well-kept, with breakfast on the roof terrace. Nearby, off the Mihmar Mehmet Caddesi at Adliye Sok 4, is the clean but rather antiseptic **Alp Guesthouse**, ✆ 517 9570. The ★★**Hotel Hali**, Klodfarer Caddesi 20, ✆ 516 2170, is well positioned for the sights, with a view of the Blue Mosque from some of the rooms. The ★★★**Hotel Pierre Loti**, ✆ 518 5700, ✉ 516 1886, opposite the *türbe* of Mahmut II on the Divan Yolu, is a new establishment, bright and keen; comfortable, if charmless rooms with air conditioning and TV, and good service. Down in Sirkeci, the ★★**Hotel Erboy**, Ebusuut Caddesi, ✆ 513 3750, does its best to inject a note of decorum into the squalor of the surrounding area. It boasts a TV in every room; prices, as everywhere in Sirkeci, are reasonable. Aksaray/Lâleli has scores of hotels in this range, all in modern buildings and all much the same. One of the more expensive, and correspondingly luxurious ones, is the ★★★**Şahinler**, 10 Koska Caddesi, ✆ 518 6800. More common are utilitarian places that get a lot of businessmen and tour groups, like the ★★**Eyfel**, 19 Kurultay Sokak, ✆ 520 9788, ✉ 527 0771, or the ★★**Pisa**, also on Kurultay Sokak, ✆ 512 5940, ✉ 527 0771; both good bargain choices.

Mid-range hotels are not easy to find across the Galata Bridge. You could try the ★★**Hotel Likko 88**, Meşrutiyet Caddesi 95, ✆ 251 5957, near the British Consulate. It's relatively new, as its name suggests, and all rooms are air-conditioned. Just off Taksim Square is the ★★★**Santral**, Billurcu Sokak 26, off Siraselviler Caddesi, ✆ 251 8110, where the double rooms come with mini-bar and television.

inexpensive

Don't expect wonders here. In comparison with the rest of Turkey, hotels on the lower end of the scale tend to be higher-priced, and proprietors do not worry themselves as much about keeping them attractive. At least, there's plenty of choice. These days, the place to look first for an inexpensive or cheap room is the Sultanahmet district, south of the Aya Sofia and Blue Mosque. In the last decade, scores of places have opened up in the old residential parts of the neighbourhood—a funky and amiable place, about evenly divided between run-down flats and the hotels. In general, the further you are from the Aya Sofia, the cheaper the hotel.

Kücük Ayasofia Caddesi, at the western end of the neighbourhood, is a good place to look: here is the **Rose Pansiyon**, ✆ 518 9705, newly opened and eager to please. Also a find for comfortable, inexpensive rooms, is the **Guest House Dawn**, ✆ 517 7858, on the same street at no. 36. The ***Hotel Aya Sofia**, behind the Blue Mosque on Reşit Sok 24, ✆ 516 9446, is slightly more expensive due to its prime location. It's a cheerful hotel, clean and friendly, though it's popular and getting more expensive. The ***Hotel Klodfarer**, Klodfarer Caddesi 22, ✆ 528 4850, provides pleasant rooms in a convenient location, in between the Grand Bazaar and Sultanahmet. South of the Topkapi Saray is the **Guest House Berk**, Kutlugün Sok 27, ✆ 511 0737, a friendly and reasonably priced family concern; **Barut's Guest House**, Ishak Paşa Caddesi 8, ✆ 520 1227, is similarly priced and equally friendly but is unfortunately closed in winter.

The Sirkeci area, near the rail station, used to be the best hunting place for inexpensive hotels. There are still plenty of choices—but this dreary area should be kept in mind only if you can't find anything in Sultanahmet. The ***Hotel Istiklâl**, Muradiye Caddesi, Vezir Cami Çikmazi 4, ✆ 527 5370, is maybe a little too near the railway station for comfort, but it has nice rooms and a rooftop bar with terrific views. A similar place nearby is the old-fashioned ***Ipek Palas Oteli**, Orhaniye Caddesi 9, ✆ 520 9724. In Aksaray/Lâleli, you'll still be able to find a few inexpensive choices, such as the ***Belde**, on Kurultay Sokak, ✆ 511 2176.

cheap

Most of Istanbul's cheap hotels can also be found in Sultanahmet, places with long experience catering to student backpackers such as the friendly, well-heated **Sultan Tourist Hotel** 2, Akbiyik Caddesi, Terbiyik Sok 3, ✆ 516 9260. In the same area, the **Yusuf Guesthouse**, Kutluğun Sokak by the Topkapi Palace wall, ✆ 516 5878, and the rather grimy **Topkapi Hostel**, ✆ 517 6558, charge the same rates and are decent alternatives if the Sultan is full. Other cheap hotels abound in Sultanahmet and you'll have no trouble finding a place to stay; if you don't find them, they'll find you. Another reliable one: **Sahil Pansiyon**, also on Akbiyik Caddesi, ✆ 518 8479; clean rooms and English-speaking owner; kitchen available.

In Sirkeci, the cheapies tend to have monolingual staff and revolting rooms. A shining exception is the **Hotel Büyük Samil**, Hüdavendiğar Caddesi 35, ✆ 526 7279. It caters well for the visitor and is very reasonably priced, including a few rooms with baths. None of the cheap hotels around Taksim can be recommended with any confidence; if you want to stay in Beyoğlu on the cheap, try Meşrutiyet Caddesi, where there are a few tolerable addresses, such as the **Dünya**, at no. 79, ✆ 144 0940.

campgrounds and hostels

There are a few places to camp, all located west of the old town near the airport. The **Ataköy Kamping**, on the Marmara, is a good one, with a pool and other facilities, and convenient bus service into the city; Orbay Caddesi in Ataköy, ✆ 559 6000. Also by the sea, near a small beach, **Florya Turist Camping**, on the coastal road in Florya, would be perfect if not for the noise from the airport, practically next door; very close to the commuter rail line into Istanbul; ✆ 573 7993

Behind the Aya Sofia is the **Interyouth Hostel**, Caferiye Sok 6, ✆ 513 6150, plain and basic and freezing in winter; dorm beds cost about 50p per person and it gets very mixed reviews. Its cafeteria serves cheapish breakfasts. The depths of Sultanahmet hold a few more hostels (any place where you'll have to share a room is called a hostel here), including a reasonably well-maintained one, the **Sindbad Youth Hostel**, on Demirci Reşit Sokak, off Küçük Ayasofia Caddesi, ✆ 638 2721.

Eating Out

Eating in Istanbul is a pure delight; the city has attracted the best of the country's chefs and many places still serve old Turkish specialities, almost impossible to find elsewhere in the country. It's true that most of the finest restaurants are now out in the newer quarters north of Taksim Square, or along the Bosphorus, places where tourists have little other reason to travel. But you're not likely to starve in old Stamboul or Beyoğlu.

Do note that Istanbul is a wonderful town for avoiding hotel restaurants. Places that have them are either catering to businessmen or tour groups, and it often seems they're only spreading a table out of some vague sense of obligation. Ask the desk clerk where he'd go if he were you; maybe he'll tell you. And if you're looking for something special, beyond what we offer below, you'll probably have to ask somebody, because restaurants in this city—beyond simple *lokantas*—are surprisingly hard to find. They're all around, only a bit inconspicuous, often tucked away on back alleys and in second-storey rooms.

But who needs restaurants in Istanbul? It is entirely possible (and if you like to eat, almost inevitable) to spend the whole day grazing out on the pavements. There are the ubiquitous *simit* vendors—and with experience you'll learn that no two *simits* are alike; some are divine, others can be taken home as souvenir door-knockers. *Büfeler* ('buffets', another French word) and street vendors decorate every street corner; they offer tasty döner, sandwiches, nuts and pumpkin seeds, bowls of lentil soup, *böreks*, puddings, cookies, baked potatoes with dressing or roast corn on the cob (two new fads), not to mention an infinity of kebabs, fish sandwiches around the docks, and lots more. Between each indulgence you can sit down for a fast glass of tea to digest. And then there are the pastry shops—start frequenting these and it's all over.

expensive

Most of these accept credit cards, but moderate or inexpensive places hardly ever will.

It's hard to find anything really distinguished in Sultanahmet. The Turkish/continental restaurant at the **Yeşil Ev**, Kabasakal Caddesi 5, ✆ 517 6786, is pleasant and peaceful and will appeal to non-smokers; it must be the only restaurant in Turkey to have a no-smoking section—in a charming conservatory; £12–15/ $18–23. On Soğukçeşme Sokak behind the Aya Sofia, is **Sarnıç**, ✆ 512 4291, a truly remarkable restaurant sited underground in what was once a Byzantine cistern. Converted by TTOK, it is furnished in a strange baronial style with much wrought-iron work and an open fire big enough to roast a Volkswagen. Such surroundings don't come cheap—but one comes here more for the setting than the cuisine. The same is true for a number of

Istanbul's old standbys, such as the Greek-Turkish **Pandeli's**, above the Spice Market at the Yeni Cami end, ✆ 522 5534, with high prices (lunch only, about £13/$20) to match its old reputation. More expensive dining can be had at the lavish dining room of the **Pera Palace** £15/$23, though here the real pleasure is dressing up and playing spy. At the landmark **Galata Tower** in Beyoğlu, ✆ 245 1160, the attraction is the view, and weekend belly-dancing and music (£15/$23 and up).

At the Tünel end of Istiklâl Caddesi, the **Four Seasons**, ✆ 245 8941, has charm, sophistication, French onion soup and a very English sweet trolley. Further out, a fine lunch in sumptuous surroundings overlooking the Yildiz Park can be had at the **Malta Koskü**, an Ottoman pavilion (£13/$20, closed evenings).

Next to the fish market in Sariyer on the Bosphorus, the **Urcan Restaurant**, ✆ 242 1677, has been a seafood favourite with locals and visiting celebrities for over fifty years (most recently Helmut Kohl, but they've restocked the kitchen since). Another one with a view, and lovely seafood *börekler*, is the **Körfez**, near the Bosphorus bridge at 78 Körfez Caddesi, Kanlica, ✆ 413 4314. Both these places, as well as the myriad other seafront restaurants along the straits, pride themselves on local favourites such as sea bass baked in salt (not too salty when it's done; don't worry); expensive as they are (£25/$38 or so), they're always crowded.

On the Asian side, there are a number of seafood restaurants on the coastal Sahil Yolu in Uskudar: the **Salacak**, ✆ (216) 341 2089 serves excellent grilled fish, with windows overlooking the Bosphorus, £16/$25 and up; and the **Kiz Kulesi**, ✆ (216) 341 0403; outdoor dining in summer and occasionally live music; about £10/$15 and up. On Büyükada, one of the Princes' Islands, try **Milano**, on the waterfront (£9/$14).

moderate

Konyali's, on Ankara Caddesi 223 opposite the railway station, is long established in Istanbul and has a fine reputation for kebabs and *böreks*, serving good food for around £5/$8 and up. There is another branch in the Topkapi Saray (the only restaurant in the Topkapi Saray). **Borsa** (next to the walkway over Reşadiye Caddesi near the Galata bridge) is a chain, but it works hard to present typical kebabs and other dishes, such as *lahana dolma* (stuffed cabbage) with a little more care than the usual *lokantas*; especially good with soups and desserts (£6/$9 avg), they are becoming quite popular—and they take credit cards. Other branches are on Taksim Square, in Fenerbahçe and Osmanbey. In Sultanahmet, slightly more expensive than the average *lokanta* in the area, **Bokhara** on Yerebatan Caddesi, a block from the Aya Sofia, offers the additional attraction of outside tables and occasional live music in summer.

In the Covered Market (western side, on Gani Çelebi Sokak), **Havuzlu Lokanta**, next to the post office, has a good range of Turkish food, and is open from 11am to 6pm. *Havuzlu* means 'with pool', for the small marble pool outside the restaurant.

In Byzantine times, the **Kumkapi** quarter was the fisherman's port of the capital. Today, just by coincidence, this busy neighbourhood on the Marmara, south of the Covered Market, has become popular with the Stamboullu for its seafood restaurants. There are dozens of them on the pedestrian streets around Telli Odalar Sokak and Arapzade Ahmet Sokak at Kumkapi's centre. None really stands out, but at most you can get a fine fish dinner for £12/$18 or under; strolling around looking for something that catches your fancy (all the seafood will be on display in glass-fronted coolers) is a pleasant way to build up your appetite. Some of the less expensive places are on Gedik Paşa Caddesi, such as the **Istanbul Restaurant**; outside tables amidst swarming street life and convivial waiters. Pick a good fish out from the cooler for £8/$12, or dine for much less on soup and kebabs.

When you visit the Sulimaniye Mosque, try and plan it to make lunch or dinner at the **Darüzziyafe**, © 511 8414; housed in the Sulimaniye's *kulliye*, this is a thoroughly modern place with some extremely refined cooking. The speciality of the house is a spicy chicken in pastry dish called *tavuklu kolbörek*; avg. about £8/$12.

In Karaköy, by the cruise ship dock, the **Liman Lokanta** is a longtime seafood favourite; it's upstairs in the Turkish Maritime Lines's terminal building, © 244 1013. An old-fashioned place with a marvellous view of Stamboul, it's only open for lunch; £6/$9, more for fish. Up the hill in Beyoğlu, the **Haci Baba**, Istiklâl Caddesi 49, is now in its 73rd year and still serving delectable Turkish cuisine at around £8/$12 a head; no alcohol.

This area has plenty of other choices, though they're often hard to find. The easiest thing is to take yourself to **Nevizade Sokak/Kalyoncukulluğu Caddesi**, behind the Balikpazari, where there are scores of simple restaurants with outside tables in the £6–10/$9–15 range, most of which specialize in seafood. **Kalyoncu**, on Kalyoncukulluğu, is a nice one for grilled fish. **Asir**, on the same street, is one of the most authentic surviving *meyhaneler*, offering plates of mezes and fish along with the drinks. The newly-restored **Çiçek Pasaji** is full of restaurants. Right now they all look pretty dull but give it a look when you pass through; one of them may be finding itself. Out in Gaziosmanpaşa, north of Eyup, there is **Çimen** at Kişla Caddesi 116, where you can get a whole lamb roasted on a spit (£4/$6 for a normal portion).

If you have a car, try to make it up to the Çamlica hill park on the Asian side and the **Çamlica Café**, © 329 8191; good, typical Turkish cooking with the grandest view of all views of Istanbul. One of the best spots for *manti* and *börekler* is up the Bosphorus, on the coast road in Istinye: the **Armağan Manti Evi**; a wide choice of fillings, sweet and savoury, and you can get enough for a snack or a full meal. At **Yedi Gün**, in Sariyer, you can get a nicely grilled fish and mezes for much less than most of the places in this swank area; £7/$10; on Iskele Caddesi.

If you want to see what the other Bosphorus villages were like twenty years ago, take the ferry to the end, to Anadolu Kavaği, the only one that hasn't been totally swallowed up by villas yet (though by the time you read this it may be too late). All around the waterfront are small fish restaurants with outside tables where you can get a sweet and simple dinner for about £8/$12.

Over the Bosphorus in Asia, Üsküdar and Kadiköy are both full of good chow houses. In Üsküdar, **Kanaat** on Selmanipak Caddesi has a wide menu and specializes in gorgeous, sticky desserts £5/$8. In Kadiköy, **Iskender Kebapçisi**, Bağdat Caddesi 423, prides itself on its mixed grills; £4/$6 for a full meal. Another branch is in Üsküdar, near the dock. The coastal road in Salacak just south of Üsküdar, facing the Kizkulesi (Leander's Tower) is a good place to look for restaurants of all kinds. Just off it, at 20 Salacak Iskelesi, **Arabin Yeri**, © (216) 333 3157 is a neighbourhood favourite seafood spot, with a view over the straits; open until midnight.

While in Asia, you could do a lot worse than dine at the unnamed restaurant at the **Haydarpaşa railway station**, with its tiled and panelled walls and respectful, uniformed waiters. You may never dine at another railway station like it. And if you're anywhere nearby, it's well worth an evening excursion to Kadiköy, the neighbourhood south of Haydarpaşa, for a dinner at the **Kadife Chalet**, on Kadife Sokak ✆ 347 8596. In an old Ottoman house, the restaurant shares space with an art and crafts gallery.

Outside town, there's always the enormous **Beyti** at Orman Sokat 9 near the airport, ✆ 663 2992, with its heliport, three kitchens, and the much-imitated *Beyti kebab*; open until midnight (reasonably priced, at around £6/$9 for a full meal).

cheap

Cheap *lokantas* and kebab stands abound in Sultanahmet, most of them on the Divan Yolu. The one that stands out is the **Paris Lokanta**, on the south side of the strip: tasty stews, marble tables—Turkish diner paradise for about £3/$4.50, the going rate for the area. Second choice is the **Vitamin**, on the north side of Divan Yolu, a lively place where an idiosyncratic chef stands in the window, surrounded by tempting dishes, and tries to entice tourists in with forceful cries of 'Yes!'. Near the Vitamin, the **Can Restaurant/Pudding Shop** was the old 1960s international rendezvous point for hippy travellers on the overland route to Asia. It's inexpensive, and you'll get a free postcard, but it's lost a lot of its character. A wide choice of dishes; the *sutluç* is an absolute dream. On the north side of At Meydani (the Hippodrome), the restaurant of the **Hotel Alzer** offers a filling £3/$5 set menu—definitely worth a visit for the plate of assorted *mezeler* that starts it off; outside tables.

After shopping in the Covered Market, try lunch at **Subaşi**, on Nuruosmaniye Caddesi near the market gate; tasty *lokanta* cooking and always crowded. For a snack or light lunch after sightseeing or shopping, there is **Gözleme**, on the north side of the Divan Yolu at Çemberlitaş: very atmospheric, decorated with kilims, and a wide choice of pastries with cheese, spinach or meat, *manti*, *böreks*, puddings and desserts.

The best *lokanta* around the Spice Market is also the hardest to find: **Küçük Hüdadad**, hidden inside the Şapçi Han directly across from the market on Kömür Bekir Sokak. £4/$6 for a complete dinner of soup, kebab and dessert. In Sirkeci, there are several good *börek* houses near the railway station, where a plate of *börekler* and a cup of tea make a lovely mid-morning snack. At the time of writing, the lower deck of the new Galata Bridge isn't open yet, but several of the inexpensive fish restaurants and cafés the old bridge was famous for plan to move back as soon as they can. At any rate, you can still find fishing boats tied up along the docks on either side, where they grill the fish right after they catch it, and sell you a very tasty and very filling sandwich for next to nothing.

Elsewhere in Istanbul, cheap eating is reduced to the simple *lokantas* that are everywhere. Beyoğlu and Taksim have plenty—one on every corner on busy streets. **Felimi Baba**, on the northern end of Meşrutiyet Caddesi, has tasty *iskender* and other kebabs for £4/$6. **Yakup 2**, on Asmalimescit Sokak near the upper end of the Tünel, is a lively, fun place, a combination neighbourhood *lokanta* and *meyhane* for the artsy Beyoğlu set.

It's hard to find anything more than a simple *lokanta* on the Princes' Islands; on Büyükada, at 10 Gülistan Caddesi, **Birtat** offers kebabs and some seafood at relatively cheap prices.

alternative cuisines

If the delights of Turkish cuisine wane, there is a wide range of alternatives. The most famous of these is Russian: **Rejans**, a favourite of Atatürk's, is hidden away on Emir

Nevruz Sokak, off Istiklâl Caddesi near the Panaya Isodion, ℰ 244 1610. Founded by White Russians in the 1920s, and once the most fashionable spot in town, Rejans has declined quite a bit, but the Russian cuisine, the vodka and the tatty ambience keep it popular. For the fine wood-panelled interior and the pre-Great War ambience of hushed stealth, you'll pay around £10/$15. Istanbul's other famous Russian restaurant is in Istinye, up the Bosphorus: **Süreyya**, Istinye Caddesi 26, ℰ 277 5886. Serious borscht and caviar, also Turkish food, expensive and usually crowded. French and Italian restaurants are very popular, though there are few in the old city. Try **Le Chalet** at Tarabya, or **Ristorante Rosa**, Cumhuriyet Caddesi 131, ℰ 241 2827, good for pizzas, about £10/$15 for a full dinner. Logically situated next to the the Italian consulate at 157 Meşrutiyet Caddesi, **Pasta Villa** serves up a range of pasta dishes at lunchtime for £3/$4.50.

Oriental restaurants are becoming popular in the modern neighbourhoods—Turks are very open-minded, and have a weakness for any kind of good cooking. Out in suburban Etiler, at 4 Nispetiye Sokak, the **Seoul**, ℰ 263 6087, offers Korean seafood, hot pickle and at-the-table barbecues (avg. £15/$28) and just what you were dying for in Istanbul —a karaoke bar! Chinese restaurants abound. The poshest, with arguably the most refined and authentic cuisine, is the **Dynasty Asian**, in the Merit Hotel, on Ordu Caddesi in Lâleli, ℰ 513 9300, about £20/$30 maximum—they also do a much less expensive *dim sum* lunch. **China Restaurant**, on Lamartin Caddesi near Taksim Square, was the first in Turkey, in the '50s, and it has become an institution, still good and reasonably priced: average dinner about £8/$12.

For something really different (and expensive) have a taco and a stiff margarita at the **Café Caliente**, on Iskele Caddesi in Ortaköy near the Bosphorus Bridge, ℰ 260 9608, Istanbul's trendy pseudo-Mexican restaurant. **Café Fischer** is a German restaurant at 51 İnönü Caddesi, near Taksim, ℰ 245 2576, good for *wienerschnitzel* and chops, about £10/$15. While **Café Wien**, on Atiye Sokak in Teşvikiye, ℰ 233 7860, serves Austrian food on its garden terrace: schnitzel, lavish pastries and *kaffe mit schlag*. For Indian grub there is **Awara** at Köybaşi Caddesi 76. With all this on offer, philistines can still be satisfied: there is a **McDonalds** in Beyazit and in Taksim, and now Turkey's first drive-in, on the E5 at Merter; a **Wimpy** on Istiklâl Caddesi and a **Kentucky Fried Chicken** near the airport in Ataköy. **Pizza Hut**, at the Taksim end of Cumhuriyet Caddesi, ℰ 251 8998, will deliver.

And if you're going on a picnic, you can visit one of the city's gastronomic shops—including many of the stands in the Balikpazari, such as Şutte, one of the few places to find ham and bacon, or Konyali, near Sirkeci Station, or in the Spice Market, where you can get the finest caviar: not from Russia any more, but from the Azerbaijani Republic.

pastry shops

Don't forget to save a major part of your calorie budget for these, for Istanbul is one of the world's capitals of sweet indulgence. You'll never be more than a block away from a place where you may sit down with a glass of tea and a slice of baklava at almost any hour of the day. In addition, the big hotels here have always had a tradition of keeping a master pastry chef in the kitchens of their elegant cafés. It isn't just about baklava and other Turkish treats. With its cosmoplitan tradition (and its incurable sweet tooth), this city has embraced everything that's tasty, from Central European tortes to French pâtisserie and chocolates to American cheesecake.

Top of the list, and still an essential part of the Istanbul experience even though it's often crowded with tour groups, is the **Pâtisserie de Pera**, in the Pera Palace Hotel: a marvel of Victorian cosiness with antique decor and silver, and a view. Some of its contemporaries from the good old days have been revived along Istiklâl Caddesi: notably, the **Café Marquiz**, with its glorious tile decoration from the '20s (supposedly to reopen soon, after a long hiatus, under ambitious new owners who plan to recreate the café's original recipes) and, across the street in the Hotel Richmond, the **Café Lebon**, locally famous for its fruit pies. The **Inci**, at 124 Istiklâl, is famous for profiteroles (they claim to have invented them).

Some of the luxury hotel cafés roll out their finest confections for a five o'clock tea: the Çiragan Palace's **Gazebo Café** and the **Café Marmara**, in the Marmara Hotel on Taksim Square. For overwhelming cream and chocolate spectaculars with the Central European touch, there is the **Café Wien** (*see* under 'Eating Out'), the **Pâtisserie Gezi**, Inönü Caddesi off Taksim Square, and the **Pâtisserie Suisse** in the Mövenpick Hotel, on Büyükder Caddesi in Maslak. In old Stamboul, the pastry shops tend to be less lavish and the recipes more authentically Turkish; one of the best is **Ciğdem**, at 64 Divan Yolu.

Entertainment and Nightlife

Istanbul is well endowed with **cinemas**, and each district has at least one, usually with several screens; most of the film palaces are on Istiklâl or around Taksim Square. English-language films, though, are almost invariably dubbed. Try to check what's showing just before setting off, lest you fall prey to the irritating habit of last-minute programme changes. Istanbul has a full schedule of **concerts**, **opera** and **ballet**; the two big venues are the **Atatürk Cultural Centre** on Taksim Square and the **Cemal Reşit Rey Concert Hall** in Harbiye; other spots, including historic sights like the Aya Irene church at Topkapi, host events during the **Istanbul Festival**, which runs from May through July. Genuine Turkish traditional and classical music is a bit harder to find; you'll get some on TRT3, 88.2 FM, and beyond that consult *The Guide* or the tourist office for schedules of concerts.

Forget the images of Turkish Delight advertisements, forget the Thousand and One Nights and 'Eastern promise'; night-time entertainment in Istanbul is disappointing. What there is, is largely across the Golden Horn in Taksim, the modern and international part of the city. There are many nightclubs and discothèques along Cumhuriyet Caddesi, where the atmosphere is so muted and antiseptic you would be happy to take your mother or to let your daughter go alone. Nevertheless, a pleasant evening can be spent at **Kervansaray**, Cumhuriyet Caddesi 30, © 247 1630 (open 9pm–3am). The cost, with a meal, all drinks, a belly dance show, a singer, dancing and maybe a magician, will be in the region of £12/$18. **The Grand**, at Bella Limana Caddesi 80 in Rumeli Hisar, offers more of the same. There is less of a tourist feel to the **Eski Yeşil**, a small cabaret on Abdülhak Hamit Caddesi near Taksim, © 255 2020. Much the same, and the only cabaret on the Stamboul side, is **Orient House**, on Tiyatro Caddesi near Beyazit Square, © 517 6163. At the top of the **Galata Tower**, © 245 1160, is a restaurant which puts on a floor show which includes folk dancing. The clientele is composed almost entirely of tour groups and the menu and floor show are clearly tourist-oriented, but at least the view from the tower is good. The restaurant opens at 8pm, and the programme starts at 9.50 and finishes at midnight. The fixed, all-in price is about £16/£24.

Gambling is illegal for Turks, but the larger international hotels like the **Hilton**, ✆ 231 0300, and the **Sheraton**, ✆ 246 2021, have casinos. A passport is essential and play is in dollars. Slot machines are not considered to be gambling, and the casinos have vestibules full of Turks playing the fruit machines which beep electronically and flash multicoloured lights continuously. All the luxury hotels that have opened in the last few years include swish casinos, including the **Hyatt Regency** in Taşkişla Caddesi, Taksim, ✆ 225 7000, and the Swissotel, with its **Grand Casino Bosphorus** across from Dolmabahçe Palace, ✆ 259 0742. The only one on the Stamboul side is in the **Merit Hotel** on Ordu Caddesi in Lâleli, ✆ 511 2768.

The **Çiçek Pasaji** (*see* p.125), long the traditional place to start an evening's revelry, is now much too tame for that, but old habits die hard, and many people still turn up in the early evening before moving on to a nightclub. More popular now are the *meyhane* of neighbouring Nevizade and Kalyoncukulluğu Sokaks. You'll also find lots of bars, some with live rock or Turkish folk music, in the streets off Istiklâl Caddesi; try the **Yaga** bar, Zambak Sokak, where the house band specializes in Jimi Hendrix covers.

Around Sultanahmet, options for an evening's entertainment shrink. Opposite the Hippodrome, the **Sultan Pub** tries hard to create a dimly lit 'Rick's Bar'-type ambience that is spoiled by Humphrey Bogart having to share the wall with James Dean and Marilyn Monroe. **Rumeli Café**, just off the Divan Yolu behind the Vitamin restaurant is a quiet and serendipitous place for a drink, with outside tables and occasionally live music. Similar bars are easier to find in Beyoğlu, like the **Beyoğlu Pub** at 140 Istiklâl Caddesi, with an outdoor terrace, or the trendy **Dadaist** just up the street. A sort of coffeehouse, just off Istiklâl on Büyükparmakkapi Sokak, **Hayal Kahvesi** has rock and jazz groups until 2am. Some of luxury hotels around Taksim and the Bosphorus have rooftop bars with a view, such as the Hilton and the Marmara Istanbul; the latter's **Tepe Bar** is one of Istanbul's top jazz venues. The Laleazar Bar atop the Hilton offers a view and a happy hour from 6.30 to 8pm. The city's only proper wine bar, **Babiali**, is in the Merit Hotel on Ordu Caddesi in Lâleli; happy hour from 5 to 7pm.

A word of warning for males only. In the side-streets of Istiklâl Caddesi are 'night-clubs', usually called *gazinos*, that advertise steamy belly-dance shows. Don't go into any, no matter how ingratiating the tout who tries to entice you may be. It's the old, old story; you'll be entrapped, required to buy 'champagne' for some repulsive whore at 100 times the going rate, and you'll leave with your wallet empty and your ego in shreds. Don't imagine you can sweet-talk your way out of this with a few smiles and protestations of innocence. You can't.

If you completely want to forget that you're in Turkey, there's no place better than Istanbul's state-of-the-art discos. **Memo's**, with live music on Salhane Sokak 10 in Ortaköy, is currently the trendiest place to go, if you've got the clothes for it. Ortaköy, for that matter, is quite the hot spot these days. Other bars include **Night Calls**, nearby on Vapur Iskelesi Sokak, with live rock most nights after 11pm; and **Yelkovan**, one of the few places offering alternative music, on Muallim Naci Caddesi. Among the flash discos, another current favourite is **Escape**, Büyükdere Caddesi in Levent, done up like a prison from an old movie. For techno-madness, try **19/20**, Tanimhane Belediye Dükkanlari 73, near Taksim, and the **Paşa Beach**, overlooking the Bosphorus on Muallim Naci Caddesi in Kuruçeşme.

Edirne	151
Thracian Villages	155
The Northern Marmara Coast	157
The Gelibolu Peninsula	159
The Southern Marmara Coast	162
Bursa	165
Uludağ	172
North and East of Bursa	175
Iznik	176

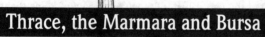

Thrace, the Marmara and Bursa

SELIMIYE MOSQUE, EDIRNE

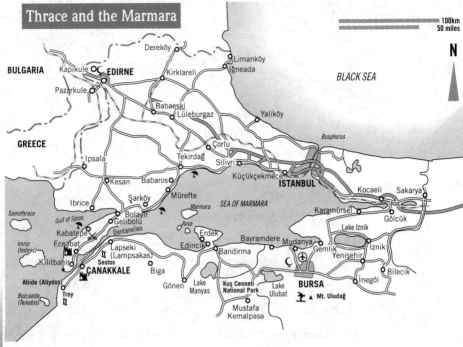

Thrace, the region Turkey shares rather uncomfortably with Greece and Bulgaria, has long held a special place in Turkish dreams and aspirations. The tribes out of the East called it Rumelia, the land of Rome that they had heard so much of and so ardently sought. Although it comprises only three per cent of Turkish territory, modern Turks, from Atatürk to the current government, pin their hopes on it being an especially magnetic chunk of real estate, capable of pulling the rest of Turkey away from the insoluble squabbles of the Middle East into the Common Market and the democratic traditions of the West.

Ancient Thrace was occupied by antiquity's most skilled horsemen, who had a special knack for splendid barbaric goldwork and uncouth religious practices. Unfortunately for them, Thrace was on the principal highway of conquerors bent on Europe or Asia. Xerxes and Alexander came this way, while the Romans, who went about their conquering more systematically, bisected it with a highway, the Via Egnatia (the modern Londra Asfalti) to speed their legions to and from the eastern marches. Many towns of Thrace's three provinces began life as Roman or Ottoman garrisons, and have known other armies as well—Goths, Bulgars, Avars, Crusaders, Russians and Greeks. Battles that have changed history have taken place here, or offshore in the Dardanelles, from the days of Homer to World War I. Until recently, much of Thrace was an off-limits military zone.

For all that, Thrace is a quiet, almost lonely place, with few monuments to show for the great events that have occurred on its soil. Most of the land is a rolling plain, emerald green in the spring, but hot and humid in the summer, and snow-blasted in the winter. As for the Marmara, it looks promising enough on the map, but don't expect anything like the sunny blue Aegean. In this part of the world, every corner seems to have its own climate, landscapes and moods, and the Marmara's tend to be somewhat sombre, more like the Black Sea than the Mediterranean. Nevertheless, there is some agreeable scenery in out-of-the-way places: the little-known Marmara Islands, around Lake Iznik, and especially up on Mt Uludağ, just a cable-car ride away from the centre of one of Turkey's most engaging cities, the old Ottoman capital of Bursa.

Edirne

Thrace's one real attraction is its largest town, **Edirne**, or Adrianople, 4 hours from Istanbul, near the Greek and Bulgarian frontiers. If you're driving from the north to Turkey, it's on the way; if you're coming from Greece, it's worth the detour from the main coastal route, for you won't find a better introduction to Turkey and its architecture—and greased wrestling, the one thing that keeps Edirne's juices flowing these days. Although the city once served as the Ottoman capital, like Bursa, it has few modern industries to keep it growing and prosperous, and today looks more or less the same as it did a hundred years ago.

History

Hadrian founded Adrianople in AD 125, on the site of Thracian *Uscudama* (Hellenistic Oresteia). Almost exactly 200 years later, his successor Constantine the Great fought a major battle nearby, a prelude to his capture of Byzantium; 1000 years later, history repeated itself when Murat won it for the Ottomans (in 1361). Since the seat of the Ottoman Empire in its early days was wherever the sultan had his divan, Edirne hosted the Ottoman court while the sultan waited for Constantinople to fall into his hands. If there was trouble in the east, the sultan stayed in Bursa; if he was interested in expanding the boundaries of Rumelia, he stayed in Edirne. Although this shuttling about ended when Mehmet the Conqueror took Constantinople, the sultans continued to bestow lavish imperial monuments on their first European capital until it reached the height of its beauty and importance in the late 16th century, before later wars and natural disasters took their toll.

Getting Around

Edirne is linked to Istanbul by Highway E5, an excellent modern road that has taken the place of the horrible old *Londra Asfalti*. Several coach lines compete for your custom on the Edirne–Istanbul run, a 3½-hour trip, and both frequency and service are excellent; this may be the run on which you're most likely to get tea and cakes and television. On the other hand, it's rather difficult to get anywhere else from Edirne. There are a few **buses** a day for Çanakkale, by way of Tekirdağ (you'll need to take a taxi from the centre of Tekirdağ to the *otogar* on the E5 to make the connnection).

There is also **rail** service from Istanbul's Sirkeci Station, but the bus is by far the better bet. The daily Balkan Express from Istanbul stops in Edirne on its way to Sofia. Edirne's rail station is out near the *otogar* on the E5. From both, there is a convenient dolmuş service to the centre.

Both the train station to the south and the bus station to the east of Edirne are too far to walk with luggage, and you may want to take a taxi or dolmuş into the centre (some bus lines, though, do stop in the centre). Edirne has Bulgarian (on Talatpaşa Caddesi) and Greek (Cumhuriyet Caddesi) consulates to help with any border difficulties.

There is an hourly **dolmuş** service from the centre of Edirne to Kapikule on the **Bulgarian border**. For **Greece**, take a dolmuş or city bus (both from Hurriyet Meydani) to the small village of Karaağac from where it is a 2½-mile (4km) taxi ride to the frontier at Pazarkule. According to the locals the Greeks have been behaving themselves lately and the usual border hassles are infrequent.

Tourist Information

Edirne: Talatpaşa Caddesi 76, west of the town centre, ℂ (284) 225 5260. In summer a central branch may be open, also on Talatpaşa, near central Hurriyet Meydani.

Kapikule: at the Bulgarian border, ℂ (284) 238 2019

Ipsala: at the Greek border, ℂ (284) 616 1577

Kirklareli: Vilayet Binasi, ℂ (288) 214 1662

Selimiye Mosque

The crowning achievement of the sultans' 16th-century building spree—itself set like a crown over Edirne—is the grand **Selimiye Mosque**, built by Mimar Sinan for Selim II. Sinan finished the mosque, which he personally considered his finest, in 1575, when he was over 80 years old. According to legend it has 999 windows and its dome is slightly larger than the Aya Sofia's; its four identical 225ft minarets, girdled with three balconies, are the tallest outside Mecca, and were supposedly aligned to appear as a single one from the distance, to deceive enemy artillery. Unlike most mosques of its stature, the Selimiye is uncluttered with a large complex of religious foundations, and those it does have are all on one side, allowing impressive views of the mosque itself from three sides.

But it was in the interior that Sinan worked his best magic. The great dome hovers at 145 feet on eight massive piers over a marble fountain symbolizing the waters of a legendary source called Zem-Zem, while at floor level the eye is drawn towards the exquisitely carved marble mimber and mihrab, the latter set back in an apse with walls adorned by Iznik tiles; it is perhaps the only one in Turkey with a window opening towards Mecca. An even lovelier display of Iznik tiles decorates the **imperial loge**; if you weren't able to get into the harem of the Topkapi Saray, here's a chance to see what you missed.

The medrese, in typical cloister style, now houses Edirne's **Museum of Turkish and Islamic Art** (*open daily 8.30–5, closed Mon pm; adm*), with items from the local *tekke* of whirling dervishes, calligraphy and charming photographs of great greased wrestlers from Edirne's past. A new **Archaeological and Ethnographic Museum** (*open daily exc Mon, 8.30–12, 1–5.30; adm*), with a small collection of costumes, kilims and carpet saddle bags, artifacts from ancient Trakya (Thrace) and ancient coins, is behind the Selimiye. The arcade of shops along the west flank of the mosque, the **Kavaflar Arasta**, was built exclusively for Edirne's cobblers; as with so many other arcades, the idea was to let the rents go to the upkeep of the mosque.

Other Mosques

Just below the Selimiye, off central Cumhuriyet Meydani, are two older imperial mosques, textbook examples for studying the development of the classical Ottoman style. The **Eski Cami**, a plain square encompassing nine vaults, was begun in 1402 by the three sons of Yildirim Beyazit after their father's collision with Tamerlane; during the next 11 years, as the mosque was erected, the three brothers fought for control of the empire. The winner, and sole survivor, Mehmet I, had the honour of dedicating the mosque. One distinct feature of the Eski Cami are the great Arabic letters painted on the outer walls, giving the mosque a curiously primitive appearance.

The second mosque, the innovative **Üç Şerefeli Cami**, was built in 1447 by Murat II; its name 'three balconies' derives from one of its asymmetrical minarets, which at 218 feet was the tallest the Ottomans ever built—until Sinan's slender rockets went up around the Selimiye. Each of the mosque's minarets is a delicately carved work, and each is different—one straight, one spiral, and one in zigzag patterns. Üç Şerefeli, the last great imperial mosque built prior to the capture of Constantinople, is covered with the largest central dome the Ottomans had yet dared and a clutch of smaller domes; inside, the architect achieved a surprising airiness. Although its other foundations are derelict, the mosque's **Sokullu Hamam**, built by Sinan in the 15th century and one of Turkey's most elegant, has been restored and serves as a bath today. Sinan's finely restored **Rüstem Paşa Kervansaray**, adjoining the Eski Cami, has also regained its original function, as a hotel (*see* below).

Other Monuments

In the Cumhuriyet Meydani, Atatürk has to share space with a peculiar statue of two wrestlers, each of whom has two faces, so the work has no 'back'. Also here are the two covered bazaars, the Bedesten (1405) and Sinan's **Ali Paşa Çarşi**. Both are fun to visit, especially if you need a plastic bucket or saucepan.

Besides these, Edirne contains literally hundreds of other Ottoman buildings in its cobbled lanes. Especially interesting (and especially in danger of collapsing) are the great wooden Ottoman houses, typically unpainted, but adorned with folk motifs carved on the gables and balconies. Edirne is one of the few places outside Istanbul where you see many of these; a couple have been converted into rather shabby pensions, in the back streets behind the Ali Paşa bazaar. When built, however, each had separate quarters for the men and the women.

If you haven't yet seen enough mosques, one of the best is up on the hills above the Selimiye, off Mimar Sinan Caddesi: the charming **Muradiye**, a landmark visible from almost everywhere in Edirne. Murat II founded the mosque in 1435 for the Mevlevi dervishes and spared no expense on its exquisite Iznik tiles. Like the Green Mosque in Bursa and many others, the Muradiye is built in a T-shape; the two rooms on either side of the mosque proper were for travelling dervishes to spend the night.

Ottoman Monuments on the Periphery

Several other imperial mosques lie on the outskirts of Edirne, mostly along the willowy banks of the **Tunca**, a tributary of the Meriç (the Greek Ebros) that forms the border between Greece and Turkey. A walk around them on a nice day is one of the most pleasant things you can do in Edirne; there are several good picnic spots around the riverbank.

Start the tour by walking to the end of Talatpaşa Caddesi. The **Gazimihal Bridge** over the

MERIÇ BRIDGE

Tunca, an Ottoman work on Byzantine foundations, commemorates a Greek who turned Turk and became a redoubtable general for the Ottomans; at the end of the bridge, the 1421 **Gazimihal Mosque,** closed and awaiting a long-overdue restoration, has a graceful portico and carved minaret. Further down the road is the 1361 **Yildirim Camii,** but you may wish to turn right, following the riverbank; not far away stands the **Ikinci Beyazit Külliyesi,** founded by Beyazit II in 1484 and endowed with a record number of religious foundations, now mostly empty but occupied in part by the University of Thrace. It includes a hospital and *timarhane* (an insane asylum) considered among the most progressive and well equipped of their day, with a sumptuous therapy ward (*darüşşifa*), a medical school, bakery, two hospices, and baths. Architecturally the complex is an important stepping-stone towards the grand imperial style of Istanbul: a lovely ensemble including a square mosque, decorated with simple patterns of windows, surrounded by an asymmetrical arrangement of domed buildings, set off with attractive small lanterns and chimneys. The six-arched **Beyazit Bridge,** built at the same time, connects the complex to Edirne. Several other fine 15th-century Ottoman bridges span the Tunca and Meriç; two of them connect Edirne with the island in the Tunca called the **Sarayiçi,** just north of the Beyazit Külliye. The name comes from the Edirne Sarayi, or sultan's palace, a pleasure dome built here by Murat II but blown to bits by the Turks in 1877 to keep the explosives they had stored there out of the hands of the invading Russians. Today the island is home to Edirne's biggest annual event, the **Greased Wrestling Tournament** (*Yağli Güreş*), which takes place in late June/early July, depending on Ramazan.

The Greased Wrestlers of Edirne

The Turks call the tournament the *Kirkpinar* ('forty spring'); according to tradition, the bouts began in the 14th century, when Süleyman Paşa, son of the second Ottoman sultan, Orhan Gazi, brought his forty heroes to campaign in Europe. In between battles, they amused themselves by wrestling. Two contestants were so equally matched they wrestled to death and were buried by their companions. The next day a spring appeared by the tombs, which became known as the 'spring of the forty'.

The Kirkpinar (now caged up in a modern stadium) attracts thousands of competitors from around Turkey. The contestants, dressed only in their leather breeches, or *kispet*, rub their skin with olive oil and warm up to drums and a wailing oboe. Next the announcer, or *cazgir*, leads a prayer and introduces the pairs of wrestlers; part of the

Turks' enjoyment of the matches is hearing the *cazgir*'s recitation of each wrestler's claim to fame and his best tricks. The free-style bouts last until one contestant is pinned down or simply keels over. Wrestlers compete in four categories, classed by age and prowess. A grand champion (*Baş Pehlivan*), who retains the title for three years straight, is awarded the highest honour, the Golden Belt. One who won it around the turn of the century, Koca Yusuf ('Enormous Joe'), has become a legend in Edirne: he went on to challenge and defeat the greatest champions of Europe and the US, but was drowned on his return voyage from America when his ship sank, finally, as the Turks sigh, 'beaten by his own bad luck'.

North of here, in an unmarked battlefield, Visigothic horsemen devastated Roman infantry in one of the climactic battles of history, the 378 AD **Battle of Adrianople**. The Visigoths had peacefully settled much of Thrace in the 4th century, and they were only rising up in revolt against the oppression and taxes of Roman rule. But the battle was a landmark in military history, demonstrating conclusively the superiority of cavalry over the Roman legions: in horses the Roman Empire was sadly lacking, while the Germans had plenty. Adrianople was the first big crack in Rome's defences, and the beginning of the end for the empire; after it, the Visigoths went on the move, raiding through Greece and the Balkans. In 410, they would sack Rome itself.

Thracian Villages

The Thracian interior isn't holiday country—mostly rolling, featureless farmland full of wheat and sunflowers that turns golden-brown in late July and August. The villages offer few sights, but on the whole they are happy and prosperous places. Two things you'll come across are tumuli, the preferred mode of burial of the ancient Thracians (some can be seen from the E5 around Lüleburgaz) and Ottoman-era bridges. The roads here were crucially important to the 15th-century sultans, consolidating their hold on the Balkans. The most impressive of their works is in **Uzunköprü**, a village near the Greek border, the name of which means 'long bridge': a 174-arch, 4400ft span completed in 1444 that for its time was probably the longest in Europe.

The Yildiz Mountains mark the boundary between Bulgaria and Turkey. Local beauty spots in the area are the frontier post of **Dereköy** and the Black Sea village of **Iğneada**, both surrounded by forests. A new road has been built here, and Iğneada's port, the village of Limanköy, has beaches and a number of family *pansiyons*.

Inland, each of a triangle of small towns in central Thrace has its Ottoman ornament: **Kirklareli**, with its 1407 Hizir Bey Cami and old hamam; **Babaeski**, with its Cedit Ali Paşa Mosque, built by Sinan; and **Lüleburgaz**, ancient Arcadiopolis, with another of Sinan's works, the Mehmet Paşa Mosque and its large collection of religious foundations, including baths and a soup kitchen.

Edirne ℗ (284–) ·

Where to Stay

expensive/moderate

In Edirne, the improbable conversion of a historic han into a modern luxury hotel resulted in the **(O) Hotel Rüstempaşa Kervansaray**, right in the centre on Iki Kapili Han Caddesi 57, ℗ 212 6119, ℗ 212 0462; the windows are a bit small and front-facing rooms can be noisy, but it all comes off well, and this is your only chance to spend the night in a building by Mimar Sinan. Prices are £50/$75 (negotiable) for a double and amenities include a disco, two bars and a hamam that stays open 24 hours a day. The next best is the gleaming, modern **Balta Oteli**, Talat Paşa Asfalti 97, © 225 1011, out of town on the road to the bus station; doubles £15/$22. Back in the centre, on Talatpaşa Caddesi, the **Sultanotel**, © 225 1372, offers comfortable rooms but a gloomy restaurant.

inexpensive/cheap

Edirne not being much of a tourist destination, you can usually get a room for under £10/$15 in a nice hotel that would be twice as much in Istanbul or on the coast. The best choice is the *Şaban Açikgöz, © 213 0313, near the Kervansaray in the Tahmis Çarşisi (look for the yellow sign): pleasant airy rooms with television (though all you can pick up is MTV). Out on the Talatpaşa Asfalti (the Istanbul road), the slightly more expensive *Kervan Oteli, © 213 8491, has a seen-better-days sort of appeal; £11/$16. The *Park Hotel, Maarif Caddesi 7, © 213 5276, is comfortable enough; doubles also around £10/$15.

For anything less than these, the situation is grim. Almost all of them are on Maarif Caddesi off Talatpaşa Caddesi by the central tourist office. Most are dives, though the **Konak** at no. 6, © 225 1348, and the **Ayvazoğlu**, around the corner on Talatpaşa, © 225 1346, are decent enough. Both are very basic, with common bathrooms. There are several campsites in the area, including the **Kervansaray Ayşe Kadin Mocamp**, © 221 1290, with a pool, on the Istanbul road just outside Edirne.

Eating Out

As every Turk knows, Edirne is famous not only for wrestling, but for liver, especially meatballs—*ciğ köfte*. Done properly, they're nearly raw and very spicy; aficionados say they're only right if you throw them at the wall and they stick. Many will find them an acquired taste, but be brave; the centre of town is full of *ciğer* (liver) parlours where the proprietors will be happy to initiate you—they also like liver kebabs, fried liver, and Allah only knows what liver else.

Outside of that you're not likely to find anything unforgettable in Edirne. There are plenty of cheap *lokantas* around Şaraçlar Caddesi, such as the **Polat**, across from the Şaban Açikgöz Hotel (a favourite of soldiers in from the nearby base—poor devils who can't get more than a 50p lunch on Turkish Army pay), and just around the corner, truly good *döner* at the **Siri Kebab**. Serving alcohol, and occasionally seafood, the **Çati Restoran** has a pleasant terrace set above Talatpaşa Caddesi; about £5/$8. There are also unexceptional restaurants in the Rüstempaşa and other hotels.

Sweet teeth need not go unindulged in Edirne; there is a wide range of delicious southeastern-style pastries at the **Gaziantep Baklavacisi** on Talatpaşa, and two more tempting pastry shops across from the post office on Şaraçlar Caddesi, the **Roma** and the **Zogo**. And alcohol isn't that hard to find either, though Turkey's only entirely European city is a surprisingly conservative place. Just look up; around the central squares bars are everywhere, on the first or second floors.

The Marmara Coast and Gelibolu Peninsula

Getting Around

Buses from Istanbul and Edirne go to Tekirdağ, and there is also a frequent service to Çanakkale via the Eceabat ferry. Tekirdağ's bus station is on the coastal road, about 2km north of the centre, but for some Istanbul–Çanakkale runs you'll have to flag down the bus on the road; they don't come into the station. In summer, there are weekly Turkish Maritime Lines ferries from Tekirdağ to Marmara Island and Erdek.

The two car ferries, Eceabat–Çanakkale and Gelibolu–Lapseki, cross the Dardanelles every two hours, until midnight.

Tourist Information

Tekirdağ: Rüstempaşa Çarşisi, 45 Atatürk Bulvari, ✆ (282) 261 4346

The Northern Marmara Coast

Tekirdağ, ancient Bisanthe, is the largest town on Thrace's Marmara coast, and one aspiring to become a resort, with nearby beaches at Kumbağ and Değirmenalti. Although mostly concrete modern, Tekirdağ is spread attractively over the hills, and has two works by Sinan: the Covered Bazaar and **Rüstem Paşa Mosque**. On the seaside promenade stands one of the best Atatürk statues, depicting the father of his country with his famous chalkboard and pointer, teaching two earnest citizens their vowels. A mile to the west of here lived the Hungarian patriot, Prince Ferenc II Rakoczy, who spent a career leading his countrymen against the Hapsburgs in the Hungarian War of Independence; in 1717, the Ottomans granted him political asylum in Tekirdağ, where he lived until his death in 1735. The song Rakoczy's troops sang in battle, the *Rakoczy March*, has roused Hungarian patriots ever since; once, when Liszt played it as encore to a recital, it caused a riot. In 1932 the Hungarian government made the house into the **Rakoczy Museum**, on Barbaros Caddesi, containing Rakoczy's flag, documents, Hungarian weapons, and paintings from the era.

East of Tekirdağ, there's a beach at **Marmara Ereğli**; to the west, the road to the Gelibolu peninsula passes through vineyards to other beaches at Barbaros, Mürefte and **Şarköy**. The latter, with an especially fine broad, sandy beach, has grown into the biggest resort on this part of the shore; it's quite a lively place when it fills up with Istanbul families in the summer. On the narrowest neck of the peninsula, **Bolayir** overlooks both the Dardanelles and the Saros Gulf; here Süleyman Paşa, son of Orhan Gazi, and leader of the forty heroes who captured Gelibolu fortress in 1354—the Ottomans' first handful of Rumelia—is buried in a *türbe*, at one end of the village. Next to him is the grave of the 19th-century poet Namik Kemal, a native of Tekirdağ and leader of the movement to reform the Ottoman Empire at the end of the 19th century.

The Dardanelles

Gelibolu, the Turkish name for Gallipoli, is a pleasant fishing village, though one usually full of soldiers. Its **Castle** has long guarded this entrance into the straits; the walls you see today date from the 14th century, when the Ottomans captured the town. One of the two Dardanelles ferries crosses here, to **Lapeski**. If you're driving, the road to Çanakkale along the Asian shore is more pleasant, but the peninsula route has more tales to tell: from Protosilaus, the first casualty of the Trojan war, to battles in the Crimean war, the First World War, and the Turkish War of Independence. Some 9 miles (14km) south of Gelibolu, at the mouth of the stream Aegospotamos (modern **Ince Liman**), Lysander and his Spartans clobbered the Athenian fleet in 405 BC, in the decisive final battle of the Peloponnesian War.

A little further south stood **Sestos**, across the strait from ancient **Abydos**. Nothing remains of either of these but stories. Here in 480 BC, Xerxes' army, marching to invade Greece, crossed the strait on a pontoon bridge of boats while the Persian King of Kings watched from the heights of Abydos, sitting on the marble throne he had had carted along with him, and wept because none of the men labouring below would be alive in a hundred years. Here lived the famous lovers, Hero, a priestess at Sestos, and Leander, a resident of Abydos, who would swim the strait every night to visit his love, guided by her lamp. One night, a storm blew the lamp out, and Leander was lost and drowned; when his body was discovered the next morning, Hero flung herself into the sea and drowned herself, too. Romantic-minded travellers can make the swim as well, taking care to avoid the many steamers that ply the strait; Byron did it in 1810.

The car ferry crossing to Çanakkale departs from **Eceabat**, near a village called **Kilitbahir**, located where the Dardanelles are at their narrowest and most defensible. The trefoil **castle** on the shore, a striking and unique design, was constructed by Mehmet the Conqueror to cut off Constantinople before he besieged the capital. Never one to leave matters to chance, Mehmet built another castle, across the water at Çanakkale, and slung a heavy chain between the two thus sealing the straits completely and giving Kilitbahir its name, 'Lock of the Sea'. Kilitbahir is now empty, and can be explored.

Jason and the Argonauts

So many and tangled are the influences and sources of this cycle of myths that its origin can hardly be found. Homer only mentions Jason once, indirectly, and the earliest versions of the tale have Jason sailing not to the Black Sea, but up the Adriatic in search of the Golden Fleece.

Pelias, the usurper of the throne of Iolcus, would have murdered the infant heir Jason, but his mother took him secretly to Mount Pelion, where he was raised by Chiron the Centaur. When Jason arrived to regain his kingdom, Pelias promised to relinquish it on completion of this quest. The fleece had belonged to a flying golden ram sent by Zeus to rescue an ancestor, Phrixus, from execution; the ram carried him to Colchis, the farthest eastern land known to the Greeks. Jason accepted the job, and got Argus the Thespian to build him the famous *Argo*. The list of companions he collected included heroes from all over the Greek world: Heracles, Castor and Polydeuces, Mopsus the Lapith—who later founded so many cities on Asia Minor's southern shore, Atalanta the speedy virgin, even Orpheus the poet (an inscription bearing Mopsus' name has recently been discovered in Cilicia, making him the first Greek hero to be documented as a historical person).

After dallying with the women of Lemnos (who had murdered their husbands) and repopulating the island, the Argonauts sailed through the Hellespont. Heracles' beloved squire Hylas disappeared on the coast of the Marmara near Bursa, and Heracles, who had just defeated Jason in a rowing contest, was marooned there by the captain as he searched for Hylas. At Salmydessus in eastern Thrace, the Argonauts chased off the Harpies that were plaguing King Phineus, and received in return advice on how to navigate the Symplegades, the 'clashing rocks' (probably ice floes that floated down from Russian rivers), that destroyed all ships attempting to pass the Bosphorus.

Along the Black Sea, they stopped at Mariandyne (somewhere near Akçakoca). Had Heracles still been with them, he could have shown them here the opening into Hades, from which he had dragged out the captured dog Cerberus on his twelfth labour. At Sinope they picked up new crew members, and from there they passed into the lands of the iron-smelting Chalybians, the Amazons, and the promiscuous Mosynoecians. Soon afterwards, they crossed the Georgian border (Colchis lay north of modern Batum) where destiny and Medea awaited them. Their journey had as yet only begun.

One source of the tale was the Greek voyages of exploration in the Black Sea c. 1000 BC. The fall of Troy had, probably, opened up this new trade route to them, and they went in search of amber, iron, and furs from the east. Every Greek city in classical times wanted its trading sites there justified, and no doubt a few paid off the early poets to make sure their heroes were included among the *Argo*'s crew.

The best version of the tale comes in the 3rd-century BC poem by Apollonius of Rhodes—the *Argonautica*. There are several good translations in English.

The Gelibolu Peninsula

There is a sad, melancholy loveliness to the lush and undulating Gelibolu peninsula. Over 200,000 young men lie buried in this thin pine-clad strip of land. In spring, the hills here bloom with wild flowers; appropriately, the most numerous are poppies.

The Battles of World War One

It is easy to forget that behind the ill-fated Allied attack on the Dardanelles in April 1915, there existed a sound strategic rationale; had it succeeded the Great War may well have ended within that same year. The seeds of the assault were sown only a few months after the assassination at Sarajevo in November 1914: on the western front both sides were already dug in for the four terrible years of stalemate trench warfare that were to follow. On the eastern front, however, the Czarist Russian army was crumbling before the power of the Kaiser's well-disciplined, well-equipped forces. In desperation, the Russians called for a mammoth resupply of arms and equipment from their British and French allies.

Britain and France were anxious to comply but this was no easy request. The way overland to Russia was blocked by the German army, the way by sea from the north by the German navy. Only the sea route from the south remained viable—from the Aegean, through the Dardanelles and Bosphorus to the Black Sea ports on the Crimea. It was a route blocked by Turkey, Germany's ally, but it was the only option open to Winston Churchill, First Lord of the Admiralty. It held an additional attraction in that success would not only resupply Russia; the capture of Constantinople would enable Allied troops to drive north through the Balkans, leaving the Central Powers fighting an ultimately hopeless war on three separate fronts. So, in November 1914, Churchill ordered the ships of an Anglo-French fleet to charge the Dardanelles.

The assault was a disaster, the naval equivalent of the Charge of the Light Brigade. The Turks had mined the straits. Three warships were sunk, three crippled; thousands of sailors lost their lives. Later attempts to sweep the straits of mines were foiled by Turkish heavy guns positioned on the peninsula. To Churchill and his generals it was clear; the Dardanelles could not be breached by sea until the Turkish army was removed from the Gelibolu peninsula.

To achieve this, two simultaneous amphibious landings on the peninsula were planned, one at Cape Helles at the entrance to the straits, the other at Kabatepe beach 8 miles north. An Anglo-French army was to conduct the former, an ANZAC force (Australian and New Zealand Army Corps) the latter. The two were to drive inland, link up and together push the Turks and their heavy artillery off the peninsula. Allied troops were assembled in huge numbers on the Greek island of Limnos and at dawn, 25 April 1915, the first landing boats hit the beaches.

By noon of that same day the Allied strategy had gone horribly awry. At Cape Helles the Anglo-French contingent had encountered massive opposition and established a beachhead only after horrific losses; the ANZAC force was hit even harder. A signals failure had directed their boats not to wide, spacious Kabatepe but to a small, narrow cove backed by sheer, towering cliffs. ANZACs died in their thousands before gaining a tentative toe-hold but that was all that was needed. More troops were landed. The push inland began. Some small advances were made. Then they were stopped.

The Gelibolu campaign was to last eight months, conducted in the steal-a-yard, lose-it-again manner of the western front. Much of the fighting was centered around Çonkbayiri Hill, the peninsula's highest point, and it was here that Lieutenant-Colonel Mustafa Kemal, the commander of the elite Turkish 57th Regiment, acquired a reputation as a brilliant, tireless leader, not afraid to risk death by his men's side—a reputation that was to serve him well when Kemal was metamorphosed into Atatürk.

In January 1916 the Allies pulled out. Ironically, their retreat was the most successful manoeuvre of the entire campaign; tens of thousands of men were evacuated under the cover of night without a single loss. Czarist Russia was never resupplied and in 1917 fell first to the Germans and then to the Bolsheviks. Churchill was dismissed and was not to hold government office for another 24 years. Yet his moment was to come, as was that of his adversary, Atatürk, the man who, quite rightly, had the last words on the Gelibolu campaign.

> *Those heroes that shed their blood*
> *And lost their lives*
> *You are now lying in the soil of a friendly country*
> *Therefore rest in peace*
> *There is no difference between the Johnnies*
> *And the Mehmets to us where they lie side by side*
> *Here in this country of ours*
> *You the mothers*
> *Who sent their sons from far away countries*
> *Wipe away your tears*
> *Your sons are now lying in our bosom*
> *And are in peace*
> *Having lost their lives on this land they have*
> *Become our sons as well.*

Touring the Peninsula

It is impossible to see all the monuments, museums and battlefields by public transport alone. This means that, unless you have a car or are prepared to hire a taxi for the best part of a day, a guided tour is the only option available. These are instructive although tour operators tend to concentrate almost exclusively on the ANZAC-related sites. Hopefully, this will soon change.

With one of the finest beaches on the peninsula, **Kabatepe** is the best place to begin any tour. Here a small, spaceship-shaped **museum** (*open daily 8.30–5; adm*) overlooks the beach and contains a sad collection of memorabilia, from an English Tommy's last letter home to the skull of a Turkish soldier ('martyr' in the Turkish vernacular), with a bullet still embedded in the centre of his forehead. From here it is a short drive to **ANZAC Cove** where you can see just why the landings were doomed from zero hour one. The hills above are dotted with ANZAC cemeteries and memorials, all immaculately maintained by the Allied War Graves Commission. Trenches remain intact at **Lone Pine**, the main Australian cemetery, and on the heights of **Çonkbayiri Hill** where five huge Turkish monoliths recount the crucial battles fought there, each stone positioned so as to represent the fingers and thumb of a man's hand, raised, pleading to God.

At **Cape Helles** the British memorial towers high, in memory of the 20,761 men of the empire who have no known grave. There are six British and French cemeteries in this area and two significant **Turkish monuments**, the First Martyrs Memorial and that huge, *pi-* shaped structure, at once a **museum** and the headstone of the literally countless Turks buried on the peninsula. Unlike the Allies, the Turks kept no records of their dead; the slain were simply shovelled into mass graves, unmarked and unknown.

Where to Stay

luxury

A remarkable establishment has recently appeared on the Marmara shore at Silivri (34930), east of Tekirdağ—close enough to Istanbul to attract the city's elite. The ★★★★★**Klassis**, © 727 4050, @ 727 4049, is a striking ensemble of neo-Ottoman buildings set high over a huge, dreamy pool. They lay it on thick here: private beach, casino and disco, every sport from squash to water skiing (a golf course is currently under construction).

expensive/moderate

In Tekirdağ, the new and modern ★**Yat Oteli**, Yali Caddesi 8, has sea views and single rooms for £10/$15. Right in the centre, the cheaper ★**Akbulut** on Muralti Caddesi offers little more than balconies above the traffic. Kumbağ beach, to the east, has the **Miltur Turistik** (M1), open April–Oct, with swimming pool, tennis courts and other recreational offerings; £18/$27.

inexpensive/cheap

Pensions are easily found at both Tekirdağ and Kumbağ beach, while in Gelibolu there is moderately priced accommodation near the ferries; one such is the friendly **Yilmaz Otel**, Tüğsavul Caddesi 6, © (286) 566 1256, charging around £4/$6 per person. Like most of the hotels in Gelibolu, they can arrange inexpensive tours of the battle-fields. Most people who come to Gallipoli, though, find it more convenient to stay across the Dardanelles at Çanakkale (*see* p.186).

There is a wide choice of campsites around the Gallipoli peninsula, including the big **Patiş Kum Motel Camp**, © (286) 814 1455, at Saros near Eceabat, with all the facilities, and the smaller and less expensive **Mocamp Seddulbahir**, © (286) 814 1429, also near Eceabat at Seddulbahir.

In Tekirdağ, try the spacious **Sahil Dörtler**, near the waterfront, across from the tourist office, with fish and meat specialities averaging around £4/$6. Gelibolu's eateries are mostly gathered around the harbour; the **Gelibolu** has outside tables, and will provide a satisfying dinner for £4/$6, slightly more for fish.

The Southern Marmara Coast

Although the scenery along the south shore of the Sea of Marmara is quite beautiful and blessed with beaches, it doesn't feature on many foreign visitors' itineraries. As far as Biga, you'll see lush green countryside with muddy fields and mules, broken by little villages lost among the trees, their presence betrayed by a single minaret sticking up. Most of its ancient sites have little to show for themselves today; nothing remains of ancient Abydos or Lampsakas (modern **Lapseki**, the second ferry crossing), although to the east two famous battles of antiquity occurred: **Biga**, where Alexander first defeated the Persians in 334 BC at the mouth of the River Granicus (Biga Çayi), and further east at **Edincik** (ancient Cyzicus), where Alcibiades and the Athenians defeated the Spartans in the Peloponnesian War. **Bandirma**, the biggest town before Bursa, is a sorry industrial settlement that was largely ruined in the war of 1922; you'll have to pass through it to get to Erdek and the Marmara Islands.

Alexander the Great

Before moving on to Egypt, Persia and India, Alexander polished off the Persian King Darius's satrapies in Asia Minor for practice. With some 40,000 men, including 5000 cavalry, he crossed the Hellespont in the spring of 334 BC, sacrificing a bull to Poseidon in mid-passage. After visiting Troy, and paying homage to the Homeric heroes, he and his men were immediately confronted by an army commanded by the Persian satraps (governors) of Phrygia and Ionia. At the River Granicus, they boldly stormed across the water into the Persian lines and routed them, setting the tone for the rest of the campaign.

Then the Macedonians marched down the Aegean coast, taking Sardis, Ephesus, and Miletus. In Ephesus Alexander threw out the pro-Persian aristocracy and restored democratic institutions, and by so doing made himself popular with all the Greeks of Asia Minor not in the Great King's pay. Taking auguries at Miletus, Alexander saw an eagle flying towards the shore, and took it to mean he would conquer the Persians by land, not by sea. Accordingly, he sent his Greek navy home—he couldn't afford it anyway—and marched across the Mediterranean coast to take the Persians' naval bases away. Termessos alone refused an alliance, and survived when Alexander decided it wasn't worth a siege. Perge, Aspendos and Side were brought into line, and then the Macedonian force split up, the great general Parmenion taking half the force to reduce the Cilician coast while Alexander headed north to chase the Persians out of Phrygia. Here, as recorded by his chronicler Arrian, he cut with his sword the famous Gordian knot. The two forces met again at Tarsus, where the always fragile Alexander took ill from a swim in the cold River Cydnus. He recovered just in time to meet Darius, the Great King himself, at Issus near today's Iskenderun. The Macedonian victory, at a disadvantage of perhaps five to one, opened the way for the conquest of Persia and Egypt.

South of Bandirma is the **Kuş Cenneti** (Bird Paradise) **National Park**, a sanctuary for migratory waterfowl, especially pelicans, grey and white herons, and cormorants, who come to nest along the willow-shaded banks of Lake Manyas between February and October, and then fly south to India and Africa in the winter. In all, 179 different species of birds have been spotted in the sanctuary. Just west of here, at **Gönen**, other airborne creatures—namely, tens of thousands of bats—have taken up residence in the Dereköy Caves. Gönen also has one of Turkey's major thermal spas for rheumatism.

Getting Around

Towns on the south Marmara shore are easily reached by **buses** travelling between Bursa and Çanakkale, a trip of about 4hrs. From Bandirma and Erdek minibuses serve the surrounding towns and beaches. Note that Bandirma has two *otogars*. The main one, south of town, serves Bursa–Çanakkale and other main line buses. To get from there to the waterfront station where the Erdek buses start, you can take a taxi or die waiting, possibly, for a city bus or dolmuş. Avşa and Marmara islands are served by **ferry** from Istanbul, daily in the summer, and once a week in the winter. Services also run from Erdek, from where in summer there are daily boats to Avşa and Marmara, and a twice-weekly crossing to Paşalimani. In all the ports, look out for the fellows with boats who run informal private ferry services, or ask anyone. On these very laid-back islands, the locals use these much more commonly than the infrequent Turkish Maritime Lines service; they are much more convenient and somewhat cheaper.

Tourist Information

Erdek: Cumhuriyet Meydani, ✆ (266) 835 1169
Avşa Island: a booth in summer by the docks at Türkeli.

Erdek and the Kapidaği

The road into the Kapidaği peninsula is not promising at first, passing scrapyards, gravel pits, and best of all a festering sulphuric acid plant. But persevere; it gets better. **Erdek**, the capital of the Kapidaği, is a very modest though very agreeable resort, popular with the people of Bursa. In the lively village centre, cafés in shady gardens cluster around the shore; from here a pretty pedestrian walk leads out to the beach and the strip of modern hotels that follows it. There are less crowded beaches to the north at Ocaklar and Narli, both with small but growing collections of cheap *pansiyons* and restaurants (and for all the industry nearby, the water seems clean enough). Another beach, one of the few accessible by paved road, is north of Karacabey, at **Bayramdere**.

The Marmara Islands

Before 1923, this miniature archipelago was largely inhabited by Greeks. They are nearly all gone now, and like much of the areas around the Marmara the islands have a slightly rough, just-settled air to them. Lately, people from the capital have been buying or building houses as summer retreats, but outside of Avşa Island don't expect much of the trappings of tourism. There are a few small beaches and secluded coves, and absolutely no sights to visit. The peace and quiet is seamless when the cement mixers aren't going, and your creditors will never find you here.

Of the four inhabited islands of the Marmara, **Paşalimani**, with its five small villages, is nearest to the mainland. There is a ferry from Erdek to its tiny capital, Balikli (means 'fishy'), and private boats make regular crossings from Narli, which can be easier. Paşalimani welcomes few visitors; there's really very little there, not even a beach, but at least you'll be guaranteed a peaceful stay. **Avşa**, the next nearest, is its antithesis. Loved by Turks from the cities, it is green and undulating and has some good beaches, particularly around its capital Türkeli (Avşa appears on many maps as Türkeli Island). Avşa has become a bit overbuilt in the last decade—at least there'll be no problem finding a place to stay. **Ekinlik**, north of Avşa, is the smallest of the islands, no more than a village where there's even less to do than on Paşalimani. The largest of the group is **Marmara** (Greek *Elafonisos*), stonier than Avşa and lacking that island's beaches, but still well patronized by Turks on vacation. There is a beach just north of Marmara village at Çinarli, reachable by dolmuş.

Where to Stay
expensive/moderate

In Erdek, the **★★Gül Plaj Moteli** on Kumlu Yali Caddesi 86, ✆ (266) 835 1053, is clean and on the beach, with doubles for £14/$21, all with private bath (open June–Sept). Similarly priced is the **★★Artek Oteli**, Ali Haydar Sahil Parki 216, ✆ (266) 835 3336. Erdek has many other hotels, though hardly any are open all year. Hotels near the thermal baths in Gönen are open all year, such as the **★★★Yildiz Oteli** on Kaplicalar Sahasi, where in addition to the baths there's a sauna, a hamam, and a pool.

In Marmara, the **Marmara Otel**, ✆ (266) 896 1185, is the best the island can do, though open in season only. Double rooms with private bath go for £6/$9. The **Otel Temizel** on Avşa, ✆ (266) 896 1134, is pleasant, and typical of what's on offer; £8/$12. The height of luxury here doesn't go very high—the rooftop bar at the **★★Ayberk**, ✆ 896 2578, with light, airy rooms with balconies overlooking the beach; doubles with bath £20/$30.

cheap

Being stuck in Bandirma need not make you miserable; the **★★Asuhan**, on Atatürk Caddesi near the main *otogar*, has comfortable rooms and a passable restaurant; there is also the less expensive and tidy **Özgür**, next to the mosque by the ferry landing.

Erdek's cheaper establishments are clustered around the port, most in the form of pensions charging around £3/$5 ; one of the nicest is the **Ümit**, ✆ (266) 835 1092, on Balikhane Sokaka, a quiet backstreet near the port. There are also inexpensive choices along the beach strip, including the clean and well-kept **Yat Otel**, closest to the centre, and the **Gün Motel**, where all rooms have a shower or bath, for £5/$8. On Ocaklar beach, the **Arseven Pansiyon**, ✆ (266) 835 1464, is slightly more expensive, but still good value for money, with spotless rooms with en suite facilities. There are a number of pensions in Marmara town and around the beach at Çinarli. Avşa has lots of them, all pretty much the same.

Eating Out

There are several small *lokantas* along the coast and on the islands, though many close in the winter. In Erdek, you'll have a choice of seafood places with outdoor tables around the port: **Kafkas Restaurant**, not Kafkaesque at all, will bring you out some *böreks* and a fine grilled fish for £5/$8 and up, depending on the fish.

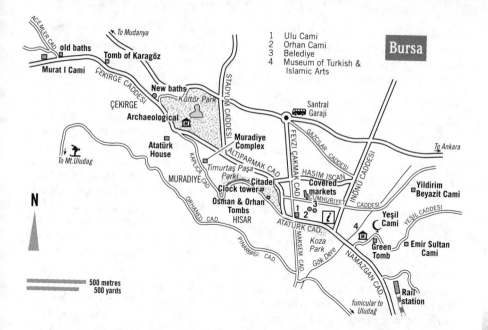

All of us old people here dream that one morning we will open our eyes and all the factories and cars will be gone, and Bursa will be as it was before.

So said the elderly gentleman we met in the tourist office, lamenting the strange fate that has overtaken this most refined of all Turkish cities. In the last decade or two, prosperous, well-run Bursa has become a victim of its own success. They wanted to attract industry, and they got it: Türk Fiat and Renault plants and scores of others. The jobs they provide have attracted vast numbers of migrants from all over Turkey, especially the Black Sea area and the far northeast. The population has more than doubled in the last decade, and now stands at over a million.

All these people, necessarily, have to stuff themselves into a ribbon-shaped medieval city built on the side of a mountain. Atatürk Caddesi, the only big street through it, has become a boiling, deafening motorway capable of giving anyone a headache after walking only one block. Everywhere else, crowds of people and cars make life pretty much unbearable. They have started building a metro (currently delayed by lack of funds), but it won't be enough. Bursa is faced with the task of redesigning and rebuilding itself from the ground up, which will take decades.

Not that we want to discourage you from coming. On the contrary; for all the commotion, Bursa is still an obligatory stop, with its medieval Ottoman monuments, a covered market second only to that of Istanbul, and its friendly, alert population. Bursans in many ways seem to be a step or two ahead of the rest of the Turks. Not the least of their virtues is a resolute civic pride, which manifests itself in surprising ways even in these difficult times. Another reason for coming is Uludağ, a breath of fresh air both figuratively and literally. This 8300ft massif is just a cable-car ride away from the centre of the city. With the snow on its peaks lingering well into the summer, the traffic and noise seem far away. Added to this Muslim alpine setting are famous thermal baths, a huge and lovely park, and plenty of trees. Bursa is the only city we have ever seen where the town council operates a flower shop. Its citizens call it *Yeşil* Bursa, 'Green Bursa', a title, unfortunately, that Bursa will have to struggle to hold on to.

History

King Prusias I of Bithynia founded Bursa—then *Prusa*—in the 2nd century BC. Although today Turkey's sixth-largest city, in ancient times Bursa was never more than a minor provincial centre. What little is known of it comes from the letters of Pliny the Younger, the governor under Emperor Trajan. To the Byzantines, the town was a fashionable resort for its baths, but the Ottomans put Bursa on the map. Sultan Orhan captured it in 1326 and made it his capital, a position it held on and off until 1453. Here the Ottomans began to sponsor great religious architecture. Drawing on the traditions of the Selcuks and Byzantines to develop a style that would be a fit heir to the past, and complement the ambitions of the sultans, their architects crowned Bursa with mosques, schools, and mausoleums solidly and honestly medieval, possessed of an austere but very present spirituality that earns them a place beside the more elaborate creations of Istanbul.

Throughout the centuries of Ottoman rule, Bursa lived quietly and polished its arts and manners; culturally it has always been the second city of Anatolia, after Istanbul. The city's career as a thermal resort blossomed under the Turks, and a spin-off, the manufacture of bath towels, gradually grew into a fully-fledged textile industry that is still important today. Particularly, the city is known for silk and for its beautifully embroidered linens (the silk industry probably goes back to Emperor Justinian, whose spies managed to steal some cocoons from the Chinese and break their monopoly). Serious industry came only after 1950. Now, along with the towels, Turkey's second-largest industrial centre ships out tons of soda-pop, bathtubs, clothing, knives, cars and trucks, cannons for the army and hosts of other products.

Getting Around

Bursa is often described as a day trip from Istanbul. This is possible but not much fun—4 or 5 hours one way by road. Bursa deserves more than one day anyhow. Most **coach** companies have 'express services' that make use of the Yalova–Kartal ferry; these are comfortable, but only nominally faster (about 45 min). Bursa's main station, the *Santral Garaji*, is north of the city centre on the E23, a 20min walk from the centre along Fevzi Çakmak Caddesi. You'll never have to wait long for a bus to Istanbul or any other western city; if you want to plan ahead for any trip, talk to the Bursa-based *Uludağ* company, a good line which has the most connections in this part of Turkey (and they use flash double-decker buses on some of their runs).

If you're really pressed, though, **Sönmez Airlines** offers two daily flights to and from Istanbul. In Bursa their office is in the Kizilay Pasaji, Cemal Nadir Caddesi, ✆ (224) 221 0099.

Fortunately, the main sights are within easy walking distance of each other in the centre; the other old quarters, the Hisar, Muradiye and Yeşil, are removed a bit from the traffic and still fun to walk. Atatürk Caddesi, even though it changes its name three times (*see* map), is the main axis of Bursa, and the route of many **buses** and **dolmuş**; terminus for most routes is the *Heykel* ('statue'), the Atatürk monument on the western end of Atatürk Caddesi. As in Istanbul, bus tickets are purchased at the kiosks by the major stops. Buses for the Uludağ *teleferik* (cable car) start from Heykel (route 3A). The *teleferik* itself runs every half hour, weather permitting, until 10pm, 9pm in winter. Taxis are easy to find anywhere in the city centre.

Tourist Information

Orhan Gazi Parki, Atatürk Caddesi, ℗ (224) 220 1848. Competent and helpful as ever, though the otherwise good city map they hand out pictures the city upside down, which can be a bit confusing. In summer a branch is open just outside the bus station.

Tourism Police: Çarşi Karakolu (the covered market police station), on Cemal Nadir Caddesi (extension of Atatürk Cad.) by the big overpass.

Seeing Bursa: The Market Area

A good place to begin a tour of Bursa is at the **Ulu Cami Park** (also called Koza Park), focal point of the city, with the tourist office and the entrance to the covered market. Facing these is Bursa's first Ottoman mosque, the **Orhan Camii**, built by that sultan in 1335, and restored after a Karaman invasion damaged it in 1413. This small but lovely mosque is the pattern for later works in Bursa; its best features are its simple but graceful porch and fountain. Inside, the central dome is supported, not by pendentives, but by semi-domes in the corners. In some ways, this is the structural system of older buildings like the Aya Sofia turned inside out; it would not work with a larger dome. The outlandish geometry that decorates the semi-domes is just that, decoration, not part of the structure. Such polygons run amok are a recurring conceit in Bursa's mosques.

Just across the street, Bursa's **Belediye** (City Hall) is not in tourist brochures, but it's probably the largest piece of folk-art in Turkey, and the prettiest city hall. Its construction of half-timber, with horizontal, vertical and diagonal beams in a seemingly haphazard manner, with bricks in between, is common in the older village homes. Here, with its painted designs of flowers and trees, and occasionally illuminated with strings of coloured lights, it's one of the unexpected delights of Bursa. Also here, on Atatürk Caddesi, is the Grand Mosque, the **Ulu Cami**, completed in 1396 by Yildirim Beyazit and twice restored. Here twenty domes, two graceful minarets, and the more than usual austerity of the outside give way to a virtuoso display of Arabic calligraphy and a famous carved mihrab within.

Next to the Orhan Camii on the northern side of the park are two lovely 15th-century *hanlar* that mark the entrance to the bazaar, the **Ipek** ('silk') **Han** and the adjoining **Koza Han** with a little *mescid* built over a fountain at the centre. Under the Ottomans Bursa was famous for silk; the trade is experiencing something of a comeback today, and each year in late June there is a big silkworm-cocoon market here. The rest of the year, this is the fancy end of the market, largely given over to leather and designer clothing shops; the jewellery and serious antiques await nearby in the **Bedesten**.

The rest of the market district encompasses everything north of Atatürk Caddesi, nearly a square kilometre in size. The network of covered bazaars and *hans* is not quite as large as Istanbul's, with less jewellery, and more bath towels and tea sets. Just the same, it's tidier and has better bargains. You can find just about anything you want here, but the real prize is the embroidered bed linens, bathroom sets, etc. Whether hand-embroidered on silk or done on a machine, it is some of the most beautiful work you'll see anywhere, and quite inexpensive; save some room in your suitcase.

Like any good Turkish bazaar, this one is a labyrinth, a web of long arcades, with streets and *hans* tucked in between. Many of the arcades were destroyed in a 1955 fire, but the Bursans have rebuilt them exactly as they were. As in Istanbul, many of the surrounding streets are given over to a particular trade; Demirciler Caddesi, as its name implies, is a whole street of smiths, hammering away in ferrous harmony.

The Citadel

To the west, Atatürk Caddesi curves around the old **citadel**, which is in an extremely strong position. Undoubtedly it had much to do with maintaining Bursa's peace and quiet over the centuries. Not much remains of the old walls built by the Ottomans, but on the slopes down to Atatürk Caddesi, modern Bursa has turned the old fortress into a modern-day version of Nebuchadnezzar's hanging gardens, called **Timurtaş Paşa Parki**; the slopes, with stairways and terraces full of trees and flowers, and bits of Byzantine arches, give ever-changing views over the old city. There are also many cafés, in which the people of Bursa practically live; wherever there's a beautiful view, common enough in the neighbourhoods on the heights, you'll find a pleasant spot to sit and reflect.

The citadel area contains the oldest houses in the city. Many are in disrepair, but more than other cities, Bursa has made an effort at historic preservation, noticeable in such streets as **Kale Caddesi**, lined with homes of the 17th to 19th centuries. Near the **clock tower**, a landmark visible from most of Bursa, are the tombs of the first two great Ottoman sultans, the **Osmangazi Türbe** and **Orhangazi Türbe**, both restored after heavy damage in the earthquake of 1855. Orhan's sarcophagus lies beside that of his wife, Nilüfer Hatun, a Byzantine princess married off for reasons of political expediency who became the first of the great ladies of the Ottoman Empire; the building she founded for travelling dervishes in Iznik now contains that city's municipal museum.

Two routes lead down from the citadel, one through the meandering streets westwards to Kaplica Caddesi, leading eventually down to the Kültür Park and suburb of Çekirge (discussed below), the other going back through the hanging gardens. From here, the abominable **Atatürk Caddesi**, the modern business street, continues eastwards around the market district. Just beyond Atatürk's statue, the street goes over a small bridge that crosses the narrow chasm of the **Gök Dere**. Small cafés overlook the stream, with lawns and flowerbeds arranged in patterns and scrolls, but you can't get to them from the cliffs. Just beyond, in a little square overshadowed by an enormous plane tree, a road branches off to the left for the **Yeşil** ('the Green'), one of the loveliest of Bursa's neighbourhoods though it too is somewhat tarnished by the traffic. This road, the Yeşil Caddesi, goes to the Green Mosque and the Green Mausoleum. Even the street signs here are green.

Yeşil Cami

The **Yeşil Cami** (Green Mosque) stands among the finest mosques in Turkey, a marvel not only in the perfection of its form and decoration, but for the way these two elements, the simple structure and the lavish stonecarving and coloured tiles, are combined into a harmonious work of art.

We read in the history books of the early Ottoman Turks as grim and resolute Gazi warriors, still attached in many ways to the kind of life their nomadic forefathers led out on the Asian steppe just a few generations before. Their detractors, historians like Gibbon and the Byzantine apologist Steven Runciman, paint them as semi-barbarians who could build an empire but didn't know what to do with one. Such a building as this makes us pause to reconsider. Mehmet I had the Yeşil Cami built in the second decade of the 15th century, at a time when all the Ottomans' resources must have been needed for the reconstruction of the state, so soon after Sultan Beyazit's disaster at the hands of Tamerlane. Nevertheless, the necessary money and attention were found to construct this masterpiece.

Mehmet's architect, Haci Ivaz Paşa, attempted no radical departures here; the Ottomans had been building in this style for a half-century already, in Bursa and elsewhere. Rather, this mosque represents the culmination, the perfection of that style. If the Ottomans had met an early end like the Selcuks, if they had never captured Constantinople and acquired the resources to build so many copies of the Aya Sofia, the Yeşil Cami would have its page in the art histories as the greatest work of the deceased nation; we would mourn the Ottomans as we do the Selcuks, thinking, 'If only they had been around to build more.' Decadence is a subtle disease; nations do not always reach their political and artistic peaks at the same moment.

The Green Mausoleum

Most visitors come down Green Avenue to the place where the Green Mosque and the **Green Mausoleum** face each other across the street and immediately head for the latter, their eyes caught by the masses of green tile. Tile from Iznik, in the very same beautiful sea-green, is used around the windows of the mosque, though sparingly, to call attention to the excellent carved stonework. No windows like these exist in Istanbul and certainly nothing like their flowery decoration, an inheritance from the Selcuks, as is the fine gateway with its concave 'stalactite' recess. Similar entrance gates are the principal adornment of most of the older Turkish mosques.

Inside, any impression that Mehmet was being cheap with the Iznik tiles is immediately dispelled. The mihrab, the ceilings, the upstairs galleries, and all the walls up to 6 feet are covered with them, in blue and green, many with floral designs. The plan is a simple one: a central hall under two shallow domes, one slightly higher than the other, a common form for the smaller early Ottoman mosques, as in the Orhan Camii. The Islamic fascination with geometry is here on display, from the unusual three-dimensional shapes that support the domes to the intricate patterns, carved into the walnut doors, shutters, and mimber, and the geometric medallions intertwined with Koranic calligraphy along the walls.

Some features are unusual. The ribbed interior of the domes shows a Greek influence, recalling the Istanbul Byzantine churches like the Kariye. In the dome near the entrance an oculus sends down a sunbeam at high noon over an exceptionally beautiful fountain, carved from a single piece of marble. The galleries around it, with some of the best Iznik tiles, were meant as private boxes for the sultan and his harem. Two *eyvans*, or chambers, flank the central hall, once used for the reception and repose of travelling dervishes.

Mehmet I, who put up the work, did not command the respect of the other early Ottoman sultans, preoccupied as he was through most of his reign with defeating the intrigues of his brothers and cousins, and with reunifying and rebuilding his shattered state. His conquests were few, but his achievements, in the worst of times, have earned him more than he usually gets. His grandfather, the first Murat, had been illiterate, but Mehmet can be accounted the first cultured man among the sultans. He had expressed a wish to be buried here, beside his great mosque, and during the reign of his son Murat II, the Green Mausoleum was built for his remains.

If the mosque had been for Allah, this was for the family. The architect was the same, Haci Ivaz Paşa, but although he and Murat were not able to confer the same perfection of spirituality upon this tomb, at least in the best family manner they spared no expense, pouring in the rich Iznik tiles in numbers exceeded only in the Blue Mosque in Istanbul. There are almost as many inside, sheathing Mehmet's immense sarcophagus, painted with sayings of the Prophet in a bold flowing calligraphy.

The Green Medrese

A third and equally worthy member of this complex stands just a block away on Yeşil Caddesi; the old theological school called the **Green Medrese** has lately been restored and converted to house Bursa's **Museum of Turkish and Islamic Arts** (*open daily 8–12, 1–5.30; adm; closed Mon pm*). The large ethnographic collection occupies the students' cells and the central courtyard; outside there's a pretty garden with a view over the Gökdere stream and the rest of Bursa. Inside are fine silver, carpets, and swords, Iznik ceramics, Selcuk architectural decoration, books and almanacs, and some very unusual 19th-century pottery from Çanakkale, a centre of the ceramic craft after it had died out in Iznik. Overhead in some of the domed ceilings around the cloister is more first-class tile work.

One speciality of the museum is figures from the old Turkish shadow play, *Karagöz*. Bursa likes to claim Karagöz and Hacivat, the traditional Punch and Judy of this ancient entertainment, as its citizens; their 'tomb' is in the suburb of Çekirge. On one puppet you can see the mechanism whereby Karagöz's hat pops up whenever he is surprised, revealing his bald head.

The Mosque of Yildirim Beyazit

Continuing beyond the Yeşil into the eastern edges of Bursa, there are two mosques of the same era, both set up on hills among the rambling cottages and stone walls of this delightful area. The **Emir Sultan Camii** (1431) stands on the street of the same name, off Yeşil Caddesi; it was built by one of the daughters of Yildirim Beyazit in honour of her deceased husband. From here, Davutkadi Caddesi heads northward some ten blocks to that sultan's own complex of religious buildings, the **Yildirim Beyazit Camii** (1395). In both of these, it's interesting to make architectural comparisons with the Green Mosque, but we can only guess at their original decorative scheme. Like the tombs of Osman and Orhan, and indeed almost everything else in Bursa, these mosques were hit hard by the 1855 earthquake; apparently the city only had resources enough to do a complete job of restoration on the Green complex, and as a result, Beyazit's and Emir Sultan's foundations were left with plain interiors that go well with the structure's formal simplicity, but are no substitute for the original.

Beyazit's mosque may have been an especially good one. Its *eyvans* and uneven twin domes recall the Yeşil Cami, and its arched portico and single slender minaret are fine elements. Before the earthquake, this mosque was the centre of a well-endowed *külliye*, a complex that included a hospital, schools, and dervish communities. Of the original eight buildings only the mosque, medrese, and Beyazit's tomb are left. This tomb, small and severe, is probably the most fitting memorial to the most ambitious and least cautious of the Ottoman sultans. Undoubtedly, it would have been grander had not Beyazit's 14-year reign ended so ignominiously at the Battle of Ankara; here, the mercurial warrior, who expected to become the lord of Europe and Asia, instead ended up as lunch on Tamerlane's table. The Turks accepted it, as the Greeks would have, as divine punishment for hubris—how else could the Mongols have been explained, but as a scourge of God? Later sultans, for a while, took the lesson to heart.

The Muradiye

Returning to the citadel, and beyond it to the west end of Bursa, you may visit the works of a more fortunate monarch, Mehmet II, the Conqueror, at the **Muradiye Complex**, along

Kaplica Caddesi just off the main street which, at this point, has changed its name to Çekirge Caddesi. Among the eleven buildings are a mosque, tombs, and schools, all plain, all made of sandstone and narrow brick. There is none of the marble and fine sculptural detail of the earlier mosques here; this no doubt reflects the attitude of Mehmet, always with his eye on Constantinople. If he did not choose to embellish his *külliye*, at least he had himself buried here—next to his father, Murat II—who is interred in a simple *türbe* supported by ancient Corinthian columns with a wide oculus in the dome; Murat had requested that his tomb be open to the sky. The most elaborate tomb here, ironically, belongs to the celebrated upstart Cem Sultan, Mehmet's younger son, who rebelled and intrigued for years against Beyazit II, his brother. Cem's career as Ottoman pretender would have been an ideal subject for a novel by Sir Walter Scott, but one with a sad end for his partisans. Beyazit finally managed to pack him off to exile in Italy, in the care of Pope Alexander VI. Even though Beyazit was paying huge sums for his brother's room and board, the Borgia pope eventually tired of his exotic guest, and had him poisoned. As if in compensation, the sultan brought him to this beautiful mausoleum, with its tiles and painted details in fairyland colours.

Çekirge

'Çekirge' means 'locust' in Turkish, and there are certainly enough of them in the woods that cover this slope of Uludağ. In the days of the sultans, Çekirge, with its famous therapeutic baths and lovely views, was the favoured residence of the imperial families. Today it's Bursa's wealthy suburb, with 2 miles of hotels and smart new apartments spreading westward from the city.

The people of Bursa like to come here to play at the **Kültür Parki**. Turks in the big cities use their parks the way we would have a century ago, and it's charming to see the families in their Sunday best, dragging their children along and they, in turn, their balloons, all coming to see and be seen, to eat ice cream and inspect the flower beds. Here there is a blue lagoon with a fountain where young couples paddle canoes, an amusement park that must have half the neon in Turkey—its two giant Ferris wheels are among Bursa's landmarks—a football stadium, and acres of garden paths. Bursa's **Archaeological Museum** (*open daily exc Mon 9.30–12, 1–5.30; adm*), in the centre of the park, has a smattering of mainly Roman artefacts, and a large jewellery and coin collection.

In the same Victorian atmosphere are the fine homes built a century ago in the streets across Çekirge Caddesi. Most are in the typical old Bursa style, in pastel plaster with enclosed wooden balconies, but a few, like the summer houses along the Bosphorus, could easily pass for American Queen Anne homes of the 1880s, with more than a touch of Hansel and Gretel thrown in. The city put President Atatürk up in the best of them whenever he came to town, and it has been preserved as the **Atatürk Museum**.

If Çekirge has been the fashionable end of the town ever since Roman times, the springs and thermal baths are the reason, widely prescribed for all manner of ailments and for general well-being besides. Most of Bursa's tourist trade comes for the waters, and several hotels in the district have their own springs. Two Ottoman foundations, called locally the **Eski Caplica** (old spring) and the **Yeni Caplica** (new spring), the latter in a nice garden next to the Kültür Parki, are open to the public and are quite popular. Even if you aren't troubled by rheumatism or gout, these are worth a visit. The Yeni Caplica was last rebuilt by Süleyman the Magnificent; parts of the Eski Caplica go back to Byzantine times. Both are open all day for both men and women.

Further west in Çekirge Caddesi, you pass a little monument called the **Tomb of Karagöz**

and Hacivat. One story from old Bursa relates that these incorrigible clowns (the shadow-play figures) were workmen in the service of the sultan, helping to build the Birinci Murat Camii; not only did they never do their own jobs, but with continual arguing and joking, they so distracted the other workers that the sultan was eventually obliged to put them to death. In fact Karagöz and his friend could probably trace their origins back to the ancient Greeks, and they have a surprising lot in common with their 14th-century contemporaries, Harlequin and Puncinello of the Italian *commedia dell'arte*.

Nearby, at the very end of the city, stands the oldest of the imperial mosques, the 1367 **Birinci Murat Camii** (Birinci means *the First*). At that time, Turkish architects had not yet found their classic style; this building, good as it is, can be considered an experiment on the way. Roughly square, the mosque occupies only the first floor, with one squat minaret in a corner. The second floor, behind a graceful loggia, was a theological school. The tomb of Murat I in the grounds has been restored too often to be of much interest, though Murat himself was a great soldier and statesman who contributed much to the growth of the Ottoman state with his Balkan conquests and rationalization of the government. A Serbian prisoner stabbed Murat in the back in the Battle of Kosovo, his greatest triumph, and his son Beyazit brought him here to this *türbe*.

Uludağ

If not for the waters, or the charms of the city itself, visitors come to Bursa to see **Uludağ** (8300ft), literally 'great mountain', the tallest peak in northwestern Turkey. From Bursa, the mountain may not at first seem impressive, only a steep emerald ridge enfolding the city and stretching to no great height. Take either of the roads around it, however, towards Eskişehir or Kütahya, and you'll see the true Uludağ, standing high above the surrounding plain in the same manner as the much taller mountains of eastern Anatolia. The peak visible from Bursa is only the first of a series, stretching peak after peak into the southeast, with forests, meadows and mountain streams in between. The highest will be covered with snow well into the summer. Uludağ is a national park, with alpine scenery, hiking trails, ski resorts with properly alpine lodges (the season runs roughly from December to March), and several hotels. You can get up there, either by the road off Çekirge Caddesi that runs for 20 miles (32km) almost to the highest summit, or by the long **funicular railway** (the *teleferik*), with a continuous service from the eastern edge of Bursa.

The ancients called Uludağ Mt Olympus, the Mysian Olympus, one of eight or so peaks around the Mediterranean with that name. The religious syncretism of the sophisticated Hellenistic world led men of letters to look for similarities in all the local cults and myths that soldiers and travellers brought back to them from the ends of their rapidly expanding world. Any mountain credited with being the home of the gods by the natives, as Uludağ was, became an 'Olympus', less a name than a category.

Bursa and Çekirge © (224–) **Where to Stay**
expensive

The tourist office lists two prices for the city's expensive and moderate range hotels, regular and 'reduced'. Theoretically these are for the off-season, but in many cases you can get the reduced rate anytime, from a quarter to a third off the price. It doesn't hurt to try—though don't expect much from the five-star places, which get a steady business from Istanbul and from the Arab world.

Most of the city's finest establishments are near the hot springs in the Çekirge suburb, a mile west of the centre. Many of the hotels here boast thermal baths; the oldest and most renowned of these is the ★★★★★**Çelik Palas** at Çekirge Cad. 79, ℗ 233 3800, @ 236 1910. Its name, 'Steel Palace', comes from the great steel dome that covers the baths. It also has tennis courts, an indoor pool, a casino and disco and nearly every other amenity for a bargain £65/$95 for a single, £80/$120 a double. The ultra-modern ★★★★★**Hotel Kervansaray-Thermal**, Çekirge Meydani, ℗ 233 9300, @ 233 9324 is more opulent still, boasting a health centre and a casino amongst its attractions; all rooms air-conditioned, with satellite TV; £115/$170. The ★★★★**Dilmen Oteli**, Murat Cad. 1, ℗ 233 9500, also has thermal baths but fewer luxuries; £30/$45, reduced rates for children. One choice in the city centre is the ★★★**Kent Oteli**, Atatürk Caddesi 119, ℗ 221 8700, big and bright, a typical businessman's hotel with doubles for £43/$65.

moderate

Two hotels in this category have thermal baths, the ★**Adapalas**, Murat Caddesi 21, ℗ 233 3900, charging £15/$22 for a double, and the ★★★**Termal Otel Gönlüferah**, in a quiet location at 1 Murat Caddesi, ℗ 233 9210; nice rooms with TV for £30/$45. Both are in the Çekirge suburb. One good choice in the centre is the ★★**Dikmen**, above all because it is on a relatively quiet side street: Maksem Caddesi 78, just north of Atatürk, ℗ 224 1840; rooms with TV, minibar and balcony for £30/$45.

cheap

There is a dearth of cheap hotels in the centre of Bursa, a situation recently made worse by the closure of the city's youth hostel. However, you could try the **Saray Otel**, Inönü Caddesi, Matbaa Çik 1, ℗221 2820, which charges £5/$8 for doubles without bath. It's next to the main square and very noisy. Slightly better are two hotels next to each other on Inebey Caddesi; the very pleasant **Otel Çamlibel** at no. 71, ℗ 221 2565, and the **Hotel Çağlayan** at no. 73, ℗ 221 1458. Both charge in the region of £6/$9; some rooms have private bath. One street away is the similar **Çeşmeli**, on Gümüşçeken Caddesi, ℗ 224 1512.

In Çekirge the **Temizel**, on Murat Caddesi, ℗ 236 3125, is simple but adequate. The biggest collection of inexpensive rooms in town can be found near the bus station; right across the street on Çelik Sokak, one good one is the **Terminal**, ℗ 254 7220—a bit old and raggedy perhaps, but friendly enough and they do their best to keep it up; baths in most rooms, and a hamam downstairs. Slightly more expensive is the **Kardeş**, Santral Garaj Çarşisi, ℗ 254 8003; friendly and well kept, but like all places near the bus station, it is deafening; £6, slightly more with bath.

Gazcilar Caddesi, a relatively quiet street of old buildings across the wide square from the bus station, has a wide choice of cheap rooms. The best is probably the **Belkis**, Gazcilar Caddesi 168, ℗ 214 8322, charging £3/$5 per person, with common shower and toilet. For a campsite with all the amenities, including a swimming pool, there is the **Kervansaray Kumluk**, on the Yalova road, ℗ 254 8968.

On Uludağ

Accommodation on Uludağ is mostly in chalet-style ski lodges like the **Alkoçlar** in the national park, ℗ 285 2130, open Dec–April; £25/$38. The ★★**Uludağ Büyük**, ℗ 205

2216, provides a swimming pool and tennis court as well as winter sports; in the summer (if they're open) you can get a discount on the rates of £63/$95. In the mountain village of Inkaya, on the road from the city, the plain but pleasant ★Akçam, ℗ 236 8303, has rooms for £20/$35 in a pretty setting. The least expensive of the hotels on Uludağ is the **Kar Oberj**, in the national park, ℗ 285 2121. Most establishments on Uludağ are closed outside the winter months and that full board is usually mandatory.

Eating Out

Bursa is the home of the *Iskender kebab*, a mixed grill with a tomato-based sauce, and you can sample it at the restaurant that claims to have first created the dish, the **Iskender Kebapçi** at 60 Atatürk Caddesi. Founded in 1867, it's an odd-looking place, with an exterior like a wild west saloon and an interior like the Blue Mosque, but you'll eat well for £6/$9 with a soft drink. Other *Iskender kebab* places are all over town, charging an average price of £3/$5. The **Haci Bey** chain is very good, with branches in Çekirge and on Atatürk Bulvari, west of the post office. In Çekirge, the **Çiragan** restaurant on the main street is where the beautiful people of Bursa go for a meal and a beer and to watch the sun go down over their city; £5/$8. There is also an inexpensive local favourite, the **Nazar Restaurant**, £2/$3, in the Iç Koza Han in the bazaar area.

Bursa's answer to Istanbul's Balikpazari is **Sakarya Caddesi**. As you follow the main street, here called Altiparmak Cad., as it curves around the Hisar, Sakarya branches off to the left. This pedestrian street, lined with restaurants and bars with outside tables, is definitely one of the two places to go in the evening. Many of its restaurants specialize in seafood, such as the **Havuk**, where you can get a grilled fish and mezes for £5/$8 and up. Outside of dining hours there will be plenty of places open for beer and snacks.

The other place to go is the **Kültür Parki**, where half of Bursa comes on any given night to row boats around the lagoon and inspect the little pavilions of the permanent industrial exhibition, featuring Turkish-made cars, eggbeaters and double-glazing. There are a number of agreeable outdoor restaurants, which double as beer gardens in the off hours. One of the least expensive is the **Oçakbaşi**, near the lagoon, with a wide choice of kebabs, a delicious, thin home-made *pide* and a pretty fruit plate for dessert; £4/$6. For a bit more you can enjoy the wide choice of mezes at the **Akarsu**, overlooking the lagoon—come on a Saturday night and there may well be a wedding party in the place, which can be more entertaining than you would expect.

Even the corner diners of Bursa keep high standards. In the home of *iskender kebab*, you needn't pay more than pocket change for the genuine item at lunchtime—look for places like the excellent **Çarşi Kebabcisi**, near the Atatürk Caddesi entrance to the covered bazaar: genuine ambience of shiny formica tabletops, Coca-cola and a huge plate of meat drenched in melted butter for £1; two or three of the owner's sons wait to see who can light your postprandial cigarette first. There are a number of good *lokantas* by the bus station. For £2/$3 you won't do better anywhere than the **Lezzet Lokantasi** on Çelik Sokak, tasty soups and *iskender*; open until 11pm.

As you would expect, Bursa has its share of fancy pastry shops. At the **Ulus**, by the post office on Atatürk Caddesi, you can pick out dainties from a wide assortment of sweets, from chocolates to chestnut cakes and pastel-coloured *lokum*, and wash it down with a glass of kiwifruit juice. A few doors away on Atatürk, Bursa's postmen, old geezers, and a surprising number of young folk light up a poisonous wad at the **Çay ve Nargile Salonu**, a convivial working-hours hideout.

North and East of Bursa

Few cities enjoy such a paradisical hinterland. To the south there's Uludağ and its mountain forests and lakes; any other direction takes you through landscapes so green and lush they will make you drowsy looking at them (Uludağ stops all the weather fronts pouring down the Black Sea and Marmara and catches all the rain). Turkey's careful farmers have made good use of this land; all along the main roads they have set up stands to sell you incredibly colossal and juicy peaches, perfect sour cherries or whatever else is in season.

Getting Around

Regular **buses** from Bursa make the one-hour trip to Iznik, taking the scenic route along the southern shore of the lake. If you're driving, consider carefully any trip from Bursa east to Yalova and points west; traffic can be as intense as in Bursa's centre. Mudanya has infrequent car ferries and summer hydrofoils to Istanbul, though for car and coach travellers it will usually be more convenient to take the short Yalova–Kartal ferry to get to the city.

Tourist Information

Iznik: Kiliçaslan Caddesi 73, ✆ (224) 757 1933

Yalova: Iskele Meydani, ✆ (216) 814 2108

Directly north of Bursa is **Mudanya**, a large, gloomy port that saw the signing of the armistice ending the Turkish War of Independence in 1922. Further on, past Gemlik and Gemlik Bay, you'll come to **Termal**. Emperors Constantine and Justinian enjoyed the thermal baths from which the town draws its name; you can do the same, although there's no other reason to stop. The road continues north to meet the sea at **Yalova**, from where ferries cross to Istanbul. It's a bright and breezy town, with yet another product of the Atatürk statue factory in its square; this one is more dramatic than most, depicting the Great Man in strident pose, arm upraised as if to strike. Should you wish to risk swimming in this less-than-clean stretch of the Marmara, there are beaches at **Çiftlikköy**, **Koruköy** and **Çinarcik**, all west of Yalova. The water at **Armutlu**, on the western edge of the peninsula, is clearer but the beach is nothing special.

Ancient *Mysia* was the province stretching from Bursa towards the east, including much of the southern shore of the Marmara and the city of Balikesir, the ancient Paleokastro. Ancient geography, as is usual in Asia Minor, was never too clear about boundaries; for a while the Romans were wont to call the area around Bursa *Phrygia Minor*, and the city itself, along with the territory to the east, *Bithynia*. Today these lands along the valley of the Sakarya River, the ancient Sangarius, are in one of the more fortunate corners of Turkey, even if they no longer have a sense of being a distinct region. The countryside is green and good, and cultivated with loving care; the villages, with their characteristic brick and timber dwellings, drift through the decades in a permanent state of genteel dilapidation. **Bilecik** would have been the most interesting, had it not been destroyed in the War of Independence. Of its early Ottoman monuments only the Karasu Bridge, reputed to be the work of Mimar Sinan, remains.

Inegöl, to the west, is an agricultural town famous throughout Turkey for spicy meatballs, *Inegöl köfte*, while in Söğüt, you may visit the **tomb of Ertuğrul**, the father of Osman, founder of the Ottoman dynasty. In a way this Sakarya valley is the original Ottoman homeland, a secure and uncontested spot in the 13th century, a perfect place for an ambitious band of roving warriors to await its opportunities with patience. The Byzantines were too feeble to trouble them, and no serious enemies appeared from the east either; despite all the talent of the early Ottomans, one can perhaps attribute much of their early success to a lucky choice of locations. And maybe the spot is always lucky for the Turks; just a couple of miles south of Söğüt, the climactic battle of their War of Independence was fought at **Inönü** in 1921. A few years later, when Atatürk decided that all Turks should have Western-style surnames, he himself conferred one upon the general who had won the battle and halted the Greek offensive. Ismet Paşa now became Ismet Inönü, later to be the second president of the Turkish Republic.

Iznik (Nicaea)

Between the Sakarya and Gemlik Bay, an inlet of the Marmara, a circle of wooded hills isolates a large lake, **Iznik Gölü**, named after the ancient city on its eastern shore. Iznik, the ancient Nicaea, was founded in the 4th century BC. For a while it was the capital of the Kingdom of Bithynia, before the Romans swallowed it up, but it wasn't until the Christian era that the city achieved its fame, or perhaps its notoriety, as seat of the two great church councils. First in the 4th century and again in the 8th, the querulous bishops and bureaucrats of early Christianity met here to argue, anathematize their enemies or smash them with bats, and run up uncollectable bills at the local hostelries.

The Church Councils

Constantine himself first summoned the church councils in 325 to decide the insoluble conflict between the Arian and Athanasian sects. His favourite, St Athanasius, came all the way from Alexandria to lead his partisans in the attack, demanding that every Christian admit both the divine and mortal natures of Christ. Arius, who has been called a 'unitarian', wished strongly to avoid having the godhead cluttered with extra, inessential 'essences', and got himself murdered here for his trouble, though his party won a short-lived victory. Nicaea, a beautiful resort city in a strategic location, central for the eastern half of the empire, had already been a residence of Emperor Diocletian; the Church Fathers found it a wonderfully agreeable locale for conventions and they came often, most importantly for the great council of 786, when the bishops codified rituals and beliefs into the form still observed by the Greek Church today.

Empress Irene, who almost married Charlemagne but could not bear to part with the intrigues and luxury of Constantinople, may have been an outrageous tart, but she is remembered fondly by the Orthodox for calling this council to put an end finally to the iconoclastic struggles that had so bitterly divided the empire. Convening at Nicaea's church of Aya Sofia, the bishops from as far away as Italy decided once and for all that holy images 'stimulate spectators to think of the originals', and therefore deserved at least an indirect sort of adoration.

Nicaea's finest hour, however, came in the dark days following the Sack of Constantinople in 1204. A die-hard, Theodore Lascaris, brought the remnants of Greek resistance here and became emperor-in-exile; he and his successor, John III Vatatzes, reconstituted the empire, carefully rebuilding its finances and its army for the day when Constantinople would once more be theirs.

The Selcuk Turks held the city and made it their capital for a brief period in the 11th century, and it fell again, finally, to the Ottoman leader Orhan in 1331. As a Turkish city, Nicaea, now

Iznik, gained fame throughout the Islamic world for its hand-painted ceramic tiles, made with a quality of colour and design that cannot be imitated today. Expensive though they must have been, all the early Ottoman sultans demanded them in enormous quantity for their mosques, and today they can be seen on buildings across Turkey wherever earthquakes and decay have spared them. They can be approximately dated by colour and pattern. Until 1520, all Iznik ceramics were exclusively dark blue and white. About that time, turquoise was added. A kind of red, always difficult in glazing, was achieved in the 1600s. Throughout the 17th and 18th centuries, designs grew less abstract and more naturalistic; floral designs predominated in the Tulip Period and after, and even human and animal figures were appearing near the end in the early 1800s.

As the finances of the empire declined, the market for these tiles disappeared, and the city with it; by the 19th century only a dismal village was left inside the old Byzantine walls; even that remainder suffered grievous damage in the fighting of 1922.

Iznik Today

Today, some leftover grace from its days of greatness keeps Iznik free of the usual sadness that accompanies ruins. The town is simply too full of roses and children and green gardens to be melancholy. Indeed, the modest agricultural centre that Iznik has become cannot nearly fill the square mile or so within its Byzantine walls, and its people wisely use the remaining space for vegetable plots and olive groves. Not much happens here now, and whatever talent is left from the long-gone ceramic industries is devoted to making cinder blocks and roof tiles.

Even though the foundation of the city predates the Romans, Iznik has the plan of a typical Roman provincial town: two broad main streets meeting at right angles in the centre, connecting the four main gates. Nearly all of Iznik's **walls** can still be seen, in various stages of decay, and along the garden paths and sheep trails you find the occasional arch or Greek inscription, towers, sally-ports and storage rooms. Two of the **gates**, the northern or **Istanbul Gate** and the western or **Lefke Gate**, survive, with Roman triumphal arches between their inner and outer parts, inscriptions in Greek and Latin commemorating the visit of the Emperor Hadrian, and remains of marble reliefs. The Lefke Gate is the better preserved, and near it are parts of a much-weathered decorative frieze. Also carved, inconspicuously, on the inside of the gate is something that is obviously a layout for the game of Nine Men's Morris (others can be seen on the steps of the Basilica Julia in the Roman Forum, the Basilica of St John at Selçuk, and in scores of sites across the Mediterranean; this must have been the favourite game of classical antiquity for people with time on their hands). Outside the gate, the **Byzantine aqueduct** has suffered little from time, although it is no longer in use.

OLD CITY WALLS, IZNIK

Inside the walls, little remains of ancient Iznik. Near the ruined Yenişehir gate at the south entrance, the half-excavated ruins of the **Roman Theatre** are visible behind a fence, and exactly in the centre of the town stands the derelict **church of Aya Sofia**, an 11th-century structure that replaced the earlier church from the era of Justinian that hosted the two ecumenical councils. Some fragments of mosaics and frescoes can still be seen. The conquering Ottomans added a minaret, and its stump is currently the home of one of Iznik's numerous storks.

Storks, surprisingly, spend their summers in Turkey. These have little to do with their North European cousins, and they spend their winters in eastern or southern Africa. Minaret stumps make perfect bases for their nests, combining good drainage, peace and quiet, and inaccessibility to weasels. Another nest may be seen on a ruined minaret near the Istanbul Gate, next to the Nilüfer Hatun Imareti, a 14th-century hospice for travelling dervishes that now serves as the **Iznik Museum** (*open daily exc Mon, 9.30–12, 1–5.30; adm*). Here a selection of artefacts, from recent Turkish crafts going back to Paleolithic tools, proves the long continuity of this site; more interesting are the grave steles and architectural fragments arranged in the garden outside. Ranging from the early Hellenistic to the late Byzantine, the steles provide a kind of glossary of symbols, a complete guide to the inexhaustible iconography of death that so long occupied the Greek world's fancy.

Not surprisingly, the most important part of the museum's collection is devoted to ceramics, some as old as 2500 BC, as well as the best Islamic work. A city map on the wall of the museum helps in finding your way through the village to the ancient sites and around the walls. Ask at the museum about a possible excursion to the **Yeralti Mezar**, north of town, a 6th-century Byzantine tomb with some fine frescoes; they have the keys. Across the street from the museum, the **Yeşil Cami**, built in the 1380s, will catch your eye with what may be the prettiest minaret in all Anatolia. The blue and green tiles that cover it are not original Iznik work, however; during restorations in the last century it was necessary to replace them all.

There are no good **beaches** on Iznik's lake shore, but people still come here, particularly from Bursa, to walk along the promenade outside the town's ruined **Lake Gate**, and to eat fresh fish in the restaurants on the water's edge. If you come on just the right day in the spring, you can ski down Uludağ in the morning and swim in Lake Iznik or the Marmara in the afternoon.

Iznik © (224–)

Where to Stay
moderate

In Iznik, the **Çamlik Motel**, © 757 1613, is the best available, right on the lake shore at Göl Caddesi 1. It's a friendly, family motel where rooms are clean but modest at £10/$15 for a double with bath; there's also a good restaurant. Yalova has the **Otel Fatih**, Cumhuriyet Caddesi 27, which is cheerful, comfortable and good value at £13/$18.

cheap

In the centre of Iznik, the **Hotel Babacan**, Kiliçaslan Caddesi, © 757 1623, has double rooms for £5/$8 without bath, £7/$11 with. Yalova has a wide choice of cheap pensions, all near the ferries.

Eating Out

In Iznik, fish are easy to come by in a number of restaurants along the lakeside promenade, including the excellent **Savorona**. In the town, on Kiliçaslan Caddesi between the tourist office and the Aya Sofia, the **Bülbül Lokanta** is cheap, clean and friendly. There are several basic restaurants by the harbour in Yalova; most stay open late.

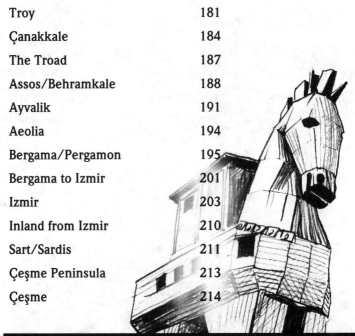

Troy	181
Çanakkale	184
The Troad	187
Assos/Behramkale	188
Ayvalik	191
Aeolia	194
Bergama/Pergamon	195
Bergama to Izmir	201
Izmir	203
Inland from Izmir	210
Sart/Sardis	211
Çeşme Peninsula	213
Çeşme	214

The North Aegean Coast: Troy to Izmir

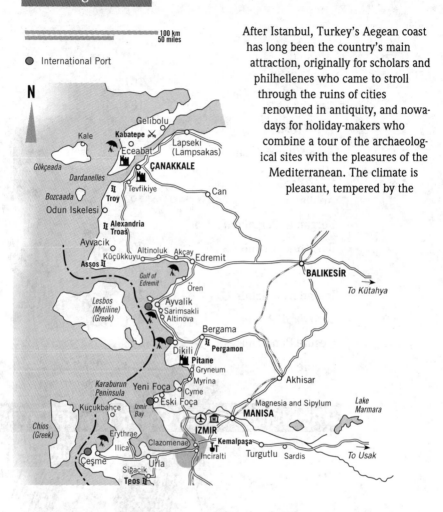

100 km
50 miles

● International Port

N

Gelibolu
Kale   Kabatepe ✕
○   Eceabat   Lapseki
Gökçeada   (Lampsakas)
    Dardanelles   ÇANAKKALE
Bozcaada   Tevfikiye
    Troy   Can
Odun Iskelesi ○

    Alexandria
    Troas
Ayvacik ○
    Küçükkuyu Altinoluk Akçay Edremit
Assos   BALIKESIR
            Gulf of
            Edremit   Ören   To Kütahya
Lesbos   Ayvalik
(Mytiline)   Sarimsakli
(Greek)   Altinova
                Bergama
        Dikili   Pergamon
        Pitane
Karaburun   ○ Gryneum
Peninsula Yeni Foça ○ Myrina
    Kuçukbahçe ○ Cyme   Akhisar
            Izmir Eski Foça
Chios   Bay   Magnesia and Sipylum   Lake
(Greek)   MANISA   Marmara
            IZMIR
        Erythrae
        Ilica Clazomenae   Kemalpaşa
Çeşme   Inciralti Turgutlu Sardis   To Usak
    Siğacik Urla
    Teos

After Istanbul, Turkey's Aegean coast has long been the country's main attraction, originally for scholars and philhellenes who came to stroll through the ruins of cities renowned in antiquity, and nowadays for holiday-makers who combine a tour of the archaeological sites with the pleasures of the Mediterranean. The climate is pleasant, tempered by the

sea in the summer and winter; olives and vineyards cover the fertile valleys and coastal plains. Mountains are never far away, nor are beaches, some in the throes of becoming major resorts, others quite deserted. Of all Turkey's regions, the Aegean coast has the best hotels, and more sprout up every year.

The northern part, Mysia and Lydia in ancient times, is a bit less touristy than the south—no fleshpots like Bodrum and Marmaris, but serene, laid-back resorts such as Behramkale and Ayvalik. The major attractions are archaeological: Troy of course, and Pergamon (Bergama) one of the great cities of the Hellenistic Era.

Getting Around

Çanakkale is connected by bus to Istanbul, Bursa, Izmir, and Edirne; the ferryboat crosses the Dardanelles from Eceabat hourly between 6am and midnight. The crossing takes 25 minutes and is ridiculously cheap, and it carries the very regular dolmuş from Kilitbahir, as well as buses to Tekirdağ and Istanbul. There are also informal ferries between Çanakkale and Kilitbahir, if you want to have a look at Mehmet II's unusual castle. These are small, usually unmarked boats that go whenever there's enough people; ask around.

From Çanakkale's *otogar*, a few streets south of the port on Atatürk Caddesi, frequent minibuses go to Troy and the neighbouring villages; buses from across the straits of course stop in the centre too, on Iskele Meydani. Çanakkale is the most popular base for exploring both the Gelibolu battlefields and ancient Troy and two travel agencies offer tours of both, **Troy-Anzac**, ✆ (286) 217 5047, and **Ana-Tur**, ✆ 217 5482. Both can be found near the clocktower and both charge the same rates, about £7/$10 per person. Be wary of unlicensed guides at both sites, who may or may not know the first thing about them.

Tourist Information

Çanakkale: next to Abdülhamid's clock tower at Iskele Meydani 67, the main square by the port, ✆ (286) 217 1187

Troy

From the time of Alexander the Great, travellers have come expressly to see **Troy**. No place is so highly charged in the Western imagination; after two and a half millennia, the wrath of Achilles, the beauty of Helen, the death of Hector, the ploy of the wooden horse, the sack of the high-walled city, and the misfortunes that dogged the victors in Homer's *Iliad* and *Odyssey* have retained their poetic resonance, each character and event an evocative, ambiguous symbol deeply embedded in our culture. For the ancient Greeks, the *Iliad* 's account of the Olympian gods was the source of their religious beliefs. And who can argue with Herodotus, who saw the Trojan War as the root and mirror of all later antagonisms between East and West.

Few ancients doubted the veracity of Homer's Troy; Alexander even exchanged some of his own armour for trophies from the Trojan War still hanging in Athena's temple. But by the 6th century AD the city was abandoned, its port silted up, the Anatolian dust thickening over it until the physical Troy vanished from all memory. Outwardly the site resembled a hill, which the Turks called Hisarlik; scholars argued over where the city might have stood, had it ever really existed. Byron was one of many who visited the Troad (the region around Troy), and one of very few who came away believing in more than poetic truth. In *Don Juan* he wrote,

> I've stood upon Achilles' tomb,
> And heard Troy doubted; time will doubt of Rome.

Another believer was Heinrich Schliemann, a merchant who made a fortune from the California Gold Rush and the American Civil War. In 1868, 46 years old and tired of wheeling and dealing, he came to the Troad, where he met an Englishman named Frank Calvert, who had dug a trench in Hisarlik and showed Schliemann his finds: part of a classical temple, and deeper down, signs of older civilizations, layered one on top of the other. Schliemann was hooked, and the former businessman became the greatest dilettante archaeologist of all time, one destined to unearth Troy, Mycenae and Tiryns, a series of spectacular finds that electrified the world. Subsequent archaeologists, especially Schliemann's assistant Dörpfeld and the American Carl Blegen, uncovered further proof that Hisarlik is indeed the site of the ancient city of Troy.

Recent Theories

As Calvert had brilliantly surmised, Schliemann found layer upon layer of civilization, which he numbered from Troy I—the oldest, dating back to 3600 BC—to Troy IX, the Hellenistic city of Ilion, founded by Alexander's general Lysimachus. Although Schliemann's aim was to discover the Troy of Priam and Hector, he uncovered a fascinating chronicle of people building over and over again on the same site. Was one of these Troys the Troy of Homer? Most scholars date the Trojan War to c. 1250 BC, just before the decline of the Mycenaean empire; Troy VII coincides rather neatly with that date, and it perished in a terrible conflagration. However, the city preceding it, Troy VI, was far more imposing and better fits the epithets Homer used in the *Iliad*—but it was destroyed by an earthquake.

Turkish archaeologists resolve the contradiction by seeing magnificent Troy VI as the citadel that Agamemnon's Achaeans unsuccessfully besieged for ten years; rebuilt shoddily after the earthquake, it was then easily captured. The Wooden Horse, it follows, was an offering by the Achaeans to Poseidon, the sea god and earth-shaker, whose assistance proved crucial in their sack of Troy. Others believe the *Iliad*, composed some 500 years after the traditional date of the war, recalls not one particular event but several Mycenaean raids on the Anatolian coast; or perhaps even recalls the last great twilight expedition, recited for latter-day kings by their bards to evoke the good old days.

In any event, no proof has ever been discovered in Troy that the Trojan War took place, although many recent discoveries, especially in Miletus, prove that the Mycenaean Greeks were in Asia Minor as early as the 15th century BC; in 1984 some of their tombs were discovered on an ancient beach at Besike Bay, one of the possible sites of Troy's long-vanished harbour.

But what has kept the debates on the Trojan War on the front burner since Schliemann is the finding of references to Troy in the dead languages of Anatolia. In the 1920s, scholars read about the Ahhiyawans—probably the Achaeans—when translating tablets from the 15th-century BC Hittite archives at Boğazköy. The archives also refer to a place called Wilusa, believed to be Ilios, Homer's other name for Troy.

Then, in 1984, some very suggestive evidence turned up in Luvian—an ancient Indo-European language, possibly the language of the Trojans—referring to 'steep Wilusa' and men named Priya-muwas (Priam ?) and Paris. If you add the fact that linguistically some lines of the *Iliad* have been shown to be older than the traditional date of the Trojan War (1250 BC), the problem becomes even more complicated. Recent scholarly symposiums in England and America and Michael Wood's excellent BBC series on Troy have heightened interest in the question: did the Trojan War take place as Homer recounts?

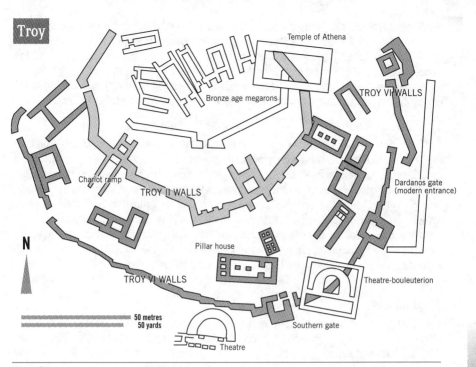

Temple of Athena

Bronze age megarons

TROY VI WALLS

Chariot ramp

TROY II WALLS

Dardanos gate
(modern entrance)

N

Pillar house

TROY VI WALLS

Theatre-bouleuterion

50 metres
50 yards

Southern gate

Theatre

The Site

The Trojan horse is certainly still there, or at least its modern Turkish descendant. It's the first thing you see at Troy and the only thing most tourists take pictures of. For, in all honesty, the site itself is bewildering, 'a ruin of a ruin' as some call it, a victim of 19th-century archaeology. The University of Cincinnati, the most recent archaeological team to work the site, determined that Schliemann's original nine layers contained some 46 substrata. What you see as you walk through the excavations are fragments of a *millefeuille* pastry of Troys.

The tall Mycenaean walls of Troy VI are the most impressive sight and among the most beautiful of the ancient world. They fit the Homeric descriptions of 'beetling' and 'steep', and at one point in the *Iliad* (Book XVI) Homer refers to their most unusual feature—angles or offsets that divide the wall into several sections. Here, too, are the foundations of a mighty bastion, perhaps Homer's 'great tower of Ilios'. Yet as splendid as these walls still are, they are not of any great extent: this eminence was the citadel of Troy, not the city. The South Gate (Homer's Scaean gate?) facing the plain was the most important; the so-called **Pillar House** above it is the most popular candidate for Priam's Palace.

Near the entrance you can walk up a surviving section of the old Hisarlik mound, for a view that evokes Homer perhaps even better than the old stones; for there, on a clear day, is Mt Ida to the southeast, from where Zeus watched the war; to the west, on a *very* clear day, you can make out Mt Fingari (Moon Mountain) on the island of Samothrace, where Poseidon sat. In the plain below wanders the Scamander River, whose god tried to drown Achilles for turning the water red with the blood of the Trojans. The two mounds near the river's mouth at Sigeion Point are by tradition the tombs of Achilles and his friend Patroclus, whose death at the hand of Hector finally roused Achilles from his sulking wrath to return to the battlefield. On most days, you are also aware of another Homeric epithet—'windy'. Much speculation has gone into determining the location of Troy's harbour, where the 'beaked ships' of the Achaeans were beached for the duration of the war. Certainly much of what is dry land was once a shallow bay or flood plain and marsh; if the Argives had to commute to the battlefield every day from any contemporary harbour, they would hardly have had time to fight.

The Chariot Ramp

The path through the excavations leads past the ruins of the temple of Athena, last rebuilt by the Romans, to the great flagged **chariot ramp**. It was near here that Schliemann unearthed the controversial 'Jewels of Helen', the one really splendid treasure found on the site. The jewellery convinced many sceptics that this was indeed the Troy of Homer, and Schliemann was so proud of his find that he couldn't resist smuggling the baubles out of Turkey to adorn his wife at Athenian parties. Finally he gave the jewellery to the Berlin Museum, where it disappeared in 1945, by all accounts, pillaged by Soviet occupation forces. Both the 'Jewels of Helen' and the chariot ramp, however, date back to Troy II (2600–2300 BC), which, though a glorious city in its day, predates the commonly accepted date of the Trojan War by a thousand years.

The Romans

The other prominent remains belong to Troy VIII, the Greek Ilion (700–300 BC), and Troy IX (300 BC–4th century AD), respectively, the Hellenistic and the Roman New Ilium. You can see a partially restored shrine, Roman theatre and bouleuterion. Neither of these cities was very large, although as the successors of Troy they enjoyed a certain renown. Julius Caesar, like many modern visitors, was disappointed by the meagre ruins; Emperor Julian the Apostate was delighted to find that Christianity in AD 354 had not yet done away with sacrifices on Achilles' tomb. Yet it was the voice of the East that has had the last word. After conquering Constantinople, Mehmet II came to Troy and declared:

> It is to me that Allah has given to avenge this city and its people ...
> Indeed it was the Greeks who before devastated this city, and it is their
> descendants who after so many years have paid me the debt which
> their boundless pride had contracted—and often afterwards—towards
> us, the peoples of Asia.

Çanakkale

Troy, or *Truva* as the Turks call it, is 17 miles (27km) from **Çanakkale**, which most visitors use as a base for visiting the excavations. On the way you can stop at **Tevfikiye**, the only oasis of tackiness Troy has produced, with its trinket shops and 'House of Schliemann'; actually, the whole village was built of materials quarried from Schliemann's dig.

Çanakkale, at one of the Dardanelles' ferry crossings, is a pleasant, slightly faded provincial capital, the ancient Greek *Abydos*, successor to Troy. Its name in Turkish means 'saucer castle', 'saucer' recalling the town's old ceramics industry which once produced florid Turkish Art Nouveau—though the town lives more from tourism and tuna fishing today. The **castle**, one of several built by Mehmet the Conqueror to hem in Constantinople, still guards the Hellespont, housing soldiers and a small **Military Museum** with a special display devoted to the heroics of Atatürk during the Gelibolu campaign. Nearby is the small **Piri Reis naval museum**. Outside the castle is a mock-up of the *Nusrat*, the Turkish minelayer that sealed the straits to Allied destroyers, thus precipitating the landings. (One bit of naval history they missed is that Çanakkale was probably the spot where the Persian King Xerxes made his famous bridge of boats, in 483 BC when his vast horde was marching to invade Greece). The excellent **archaeological museum** (*open daily exc Mon, 8.30–5; adm*) is 1 mile from the centre, and stars finds from the Dardanos Tumulus. This, dating from the 4th century BC, was discovered 6 miles south of Çanakkale in 1959 and produced golden diadems, ivories, gold jewellery, votive statuary, and the remains of a wooden harp.

The best thing about Çanakkale is its lively waterfront, where the whole town along with the visiting ANZACs comes each evening for a promenade and a fish dinner. The nearest beach to Çanakkale is the thin strip of sand at **Kepez**, 4 miles (6km) west of town. The beach at **Dardanos**, 3 miles (5km) further on, is better. **Güzelyali**, a small fishing village-cum-resort 11 miles (18km) west of Çanakkale, also has a beach.

Turkey's Aegean Islands

Getting Around

Kabatepe, on the Gelibolu peninsula, is the port for Gökçeada, though in summer there are also services from Çanakkale. Boats for Bozcaada depart from Odun Iskelesi south of Çanakkale; it's a trip of less than half an hour, but first you need to get to Odun Iskelesi, an hour's minibus ride from Çanakkale. Services to both Aegean islands can be infrequent, particularly in the winter.

Gökçeada and **Bozcaada** are Turkey's sole possessions amongst the Aegean islands, both of them wrested from the defeated Greeks in 1923. Strategically, they are important, guarding the mouth of the Dardanelles, and both are heavily militarized, staring across the sea at the equally well-defended Greek islands of Samothraki and Limnos. Historically and ethnically, the islands are more Greek than Turkish and were exempted from the population exchange. Since the Cyprus conflict, many of the indigenous Greeks have left, driven out by years of nagging Turkish oppression (mirrored by the treatment of ethnic Turks in Greek Thrace). Only in the last few years have the islands become accessible to foreigners

Gökçeada (the Imbros of the Greeks and Imbroz of Homer) is a green, lumpy island whose few visitors tend to head straight for Kale in the north where there are beaches, pensions and restaurants. The island is the birthplace of Bartholomeos, the current Greek Patriarch in Istanbul (patriarchs are required by law to be Turkish citizens). Above the village is a ruined Ottoman castle, built by Süleyman the Magnificent. There's not much else, save for a prison and some pleasant walks.

Bozcaada is flatter and smaller, and fringed with beaches. Its one town seems very Greek, with white-washed houses, overhanging upper storeys and narrow, serpentine streets. Its **castle**, vast and explorable, has been there since Byzantine days, and now guards the islanders' goats and sheep. Bozcaada (ancient Tenedos) was, according to epic tradition, the Achaean base where the Greeks hid their ships, waiting for Odysseus to emerge from the belly of the wooden horse and signal that the sleeping Troy was theirs for the taking. Up until the 15th century, Greeks living on the island would act as tour guides for foreigners seeking Troy.

expensive/moderate

In Çanakkale the most comfortable, and most expensive, hotel is the ★★★★**Akol Hotel** on Kaysereli Ahmetpaşa Caddesi, ☎ 217 9456, 📠 217 2897, where £65/$100 buys a plush double room with air-conditioning, TV and so on. On the same street the ★★**Büyük Truva**, ☎ 217 1024, is nice without being wonderful; fewer amenities for about half the price. The ★★★**Otel Anafartalar**, Iskele Meydani, ☎ 217 4454, has rooms with balconies that gaze across the Dardanelles to Kilitbahir; doubles £16/$24. The less expensive ★**Kestanbol**, just around the corner from the bus station on Hasan Mevsuf Sokak, ☎ 217 0857, has some rooms with balconies and television.

Güzelyali, 15km from Çanakkale, has several comparatively swank hotels, popular with holidaying Turks. The best is the ★★★**Iris Oteli**, Mola Caddesi, ☎ 232 8100, where doubles with breakfast cost £35/$52. It boasts the town's only disco, as well as its own stretch of beach, and water sports. The ★★★**Tusan Oteli**, ☎ 232 8210, in a pretty setting in the woods, is new and bright and slightly less expensive, also with a private beach, windsurfing and water skiing, etc. A simpler, inexpensive choice is the **Taşkin**, ☎ 232 8138; £8/$12.

cheap

Çanakkale can seem like a '60s time capsule in summer, loaded with bright-eyed, clean-cut backpackers. The vast majority, as you will soon discover, hail from the antipodes, and there are plenty of places that specialize in accommodating them. Descending from the coach you will most likely be met by an employee of the **Anzac House**, Cumhuriyet Meydani, ☎ 217 0156. Rooms can be a bit funky, but the friendly and very helpful staff serves up beer and Vegemite sandwiches (would we lie?) and continuous battle documentaries on video; everyone has a good time. Like many other Çanakkale hotels, they arrange tours of the battlefield.

Among the other nice cheapies, on a quiet side street just off Cumhuriyet Meydani, is the **Koç Pansiyon**, Kizilay Sokak 7, and even better, the **Hotel Efes**, ☎ 217 3256, with its peaceful garden complete with gurgling fountain. It is quieter than most too, set back from the main street on Aralik Sok 5. Rooms with private shower cost £4/$6 per person. The **Hotel Kervansaray** on Fetvane Sokak, ☎ 217 8192, is cheaper still. Also on Fetvane Sokak, near the clock tower, there's the **Oteli Konak**, ☎ 217 1578, a little faded but perfectly acceptable and charging, for a room with shower, £5/$8.

If you are mainly interested in Troy, as an alternative to Çanakkale you might stay in Tevfikiye, though there are only a few very modest *pansiyons* there and a *lokanta*. Güzelyali has a handful of *pansiyons* and there are campsites at Kepez and Dardanos.

On Gökçeada the **Gökçe Otel**, Fevzi Çakmak Caddesi 14, ☎ 697 1473, is pleasant and eager to please, charging £3/$5. The ★★**Koz Otel**, ☎ 697 8189, on the waterfront in Bozcaada town, charges £8/$12, breakfast included. Like most of the hotels and pensions on the Turkish Aegean islands, both are open June–September only. Outside of these months, you may be able to find a room to let in a private house.

There is certainly no shortage of campgrounds around Çanakkale, from the large and well-equipped **Truva Mocamp** at Güzelyali, ☎ 232 8025, which has a restaurant/

canteen, to the simpler **Paradise Camping**, ✆ 263 6178, near the beach at Dardanos. At Kepez, 5km from Çanakkale, the **Şen Mokamp**, ✆ 263 6888, has campsites under the pines on the beach. There are two modest campgrounds on Gökçeada.

Eating Out

Çanakkale is a great place for a fish dinner; there are a number of good restaurants competing for your trade, all in a row near the castle, and all with outside tables facing the harbour. For excellent value, try the **Entellektüel**, with fixed-price menus including a grilled fish, chips, salad and a beer for as little as £2/$3. It's all a matter of what fish, of course; you could splurge and spend as much as £8/$12. Also good, and popular with the locals, is the very similar **Rihtim Restoran** next door.

Less expensively, you can get tasty kebabs and *köfte*, and and sometimes grilled fish, at the **Ömur Köfte Salonu**, on the waterfront near the Hotel Bakir. The **Trakya Restoran**, a good and inexpensive *lokanta* across from the Anzac House, is more than used to entertaining tourists, as is the **Aussie and Kiwi Restaurant**, around the corner on Yali Caddesi. For a filling *manti* lunch, there is the **Tutku Manti Salonu**, just down the street from the Trakya on Demircioğlu Caddesi.

The Troad

The bulging peninsula south of Troy to Mount Ida is known as the Troad, famous in ancient times for horse breeding. Highlights include the awe-inspiring walls of ancient Assos and the sumptuous Gulf of Edremit. It's a dreamy, beautiful country, full of maples and olive trees; farmers set up stands all along the roadsides selling olives—some of Turkey's best—olive oil and homemade relishes. The best time to come is June, when the deep red blankets of poppies make an unforgettable sight.

Getting Around

Buses and **minibuses** between Çanakkale and Izmir serve the coast well, and there should be no difficulty getting to and from Assos or anyplace else (Assos minibuses always bear the destination sign *Behramkale*). During the day, minibuses run continuously along the northern edge of the gulf to Edremit. To reach Ören you may have to take a dolmuş from Edremit to Burhaniye and then a local bus to the coast. In summer, Ören is linked by boat to Ayvalik (*see* below), with four crossings a day.

Travelling between this part of the coast and the Marmara shore or points east will require a bus change in Balikesir (and if you ever get tired of lemon cologne, Balikesir's bus station has a shop that will sell you cologne in a few dozen other flavours).

Tourist Information

Akçay: Edremit Caddesi, Karabudak Apt 20, ✆ (266) 384 1113
Ören: town centre, ✆ (266) 422 2870

Alexandria Troas

South of Troy lie the ruins of the city that superseded it in Hellenistic times, **Alexandria Troas**, a few miles south of the sandy beach at **Geyikli**. Many early travellers to the Troad mistook its ruins for Troy itself. The city was founded by Antigonus the One-Eyed at the end of the 4th century BC, but achieved its greatest glory after another of Alexander's generals, Lysimachus, killed Antigonus in battle and renamed it in memory of his old commander. He made it the main port in the Troad and one of the richest commercial centres on the entire coast. In Hadrian's time, Herodes Atticus, the Rockefeller of his day, endowed it with a monumental bath complex and aqueduct. Its convenient position on the main sea route later brought about its demolition, as the builders of Istanbul's imperial mosques cannibalized it, block by block. Today the most impressive remains, besides the baths, are the great broken stones scattered on the beach.

Before you get to Assos, the dolmuş from Çanakkale passes through Ayvacik, a ramshackle village worth a stop only if you're hunting for Turkish carpets; Ayvacik is the home of DOBAG, a cooperative run by weavers dedicated to doing things the traditional way.

Assos/Behramkale

South of Alexandria Troas, on the north shore of the lovely Gulf of Edremit at the new resort of **Behramkale**, is the imposing site of ancient **Assos**. Take the paved road from Ayvacik, crossing a charming 14th-century Ottoman bridge, from where you can see Behramkale/Assos hugging the top of an extinct volcano, some 785ft over the sea. The thoroughly relaxed resort, down beneath the ruins, is becoming increasingly popular—perfect for a day or two on the beach and a look at the ruins; enterprising locals are already getting up day trips to Troy from here.

History

Some archaeologists believe the Hittite King Tudhaliyas IV established his colony of Ashachuva on the commanding height, in the 13th century BC, to keep an eye on the Mycenaeans troubling his western frontiers. Greek Assos was founded by Aeolians from Methymna, Lesbos, in the 1st millennium BC. The city was famous for its great archaic Doric temple of Athena (540 BC), that once crowned the very summit of the acropolis.

Assos passed through several hands—Persians and Athenians—and was once governed by a banker and by a eunuch. The latter was Hermias, a student of Plato at the Academy, who had a chance to apply his teacher's theories of an ideal city-state to his own realm of the Troad and Lesbos. He invited other students of Plato to found a branch of the Academy in Assos, and for three years, Plato's greatest student, Aristotle, lived here, busy founding the sciences of biology and botany, and marrying Hermias' niece. Aristotle's pupil, Alexander, later captured the city; after that it came under the kings of Pergamon. Several Crusaders' battles took place nearby, until the Ottomans captured Assos in 1330, and at once began to quarry the site to build a mosque and bridge over the Tuzla. The villagers of Behramkale took up the stones when the Ottomans left off; one anonymous Turkish writer describes Behramkale as 'a rusty dagger piercing the walls of Assos'. Perhaps because of this Assos is one of the more dishevelled gardens of weeds along the coast; be prepared to scramble through the prickles to see the remains.

Walls of Assos

Most remarkable, especially in light of the quarrying on the site, are the **walls**, among the best preserved in the whole eastern Greek world. Stretching some 2 miles, they stand 46ft high in places; they include some excellently preserved gates, each done in a different style. They date back to the mid-4th century BC, perhaps built under the rule of Hermias. Inner walls surround the acropolis and the **Temple of Athena**. Of this once magnificent structure little remains but its platform and a few decorative elements; its Doric friezes are scattered in museums in Paris, Boston, and Istanbul. The bird's-eye view of Lesbos and the Gulf of Edremit on one side and the valley of the Satnioeis on the other makes the climb worthwhile.

Other remains, all in the lower town, include two stoas of the agora (3rd century BC), an agora temple, a Hellenistic bouleuterion, gymnasium, and theatre. Architecturally, they resemble the Pergamon style—note the location of the temple in relation to the agora, and the unusual mix of Doric and Ionic orders in the decorative scheme. Outside the main gate, in the Hellenistic-Roman **necropolis** are numerous broken sarcophagi; Assos exported similar ones through the ancient world. If you're energetic you can hike down to the fine white pebble beach for a swim and a look at the remains of the ancient breakwater.

Gulf of Edremit

The **Gulf of Edremit** is one of the loveliest places in the whole of Turkey. Here are fine sandy beaches, writhing olive groves, dark pine forests, and sparkling white seaside villages. To the east loom the bosky slopes of Mt Ida (*Kaz Dağ*) and in the gulf the emerald Alibey islets float in a crystal sea, with the shapely green outline of Lesbos as a backdrop.

The beach resorts that line the gulf get better the further east you go. The first, **Küçükkuyu**, looks idyllic from afar, its harbour filled with bobbing fishing smacks, but closer inspection reveals a grubby, ramshackle little town with little to boast of save a small beach to the west. **Altinoluk**, 6 miles (10km) east, is a definite improvement. Clean and bright, it caters well for the visitor and has a nice, if small, beach. Halfway between Altinoluk and the next resort, Akçay, the village of Güru will, for a small fee, soothe your aches away in warm, mineral-filled waters.

Above Akçay looms Mount Ida, venue of the world's first beauty contest where the judge, Paris, chose Aphrodite as the fairest of the goddesses, after she bribed him with the promise of Helen, an ill-fated selection that led ultimately to the Trojan War. **Akçay** itself is another Altinoluk, open and breezy with a welcoming aura, a resort that has so far refrained from the mass, crass commercialism that so bedevils **Ören**, 15 miles (25km) south at the gulf's epiglottis. The reason for Ören's overdevelopment is quite simple; the beach is the best along the gulf, huge and wide and sandy, backed by a grassy verge that billows with flowers in spring.

Inland between Akçay and Ören, the humble town of **Edremit** can at least pride itself on its antiquity. This was ancient Adramyttium, sacked by Achilles in one of his raids along the coast. It was in Adramyttium that Achilles captured Chryseis, daughter of the priest of Apollo, and gave her as a prize to Agamemnon. The *Iliad* begins with Agamemnon's refusal to accept the father's ransom for the girl. The main road east from here will take you to **Balikesir**, the equally humble provincial capital of all this area, a city with a grumpy air that seems to be wondering why it is stuck out in the middle of the piney-wood mountains while all the other towns in the province are having fun on the beach. Balikesir was the ancient Greek *Paleokastron*, though most of its monuments are Ottoman mosques and tombs from the 14th and 15th centuries.

Where to Stay
expensive/moderate

Quite a bit of top-quality accommodation available has opened in Behramkale in recent years, notably the palatial ★★★★**Assos Eden Gardens**, ℭ (286) 752 9400, ✆ 752 9404. It's right on the beach, and there is also a huge pool, hamam, jacuzzi, fitness gym and every other conceivable amenity; almost all rooms have a sea view; £65/$98. The same management also runs the much less expensive ★★**Assos Eden Beach**, ℭ (286) 752 7039, also on the beach, with windsurfing and sailing on offer; £32/$48 for a double. Also in Behramkale, the ★★★**Behram Hotel**, ℭ (286) 721 7016, is one of the nicest on offer, and charges about the same rates.

Besides its beach hotels, Altinoluk has a Turkish rarity—a pretty country inn, decorated with Ottoman antiques: the ★★★**Chalet Chopin Pension**, ℭ (266) 396 1044, is set on a wooded hill above the beaches, next to an old windmill; there's a swimming pool, and a good restaurant; £32/£48. Also in Altinoluk is the ★**Hotel Özsay**, ℭ (266) 384 1190, whose rooms have sea views; doubles £13/$20.

In Ören the ★**Otel Urgut 2**, ℭ (266) 422 1205, has a swimming pool, a bar and a restaurant; rates for a double room are £14/$21.

Only a malevolent twist of fate would condemn you to a night in Edremit, but at least there's a good hotel there, the ★★**Otel Bilgiçler**, across the street from the pretty town park at Menderes Bulv 63, ℭ (266) 372 2255; £14/$21.

On the beach in Akçay is the ★**Öğe Moteli** on Oruçreis Caddesi, with a restaurant and motorboat for guests' use; £15/$22. On the road to Edremit, the **(TK2) Turban Akçay Holiday Village**, ℭ (266) 422 1217, offers many sports facilities, tennis, swimming pool, and water skiing, and reductions for children; £33/$50, or you can rent your own beach house for £50/$75. There is also a fully-equipped campground as part of the complex.

cheap

Behramkale seems determined to become an upmarket resort, and inexpensive choices are few: the **Şen Pansiyon**, ℭ (286) 781 7209, a block from the harbour is the first place to look; £5/$8. In Küçükkuyu the **Nür Motel**, behind the harbour, charges only £3/$5 per person for a spartan room with bath.

There are pensions galore in Altinoluk and Akçay, all charging in the region of £5/$8—£7/$11 for a double room with en suite facilities. A good choice in Altinoluk is the ★**Hotel Sahin**, Barbaros Caddesi, ℭ (266) 396 1388; rooms are large and priced £8/$12. Prices are slightly higher in Ören. The only cheapie in Edremit is the wretched **Otel Sato**, Park Karşisi; as a rule, any hotel in Turkey called the Sato should be avoided, though don't ask us why.

Just east of Küçükkuyu is a strip of campsites, including the shady and quite inexpensive **Truva Camping**; ℭ (286) 752 5206.

Eating Out

As a rule, restaurants in the region are simple though often excellent. The **Nür Motel** in Küçükkuyu has a restaurant where you can eat well and cheaply for around £3/$5 while admiring the flying ducks pinned to the wall. Edremit's favourite since 1924 is the inexpensive **Omür Lokanta** on Menderes Bulvari, with a wide choice of stews and kebabs. In Altinoluk, the **Doba** restaurant serves fine fish meals for £4/$6 or less if you haggle hard, and likewise at the **Beyaz** restaurant in Akçay. Ören is full of similar restaurants.

Ayvalik

The southernmost of the gulf resorts, **Ayvalik** is largely bypassed by visitors from overseas, inexplicably so. The town has excellent beaches close at hand, several local curiosities to view and the loveliest setting on the gulf, surrounded by an entourage of 25 islands and islets, most uninhabited, all verdant, all rising from the sea like the lost cities of antiquity. Beyond them, its pine-draped cliffs bristling on the horizon, looms the Greek island of Lesbos.

Getting Around

Ayvalik's bus station, 1km outside the centre on the road to Edremit, has services to most major towns in western Turkey. Most minibuses, however, including those to Izmir, Küçükköy and Bergama, start from the central square by the port. In season there are also very frequent minibuses to the beaches around Sarimsakli.

In summer, boats cross the gulf to Ören four times a day. The boat service to Greek Lesbos operates daily in summer but only once or twice a week in winter.

Tourist Information

Ayvalik: in a booth by the harbour, ℗ (266) 312 3158; ✉ 'Alo Ayvalik'. The extremely helpful office here has deals including a 20% discount on rooms, camping and rental cars if you contact them in advance. The Geylan Bookshop, in the Süner Pasaji on Talatpaşa Caddesi, has a selection of English books and books about the area.

Ayvalik itself was predominantly Greek before 1923 and still retains a faintly Hellenic aura, particularly in its churches, even though most have since been converted into mosques. Unlike most of the other resorts on this stretch of coast, it is an old and sizeable town, with a charming centre of narrow streets of brightly painted houses, and little squares with plane trees. Most of the tourist activity is confined to the port area, lined with cafés, restaurants and excursion boats; from the here you can see the long peninsula of **Sarimsakli** to the left, where the best beaches are, and to the right the conical island of Alibey, Greek Lesbos, and on a reasonably clear day Mt. Ida.

Two of the churches in particular are worth a look, if only to see what a neo-Gothic church looks like with a minaret attached; the **Çinarli Cami** (once *Agios Ioannis*) and the **Saat Cami** (*Agios Georgios*). The latter is the 'clock mosque', so named for the large timepiece that adorns its exterior. Another church, the **Taksiyarhil**, contains a unique collection of icons painted on dried fish skins, although since its doors are permanently locked, there seems to be little hope of ever seeing them. Pester the tourist office enough and they might—just might—be able to arrange a visit. See the icons now, if you can, for plans are already under way to claim this church too, for Islam. Ayvalik has an organization dedicated to the preservation of its old quarter and the churches, but for the moment resources are scant and little can be done.

Try to be in Ayvalik on Thursday, for one of the busiest and most colourful **markets** on the

Aegean coast—few tourist trinkets, but dozens of back streets lined with gorgeous produce; all the country folk for miles around come in to see and be seen.

Around Ayvalik

A dozen or so cruise boats haunt Ayvalik's harbour, waiting to carry you off to the dozen or so islands and a number of good beaches. One of the prime attractions is **Alibey Island** (also called Cunda Island by the locals), the largest of the island group (for this you really don't need a boat; the island is also connected to the mainland by a causeway). Opposite Ayvalik, it curves around from the north in the shape of a badly drawn treble clef, it furnishes Ayvalik with a perfect sheltered harbour and is a popular spot with day-trippers. You can see the island's old Greek houses, now in a desperate state of repair, but most people come here for the beaches. Two miles south of Ayvalik, the leafy suburb of **Çamlik** is also blessed with a beach but the first prize for sea and sand epiphanies goes to **Sarimsakli**, 3 miles (5km) beyond Çamlik. Sarimsakli may not be to everyone's taste—lots of breezeblock hotels and overpriced restaurants—but its beach is monster-sized and utterly enticing. Yet another huge beach is at **Altinova**, a further 5 miles (8km) to the south.

A short dolmuş ride from Ayvalik or Sarimsakli, a couple of geological oddities lie in wait: the **Devil's Dinner Table** (*Şeytan Sofrası*), a large, flat, round rock on a promontory protruding into the Aegean, and, on the hill adjacent, another flat rock from which two slender outcrops rise vertically to a height of 13ft. They look like **rabbit's ears**, hence their name. Inland from Ayvalik, on the road to Bergama, you'll be skirting the truly imposing massif of the Madra Daği, a beautiful and totally unspoiled area (if you have a car that can take it, consider continuing on to Bergama via the bad, partially unpaved mountain road through it instead of the coastal route).

Lesbos

Greece's third-largest island, Lesbos is also commonly called Mytilini after its capital, the destination of the little ferries from Ayvalik. The island has its charms, but it isn't really the place to go for a day trip unless you simply want a taste of Greece—it's fine for that, being one of the less touristy islands; Lesbos is more concerned with its olive trees, of which there are about eleven million. Mytilini, under its Byzantine–Genoese castle, is an attractive town, with antique shops, a Hellenistic theatre and a number of interesting museums, including one dedicated to the works of Theophilos, Lesbos's famous naive artist.

Most visitors to Lesbos stay a few days and tour the quiet rural parts, where sights include ruins of a Roman aqueduct, several beaches, yet another Mt Olympos, a few Byzantine churches and monasteries, and of all things, a petrified forest, at Sigri in the northern part of the island.

Ayvalik and around ✆ *(266–)*   **Where to Stay**

expensive

The plush hotels here are all out by the big beach at Sarimsakli. One especially nice one is the **Büyük Berk Otel**, ✆ 324 1045, 🖅 324 1046. Set on the beach, double rooms with balconies go for £30/$45. 15km from Ayvalik at Tuzla Mevkii, the ★★★**Club Washington**, ✆ 324 1779, 🖅 324 1551, offers plush rooms around a huge pool and a wide stretch of beach in a wooded, isolated setting. All water sports from scuba diving to windsurfing are available, and there are tennis courts and a gym; £42/$63.

On Alibey Island, the attractive ★★★**Cunda**, ✆ 327 1598, @ 327 1943, is a low, motel-style place with balconied rooms right on the beach; opportunities for water sports; £30/£45.

moderate

Ayvalik has plenty of good hotels but none that is truly outstanding. At Balikhane Sok 7 near the harbour, the ★**Kaptan Hotel**, ✆ 312 8834, has views of Alibey Island and double rooms with bath for £12/$18; the friendly proprietor speaks English. The ★**Hotel Kantarçi**, Inönü Caddesi 74, ✆ 312 1166, has doubles with bath for £10/$15.

On Alibey Island, the choice is between the **Ortunç** and the **Sayilgan Motel**, ✆ 327 1629, both simple places near the beach that will ask about £10/$15. The Ortunç also has a campground.

Sarimsakli's hotels tend to be a little more up-market, although not necessarily better; most are hastily slung-up budget constructions that suffer from over-exposure to tourists; the ★★**Ankara Hotel**, ✆ 324 1195, is one of the better ones, with a terrace bar and television in some rooms; £13/$20. For a little bit more, you can get a pool and rooms with balconies at the ★★**Billurcu**, ✆ 324 1189.

cheap

Almost all the accommodation in this class is found in the centre of Ayvalik. Near the harbour, the **Yali Pansiyon**, ✆ 312 2423, is a charming, family-run establishment. Housed in an old Greek mansion, with a grandiose staircase and delicate ornamentation, its cavernous rooms go for £4/$6 per person. There are only four of them, however, so it's best to phone ahead. Bathroom facilities here are shared. Second choice on the harbour is the **Kiyi Motel**, ✆ 312 6677, at about the same rates. Just off the Kordon Boyu on Motor Sokak near the town centre, the friendly and chaotic **Çiçek Pansiyon**, ✆ 312 1201, also offers good value for money; £5/$8. The cheapest is the shabby **Yürt Otel**, ✆ 312 2109, on the main square, with sagging beds for £2/$3.

Anything under £10/$15 is hard to find in Sarimsakli. There are a number of inexpensive *pansiyons* on Alibey Island, including the **Güney Motel**, by the port, which also has a nice, simple restaurant; ✆ 327 1109. In a peaceful, isolated setting on the far end of the island is the **Ada Camping**, ✆ 663 7121, with shade, a restaurant and a beach. In Altinova, near the beach, the **Kazan Motel**, ✆ 338 1430, is quiet and comfortable; £6/$9 with bath.

Eating Out

There are several good restaurants clustered around the Atatürk statue, at the angle of the port, one such being the **15 Kardeşler**. The name means 'fifteen brothers' and they aren't kidding; a few of the boys will be around to practise their English, bring you your kebab, peppers, *pide* and chips (very tasty, for about £3/$5) and tell you the family story (dad is still doing well, but he wore out two moms to produce all fifteen of them). The boys have plenty of competition around the harbour, including the **Elif 2** where a full fish meal costs about £5/$8. Also good for fish is the **Öz Canli Balik**, Sahil Boyu 3 (about the same price, including a glass of wine). A cheap place to eat excellent *iskender kebab* is the tiny **Körfez Salonu** on Gümrük Caddesi.

The causeway between the mainland and Alibey Island is one long row of bright fish restaurants. On Cumhuriyet Caddesi in the village, the **Lyra** offers a wide choice of mezes and seafood and an outdoor terrace; £4/$6 and up. This area of the coast is heaven for oyster lovers—most of Turkey's small crop is farmed here—and many places specialize in the mollusc, one of the best being the **E Restoran** in Altinova; £5/$8.

Aeolia

PASTRY MAKERS

The Aeolian Greeks came from Thessaly or Boeotia, perhaps as early as the 12th century BC, and until the Persian conquest Aeolia survived as a quiet little nation, with its capital at Mytilini on Lesbos. Aeolia was famed in antiquity for the fertility of its soil, so fertile, it seems, that the early Greek colonists spent all their labours tilling it, with little time left over for the intellectual pursuits and adventures that preoccupied the Ionians to the south. But it is here in Aeolia that we find Bergama, ancient *Pergamon*, a city that rivalled Athens and Alexandria as a cultural centre in its day.

Getting Around

Bergama is the minibus transportation hub of the area, although if you go there on any bus that doesn't end its run there, you'll be left on the highway 4½ miles (7km) from town and have to catch a minibus in, which can be a problem. And if you mean to come here on a day trip, arrange your transportation back in advance, or you may be stranded in the evening.

From Bergama's *otogar* there are minibuses every half-hour to Dikili; Dikili has a weekly ferry to Lesbos in summer. Direct buses from Bergama and Izmir also serve Eski Foça but they are infrequent. You may have to take an Izmir-bound bus from Bergama: ask to be let off at the Eski Foça junction and trust to either luck or a dolmuş to carry you the remaining 16 miles (26km).

Tourist Information

Bergama: Zafer Mah. Izmir Cad. 54, on the main road into town, ✆ (232) 633 1862

Eski Foça: Atatürk Bulvari, on the entrance to town, ✆ (232) 812 1222

In the last two centuries BC, Pergamon may well have been the most beautiful and sophisticated city in the Mediterranean world. It was not an original Aeolian foundation, but rather a Hellenistic city state, a creation of Alexander's heirs. Although inhabited before Alexander, the site never amounted to much—a minor Greek–Persian satrapy, first mentioned in 399 BC in Xenophon's *Anabasis*. Doubtless, had it been nearer the sea, it would have thrived much earlier, for few cities could boast such a splendid defensible site, a citadel 1300ft above the surrounding plain, with streams flowing below on two sides. When Alexander's general, Lysimachus, came into a fabulous fortune—9000 talents, the spoils of war in the Troad—Pergamon seemed the perfect place to safeguard the treasure. Lysimachus died without an heir in 281 BC, and the man he set to watch over the loot, a certain Philetairos, simply kept it, using the money to wine and dine friends and build monuments in Pergamon. His adopted son Eumenes is the first of the famous Kings of Pergamon; Eumenes' adopted son, Attalus (ruled 241–197 BC) gave the rulers their dynastic title, the Attalids.

Attalus I

Attalus I was audacious and spent much of his reign fighting for more territory; most notably, he stood up to the bellicose Gauls of Galatia, who were running a proto-protection racket in Anatolia. Upon his refusal to pay, they came to collect, fierce and more numerous than the Pergamene defenders, who were reluctant to fight against the odds. However, Attalus ordered a sacrifice to the gods, and miracle!—plainly written on the victim's lungs was the word 'Victory'. Inspired, the Pergamenes soundly thrashed the Gauls. Only later was it discovered that the priest offering the sacrifice, or more probably Attalus himself, had written the word backwards in ink on his hand and pressed it on the entrails when no one was looking. But even if the augury was a cheat, Attalus had freed western Greece from a serious threat, and in honour of the victory over the barbarians, his successor, Eumenes II, erected the famous Altar of Zeus.

Eumenes II

Eumenes II ruled Pergamon at the height of its power and influence. But just as the city owed its initial prosperity to the luck of a treasure deposit, it owed its great rise in prestige to a second lucky break. Attalus had kindly sent the superstitious Romans the meteorite-cult statue of Cybele, the Great Mother Goddess of Asia (the Romans hoarded cult statues of their conquests, to keep the gods of conquered provinces in line), and in return the Romans, upon defeating Antiochus the Great at Magnesia (190 BC), gave Pergamon Antiochus' provinces of Asia Minor, stretching from the coast to Konya. Relations between Rome and Pergamon became even closer as Eumenes assisted Rome militarily against its enemies, including the most worrying, Hannibal, who ended up in Bithynia after his defeat at Zama, and according to tradition, died and was buried in Iznik. Eumenes' brother, Attalus II, continued his policy of helping Rome, especially in the subjugation of Greece.

Attalus III

But it was his nephew, Attalus III, who recognized the inevitable, and amazed the classical world by willing Pergamon to Rome when he died in 133 BC. Some accounted it a Roman trick, and perhaps, as a result, a body of stories has grown up, attesting to Attalus III's eccentricities, that he loved his mother so well that he took the title 'Philomater', that he was obsessed with poisonous plants, which he fed to condemned criminals to try out his antidotes, and that he never went out in public except to work on his mother's tomb, where one day, in the heat, he fainted and died, only five years into his reign. Rome had no problem in accepting Attalus' bequest, and according to the terms of the will, left Pergamon a free city. This state of affairs lasted until 88 BC, when Mithridates Pontus came to 'liberate' the Greek states from Rome and ordered all Romans massacred, an order the Pergamenes carried out with great zeal.

When Rome, in return, defeated Mithridates, Pergamon lost all its rights; 40 years later, it even lost its greatest treasure, its library, when Antony looted its 200,000 volumes and gave them to Cleopatra, ending once and for all the rivalry between the libraries of Alexandria and Pergamon. Pergamon gradually dwindled after that; while up on the acropolis, any walls of cheap mixed brick and stone you see probably date from Byzantine or Selcuk times.

The Site

Open daily 8.30 until sunset; adm.

The average visitor is attracted first to Ephesus, where the ruins are more substantial, or Troy, where there's a story everyone knows. But use your eyes and your imagination a bit, and you may find Pergamon the most totally captivating site of all classical cities. The key to everything is the tremendously high acropolis. Try to catch sight of it from wherever you are in the town or on the plain, and imagine it as it was under Eumenes or Attalus, crowned with spectacular marble temples, and a plume of smoke continually rising from the Altar of Zeus.

At its height, Pergamon had a population of well over 100,000. It spilled down the precipitous slope, making nearly every building visible from the valley and creating the impression of a single work of architecture. The city was blessed not only with its natural setting, but also unreasonable portions of wealth and talent. Its architects and sculptors were among the finest in the Hellenistic world. To see the best of their creations you have to go to the Pergamon Museum in Berlin (where much was damaged in the last war), but the assiduous Germans left enough behind for us to at least conjure up an image of this fantastical city of dreams.

To see the ruins of Pergamon in a day without a car, you'll probably have to invest in four taxi trips: to the acropolis and back, and to the Asklepieon and back. If you only have one day, the best thing to do with it is to take a taxi up to the acropolis, then walk back down along the ancient main street. It isn't easy finding the path, but it can be done and it's worth the attempt.

Acropolis

The majestic **acropolis** looms behind the modern town, from which there is a paved road to the top (it's a stiff climb of over 3km, so you may want to spring for a taxi). Since 1878, when a German railway engineer and amateur archaeologist named Karl Humann began digging here, the Germans have completed four major excavations in Pergamon, and currently a fifth is under way. One project in the works is the reconstruction of the columns of the **Temple of Trajan**, at the highest level of the acropolis; it is the only structure dating wholly from Roman times. Both Trajan and his son Hadrian were remembered here; their two huge marble heads, found in the temple, are now in Berlin. Hadrian, one of the most cultured of the emperors and a great friend of Pergamon, built the Temple as centrepiece of an important complex, modelled after the great Forum of Hadrian in Rome. It may have included a library, as in Rome—perhaps intended as recompense for the Roman theft of the original. The pseudo-Egyptian capitals around the stoa are an unusual touch.

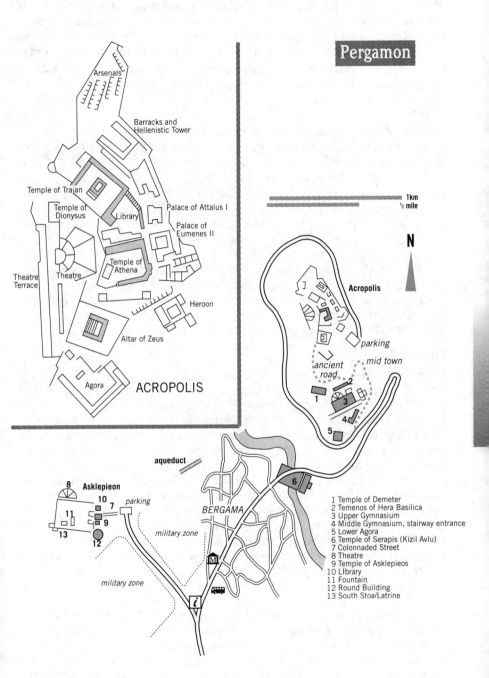

Pergamon

Arsenals

Barracks and
Hellenistic Tower

Temple of Trajan

Temple of
Dionysus   Library

Palace of Attalus I

Palace of
Eumenes II

Theatre
Terrace   Theatre

Temple of
Athena

Heroon

Altar of Zeus

Agora   ACROPOLIS

1km
½ mile

N

Acropolis

parking

mid town

ancient
road

1

2

3

4

5

aqueduct

6

8   Asklepieon

10   7
11   parking
         9
13
    12

BERGAMA

military zone

military zone

M

i

1 Temple of Demeter
2 Temenos of Hera Basilica
3 Upper Gymnasium
4 Middle Gymnasium, stairway entrance
5 Lower Agora
6 Temple of Serapis (Kizil Avlu)
7 Colonnaded Street
8 Theatre
9 Temple of Asklepieos
10 LIbrary
11 Fountain
12 Round Building
13 South Stoa/Latrine

Directly behind the temple stood the Hellenistic **barracks** and **tower**, perfectly located for the view over the plain. Adjoining the barracks to the south were the two **palaces**, peristyle mansions of the kings of Pergamon, of which not much remains except walls and cisterns. Water was always a headache in the citadel, and anyone caught polluting the reserves was punished.

Up on the acropolis, you'll notice one telling clue of Pergamon's early decline. The tops of the walls, built under Roman rule, use plenty of recycled marble from Greek buildings.

Library

Southwest of the palaces stood the renowned two-storey **library** begun by Attalus II, which at its height had some 200,000 volumes. Eumenes II in particular was obsessed with acquiring books, and had a naughty habit of borrowing and not returning. For books by Aristotle and Theophrastus he is said to have paid their weight in gold.

The Pergamene library became so great that it excited the jealousy of the Ptolemies in Egypt, whose library at Alexandria was its only serious rival. As a result Egypt banned the export of papyrus. All books at the time were written on long scrolls of this brittle stuff; but Eumenes, undeterred, offered a large reward to anyone who could come up with a replacement. A certain Crates of Smyrna recalled the old Ionian custom of writing on sheepskins treated with lime and dried. This 'Pergamon paper' became known as parchment, and as it was too thick to roll up like papyrus, the codex, or modern paged book, was invented. Pergamon's library survived in Alexandria until the 7th century; the Christians have a story that the Arabs used the books to stoke the fires in their baths after they conquered the city, while Muslim historians say that Christian fanatics had torched them all long before.

The Theatre

A **temple of Athena** stood next to the library, of which little more than the foundations remain. The Athena of this temple was Athena Nikephoros, or 'she who grants victory' and it is thought that the original of the famous 'Dying Gaul' now in the Capitoline Museum in Rome once stood in its precincts. From the temple a narrow stair-passage descends to the **Greek Theatre**. It's not unusual to find ancient theatres carved into hillsides, offering spectators not only a view of the stage but a panoramic backdrop as well, but this is an extreme case; nowhere will you find a theatre so dizzyingly steep and dramatic, resembling an immense fan cut into the rock. Its 80 rows of seats could hold 10,000 spectators. A **Temple of Dionysus**, the god of wine and theatrical festivals, stood off to the audience's right, closing one end of the long promenade of the **Theatre Terrace**; since the stage of the theatre was portable, it could be removed at the end of a performance to permit access to the terrace (where the post holes for the wooden set can still be seen). Architecturally, the Dionysus Temple (also known as the Caracalla) is considered a landmark—set high on a platform, closed on three sides, it is the prototype of many later temples in Rome.

Altar of Zeus

As you walk over the acropolis, consider the method behind the Greek planners' seemingly haphazard arrangement of monuments. The great **Altar of Zeus** stood on the terrace below the temple of Athena. Built during the age of Eumenes II, this was one of the outstanding monuments of the Hellenistic age, shaped like a horseshoe and covered with the famous high reliefs portraying a battle between the Olympian gods and the Titans, symbolic of Pergamon's (or civilization's) victory over the barbaric Gauls. There was another connection. With the presumption possible only to the heirs of Alexander, Eumenes and his family pretended that Telephos, the son of Hercules (who figures prominently in the reliefs) was the founder of their dynasty. These reliefs are in Berlin; all that remains on the acropolis are the altar's foundations. The Turkish government and the city of Bergama have been trying to get them back for decades, without much success.

To the south of the altar, on a lower terrace, are the remains of the **Upper Agora** and its temple, in a mixture of Ionic and Doric orders, a common trait of Pergamene buildings that spread throughout the Mediterranean world. The Altar of Zeus was Karl Humann's greatest discovery (he found it incorporated in a Byzantine wall); a life-size reconstruction, along with those reliefs, is the star attraction in the Berlin museum. Humann is buried here, just below the Upper Agora.

Mid-town Pergamon

Recently much of the **Ancient Road**, connecting upper Pergamon to the **mid-town area**, has been cleared. While the acropolis was reserved for the kings, nobility and officers, regular citizens lived in the mid-town, which also has several important public buildings. Excavations in 1973 uncovered the **Odeion** and a 'Marble Hall' which have been reconstructed—a fascinating sight few visitors to Pergamon ever see. Further on, mysteries (initiations) similar to those at Eleusis took place in the enormous **Temple of Demeter**, erected by Philetairos and later enlarged by the wife of Attalus II, Apollonia. The temple—with its pit for the blood of sacrifices, fountain, and rows of seats for spectators of the mysteries—has unusual archaic palm leaf capitals. Near here are three terraces, each with a gymnasium. Young men trained and studied in the huge **upper gymnasium**, which doubled as an auditorium for ceremonial occasions with its small theatre; Attalus II created it, though what you see is largely a Roman-era rebuilding. The **middle gymnasium** was reserved for adolescent boys, and the third served as the children's playground. The **stairway entrance** connecting the lowest level to the second is one of the finest pieces of workmanship in all Pergamon, an early and well-preserved example of vault and arch construction.

The main street through the mid-town was remarkably narrow, though paved with massive blocks, worn by pedestrians and scored by chariot wheels. Along it are the ruins of shops and houses. Especially interesting here is the peristyle **House of Attalus**, a fair example of how the upper classes of Pergamon lived. Beyond the house in the **Lower Agora**, the famous head of Alexander, now in the Istanbul museum, was discovered.

If you've made it this far down, you'll already see the edge of modern Bergama below. The rest of the ancient street is unexcavated and unmarked, but steep as it is, you should be able to pick your way down, finally ending up in some woebegone, cobbled back streets near the Temple of Serapis where the children and dogs will stare at you as if you had just dropped down from Mars.

Remains in the Modern Town

Modern Bergama has engulfed lower Pergamon, with one monumental exception. The Turks call it *Kizil Avlu*, the Red Courtyard. This red brick mastodon originally served as a **Temple of Serapis**, or Osiris, the resurrected Egyptian god. According to legend, the thousands of bricks in the temple were relayed to the site from hand to hand in a great human chain, so they would neither be on earth nor in the sky; indeed the whole temple is built over the Selinos stream, which still runs through an ancient tunnel below. Other underground chambers and tunnels had a religious significance. One of the temple's two massive towers now contains a mosque. The whole building was converted into a basilica by the early Christians. The church of Pergamon was one of the seven churches of Asia addressed by St John in his *Apocalypse* (*Revelations*), singled out as possessing the 'throne of the Devil'—interpreted as the Altar of Zeus, or more probably as the seat of Roman authority.

Modern Bergama itself is a shabby and dusty sort of town; at first glance you would guess it was built around a factory rather than a major tourist attraction. It does have a fine little **Archaeology and Ethnographic Museum** (*open daily, 8.30–5.30; adm*), where there is a small model of the Altar of Zeus and some finds from the site, including two statues of hermaphrodites. The courtyard is filled with reliefs and other architectural fragments; look out for a wonderful figure of Cerberus, the three-legged hound of hell, and another relief with a poppy. Inside, there are some lovely terracotta ex-votos to Asklepieos—an ear or a finger to show what part the god cured, and a Roman mosaic with the head of Medusa. Also present is that staple of all Mediterranean archaeology museums, a big nude statue of Emperor Hadrian (one of the greatest and most useful of all Roman rulers; unabashedly gay, and *such* a tease).

Asklepieon

A few arches of an aqueduct remain in the modern town; if you walk up the maze of streets towards them you'll eventually find the short-cut to ancient Pergamon's **Asklepieon**, the sanctuary of healing (*open daily 8.30–5; adm*). You can drive there by taking the road that branches off next to the tourist office, passing a large military base.

Pergamon had the most renowned Asklepieon in Greek Asia, and produced one of the best physicians of the ancient world, Galen (AD 131–201), personal doctor of Marcus Aurelius. Asklepieos, the god of healing, was the son of Apollo, and his priests, like Galen, treated the faithful with surprisingly modern methods—diet, baths, music and exercise in a lovely environment, combined with dream interpretation and auto-suggestion. Over the entrance of the sanctuary were inscribed the words, 'By order of the gods Death may not enter here'.

The sanctuary in Pergamon predates the kings of Pergamon and reached its greatest extent in the 2nd century AD, when the hellenophile Emperor Hadrian endowed it with most of the structures you see today. The **Sacred Way**, a wide colonnaded street that led to the Asklepieon from the Roman town, leads you to the entrance gate, or **Propylon**, of which only a few steps remain. Within an open space is the circular **temple of Zeus–Asklepieos**, at one time covered with a dome, modelled after the Pantheon in Rome—another of Hadrian's works.

Beyond lie the main grounds of the Asklepieon itself, encompassed by three long stoae; there, patients could sit in the shade or be sheltered from the rain. When bored, they could use the library, a square building north of the temple. The sanctuary's theatre, off the end of the north portico, could seat 3500 and is believed to have been used to entertain both patients and locals. A sacred spring flowed in to the nearby fountain with marble steps. Such water was very important in the healing process: an analysis in the 1970s found it to be mildly radioactive. There are two other fountains in the sanctuary: a drinking well near the entrance of the sacred Tunnel, and a carved rock pool near the west stoa, used for the frequently prescribed mud baths.

The Sacred Tunnel

The **Tunnel**, 266ft long, leads from the centre of the sanctuary to a mysterious two-storey brick structure, built in Roman times, and believed to be a **Temple of Telesphoros**—a minor doctor deity. Another treatment centre, it was added on to the original Asklepieon rather like a modern hospital annexe. The tunnel itself was more than a passageway: while patients walked through its shadows, the doctor-priests would whisper healing suggestions.

The **south stoa** near here had to be supported on columns to attain the level of the rest of the sanctuary, producing a cryptoporticus you can walk through; at the far end is a luxurious marble **latrine** for men, and a small, less well-appointed one for the women; both, however, had to use mussel shells as toilet paper. The central Asklepieon proper had shrines to the several gods of healing—Hygiea and Apollo among them, and incubation chambers, where patients slept, hoping for a dream from the god to guide them in their cure.

Dikili

Cruise ships call at **Dikili**, the port of ancient Pergamon and the nearest beach which is safe for children. Though it's a growing resort, there's not much else to Dikili, other than some mildly attractive back alleys, a simple monument erected in memory of the assassinated Swedish Prime Minister Ölaf Palme (who visited Dikili in 1968) and a string of waterfront bars. South of Dikili, there is a quieter, smaller resort at **Çandarli**, set under a Genoese castle that has been so enthusiastically restored it seems a stage prop.

Bergama to Izmir

Between Bergama and Izmir, the coast is dotted with Aeolian cities, of which little remains beyond their names: Pitane, northernmost of the Aeolian Confederacy (modern **Çandarli**), has a picturesque 13th-century Venetian castle next to the small beach. To the south stood Gryneum (**Temasalik Burnu**), once renowned for its temple and oracle of Apollo, of which only a mound in a field now remains. Continuing south, **Myrina** was reputed to have been founded by the Queen of the Amazons, and beyond that, on the coast, stood the once-great **Cyme**. Both contributed too much building material to modern **Ali Ağa** to be of any interest today.

Eski Foça

In the *Odyssey*, Homer tells of the Sirens, whose beautiful songs would lure sailors to their death. The cunning Odysseus, who had to sail past the Sirens on his voyage home, managed to evade disaster yet still enjoy their singing by ordering his crew to bind him to the mast and then to block their own ears with beeswax. Of the many places across the Mediterranean that claim the Sirens, **Eski Foça** puts in one of the better bids with its jagged **Siren Rocks** just off the shore that whine and howl when the wind blows through them. How the sailors could have found such a banshee-like wailing so enchanting is another question entirely, but that's Eski Foça's story and they're sticking to it.

Today, tourists sunbathe on the Siren Rocks, as they do on the beaches near Eski Foça, for this little town, occupying a promontory between two deeply indented bays, is now an attractive resort. The town was not been swamped, however, and still retains a workaday atmosphere, thanks to the good fishing off its shores. The fishermen are not the only ones who appreciate the rich fishing grounds off Eski Foça: it is one of the last habitats of monk seals, and in 1991 the town and its sea were declared a protection zone for these lively but reclusive beasts. Eski Foçians take this responsibility seriously, to the extent that the obligatory statue of Atatürk in the main square has been replaced by a stone seal.

Eski Foça was ancient Phocaea, the northernmost Ionian city, and unlike its Aeolian neighbours always looked to the sea, boasting one of the best harbours in the area. The seafarers of Phocaea founded numerous colonies, most famously Marsalla (Marseilles) and Elea in Italy (where Zeno wrote his nasty paradoxes). Again, almost all the stone that remained of ancient Phocaea went into the medieval castle on the shore. Still standing, oddly enough, is the so-called **Taş Kule**, a mysterious 8th-century BC tomb, believed to have been built by the Phrygians or Lydians. It's along the Eski road, where you just might mistake it for an Art Deco petrol station.

Yeni Foça, little sister of Eski, is some 12 miles (20km) to the north, a pleasant village with pleasant beaches that attracts the likes of the Club Méditerranée.

Bergama and Dikili ©(232–) **Where to Stay**
moderate

Bergama has a few good hotels—but when it's crowded in summer the best way to do the sights might be as a day trip from Ayvalik. On the other hand, rooms are cheaper here than anywhere along the coast, and there are some real bargains. £16/$24 gets you your choice from the town's three top establishments: the ★★★**Berksoy**, just outside town on the Izmir road, © 633 2595, ⊗ 633 5346, no doubt the best of the lot, with balconied rooms facing a park, pool and tennis, satellite TV in each room. If they're full, settle for the ★★★**Iskender**, also on the Izmir road, © 633 2123, where some rooms have air conditioning and TV. For £10/$15, the ★★**Efsane**, © 632 1614, has a swimming pool; it too is on the Izmir road, Bergama's main street.

Dikili has the ★★**Perla Oteli**, Şehit Sami Akbulut Caddesi 97, © 671 4145, similarly priced. It's the same story with Eski Foça, despite its resort status; the best is the ★★**Hanedan Oteli**, Büyükdeniz Mevkii, © 812 1515, near the beach with its own restaurant; doubles go for £18/£27. Eski Foça does have some lovely pensions, however; two of the nicest, on Hükümet Caddesi, are owned by Zeki, a friendly Kurd from Erzurum—the **Zumrut** and the **Zeki**, © 616 1280 for both. Prices, including breakfast, are £7/£11 at the former, £9/$14 at the latter. The **Karacam**, Sahil Caddesi 70, © 812 3216, offers nice rooms in a restored old house; £17/$26.

cheap

In Bergama, almost everything is along the main Izmir Caddesi around the bus station: the **Aktan**, © 633 3400 and the **Sayin** are both clean, modern places with rooms for about £4/$6, and both have some rooms with baths. Closer to the ruins, the **Athena**, © 633 3420, occupies another old Greek house. The **Pergamon Pansiyon**, © 633 2395 (*see* below) has a very friendly management and nice rooms, some with showers; it's at Bankalar Caddesi 3 (the main street's name in the centre), convenient to the ruins. The **Berksoy Hotel** (*see* above) has a well-equipped campground, © 633 2595—you get to use their pool, too. The less expensive **Bergama Camping**, © 633 3902, also has a pool.

Dikili has some nice pensions north of the bus station and some filthy flea-pits on the main road towards the harbour and in the old town. In Eski Foça, the **Kahraman**, © 712 7273, Dalyan Caddesi 23, is a good bargain at £8/$12. If you're on a tight budget, the **Aydin Pansiyon**, Fevzi Paşa Mah 2, © 812 2941, is a much better alternative; £4/$6 per person for a large, spotless room with private shower and toilet.

Eating Out

Bergama has a pitiful few inexpensive *lokantas*, almost all just south of the bus station on Izmir Caddesi, such as the **Ozan 2**, with decent *pide* and soup. A few gruesome locations try to tempt tourists with signs like 'Flat Bread with the Soup; Meatball in the Tile!' But just when you think you're going to starve to death here, you find the **Pergamon Pansiyon** on Bankalar Caddesi (the main street's name in the town centre), and one of the most gratifying dining experiences to be had in these parts, for about £3/$5. The restaurant is in an enclosed courtyard, with two fountains and lots of cushions everywhere, Ottoman-style. Excellent *börekler* and other mezes; the kebabs are damn spicy all right, and they serve beer. All Bergama seems to come here in the evenings.

Dikili has a good selection of waterfront restaurants serving fresh fish. Being a resort, Eski Foça provides good fare, particularly at the **Ali Baba Restaurant** (£4/$6) on Atatürk Meydani and at the **Pizza Milano** at Kücükdeniz Sahil 58 (pizza and a glass of wine £3/$5).

Izmir

Of all the ancient Greek cities on the coast of Asia Minor, only **Izmir** (old Smyrna) has survived as a city into modern times. Why Izmir, and not Sardis or Pergamon or Ephesus or Miletus?—partly because of a good deep harbour that can't silt up, and partly simple luck of the draw; while the city has suffered much from history and earthquakes, it has never been destroyed completely like so many others. Few cities can boast such a splendid situation, at the head of a long narrow gulf, spread out beneath the flat-topped hill known as Mt Pagus by the Greeks and more picturesquely as the Velvet Castle (*Kadifekale*) by the Turks.

Now Turkey's third city, with over three million people, Izmir is still a new, rough creature, rebuilt from the ground up after the fire and population exchange of 1922. Understandably, it is still a city in search of an identity. To get an idea of what up-to-date, hard-working Izmir thinks, ask someone there what they think of Ankara or especially Istanbul. You'll learn a new word in Turkish: *yaramaz*, or useless. "Istanbul *yaramaz*!"

History

Surprisingly, when the Aeolian colonists arrived in the 10th century BC, they chose not the present site of Izmir but a small peninsula at the end of the gulf, called Bayrakli. One day, while the entire city was out celebrating the Dionysia, Ionians from Colophon sneaked in and took over. According to one ancient tradition, Ionian Smyrna was the birthplace of Homer, said to have been born on the banks of the River Meles (*Halkapinar Suyu*). Ancient Smyrna was plagued by the Lydians and never thrived until Alexander the Great, while hunting on Mt Pagus, dreamt that Nemesis told him to found a city there. The inhabitants on the peninsula moved to the hill, and the new Smyrna prospered and was eventually welcomed into the exclusive confederacy of Ionian cities as its thirteenth member. Strabo and many other ancient authorities referred to the city's charms, and 'beautiful Smyrna' is a name that has stuck through the centuries, despite frequent disasters.

In the late Ottoman Empire, Turks referred to the city as *gavuz Izmir*—'infidel Smyrna', for its overwhelming majority of Greek and Armenian Christians, and Jews. In those days it was the unquestioned cultural and good-time capital of the eastern Mediterranean, full of blooming Art Nouveau buildings, buzzing with deals being made in a score of different languages, and quite seriously looped on hashish and opium; among the city's creations was the intense, heavy style of Greek popular music called *rembetiko*, born in Smyrna's bars and drug dens. All this came to a tragic end in 1922, when Atatürk's defeat of the Greek army led to a mass exodus of Greek civilians from the city. As is traditional, the Greeks blame the Turks and the Turks blame the Greeks, but for whatever reason, while hundreds of thousands of Smyrna's citizens waited on the docks for transit to Greece, it caught fire and over eighty per cent of its buildings burned to the ground.

Atatürk's government wasted no time in rebuilding it, in a dreary modern plan of wide, straight boulevards and traffic circles. After the last war it became the headquarters for NATO's southern command. Trade has gradually returned, and the new all-Turkish Izmir is flourishing, the most thoroughly modern and Westernized city in Turkey and its busiest port.

Getting Around

The main **bus** terminal (Yeni Garaj) is northwest of the centre in Halkapinar, on Şehitler Caddesi. However, Halley's Comet appears more frequently than the no. 50 bus that is supposed to ferry passengers into the city centre: if you can find a dolmuş that's not crammed to the hilt, take it; otherwise, hail a cab. Another terminal, serving Çeşme and other nearby southern destinations, is in suburban Uçküyülar; to get there, take the 249 or 250 bus from Alsancak Station, Lozan Meydani or Konak (next to Uçküyülar, incidentally, is a big field where people come to sell cars on weekends—if you're tired of riding buses here's your chance to pick up a '59 Chevy and do the coast in style). Two more stations to know: the **Orcaner** bus station out in the suburbs, where some services to Kuşadasi, Pamukkale and Selçuk begin and end, and the **dolmuş stop** near the tourist information office on Gaziosmanpaşa, where there are minibuses to the beaches at Altinkum and Çiftlik.

Izmir's new **Adnan Menderes airport** is served by frequent flights from Istanbul and Ankara, as well as weekly direct THY flights from London, and numerous charters from abroad. The THY terminal is next to the Tourist Office on Gaziosmanpaşa Caddesi, and is connected by bus to the airport one hour before every flight. From Izmir's central Basmane Station, at the head of Fevzipaşa Bulvari, there are **rail** links with Aydin, Denizli, Konya, and Ankara. The overnight *Mavi Tren* special to the capital is a relatively fast and luxurious run if you're headed that way (though still not as good a deal as the bus).

The Yeni Liman at Alsancak, on the northern tip of the city, is the port for **ferryboats** and the Turkish Maritime Lines cruise boats; in Izmir their address is Atatürk Bulvari 125. Once a week (on Wednesday at 4pm), a car ferry leaves for Venice; the return leaves Venice Saturday night, and both ways there is a stop in Çeşme. It arrives on

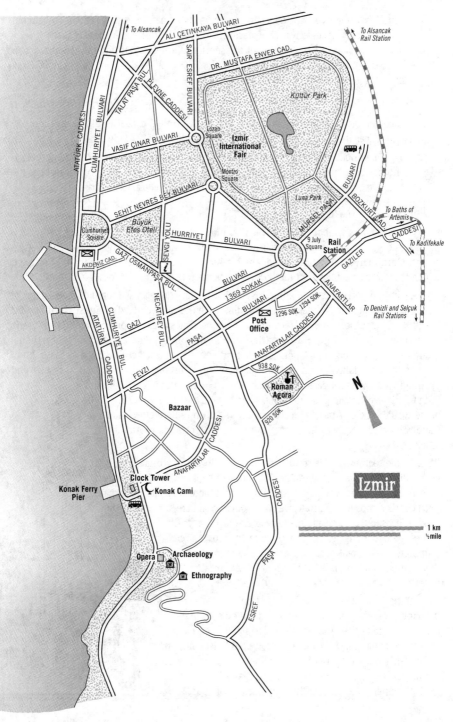

Tuesdays, when you can take it on to its final destination, Antalya. Boats to Istanbul leave at 2pm on Tuesdays, Thursdays and Saturdays. In summer there is also a weekly Stern Line boat to Bari. Ferries for the short ride to **Karşiyaka**, Izmir's suburb across the bay, leave regularly from the Konak docks (Konak Iskelesi) and Alsancak Iskelesi, on the Kordon.

Tourist Information

Gaziosmanpaşa Bulvari next to the Büyük Efes Hotel, © (232) 489 9278; there are also offices in Alsancak, Atatürk Caddesi 418, and at the ferry docks, © 251 5480.

The main **post office** (and poste restante pickup) is on Cumhuriyet Meydani; there is another big office on Fevzipaşa Bulvari near Başmane station. For English **books**, the best bet is the Dünya Bookshop on Akdeniz Caddesi, off Gaziosmanpaşa.

A Tour of the Town

Izmir's pride and its symbol is the **Kordon** (Atatürk Caddesi), the shorefront boulevard where the waves of the Aegean beat almost against the doors of swank blocks of flats and cafés. At its centre, **Cumhuriyet Meydani**, stands the big Atatürk Monument and the Büyük Efes Hotel, which thanks to a peculiarity of the '20s plan has the role of being the focal point of the city.

To the south, especially on and around Necatibet Bulvari, you can see some of the remains of old Smyrna, lovely turn-of-the-century buildings like the restored **Kizlar Ağasi Hani** on 902 Sokak, at the southern end of Necatibey. One of few blessings the planners left Izmir is the great green expanse of the **Kültürpark**, Izmir's fairgrounds, where the Izmir International Trade Fair is held from mid-August to mid-September (a time when it is hard to find a hotel room in the city). Like the similar Kültürpark in Bursa, this one is the place to go on weekend evenings, with outdoor restaurants, dance halls, horse-drawn carriages and a 'Luna Park' with some good rides. Of course, no Turkish city worthy of the name would lack an **Atatürk museum**: Izmir's is on (where else?) Atatürk Caddesi towards Alsancak and contains the usual assortment of Atatürkish knick-knacks.

Back on the seafront, at the southern end of the Kordon is **Konak**, name of both a district and its central square distinguished by its lovely **clock tower**, built in the 19th century by Sultan Abdülhamid, and the small but ornate 18th-century mosque, **Konak Cami**. From the square an underground passage leads to the shore and the ferry docks; if you have time to kill in Izmir one of the best things to do is take the ferry across the bay from here to **Karşiyaka**, not only for the views around the bay from the boat, but for the suburb's very pleasant waterfront park, full of snack stands and cafés.

Everything inland from Konak is Izmir's **bazaar district**, a maze of narrow streets and cul-de-sacs that predate the great fire. Anafartlar Caddesi is the main drag, and while Izmir's market can hardly compare to Istanbul's or Bursa's, it's still worth a visit for unexpected things like the Şunnet Çarsisi, a pretty courtyard next to an old *han* where garden supplies are sold, or the huge glass-roofed arcade at

THE CLOCK TOWER, IZMIR

913 Sokak and Gaziosmanpaşa Bulvari, a pre-1922 monument now come down in the world, selling cheap clothes.

Just south of the bazaar (take 838 Sokak south of Anafartlar) are the excavations of the **Roman agora**, a rebuilding financed by Emperor Marcus Aurelius after a terrible earthquake (*open daily 8.30–5; adm*); here you can see two rows of colonnades and three statues discovered on the site: Poseidon, Demeter and half of Artemis.

The Museums and Kadifekale

South along the waterfront from the clock tower a new three-storey building houses Izmir's **archaeology museum** (*open daily 8.30–5; adm*), with an extensive collection of artefacts from the region. If you're on your way to Ephesus, you should definitely stop in here first; there are models and plans of the Meryemana Kilise and St John's, and a number of finds from the sites. In any case, this museum is worth the trip, a treasurehouse of expressive sculpture from Archaic times through the Classical and Hellenistic. In the latter, expecially, you may appreciate the soft reflectiveness of the portraits of a *nun of Isis*, and *Aspasia*. Some of this sensibility carried on into Roman times; there's a basement full of fine Roman portrait busts, though all are larger than life and a bit Felliniesque. Some of the best works are outside in the gardens: grave steles with the common motif of death's door, friezes from Aphrodisias, and a fanciful, delightful Roman frieze from Miletus, showing almost naive hunting scenes with grinning goats, dolphins and ostriches.

Next door, the **ethnography museum** (*open daily 9–12, 1–5.30; adm*) has more to offer, with well-thought-out displays on Ottoman life ranging from a feature on camel wrestling to a mock-up of a Turkish boy's circumcision ceremony, complete with a mannequin of a suitably anguished adolescent. Almost directly above the Roman agora looms Mt Pagus, or **Kadifekale**, the Velvet Castle crowned with fortifications begun by Alexander the Great, and rebuilt in turn by the Byzantines and Ottomans. The view of Izmir from the walls or one of the nearby cafés is vertiginous.

East of the central city, on Gaziler Caddesi, the *Halkapinar Gölü* has been identified as the ancient **Baths of Artemis**, where a statue of the goddess was discovered. This spring-fed pool, now in the grounds of the Izmir water company, supplies the entire city, and is believed to be the source of the ancient River Meles. A Homeric hymn refers to a pool of Artemis in the vicinity, and, according to tradition, Homer sat on its banks and composed his iambic verse. The pool is still a charming, poetic oasis in the big city, and visitors are welcome.

Izmir ⓒ (232–)

Where to Stay

luxury

In Izmir, the ★★★★★**Büyük Efes**, ⓒ 484 4300, ✆ 441 5695, is an institution, its enclosed garden occupying a large wedge of the city's most expensive real estate, on Cumhuriyet Meydani. Although ageing, it has all the amenities, from sauna to tennis courts, television to refrigerators, Turkish bath to swimming pool. In recent years the Hilton chain has trumped this with a hideous but inescapable 500ft skyscraper, visible from almost anywhere in town; the ★★★★★**Izmir Hilton**, at Gaziosmanpaşa Bulv 7, ⓒ 441 6060, ✆ 441 2277, has two presidential suites, in case two presidents happen to pass through at the same time, a non-smoking floor(!), a casino, 24hr room service, pool, health club, sauna, tennis and squash courts, and on and on. At Cumhuriyet Bulv 138, the ★★★★**Pullman Etap Izmir Oteli**, ✆ 489 4090, 🖷 489 1709, is another top-class establishment, near the Büyük Efes.

expensive

A new addition to this list is the ★★★**Marla**, Kazim Dirik Caddesi, off Gaziosmanpaşa, ✆ 441 4000, 🖷 441 1150, posh air-conditioned rooms and a health club downstairs, in a striking postmodernist building decorated with a bizarre sort of totem pole of goddesses all the way to the roof. If you're not staying there, at least have a look.

Near the city centre are the ★★★**Anba Oteli**, Cumhuriyet Bulv 124, ✆ 484 4380, and the ★★★**Izmir Palas Oteli**, Vasif Çinar Bulv 2, ✆ 421 5583; both have air-conditioned rooms with balconies and TV for about £42/$63, but the Izmir Palas is on the Kordon and some rooms have sea views. Prices may be lower in the off season. Nearby, in a quiet location off Gaziosmanpaşa Bulvari , is the ★★★**Karaca Oteli**, 1379 Sokak 55, ✆ 489 1940, modern and swish, at about the same rates. Also for about the same, you can stay outside town at Balçova at the ★★★**Balçova Thermal Hotel**, Hüseyin Öğütcan Caddesi, ✆ 259 0102, a resort complex built around hot springs: air-conditioning, tennis, two big pools and plenty of other sports activities.

moderate

Most hotels in this category are rather drab modern places intended for travelling salesmen. The nicest is the ★★**Tanik**, on 1364 Sokak off Gazi Bulvari, ✆ 441 2007, fine rooms with bath and TV (quieter if you ask for one away from the boulevard); £22/$33. Next, the ★**Babdan** at Gaziomanpaşa Bulvari 45, ✆ 483 9640, for about the same rates (it's a bit noisy though). In Basmane, a stone's throw from the railway station, is the ★★**Billur Oteli**, Anafartalar Caddesi 783, ✆ 483 9732, priced at £18/$27, breakfast included. Rooms facing the rear are quieter. The ★**Nil Oteli**, Fevzi Paşa Bulv 155, ✆ 483 5228, also suffers from street noise but its rooms are very pleasant and relatively inexpensive; £11/$17 for an en suite double.

cheap

Rather than pay more for one of the above, you'll do just as well in one of the perfectly acceptable inexpensive hotels on **1369 Sokak**, the traveller's best friend in Izmir. The street is located near the rail station, just north of Fevzipaşa Caddesi, and it holds everything you will ever need (*see* 'Eating Out', below). First choice is the **Oba** at no. 5, ✆ 483 5474, the furthest hotel from the station, but one with clean, modern rooms with bath, some with TV, for £6/$9. At the opposite end is the **Özcan Oteli**, 1368 Sokak 3, ✆ 483 5052, very much the same in quality and price. Tolerable places for slightly less on the strip include the **Kent** and the **Güven Palas**, and the **Fatih**, around the corner on 1366 Sokak.

One step lower than 1369 is its mirror-image street on the other side of Fevzipaşa Bulvari, 1294 Sokak. Hotels here are the cheapest in town; there are loads of them, some nice and some a bit rough. Two of the best-kept are the **Yildiz Palace**, at no. 50, ✆ 425 1518, and the **Balikli**, at no. 20, ✆ 484 2560. The **Güzel Konya**, not quite as good, has more character, in a ramshackle wooden pre-fire building.

For a different look at Izmir, stay in the **Yeni Şükren Oteli**, on Anafartlar Caddesi, a very basic but friendly establishment in the middle of the bazaar.

Eating Out

For dinner in Izmir, you may do as the locals do and take yourself to the trendy district of Alsancak, where most of the restaurants are. These tend to be agreeable, informal place with tables out on the pavement; on any evening, and particularly on weekends, it's the best scene Izmir has to offer. **Gazi Kadinlar Sokak**, a pedestrian street of surviving pre-1922 houses just off the Kordon, is one of the first places to look. The attractive Greek houses with their bay windows have been largely restored, and most of them now house seafood restaurants. Most have simple menus of mezes and the day's catch of fish, such as the **Cipa Restoran**; £6/$9. For kebabs and typical Turkish fare the **Sardanya** will set you back £5/$8.

Almost every big streetcorner in Alsancak seems to have some sort of outdoor fast-food joint, Turkish-style, with big Coca-Cola signs to prove they're hip. Some of these can be surprising, such as the **Fil Kafeterya** on Ali Cetankaya Caddesi: pizza on a plank, fresh-squeezed orange juice, soft ice cream, burgers and kebabs; a quite acceptable pizza and a drink for less than £2/$3. The fancy places are along the waterfront on and around the Kordon, where seafood is the speciality. You could try the **Remzi Baba** at no. 282 or the **Golden Restaurant** at no. 314. Both have music, dancing and set meals for around £8/$12 a head, wine included. For something different in the centre, there is the inexpensive **Vegetaryen Restoran**, on 375 Sokak in Alsancak near the American Hospital.

The obvious place to look for inexpensive chow is around the railroad station and that ever-friendly 1369 Sokak. On this pedestrian street, plenty of bars put out tables and grill kebabs outdoors (some have live music on weekends); chestnuts and mussels are on offer, and violinists and girls with roses ply the tables. There are also proper restaurants, notably the **Dört Mevsim**, with truly good kebabs and incredible homemade *pide* blown up like a balloon, £3/$5. Directly across from the station, the **Başmane Kebab Salonu** packs them in for a wide choice of grills at low prices; chicken too. Among a score of steam-table *lokantas* on the station square, the **Tokat Lokanta** stands out. Plenty of street-front stands in Izmir specialize in *böreks* and other sorts of Turkish savoury pastries that everybody's mom makes, but you'll hardly ever see in restaurants. Some of the best come from a tiny local chain facetiously named **McZeki's**; there's one on Fevzipaşa Bulvari near the post office.

Looking for something cheap and decent around Gaziosmanpaşa Bulvari can be a problem. The **Amazon Bar–Restoran**, hidden away next to a playground behind the Hilton, offers seafood pizza, roast chicken and such; £3/$5 for a full meal. On Anafartlar Caddesi, the main street of the bazaar neighbourhood, the **Şükren Lokanta** provides a welcome oasis amidst the bustle; the food's nothing special but you won't do better here. An equal choice just nearby is the **Meşaret Kafeterya**, in the courtyard of an old *han* with a marble fountain.

Restaurants in the business centre, around Gaziosmanpaşa Bulvari, are scarce, but for seafood there is the simple, popular **Çanli Balik** on Cumhuriyet at Kemalettin; £4/$6. For something different, there's the rather unimaginatively named **Chinese Restaurant** at 1379 Sok 57, off Gaziosmanpaşa Bulvari near the Hilton. A full dinner will set you back about £10/$15, with lunch menus for less. For the simple *lokantas*, search in the area between Konak and the market. Many of the city's *meyhaneler* are on or around Akdeniz Caddesi, dark dives with outside tables under a canopy where they usually grill some kebabs in the evening. Also here is the **Café Izmir**, on Akdeniz, where you can puff on your *narghile* in a strangely modern setting.

Inland from Izmir

Getting Around

Both Manisa and Sardis are connected to Izmir by rail and bus (1½ hours). For Sardis, take any bus or minibus/dolmuş for Salihli or Sartmustafa.

Tourist Information

Manisa: Doğu Cad 8, Eylül Işhani, ✆ (236) 232 7541

Manisa

East of Izmir is **Manisa**, ancient Magnesia ad Sipylum, which began its life as the westernmost outpost of the Hittites. Much later, as a Greek city, Magnesia was mentioned in Homer and in mythology—though it *isn't*, sorry, the Magnesia that gave its name to magnesium and magnets; that one is a region in Thessaly. Magnesia was, however, the birthplace of our forebear Pausanias, whose scholarly *Guide to Greece*, written in the reign of Trajan, was probably the world's first travel guide. Manisa became Ottoman property in the early 14th century, and was favoured under the sultans, particularly Süleyman the Magnificent, who served as governor here before his accession to the throne. In 1922, retreating Greek troops destroyed most of the city, leaving this provincial capital modern and a bit dull, with little to show the visitor.

Finds from Magnesia and Sardis can be seen in the **Manisa museum** (*open daily exc Mon, 8.30–12, 1.30–5; adm*), among them a fine Roman statue of a young girl and inscriptions from a synagogue discovered in Sardis in 1962. The museum is in the medrese of the **Muradiye Cami**, a work of Mimar Sinan and noted for the tiles and goldwork in the interior. The 14th-century **Ulu Cami**, halfway up to the derelict Byzantine fortress on the ancient acropolis, has a Selçuk-style minaret, with coloured tiles and columns from an ancient temple. A third mosque, the 1522 **Sultan Cami**, built by the mother of Süleyman the Magnificent, is the most famous in Manisa, for here, at the end of May, the Mesir festival takes place. *Mesir* is a paste, a concoction of some 41 ingredients and spices, reputed to be a cure-all. It is tossed in paper wrappers from the top of the minaret. According to popular belief, it only works if you scramble for it, and hundreds of people do so, every year.

Food for the Gods

Just east of Manisa, at Akpinar, there is a carved relief of the great Mother Goddess Cybele on the side of Mt Sipylus. This region is closely identified in mythology with Tantalus, his sons Pelops and Broteas, and his daughter Niobe. Broteas, the ugliest man in Greece, is credited with carving the Cybele, while Pelops, less talented, got chopped up in a soup at the banquet Tantalus prepared for the gods on top of the Mt Sipylus. The gods (except for the earth goddess Demeter, who was mourning for her lost daughter Persephone and carelessly ate a bit of shoulder) recognized the meat for what it was and punished Tantalus in Hades with eternal thirst and hunger, always keeping water and fruit just out of his reach (hence 'tantalize'). Zeus put Pelops back together again (with an ivory shoulder), and he went on to conquer southern Greece and give it his name—the Peloponnese.

It's difficult to know what to make of all this, but we have definitely hit a nerve; the story of Tantalus is one of the myths where the ghosts of ancient belief and ritual glare out from behind the civilized veneer laid down by the classical-era storytellers. A 'Feast of Tantalus' was an important midwinter holiday in western Asia Minor, celebrated by an *eranos*—a pot-luck banquet, like the one Tantalus threw for the gods. It may contain a memory of an actual human sacrifice and even cannibalism, rites suppressed in the later stage of religious evolution represented by Zeus and the Olympian gods; there are plenty of dark hints toward this in Arcadia, in Pelops's own Peloponnese. Or else, the fate of Pelops may have been strictly metaphorical. We may think of him as the typical sort of sacred king, whose career, representing the sun's, begins at midwinter (the New Year's baby of popular art is a survival of this). His death and rebirth recalls the cycle of the year. Somewhere on the slopes of Mt Sipylus is a small ruin of a tholos tomb that the ancients called the 'Tomb of Tantalus'.

As for poor Niobe, she had seven daughters and seven sons, but was rash enough to boast that she was a better mother than Leto, who had only two children, Apollo and Artemis. These two stern archer gods then avenged their mother by slaying Niobe's fourteen. Niobe's grief was so great that Zeus took pity on her and turned her to stone. A natural rock formation southwest of Manisa is believed to be the Niobe referred to by ancient writers; it lies along the road to Karaköy, near a picnic ground, one of the many scenic spots in the region.

Sart/Sardis

A little more than an hour east of Izmir is the 20th-century village of Sart, built over the ruins of the ancient capital of Lydia, **Sardis**. Situated below the steep Mt Tmolus, dominating the fertile plain of the River Hermes (the *Gediz Nehri*) and located on the great Royal Road of the Persian Empire (the western part of the road may go back to Hittite times), Sardis from the 7th to the mid-6th century BC was the world's richest city. A good part of its wealth was in gold washed down from the mountain by the River Pactolus, which the Lydians collected in sheep-skins spread in the shallows—perhaps the source of the legend of the Golden Fleece.

The Lydians

The Greeks were fascinated by the Lydians, and their fame went as far as the Assyrians who called them the *Luddi* in their inscriptions. The Lydian race was a mixture of native Anatolian and Western invader; their language used many Greek letters and was related to Phrygian and, curiously, Etruscan (Herodotus writes that Etruria was a Lydian colony, and the mysterious Etruscans themselves claimed to have originated in Asia Minor). Besides building giant mounds for their deceased rulers, the Lydians were also famous for condoning prostitution; it was the way a good Lydian girl earned her marriage dowry.

There were three Lydian dynasties. At the end of the second, the Heraclid, the Lydians gained ascendancy as the Hittites in the region declined. The last Heraclid king was

Candaules (700 BC), who, it is said, was so proud of his wife's beauty that he contrived for his trusted minister Gyges to see her naked. The queen, however, saw the unwitting voyeur and the next day gave him a choice: either kill her husband and marry her, or die on the spot. Gyges chose the more pleasant alternative, and founded a new dynasty, the Mermnad, that brought Sardis and Lydia, literally, a golden age. By the time of Croesus (563–546 BC), Sardis controlled the whole of Asia Minor, which Croesus ruled with a very benevolent hand. Lydia had been the first nation in the world to mint coins, and Croesus the first to issue them in pure gold and pure silver. His reputation for wealth has come down to us, but did little to impress the visiting Athenian lawgiver Solon, who, after touring the fabulous treasuries, merely commented, 'No man can be reckoned happy until the end'.

A few years after Solon's visit, the Persians under King Cyrus menaced Lydia's borders. Croesus asked the Delphic oracle whether or not he should attack and the oracle coyly replied that if he crossed the River Halys he would 'destroy a great empire'. Encouraged, Croesus took the offensive, only to meet defeat. Cyrus chased the Lydians back to Sardis. After a two-week siege the city fell, and Croesus realized too late that he had destroyed his own empire. Condemned to be burnt at the stake, Croesus groaned 'Solon, Solon!' as the fire was lit, and Cyrus asked what he meant. Croesus told him what the Athenian had said and, moved, Cyrus ordered his life to be spared.

Cyrus made Sardis the capital of a satrapy and, as such, it was sacked when the Ionian cities revolted against the Persians in 499 BC. It recovered in the Hellenistic era, until the earthquake of AD 17 flattened it. Tiberius had it rebuilt, and it became an early centre of Christianity, one of the seven churches of Asia and an important bishopric under the Byzantines. In 1401, Tamerlane destroyed Sardis so thoroughly that it was never rebuilt; when excavations began in the early 20th century, the archaeologists had to dig down 30ft in places, so thickly had the soft rock of the acropolis silted down over the lower city.

The Site

One thing the excavators have discovered is that Sardis was at its most extensive under Croesus, and it takes some walking to see it all. The **Temple of Artemis**, most famous of ancient Sardis' monuments, is about half a mile up the Pactolus valley; although the sanctuary was founded in the 5th century BC, the temple wasn't begun until the 3rd. Its two Ionic capitals are among the finest anywhere; thirteen others have been re-erected to give an idea of the temple's shape. In Roman times the temple was divided into two, half dedicated to the worship of Artemis, the other half to Faustina, wife of the Roman emperor Antoninus Pius. Along the road to the centre of Sardis, an altar to Cybele was discovered, as well as the workshops where the Lydians worked the gold they 'fleeced' from the river.

Equally impressive are the Roman gymnasium and baths from the 2nd century AD, just off the highway; shops and a synagogue complete the complex with the **Marble Court** in the centre. Nearby, part of the Royal Road has been uncovered, and, most interestingly, what appears to be a prototype bazaar dating back to the 7th century BC, giving rise to the theory that wealthy Sardis was the first city to practise organized retail trade. Next to this, the **House of Bronzes** (6th century AD) was perhaps the residence of the bishop of Sardis.

If you're reasonably energetic you can walk up the acropolis, one of the most dramatic in Asia

Minor, its sheerness accentuated by the dagger-shaped rock formations around it. The walk from the valley takes less than an hour; on top the surviving fortifications are mostly Byzantine. Six miles (10km) north of Sardis are the Bin Tepe, or **Thousand Hills**, actually some 100 earthworks built by the artisans, merchants and prostitutes of Sardis. The largest is the **Tomb of Alyattes**, the father of Croesus. At three-quarters of a mile in circumference and 260ft high, it's the largest mound in Turkey, perhaps in the world.

Kemalpaşa

Between Sardis and Izmir, **Kemalpaşa** is the ancient town of Nymphaeum, where Andronicus I Comnenus built the **Palace of Nymphaeum** in 1184, the ruins of which are just outside town. In **Karabel**, on the main road south of Kemalpaşa, there is a second **Hittite relief** similar to Manisa's Cybele, this one of a large warrior; Herodotus referred to it, although, like all Greeks in the classical era, he knew nothing of the Hittites, and assumed it was Egyptian.

Çeşme Peninsula

Getting Around

There are frequent buses (lines 249 and 250) from Izmir's Cumhuriyet Meydani and Konak Meydani to Üçkuyular bus station from where buses leave regularly for Çeşme. From that town's tiny *otogar*, on the port, minibuses depart for the beaches and villages around the peninsula. Between November and April there are usually one or two boats a week between Çeşme and the Greek island of Chios; in season they go every day and can take up to 10 cars.

Tourist Information

Çeşme: Iskele Meydani 8, at the harbour, ✆ (232) 712 6653

The peninsula west of Izmir has several popular beach resorts and thermal spas. **Inciralti** is the closest to Izmir and thus the most crowded; just to the south, the **Baths of Agamemnon**, in use since antiquity, are noted for treating rheumatism. Further west, near **Urla** and another beach, a causeway leads out to an islet where once stood the ancient city of **Clazomenae**. The original causeway, constructed by Alexander the Great, can be seen just below the surface of the sea; otherwise little remains of this Ionian city that produced the great philosopher Anaxagoras, the precursor of Socrates, in the early 5th century BC.

Sığacik

You can go south from Urla to Seferihisar and from there to **Sığacik**, the prettiest village on the peninsula, its old houses clustered around an old Genoese fortress and small port. Here, by the lovely white beach of **Akkum** stood ancient **Teos**, one of the wealthiest Ionian cities on the coast. Teos was the birthplace and home of the lyric love-poet Anacreon; it is also the site of a famous Hellenistic **temple of Dionysus**, with an unusual trapezoidal enclosure. Some columns have been re-erected, to make a picturesque tableau in the olive grove. Nearby is the **theatre** which, though in poor condition, offers a fabled view from its upper seats. Better preserved is the **Odeon**, with its eleven rows of seats, where concerts were performed.

At the tip of the peninsula, facing the Greek island of Chios is **Çeşme** ('fountain'), named after its numerous hot springs. It is the westernmost town in Turkey, a distinction that has an added significance during Ramazan, when the pious Muslims of Çeşme have to wait longer than anyone else to eat supper. Çeşme makes its living as a resort, though one totally lacking in the glamour or intensity of resorts further south. It is a serene family spot to sit on the beach; that's all.

An attractive town, with red tile roofs, Çeşme is dominated by a large, sloping Genoese **castle** captured and restored by Yildirim Beyazit in 1400. Beyazit's engineers evidently discharged their duties well; the castle is in good shape and housed within the crenellated walls is a theatre, a restaurant and a small **museum** displaying the finds from ancient Erythrae (*open daily 8.30–12, 1.30–5; adm*). Two important naval battles took place off Çeşme: the decisive Roman defeat of Antiochus III in 190 BC, which gave the Romans a free hand in Asia Minor, and the destruction of the Ottoman fleet by the Russians in 1770.

Çeşme faces the Greek island of Chios, much favoured by the sultans for its breath-sweetening mastic, some of which went through the **caravanserai**, built in a U-shape by Süleyman the Magnificent in 1529; it has been restored and is now a hotel (*see* below). As in all Turkish resorts, the port is lined with cruise ships, pretty wooden sailing craft waiting to take you away on a trip around the peninsula and its islets; going rate for a half-day excursion with lunch is about £10/$15.

Around Çeşme

Çeşme has a small beach but better bathing is to be had elsewhere. South of town there are beaches at nearby **Çiftlik**, much better ones at fast-developing **Altinkum** and more at **Ovacik** and **Güverçinlik**. For real seclusion head for tiny **Alaçati**, a village 4½ miles (7km) east of Çeşme, and then walk south 2 miles (3km) to find the beach. At offshore **Donkey Island**, so named for its population of wild donkeys, there are several nice swimming spots; Çeşme's travel agents regularly organize day trips.

Dalyan, a fishing village north of Çeşme, is pleasant and pretty but its beach is poor, unlike the mammoth stretch of white sand that can be found at **Ilica** to the east. Fronted by four large windmills, and famous for its thermal springs, Ilica has pretentions to becoming a popular resort in its own right, unfortunately leaving the impression that the town is just one big building site. Other beaches are at **Buyuk**, **Şifne** and **Ildiri**.

Ildiri is near ancient **Erythrae**, a member of the Ionian Confederacy, set at the foot of the rugged Karaburun peninsula. Unfortunately the site was so well quarried in the 19th century that little remains in the picturesque spot beyond some well-built walls and a ruined theatre. In ancient times Erythrae was famous for an archaic statue of Hercules which floated on a raft from Egypt to a point between Chios and Erythrae. Both wanted it, but the raft couldn't be budged until a blind man in Erythrae dreamed that the statue could only be towed away with a rope of women's hair. The women of Erythrae refused to part with their locks, but their Thracian slaves used theirs to make the rope that did indeed pull the raft to their city. The statue restored the blind man's sight, and in the sanctuary subsequently built for it, no women were allowed except Thracians. It's now impossible to tell which of the remains was Hercules' sanctuary, but a stream that tastes bitter still flows in the walls and, according to Pliny—a notorious story-teller—it causes hair to grow all over the body.

A Trip to Chios

There's plenty to see on this island if you want to cross over for a day or two. Chios (*Sakiz* in Turkish) is famous for its rich shipping magnates and for mastic—chewing gum, from lentisk bushes, a favourite of the Ottoman Turks. **Chios** town, impressively modern and prosperous, is the capital, with an excellent white sand beach just to the north at Karfas; or else, you might take an excursion up into the mountains to **Nea Moni**, a fascinating 11th-century monastery in a beautiful setting, with Byzantine mosaics. Chios does not see vast numbers of tourists; it's especially fun to bicycle around, exploring picturesque medieval villages such as **Pirama** or **Pitios**, which like Izmir claims to be the birthplace of Homer. Aound **Sklavia**, there are a number of villas and gardens from the time Chios was ruled by the Genoese. The most memorable sight Chios has to offer is undoubtedly **Pirgi**, a village with a long-standing custom of decorating its buildings with complex, geometrical *sgraffito* façades in black and white (this was a habit in many of Anatolia's Greek villages too, before 1923, and you'll see a few forlorn examples as you travel around the coast).

Çeşme Peninsula ① *(232–)*

Where to Stay

Çeşme's **Hotel Cooperative** has booths at the entrance to town and near the *otogar* and tourist office; they can help you find a room in summer when things are packed.

expensive

Around Çeşme, the top beach resort hotel is the Golden Dolphin, in Turkish the **(TK1) Altinyunus Tatil Köyü**, ① 723 1250, ◉ 723 2252, with 515 bungalows and nearly every possible recreational facility, including horse riding, water skiing and thermal baths; £58/$87. In Ilica, among the many small hotels with thermal establishments is the elegant ★★★★**Turban Çeşme**, ① 723 1240, open in season only, with tennis and swimming pool. In Çeşme, the peaceful ★★★**Kervansaray Hotel**, ① 712 7177, was once the town's caravansaray, now completely redone and elegantly furnished. At Kalyan, the ★★★**Çeşme Ladin**, ① 724 8327, offers a private beach and a pool, and rooms with TV and balconies, most overlooking the sea; the emphasis here is on sports, with a pool, gym and all imaginable water sports accommodated.

moderate

Next to each other near the harbour at Çeşme on Cumhuriyet Meydani are the ★★**Ertan**, ① 712 6795, and ★★**Ridvan**, ① 712 6336, both very much alike, with private sections of beach and double rooms for about £18/$27. Both are conveniently located but are closed out of season. The ★**Kaptan**, Adnan Menderes Bulvari, is owned by Mustafa Denizli, manager of Istanbul's Galatasaray football team; it has a swimming pool. In Ilica the staff at the ★★★**Hotel Delmar**, Izmir Caddesi 154, ① 723 4300, are helpful and the hotel is on the beach and has its own thermal pool.

cheap

Just follow the signs for Çeşme's cheap pensions—there are 114 of them on the peninsula. If you're looking for accommodation in this category, though, try to avoid arriving in Çeşme over the weekend in summer, when the town fills up with holidaymakers from Izmir. Most of the *pansiyons* are located on the hill above the port, pleasant, family-run places such as the **Begovilya** and the **Sahil** ① 712 6934, both overlooking the port. Another one nearby is the **Koroğlu**, ✆ 712 6086. In the centre of Çeşme, top choice is the **Alim Pansiyon,** near the hamam, ✆ 712 7828, where a sparkling clean room with private shower awaits you for only £3/$5. The nearby **Kervan Pansiyon**, ✆ 712 6061, is also good value, and similarly priced.

There are camp sites near the town and on the peninsula, notably the **Vekamp**, in a pleasant location near the beach at Ilica; it also has a swimming pool fed by natural hot springs; ✆ 723 1416. A very simple and inexpensive campsite is the **Altin Kum**, on Altinkum beach.

Eating Out

You can get all the kebabs and sandwiches you need, but whether in Çeşme or anywhere else on the peninsula anything above the tourist common denominator is hard to come by. At any rate, there will be no problem finding good seafood; the **Rihtim Restaurant** on the harbour in Çeşme offers *midye* (stuffed mussels), and uncommon treats like octopus (£5/$8), the best deal among the generally overpriced harbourfront places. Next door, the **Dolunay Café** has a £5/$8 set menu including a fish or kebab plate and wine. Popular with tourists, the **Castle Restaurant** is unusually located within the precincts of the castle itself; £5/$8. For a break from Turkish food, Çeşme can offer the **Meydan Chinese**, behind the playground at the centre of the harbour; not-too-adventurous Chinese cooking for £9/$14. On Yali Caddesi, the **Buhara**, with outside tables, specializes in spicy Gaziantep-style kebabs and other grilled meats; £4/$6.

In Ilica, the **Anilar Restaurant** has good food (£4/$6) and, as night falls, music and dancing. Dalyan has several good fish restaurants, as has Altinkum, although on the rest of the peninsula you'll be fortunate to find anything beyond the basic *lokanta.*

Kuşadasi Bay   218

Selçuk   220

Ephesus   222

Kuşadasi   228

The Cities of Ionia   231

From the Coast to Lake Bafa   231

Priene   231

Miletus   234

Didyma   236

Along the Maeander to Pamukkale   238

Aphrodisias   240

Pamukkale   242

Caria   244

Bodrum   248

Bodrum Peninsula   251

Marmaris   256

The South Aegean Coast

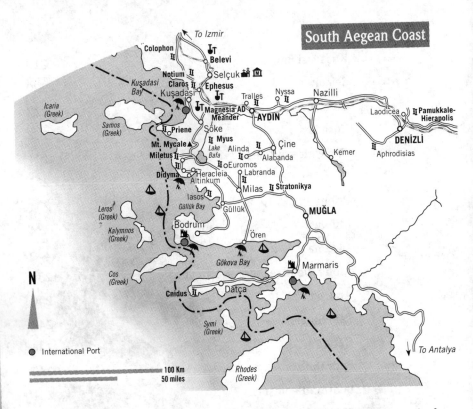

Map labels:

To Izmir

Colophon

Belevi

Notium · Selçuk

Kuşadası · Claros · Ephesus

Bay · Kuşadası · Tralles · Nyssa · Nazilli

Icaria (Greek) · Magnesia AD · Meander · AYDIN · Laodicea · Pamukkale-Hierapolis

Samos (Greek) · Priene · Söke · Çine · DENIZLI

Mt. Mycale · Myus · Alinda · Kemer · Aphrodisias

Miletus · Lake Bafa · Alabanda

Didyma · Heracleia · Euromos · Labranda

Altınkum · Iasos · Milas · Stratonikya

Leros (Greek) · Güllük Bay · Güllük · MUĞLA

Kalymnos (Greek) · Bodrum · Ören

Cos (Greek) · Gökova Bay · Marmaris

N

Cnidus · Datça

Symi (Greek)

International Port

100 Km
50 miles

Rhodes (Greek)

To Antalya

This section of the coast encompasses most of ancient Ionia, where much of western civilization was born in the 7th and 6th centuries BC. But the region is blessed with more than the remains of great cities and past glories. As Herodotus, a native of the region, wrote, the climate of Ionia is the fairest in the world, and it is endowed with a light-filled Aegean beauty—'all repetitive variations, outline beyond outline, like the tones of a voice beyond words', as Freya Stark put it.

Names like Kuşadası, Bodrum and Marmaris, only a few years ago sounding strange and exotic, now roll off the tongue of many a travel agent, yachtsman (the jagged coast is exceptionally well suited for sailing) and even the most timid package-tourist. Yet, as modern and trendy as the south Aegean coast has become, it is paradoxically the only place in Turkey where you're likely to see a camel or, in winter, that most exotic of Turkish sporting events, camel wrestling.

Kuşadası Bay

This gently curving bay, *Kuşadası Körfezi*, has become one of the hot spots for tourism on the Aegean coast. Its two poles, Kuşadası and Selçuk, maintain a neatly symbiotic relationship to keep all the visitors happy; together they do their best to fill the shoes of neighbouring Ephesus, one of the great metropolises of the ancient world and now one of its most evocative ruins. Kuşadasi, an improbable, noisy and overbuilt resort, supplies the beaches and seafood; Selçuk, an amiable modern town, offers itself as the most convenient base for seeing Ephesus and the other classical remains in the area.

Getting Around

Colophon and Claros are difficult to reach by minibus from Selçuk or Kuşadasi, but it can be done—better if you have your own transportation, and can combine the ruins with a spell on some of the isolated beaches in the area. Selçuk and Kuşadasi can easily be reached by bus from anywhere, and there is also a typically slow rail connection to Selçuk from Izmir. For Belevi, there is an infrequent dolmuş from Selçuk. There's no problem exploring Ephesus from Selçuk; you could take a dolmuş there but the 2-mile walk is very pleasant and passes the Temple of Artemis. The only way to get to the House of the Virgin Mary, 5km from town, is by taxi.

Selçuk's bus terminal is exactly in the town centre, on Atatürk Caddesi (the main Izmir–Muğla road). Through buses from either direction, however, do not usually stop in the station, but just outside it on Atatürk Caddesi facing the town park. From Selçuk there are frequent connections to Pamukkale and to Aphrodisias (*see* below); the Palâle line has ten buses a day to the village closest to the latter, Karacasu. If you want a look at the ancient Carian cities to the south, ask around at Selçuk or Kuşadasi; bus arrangements change frequently, and in summer there are often tours on offer.

Tourist Information

Selçuk: in the park in the town centre, facing Atatürk Caddesi, opposite the museum, ✆ 892 6945.

Colophon

One Ionian city splendid in its own day, but almost forgotten now, is **Colophon**, most easily reached by heading directly south from Izmir. It was the only city built far from the sea, and the home town of Plato's courtesan Archeanassa ('Even upon her wrinkles there rests a bitter passion'). Colophon was renowned in antiquity for its horses and mighty cavalry, and for its fierce dogs trained to fight in battle; yet it was also one of few places in the ancient Greek world where dogs were sacrificed (the only deity that demanded dogs was Hecate, the underworld deity who may have originated in Caria). Because its land was incredibly fertile and its fleet powerful, it became so wealthy that the men wore kingly purple robes daily, drenched their hair with musk, and ate 12-course meals. Lavish living made them soft, and Colophon was one of the first Greek cities to fall to the Lydians. In the Hellenistic age, it became a backwater as Ephesus stole all the trade; eventually it was destroyed by Lysimachus, and its inhabitants relocated to his newly-refounded Ephesus. Today little remains of Colophon except a few scanty walls.

Notium and Claros

Notium nearby was the port of Colophon, and although mainly visited these days for its sandy beach, it has some well-preserved sections of wall, the foundations of a temple and stoa and a small theatre. What really makes the trip to the area worthwhile are the excavations at

Claros, a 20-minute walk from Notium. Here stood the famous temple and oracle of Clarian Apollo, visited from as far away as Britain and southern Russia.

The valley of the temple is flooded every year, and over the ages the temple disappeared in the mud. In the 1960s it was rediscovered and excavated by the French, although in the winter good parts of it will be underwater. The lower chamber, to which the priest would descend to drink the sacred water and utter the oracles, is all flooded, but you can make out the purposely disconcerting maze-like corridor that led to the Adyton, the sacred oracle chamber. The temple was built in the Doric style, surprisingly, because Doric was usually reserved for temples on heights, where it showed to better advantage. A sacred way led to the entrance from the monumental **Propylaea**, or gate. Around the temple, fragments of three colossal statues—of Apollo, Artemis, and their mother Leto—lie strewn about; Apollo's leg alone measures over 10 feet. The **altar**, just east of the temple, is some 60 feet long, half dedicated to Apollo, and half to Dionysus, who, as at Delphi, took over the temple during the winter months, when the sun god went to frolic with the Hyperboreans in Britain. Near the temple there's a **sundial** dedicated to Dionysus and a smaller **Ionic temple** dedicated to Apollo's twin, Artemis, lies northwest of the main temple.

Although the structures date from the Hellenistic age, Claros had been a sacred spot for hundreds of years before. The weary, pregnant Leto stopped here as she fled the relentless jealousy of Hera, before giving birth to Apollo and Artemis on the island of Delos; and here the famous Sibyl, Herophile, predicted that both Asia and Europe would be destroyed because of Helen.

Selçuk

Selçuk, the small but attractive successor to ancient Ephesus, is a happy town, grown prosperous on its proximity to some of the finest attractions of western Turkey. Ephesus is an easy walk away, the bustling and overripe Kuşadasi a half-hour drive. Priene, Miletus and Didyma can all be seen by day trip. Add that to the sites and charm of Selçuk itself, and after a day or so, you may not want to leave. Because of the area's religious associations—including the home of the Virgin Mary herself—it is extremely popular among Christian tourists and groups; everybody comes here, even the pope (1979).

Selçuk has an exceptionally fine **archaeology museum** (*open daily exc Mon 8.30–12 and 1–6.30; adm*). Besides the two famous *cult images of Ephesian Artemis* (*see* below), look for a dramatic tableau of Odysseus blinding the Cyclops, some lovely carved ivory furniture, erotic statuary from the brothel, and a frieze from the altar of the Temple of Domitian in a style that can only be called Roman Art Deco. From Domitian's statue in the temple a weird colossal head and arm have survived, looking like lost props from a Fellini film. Note the 6th century AD statue of the city's consul Stephanos. His head is only the last occupant of the body; the townspeople would change it whenever a new one was elected.

Out in the courtyard is more sculpture, including a memorable 2nd century BC stele with a relief of a sexy Dionysus, and a sarcophagus with the nine Muses on it.

Moods of a Goddess

The star attractions of the Selçuk museum are undoubtedly the two statues of Ephesian Artemis, so covered with hanging, breast-like thingumabobs that she resembles a pine cone. No one knows what they really were intended to represent, but they certainly aren't breasts—the image of Zeus Stratius at

Labranda had them too. The earliest cult images in Greek temples were weird, primitive objects dating back to remotest antiquity: conical wooden figures, shapeless stone lumps or even meteorites. The Selçuk statues, products of a very sophisticated age, nevertheless offer plenty of clues to the primeval sources; they rank among the most striking images of a deity ever produced in antiquity, and are worth looking at in detail. One Artemis wears a *polos*, a kind of crown suggesting a wall and towers that is often worn by Athena, or by the tutelary goddess of any city, which was certainly Artemis's status in Ephesus. The other has a necklace with the signs of the Zodiac, pictured just as we know them today. Astrology first came into the west in Hellenistic times, brought back from Babylon after Alexander's conquest, and it was the fascination of the age.

Note the animals, in ranks of three, that adorn much of the statues' surface, betraying this Artemis's true meaning as just a Hellenized, up-to-date name for the primeval Anatolian goddess, the mountaintop *potnia theron*, or 'mistress of the wild things'. One statue has plenty of bees on it, which to a Greek mind would be more appropriate to Aphrodite—but then, this lady does not have much to do with the tenets of classical Olympian religion. An outlandish but currently popular theory says that Artemis's 'breasts' are really testicles. Cybele, another aspect of the same Anatolian goddess, presided over an orgiastic cult whose priests offered her the ultimate ex-voto; they castrated themselves (this cult eventually spread as far west as Gaul. In the last centuries of ancient Rome it was quite popular among the city's poor).

The consciously sanitized version of Artemis that we see in Greek mythology—the virgin huntress revelling with her nymphs, may be unpredictable and a bit dangerous, but she's never a serious threat to the reasoned order of Zeus and her brother Apollo. She is the poetic creation of a very civilized age. But as the aspect of the Great Goddess who delights in untamed nature, and rules the hunters who live from it, her origins may go back as far as the Paleolithic. As Artemis, she first appears in a Linear B inscription from Minoan Crete. The Greek colonists in Asia Minor melded her image onto the transcendant goddess already worshipped everywhere in Anatolia. Everywhere, though, her rituals carry dark hints of a violent, half-remembered past. In many Greek cities, they included the drawing of human blood, likely a sublimation of what was once human sacrifice. More commonly, Artemis would demand a vast sacrifice of living things, hung on trees or columns and incinerated in a great bonfire. As Pausanias described one: '...all manner of victims, also wild boar and deer and fawns and some even bring the cubs of wolves and bears, and others full grown beasts... Then they set fire to the wood. I saw indeed a bear and other beasts struggling to escape from the first force of the flames and escaping by sheer strength. But those who threw them in drag them up again on the fire. I never heard of anyone being wounded by the wild beasts.'

In any case, not a goddess to be taken lightly. You'll meet her everywhere in Anatolia, as Cybele or Artemis or Aphrodite or whatever—originally it's all the same. And in one form or another she will always be around. Currently, the people of Selçuk are so taken with their Artemis that they have reproduced her in larger-than-life marble on a fountain facing Atatürk Caddesi, just north of the town hall. That will give the archaeologists of the future something to think about.

Dominating Selçuk is the old acropolis of Ephesus, which Justinian crowned with the **Basilica of St John**. The Apostle John spent his last years in Ephesus writing his Gospel, and his burial spot is marked by a slab of marble. The church was in the form of a cross, covered by a large central dome with several smaller domes forming the arms—before the whole was shattered by earthquakes. Today the entrance is through the **Gate of Persecution**, a Christian misinterpretation of a relief of a battle scene: the baptistry and apse with some surviving 10th-century frescoes have been reconstructed. Directly above towers the **Citadel of Ayasoluk**, with its Byzantine–Turkish fortifications and grand views (*often closed*). Just below the church stands a key work of the Selcuk Turks, the **Isa Bey Mosque** (1375). Isa Bey was a prince of the Aydin Turks who briefly ruled western Anatolia, and his mosque was the first to be built with a courtyard and stalactite vaulting, anticipating the later Ottoman style.

Ephesus

Thanks to its proximity to the coastal resorts, more tourists come to visit Ephesus than any other site in Turkey. But it isn't a genuine city of classical Greece you'll see here, but a relative late-bloomer, a conveniently situated city that the Romans transformed into the capital of their Province of Asia. That was an opulent time for Ephesus, and most of the ruins on display are the magnificent public buildings of the 1st–2nd centuries AD. Compared to the older sites, such as Priene or the Carian cities, Ephesus can seem strangely modern and familiar. Its remains are those of a rich, comfortable place, living on the crest of the wave of classical civilization, centuries after the great centuries of Greek cultural achievment. When you get to know it, you'll certainly notice a kinship with the cities we live in today.

History

Ephesus was first settled by the Lydians and Carians who worshipped the great Anatolian goddess Cybele. When the Ionians arrived, around the 10th century BC, they combined the ancient cult of Cybele with their own of Artemis, a syncretism that had unusual success. But Ephesian Artemis has little in common with the virgin goddess of the hunt; she is an oriental, mysterious, fertility figure. From the start, the cult attracted devotees from across the Mediterranean and its temple was the one constant in the city's history, for Ephesus itself moved no fewer than four times. The early Ionian settlement was on the slopes of Mt Pion (*Panayir Daği*), above the theatre, and its harbour was near Selçuk. The greatest of all the presocratic philosophers, Heraclitus, was born here. Croesus, King of Lydia, conquered Ephesus in 550 BC, but refrained from destroying it when the artless Ephesians tied a rope around the town and bound it to the temple of Artemis. He did however force them to relocate to the defenceless plain near the temple. Lysimachus, Alexander's general and heir to Ionia, noticed that the River Cayster was silting up the port and induced the Ephesians to move again by building new houses downstream and flooding the old with tons of sewage—a convincing argument for those who had wanted to stay put.

In its new location, in the valley between Mts Pion and Coressus, Ephesus became the boom town of Asia Minor. The population doubled when Lysimachus removed the populations of

Ephesus

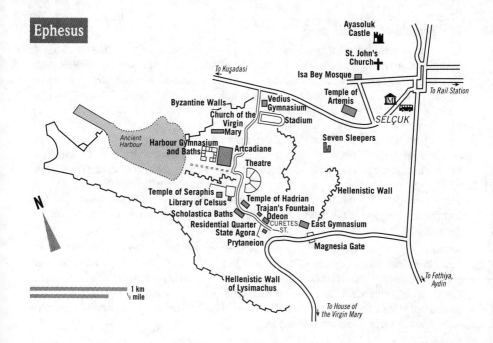

Colophon and Lebedos to Ephesus. In Roman times, it became a provincial capital of the province of Asia, the banking and trade centre of the east, and, with some 500,000 inhabitants, the largest city in Anatolia,

> *devoted to dancers and taken up with pantomimes, and the whole city was full of pipers, and effeminate rascals and noise.*

Philostratus, 1st century AD

Or as Heraclitus, Ephesus' native son, had earlier put it: 'May wealth never leave you, Ephesians, lest your wickedness be revealed.' Four different Roman emperors granted the Ephesians permission to construct a temple for their own worship—a great state honour. Yet Ephesus' prosperity was undermined by one constant vexation: the silting up of its harbour. Several dredgings and other solutions were attempted, with only temporary success; today the sea is more than five miles away.

St Paul

Ephesus in its prime witnessed some of the events that marked the great religious conversion from the goddess Artemis to the new God of the Christians. The Apostle John converted many of the natives even before St Paul came to live in the city. After three years, St Paul left memorably: his preaching attracted so many adherents that the local silversmiths, who made cult figures of Artemis, felt their livelihoods threatened and started a riot, packing the great theatre with people shouting, 'Great is Artemis of the Ephesians!' St Paul left shortly afterwards. With the decline of Rome and the silting of its harbour, Ephesus dwindled, and in the 6th century the city was abandoned for a new site—modern Selçuk.

The Temple of Artemis

Most of what remains in Ephesus today is Roman, except for the melancholy remains of the **Temple of Artemis**, about half a mile from the excavations on the Kuşadasi–Selçuk road. This, one of the Seven Wonders of the Ancient World, is now marked by a single column re-erected on a ruined foundation in the middle of a swamp, its tip a favourite nesting place for storks. At least three temples have stood on the site. The original, built around the 7th century BC, was replaced in the 6th with a far grander edifice (significantly bigger, for the sake of status, than the temple of Hera, under construction on the nearby island of Samos). The temple measured 179 by 374 feet, larger than a football field, and four times the size of the Parthenon, surrounded by a forest of 129 columns. For all their sophistication, the Greek cities loved to compete in the same boosterish way American cities do with their skyscrapers today. The Artemision was undoubtedly planned to be the biggest temple in the world, just a few feet longer and wider than the then-reigning champ, the 175 by 367ft Temple of Olympian Zeus in Akragas (Agrigento, Sicily).

Amazingly, the whole thing was made of marble, except for the wooden roof and inner architrave. In 356 BC, on the night of Alexander the Great's birth (or so they say), a mad arsonist in search of immortal fame burned it down. It lay in ruins until Alexander himself came and offered to pay for its restoration. The Ephesians politely declined, with the excuse that one god should not build a temple to another. They then rebuilt it themselves on the same massive scale, and filled it with treasure and statues.

Gigantic as it was, by the mid-19th century, when the British railway engineer J. T. Wood tried to find it, not a trace remained: Justinian had quarried most of its marble for the Basilica of St John (*see* below) and the rest had receded into the mud. For nine years, Wood searched for the temple, until 1874 when an inscription was discovered, giving directions to the Sacred Way. Wood excavated the road and followed it to the great temple.

The Main Excavations

Excavations of Lysimachus' Ephesus were begun in 1895 by the Austrians and continue to this day. Along the road from the parking lot lies the vast **Gymnasium of Vedius**, built in AD 150 by a prominent citizen, Publius Vedius Antonius; the structure includes well-preserved baths and a latrine. Next to it is a partially excavated **stadium**, much quarried by the Selcuks for their castle. Across the road are the few remains of a temple from the time of Croesus; south of this are ruined Byzantine baths and the long, narrow **church of Agia Maria**, built in the 2nd century as a bank and market. In the 3rd century it was converted into a church dedicated to the Virgin Mary—the first church anywhere consecrated to the Mother of God. In AD 431, the Emperor Theodosius II convened the Third Ecumenical Council here, which declared Jesus to be both the son of Mary and the Son of God.

The Theatre

Beyond the parking lot and the ticket booth are the remains of the **Harbour Gymnasium, Palaestrae and Baths**, the largest surviving structure in Ephesus, only part of which has been uncovered. It gives on to the **Arcadiane**, the street to the harbour, named for its builder, the Byzantine emperor Arcadius (d. 408). Paved with marble and lined with colonnades and stoas, this was one of the few thoroughfares in antiquity to be furnished with street lamps. At the end of the street rises the majestic **theatre** carved into the flank of Mt Pion, built in the

Hellenistic era and remodelled by the Romans under Claudius and Trajan. In classic Greek theatre, all the action took place in the orchestra, but by the Hellenistic age, the actors performed on a small raised stage, leaving the orchestra to the increasingly irrelevant chorus. By Roman times, fashion had moved all the drama to the stage, which reached grand operatic proportions in Ephesus—three levels with an ornate façade, adorned with statues and columns. The theatre seats 24,000, and has been restored with a heavy hand for the annual Ephesus Festival. The top seats offer a fine view of the ruined city.

Along the Marble Road

From the theatre, the **Marble Road**, grooved with deep cart ruts, was the main street of Ephesus. Following it will bring you to a 1st-century **Doric stoa** and, the most elegant of Ephesus' buildings, the **Library of Celsus**, with its lovely white marble façade, fine carvings and statues. This was built in AD 110 by the consul Gaius Julius Aquila as a temple-tomb for his father, Gaius Julius Celsus, whose unopened lead casket is still in its sarcophagus in the grave chamber. The reading room of the library had three floors; as in Pergamon, niches in the walls mark former shelves for the scrolls. Although the reading room was burned by the Goths in AD 262, the façade survived unharmed, and in the 5th century the depression around it was filled with water to make a reflecting pool. Behind the **agora** (currently being restored) stood the **Temple of Serapis**, built in the 2nd century, perhaps by the Egyptian residents of the city, although the god Serapis had a cult following among Greek and Roman alike, and provided serious competition for Christianity in its early days. Like the Temple of Serapis in Pergamon, this one was massive; each of its eight monolithic columns weighed 57 tons.

Street of the Curetes

At the library the street turns and becomes the **Street of the Curetes**. According to the Ephesians, Artemis was born nearby, at a place called Ortygia; her mother, the goddess Leto pursued by Hera, was able to deliver her here thanks to the Curetes, the young men who frightened the vindictive Hera away by banging on their shields. The Curetes had performed a similar service in Crete, at the cradle of the infant Zeus, where their banging kept his cannibalistic father Cronos from hearing Zeus' cries. Their presence in Ephesus, and the fact that an order of priests in the Artemision were called the Curetes, suggests that the cult of the Ephesian Artemis long predates her first temple.

The **Baths of Scholastica** (2nd century AD) were renamed after a Christian lady who remodelled them in the year 400. Her headless statue still presides over the entrance; inscriptions indicate that the baths also served as the town brothel. Much of the stone Scholastica used for her remodelling came from the neighbouring Corinthian **Temple of Hadrian**, which had partially collapsed in an earthquake. Part of it has been reconstructed, and with its four reliefs (the originals are in the museum), this shrine to the good gay emperor is one of the most attractive in the city. Opposite, on the slopes of Bülbüldağ (Mountain of the Nightingales), a large **residential quarter** (*separate admission*) has recently been excavated, bringing to light

LIBRARY OF CELSUS

many luxurious mansions owned by Ephesian merchants, complete with mosaics and frescoes.

Curetes Street continues to the fountain of Trajan, or **nymphaion**. A colossal statue of the emperor once stood over the fountain, and what remains—his giant feet, one resting on the world—suggests a Rome already too big for its britches. The street continues past numerous small buildings, some reliefs and fountains, to Domitian Street, leading to the ruined **Temple of Domitian** (1st century AD), the first of the four temples consecrated to imperial worship. A huge statue of the sporty but paranoid Domitian stood within, enjoying a splendid view from the temple's platform. Little survives of the **state agora** next to the temple. Adjoining the north stoa of the agora is the **prytaneion**, or city hall, and the **odeon**, which was probably used for government meetings rather than concerts. An eternal flame was kept burning in the Prytaneion and it was here that the museum's two statues of Artemis were found, carefully buried—perhaps by a secret worshipper to hide them from the Christians.

The Seven Sleepers

The road continues past a great fountain, another bath and the **East Gymnasium** (all 2nd century AD) on its way to the ruined **Magnesian Gate**, one of the two main gates built by Emperor Vespasian *c*. AD 75. The Sacred Way to the Temple of Artemis passed through here and around Mt Pion. Following the track, you pass a large, early Christian cemetery that surrounds a church and the graves of the **Seven Sleepers**, a popular motif in Christian and Turkish folklore. In the mid-3rd century, seven young Christians of Ephesus hid in a mountain cave to escape the mandatory imperial worship. They fell asleep, the cave was sealed up, and when they were shaken awake by an earthquake, discovered that they had slept for 200 years. When they died the Ephesians buried them here, and a church was built over their graves that became a popular pilgrimage site—an echo of the myth of Endymion (*see* below). In fact there were really eight Sleepers; one of them had his dog with him.

The track continues to modern Selçuk. (The track to the right from the Magnesian Gate leads to the **Walls of Lysimachus**, well preserved in many places.)

The House of the Virgin Mary

In a municipal park 5 miles (8km) southeast of Selçuk is the Panaya Kapulu, or **Meryemana**, the house where Mary, who accompanied St John to Ephesus, is said to have lived and died *c*. AD 37–45. While the site has always been associated with the Virgin, the house was unknown until a German invalid called Catherine Emmerich (1774–1824), who had never been to Ephesus, had a series of visions which enabled her to give exact directions to the house and a detailed description of its appearance. In 1891, the Lazarist order of Izmir found it exactly where and as she had described it: a brick house of the 6th century, its foundations dating back to the 1st. (The story curiously parallels Mehmet Fatih's dream discovery of the grave of Mohammed's standard-bearer Eyüp near Istanbul.) In 1967, Pope Paul IV gave the house its certificate of authenticity and it was recently visited by Pope John Paul II. The Virgin's tomb, according to Catherine Emmerich, is about a mile from the house, but has never been found. The house is a busy pilgrimage site; both the Orthodox and Catholics (as well as many local people) gather here to celebrate the Assumption of the Virgin on 15 August. Mass is celebrated every Sunday, at 10.30.

The Church does tolerate some competition in Virginal abodes. In Loreto, the famous pilgrimage site in central Italy, you may visit Mary's original home from Nazareth. As the story goes, the house was divinely transported to a hill in Istria (in Slovenia today), but God changed his mind and airmailed it to Italy in 1294, just coincidentally at a time when the pope was trying to drum up interest in a new Crusade.

Belevi

Ten miles (16km) northeast of Selçuk, on the Izmir road, the village of **Belevi** has two unusual monumental tombs. One, known as the **Belevi Mausoleum**, is just off the road; it stands on a massive square base carved from living rock, topped by a chamber of marble, surrounded by columns and reliefs of the battle of lapiths and centaurs; the sarcophagus, however, was hidden in the base in an effort to foil grave robbers (it is now in the Selçuk Museum). Many believe the man buried here was the Seleucid King Antiochus II who died in Ephesus in 246 BC, poisoned by his wife. The other tomb, a hilltop tumulus surrounded with a wall of fine masonry, probably dates from the same century.

Selçuk © (232–)

Where to Stay
expensive/moderate

Accommodation in Selçuk is more than ample, though there is little that really stands out. If you really want to see the sights in style, it can be done just as conveniently from one of the resort hotels at Pamucak, on the way to Kuşadasi (*see* below).

Very near to the entrance to Ephesus, and set in an attractive garden, the **(M1) Tusan Efes Moteli**, Efes Yolu, © 892 6060, is quiet and comfortable; double rooms go for £10/$15. In Selçuk itself, the pick of the bunch is the **(M2) Kalehan**, Atatürk Caddesi 49, © 892 6154, a renovated, charmingly decorated stone inn with a swimming pool; £12/$18, for a bit more there are four luxury suites. The hotels **★★Atadan**, Atatürk Caddesi 6, © 892 6297, and **★★Mekan Hotel Villa**, Atatürk Mah 1, © 892 6299, are both newer buildings with balconies and charge about £15/$22, breakfast included.

Two otherwise unremarkable hotels facing the aqueduct are very popular with tourists for their rooms with views of the nesting storks along the way: the **★★Aksoy**, © 892 6040, and the **★★Victoria**, © 892 3203, both with rooms for about £7/$12. Some places in Selçuk seem to be in the business of exploiting tourists, so be a bit selective about letting someone lead you away from the bus station.

cheap

In Selçuk there are more than 70 pensions to choose from, the vast majority being clean, comfortable and cheap. Most convenient for Ephesus are those in the back streets behind the museum, such as the **Australian Pension** at Prof Miltner Sok 7, © 892 6050, which charges £4/$6 for a double room with a free ride to Ephesus thrown in. It fills up fast in the summer with backpackers, so it's best to phone ahead. Also noteworthy are the nearby **Barim**, an old Greek house with a stork on its chimney on Turgut Reis Sokak, © 892 6927, and the friendly, very basic **Bolero**, Okul Sok 9 off Atatürk Caddesi, © 891 8422, both charging about £3/$5. Next to the Barim on Turgut Reis, the **Kirhan** offers agreeable small rooms and lifts to the ruins and beaches, for what must be among the lowest rates in town.

Camping choices are limited; it seems a choice between the simple **Garden**, out near the Isa Bey Cami, which has a pool but little else, and the better equipped **Pamucak Turistik Tesisleri**, just off the beach in Pamucak, © 897 3636.

Eating Out

The pedestrian streets in the centre of Selçuk make a lively scene on summer evenings; there are a number of restaurants geared towards the tourist trade, of which the best is the one with the attractive kilims spread over the tables out on the street, the **Tat Restoran** on Cengiz Topel Caddesi, run by a friendly young fellow from out East; a very good selection of mezes, and *saç kavurma* done at your table; £4/$6 or less. One of the nicest places to dine in Selçuk is the **Park Restoran**, in the park at the town centre: outside tables underneath the trees, and kebabs and moussaka for about £3/$5.

Kuşadasi

In the early '70s, **Kuşadasi** was still a sleepy little port town; today it holds the dubious distinction of being one of Turkey's slickest and most expensive resorts, where seven or eight cruise ships call each day, and luxury yachts under many different flags bask in the marina. More than any other resort in Turkey, this town was built by package tourism.

Getting Around

To reach Kuşadasi, take either a direct bus from Izmir or a minibus from Söke or Selçuk. Minibuses trundle continually up and down the coast, linking the resort to all the beaches, and you'll be able to catch one on Atatürk Caddesi near the harbour for most points. Minibuses to Selçuk, Dilek National Park and more distant points begin from the little station on Adnan Menderes Bulvari, three short streets east of Inonu Bulvari. The big buses, for Izmir and more distant points, use the Yeni Garaj, south of the centre on Çevre Yolu (the road for Söke).

Most of the coastal and Greek Island cruises stop here, and Kuşadasi is also linked year-round with the Greek island of Samos. This is probably the busiest of the cross-border ferries; except Sundays, there will usually always be a morning and afternoon boat, and more if demand warrants it. In the summer as many as five boats make the crossing each day—often tiny, cabin cruiser-type boats with room for just a few people. With the bizarre winds that frequent this part of the Aegean, this can be an exciting crossing, even in summer.

Tourist Information

Liman Caddesi, near the quay, © (256) 614 6295

Kuşadasi means 'bird island' in Turkish; off the shore is an islet called Pigeon Island, the site of a Genoese castle, where cafés and the garden are dotted with pigeon houses. The town itself has grown up into a rather unlovely city, with the resort strips stretching out for miles in either direction. At the centre, the **Kale**, most of the streets have been taken over by *pansiyons*, souvenir shops and such; the best indication of what Kuşadasi has become is the rather incredible thoroughfare renamed **Barlar Sokak**—Bar Street—where hordes of indistinguishable t-shirted northerners stumble about aimlessly until 3am any summer night. The city has an entertaining and not at all touristy market on Friday mornings.

The nearest beach is **Kadınlarplaji**, 'Ladies' Beach', 2 miles (3km) south and backed with all the usual trappings of mass tourism. Further on is the aptly named **Long Beach** and beyond that **Silver Beach**. **Kustur Beach** and **Pamucak Beach**, probably the best and least crowded of them all, are north of town off the road to Selçuk.

In 1985 the forests above Kuşadası and Ephesus were hit by a devastating forest fire, but beautiful **Dilek National Park** on the peninsula 20 miles (32km) to the south was spared (*open daily 8–5, later in summer; adm*). The park encompasses beautiful Mt Mycale (modern Samsundağ), its 4082 feet plunging down into the strait facing Samos; it has abundant wildlife, caves, beaches, springs, and a castle. There are camp sites and picnic grounds and paths up the mountain (although visitors are advised not to go walking alone because of the bears). The beaches on the peninsula's northern coast are quieter than those at the resort; they can be found at **Aydinlik**, **İçmeler** and **Kalamaki**, and also near the village of **Güzelcamli**, the closest village to the park.

Samos

Now, as in ancient times, Samos holds its place as the richest and most important Greek island after Crete. Back then, the island produced famous men such as Pythagoras and the astronomer Aristarchus; its great Temple of Hera was known across the Mediterranean—fittingly so, as the goddess herself was born on Samos. Lush and green compared to other islands, Samos sees plenty of tourists throughout the season, so prices can be high. In July or August there will usually be a festival in one of the villages, along with the Wine Festival in August; Samos has been known for its wines since antiquity.

Samos is also the name of the island's capital, the destination of the ferries from Kuşadası. This slick and modern town can offer a museum of archaeology, and good beaches just to the south at Possidonion and Psili Ammos. **Pythagoria**, not far from Samos but on the southern shore, is the biggest draw, with ruins including Hera's temple, walls and a unique half-mile tunnel, built in the 6th century BC.

Kuşadası ✆ (256–)   ***Where to Stay***

There are quite literally hundreds of hotels and pensions in Kuşadası and finding a room is rarely a problem. However, many of the more up-market establishments tend to be block-booked by tour operators in summer, and closed in winter.

luxury

The really exceptional places are not in Kuşadası itself, but on the beaches to either side. At Pamucak, 6km to the north, near Selçuk: the ★★★★★**Ephesus Princess**, ✆ 892 7052, ✆ 892 7079, offers plush air-conditioned rooms, an enormous pool, sauna and hamam and all sports facilities imaginable; in addition to the main building there are also rooms in separate bungalows and some self-catering accommodation. Very similar in amenities and style, the ★★★★**Club Ünlü**, ✆ 892 6731, ✆ 892 5129, is slightly less expensive, and offers a good restaurant on its rooftop terrace.

Other self contained pleasure palaces on the periphery include the ★★★★★**Korumar**, ✆ 614 8243, ✆ 614 5596, a Miami Beach-style complex on a cliffside facing two small coves with beaches. There is a casino and disco, hamam and sauna, two pools and water sports. The ★★★★★**Fantasia Hotel**, Söke Yolu, ✆ 614 8600, 📠 614 2765, is 3 miles (5km) out of town on the road to Söke and has restaurants, bars, a disco, recreational facilities and everything else you would expect for £75/$115.

Slightly less expensive than these, on one of the busier parts of the beach, the ★★★★**Tusan Oteli**, ✆ 614 4495, 📠 614 4498, offers a wide range of recreational facilities and in-room satellite TV; £63/$95.

expensive

Staying in the centre of Kuşadasi isn't much fun, unless you do it at the elegant ★★★**(S) Club Caravanserai**, ✆ 614 4115, open April–Oct, located in the centre of town in a 17th-century caravanserai, with a beautiful garden restaurant in the courtyard; £38/$57. If you'd prefer something nearer the beach, the ★★★**Minay**, Alitepe Sitesi at Kadinlar Beach, ✆ 614 8804, is open all year and a good bargain: air conditioned rooms, some with TV, a hamam and gym.

In a isolated setting (by Kuşadasi standards anyway) 3km from the centre, the ★★★**Zinos**, at Eski İçmeler Mevkii, ✆ 614 3059, has a private beach, restaurant pool and sports opportunities; motel-style rooms with balconies are simple but comfortable. Somewhat similar, with plenty of trees and its own marina is the ★★★**Kismet**, at Akyar Mevkii, Türkmen Mah., ✆ 614 2005.

moderate

These can be a pretty undistinguished lot: an endless supply of concrete chunks with only the names to tell them apart. In the town, and open year-round is the ★★★**Efe Oteli,** at Güvercin Ada Cad. 37, ✆ 614 3660, where a double with bath goes for £18/$27; some fancier rooms go for more. The nearby ★★★**Atine Oteli**, Atatürk Bulv. 38, ✆ 614 7608, is swisher but rather soulless; doubles £28/$42. On a hill overlooking the harbour, the ★★**Stella Oteli**, Bezirgan Sok 44, ✆ 614 1632, has a lofty charm; double rooms with breakfast cost £28/$42. In the centre of town, the **Bahar Pansiyon**, Cephane Sok 12, ✆ 614 1191, is colourful and has a restaurant on the roof; £12/$18. Close to Kadinlar Beach, the ★★**Turkad**, ✆ 614 1405, has a garden and tennis courts.

cheap

As is so often the case in Turkey, most of the cheap hotels and pensions are clustered together in the same area; in Kuşadasi this is one block south of the post office on and around Arslanlar Caddesi. Along this street are the pensions **Su**, ✆ 614 1453, and **Rose**, ✆ 614 1111, both clean and charging about £4/$6; both have common bathroom facilities. On Bezirgan Sokak, the **Eniste**, ✆ 614 2171, and the **Hasgül**, ✆ 614 3641, both have clean simple rooms, some with balconies overlooking the harbour.

Another happy hunting ground for cheap digs is in the streets behind Kadinlar Beach. In this area, the **Emek Pansiyon** (follow the signs from the beach road), ✆ 614 1731, offers good value for money—very clean and airy rooms with private shower and toilet at only £4/$6. One surprisingly nice alternative to Kuşadasi is to spend some time at the village of Güzelcamli, on the boundaries of the Dilek National Park. A number of *pansiyons* have opened here, including the **Aydin**, ✆ 614 8616. The most pleasant of the campsites around Kuşadasi is out on the Izmir road, **Önder Camping**, ✆ 614 2585, which also offers cabins and a restaurant.

Kuşadasi has many expensive fish restaurants on the waterfront, and nothing particularly distinguished. Generally, the further you go from the sea, the less you will have to pay. At the harbour, the **Kazim Usta Restaurant** has a fish tank out front from which you select your hapless dinner; it's not cheap, a full meal with wine costing around £10/$15. In a similar price bracket is the much-praised restaurant at the **Club Caravanserai** (*see* above). A good, inexpensive restaurant with a more authentic Turkish ambience (a rarity in Kuşadasi) is the **Konya Pide Salonu** at Kahramanier Caddesi 65, where a meal of grilled meat, rice, salad and a soft drink should come to no more than £3/$5.

The Cities of Ionia

In ancient times, the heartland of this most gifted province was the valley of the Maeander (modern Menderes), the largest and most important river of western Asia Minor. Its often changing course gave us the word 'meander'; yet as much as the river contributed to trade and the fertility of the soil through its annual, Nile-like flooding, it proved as much a curse as a blessing to Priene and Miletus, the two cities at its mouth. Like Ephesus, both once stood on the coast, but the tons of silt the Maeander carried down to the sea each year filled their harbours, and caused them to be abandoned. Today both are miles from the sea.

From the Coast to Lake Bafa

Getting Around

The village of Söke, with regular connections to Kuşadasi, is the transportation hub for the coastal area, with frequent minibus service to Priene and Didyma. There's no public transport to Miletus, though a Söke minibus goes to Yeniköy, 5km away. To reach Lake Bafa, take any bus from Söke to Bodrum and ask to be let off at the lake (*Bafa Gölü*, also called *Çamiçi Gölü*). From the campgrounds, you can take a boat to Heracleia.

For seeing Priene and Miletus, transport is convenient enough (via Söke) if you use Kuşadasi or Selçuk as a base. Another possibility, especially if you have a car, is the resort at Altinkum, near Didyma.

Tourist Information

Altinkum: a booth on the beach at the centre of town is open irregularly in summer.

Priene

Priene was never a large city; estimates of its greatest size range from 4000 to 6000 free citizens. Nor did it play much of a role in the politics of the age. In late Roman times, as its harbour gradually became unusable, the city dwindled, and after the 6th century nothing more is heard of it. Even so, you may well find its ruins more alive, more evocative of the ancient world than any other city in Asia Minor. Despite its small size, Priene had a reputation for talent and accomplishment. The site, largely excavated, reveals a well-built and beautiful city, especially its residential quarters. Also, Priene's very lack of prosperity under the Romans make it, in one sense, unique. Unable to build on the scale of Ephesus, Priene changed little

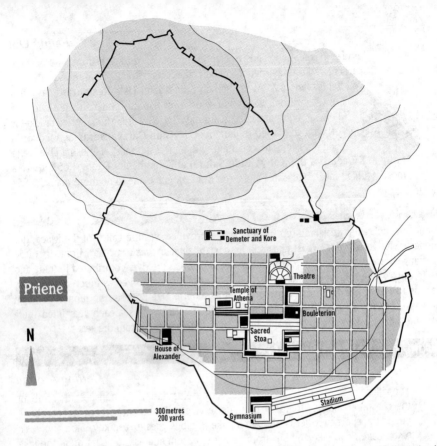

Priene

N

300 metres
200 yards

Sanctuary of Demeter and Kore

Theatre

Temple of Athena

Bouleterion

Sacred Stoa

House of Alexander

Stadium

Gymnasium

after the 4th century BC; outside Greece itself, it remains the best example of a Hellenistic city. Nothing remains of the first Priene, founded at the same time as the other Ionian cities. Its site on the muddy Maeander hasn't even been found. By the 4th century, the advancing coastline made a new foundation necessary, and with the support of Athens, a new Priene was laid out on the slopes of Mt Mycale. Following the precepts of the geometer Hippodamus of Miletus, the steep and difficult site was forced into a strict gridiron plan of narrow streets, with a broad central avenue connecting the major buildings and agoras. The plan has an elegant simplicity, but it's a matter for conjecture whether the Prieneans used it for art's sake or simply to make land surveys easier.

The Site

After a fair climb up from the parking lot, you enter Priene through the northwest gate. Continue across the unexcavated portion of the town to one of the finest extant examples of a classical Greek **theatre**. Unlike the theatres elsewhere in Turkey, built or remodelled under the Romans, this one is small and horseshoe-shaped, leaving ample space for the orchestra and chorus, the centre of attention in a classical Greek play. The seats around the orchestra were for the nobles of the city, a kind of ancient dress circle. At the centre is an altar, dedicated to Dionysus. Also unlike later works, there is no elaborate stage building. The small colonnaded structure, the **proskenion**, dates from the 2nd century BC. Originally, the three doors were used for the entrance of actors, and the spaces between them covered with painted boards for scenery. The roof of the proskenion, used for the *deus ex machina*, took more and more of the action as drama evolved; eventually it came to hold the action, and the proscenium became what we know as the stage. Facing it, at the right-hand end of the first row of seats, is a square stone base that held a water clock; as Greek theatres also served for political meetings, and occasionally for important trials, the water clock controlled the time allotted to each speaker.

Immediately below the theatre are the foundations of a Byzantine church and a gymnasium. Below these lies the **agora** and centre of Priene. On its north side, the **sacred stoa**, according to its inscriptions, was built as a gift of King Ariarthres VI of Cappadocia. Behind it, the well-preserved **bouleuterion** or council hall (200 BC) was the subject of a beautifully drawn reconstruction that appears in most books on ancient Greek architecture. Even among its ruins, you can gain an insight into the public life of an ancient Greek democracy. In the bouleuterion, there were seats for 600–700 citizens, who discussed matters not crucial enough to submit to the entire citizen assembly. Speakers stood next to the altar that held an eternal flame, symbolizing the purity and continuity of Priene's civic life; as they spoke, their peers, on three sides, were close enough to look them in the eye. Next to the bouleuterion is the **prytaneion**, where committees delegated by the council dealt with routine city business.

The Temple of Athena

The agora was the central square of Priene, devoted to commercial and religious affairs as well as political. The small square just to the east was the city's food market, while the sanctuary of Zeus Olympios, now gone, occupied the square's eastern face. Just to the northwest of the agora, stairs from another stoa lead up to the most important building of Priene, the **Temple of Athena**, a classic example of the Ionian order. Its architect, Pytheos, also designed the Mausoleum of Halicarnassus, but thought more of this temple, so much so that he wrote a book about it which was used as a textbook by architects throughout the Mediterranean. Several of the columns have been re-erected, and it's not hard to imagine how the temple must have appeared looming over the agora, Priene's most conspicuous landmark, visible for miles around. Here, as in all the city's buildings, the grey weathered surface of the stone hides a luminous cream-coloured marble from Mt Mycale, which the Greeks painted bright colours.

An inscription on the temple of Athena relates that Alexander the Great financed its completion. For this, and for their liberation from the Persians, the Prieneans devoted a small shrine to him, in the company of the other gods. The **House of Alexander** is near the western gate of the central avenue. Along the way, you'll pass the excavated residential district of Priene. Although this was laid out in a rigid grid plan, there was a remarkable individuality in the inner plans of the houses: nearly all had a central courtyard and columnar porches, and many had second floors. The finest ones are just a few squares west of the theatre.

Other sites on the north and south sides of town require some climbing. In the northern heights, not too far above the theatre, is the oldest temple in Priene, the **Sanctuary of Demeter and Kore** where the *temenos* wall, benches to hold votive statues, and the sacrificial pit can be seen. To the south, just below the agora at the city's walls, are the **gymnasium**, with its well-preserved washrooms, where the water poured out of lion-headed spouts, and the **stadium**. Like the theatre, this is a rare example of the earlier Greek style, and was never remodelled into a Roman extravaganza. Seats are on one side only, and the course is a short and simple one-way track. Remains of the starting gate are near the entrance from the gymnasium: the Greeks started their runners as we do horses.

Miletus

Priene stood on the northern edge of the Latmian Gulf, the inlet now filled by the advancing delta of the Maeander. On the southern shore was **Miletus**, first among the Greek cities until the rise of Athens in the 5th century BC. Few cities have ever achieved such power and brilliance, and left so little to show for it. The river again is to blame. Of the original Miletus so few traces remain that scholars still dispute its precise location. The present ruins date from the second foundation, after the original city was devastated by the Persians in 495 BC.

History

Miletus' origins are shadowy, though recent excavations have produced finds that go back to *c*. 1600 BC. Ancient writers variously claimed its founding as the work of Carians, Lycians or Cretans. The city was probably the *Millewanda* that appears in Hittite records of the 14th century, a thorn in the side of Hittite King Mursilis II. Millewanda was the capital of a people known as the Ahhiyawans—probably the origin of the 'Achaeans' in Homer. Mythology credits an eponymous founder, a mortal son of Apollo who sailed from Minoan Crete and made Miletus an important seaport. With the collapse of the Minoans, Miletus was occupied by the Mycenaeans; when the Ionians seized the town, they killed all the Cretan men and married their wives, lousy but typical behaviour for the period. By 700 BC, Ionian Miletus began to prosper, controlling the Aegean trade routes and sending out more colonies than any other Greek city—90 of them, from Naukratis on the Nile delta to Sinope on the Black Sea.

Miletus' greatest colony, however, was the human mind. The Milesians were the first to look at the world from a detached, universal viewpoint. Thales, foremost among the Seven Sages and the first philosopher, suggested that water was the origin of all life; his follower Anaximander declared all things were infinite in substance, that the earth hung free, only one of infinite worlds; while the third great Milesian philosopher, Anaximenes, understood everything to be made of air, either rarefied or condensed, which encompassed the world like a human soul.

As the Persian menace grew, Ionian thinkers began to immigrate to the growing city of Athens, keeping philosophy alive after Miletus suffered its fatal defeat in 495 BC. It broke the heart of the ancient world: when a play called *The Fall of Miletus* was performed in Athens, it caused the whole audience to burst into tears, for which the dramatist was fined a thousand drachmae.

Miletus was rebuilt immediately after the Persians flattened it, on a new site and on a new grid plan according to the precepts of its native son, the geometer Hippodamus. Its arrangement of agoras and public buildings was a triumph of Greek urban design, but you can't see that from the ruins. If Priene is the most evocative Greek city, Miletus is the biggest archaeological disappointment of Turkey. So thoroughly has the Maeander scrubbed away and silted over its ruins that little beside the theatre remains. It is even difficult to tell where the coastline was, and the city that contributed so much to western civilization has become a creepy desolation of muck and prickly weeds.

In Aristotle, we read that the great Miletan philosopher Anaximander believed that the water was gradually drying up from the earth—it has been suggested he got the idea from watching his city's harbour gradually silt up.

Philosophy Starts Here

According to Aristotle's follower Eudemus, Thales, one of the 'seven wise men' of antiquity, brought geometry into Greece from Egypt, and he showed how to use angles to find the distance from the shore to a ship in the harbour. Besides Egypt, he may also have visited Babylon, or perhaps he learned his astronomy only from contacts with the east, connections for which the cosmopolitan trading city of Miletus was well placed. His famous trick was to predict the solar eclipse of 585 BC. Though other peoples, the Chinese and the neolithic Britons, had done this long ago, it was quite a stunt for a 6th-century Greek, and it made his reputation for wisdom. 'The man's a Thales!', says a character in Aristophanes' *Birds*, written two centuries later.

Thales' successor, and possibly his student, was Anaximander, who drew the first maps among the Greeks and built the first model of the heavens and the first sundials. His student Anaximines, yet another Milesian, speculated on the cosmos and the nature of matter. From nearby Samos came Pythagoras, whose monumental contributions to mathematics are familiar enough; his brand of mathematical mysticism, in which all things could be reduced to numbers, dominates the thinking of scientifically-minded people today. All of these founders of philosophy wrote in verse, and only tantalizing fragments of their work remain—as with Heraclitus of Ephesus, the deepest and strangest of all, who left behind fascinating epigrams in the spirit of Zen :

> *This most beautiful cosmos is a pile of things poured out at random.*

> *It is not possible to step twice into the same river... it scatters and again comes together, and approaches and recedes.*

The lives of the Ionian philosophers covered only a few generations. By the 5th century the leading lights of philosophy, such as Zeno and Empedocles, were coming from the distant colonies in southern Italy and Sicily. Until the time of Plato and Aristotle, very few Greek thinkers came from Greece itself. Ionia, like Italy, was the 'new world' for the Greeks, a wide-open society of booming cities where free thinking was considerably easier than in the tradition-bound homeland.

The genuinely subversive contribution of the Ionian thinkers comes through in their attitude towards religion. As Xenophanes of Colophon put it, in one of the few surviving bits of his poetry:

> *Ethiopians say their gods are flat-nosed and dark,*
> *Thracians that theirs are blue-eyed and red-haired...*
> *If oxen and horses and lions had hands*
> *and were able to draw with their hands and do things the same as men,*
> *horses would draw the shapes of gods to look like horses,*
> *and oxen to look like oxen...*

Never before had anyone looked upon sacred things with such a critical eye. But the first philosophers were not trying to destroy religion, but to make faith square with what could be understood by reason. Their consensus was that God is one. Ideas make their way slowly, and the Ionians could not know they were paving the way for the acceptance of Christianity many centuries later. But that, however significant, was only a small part of their achievment. The Ionian philosophers' great discovery was a perception of order at work in the world, an order comprehensible to the human mind. Their speculations marked the beginnings of philosophy, and also of science—the beginnings of western civilization, no less.

The Site

With a map from the small **museum** half a mile south of the ruins (*open daily 8.30–5; adm*), you can locate a few landmarks. Miletus' great **theatre**, then as now the most conspicuous landmark, rises on a hillside above one of the city's five harbours, well preserved above the floods of the Maeander. The Roman theatre, with seats for 15,000, was built around the earlier work of the 4th century BC that seated only a third as many. The columns that marked the 'royal box' still stand. Scanty ruins of an agora and the stadium occupy the former harbour's opposite shore. From this side of Miletus, you have a good view of the island of Lade, now a mere lump in the Maeander Plain. Here, in 495 BC the Persian navy destroyed the combined fleets of the Ionian cities and put an end to their rebellion. As leader of the revolt, Miletus' destruction was assured. Ironically, the Persian garrison later took refuge here when Alexander the Great stormed the town.

Climbing over the hill of the theatre will bring you to the **city centre**, a network of stoas, avenues, and agoras around the narrow **Bay of Lions**. In wartime this harbour had special significance; it needed no fortifications on the shore, as a chain could easily be extended across it to protect both the town and the fleet. Some searching among the weeds will reveal the two stone lions that stood on either side of the harbour. Inside the harbour, a large triangular base once held a **monument of Augustus,** commemorating his victory over Cleopatra and Mark Antony at Actium in 31 BC.

Around the harbour, the only structures of interest lie along the wide processional avenue; the first, the **Temple of Apollo Delphinius**, has the foundations of a colonnaded sanctuary with statue bases and a curious circular temple. On the same side of the avenue are the **Capito Baths**, the **gymnasium**, a **nymphaion**, and a 5th-century **church**. If you follow the avenue south through the enormous **south agora**, you'll find a fine 15th-century mosque, **Ilyas Bey Camii**, made of coloured marble salvaged from Miletus, belonging to the nearby village of Yeniköy. The low hill beyond the city's southern walls called *Kalabak Tepe* was the acropolis of the original Miletus founded by Crete, where a few old stones have been found.

Didyma

If Miletus disappoints, **Didyma** won't. Didyma, south of Miletus and in its territory, is a temple complex and not a city. Yet few in western Asia Minor are so well preserved or impressive.

Didyma was a holy site before the Ionians ever arrived, and was believed to be the oldest of the 19 oracles in Asia Minor. The Greeks rededicated the Anatolian cult to their own god Apollo and continued the oracle. When Croesus, the King of Lydia, was considering his invasion of Persia, he wanted the advice of an oracle, but first decided to put three of them to the test. He sent ambassadors to ask each of them, on the same day, 'What is King Croesus doing?' Only Delphi knew he was boiling a lamb and tortoise stew. Didyma failed the test utterly, and when the Persians sacked Miletus they also burned the temple and carried off its statue. The oracle fell silent for 150 years, until it predicted Alexander the Great's victory at Issus. Then the sacred spring suddenly flowed again. A grateful Alexander sent some money, his lieutenant Antiochus brought the statue back, and the oracle declared Alexander to be the son of Zeus.

Seleucus I of Syria and the Milesians started to rebuild the temple on a massive scale, planning to make it the largest in the world. Work continued in fits and starts for some 500 years but was never completed. As with so many other things in the time of Alexander and his successors, the ambition of the original work seems to have overreached all common sense; the technical difficulties in building column-and-lintel architecture on such a scale might well have doomed it from the start. Completed, it would have surpassed even the Artemision at Ephesus. As it is, the temple provides a wonderful lesson in the transience of glory. You may never have heard of Seleucus I, but he ruled an empire that stretched from the Aegean nearly to India, building it a piece at a time with lands snatched from the other generals of Alexander, his former comrades-in-arms. Undoubtedly Seleucus' interest in the temple was in part as political propaganda, and as a monument to himself. Soon after it was begun, Seleucus moved to expand his empire westwards. He landed in Greece, and was assassinated as he stepped out of his boat.

As it was, the unfinished temple was considered by the ancients as one of their greatest works of architecture. In design it is comparable to the Artemision in Ephesus, encompassed by a double row of columns, some 120 in all. The cella, with its 70-foot walls, was too large to be roofed over, so the cult statue of Apollo was kept in a smaller temple behind the cella. Many columns have been re-erected by the excavators. Because the temple was never completed, some are unfluted, and many stone blocks still bear their masons' marks. Every five years the Didymeia—sports, drama, and music contests—was held at the sanctuary and in the **stadium** next to it; names carved in the steps of the temple are those of spectators with reserved seats.

Lake Bafa and Heracleia

Near Didyma are a pair of beauty spots. On the tip of Didyma's peninsula, **Altinkum** boasts fine sandy beaches, and an ambition to someday usurp Kuşadasi as the coast's busiest resort. On the main north–south highway, the lake of **Bafa** was once part of the sea, but the silt-bearing Maeander dammed it off so long ago that its waters are more fresh than saline. Overlooking the lake looms the jagged form of Mt Latmos (in Turkish, the 'Hill of Five Fingers'), where the beautiful shepherd Endymion slept, made love to by the moon goddess Selene and blessed by Zeus with perpetual youth. Few places in Turkey are so hauntingly beautiful under a full moon.

Beneath the mountain stood **Heracleia**, a Carian city (the Carians, like the Lydians and Lycians, were a native people of Anatolia Hellenized by the Greeks). Heracleia was never very important, but is a must for all romantics, who, for the full effect, should sail there across the lake from the camp site on the shore (a new road also leads around the lake to the site). The ruins are impressive, especially the walls and defensive works built by Lysimachus in the 3rd century BC that twist and clamber up the slopes of Mt Latmos. The setting lends the towers, gates, stairs, and parapets an other-worldly air.

In the city, the cella walls of the **Temple of Athena**, high on a bluff, dominate the other monuments. The **agora** behind the temple is also fairly intact, especially its fine south wall. The theatre, nymphaeum, and bouleuterion have not held up so well, but in the southern part of Heracleia is an unusual temple identified as the **Sanctuary of Endymion**, partially cut into the rock, rounded in the back, with a row of columns in the front. In the 7th century, Christian refugees from the Sinai built monasteries and hermitages on the lake islets and around Mt Latmos, and venerated Endymion as a mystic saint, who spent his life on Mt Latmos meditating on the moon, seeking the secret name of God. When he finally learned it, he died and was laid to rest here. Once a year the Christians would open up Endymion's coffin, and his bones would hum, trying to communicate the holy name. Further south, beyond the **Byzantine castle** is a **Carian necropolis**: the economy-minded Carians used natural pits in the rock and covered them with crude stone slabs. Some lie under the surface of the lake.

Altinkum/Priene ✆ *(256–)* **Where to Stay**

Two decades ago, the swampy, formerly malarial wastelands at the mouth of the Menderes were one of the emptiest corners of the Aegean coast. Now the growing new resort on the fine beach at Altinkum ('golden sand') has over a score of hotels and *pansiyons*.

expensive/moderate

To do Altinkum in style, stay at the ★★★**Orion Hotel Didim**, a nicely flagrant piece of resort architecture right on the beach; all rooms with balcony and sea view and satellite TV; there's a pool and garden. For about £12/$18, you have a choice of two well-kept, very similar establishments with swimming pools, the ★★**Göç**, at Göç Caddesi, ✆ 813 1054, and the **Orchidea**, 1 Çağlar Sitesi, ✆ 813 4548.

If you want to base yourself close to Priene and Miletus, there is a simple and quite comfortable hotel in Söke, the **Haymanali**, near the bus station at 55 Santral Garaj Yolu, ✆ 512 0322; some rooms with TV and balconies.

cheap

Altinkum's cheap pensions are gathered together behind the harbour: about a dozen family-run places, all charging charge roughly £4/$6 and all much the same; take your pick. For something different, stay at the only *pansiyon* in Priene, the **Menderes**, all alone on the road up to the site—it's two rooms in a private home, with meals provided. On beautiful Lake Bafa there are several places to camp, the best being **Çeri'nin Camping**, ✆ 512 4498; it is next to some Byzantine ruins and has a decent restaurant, as well as several spartan rooms to let for £5/$8 per person; tours of Heracleia are arranged from here.

Eating Out

Right below Priene and next to the waterfall is the **Şelale** restaurant, a wonderful oasis after clambering over the ruins in the sun, where you can eat for around £4/$6. At Didyma, occupying a tremendous spot overlooking the temple, is the **Kamaçi Restaurant**, renowned for its fish. There are many more restaurants and *lokantas* by Didyma, and at Altinkum—typical resort town seafood places here, none of which seem to stand out. Everywhere else, take what you can find; some informal outdoor places with lake fish open up in the summer around the shores of Lake Bafa.

Along the Maeander to Pamukkale

Getting Around

Trains run frequently from Izmir and Selçuk to Aydin and Denizli; the overnight 'Pamukkale mototreni' connects Denizli with Istanbul and Ankara. Aydin's *otogar* is south of town on the E 24 highway; buses run from here every 30 minutes from Izmir and there is a regular service from Selçuk too, as well as Denizli and Bodrum. Minibuses use the old station in the city centre on Gazi Bulvari, and there is a dolmuş connecting service between the two. From Denizli, frequent minibuses go up to Pamukkale—some wait until they have a load of passengers. Denizli city buses also make the trip, from the big square south of the *otogar*. In summer there are services direct to Pamukkale from all the nearby resorts (as many as ten a day), and also from Selçuk.

Getting to Aphrodisias can be a problem. Accommodation is scarce, so if you mean to do it as a day trip make sure you have return transportation arranged in advance. Minibuses provide a service to Aphrodisias from Nazilli, though most only go to the village of Karacasu, 7 miles (12km) away, from which you would have to take a taxi. In summer you might find a direct bus from Izmir to Geyre, or Karacasu, with a dolmuş service to Geyre. Even so, the easiest way to do it without a car is to get on a tour from Pamukkale.

Tourist Information

Aydin: Yeni Dörtyol Mevkii, ✆ (256) 225 4145
Denizli: 8 Atatürk Caddesi, ✆ (258) 264 3971
Pamukkale: Örenyeri, ✆ (258) 272 2077

Myus and Magnesia ad Maeander

Up the Maeander from Lake Bafa's north shore are the scanty remains of one of the twelve Ionian cities, **Myus**, near the modern village of Avşar; although it once had a harbour bristling with 200 warships, it was later best known for malaria and for having once been traded away by Philip V of Macedon in exchange for some figs given him by Myus' upriver rival, **Magnesia ad Maeander**.

Lying between modern Söke and Ortaklar, Magnesia ad Maeander, like Turkey's other Magnesia (now Manisa), was founded by settlers from Greek Magnesia, who lacked imagination when it came to place names. Under the Persians, Magnesia itself had been given away to their old enemy, Themistocles, hero of the great Athenian victory over the Persians at Salamis in 480 BC. Towards the end of his career Themistocles lost the favour of the fickle Athenians and went to Persia, where King Artaxerxes had offered a reward to anyone who brought him Themistocles. The charming Themistocles claimed and received the reward himself. Artaxerxes then gave him Magnesia (for his bread), Lampsacus (for his wine) and Myus (to go with his bread). Themistocles lived in Magnesia, and when forced to choose between his native Athens and Persia's ally Sparta in the Peloponnesian War, he committed suicide by drinking bull's blood, while sacrificing at the **Temple of Artemis Leucophryene**, the only monument of Magnesia that has survived. The temple dates from the 2nd century BC, after the goddess herself made a miraculous appearance in the city. Because of this, Magnesia was considered sacred, and had no walls.

Tralles (Aydin) and Nyssa

Continuing up the fertile Maeander valley, the large town of **Aydin** is the descendant of ancient Tralles, which lies just to the west. A military installation now occupies the site, and it can only be visited with special permission. It had two claims to fame: the 'Tralles stone', the most complete record of Greek musical notation, and its son Anthemius, mathematician and co-architect of the Aya Sofia. Aydin has a 17th-century mosque, the **Bey Cami**, and a small **museum** displaying some of the finds from Tralles, but nothing else to detain you. Twenty miles (32km) to the east, a sign points the way to ancient **Nyssa**, lost in the olives a mile from Sultanhisar. The city, in a lovely, picturesque gorge beneath Mt Messogis, was founded by Antiochus I in the 3rd century BC; most of what we know about it comes from the geographer Strabo, who studied there. He described Nyssa as a 'double city', split half the year by a torrential stream; he also wrote that the water was so greasy that the young men could dispense with oiling themselves after bathing. The imperial Roman **theatre** and the semi-circular **bouleuterion** (2nd century BC) are the best-preserved monuments in the city. Strabo described the 350-foot vaulted **tunnel** that helped to drain Nyssa's spring torrents and support the city's main square and the current parking lot. Two Roman bridges spanned the gorge; nearby, a pile of stones once formed a **stadium**, although its seats were destroyed by flooding—flooding that was an original feature of the building, for the staging of *naumachiae*, or simulated sea battles.

Aphrodisias

Ancient **Aphrodisias**, on a lofty plateau below the slopes of Mt Cadmos, now Babadağ ('Mt Dad'), is a 44-mile (70km) detour south of the Maeander, but one well worthwhile. Dedicated to the goddess of love, this city is one of most exciting recent excavations in Turkey, begun in 1961, by Dr Kenan T. Erim and the University of New York, partially financed by the National Geographic Society (*see* the October 1981 magazine). The monuments and statues of Aphrodisias owe their state of preservation, in part, to earthquakes in the Middle Ages that covered the city and its approaches.

The site was always sacred, perhaps as early as the Neolithic age; Aphrodite's predecessor may have been the eastern goddess Ishtar or Astarte; the city's original name had been Ninoe, for the legendary King Ninus of Assyria, and it is believed the Assyrians at some remote date founded a sanctuary of Ishtar here. By the Hellenistic age, Ishtar had become Aphrodite. History tells us little about Aphrodisias, except that Julius Caesar, whose family claimed descent from the goddess, preserved the sanctity of the great Temple of Aphrodite; the young Octavian was so impressed with it that he declared, 'I choose this city from among all those in Asia for myself...' By Byzantine times, the town was known simply as Caria, as it was the chief town in the province, and this was corrupted into Geyre, the name of the Turkish village at the site; a series of strong earthquakes depopulated it gradually, and by the 13th century the city was abandoned.

From the quantity of excellent statuary found, made of the fine bluish marble from Babadağ, archaeologists have discovered a whole new school of sculpture, one that adorned Aphrodisias and exported works throughout the Mediterranean; signatures on statues found elsewhere are now identified with the 'Aphrodisian school'. The city's festivals featured sculptural competitions, something unique in the ancient world. A small museum has recently opened on the site to house these marble goddesses, gods, satyrs and emperors.

The Site

Still under excavation (no photos, no dallying off the prescribed path), Aphrodisias is little more than a third uncovered. The circular tour begins with the **theatre**, with a seating capacity of 10,000, dug into the flank of a tell, or mound, in which are buried layers of earlier Bronze Age settlements. A small bath stood here, while to the north are the much more lavish

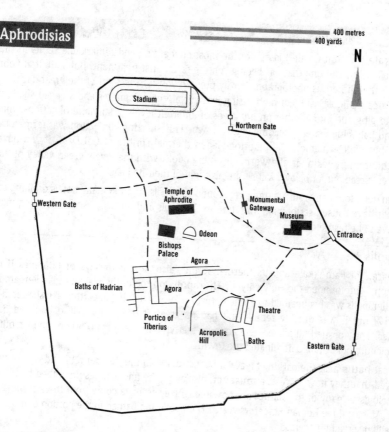

Aphrodisias

400 metres
400 yards

N

Stadium

Northern Gate

Western Gate

Temple of
Aphrodite

Monumental
Gateway

Museum

Odeon

Bishops
Palace

Entrance

Agora

Baths of Hadrian

Agora

Theatre

Portico of
Tiberius

Acropolis
Hill

Baths

Eastern Gate

Baths of Hadrian, complete with huge galleries, heated rooms and a palaestra, still retaining some tiles and mosaics. The grand **Portico of Tiberius** separates the baths from the **agora**, a pair of squares decorated with Ionic and Corinthian columns set in a poplar grove. To the north is the former palace of the Roman governor, converted in the 5th century into the **bishop's residence.** Nearby is an **odeon** with a frequently flooded mosaic floor. Beyond is the **Temple of Aphrodite,** built in about 100 BC over a sanctuary at least 600 years older; 14 of its Ionic columns still stand. Hadrian added the **monumental gateway** that led into the temenos, or sanctuary area. The Byzantines made the whole into a basilica. North of Aphrodite's temple is the **stadium,** perhaps the largest, and certainly one of the best preserved ever discovered. It stretches 865 feet from end to end and could seat 30,000; one side was enclosed for Roman gladiatorial bloodshedding.

Denizli

Returning to the main highway, the E24, you'll pass **Laodicea,** chiefly remembered today as one of the Seven Churches of Asia addressed by John in *Revelations* and as the last residence of Cicero. At the head of the Maeander valley is the major market town of **Denizli,** unremarkable except for two large statues of chickens, the bird to whom the city owes its present prosperity, one in the centre of town and one on the roundabout on the road to Pamukkale.

Pamukkale ('Cotton Castle') is one of the most enchanting and remarkable sights in the whole of Turkey, and one that has been given the full tourist treatment. But snub it at your own loss: the numerous photographs hardly prepare you for the sight of the great dazzling white plateau, almost 400 feet high, rising in a curtain of stalagmites and stepped shallow pools, merging one into another on hundreds of different levels, a fairyland of cotton-white forms and pale blue water cascading gently down. This amazing confection was formed by nothing but water—namely the limestone-laden thermal springs of Çal Daği. If you have young children, frolicking in the warm glistening pools, with the lovely green valley of the Maeander spread out far below, will be the highlight of their holiday.

Unfortunately, too many tourists tramping around the pools, and too many hotels draining off the water have caused serious deterioration in the pools and terraces. Access to them may soon have to be restricted.

Hierapolis

The charms of Pamukkale and its thermal springs also caught the eye of Eumenes II of Pergamon, who founded the Holy City, or **Hierapolis** on top of the plateau. Like Pergamon itself, Hierapolis was bequeathed to Rome in the will of Attalus III. An earthquake shattered it in AD 17, but it was quickly rebuilt and had its greatest prosperity in the 2nd and 3rd centuries. The Apostle Philip lived here and was martyred in the year AD 80: in the Byzantine era, the church of St Philip dominated the town.

The great **baths** near the parking area were constructed in the 2nd century and are so well preserved that they now serve as a **museum**, displaying the fine marbles unearthed by Italian archaeologists; many of the statues are now recognized to have come from the Aphrodisian school. At least three Roman Emperors visited Hierapolis and bathed in the portion of the bath especially reserved for them.

Behind the bath stands a **temple of Apollo**, chief deity of the city, a **fountain**, and a small grotto called the **Plutonium**, a sanctuary of Hades (Pluto), the god of the Underworld; a sign warns of poisonous vapours, the same that instantly killed sparrows in Strabo's day, but was harmless to eunuchs.

The impressive and recently restored **theatre** dates from the 2nd century AD, and is especially interesting for the fine reliefs of Apollo's twin, Artemis. Behind the theatre and outside the Roman wall is the **Martyrium of St Philip the Apostle** of the 5th century. From the bath, the road leads to the other excavations: a **colonnaded street** erected by Domitian, a monumental **gate** of the same period, another **bath**, and stretching on for over a mile, the **necropolis** with a fascinating variety of tombs and sarcophagi dating from Hierapolis' foundation up into Christian times.

Many of the hotels in Pamukkale have their own thermal springs; one, the Pamukkale Motel, captured the prize of the lot: the ancient **Sacred Pool**. The water is warm and slightly effervescent and a lovely garden surrounds the pool; for a small fee, non-residents can while away an afternoon in this dreamland.

There's little reason to overnight in Aydin: if you do, the ★**Orhan**, ℗ 212 1713, is the best available, with double rooms with private shower costing £12/$18. Denizli has several pleasant hotels although, again, there's no reason to stay there unless Pamukkale is packed—a common enough occurence in summer. The best in town are the ★★★**Pişkin**, 10 Atatürk Caddesi, ℗ 264 5648, and the ★★★**Palaz**, Kayalik Caddesi, ℗ 263 0566; both have comfortable rooms with satellite TV and air conditioning. Skip the air conditioning and you can get by for less at the very pleasant ★★**Kuyumcu**, 136 Atatürk Caddesi, ℗ 265 0545.

The best hotels in Pamukkale are on the top of the ridge near the falls. All have comfortable rooms, swimming pools and a tourist conveyor-belt atmosphere. An exception to that last comment is the ★★★★**Colossea Thermal**, outside Pamukkale at Karahayit village, ℗ 271 4156, 🖃 271 4250, an impressively stylish complex built around a courtyard with a huge pool: lavish rooms, a hamam, and night clubs and sports to keep you busy. You can stay in Pamukkale itself, around the Sacred Pool in the **(M1) Pamukkale Motel**, ℗ 275 1024; the pool is beautiful and you can splash around in it as much as you wish, although you'll splash with countless others in high season; £18/$27 double. The ★★★**Koçak**, ℗ 272 2099, is right behind some of the nicest pools and charges similar prices to the Pamukkale. Down in the village (a path leads down from the cliff), **Ali's Travellers Resthouse**, ℗ 272 2065, is a famous institution, with everything from a campground to private rooms, a restaurant to a swimming pool; £10/$15, breakfast included. The village is full of *pansiyons*, though many of these have improved themselves into proper little hotels, where a room with bath usually goes for £8/$12. Two of these are the **Kervansaray**, ℗ 372 2209, English-speaking, with a good restaurant; and the **Halley**, ℗ 372 1204.

cheap

Most of the *pansiyons* in Denizli cluster around the *otogar*, such as the family-run **Murat**, ℗ 261 2018, on Deliktaş Sokak, and the friendly, slightly more expensive **Denizli**, ℗ 261 8738, on the same street. There's nothing around Aphrodisias, only a few rooms at the campsite **Chez Bayar** in the village of Geyre.

In the village below Pamukkale (Pamukkale Köyü) there are dozens of cheap *pansiyons*. It's an inferno; their representatives will accost you the moment you clamber out of your car or off the bus. Most are fair for the price, and many have swimming pools (although some are no bigger than a fair-sized bucket), but this is a place where you can afford to be choosy. One of the nicest is the new **Muhammet Pansyon**, set among the fruit trees; rooms are decorated with Turkish carpets and all have showers. The **Anatolia** is clean and welcoming and a good bargain.

Eating Out

If you're driving, the **Doyurum Restaurant**, 10km out of Karaçasu on the road to Pamukkale, is a nice place to break the journey, where you can eat very well for £4/$6. In Pamukkale, nearly all the restaurants are attached to the hotels and are somewhat overpriced; the one in the **Pamukkale Motel** (*see* above) is one of the better ones, with tables around the famous pool. In the village below, what is not a pension will almost certainly be a restaurant. The **Pizzaria** is a popular place, although it's not particularly good, but there again, neither are its competitors.

In Denizli, the place to go is the **Denizli Evi**, a beautifully restored Ottoman house on Istiklal Caddesi: a wide choice of mezes, grills and seafood, and sometimes live classical Turkish music for accompaniment; well worth a splurge at about £8/$12.

Caria

This section of the southwest coast, between Lake Bafa and Bodrum, once belonged to the Carians, yet another native people more or less Hellenized by the time history discovered them. Halicarnassus (Bodrum) was their largest city, the birthplace of Herodotus and capital of King Mausolus, who gave the world a new name for tombs.

Getting Around

It won't be easy to see any of these minor sights without a car. For Euromos, take any bus from Söke to Bodrum and ask to be let off at Selimiye, the nearest village; Selimiye is also served by infrequent minibuses from Milas. For Alinda, take the minibus from Aydin to the village of Karpuzlu, within walking distance of the ruins; this will be a rather long day trip. For Alabanda and Gerga, you'll have to make a deal with a taxi driver if you don't have a car. Labranda can be reached by car or taxi on a nasty dirt road from the village of Kargicak, north of Milas.

To reach Güllük, take any Milas–Bodrum bus and get off at the Güllük junction, where you can either hitch or wait for one of the very regular minibuses from Milas dolmuş terminus to pass by. In Güllük, you can get a party together and rent a boat for an inexpensive day trip to Iasos. Ören is linked by bus to Milas.

Tourist Information

Muğla: Marmaris Bulvari 24, ☎ (252) 214 1261

Inland: The Carian Heartland

Even in Roman times, cultural Hellenization of Caria was largely limited to the coasts. Come up to the heights between Aydin and Muğla, to the heart of this lost nation, and you will find a remarkable little flock of stone cities, testimony to a Caria that was prosperous and densely populated through Roman times, and has been a desolation ever since. The architecture—for the surviving ruins are substantial—and the entire feeling of the more isolated sites seems a world away from sophisticated Ephesus or Pergamon.

There are few good roads in these parts, and it's as easy to get lost in the hills as it is to become totally confused over all these sites with exasperatingly similar names. **Alinda**, near the village of Karpuzlu, about halfway between Aydin and Muğla, was once the outpost of Queen Ada, sister of King Mausolus (one that he didn't marry). She kicked up a fuss in the dynastic squabbles following Mausolus' death, and found her knight in shining armour in the person of Alexander the Great. Ada promised to support Alexander if he helped her capture Halicarnassus, and the two spent weeks plotting in Alinda.

Never excavated, Alinda is one of the most attractive ruins in which to explore. The ancient town is on a dominating height. In the centre, there is a market building the size of a department store bordering its agora (two of the three floors are still intact), a theatre and watch tower, all in a good state of preservation. From the tower it is a short climb up to the second, upper acropolis, with walls and a gate in equally good shape; oddly this one contained no temples, but only houses. If you have more time for exploring there are necropoli all around the town, and the handsome arcade of an aqueduct, visible from the acropolis.

Less remains of **Alabanda**, 5 miles (8km) from modern **Çine**. This city was also briefly capital of Caria, and still has its fine wall and bouleuterion, but no trace of a temple of Apollo mentioned by Vitruvius. The River Çine Çay, with its gorge, is ruggedly picturesque, especially along the road between Çine and Yatağan Göktepe. In antiquity the river was called Marsyas, after the flute-playing satyr who had the audacity to challenge Apollo and his lyre to a musical contest, with the Muses as judge. When the god was proclaimed victor, Apollo, never known for his sense of humour, flayed Marsyas alive and hung his skin on a tree at Calaenae to the south, the source of the Çine Çay.

Southeast of Alabanda, on the opposite side of the Aydın–Muğla road, you can visit **Gerga**, no doubt the most bizarre ruin in western Turkey—but it won't be easy. Along the Aydın-Muğla road north of Çine, you'll see the ruined 16th-century Incekemer ('slender arches') Bridge; from here, it's a two hour walk, not signposted, up to the village of Incekemer and from there to Gerga. The big mystery here is the endless Greek inscriptions on every monument and bit of exposed rock—'Gergas' or 'Gergakome' (Gerga village), as if the inhabitants wanted to make sure you know where you are. Some of these are in letters three feet tall; nothing similar is recorded in any other ancient town. In fact no one knows whether this was a real town, or perhaps an important Carian religious sanctuary, or whether Gerga was its name or the name of a deity worshipped here. The major attraction is a temple, almost perfectly preserved, that seems almost a parody of Greek architecture, with a stone roof carved to mimic a wooden one. Nearby is a huge fallen statue, also marked 'Gergas'. There is another fallen statue to the west, along with two oil presses and a pair of tall pyramidal monuments. Everything in Gerga most likely dates from Roman times. No ancient writers mention this town, neither has any part of it been excavated. What it was, and the meaning of its enigmatic monuments, remains a total mystery.

Muğla, and More Carian Cities

The road to Marmaris and its peninsula begins at the provincial capital, **Muğla**, a modern and surprisingly attractive city that seems a world away from the tourist fleshpots of the coast. There is little to go out of your way for, but you can explore the pretty, well-maintained 18th-century residential neighbourhoods reminiscent of those in Bursa, clinging to the hillsides to the north of the bazaar. Market day is Thursday.

Muğla is also the base for visiting the Hellenistic/Roman ruins of **Stratonikya** (*Stratoniceia*), 22 miles (36km) to the west, near Eskihisar and a lignite strip mine that has devoured the necropolis. This city began as Chrysaor, centre of the Chrysaoric Confederacy to which all

Carian cities belonged. It was refounded by King Antiochus, and named for his wife Stratonice, who had previously been his stepmother (a little present from his dad, Seleucus I; women didn't get much respect from Alexander's generals). The city belonged off and on to Rhodes before Roman rule, and it prospered greatly until Byzantine times. At the centre of the site stands a building that is often called the 'Temple of Serapis', but may really have been the bouleterion, bordering what was the agora. Other remains include parts of the walls and gates, a Roman gymnasium, and a substantially intact theatre; there's a small museum of finds and further excavations here are currently underway.

Lagina, north of Stratonikya near the village of Turgut, is the site of the **Hekateion**, an important Carian sanctuary to Hecate, the witchy Queen of the Night. Her sacred spring can still be seen near the ruins.

Another collection of lost Carian cities can be visited south of Lake Bafa. **Euromos**, the northernmost of them, is also the easiest to find, just off the road from Lake Bafa to Milas. It is notable these days for its majestic, magnificently preserved **Temple of Zeus** (2nd century AD), lying tantalizingly close to the highway (Rt 525). Paid for by Hadrian, it's one of the few Corinthian temples along the coast, and one of the best-preserved in Turkey; 16 of its elegant columns and their architrave still stand in place. Other ruins include a theatre and Roman-era baths.

Much more substantial is **Labranda**, a town that usually belonged to neighbouring Mylasa. It was known for its sanctuary of the double axe (a *labrys*, as in ancient Crete) dedicated to Zeus Statius, where the oracle was a pool of tame fish who, if ancient writers are to be believed, wore golden earrings and necklaces (the answer was favourable if they fish ate the petitioner's breadcrumbs. A similar oracle survives way out in eastern Turkey, at Urfa; now it is an important Muslim pilgrimage site, but you can still feed the fish). The remains here, tidily excavated by a Swedish team and marked on a placard, include the Temple of Zeus, adjacent priests' houses and well-preserved *androns* (palaces reserved for sacred banquets) notable for their unusual windows. Another excavated section to the east includes a monumental stairway leading up to a Byzantine church. Behind this, a small building is thought to be the location of the oracle.

Milas (Mylasa)

A Sacred Way linked the 10 miles between Labranda and the city of **Mylasa** (modern **Milas**) in the 4th century BC. Mylasa, long the most important of the Carian cities, was the home town and capital of Mausolus. It had an ancient reputation for its fine temples and public buildings, partly thanks to a nearby marble quarry. Milas has been continuously occupied since ancient times—the only one of these Carian towns to survive, and consequently little remains. Bits and pieces of its ancient buildings can be seen in the town's fine collection of medieval mosques, notably the **Firuz Bey Camii**, built by the Ottomans in 1394, shortly after they captured the city. Earlier mosques, the **Orhan Bey Camii** and the **Ulu Cami**, are the work of the Turkish Menteşe emirs, who founded a little state here a century before the Ottomans. Across from the Ulu Cami is a small **archaeological museum**.

The large **Baltali Kapi**, the Roman-era gate 'of the axe', marks the beginning of the Sacred Way, around the corner from the Orhan Bey Camii. South of here on Tabakhane Caddesi, the site of the **Temple of Zeus** is marked by a single Corinthian column, currently occupied by a stork. This is the edge of Milas's charming bazaar district, a pocket of narrow streets that contains a wonderful medieval *han*, the **Çölluhani**, just off Cumhuriyet Caddesi. The best time to visit Milas is a Tuesday, when there is a big farmers' market. Old streets around the edge of the bazaar and on the riverbank have a number of pretty Ottoman mansions from the 18th century, in varying states of decay.

West of the centre on Gümüşkesen Caddesi, a tomb called the **Gümüşkesen** (2nd century AD) is believed to be an exact miniature of the great Mausoleum of Halicarnassus. For a tip the caretaker will let you climb up to the roof for a view over the city. It's ironic that Milas was the only one of these cities to survive, because it is the only one on the plain, not on a defensible hilltop. A Roman governor once remarked that 'the people who founded this city must have known no fear'. The Mylasans' citadel, now called **Peçin Kale**, lies 5km east of the city. Its castle, built by the Byzantines and remodelled by the Menteşe Turks, now contains the ruins of a later Turkish village. The Menteşe governors built a complex of buildings further up the hill, including a mosque, a *han*, and the **Medrese of Ahmet Gazi** (1375), the last governor, who withstood an Ottoman siege of over a year and who is buried inside.

Back on the coast, **Iasos** (modern Kiyikizacik), famous in antiquity for the best fish along the coast, has recently been excavated to reveal the best-preserved Carian city, although that's not saying a great deal; most memorable here is the restored Roman-era **mausoleum** on the outskirts. For a while splendid mausoleums were the fad in Caria, inspired by the great model in Halicarnassus. Excavations at Iasos have turned up pottery going back to Minoan times. An ally of Athens in the Peloponnesian War, the city was destroyed by a Spartan-Persian force and thereafter refounded. Its coinage showed a boy riding a dolphin, and there was a story to go with it of a boy who had befriended one, and was brought before Alexander and made a priest of Poseidon (similar legends were told in many Greek cities, such as Puteoli, near Naples). The scanty remains of the town itself, on a small peninsula, include a Roman-era bouleuterion, a colonnaded agora, walls and gates, a Temple of Demeter and Kore, and a Roman villa with some floor mosaics. Much of the rest of Iasos was cannibalized by the Ottomans; there are good views across the coast from the castle, founded by the Knights of St John when their headquarters were on nearby Rhodes.

Güllük and Ören

An oasis on its own small gulf, **Güllük** was for years the sole preserve of locals and Germans. Now it is fast learning to live with tourism. This diminutive fishing village has been earmarked for development, and already the hulks of soon-to-be holiday homes fill the hills to its north. There's no real nightlife to speak of, yet, and recreation is thus far limited to swimming off the miniscule beach or crossing the gulf to Iasos, an hour's sail away.

Ören, the only village on the northern coast of the gulf of Gökova, is much the better resort choice here, despite the smokestacks of several Polish-built power stations nearby. Yet it is pretty, with a good beach, and it sees very few foreign visitors. Even in summer, you may well be the only non-Turk in town.

Muğla/Güllük ⓒ (252–)   ***Where to Stay***

Accommodation in this area is of a modest nature, clean and comfortable but with very few frills. Don't expect to stay around the Carian ruins; there are no hotels in Karpuzlu or anywhere else nearby.

moderate

For anything more than a simple *pansiyon*, you'll have to stay in Muğla, where

there are a few comfortable hotels, such as the **★Yalcin**, ✆ 214 1050, facing the
otogar; £12/$18.

cheap

The **Kordon Motel** next to Güllük harbour, ✆ 532 1356, has rough-and-ready
doubles for £4/$6. In the centre of the waterfront, the Kaptan, ✆ 532 1006, offers
more of the same. To reserve a room at the comfortable **Yiltur Pansiyon**, on the
beach in Ören, call ✆ 532 2108; £5/$8. Milas has a handful of pensions, should you
happen to be stuck there for the night.

Eating Out

Attached to the motel, the **Kordon Restaurant** in Güllük is typical of the
eateries here; good, friendly and inexpensive, charging £4/$6 for a fish meal
with a side dish and a drink. A short walk away along the quayside, the **Deniz**
is also good. Ören has several nice fish restaurants near the harbour and some
simple *lokantas* further back. Nothing in Milas is particularly wonderful,
excepting the extremely cheap **pide salonu** at the bus station, useful if
you're just passing through.

Bodrum

Whitewashed and flower-decked **Bodrum** is the most sophisticated resort on the Aegean coast
(even though its name means 'dungeon' in Turkish). Anchored to the southern shore of the
Bodrum peninsula, it lies in a sunny region of spectacular scenery and sandy beaches; when
approached by land, it makes an unforgettable impression, even at night when its great landmark, the Castle of St Peter, is bathed in a golden light.

Bodrum is big business. Costa del Sol-style holiday villages and timeshares become more in
evidence with each passing year. If you've booked a 'Blue Cruise' from overseas, your voyage
may well begin in Bodrum; if you'd like to initiate your own sailing holiday while in Turkey,
this is a good place to do so. The diving is excellent, and you can learn if you don't know how
at one of several scuba-diving schools. What really sets Bodrum apart from the other resorts is
its nightlife; it's the only town in Turkey that truly stays up all night, with a scene that is
brasher and louder than anywhere.

History

Bodrum occupies the site of ancient Halicarnassus, a Carian city colonized by the Dorians
from the Peloponnese *c.* 1000 BC. It belonged to the Dorian 'Hexapolis', a typical Greek
confederacy of cities that included Kos, Cnidos and the three cities of Rhodes. In the 6th
century BC, the other five members gave Halicarnassus the boot: it was too ambitious, and
too susceptible to Ionian free thinking. Although the city soon came under direct Persian
rule, the spirit of inquiry survived to inspire Herodotus (485–420 BC), the 'father of history',
the first to chronicle events (the Persian wars) without resorting to the gods for an explanation. Halicarnassus' most glorious period came late, under the Hellenophile satrap Mausolus
who made himself king of a powerful, independent Caria from 377 to 353 BC. He was so
pleased with himself that he began the Mausoleum to himself, which his widow (and sister)
Artemisia II finished as a tomb to beat all tombs, one of the Seven Wonders of the World.
Artemisia declared herself Queen of Halicarnassus and militarily baited the Greeks so much

that they put a price on her head, 'thinking it a matter of great shame for a woman to make war on Athens'. It was her younger sister, Queen Ada of Alinda, who became a good buddy of Alexander and encouraged him to attack Halicarnassus in 334 BC: for Ada's sake, Alexander spared the Mausoleum but little else.

When the Knights of St John lost their castle in Smyrna to Tamerlane in 1402, they came here; finding the Mausoleum toppled by an earthquake, they used it as material to build their Castle of St Peter. Together with their fortifications on the islands of Kos and Rhodes, the Knights dominated the southeastern Aegean, running a hospital for passing pilgrims and ruling the seas as privateers in their swift vessels.

One of the most interesting people to reside in St Peter's Castle was the Ottoman Great Pretender, Cem Sultan, younger brother of Beyazit II. Cem thought the Knights would assist him in his frequent attempts to defeat and depose his brother, but the Knights, paid off handsomely by Beyazit, had other ideas, and kept him as a hostage. They handed him over to Pope Alexander VI Borgia, who made a small fortune on the ransom before poisoning Cem. The Knights themselves were forced to move on to Malta when Süleyman the Magnificent captured Rhodes in 1523, making their citadel at Bodrum untenable.

Getting Around

Bodrum is easily reached by bus from anywhere on the coast, though it will always be a long and roundabout trip by way of Milas or Muğla. Minibuses serve most of the towns on the peninsula, and all of them leave from the *otogar* on the main Cevat Sakir Caddesi, a mile north of the centre. Some of the more tucked-away beaches are best visited by the boat taxis (*dolmuş motorlari*) that depart from Bodrum harbour. Boats ply between Bodrum and the island of Kos regularly from spring to autumn, less frequently in winter, and it's a port of call for many cruise ships. In addition, the summer brings daily ferries to Rhodes, Datça and Altinkum, and at least two a week to Didyma, depending on demand. Occasionally there are even services to Patmos, Dalyan and Caunos; see any travel agent or Bodrum Express Lines on Kale Caddesi, © 316 1087, near the port for details. Some of these take cars, but hydrofoils are increasingly used.

An airport is currently under construction near Güllük, but it may be a year or two before flights begin—the financially strapped national government has suspended all such projects for the moment. There is a small airport in operation at Mumcular, and an airline called Maş Air provides daily flights to and from Istanbul in season. Call © 231 1072 in Istanbul, or © 316 0969 or © 373 6370 in Bodrum.

Tourist Information

Eylül Meydani 12, right on the harbour; © (252) 316 1091.

Bodrum Babylon

The town follows the classic Turkish resort plan closely: castle in the middle, next to a harbour lined with seafood restaurants and full of attractive excursion boats waiting to take you on cruises around the peninsula. Farmers bring in camels for the tourists to ride. Just north of the castle is the frenetic **bazaar district**, where mountains of gold and hecatombs of leather await the tourists. Shopkeepers keep a sharp eye on the arcades, ready to pounce on anyone who stops to look in the window. At the centre, with some of the swankiest shops, is the restored 18th-century **Hacimolla Hani**.

The castle of St Peter, on its tiny neck of land, neatly divides the harbour into two. Dreadnoughts of the wealthy tie up at the yacht marina in the **West Harbour**, but the action is to the east, along pedestrianized **Dr Alim Bey Caddesi/Cumhuriyet Caddesi**. Here the real tourist inferno begins—a rather jolly one, as tourist infernos go, with more food and carpets and jewellery lurching out at you from every shop window, cosmopolitan crowds of happy campers, and a babel of signs like the one promising 'Constantly Hot Water Speaking English and Greek.'

On Thursday afternoons and Friday mornings, there is a busy and colourful (but more than a bit touristy) market.

The Castle of St Peter

The Knights' castle (*open daily exc Mon, 8–12 and 2–6; adm*) stands high on a small rocky peninsula over the original Carian settlement. Because the Knights ruled the seas, they concentrated their defences on the landward side. The first of seven gates to the castle is at the top of the ramp near the tourist office. This leads into the Northern Moat, site of the annual Bodrum Festival. Near the gate you will see the first of some 250 knightly coats of arms carved into the castle walls, as well as numerous reliefs and other architectural embellishments salvaged from the Mausoleum. A wooden bridge replaces the drawbridge leading into the outer citadel, where peacocks patrol the courtyard. Here, the small Gothic **chapel of the Knights** contains a collection of Bronze Age artefacts from the area. This begins the castle's archaeological collection, much of it recovered from offshore wrecks: an exhibit on under-water archaeology explains how it's done.

Finds in other rooms include a bronze statue of an African child, a bronze statuette of the goddess Isis, Roman glass, coins, jewellery, a Byzantine steelyard, and other items salvaged from a 7th-century wreck. The **Snake Tower** (named for the relief over the door) has a small theatre full of amphorae.

The Knights of St John, or Knights Hospitallers, were most often the second and third sons of noblemen. They divided themselves into different *langues* (languages), each *langue* being responsible for defending a certain area of the walls. St Peter's Castle had four *langue* towers. The **German Tower**, near the Snake Tower, has been restored, along with the nearby **hamam**, built for the prisoners when the castle was made into a state prison a century ago; the **Italian Tower**, and the **French Tower**, the highest of all, offer wonderful views of Bodrum and the two harbours formed by the peninsula. The **English Tower**, on the south corner of the castle, has been done up to its medieval hilt, with tapes of medieval music and glasses of wine served by young Turks dressed as knights and ladies. On the west wall, notice the relief of a lion and the arms of Edward Plantagenet; inside on the marble windowsills are names and dates carved during the many long hours of idleness. Perhaps they were relieved when England was expelled from the Order upon Henry VIII's divorce from Catherine of Aragon.

Further chambers in the castle have been arranged to display collections of ancient and medieval glass, coins and jewellery; best of all is the **Hall of the Carian Princess**. In 1989, a sarcophagus was discovered in Bodrum, belonging to a woman who was probably member of the Hekatomnos dynasty, the family of King Mausolus, sometime in the 4th century BC.

Besides some rich jewellery and furnishings, enough of the body and clothing remained for a medical team from Manchester University to attempt a reconstruction of the poor girl in clay. They've got her standing up in a niche, wearing a rich Hellenistic ball gown and looking for all the world like Imelda Marcos.

The Mausoleum

What remains of the **Mausoleum of Halicarnassus** is a bit outside the bustling trendy centre of Bodrum, on Turgutreis Caddesi to the west of the ancient harbour. Designed by the great Ionian architect Pytheos, only the massive foundations remain, capable of supporting a 200ft pile. Models on the site tentatively reconstruct the form of the Mausoleum, and there are a few copies of its reliefs—most of which were carted off to the British Museum in London.

The Mausoleum was the biggest tomb ever built by the ancient Greeks, and not just its name has come down to us: it has been imitated ever since (as in the Masonic Temple in Washington DC, a full-size copy). The best copy, however, is in Milas (*see* p.246). The only ancient monument of Halicarnassus to survive is the restored **amphitheatre**, with an original seating capacity of 10,000, north of the Mausoleum on Göktepe.

Bodrum Peninsula

As resorts go, Bodrum has everything—everything except a beach. But there are plenty of those minutes away around the peninsula. Shaped like a badly drawn map of Africa and Asia, the Bodrum peninsula contains several burgeoning resorts, some attractive fishing villages and the ruins of ancient Myndus. It can be toured by dolmuş or by chartering your own caique.

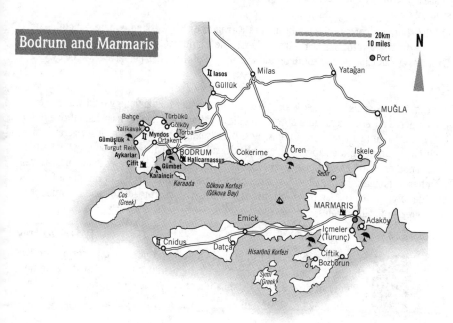

Bodrum and Marmaris

West from Bodrum: Gümbet, 3km outside town, is the closest and busiest beach resort, a rather characterless place with plenty of plastic hotels and evidence of more in the offing. The beach is good, however, and fitted out for every possible water sport, although windsurfers prefer **Betiz**, further west. The inland village of **Ortakent**, brooded over by the hulks of abandoned windmills above it, has a lazy charm; its beach, 6km south, is the peninsula's longest, 3000 yards of sand and pebble stretching westward. Even nicer are the beaches at **Bağla** and sheltered **Karaincir** to the south, with their lovely, fine sands and (usually) lack of crowds. At the southern tip of the peninsula, opposite the Greek island of Kos, a resort is fast being slung up around the fishing village of **Akyarlar**.

The western tip: In spite of its rather inconsequential beach, **Turgut Reis** is a heavily developed resort. It is named after the 16th-century Admiral Turgut (Dragut), who was born here to Greek parents; his mentor Barbarossa, another Greek who 'turned Turk', in a moment of unusual humility declared that Dragut was ahead of him 'both in fishing and bravery'. Together the two of them terrorized the Mediterranean through much of the 16th century. Dragut led the great siege of Malta in 1565 and died there, and Süleyman's fleet and army had to return empty-handed, the first important military setback for the Ottoman Empire. Two fine beaches lie on either side of Turgut Reis: **Akyar** at a fishing hamlet, and silvery **Gümüşlük**, the site of ancient Myndus. Development of Gümüşlük village has been deliberately restrained due to its proximity to ancient Myndus, and the village is perhaps the peninsula's most charming. Just south of here is **Kadikalesi**, another attractive little village, with an abandoned Greek church on the hill above it.

The northern shore: This side of the peninsula is blanketed with pine forests that reach the shore in many places. **Yalikavak** is a scenic settlement, where many windmills still function, but its beach is poor, typical of those along this mostly unspoilt stretch of coastline. The villages of **Gölköy** and **Türbükü** do their best for bathers, making the most of their narrow strips of sand.

Off the southern coast of the peninsula lies **Karaada** or Black Island, where mineral waters flow into a sea grotto, popular with bathers. The island can be reached by boat trip from Bodrum, as can Cnidus, due south on the western tip of the Datça peninsula (*see* below).

Kos

Bodrum itself is so like a Greek island resort, it's a wonder that anyone would want to cross the border. And Kos offers more of the same; its location near Rhodes has made it one of the busier tourist destinations among the islands. In season, everything will be just as crowded as Bodrum (and much more expensive). Nevertheless, Kos can invite you to some ancient attractions: another **castle** of the Knights of St John, a restored **Roman house** with mosaics, as well as other Roman-era ruins, all in Kos town, the island's capital. You can bicycle a few km outside town to see the famous **Asklepion**, a centre of ancient medicine and a reminder of Kos's great son, Hippocrates.

Bodrum ℗ (252–) **Where to Stay**

Bodrum is blanketed in endless hotels and pensions; prices are on the high side, but that doesn't keep them from filling up in the summer. Plenty of new luxury establishments have opened in recent years, but though the trend is upmarket the overwhelming majority are still resolutely middle-range. Virtually every town and village on the peninsula has places to stay, although in some of the less-frequented villages on the northern coast, there may only be basic pensions.

If you're the type that sleeps nights, the important thing about staying in Bodrum is to find a place not too near the nightclub strip: Dr Alim Bey Cad/Cumhuriyet Cad, in Kumbahçe, which can be deafening until dawn. Most of the *pansiyons* are in this area, as well as more expensive places. Some of the noisiest places are quite nice and do their best to compensate (on the other hand, if you're looking for people who dance nights and sleep days, this is definitely the place). Also note that half pension is required in almost all of the three-and four-star places, and in some of the two-stars.

luxury

There are a few of these, most of them spread around the peninsula in peaceful settings. At the top of the status totem-pole, the ★★★★★**Club Hotel M**, Değirmen Mevkii, Haretman, ⍉ 316 6100, ⍉ 316 2581, is a small and lavish place, designed with touches of Cecil B. DeMille (like the colonnaded pool); all imaginable amenities, disco, casino, beach and water sports. Next best is at Gümbet: the ★★★★**Grand Iskandil**, ⍉ 316 4762, ⍉ 316 4765, with comparable facilities; besides the hotel there are 40 private apartments in the complex; no beach, but maybe the most spectacular pool on the coast.

expensive

One of the longer-established holiday villages, the **(TK1) Club Ora**, 4 miles (6km) east of town on Milas Yolu, ⍉ 316 7591, with tennis courts, swimming pools and plenty of other recreational facilities. Half-board is compulsory. Also to the east, but closer to the town, is the ★★★**Manastir**, Mev. Kumbahçe, ⍉ 316 2854, with a swimming pool, on a pretty terrace overlooking the sea, as well as a gym and tennis courts. The most comfortable in town is the ★★★**Bodrum Maya**, Gerence Sokak, ⍉ 316 4741, which offers a pool and its own parking, always a consideration in this crowded town. For recreational facilities in Turgut Reis, try the holiday village **Gökçe Club Armonia**, ⍉ 393 6481, on the beach at Akyarlar, at £34/$50, typical rates for this category; there's a nice stretch of private beach, plenty of sports opportunities and a hamam; they arrange babysitting and entertainment for children. Gümbet beach, 2km west of the centre, is lined with a wide selection of three-stars, good places to look for bargains when they aren't full of package tours. The ★★★**Anka**, Eskiçeşme Mah, ⍉ 316 8217, ⍉ 316 6194, and the ★★★**Club Hotel Flora** are both air conditioned and next to the beach, and both can set you up with equipment and lessons for windsurfing, the current craze here, and other sports.

On Mümtaz Ataman Caddesi at Kumbahçe, the ★★★**Hotel Naz**, ⍉ 316 1365, has a pool and a garden full of orange trees; it's a few streets from the strip but not too noisy.

moderate

In the centre of Bodrum are a number of excellent, moderately priced hotels, including the ★**Emirhan**, Kumbahçe Mah, Adliye Sok, ⍉ 316 6830,with a swimming pool. Two of the nicest are on the strip, and will be perfect if you're coming to Bodrum for serious partying: the ★**Karya**, 127 Cumhuriyet, ⍉ 316 1535, and the ★**Dinç**, next door at no. 123, ⍉ 316 1141. The ★★**Seçkin Konaklar**, Neyzen Tevfik Caddesi,

© 316 1351, enjoys an ideal location by the West Harbour—close to the action but not too entirely noisy. It's a low-rise complex with both rooms and apartments, and a pool. Also on Neyzen Gevfik Caddesi, at no. 224, the **Hotel Gala**, © (614) 122 16, is a no-frills, central hotel with a bar and a pleasant garden; £20/$30. Gümbet has a few one-star places that are practically indistinguishable from the more expensive ones. The *Melisa, Eski Çeşme Mevkii, © 316 1044, has simple rooms and a pool for about £15/$23.

Out on the peninsula, the **Toloman**, © 343 1226, at Bitez is a pleasant and restful place directly on the beach. Besides the rooms there are a dozen apartments for rent. The Turgut Reis area has several hotels in this category, including the **Yaprak**, at Kadikalesi, © 382 3801, a very pleasant and well-run establishment. On Ortakent beach, the **Yildiz Motel**, © 316 3195, has a pool and spartan double rooms with bath for £10/$15.

cheap

Most of Bodrum's *pansiyons* are located in Kumbahçe, what seems a whole city of them on the back streets behind the bar strip of Dr Alim Bey Caddesi; there isn't a lot of difference from one to the other. Try the **Billur Pansiyon** off Cumhuriyet Caddesi, © 316 4849; rooms with bath for £5/$8. If it's not full, the management is amenable to bargaining. Nearby is the **Kemer Pansiyon**, Uşlu Çikmazi 36, © 316 1473, where rooms are basic but clean; £3/$5 without bath. Avoid the rip-off Burak Pansiyon on Dere Sokak, which always has a minion around the bus station.

Around the West Harbour area is another concentration, including the pleasant **Istanbul Pansiyon**, on 1017 Sokak. Relatively quiet is the **Ataer Pansiyon**, Neyzen Tavfik Caddesi 102, © 316 5357, a pleasant place run by a pleasant family and charging £4/$6. In Turgut Reis, the **Aydin Pansiyon**, © 382 3082, is attractive and comfortable; doubles £9/$14 with breakfast. Gümüşlük has several very pleasing pensions, all charging £4-6/$6-9. The region has a handful of camp sites, of which the best equipped are **Zetaş Camping** in Bodrum, © 316 1407, and the **Irem Motel Camping** at Bites Koyu; other, more informal places, often on far nicer sites, are near the beaches nearly everywhere on the peninsula.

Eating Out

Like the other resorts, only more so, Bodrum has a waterfront lined with outdoor restaurants. In general, these are the last place to go—expensive, tourist-orientated places cobbled together each season with temporary staff. Still, there are plenty of places to get a good dinner. The **Han** restaurant, in an 18th-century caravanserai at Kale Caddesi 29, © 316 7951, has the most original surroundings, and possibly the finest cuisine in town, with dishes like shrimp and avocado cocktail and chicken stuffed with pistachios; original desserts too, and a bar upstairs with live Turkish music; average £8/$12.

One reliable place for seafood is the **Gemibaşi**, with outside tables facing Neyzen Tevfik Caddesi; £8/$12 average. Bodrum, at least, is one place where you can get a change from Turkish food: there are Chinese restaurants, such as the **Sandal**, the

'Authentic Thai and Chinese Restaurant', Atatürk Caddesi 74; its menu features no less than 139 items but those confounded by the agony of choice can always order the set meal, for £8/$12. Another, for slightly less, is the **Uzakdoğu** (means 'far east'), 146 Neyzen Tevfik Caddesi, with a branch at Gümbet; £10/$15. **Picante**, a bar/restaurant with Tex-Mex cooking and margaritas, is at 8 Külcü Sokak; £8/$12.

For something unexpected and memorable, head north from the town hall and seek out the **Buğday Vegetarian Restaurant** on Türk Kuyusu Caddesi, a back street far from the tourist strip. Lovely cooking, all natural ingredients, and a pretty enclosed garden (occasional music and even art exhibits); £4/$6 or a little more. In the middle of the bazaar on 7 Sokak, **Ağan Bolu** offers surprisingly good food at kebab-stand prices: £3/$5, or a bit more for their special shrimp or octopus casseroles (well worth it). Off Dr Alim Bey Caddesi on a side street (sorry, it didn't have a street sign), the **Geren Restaurant** has outside tables just far enough away from the action on the strip; £4/$6, more for seafood. **Sünger Pizza**, at the end of the strip near the Halikarnas disco, offers a wide choice of creditable Italian pizzas and beer for about £4/$6. And if you want to support the local side, patronize the convivial **Club Bodrum**, in a garden behind the castle. Good simple food and outside tables in a nice location—and it's run by the local football club, Bodrum Spor, to meet their expenses.

Restaurants on the peninsula range from the fancy at Gümbet and Turgut Reis to the plain at Ortakent and Yalikvak. The popular **Vira Cafe** at Ortakent does pizza in addition to the usual Turkish fare; £6/$9 for a full dinner; they also have rooms to let. Bitez has some good simple places: the inexpensive **Çardak** near the Bitez Han hotel is popular locally for its chicken casserole. At Kadikalesi, the **Kilçik** in the Yaprak Hotel offers mezes and grilled fish for £6/$9. If you're staying at Gümüşlük, by all means stop in at the **Bati**, near the beach; everything from *pide* snacks to full dinners for about £5/$8; excellent lamb and seafood casseroles and outside tables by the waterfront.

Entertainment and Nightlife

Almost everything is on the joyous pedestrian strip of Dr Alim Bey Caddesi/Cumhuriyet Caddesi, but it's a potent and concentrated mixture, with everything from slick discos to quiet bars with folk music to watering holes that seem to be specially designed to attract northern lager louts and get them off the streets. Pool halls, hippie trinket dealers and sidewalk portrait painters decorate the streetscape. At the top of the list is a Bodrum institution, the disco **Halikarnas**, at the far end, which claims to be the biggest in Europe. You can't miss it; its laser light shows bounce off the castle and around the town all night, giving the impression of an invasion from Mars. Dress up; it's £5/$8 to get in, which after a while in Turkey may seem like a fortune. Another flash disco, currently very popular, is the **Hadigari**. Closer in, you'll encounter the **West Side Bar**, one of the cooler places to be, with a shady courtyard and an up-to-date tape collection. The **Red Lion Bar** is for serious guzzling, and it generates the highest decibel levels east of Mykonos. There are some agreeable holes-in-the-wall featuring whatever live folk, jazz or blues music floats into Bodrum, such as the **Club Mani**, and the **Jazz Cafe**, near the Halikarnas. Bodrum also has two **casinos**, one at the Club M Hotel out at Haretman, and another in the Karia Princess Hotel on Canlidere Sokak.

Marmaris

The scenery between Muğla and Marmaris is reminiscent of California and becomes spectacular as you descend to the lovely pine-clad **Bay of Marmaris**. The town itself was devastated by an earthquake in 1958, and little of architectural interest remains apart from the fortress built by Süleyman during his siege of Rhodes. However, its lovely setting on the deeply indented coast, its access to the bay's beaches, and its fjord-like scenery have made it one of Turkey's major yacht ports and one of its most popular and well-known holiday resorts, though one where the concrete mixers have definitely got out of hand. Superficially, at least, Marmaris is practically identical to Bodrum. For you package trippers who can't tell which you're in, Marmaris is the one with the smaller castle, and the marina on the east side instead of the west.

History

The Carians were quick to appreciate the natural harbour of Marmaris, or Fyskos as it was then, and used it as a base from which to terrorize the Phoenicians on Rhodes. After the eclipse of the Carians, the town was passed around among various powers—Egyptians (Ptolemy's empire, after Alexander), Ionians, Dorians, Romans—before becoming part of the Ottoman Empire in 1425. It remained a forgotten outpost for nearly 100 years until Süleyman the Magnificent, irritated by the Knights of St John on Rhodes, who pillaged Muslim pilgrim ships and let Christians pass freely, followed the Carian example and used the town as his base to besiege the island. When the Knights finally surrendered, Süleyman was so pleased with his success that he ordered a castle to be built in the town. The result was a typically quaint Ottoman affair, almost cute, its battlements affording one of the coast's loveliest vistas. However, Süleyman didn't like it. '*Mimar as*', he grumbled when he saw it—'Hang the architect'. Hence the town's name. Or so they say.

Getting Around

Marmaris has one of the most reliable ferry services to a Greek island—Rhodes, daily, most of the year round.

Dalaman airport at Muğla is the closest airport, about a 90-minute drive from Marmaris. Buses run every half-hour in season to Marmaris's main *otogar*. The airport has regular domestic flights from Istanbul, Izmir, and Antalya, and an increasing number of international charters—including daily connections to London, Amsterdam and even New York, all via Istanbul.

Marmaris's *otogar* has a convenient central location on Cevat Şakir Caddesi behind the east harbour, though most buses also stop at the circle on Atatürk Caddesi, by the west harbour. There are frequent bus connections from Bodrum, and from Izmir and Fethiye; minibuses provide transport along the serpentine road to Datça and Cnidus. Those for Içmeler and points west begin from the centre of the harbour, by the Atatürk statue (one of the new model Atatürk statues, with a top hat), as do the seasonal boat dolmuşes for Turunç and the many fine beaches and islets around the bay. Minibuses for Yalanci and Boğaz beach leave from Mustafa Münir Elgin Bulvari, behind the marina.

Marmaris: Iskele Meydani 2, on the west harbour, ℗ (252) 412 1035; there is a hotel reservation booth open in season here.

Datça: Hükümet Binasi, ℗ (252) 712 3546.

Around the Town

The Knights' **castle of St Peter** (*in summer daily 8–12 and 3–7 pm; adm*) has since been restored and converted into an ethnographic museum with the standard collection of kilims, daggers, etc, as well as a room given over to holiday snaps of Cappadocia. The castle is reached through a convoluted series of back streets that offer some hints as to what Marmaris was like 50 years ago, when the town's income was derived from that most hazardous of occupations, sponge-diving. The divers would set sail every spring and return several months later, usually minus a few poor souls. The women and children would see the boats coming in and gather anxiously on the quayside. The **statue** of the woman and child at the harbour commemorates those who looked in vain (currently, there are hardly any sponges to be had here or anywhere else in the Mediterranean, thanks to an epidemic of 'sponge blight' in recent years).

Behind the statue the town's **bazaar** begins, one of the more pleasing touristic markets in Turkey, bustling and cheerful. From here the town's spacious **beach** is a short walk away, to the west of town.

East of Marmaris, over the wooden bridge, is **Günnücek Park**, a picnic spot within a grove of rare frankincense trees. You can swim off the small platform here. For better swimming, go to the islet of **Sedir** on the other side of the peninsula in Gökova Bay. The islet is only half a mile long but very popular for its unusual snow-white sand with perfectly round grains, shipped to the islet from the Red Sea some 2000 years ago for Cleopatra. Then, a city called Cedrea stood on the islet; the ruins of walls and a theatre remain.

For yet more beaches, and for **thermal springs,** head south of Marmaris to **Içmeler**, a fast-developing resort. It is near the village of **Turunç** where the beach is less crowded; across the bay are the **Phosphorescent Caves**, where the water glows when disturbed.

SPONGE SELLER

South of Turunç lies the **Rhodian Peraea**, the only mainland territory of that once-powerful island-state. The Rhodians made little use of this little peninsula, spreading between the islands of Rhodes and Kos, and there's little to see. A steep climb up from **Kumlubük**, another village with a sandy beach, leads to what remains of ancient **Amos**: fragments of some walls, and of a theatre and a temple. The ancient towns of **Saranda**, near **Sügut** village, and **Bybassios**, on the road to small but teeming **Bozborun**, have scanty remains, likely to appeal to specialists only.

Rhodes

The largest and greenest of the Dodecanese is also one of Greece's most flagrant tourist play-grounds—prices will be a shock after Turkey. Rhodes has had a fascinating history: a power in its own right in Hellenistic times, home of the famous Colossus. Like Bodrum, the island was controlled by the Knights of St John for two centuries after 1306, and the Italians ruled it from 1912 until 1945.

The ferry from Marmaris lands at **Rhodes** town, the island's capital, where there are the castle and walls of the Knights to explore, as well as architectural contributions from ancient times up to Süleyman the Magnificent and Mussolini. The town is a major resort, with a casino, busy nightlife and even a golf course. From the capital the most common excursion is to beautiful **Lindos**, the island's second city, with the ruins of its magnificent acropolis. A number of villages haven't yet been too spoiled by tourism, notably **Lardos**, on the coast near Lindos; **Embona**, up in the mountains above Rhodes, and **Kamiros**, the third of the island's Doric 'three cities'. Along the west coast are a number of resorts and a famous beauty spot, the **Valley of the Butterflies**.

Datça and Cnidus

West of Marmaris, the road makes quite a dramatic ascent up to the top of mountains, before dropping down to **Datça**, one-time Doric city, now small-time Turkish resort. Built around a horseshoe bay, Datça has beaches but there are better ones further west along the peninsula, and local tour operators will happily sail you to them. They'll also take you to ancient Cnidus.

Cnidus, at the very tip of the peninsula, was the headquarters of the Dorian Hexapolis (a loose confederacy of towns in Asia Minor that had been settled by Dorians). In ancient times, it was famous for a statue of Aphrodite by the great Praxiteles, modelled on the renowned courtesan Phryne (whose name means 'Toad', although she won a court case by baring her bosom before the judges). This first 3-D female nude was originally commissioned by Kos, but the islanders were too prudish to keep such a bombshell, and Cnidus picked it up and made the 'Aphrodite of Cnidus' the main tourist attraction of the coast, set in a temple to be viewed from all angles and tended by a lusty crew of priestess-prostitutes. The base of the statue has recently been discovered in the circular foundations of a Corinthian temple in the city. The streets of Cnidus were laid out in a grid over a number of terraces; the walls and the Hellenistic theatre are the best preserved of the remains. The lovely statue of Demeter in the British Museum came from here, and although excavations are currently under way, no one has yet found the observatory of Eudoxus, a native of the city, student of Plato, and a pioneer in astronomy and geometry.

Marmaris and around ℰ (252–)   **Where to Stay**

The only time of the year when it may be difficult to find a room in Marmaris is during the regatta, held in the second week in May.

luxury/expensive

The ★★★★★**Marmaris Altinyunus Oteli**, ℰ 455 2200, 3 miles (5km) west of Marmaris, offers almost every conceivable form of recreational activity including a fitness room, swimming pools, private beach, nightclub and so on. The **(TK1) Marti Holiday Village**, ℰ 455 3440, ℰ 455 3448, offers more of the same but is somewhat cheaper. The emphasis is on water sports here; there are indoor and outdoor polls and a broad stretch of beach. Both of these have their own casinos. In Içmeler, ★★★★★L'Etoile, on Kenan Evren Bulvari ✆ 415 3570, 🖅 415 3574, is very new and very plush; lovely rooms with satellite TV and balconies over-looking the beach; hamam, pool and all sports facilities.

moderate

In Marmaris, at Atatürk Caddesi 10, the ★★★Yavuz Oteli, ✆ 412 2937, has a rooftop pool with terrific views; £18/$27—good value for money. The ★Ayce Oteli, Çam Sok 4, ✆ 412 3136, has doubles for £14/$21. It's off the main street and therefore quieter than most. To the west of the town, the ★★★Lidya, Siteler Mah 130, ✆ 412 2940, is one of the most ambitious establishments in town, with opportunities for all water sports and speedboat rental, a piano bar and a night club with a wild floor show; there is a variety of accommodation available, from rooms to apartments. There are plenty of hotels near the beach, on Atatürk Caddesi and the back streets behind it. One of the better bargains is the air-conditioned ★★Çubuk, 1 Konti Sokak, ✆ 412 6774. Right in the centre of the action on Haci Mustafa Sokak, the ★Begonya, ✆ 412 4095, with its wooden-lattice shutters and well-furnished rooms, must be the prettiest hotel in Marmaris; the only drawback is noise from all the bars around it.

The ★★★Mare in Datça has a solid reputation, a beachside location and a swimming pool. Turunç, with its long beach, has a number of adequate mid-range hotels; two that place a special emphasis on sports, with excellent facilities, are the ★★Diplomat, ✆ 476 7145, and the ★★Mavi Deniz, ✆ 476 7190. The Diplomat has a nicer section of beach; both have apartments to rent also.

cheap

Marmaris does not have as many *pansiyons* as Bodrum, and it can be crowded in summer; it's best to arrive early in the day and check the hotel reservation booth by the tourist office. Otherwise, the best place to look is not in the old town, but in the new streets to the west behind Atatürk Caddesi. There, where the paint is hardly dry and the streets have no names, you'll find family-run places like the friendly, English-speaking **Maltepe**, ✆ 412 1629; nice rooms with bath for £4/$6.

The **Keskin**, Karacan Sitesi Yani, ✆ 412 6170, charges about the same. It has a communal kitchen so if you're out to save money, you can cook your own food. The **Otel Imbat**, nearby on Eski Çarşi 5, is another bargain choice, where a clean double room with private shower and toilet costs £6/$9. For slightly less than the average pension, you can stay at the **Interyouth Hostel**, ✆ 412 6432, just outside town on the road to Datça, with a cafeteria and laundry.

For budget accommodation in Datça, try the **Karaoğlu**, ✆ 712 1079, among a number of similar places on the hill overlooking the bay. The nicest camp site in the region is **Camp Amazon**, ✆ 436 9111, 24 miles (39km) from Marmaris in the Bordübet National Park, with a pool, nearby beach and every essential facility.

Eating Out

In Marmaris there is a solid block of restaurants along the yacht harbour. Most of them are quite expensive by Turkish standards, although the food is delicious. Grilled fish like the wonderful *mercan* (pandora) can be had for about £8/$12 in places like the **Aksambaşi**, at the far end of the strip. For something less expensive, the **Yeni Liman Restaurant** in the bazaar has a nice selection of meats and sweets; a full meal, with a beer or a glass of wine, should come to around £4/$6. On Haci Mustafa Sokak, between the bazaar and the bus station, there are several nice restaurants huddled together in one of the oldest parts of town. The **Pizza Napoli** offers a fair approximation of the real thing, in a proper Neapolitan pizza oven, £4/$6, while the **Ezgi**, at about the same price, is an excellent place for kebabs and chops, sometimes to the accompaniment of a lute player or other music. The **Pagoda** turns out typically basic Turkish Chinese restaurant fare for £5/$8. West of the castle, one street in from Atatürk Caddesi, the **Stop Café** is a good place for *manti* or *köfte* for a light lunch or snack.

Outside town at Turban Yolu 30, the **Birol** offers some sophisticated cooking as in their special *gamgam*, chicken with mushrooms, cream and garlic butter; £6/$9. Datça has plenty of restaurants, all much of a muchness. There are two small restaurants in Cnidus, and you can get food at any of the coves with a camp ground around Marmaris bay.

Entertainment and Nightlife

Marmaris is second only to Bodrum in this department, and the centre of the action is Haci Mustafa Sokak, just behind and running parallel to the East Marina. The disco crowd fills up the attractive **Magic Garden** nightly, while more subdued entertainments can be had at places like the small and refined **Bar Fendi**, which often features a guitarist or other live music, or the **Black and White**, with a lovely garden. At the far end of the street, **C'est Ça** offers live blues or rock every night in season. Over on the harbour, the yacht set congregates at the **Scorpio Bar**.

Marmaris's best setting and view belong to the **Panorama Bar** on the height next to the castle. While you're pub crawling, watch out for the incredible stand on the harbour occasionally set up by **Lütfü Küçük**, a manic, talented caricaturist who has become locally famous from appearing on Turkish TV—the spirit of P. T. Barnum lives on.

The Lycian Coast: Marmaris to Antalya 262

Around Lake Köyceğiz 263

Fethiye 265

Kaş to Antalya 271

Antalya and the Pamphylian Coast 277

Antalya 278

East from Antalya 284

Perge 285

Aspendos 287

Side 288

Cilicia 293

Alanya 294

Alanya to Silifke 298

Silifke 300

Uzuncaburç 302

Kizkalesi 303

The Southern Coast

ANTALYA HARBOUR

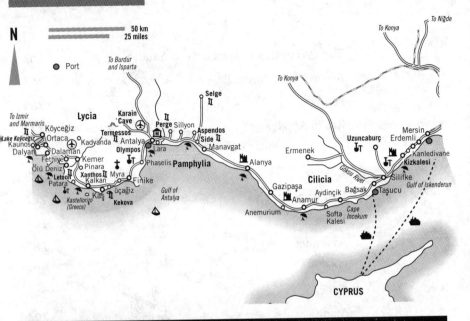

The Lycian Coast: Marmaris to Antalya

In ancient times, when the indigenous Lycian people crowned this rugged stretch of coastline with a garland of lovely cities, the area was still something of a *terra incognita* for most Greeks and Romans. Even now the difficult mountainous terrain makes the interior hard to penetrate. Lately, however, the Turkish government has completed a coastal road, stretching around the Lycian bulge from Fethiye to Antalya. It was the last unfinished section of the coast highway, and its construction has opened to tourism a land that still retains its lazy charm, a transparent sea, in every imaginable shade of blue and turquoise, magnificent scenery, and archaeological sites in varying stages of excavation, all in settings that would delight any romantic. The villages, strung around the coast, might as well be islands: on one side the sea, on the other an equally inhospitable sea of steep mountains and maquis. In such a setting, people here tend to be convivial even by Turkish standards—friendly and talkative, and never in a hurry.

The Lycians

The Lycians were a native Anatolian people. Homer says that they fought with the Trojans under their leader Sarpedon, brother of King Minos of Crete, which led Herodotus to write that they were the descendants of an ancient Cretan colony. Lycia first appears in the records of the Hittites as the 'Lukka Lands', in the 13th century BC. Most of the remains discovered along the coast, however, date back only to the 7th century BC at the earliest. Like Cilicia to the east, the rugged nature of the thickly forested terrain kept Lycia out of the pages of history, but by the time of Alexander—who captured the coast easily from its Persian satraps—its population had become more or less Hellenized, adopting many Greek letters into the alphabet, and adapting Greek sculptural and architectural forms.

The latter they adapted for their mortuary obsession, carving elaborate tombs with temple-like façades into the living rock, in some places so thick they resemble lost metropolises of the dead. Elsewhere, they made sarcophagi and tombs in the form of miniature houses of stone, remarkably graceful constructions with curving roofs. These, often on high platforms, and the beautiful tombs carved into the steep cliffs overhead are the most distinctive features of the Lycian landscape.

Around Lake Köyceğiz

Getting Around

Köyceğiz is serviced by all buses travelling east or west along the coast. For Dalyan, coming from either direction, you must alight at Ortaca and take a dolmuş from there. Alternatively, there are boats to Dalyan from Köyceğiz several times a day. Kaunos can be reached by motorboat from Dalyan; in summer you'll always be able to find someone to ferry you across.

Tourist Information

Köyceğiz: Atatürk Kordonu 1, © (252) 262 4703

Köyceğiz

Köyceğiz lives for the lake on whose northern shores it stands, and from which it draws its name. Ringed by a phalanx of foreboding mountains, with waters transparent in the shallower stretches, this lake has supported the town for millennia, its healthy stock of fish constantly being replenished via the meandering channel that connects it to the Mediterranean. Birds like the fish as much as the local fishermen do and 119 species have been spotted here, from storks to kingfishers and even, on occasion, the endangered sea eagle. Out on the lake at night, you may sight another rare creature, the softback turtle.

Köyceğiz itself is a drowsy town and Monday, market day, is the only time of the week when it shakes itself from stupor. On other days there's little to do except stroll the leafy promenade, cross the lake to the muddy thermal baths on the southern shore and enjoy fresh fish at any one of several wonderful lakeside restaurants.

Dalyan

Dalyan represents all that is gorgeous about the southern coast of Turkey, yet it has so far been spared the more tawdry trappings of mass tourism. The village can be reached by road but it is far nicer to sail there from Köyceğiz, winding through the channel on the way to the open sea. Dalyan lies midway along this channel, a village of little more than one street, a square and a harbour, bounded to north and south by barely touched countryside. Across the water the first traces of ancient Kaunos (*see* below) can be seen, rock tombs built into the sheer cliff face. No structure in the village is higher than three storeys, by order of the *belediye*, who are anxious that Dalyan remains unsullied and who reinforce this policy with loudspeaker announcements exhorting locals 'not to pester the tourists' and 'not to drop cigarette ends in the street'.

Dalyan **beach**, a 30-minute sail south, is one of the most visually stunning on the Mediterranean rim, a sand-based island at the mouth of the channel. It is totally undeveloped, thanks to the presence of giant loggerhead turtles, who have used it as a laying ground since time immemorial. Tourist development very nearly killed these turtles off. The female logger-heads would lay their eggs by night in the soft sand, in clutches of about 100; by day, sunbathers would turn up to stretch out on that same sand and poke sun umbrellas into it for shade. If the eggs managed to survive this treatment and hatch, the hatchlings were faced with a further problem; the bright lights from the hotels and bars on the beach would counteract the gleam from the sea that they would otherwise instinctively crawl towards. The baby turtles would set off in the wrong direction; inevitably, they died.

What was happening became common knowledge in the late 1980s and ignited a debate within Turkey that soon was to spread overseas. Influential environmentalists became involved and in 1991, the developers, who had previously been proposing that they and the turtles should have half the beach each, completely backed down. All structures on the beach were bulldozed and their foundations covered, and the entire area was ordered closed from 8pm to 8am, from May through to October, the main laying season. The beach is open during daylight hours but swimmers and sunbathers are asked to exercise special care.

Kaunos

Further down the channel from Dalyan is ancient **Kaunos**, the westernmost settlement on the Mediterranean coast, marking the border between that sea and the Aegean, and between Caria and Lycia. Its remains show the styles of both cultures, as well as of later civilizations: there are Lycian and Carian tombs, a wall built by King Mausolus of Caria, medieval walls on the acropolis, a Roman fountain and a Byzantine basilica. The city was eventually abandoned after its harbour silted up, a fate it shared with illustrious Ephesus.

Köyceğiz and Dalyan ☎ (252–) **Where to Stay**

In both Köyceğiz and Dalyan you can save money on hotel bills. There is nothing at the luxurious or expensive end of the market, although the moderately priced and inexpensive pensions are, as a rule, very good indeed.

moderate

In Köyceğiz, the ★★**Hotel Özay**, Ulucami Mah, ☎ 262 4300, is the best in town. It is tastefully furnished, has a swimming pool, and is on the lakeside; the management arranges sailing, sports and boat tours. Dalyan has seen a number of new hotels open up in the last few years. The status address here is the ★★★**Antik**, ☎ 284 2136, a very attractive motel-style complex with a pool set in a garden full of oleanders; some rooms have air conditioning. Another good choice, on the waterfront close to the centre, is the ★★★**Dalyan**, ☎ 284 2239, a similar complex right on the waterfront.

cheap

Köyceğiz has a clutch of pensions. The **Keramos**, ☎ 284 2914, two blocks behind the lake near the bus station, has spare and waterless rooms but the atmosphere is lively—thanks in part to the owner's ghetto-blaster—and the garden pleasantly shady. At Dalyan harbour, the **Göl Motel**, ☎ 284 3062, is clean and has en suite rooms for

£4/$6. The street leading south from the square, adjacent to the channel, is filled with small pensions, all charging around the same rate.

Eating Out

The cheerful staff at the **Çinaralti** restaurant on Lake Köyceğiz serve fish (usually sea bass or grey mullet) fresh from the lake for around *£5/$8* a head, drink and a side dish included. In Dalyan, the harbourside **Denizati** is excellent for *£5/$8*, as is the less expensive **Çiçek** on Maras Mah, with its fine selection of mezes. For a drink, try the **Han Bar** on Maras Mah, decorated with *narghiles, kilims* and Ottoman memorabilia.

Fethiye

Getting Around

The nearest airport to Fethiye, Dalaman, has regular flights to Istanbul and weekly charters from abroad; it's 50km away, with an information office and taxis to take you into Dalaman town, where there are minibuses to Fethiye and everywhere else along the coast. All buses travelling this coast stop at Fethiye; the *otogar* is a mile east of the centre on Atatürk Caddesi, at the intersection of the roads for Muğla and Antalya. Minibuses leave constantly in the summer for Çalis and Ölü Deniz from the central terminus behind the post office. In season there is also a boat dolmuş to Çaliş, every half hour until midnight.

Getting to most of the ancient sites is possible without a car, though not always easy. From Fethiye, you can take a minibus to Sidyma, Araxa, Tlos, Xanthus, and the Letoon; all will require some walking once you get there. For all those close to the coastal road, you can be fairly sure of finding some minibus or even intercity bus to pick you up on your way back.

Tourist Information

Iskele Meydani 1, © (252) 614 1527

A modern town built over ancient Telmessos, **Fethiye** has Lycia's best harbour, protected by twelve islets. Telmessos means 'Land of Light' in Lycian, and is first mentioned in the 4th century BC. Most of it lies buried under modern Fethiye (itself rebuilt after an earthquake in 1957), with the exception of the **rock tombs** cut into the cliff near the bus station; these, especially the grand Ionic temple **Tomb of Amyntas** of the 4th century BC, are among the finest in Lycia. Here and there throughout the modern town you see large sarcophagi. The oldest and most interesting of these is the **Lycian Sarcophagus** next to the post office, carved from a single block of stone. The new **museum** (*open daily exc Mon, 9—5; adm*) is near the school, and has exhibits from Lycia, and an interesting sculpture garden.

Fethiye, though modern, has a leisurely charm, and it is the best base for visiting the Lycian sites in the vicinity. After Marmaris or Bodrum, it may even look a bit down at the heels; at least it has managed to side-step the blanket commercialism of some of the resorts on the southern coast. The leather and carpet merchants are huddled together in a relatively small area behind the harbour; in the hamlets outside town, life meanders on as it always has. From the harbour most of the sailboats will be offering 'twelve island tours'; some will go wherever you want.

The nearest beach is 3km away at **Çalis**, a suburb of Fethiye that is more obviously a 'resort'. It lies opposite the islet of **Şövalye** which also has a beach. Gümlük beach, just north of Fethiye, is in a grove of styrax, or liquid-amber trees.

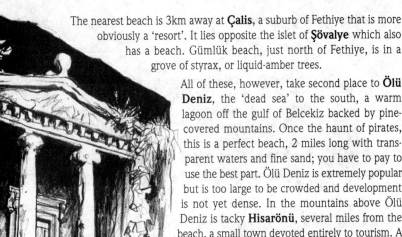

AMYNTAS' TOMB, FETHIYE

All of these, however, take second place to **Ölü Deniz**, the 'dead sea' to the south, a warm lagoon off the gulf of Belcekiz backed by pine-covered mountains. Once the haunt of pirates, this is a perfect beach, 2 miles long with transparent waters and fine sand; you have to pay to use the best part. Ölü Deniz is extremely popular but is too large to be crowded and development is not yet dense. In the mountains above Ölü Deniz is tacky **Hisarönü**, several miles from the beach, a small town devoted entirely to tourism. A 30-minute walk from Hisarönü is the Greek ghost town of **Karmilassos** (Kara Köyü in Turkish), with forlorn houses and abandoned churches; as with so many towns along the coast, when the Greeks left in the population exchange the Turks had no inclination to move in, preferring to let entire towns go to ruin; there are now some ambitious plans for restoration of the village, but besides the efforts of some private individuals, not much has happened.

Inland from Fethiye

Inland from Fethiye you can explore, literally, three seldom-visited Lycian cities. **Kadyama**, northeast of Fethiye near modern **Yeşil Üzümlü**, has a well-preserved theatre, a Doric temple, and baths, as well as other remains. **Tlos**, on the slopes of Akdağ, the White Mountain, is 30 miles (48km) from Fethiye, near modern Kaleasar, on the other side of the River Xanthus, the modern Koca-Çay. Tlos was one of the most important members of the Lycian confederacy of the 2nd century BC and remained inhabited through the Byzantine era; in the 19th century it served as the winter headquarters of the pirate Kanli Ali Ağa. As well as Lycian rock tombs, there are remains of Kanli Ali Ağa's fortress on the acropolis, Roman walls around the necropolis, a Roman stadium, baths, and necropolis, and a Byzantine church. On the other side of the modern village lies the theatre.

Pinara, another important member of the confederacy, is closer to Fethiye, on the west bank of the River Xanthus, east of **Kemer**—the *western* Kemer (there are two villages of this name, one at each end of Lycia). Pinara is one of the more romantic sites, on a height beneath the mountains, the ruins overgrown. Pinara is especially notable for its Lycian rock tombs; a Roman odeon and a Greek theatre are also easy to find. **Sidyma**, 9 miles (14km) off the coastal highway south of Pinara near Dodurga, has more rock-cut tombs.

Xanthus

Far more interesting, however, is **Xanthus**, the ancient capital and oldest city of Lycia, dating back to the 8th century BC and famous in antiquity for its great resistance to Cyrus' General

Harpagus who attacked in the mid-6th century BC. Although they fought courageously, the Xanthians were outnumbered. According to Herodotus, when they saw they were doomed to defeat, they retreated to their citadel, gathering together their womenfolk, children and slaves. After locking them inside, they set fire to the building and burned it to the ground. They then swore to fight to the death, and did. Indeed, when Xanthos was excavated, a heavy layer of ash was discovered over the ruins of that period.

Rebuilt by 50 families who had been away during the siege, Xanthos prospered up until the Roman period, when it once again suffered a terrible devastation, this time at the hands of Brutus in 42 BC; rebuilt yet again with the aid of Mark Antony and Emperor Vespasian, the city survived until the 12th century. Today it is one of the most revealing Lycian sites, most of it having been cleared to disclose the layout of the city and its imposing funerary monuments. Unfortunately they were stripped of their reliefs in 1838 but these can now be seen in the Lycian Room of the British Museum in London, along with the entire Temple of the Nereids. The Turks have replaced many of the reliefs with plaster casts.

The funerary monuments are all near the parking area, around the **Roman agora** and **theatre**; the **Tomb of the Harpies**, high on its monolith, is adorned with reliefs (plaster copies) of scenes from the Underworld. The winged female figures transporting souls, however, are not harpies but *kers*, who in true Greek religion, as opposed to the Olympian mythology, performed that function. Next to the tomb is a Lycian tomb-sarcophagus (4th century BC), high on its pillar. A similar tomb stands on the other side of the theatre. The **Inscribed Pillar** in the agora once supported the sarcophagus of a Lycian King; it bears writing in Lycian on all four sides, their longest inscription yet discovered, and although this has yet to be deciphered, other evidence has led scholars to believe it was the tomb of King Kherei, who defeated the Athenians in a battle of the Peloponnesian War. The Lycian acropolis was just south of the theatre; the palace of the Xanthian kings may have stood here, on the western end overlooking the river that locals call the '**Royal Terrace**', but the only ruins older than Byzantine times are those of a **Temple of Artemis**.

East of these ruins, part of a street can be made out, with another **agora** on one side and a **basilica** on the other; at the southern end of the street stood the **Temple of the Nereids**, which the malevolent Hyperboreans carted off to their capital a century ago as a cultural trophy. Across the path from this is an **arch** near the southern gate, donated to Xanthos by Vespasian. If you follow the street in the opposite direction, towards the northern walls, you'll come to more interesting **tombs** and a Byzantine monastery, and beyond the largely ruined walls, the city's **necropolis**.

Like the other ancient provinces of Asia Minor, Lycia had a federative sanctuary, a holy place shared by all the cities, the expression of their ethnic and religious unity. This was the **Letoon**, 2½ miles (4 km) south of the main road (the turn-off is just north of the one to Xanthos), dedicated to Leto and her children, Apollo and Artemis. Although there was a small city here, the only remains are of the temples and a small but well-preserved **theatre** on the hillside. Even though only foundations of three temples remain (the **Temple of Leto**, the largest and easternmost of the three, the **Temple of Apollo and Artemis**, and a smaller unidentified one between them), the site is one of the most pleasant along the coast. The half-sunken ruins, including a huge and elaborate semi-circular **nymphaion** and a 7th-century **monastery**, have become elegant pools for the lazy turtles and fat white ducks that abound near Leto's ancient spring, which still flows as freely as in ancient times. These peacefully share the spot with other exotic wildlife, including clouds of magenta dragonflies and frogs, straight from Aristophanes, croaking 'Brekekekex coax coax!' in the most correct classical Greek accents. On the floor of the twins' temple is a mosaic in the cella showing Artemis' bow and Apollo's lyre. Long inscriptions are everywhere; some have been removed to the nearby **museum**.

Apollo, surprisingly for a god of light and reason, proves a pretty shadowy character outside Greece proper. His mother Leto—etymologically and in religion the same as Leda, Latona, Lat, or other variations in mythology—seems to have been an old Middle Eastern version of the great goddess. Apollo, here, must appear in his role as god of the cult of Hyperboreans ('men from beyond the North Wind') centred at Delos, and extending, if the ancient historians are to be believed, from Britain to Palestine. At Patara, the next town along the coast (*see* below), an oracle of Apollo existed that functioned only in the winter, the opposite of the oracle at Claros. In the summer, Dionysus presumably took over the temple while Apollo removed himself behind the north wind, to England, specifically to the temple founded in his honour (under a different name) at Stonehenge.

XANTHOS LYCIAN TOMB

Fethiye and around ℭ (252–)

Where to Stay

expensive

As at Köyceğiz, a number of upmarket hostelries have opened near Fethiye in recent years, of which the most attractive is the ★★★**Asena**, ℭ 616 6713, 7km from town at Hisarönü Köyü: a lovely complex of low rise buildings: pool gym, hamam, riding and more on offer. 5km from town, the ★★★**Mendos** on Çalış beach, ℭ 613 1130, is a simple beach hotel with air-conditioned rooms. In Fethiye itself, there is the ★★**Hotel Mara**, Kral Caddesi, ℭ 614 9307, where air-conditioned double rooms with breakfast on the rooftop terrace go for £20/$30.

moderate

The ★**Hotel Se-Sa**, ℭ 614 4656, near the Mara on Akdeniz Caddesi, is similar to it and slightly cheaper, with en suite doubles for £16/$24. Adjacent to the tourist office is the ★★**Hotel Dedeoğlu**, ℭ 612 1606; air-conditioned rooms, and a pool. At Çalış Beach the hotels tend to lack character but the service is friendly and helpful, as at the ★★**Seketur**, ℭ 614 1060; rooms with balconies, a lovely pool, disco and sports opportunities. Hisarönü has any number of hotels charging similar prices, all new and seemingly alike. This village is not to be recommended as a base unless all you are interested in is Ölü Deniz. Directly on the beach at Ölü Deniz, the ★★**Meri Oteli**, ℭ 616 6060, is nice, set among trees, with facilities for water sports and riding; a little expensive for its rating, but worth it. Early reservations are essential.

cheap

Fethiye is where to find one of Turkey's best pensions, the **Mer Pansiyon**, Dolgu Sahasi Sahil Yolu 1, ℭ 614 1177, which would put many a two-star hotel to shame.

Rates for the spotless, en suite rooms vary according to the view, ranging from £4/$6 to £6/$9, breakfast included. For families, there is a special lockable annexe with a separate room for the kids. Not as good, but still nice, is the **Palmiye**, © 614 2140, on the shore west of the centre at Karagözler; £5/$8 with breakfast on the roof terrace. The town's cheapest pensions can be found in the streets around the bus station, with an average price of £4/$6; just follow the signs. Çalis has *pansiyons* too, the best of which is the **Anil**, on Barbaros Sokak, © 613 1192; all rooms with bath and there's a small pool. There are plenty of scrappy campsites around Ölü Deniz; **Deniz Camping**, © 616 6012, has full facilities.

Eating Out

The **Rafet Restuarant** in the harbourfront park is an old established favourite but still good and very inexpensive: good kebabs, including fish kebabs, from £3/$5 up for a full seafood dinner. The **Tahirağa** is also good, as is the **Meğri**, both on Çarşi Caddesi; the latter serves a mammoth collection of mezes, including stuffed aubergines drenched in a rich cheese sauce. Both restaurants charge around £4/$6, drink included. The lightest lunch in town is provided by the **Turkish Vegetarian Restaurant**, on Eski Mehri Sokak; very inexpensive omelettes, sandwiches and plats du jour. For a splurge, if you can make it out to Ovacik Köyü, on the road to Ölü Deniz, the **Şadirvan** offers some delicate cooking in specialities such as trout with almonds and quail (*bildiricin*) cooked in butter, as well as the usual kebabs. A full dinner with mezes and wine goes for about £10/$15, though you can eat well here for half that.

Nightlife is not as frenetic as in the other resorts; most of the few places are in the old town above the harbour: the **Yesilcan** is worth a drink at least for the view from its roof terrace, and the **Yasmin Bar**, set prominently above the harbourmasters', has live rock and blues and occasionally Turkish music.

Patara and Kalkan

Getting Around

The Fethiye–Patara–Kalkan–Kaş bus and dolmuş service is fast and regular, even out of season. In Patara, there are frequent minibuses from the village to the beach and the ancient city. Kalkan is a good place to base yourself if you are interested in archaeological sites; more than 25 can be reached within 2 hours by car. There is no proper *otogar*; all buses stop on the coastal highway at the top of the town.

Patara

There are two good reasons for visiting **Patara**, a ramshackle but welcoming village 46 miles (74km) east of Fethiye. The first is to explore the ruins of ancient Patara; the second is to enjoy the 11-mile sandy beach, the longest continual strand in Turkey and one that is, save for a few restaurants and *pansiyons*, still undeveloped.

As at Dalyan, giant loggerhead turtles must be thanked for this. These immense amphibians have long used Patara beach as a laying spot for their eggs, and it was the furore over Dalyan that raised concern in Patara as to the fate of their own turtles. Now, as at Dalyan, the beach is closed off at night and daytime bathers are warned to be careful where they lay out their beach mats, lest the eggs be scrambled. There is no development at ancient Patara either, in this case to protect the ruins.

Between sand, sea, and pines, Patara is altogether one of the most attractive sites in Lycia. Entering the ruins (*open daily 8.30–5, 7 in summer; adm*), you pass some fine **Lycian tombs** on the right-hand side, and two apsed buildings, the **Roman baths** built by Vespasian, and a later **Christian basilica**; new excavations here started in 1994. A three-gated monumental **arch**, stripped bare of its statues, adorned the town's main entrance. The **theatre** is in good shape, but partially covered by a tremendous sand dune, well over 100 feet high.

Kalkan

There's nothing much to say about **Kalkan**, despite the magic of its location at the mouth of a crystal bay, and why it has grown into a small resort is something of a mystery. It is certainly colourful enough, and has a definite charm, but if you walk from where the buses stop at the top of the hill down to the twee little harbour below, you will see all there is to see. There are no beaches here—for a swim, people go either to Patara or to **Kaputas beach**, 200 steps below a steep cliff 10 miles (16km) west of Kaş—and the nightlife is very low-key. Overall, Kalkan is a nice place to hole up for a day or two before boredom drives you on.

Patara ℂ (242–)

Where to Stay
expensive/moderate

There is very little that's fancy in Patara. The most expensive, by virtue of its swimming pool and tennis courts, is the **★★★Beyhan Patara**, at Gelemiş, ℂ 843 4096. The **Apollon Motel**, ℂ 843 5215, has a pool too and is considerably less expensive, at £12/$18. To compensate for the lack of a beach in Kalkan, the **★★★Hotel Pirat**, by the marina, ℂ 844 3178, has constructed a swimming platform only 200 yards distant. It's an elegant establishment, with air-conditioned rooms and two pools; £20/$30.

You'll need to book in advance if you want to stay. Kalkan also has several very nice pensions. At the harbour the **Akim Pansiyon**, ℂ 844 3025, is drenched in bougainvillea and charges £8/$12 for doubles with bath, less if you don't mind sharing the common bathroom. A short stroll away, the **Balikci Han**, ℂ 844 3057, is a restored mansion decorated in Ottomanesque style.

cheap

In Patara, every other building seems to be either a cheap hotel or a pension. Most are very good, such as the **Otel Mehmet**, ℂ 843 5032, with its helpful English-speaking proprietor. All rooms have a balcony and private bath. Similar in both price and quality is the **Rose**, ℂ 844 5165. A new addition, the **Patara Viewpoint**, ℂ 843 5184, has a wonderful setting on a hillside above the village and very friendly proprietors. Kalkan's cheap pensions are few; you'll find what there is in the side streets at the top of the road leading down to the harbour.

Eating Out

In Patara, at the **Ali Baba Restaurant** at the top of the village, a meal of grilled chicken and salad and a glass of wine will cost around £4/$6. On the beach there's a good place for *manti*, the **Harabe**. For good *pide* in Kalkan, try the **Ilban** near the bus stop at the top of the village. Further down, the **Kösk** is good, though expensive, with all-you-can-eat meze buffets and the house speciality, swordfish steak £8/$12; you can do just as well for half that at the **Ilyada**, on the harbour.

Kaş to Antalya

Getting Around

Kaş is easily reached by bus from anywhere on the coast; the *otogar* is on the northern edge of town, on the road to Antalya (Elmali Caddesi). Coming from inland, the only entrance is over the mountains from Isparta and Burdur, a long and tiresome journey over roads that are unpaved for much of the way. The easiest way to explore the Kaş coastline is by day trip from Kaş, though there's nothing to stop you hopping off the boat in Üçağiz, doing some hiking or some lazing, and picking up the boat the following day. Each morning at 10am a dolmuş leaves Kaş for Üçağiz, returning at 8am the following morning. To get to Aperlae, charter a boat from Üçağiz. It's an 80-minute walk from where the boat docks to the site. Also from Kaş, there are minibuses every half-hour in summer for Patara and Xanthos.

For Kyanaea, take an eastbound bus from Kaş and ask to be let off at Yavu; from there, the ruins are a hard, one-hour climb away. Be sure to get good directions as it is easy to get lost; you may want to employ someone from the village as a guide. Demre can be reached by bus from Kaş, or more expensively by boat from Üçağiz. Inexpensive tours of Kekova are arranged daily through the travel agents.

To get up to Mt Olympos without a car, you'll have to find one of the infrequently running minibuses from Kemer, but only in summer. Most coastal minibuses will take you at least within walking distance of Phaselis, though for the sites up in the mountains, Limyra and Arkyanda, you'll need a car.

Tourist Information

Kaş: Cumhuriyet Meydani 6, ☎ (242) 836 1238

Kemer: Belediye Binasi (city hall), ☎ (242) 814 1112

Kaş

Ten years ago the delightful fishing village of **Kaş**, huddled shyly under the lower peaks of 9802ft Mt Akdağ, offered perhaps the ultimate in sunny Mediterranean languor. Of course it was too good to last—even then, Saudi Arabian interests were plotting the biggest resort complex in the world here, with no fewer than 10,000 rooms. That scheme fell through, thank goodness, but Kaş has been more than overbuilt in the decade since. Today the new resort has a half-finished look about it; some of the streets to the new hotels aren't even paved yet, and bulldozers and cement mixers stand about, waiting to disturb your slumbers. Don't be put off though; it's a happy, relaxed place, and still maintains more of its village character than most of the other big resorts. And it's still the best base for seeing this delicious stretch of the Lycian coast.

Kaş was Habesa to the Lycians and Antiphellos to the Greeks, and bits and pieces from the past survive both within the town and on the cliffs behind, where several tombs have been cut into the almost vertical face. West of the harbour are the ruins of a **temple** and a 1st-century **theatre** of medium size, with 25 rows of seats. In the centre of town stands a tall, lovely **tomb**, with inscriptions in Lycian; the hole smashed in the side was made centuries before by looters, robbing the corpses of the gold and the jewellery interred with them. Another is on a hill just to the west on a narrow peninsula, and another at the harbour. All of these tombs (except the one at the harbour, which was moved by the municipality to make way for extensions), indeed all the tombs in the vicinity of Kaş, face the **island of Kastellorizo** and archaeologists and anthropologists alike are totally baffled as to why.

Just a mile offshore from the town, this lonely little island (also called *Megisti* in Greek, or *Meis* in Turkish) marks the easternmost boundary of the Greek republic, inherited from the Italians after the Second World War with the rest of the Dodecanese. This quirky backwater, which once had a population of 16,000, is still recovering from 1944, when it was pillaged and burned by retreating British troops in one of the more bizarre incidents of the war. The few Greeks who live there, heavily subsidized by the Greek government, come over to Kaş to do their shopping. A small company in the town runs unofficial day trips to the island, unofficial as Kastellorizo is not a port of entry into Greece; ask at the tourist office to find out how to get over, since conditions change all the time.

Around Kaş's **harbour** you'll find the usual array of cruise boats, offering day trips to Kalkan, Patara or Kekova and something unique, the Aquapark, a glass-bottomed boat that does tours of the partially sunken ancient town of Aperlae, as well as night cruises when weather permits. The town's other attraction is its farmers' market, every Friday.

Kaş's beaches may disappoint: two stony, ugly coves known respectively as Little Pebble Beach and Big Pebble Beach. The nearest sandy beach is **Kaputas**, 10 miles (16km) to the west, created by the Kaputas stream which has cut a big chasm through the rock wall. By land, it is accessible only via an endless flight of stone steps. To save bathers this exertion, motorboats from Kaş chug there each morning. Understandably, Kaputas gets very crowded.

Inland, 12 miles (19km) east of Kaş, are the ruins of ancient **Kyanaea**, renowned for the rows and rows of sarcophagi that dominate the site, dating back to Lycian and Roman times.

Kaş ℗ (242–)   *Where to Stay*

At the moment, Kaş is short on expensive, luxury hotels. This will change in the near future, however: establishments of this nature are already being built on the Çukurdağ peninsula outside town wherever there is a level stretch of ground.

expensive to moderate

Currently, the status adress in Kaş is the ★★★★**Aqua-park**, 5km up the coast at Cukurbağ, ℗ 836 1901, ℗ 836 1906. It's a beautiful complex, with pool, tennis and a gym; they have their own glass-bottom boat for tours around the coast. As the beaches in Kaş are poor, you may want a hotel with a swimming pool, in which case the ★★★**Ekici Oteli**, Hükümet Konaği Yani, ℗ 836 1417, is a good choice. It has a hamam too; air-conditioned rooms go for £32/$48. The ★★**Mimosa Oteli**, Elmali Caddesi, ℗ 836 1272, is about half the price but has no pool. The **Limyra**, Meltem Sok 5, ℗ 836 1716, is a top-quality pension, with pine decor, in a quiet setting; doubles £13/$20 with breakfast, and there is a big discount off-season. On Bahçe Sokak, near the post office, the new **Otel Çukurbağli**, ℗ 836 1760, has rather cramped doubles with private bathroom for £12/$18. If you need a quiet setting, the ★★**Bolel**, ℗ 836 1428, is out by itself at Çukurbağ: there's a pool, and rooms with satellite TV—some rooms have great views over the bay.

Between the bus station and the harbour on Meltem Sokak, the **Keskin Pansiyon**, Ⓣ 836 1060, offers very good value for money. Clean rooms with a bath and a balcony go for £6/$9, and are even cheaper outside July and August. Other cheap pensions are all over town, particularly north of the bus station: their representatives will wave their cards in your face the minute you arrive in town. Nice ones include the **Linda**, Ⓣ 836 1828, with rooms with a view at Küçük Çakil Mah, by the Little Pebble Beach, and the **Yali**, Ⓣ 836 1870, on Hastane Caddesi. Also at Little Pebble Beach, the **Çakil Pansiyon**, Ⓣ 836 1532, is a low-priced family concern; £6/$9, breakfast extra. Among a number of campsites, the **Kaş Camping,** Ⓣ 836 1050, on the road to Çukurdağ stands out; it's right on the sea, and besides campsites it has bungalows to rent at very reasonable rates.

Eating Out

It's difficult to find anything in Kaş that isn't either overtly touristy or else just a basic kebab house. The **Kalamar** on Şube Sokak is quartered within a colourful garden; £5/$8; while near the market on Uzun Çarşi Sokak, the **Eriş** occupies a restored old Ottoman-era house; good seafood for £6/$9 or perhaps a bit more. Next door, the English-run **Smiley's** offers a bit of everything on its menu, for about £4/$6; it's also the best place in town for breakfast. For seafood, the best inexpensive choice is the **Çinar**, on Çukurbağli Caddesi by the post office. Above the harbour by Küçükçakil Beach is the **La Villa Beach Bar**; both of these will serve you a well grilled fish, salad and drink for about £6/$9.

Entertainment and Nightlife

This can be at least slightly more intense than Fethiye, but nothing like Bodrum. The biggest and most popular disco, the **Full Moon**, lies out on the coast road towards Fethiye (they provide minibus transport in season). There are some wonderfully noisy dancing spots in the town itself: the **Deniz Alti** and the **Mavi Bar**, on the waterfront, and the **Redpoint**. For something a bit more refined, the **Sun Café** by the harbour puts on live Turkish music, while at the **Nokta Bar**, on Uzun Çarşi Caddesi, you're likely to hear anything from live blues to live flamenco.

Kekova Island and the Kaş Coastline

Heavily indented and full of isolated caves and islets, this part of the coast captures in equal measure some of Lycia's most spectacular scenery and some of its most intriguing ruins, many of which lie semi-submerged in a sea as clear as any in the world. The best are at the mysterious city that once stood on **Kekova Island**, east of Kaş; along its southern shore houses, walls and kilns can be easily identified and staircases descend from the cliffs to disappear into the ocean. On a small beach a large, arched structure stands erect, once part of a boatyard. Little is known of this city, not even the name. A local theory maintains that it was inhabited by pirates who, after indulging in the pillage and plunder that their occupation entailed, would then stash their loot in one of the many hidden caves. They lived here for centuries until divine retribution intervened in the form of a massive earthquake that shook the city into the sea and drove the brigands away.

The village of **Üçağiz**, across the water on the mainland, began life in the 4th century BC as Teimiussa. What remains of Teimiussa is spartan but striking, a plethora of **rock tombs** huddled together, many rising picturesquely out of the water—again, all facing west to Kastellorizo. For the present, Üçağiz itself exists in a time-warp, a barely touched village of fishing and weaving that until 1992 could be reached only by boat. Its setting is undeniably lovely, amidst the two bays and slender channel that give the village its name, Üçağiz being a direct translation of its Greek name, Tristomo, or 'three mouths'. As a recent fixture on the day-trip itinerary from Kaş, Üçağiz is however fast becoming a 'real' village. Restaurants line the waterfront and the first carpet shop is already open. From here a boat can be hired to view ancient **Aperlae**, a mostly submerged Lycian city.

Further along the mainland, clinging to the side of a hill, is **Kale**, descendant of ancient Simena, another member of the Lycian League. Its **castle**, built by the Lycians and renovated, so it is said, by the pirates of Kekova Island, is in good condition, its crenellations showing a variety of styles. Inside it is the **theatre** of Simena, the smallest theatre yet discovered, with only seven rows of seats—an indication of the diminutive size of Simena and also of the value placed on culture in even the tiniest Greek towns.

Demre (Kale): St. Nick's Home Town

Going northeast, the next modern town, **Demre** (which appears on many maps as *Kale*), stands on a little plain full of small farms, grown prosperous from citrus fruits and greenhouse tomatoes. Demre is the descendant of ancient Myra, home of jolly St Nicholas, a 4th-century prelate. He was actually born in Patara, but it was in Myra that he was bishop, sufficiently beloved for his generosity and good deeds to get himself canonized. Before he became Father Christmas, he was known as patron of sailors and pawnbrokers; and the Greek Church still knows nothing of the Christmas duties he has in the west. Travel brochures have lately appeared with pictures of an American-style Santa Claus in front of the ancient ruins. Let us hope this doesn't get out of hand.

Follow the 'Baba Noel' signs in Demre to the **St Nicholas Church**, a 5th-century building with extensive 11th-century additions, including a large barrel-vaulted nave and cloister. In the original structure there is some fine marble inlay work and much carved stone recycled from earlier buildings. Of the later frescoes, only one unidentified saint survives. This may well be the oldest surviving church building in Turkey.

Myra

About 1 mile outside Demre, the ruins of **Myra** include an amazing collection of **tombs** cut out of the cliffs above the city, all in the form of temple façades. There are over a score of them, arranged on the cliff in an asymmetric jumble. Most are from the 4th century BC, and many contain funeral scenes in relief. Several of the façades have roofs carved to imitate wooden beams, suggesting that they were copied in form from wooden temples or other buildings that have not survived; the same is true of the Phrygian cliff-face façades west of Ankara.

Myra's other attraction is its **theatre**, a late Roman work with some uninspired sculpture. From its huge orchestra, we can guess it was used more often for games and animal shows than for classical drama. In the vicinity are a number of Byzantine structures protruding from the surrounding farms and greenhouses, and, a few miles to the southwest, a **Roman granary**, one of many in Lycia, decorated with a relief of Hadrian, who built it.

Around Finike

From **Finike**, a nondescript agricultural town 19 miles (30km) east of Demre, you have the choice of continuing along the coast, or striking inland through the mountains. Either way will take you to Antalya, though the recently built coastal route is considerably shorter. Travelling inland, you encounter first the ruins of **Limyra**. In the early 4th century BC, this was the most powerful city of Lycia under King Perikles, founder of the Lycian League of cities and a fighter for Lycian independence against Mausolus of Caria. The site is worth a visit for the tombs—if you haven't seen enough yet—spread all over the outskirts of the ancient town. Notable among them is the **Heroon of King Perikles**, in the form of an Ionic temple, although some climbing will reveal several others that rank among the best Lycian tomb architecture.

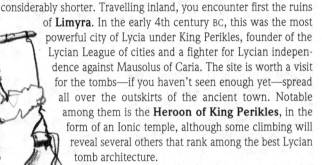

North of Limyra the road passes **Arykanda**, another ruined town. Its only distinction seems to have been a precocious and enthusiastic acceptance of Christianity, as reflected in its monuments, including remnants of an early Byzantine basilica and an even earlier temple that was converted to Christian use. The biggest ruins on the site, however, are a small **theatre**, well-preserved and beautifully situated, with a view over the surrounding hills, and a bath complex with one of its 30ft walls still standing.

Beyond this come two lakes, **Avlan Gölü** and **Karagöl**, the 'Black Lake'; its waters are held back by a natural dam, overflowing dramatically through a chasm in the cliff. If you press even further inland, into the Ak Dağlar, you'll come to the only sizeable village in these parts, **Elmali**, with some Selcuk remains, and an attractive, tiled 17th-century mosque to match its neighbourhoods of old wood-frame houses.

Olympos and the Chimaera

Along the coast, the road skirts the grand massif of the Bey Dağlari, the 'Bey's mountains' around Cape Gelidonya, a familiar landmark to sailors ancient and modern. Heading northwards, **Olympos** is another ruined town in a pretty setting, though little remains of it. If you pass at night, you will see a small flame rising from the mountains above the town. All the ancient geographers mention it, and it takes its name, the **Chimaera**, from the myth of Bellerophon. The Lycian King, Iobates, sent Bellerophon to kill the fire-breathing monster, part lion, goat, and serpent. With the aid of the winged horse Pegasus, he succeeded, and returned, after completing other tasks set by Iobates, to Xanthos where he married the king's daughter and became heir to the Lycian throne. Carried away by his success, Bellerophon tried to ride Pegasus up to Mount Olympos. For his presumption, Zeus sent a gadfly to tickle Pegasus, who threw him to earth; Bellerophon landed in a thorn bush, which put out his eyes, and he wandered the earth, blind and lame, to the end of his days.

The real Chimaera isn't at all monstrous; in the daytime it isn't even visible. Whatever combination of gases causes it has never been satisfactorily explained, but if you care to make the half-hour climb up to the spot (on a well-marked trail), you will find it can easily be extinguished, only to relight itself after a few seconds. Apparently in ancient times it put on a better show. Nearby are the ruins of a temple (of Hephaestus of course) and the old writers describe it as only one of a number of fiery manifestations on the mountain's slopes.

Bellerophon didn't have to go far to reach the home of the gods. The Lycian Olympus, one of at least three mountains of that name and fame in Asia Minor alone, is now called **Tahtali Dağ**, the highest peak of the Bey's mountains.

Phaselis

Beneath Tahtali Dağ on the shore are the ruins of **Phaselis**, one of the foremost cities of Lycia. Founded by Rhodes in the 7th century, Phaselis often stood apart from its neighbours, even to the extent of supporting Mausolus against the Lycian League. The Phaselitians, like the people of Side, had a reputation as cut-throats and schemers; once, desperate for cash, they offered Phaselitian citizenship for sale to all-comers. They met their match when a real cut-throat, the pirate Zenicertes, sacked the town and made it his headquarters, c. 90 BC. The ruins left today are all from the rebuilt city of Roman times. Its three harbours can easily be seen from the shore, also a **theatre, aqueduct** and a number of **tombs**. Now, as in ancient times, Phaselis though lovely is famous for being infested with nasty hornets. These may or may not be in the mood to annoy you when you visit.

Beyond Phaselis, the highway passes more wonderful corniche scenery through mature Mediterranean pine forests. The broad curve of the Lycian shore ends as it began, with a village called **Kemer**, its name fittingly meaning 'band' or 'arch'. From here, Antalya is just over the horizon; Kemer has absorbed much of the holiday overflow from that city, and grown into a big, brash resort built around a new marina—a startling contrast to the relatively unspoiled parts of the coast that precede it. Among the ranks of hotels are complexes like **Tukan City**, 7km away at Çamkuya, with a shopping mall, parks, horseback riding, a huge, high-tech disco, pool and casino.

Kemer and around ✆ *(242–)*   **Where to Stay**

luxury/expensive

Everything in these classes is in Kemer, which has somehow, inexplicably, become the poshest corner of the southern coast. The tone of the place is set by impressive, totally self-contained holiday complexes like the ★★★★★**Favori Aqua Resort** at Çamyuva, ✆ 824 6214, 🖨 824 6210, where everything that has ever been devised for having fun in the water is on offer, from jacuzzis to banana sailing; there's a casino, disco, gym, private beach, shopping mall and special entertainments for children. Something very similar, at Tekirova, is the ★★★★★**Phaselis Princess**, ✆ 821 4070, 🖨 821 4069; every luxury a resort could have, on a broad stretch of beach.

moderate

Demre has a very nice hotel near the Baba Noel, the ★★**Sahin**, ✆ 871 1686, where doubles with private bathroom and breakfast cost only £7/$11. You wouldn't think of Finike as a prime spot for a holiday, but if you end up there the (S) **Anadolu**, on Sahil Yolu, ✆ 855 3804, can provide an agreeable stay by the beach; simple rooms with bath for £13/$20. There are plenty of comfortable modern places in Kemer, such as the ***Dragos**, ℗ 814 2189, with a small pebble beach and pool, and some rooms with a view, but for something a bit different try the **Erendiz Ranch**, outside Kemer at Aslancakbucak, ℗ 814 3214, where the accommodation is traditional and simple and the emphasis is on horse riding (it's run by and for Germans).

cheap

Üçağiz has a woeful collection of ramshackle pensions; the **Onur**, ℗ 874 2071, by the shore, is about the best. Accommodation in Demre is a lot better, with a good selection of pleasant pensions scattered around town; both the **Lykia**, ℗ 871 2579, and the **Noel**, ℗ 871 2304, have their fans; the latter is closer to the ruins. Near the station, the cheap **Töpcü** will do at a pinch.

The closest base for seeing Olympos would be the village of Çirali, where some very modest accommodation exists. More pleasant, though, would be to stay at the tiny, nascent beach resort of Adrasan, very near Olympos village. There are a number of new *pansiyons* here, including the clean, family-run **Özcan**, ℗ 833 5220. To see the ruins at Phaselis there are a few *pansiyons* and a campsite at Tekirova, 3km to the north.

Eating Out

Üçağiz has several restaurants, none of which stand out particularly, although their waterside settings are charming; the **Marina** is a good bet for seafood; about £6/$9 and up. Along the coastal road between Kaş and Demre, the popular **Çeşme** has a lovely garden terrace; its speciality, besides kebabs, is *gözleme*, or Turkish crepes; £6/$9. Demre is full of plain lokantas and little else; at least the **Güneyhan**, near the Baba Noel, has an extensive menu; £3/$5.

In Kemer and environs, you could easily spend as much for dinner as in Paris, especially in some of the hotel restaurants—but we doubt it would ever be worth it. A couple of alternatives popular with the Turks are the **Mimoza**, in the centre on Hastane Caddesi, with typical Turkish food for about £5/$8; and the **Ulupinar**, just off the coastal road south of Tekirova: a beautiful view and excellent seafood (you can bet the trout is fresh; they raise them themselves); £6/$9 and up.

Antalya and the Pamphylian Coast

In the twilight of the Aegean Bronze Age, a time when history passes into myth, the Greeks wrote of the 'mixed multitude of peoples' set in motion by the fall of Troy; many of these found their way to the land between the mountains of Lycia and Cilicia. Historians think it likely that settlement of this region actually preceded the breakdown of civilization in the 12th century BC. The Greeks later came to call this region **Pamphylia**, 'land of all tribes'. Its ancient borders are marked by the two largest modern towns in the area, Antalya and Alanya. Its cities, Perge, Side, and Aspendos, all prospered on the fertile plain, becoming rich and thoroughly Hellenized by the time Alexander came. Although their early history was more within the Hittite–Anatolian world than the Greek, they kept stories, some from Homer, of their foundation by the seers Mopsus and Amphilochus, who had been with the Achaeans at Troy.

The coastal plain begins at **Antalya**, the Lycian mountains ending abruptly to form a spectacular backdrop for the city. Ten years ago, Antalya seemed well on its way to transforming itself from a sleepy old Selcuk town to a charming Mediterranean resort city, the capital of what people back then were fond of calling the 'Turkish Riviera' or the 'Turquoise Coast'. Somewhere along the way, however, things got out of hand. There are plenty of palm trees, and broad, fine beaches stretching away from the city on both sides, but Antalya can hardly be called a resort any more—it's Turkey's wealthiest and fastest growing city (25% annually, in the last few years), with a population already over half a million. Antalya can still be fun: stay in a *pansiyon* in one of the restored old houses in the centre, and take a big city break after all those ruins and beaches.

History

Unlike so many of the coastal cities vacated by the Greeks, Antalya has been continuously occupied, and consequently very little is left to mark its history. King Attalus II of Pergamon, given this stretch of coast by the Romans for safe-keeping in 188 BC, founded the city when Side refused to acknowledge his authority. Called Attaleia, it soon surpassed Side and the other Pamphylian cities, gaining further impetus under the Romans when Augustus settled a colony here in 6 BC. When Mediterranean civilization collapsed, Attaleia showed more resourcefulness than other cities, setting up a fleet to defend itself against pirates, Arabs, and occasionally the Byzantine taxman, and consequently survived in a reduced state despite the contraction of seagoing trade.

Recovery came with the Selcuks in the early 13th century; although various Turkish tribes had already held stretches of coastline, the Selcuks were the first to develop the area, rebuilding Attaleia and Alanya, linking them to Konya with a string of caravanserais. The sultans often spent their winters here. Had it not been for the disruptions caused by the Crusaders, and the stranglehold that Venice and Genoa kept on the eastern trade, the Selcuks might well have brought the old eastern Mediterranean world back to life with a Turkish–Muslim slant.

Getting Around

There is no rail service in the area, but no one feels the loss. Buses between Antalya and all points are very frequent (even to Istanbul, a 13-hour trip). The **bus station** is conveniently located north of the centre, on Kazim Özalp Caddesi—still about a 1km hike into the area where the hotels are, though there are minibuses and plenty of taxis about. There is a second *otogar*, the Doğu Garaji, west of the centre on Ali Cetinkaya Cadesi; from here, minibuses go to Aspendos, Manavgat and other points on the Pamphylian coast to the east (note however that the main line buses for Side and Alanya leave from the main station). The city's new **airport** receives daily flights from Ankara and Istanbul and charters from abroad; it is connected to the centre (Cumhuriyet Caddesi) by THY airline buses; a taxi will cost about £4/$6. Dozens of cruise ships stop here in season, and there is also the Turkish Maritime Lines steamer to Venice, every Wednesday from May to October (© 241 1120 in Antalya for details).

Within the city, most sites are within easy walking distance of each other; for the museum and Konyaalti beach, it's easy to take a dolmuş down the main street,

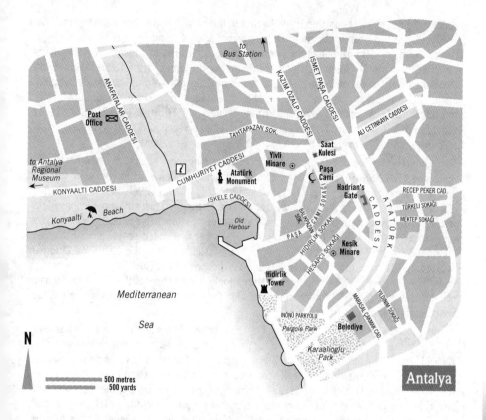

Konyaalti Caddesi (called Hastane Caddesi in the centre). Antalya has many travel agencies, such as Camel Tours, who will organize trips by coach, minibus or car, to the various sites at quite reasonable rates.

Tourist Information

Cumhuriyet Caddesi, THY Yani, ✆ (242) 241 1747; also on Mermerli Sokak, Selçuk Mah, ✆ 247 5042

The Old Town

Most of old Antalya's walls were removed long ago, but their course is followed by two modern boulevards, Atatürk Caddesi and Hastane Caddesi, separating the old and new towns. Where these streets meet, a surviving bastion of the Selcuk wall has been converted into an odd **clock tower**. To enter the old town in style, walk a few squares along Atatürk Caddesi to the restored **Hadrian's Gate**. Its three arches are decorative, but hardly a solid link in a fortification; in Hadrian's time, so secure was the pax Romana that it seemed cities would never again need real walls. In many places in Asia Minor there are purely ceremonial gates like these, or their ruins. This one was constructed in honour of Hadrian's visit in AD 130, and there would originally have been a statue of the emperor on top.

Antalya's old town was completely left behind in the growth boom that started in the '70s. Today, though still a rather poor quarter, its streets of pretty Ottoman houses have survived; in parts it seems that almost half of the houses have been restored as *pansiyons* or restaurants, much as in Istanbul's Sultanahmet. Towards the southern end is the **Kesik Minare**, the 'broken minaret' struck by lightning long ago. The mosque it serves was originally a Byzantine church built in the 5th century, rebuilt and restored many times since. Continuing further, towards the sea, you come across a squat stone cylinder, the **Hidirlik Tower**, believed to be the tomb of a 2nd-century Roman consul; traces of a carved fascia, symbol of the consuls' authority, can still be made out.

Surprisingly few Selcuk buildings remain in Antalya. The most important is the city's landmark, the **Yivli Minare**, the 'grooved minaret', typically Selcuk in its heaviness of form but unerring sense of proportion. Its lobed shaft and stalactite balcony are unique—one of the few of Turkey's fine minarets the visitor will remember. There are some surviving sections of the **walls** nearby, along with more lovely Ottoman houses. It's impossible to date the houses; the same style, with low tiled roofs, stucco or half-timber walls, and second-floor balconies, continued for three centuries; some of them were actually built in the 1920s. An Ottoman mosque, the 16th-century **Paşa Cami**, is nearby, just behind the clock tower. At the eastern end of the old town, overlooking the sea, **Karaalioğlu Park** witnesses the nightly promenade of the Antalyalilar; it's quite an elegant park, full of big trees and tea gardens where you can watch goldfish splash in the fountains.

Another job of restoration—on a grand scale—has been performed on old Antalya's **harbour**, at the opposite side of the old town from the park. Only a few years ago this entire area (called **Kaleiçi**) was falling into ruins; the city's ambitious plan for saving it has won an international architectural award. Around the newly constructed basin for yachts and other pleasure craft, new roads, fountains, hotels, parks, and terraced cafés have grown up; there are also new streets of shops crawling with carpet salesmen. At the top of the cliffs, on Hastane Caddesi, take a moment to admire the glory and grandeur of the most audacious, indescribable **Atatürk Monument** in all Turkey. May it stand forever.

Museum

West of the old town, Konyaalti Caddesi (called *Sarampol* by many locals, and on some minibus signs) heads towards the mountains, the long beach on one side, an equally long row of modern apartments on the other. About a mile out, it passes the new **Antalya Regional Museum** (*open daily exc Mon 9–6; adm*). Of all Turkey's museums, this is the most attractive in its arrangement of exhibits, and the simplest for the visitor, with clear, multilingual explanations. It contains one of the largest and best collections in the country, with exhibits ranging from the Stone Age remains from nearby Karain Cave, the earliest habitation yet discovered in Turkey, to a beautiful 6th-century relief of the archangel Gabriel. Greek and Roman sculptures fill several large halls. One great sarcophagus, carved in the form of a temple, portrays the twelve labours of Hercules. Another supposedly held the remains of St Nicholas of Myra (but don't tell your children you saw Santa Claus's grave). Merchants from Bari in southern Italy stole the body in 1087; it remains in Bari to this day, performing miracles for the faithful and oozing a mysterious holy goo that worshippers take home in tiny phials—just as it did back in Myra in Byzantine times. The sarcophagus, as you'll notice, was a bit too heavy to take along. Antique statuary in the collection includes a group of huge Olympian gods, and some equally large emperors, Hadrian, Septimus Severus, and Trajan, a relief of the twelve Lycian gods and a famous icon of the Artemis of Perge. Best of all, perhaps, is a remarkable, almost impressionistic scene of the underworld from a grave stele, hung inconspicuously behind the Hercules sarcophagus. The Byzantines are well represented in all periods. The final rooms have a very good ethnographic collection, with a special section on the Yürük nomads of Anatolia.

Beaches

Konyaalti Beach, extending for miles, is an extremely popular spot, barely visible from the street for all the restaurants, cafés and cabins. Still, there's room for all; you just need to go a little further out to be alone. Many visitors prefer the fine sand at **Lara Beach** about 7 miles (11km) southeast of town, and here also are the **Düden Waterfalls**, plunging dramatically into the sea—when there's enough water around; don't expect much of a show in summer.

Around Antalya

The northern road leads high up into the mountains from Antalya towards Burdur and Isparta. After 6 miles (10km), at a crossroads, there is a choice of excursions. The right-hand route leads past a lovely forested picnic spot, the **Düzler Park**, towards **Karain Cave**, where human remains some 50,000 years old were found. Beside the cave, which is a long climb up the mountain, there's a small museum, probably only of interest to the most fervent aficionados of the Palaeolithic.

Termessos

Up here in the mountains, we have left classical Pamphylia completely behind. Until Roman times, the influence of the Hellenized Greek cities never extended much beyond the coast; this mountainous region was known as Pisidia, the region of a fierce confederation of native Anatolian tribes who were better left alone. One of their greatest cities was **Termessos**, its ruins accessible on a new motor road 16 miles (26km) down the left-hand fork from the crossroads. The people of Termessos called themselves Solymians, giving the name to the formidable crag, Mt Solymos, under whose shelter they built their city. King Iobates, as mentioned in the *Iliad*, sent Bellerophon against the Solymians and he served them just as he had the Amazons, bombing them into submission with great boulders hurled down from Pegasus.

Other would-be conquerors did not fare as well. The Termessians liked to say they'd defeated Alexander, who abandoned a siege here on his way to Sagalassus in 334 BC. Throughout the Hellenistic era the coastal cities were constantly at odds with the Termessians, and the Romans discreetly signed a treaty declaring the city 'friend and ally of the Roman people'. Termessos remained autonomous throughout the Roman period, and showed it by not even bothering to put the emperor's picture on its coins.

The ruins, difficult to reach without a car, are well preserved, but not excavated; the difficult mountainous site is an attraction in itself, altogether different from the coastal towns. Most of the ruins are from Roman times, and in no way unusual. There is a **theatre** in good condition, an **odeon** nearby, and a small indoor theatre that also served as a bouleuterion. Like Athens, Termessos has its **Stoa of Attalus**, in the agora just behind the odeon, built by the Pergamene king. The main thoroughfare, called King Street by the Termessians, touches the western edge of the agora on its way north, where it turned into a **colonnaded street** of shops, once lined with statues of prominent citizens. All these are gone, but the inscriptions tell us that many were champion wrestlers; this sport was a speciality of the city, and of Pisidia, as it is among the Turks today.

An outstanding feature of Termessos' remains, if you have the time to search them out among the bushes, is the large number of **tombs**, all around the slopes to the east, west, and south. Some are mere sarcophagi, others elaborately built in the form of temples (the best are to the south) and yet others, on the northwest slopes, are façades carved out of the rocks in the manner of the Lycians. Most have inscriptions, but not all are tributes to the dead; many warn of the fines grave robbers or anyone attempting to reuse the tombs would incur, all mentioning specific amounts, payable to, for example, the Temple of Solymian Zeus. There are references also to the amounts payable to informers for catching the evildoers in the act.

Antalya ✆ (242–) **Where to Stay**

Antalya is full of hotels and *pansiyons*. If you're not too fussed about being near a beach, the old town is perhaps the most pleasing area: the atmosphere is convivial, there are plenty of restaurants nearby, and many places have lovely views of the harbour.

luxury

Konyaalti and the more distant beaches have more than their share of five-star behemoths. At the top of the list is the ✶✶✶✶✶**Falez Antalya** on Konyaalti, ✆ 248 5000, ✉ 248 5025, in a beautiful park-like compound with a huge three-level pool, tennis courts, and rooms with a sea view. Next door, the streamlined, futuristic ✶✶✶✶✶**Sheraton Voyager Antalya**, 100 Yil Bulvari near Konyaalti, ✆ 243 2432, ✉ 243 2462, offers the best of American chain-style comforts and lots of sports and entertainments. Neither is on the beach, though they own stretches of it and provide transport.

The best golf course in Turkey awaits you duffers 20km east of Antalya at Belek, part of the ✶✶✶✶✶**Albeach Golf Hotel**, ✆ 725 4076, ✉ 725 4099, a truly impressive complex on a big beach, surrounded by pine groves. There's every imaginable amenity in the rooms, many with sea view and balcony; besides golf, all sports from riding to windsurfing are available. The 18-hole course is open to all; green fees about £22/$33.

expensive

Some of the best places in this category are out east at Lara beach, a bit far from town but quieter. With a small private beach under the cliffs, reached by stairs, the ✶✶✶✶**Antalya Prince**, ✆ 323 3070, ✉ 323 3041, has air conditioned rooms and full facilities. Also at Lara beach, the startling modern ✶✶✶**Turist**, ✆ 349 1414, has a glass-front elevator, a hamam and pool; all rooms with satellite TV and air conditioning.

moderate

The nicest in this category is in the old town. The **(S) Turban Adalya Oteli**, Antalya Kaleiçi, ✆ 241 8066, was built in 1869 as the branch office of a bank. It is well worth visiting, even if only to see the magnificent lobby with its marble fountain; it's near the old harbour, and has a swimming pool. Another fine restoration job around the harbour has created the **(S) Argos**, Atatürk Ortaokulu Karşisi, ✆ 247 2012, all rooms with satellite TV and air conditioning, and here too there is a small pool. A more modern building in the Kaleiçi, the ****Aspen**, ✆ 247 7178, on Kaledibi Sokak, offers the same amenities.

One of the nicest hotels in the Old Town is the **(S) Villa Perla**, ✆ 248 9793, an old house on Hesapçi Sokak built around a pretty courtyard, with a good restaurant. There'll be no problem finding a moderate-range hotel in the newer quarters or at Lara beach; the problem is telling one from the others.

cheap

Nearly all of these are in the old town, and they fall into two categories: those in restored Ottoman-era houses, or more modern *pansiyons* like those in Kaş or the other resorts, usually closer to the harbour.

Among the former, two readers have written in praise of the **Ani Pansiyon**, Tabakhane Sokak just off Hesapçi Sokak, the main drag of the old town, ✆ 247 0056; spotless rooms and filling breakfasts. At the southern end of Hesapçi, one of the livelier corners of the old town after dark, the **Bermuda**, ✆ 321 1965, has so-so rooms, but it's a friendly place with a good restaurant. For a very inexpensive room with private shower and toilet, try the **Ertan Pansiyon**, Üzun Çarşi Sok 9, ✆ 321 5535. Another good, basic address in a restored building is the **Ottoman House**, on Mermerli Banyo Sokak, ✆ 247 5738. Of the latter, modern sort, one of the best is the **Özmen**, close to the harbour at 5 Zeytin Çikmazi, ✆ 241 6505; run by friendly, helpful people, nice rooms with bath, and a roof terrace with a view. The nearby **Sabah**, ✆ 247 5345, on Hesapçi Sokak, is much the same.

The cheapest places in town are clustered around the *otogar*, not necessarily the place to come away from with fond memories of Antalya. As for campsites, the place to look for them is on the main road, between Antalya and Kemer. **Denizler Camping**, ✆ 229 1316, at Sarisu, is fully equipped and set by the sea. 15km west of the city, **Kindilçeşme Camping**, ✆ 814 1065, offers shady spots under the pines; it too is on the shore.

Eating Out

Down in the far end of the old town on Hidirlik Sokak, the **Uğur Restoran** is worth the trouble it takes to find it. Excellent *saç kavurma*, outside tables under the medieval walls, and jovial waiters who can't stop giggling once you get them started; full dinner with starters for £4/$6. Almost as good, with similar food and prices, are the nearby **Villa Perla**, on Hesapçi Sokak, with a pretty enclosed garden, and the **Barbaros,** on Balikpazari Sokak, which also has outside tables. At the Karaalioğlu Park entrance to the old town, the **Yörükoğlu Pansiyon** has a very popular restaurant with a garden terrace where you can get full dinners, or else beer and *midye* (mussels) or other snacks. There are pleasant tea gardens in the park where you can have a whole samovar brought to your table if you mean to stay a while. At the end of Kazim Özalp Caddesi by the clock tower, **Parlak** has been famous for its barbecued chicken and cacaphonous ambience for decades; £5/$8. A number of kebab restaurants haunt Eski Şerbetçilar Sokak, a pedestrian street at the junction of Atatürk and Cumhuriyet; this was once the place to eat in Antalya, but now all of them may be safely ignored.

But by all means, do not miss a dinner at an unpretentious-looking kebab house nearby called the **Şanliurfalar** (because everyone there comes from out east in Şanliurfa), set in a garden on an unnamed side street just to the left as you enter the old town by the clock tower. Ask for the *Sultan'yar*, an incredible mixed grill that entirely fills the plastic bar tray they serve it on; roughly two square feet of kebab and *pide* for less than £4/$6, with salad and beer. Yet another good and cheap kebab house, extremely popular with the locals, is the **Antalya Işkembe Kebap Salonu no. 2**, on the little pedestrian street of restaurants and cafés just across Atatürk Caddesi from the old town (Hesapçi Sokak entrance); on this street you can also find hamburgers and other heretical snacks.

Antalya can't show you a lot of nightlife, surprisingly—perhaps because the resort area and beaches are so far from the centre, and partly because so many of the fancier hotels have chosen to be enclosed compounds, with their own clubs and discos. Visitors in town stroll around Kaleiçi and the back streets of the old town, where there are plenty of places for a quiet drink.

East from Antalya

The road east from Antalya does not follow the coast. It doesn't need to; the land is flat and there are farms, citrus groves, and banana plantations on either side as far as Side. Much of this land is haunted with ruins, and it is no surprise to see an ancient column sticking up in a field or along a side road, not always easy to distinguish from the concrete aeration stacks of the irrigation system. Except for Antalya and Side, all the ancient cities of this region were built inland, their ports being nothing more than a landing stage at the highest navigable point of the closest river. Consequently, all the yellow signs marking the turn-offs to sites are on the north side of the road.

Getting Around

All the sites can be reached via the busy coastal road. If you don't have a car, buses and minibuses ply the Antalya–Side route with great frequency, so you'll never have long to wait. Side is the base for seeing the other ancient sites; its taxi companies make a business of such excursions, and post their rates on blackboards in town (£16/$24 for a trip to Aspendos, for example). All the turn-offs from the main road are marked with yellow signs; at some of these, such as Aspendos, taxis wait by the roadside to take in passengers descending from the minibuses. Prepare for some rough roads if you're heading for Selge or Sillyon, but there's no other way to see them than by car (for Selge a jeep would be better; currently there are not even any tours organized here on a regular basis).

Side's *otogar* is across from the tourist office, on the coastal highway. The town has a unique service to get tourists in and out of town from it in summer—they load them in a wagon, pulled by a tractor; watching the bewildered, sunburned masses trundle by will make your day.

Tourist Information

Side: On the coastal highway at the turn-off for the town, ✆ (242) 753 1265

Perge

Perge is only a mile from the highway. Claiming Mopsus and Calchas as its founders, Perge prospered throughout the Classical period and into Byzantine times. Although its ruins do not show a city of great size, its theatre could seat 15,000, as many as Side or Aspendos. Perge's most famous citizen, the mathematician Apollonius (3rd century BC), was a follower of Euclid who did important work with ellipses and conic sections, contributing much of the background of Ptolemy's epicyclic theory of the universe.

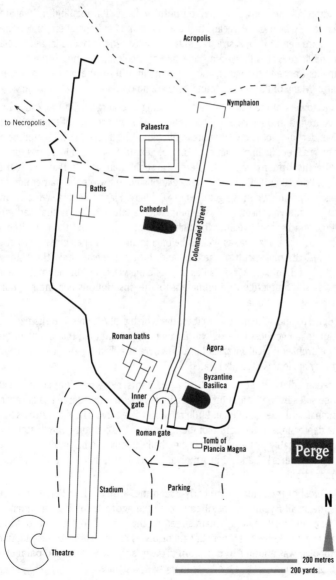

The modern road to Perge passes between the **stadium**, one of the best preserved in Turkey, and the **theatre** before it reaches the parking lot at the main gate. Although as yet unexcavated, the theatre shows promise of having been an even more impressive sight than those of Aspendos or Side. Its stage building is still present in part, along with some of its sculpted friezes; among the recognizable tableaux are scenes of Eros and Psyche, and Dionysus and Ariadne. In the stadium, the space facing the outside under the seats was rented out for shops, just as they are now in some modern Turkish stadia. Some of the runners' names and trades can still be read on the walls. Interestingly, the stadium seated fewer spectators than the theatre.

Perge's **main gate**, at the centre of the southern walls, is its outstanding feature—the Hellenistic inner gate, which the Pergeans made into a grand ceremonial entrance. The outer gate, added in the 3rd century AD, is strictly utilitarian. Between the two, a large courtyard full of monuments and statues was flanked on one side by a colonnade and on the other by the **propyla**, a formal entrance to the baths, and the fountain or **nymphaion** that looked like the façade of a theatre. Many of the statues found here are now in the Antalya museum.

To the two round towers of the gate still partly standing, the Pergeans of the 2nd century AD added another courtyard in the shape of a horseshoe, lined with statues of the city's founders. At that time, 'founder' did not necessarily mean one who had 'founded', but could be anyone who financed any great public improvement. And so, next to Mopsus and Calchas (the statues are gone but the inscriptions remain), there are such men as M. Plancius Varus and C. Plancius Varus, both identified here by their relationship to a woman—father and brother. This becomes less surprising when we get to know the lady. Plancia Magna, whose statue can also be seen in the Antalya museum, was a member of a talented family that had migrated from Italy to Perge and become wealthy through land-holdings. One of the men attained the office of Roman consul and Plancia, as well as being a great civic benefactress, was also chief priestess of Artemis, the major cult of the city, and, for a time, even held the highest civic office in Perge, that of demiurge. Great ladies in public life were not unknown in the ancient world, but for one so completely to dominate a town—inscriptions bearing her name are found everywhere—is exceptional.

In Perge, as at Ephesus and so many other cities, the worship of Artemis, a Hellenized abstraction of the old Anatolian goddess Cybele, was far more important than that of any of the male gods. One of the archaeological puzzles here is where the Temple of Artemis, a building mentioned by many ancient writers, is located.

Compact and rectangular, Perge was cut into quadrants by two colonnaded streets and enclosed on three sides by walls, and on the north by a low hill that served as an **acropolis**, probably the original settlement of Perge. Little remains there now. The main streets had to be very wide as the depressions in the centre of them between the columns were water channels, not for sewage, but probably just a unique civic embellishment, the inspiration for the similar canal that ran down Atatürk Caddesi in Antalya, before it was filled in a few years ago to accommodate more traffic.

Inside the walls most of the remains are early Byzantine, a time when Perge was still prosperous: there is the small **Byzantine basilica** next to the **agora**, adjoining the inner gateway on the eastern side, and further up the main street, on the left, the foundations of the **cathedral** remain; this may mark the spot where St Paul made his first converts. At the end, under the walls of the acropolis, was another **nymphaion**. Towards the west gate, the **palaestra** built during the reign of Claudius is one of the better-preserved structures.

Sillyon

Like Perge, **Sillyon** was first built on a low, defensible hill; you must climb a bit to see what's left there. To reach it, take the signposted road to the north, 9 miles (14km) past Perge on the coastal road. It was never a very important town, managing to avoid most of the quarrels of its contentious neighbours, and appears in history only when Alexander passed through.

The remains consist of foundations and streets and steps cut out of the rock of the hill. Some of the fortifications remain, including one complete square tower and a few well-preserved Byzantine buildings. A recent landslide swept away most of the theatre and all of the odeon.

Aspendos

The next ancient town, **Aspendos**, also lies north of the coast road on the banks of the Köprü Çay, the ancient River Eurymedon, then a much larger river than now. To get to the site, take a side road for 2½ miles (4km) from the main road, passing a beautiful arched **Ottoman bridge** over the Eurymedon. The road may or may not be asphalted: work is in progress.

In 468 BC the final battles in the long wars between the Persians and Greeks were fought here, resulting in such crushing defeat for the Great King that Persia finally abandoned its attempt to subdue the Greek world. In a single day, the boldness of the Athenian Admiral Cimon won two victories at once, on land and on sea. Both the Persian fleet and their army were concentrated at Aspendos for another assault on the Aegean. Cimon successfully drew the fleet from its harbour in the Eurymedon, and defeated it in a day-long battle, capturing many of the Persian ships; not content with this, he dressed some of his small force of marines in Persian uniforms and sent them up the Eurymedon, where they created a diversion so that Cimon and the rest of his men, secretly landed up the coast, were able to disperse or capture the entire bewildered Persian army.

Aspendos and Side were usually the two leading cities of Pamphylia, which is perhaps why they never got on well with each other. After the Romans finally made them agree, Aspendos thrived until well into the Byzantine era; little is known of its eventual abandonment; the wars and disruptions caused by the 7th-century Arabs certainly had much to do with it.

The Theatre of Aspendos

Aspendos has the best-preserved **Roman theatre** anywhere in the Mediterranean. This is no exaggeration; not only is the entire cavea intact, along with the arcade at the top, but the entire stage building has survived. Credit is given to the Selcuks for some preservation work, but no one yet knows what use they made of the building.

At the present entrance, a door in the centre of the stage building, is a small plaque with a message from Atatürk; his government made restoration of this theatre its first major archaeological project, and the inscription records Atatürk's wish that the Turks should not 'lock it up like a museum piece', but use it for performances of classical drama—and wrestling. This is not so strange; throughout this part of Asia Minor, wrestling matches were commonly staged in the theatres. Currently, plays are produced during the September festival, but wrestling, as elsewhere outside Thrace, is becoming increasingly rare.

Whichever you would prefer to imagine on the cards, stepping inside the theatre magically transports you into the past, evoking the lost Graeco-Roman world in a way few ruins ever can. Not that it is a building of any great architectural distinction—no offence to Zeno, its architect (2nd century AD)—it is simply that it has survived. Even without its marble veneer or the statues that once graced the interior of the stage building, it is easy to imagine what a night at the theatre in old Aspendos might have been like.

All the theatres of the Pamphylian cities had stage buildings; all were built in Roman times after this innovation had come into vogue. Earlier Greek and Hellenistic theatres had been open, as at Epidauros in Greece, sited with a striking natural backdrop for the action in the skene and orchestra. Later, the plays moved up to a raised stage, or proscenium, and stage buildings were used both for manipulating the sets and props, and to shut out the outside world.

Of the sculptural scheme, all that survives is a frieze of Dionysus, but on the right, some plaster with a red and white zigzag design can be made out. This has been identified as Byzantine work; there are similar designs in the castle towers of Alanya. Climbing to the arcades on top for the view, or to find a short cut into the city, is disappointing as the hill on which the theatre is hung is separated from Aspendos proper by a ravine. To see the rest of the town you must go around it; both sides lead to gates from which paths lead up to the city.

Aspendos has not been excavated, apart from the theatre, but there are remains of a few public buildings, a stoa, bouleuterion and basilica around the agora; all the more substantial ruins are Byzantine. The reason for making the climb is to see the **aqueduct**, one of the best-preserved examples anywhere, stretching from the hill of Aspendos across the plain to the distant mountains. Four long sections still stand. The two towers may seem puzzling, but it was no problem for Roman engineers to make water flow uphill, using the principles of gravity and capillary action; the towers served to regulate the pressure and allow air to escape.

Back at the bottom of the hill, you may wish to visit the two **baths**, to the left of the theatre along the access road, and the half-buried **stadium**, to its right.

Selge

Another Pisidian city that can be reached from the coast, **Selge**, was originally called by the very un-Greek name of Estlegiys; as it became Hellenized, it grew and prospered from the manufacture of storax gum, used as incense. Selge, like Termessos in a difficult but beautiful mountain setting, has a ruined **theatre** and **stadium**, and a well-preserved Roman **bridge** over the Eurymedon. It's out of the way, 21 miles (34km) north of the coast road to the village of Beşkonak; from there a track leads the last few miles up into the mountains, to the village of Altinkaya (locals call it Zerk). Nearby, a few miles north of Beşkonak, is the recently opened **Köprülü Kanyon National Park**, a natural wonderland that is now the scene of one of Turkey's biggest environmental battles—local citizens are working feverishly to keep the whole place from being swallowed up by the reservoirs of two big hydroelectric dams proposed by a private utility.

Side

All these cities, interesting as they are, must be taken only as a prelude to **Side**. First among the Pamphylian cities of antiquity, or so it boasted, Side now must be considered the first among Pamphylia's ruins; it was the first to be substantially excavated, and so a visit here will prove much more rewarding to the non-specialist.

In the 1890s, when Crete was freed from Ottoman rule, a community of Muslim fishermen came from the island to settle here. They built a village among Side's ruins, and resisted all attempts by archaeologists and the government to relocate it. They're still trying, but in the

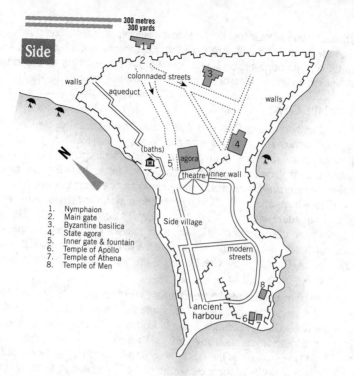

Side

300 metres
300 yards

walls

colonnaded streets

aqueduct

walls

(baths)

5 agora

theatre inner wall

4

Side village

modern
streets

1. Nymphaion
2. Main gate
3. Byzantine basilica
4. State agora
5. Inner gate & fountain
6. Temple of Apollo
7. Temple of Athena
8. Temple of Men

ancient
harbour

N

meantime the villagers have made the most of their opportunity, turning their town into one of Turkey's most improbable tourist traps. Its main street, full of ice-cream parlours, bars and trinket-stands, follows the route of old Side's colonnaded street, and the ancient residential quarters are filling up with hotels and pensions. It's pleasanter than it sounds. The beaches around Side's peninsula mainly attract Turkish and German families, the restaurants are good and the atmosphere relaxed (note that the beaches near the centre can be crowded and awful, and there's no public transport out to the good ones, which are largely divvied up among hotels anyhow). There is a noisy disco, but it's out in the ancient suburbs near the Byzantine basilica.

History

Cyme, the Ionian city near Smyrna, founded Side as a colony in the 7th century BC; it is thought that despite the Greek colonists, Side remained very much a city of native Anatolians, speaking their strange language which had been replaced everywhere else by Greek.

'*Side*' means pomegranate, and the fruit was often depicted on the city's coins, so many of which survive as to suggest great prosperity, lasting well into the 6th century AD. How they made their money is another question. Sideans, even more than the rest of the Pamphylians, had a well-earned reputation for being scoundrels, both in business dealings and in relations with other towns. In the 2nd century BC the city had an arrangement with the Cilician pirates and acted as their fence, circulating stolen goods and the pirates' captives. Until Pompey put the pirates out of business, Side ran a slave market that, if ancient writers are to be believed, handled thousands of poor souls every day.

Despite this, the Sideans never fell foul of Rome. Most of the slaves ended up in Rome, and

Sidean prosperity was not affected by the Roman takeover. By the 4th century AD, however, Side had so dwindled that it built a new wall near the theatre, reducing itself by half. After a revival in the 5th and 6th centuries, the depredations of the Arabs put an end to Side after a thousand years of urban life. Most of the inhabitants gradually resettled in Antalya.

Remains of the City

There is no difficulty in finding Side; even before the turn-off is reached, the forest of signs for restaurants and pensions springs up, growing thicker as you approach the town. The modern road enters very near the ancient **main gate**, with a small semi-circular court just inside—not for decoration, as at Perge, but for defence. The ruins just outside the gate belong to the **nymphaion** or fountain. Greek cities commonly had embellishments like this outside the gates, to water animals and/or to allow travellers to refresh themselves before entering the city. The long **aqueduct**, which passes through the wall's three towers to the right of the gate, carried the water to the nymphaion and from there into the city. Sections of the aqueduct in good repair can be seen for some distance north of the city, and its path inside the walls can be traced through the 'Quarter of the Great Gate', as the northernmost district by the baths and theatre is described in inscriptions.

Inside the gate, two **colonnaded streets** begin. That on the right, leading towards the theatre, was the main thoroughfare of Side, while the street on the left goes through the Quarter of the Great Guild, heading due south. Colonnaded streets like this were the status embellishment of Roman cities, shady arcades for business and shopping that gradually replaced the old Greek agoras as the places to see and be seen in. The two in Side, totalling over a mile in length, testify to the great wealth of the city in Roman times; no other city in Asia Minor, not even Ephesus, had as many. Most of the surviving structures in the Quarter of the Great Guild date from the Byzantine afterglow, including a huge **basilica**, on the left side of the colonnaded street, a church, and an unidentified building off to the right.

Just before reaching the inner gate, the other street passes the Roman **baths** to the right and the large **agora** to the left. This was used in the 2nd century as the slave market, and it isn't difficult to imagine the crowds of woebegone captives chained to the columns. In the centre of the agora, the circular foundation and ruins belonged, quite fittingly, to the Temple of Fortuna. Another open square, the **state agora**, stands a few hundred feet to the east, near the old sea wall. As its name implies, it was the governmental centre of Side. Most of this part of the city is partially buried under sand dunes that have accumulated over the centuries, and has not yet been excavated.

The baths, going back across the narrow neck of the peninsula, have been incorporated into the **Side Museum**, with an excellent collection based solely on the strength of what the archaeologists found here: there are lots of Roman statues, including some excellent copies of earlier Greek works; reliefs of uniforms and weapons, found near one of the city gates, probably commemorate the spoils won in a victory over Pergamon, when King Attalus tried to conquer the Pamphylian coast; some wonderful sarcophagi show the sentimental side of the ancient world's attitude to death, portraying death's door, one with the deceased's faithful dog peering out; another, a child's, is carved with birds and butterflies.

The great arch of the **inner gate** still stands, simply because, at some later time, the citizens were compelled to wall it up, leaving a smaller entrance in the centre. It is thought that a statue of an emperor in his four-horsed chariot crowned the gate, hence the name of the neighbourhood, 'Quarter of the Quadriga'. In every Pamphylian city there is evidence of gradual impoverishment; marble façades on concrete, or sarcophagi reused and statue bases with the old inscriptions blotted out and new ones added. Here, the grand **fountain** to the left of the gate was originally a monument in honour of the Emperor Vespasian, moved here from somewhere else in the city.

Here the modern village begins, built around the ruins of the old, down the colonnaded street to the end of the peninsula. The town is closed to traffic, but you may take your car if you're staying at one of the hotels or pensions. Side's well-preserved **theatre**, adjoining the inner gate and facing the agora, dominates the centre of the city. On this flat peninsula, with no natural hillside out of which to carve one, the Sideans had to build a theatre themselves. The cavea, the largest in Pamphylia with room for some 25,000 spectators, is supported by an impressive system of vaults and arches.

A 4-foot wall was built around the bottom row of seats to seal off the orchestra when combats and wild beast shows began to shove drama off the stage. The remains of two chapels, on either side of the stage building, and some inscriptions indicating seats reserved for priests, reveal that at some time in the early Byzantine era it was used as an open-air church (note the crosses carved over some of the entrances). Most of the sculptural friezes on the stage build-ings remain, but the reliefs, probably scenes from the myths of Dionysus, are so completely effaced that early Christian vandalism is suspected.

Once in the modern town, you're on your own trying to find the other homes, baths, and temples of old Side. The newer buildings, in and around the ruins, exasperate the archaeolo-gist, but make a picturesque setting. Unfortunately, in the last few years so much has been built inside the inner wall that it becomes increasingly difficult to trace the ruins; many have been fenced off into gardens. Ruins of some of the more important of the city's temples have been excavated at the very tip of the peninsula overlooking the **harbour**, now silted up. There are no natural harbours on the Pamphylian coast and Side, the foremost port city, was forced to make one out of almost nothing and dredge it continuously. 'A harbour of Side' became a figure of speech, like the labours of Sisyphus, for any unending task. Just where the water's edge once was, the platforms of the **Temple of Apollo** and the **Temple of Athena** are visible; the surrounding ruins belonged to a huge Byzantine **basilica** built over the temples, which were presumably incorporated into it. Part of the columns and architrave of Apollo's temple have been reconstructed, carved with outlandish masks on the metopes. Behind these, in what must have been a square at the end of the colonnaded street, are more ruins, of a Byzantine **fountain** and a semicircular **temple** (3rd century AD) devoted to Men, the Anatolian moon god.

Attractions near Side

While in Side, incidentally, avoid all proffered excursions to the **Manavgat Falls** in the moun-tains above Side, unless you need more souvenirs, or the prospect of a 3ft waterfall excites you. Leaving the town on the way to Alanya, you pass two well-preserved **kervansarays** of the Selcuks; at **Şarapsahan**, 9½ miles (15km) west of Alanya on the coast, and **Alarahan**, on the side road 5½ miles (9km) up in the mountains. Şarapsahan is fortified, testifying to the uncertainty of the sea lanes even in the best days of the Selcuks. Near Alarahan, the **Alara Castle** is a steep climb, but gives a spectacular view over the valley.

Three miles (5km) before Alanya, the highway department has constructed one of its **roadside**

beaches. This is cleverly designed; a steep embankment had to be built for the road, 100 feet above the sea, so they simply added steps and built dressing rooms into the side. The effect is one of perfect isolation.

Side ✆ (242–)   **Where to Stay**

Side has over 25,000 beds to let but the trick is to get one that is convenient for the beach, the town and the ruins while being quiet enough to allow you a peaceful night's sleep. With this in mind, follow the main street down to the harbour and bear left at the 'mosque' sign. Walk on into a bewildering array of side streets and several good, moderately priced hotels and pensions will present themselves. Several are noted below.

luxury/expensive

Everything fancy will not be found in Side proper, but in the beaches to either side. Locals claim the **★★★★★Asteria Oteli**, ✆ 753 1830, ✆ 753 1830, to be the best in the town and they're probably right. Two miles (3km) out of town on the western beach, it has cavernous air-conditioned rooms with satellite TV, swimming pools including a heated one indoors and plenty of recreational facilities. If you need something directly on the beach though, try the **★★★★★Turquoise**, at Sorgun Mevkii, ✆ 756 9330, ✆ 756 9345, a palatial complex built around a garden courtyard, surrounded by forests, with every imaginable luxury and every sport on offer—including a polo ground. Like the other luxury establishments, a double room at these goes for about £45/$67. For slightly less, you can enjoy much the same amenities at the **★★★★Sol Selin**, ✆ 763 6680, ✆ 763 6214, on the beach at Çolakli Köyü.

moderate

The beaches to either side of Side are graced with a number of gleaming complexes less pretentious than the above. The **★★★Hane**, ✆ 753 2445, 6km west of town, has a good stretch of beach and a pretty park, and comfortable air-conditioned rooms; a little distant, but it has everything you'll need. If you prefer to stay in the centre, there is the **★Apollo**, ✆ 753 1941; individual small bungalows near the Temple of Apollo. A bit expensive for a *pansiyon*, but worth it, is the **Hanimeli** on Turgut Reis Sokak, ✆ 753 1789, a beautifully-kept old house in a garden; £11/$17 including breakfast.

cheap

There's a fair number of *pansiyons* sprinkled around the village, almost all family-run places where the owners take some pride in keeping the place up (they're a bit more expensive than other towns, though, averaging about £7/$11); those on the eastern shore boast of a view of Side's Famous Sunrises, while the westerners tell you about the view of Side's Famous Sunsets. Next to the Hanimeli, the friendly owners of the **Şen**, ✆ 753 2989, offer clean, simple rooms with bath, and a roof terrace to relax with a view over the town. On the opposite side, you can settle for the sunrises at the **Çiçek**, ✆ 753 3849, which is just as good in every way. Yet another, similar *pansiyon* with a view is the nearby **Yildiz**, ✆ 753 1157.

Near the bus station there are several *pansiyons* if you don't mind the tractor ride or the 15-minute walk into town. There are camp sites either side of the road into the town.

Side has its share of tourist seafood palaces, and places where Germans would feel at home. For a seafood dinner without breaking the bank, head for **Koşeoğlu**, and its outdoor terrace on the east side waterfront: the menu includes things not often seen in Turkish restaurants, such as shrimp and octopus, and a full dinner can be had for £6/$9. If something simpler is called for, try the very inexpensive **Şiş Restoran**, in a garden on Mergiz Sokak. There's a wide choice of kebabs including a zingy Adana kebab, and they do pizzas too.

After doing the ruins of Aspendos, you can have lunch at the **Belkis**, on the road to the site in the village of the same name; outside tables in a nice setting, and simple but good food for about £4/$6.

Cilicia

This coastal province is ready-made for tourist brochures; the historical background is as good as even the wildest imaginings of a copywriter. Mark Antony did present Cilicia to Cleopatra as a love gift—though not just for the sensuous coastal scenery or the forests and peaks of the beautiful Taurus mountains. Cleopatra, always a sharp girl, chose in this case not to see the forest for the trees. Cilicia's timber happened to be Egypt's biggest import, and the queen simply wanted to get it wholesale. Besides, these two lovers had a navy to build.

Half of Cilicia, like Lycia, is difficult country; the ancients commonly referred to the western portion as 'Rough Cilicia' and the eastern as 'Smooth Cilicia', the latter a plain created by deltas of several rivers around the present-day metropolis of Adana. Both sections have always lacked big towns and culture; Rough Cilicia because there's nothing but mountains and trees, and Smooth Cilicia partly because of its location on a major medieval conqueror's highway through the Cilician Gates, and partly because of the mosquito. Malaria was a problem until recent times. Few of the armies that have passed through ever felt inclined to stop, and history has mainly avoided both the Cilicias. Rough Cilicia, impenetrable and indeed almost unknown to the Greeks and Romans, enjoyed its best hour just a century before Antony and Cleopatra had their fling, as the most notorious pirate's nest in the entire Mediterranean. Following the example of Tryphon the Voluptuary, a Governor of Kalonoros who turned to piracy after an unsuccessful revolt against the Seleucid King Antiochus, the Cilician pirates ruled the waves for a hundred years until the Romans decided to wipe them out; in 67 BC, they sent Pompey in with more ships and money than he asked for, and within six weeks the great Roman general had either killed, coerced, or bought off the lot of them.

Piracy made a comeback with the Arab invasions of the 7th century and Cilicia, never really prosperous at the best of times, degenerated into a beautiful wasteland. Ottoman rule did nothing to help, and until the Turkish republic, Cilicia remained the poorest, most backward and disease-ridden corner of western Anatolia. In the last 30 years, the change has been dramatic. Modern Turkey's extensive water projects have turned the once-useless coast into a garden of citrus and banana groves, with cotton the major crop on the plains around Adana.

In **Alanya**, the 'pearl of the Turkish Mediterranean', not agriculture but tourism has accomplished the work of transformation. In ancient times writers included this city sometimes in Pamphylia, sometimes in Cilicia. Its great rock of a peninsula that the Greeks called *Kalonoros* or the 'beautiful mountain' makes a natural boundary stone between the two provinces. Today, with some 50,000 people, it's by far the most important town between Antalya and Mersin. It also has some of the best beaches along the southern coast, but Alanya is a town worth visiting in its own right; no brash upstart of a resort, it has memories going back to antiquity, and some fine monuments left by the cultured Selcuk sultans.

History

Like the rest of Cilicia, ancient *Coracesium* only got in the news when pirates were using it as a base, as in the time of Tryphon the Voluptuary. But even in the worst times, the rock of Kalonoros continued to be inhabited. An almost impregnable position, it was a good place to hold. Alâeddin Keykubat discovered this to his dismay when he tried to take the citadel in 1220. Various stories still circulate as to how he finally got in; one has him marrying the commander's daughter and taking the whole family back to Konya, while another says that, in a final desperate move, he had his men tie torches to the horns of thousands of goats and drive them up the hill at night, tricking the defenders into thinking a great army was coming after them; one imagines they would have found the battle cry somewhat suspicious. The most plausible version has Alâeddin making a deal with the Armenian prince who held Kalonoros— offering him another piece of land instead, and saving them both the trouble of a siege.

Alâeddin renamed the city after himself, 'Ala' iyeh', and Atatürk, on a visit during his Westernizing campaign, changed it to the more euphonious 'Alanya'. For a while after the Selcuk decline Alanya belonged to the French Lusignan kings of Cyprus, a relic from the crusades. With the most beautiful setting along the southern coast and miles of beaches, Alanya has become a major resort, especially popular among the Germans but seeing more people from Britain every year. The lower town around the harbour and the coastal highway past the beaches on either side (those west of the citadel are less popular and less crowded) are all full of tourist clutter in the manner of Marmaris, or a Greek island. The Alanyali take refuge, as they have done from so many other invaders, up in the lovely old neighbourhoods above the citadel.

Getting Around

Although Alanya has no air or rail connection, regular buses travel to points along the coast and inland to Konya. Cruise ships call often in the summer, and there is also a **ferry** service to Girne (Kyrenia) in the Turkish Republic of Northern Cyprus, only a 3½ hour trip (about £40 return; no cars—the car ferry goes from Taşucu). In summer it usually runs daily, Wed–Sat, off season Fri only, and it's becoming an increasingly popular trip for Alanya vacationers. (The Northern Cypriots will not stamp your passport, so you won't have to worry about harassment if you pass through Greece later on.) Around the harbour you'll see plenty of **tours** on offer, to the caves and other sights around the mountain, inaccessible by land; the average rate is about £8/$12 a boatload, so you might look around for companions to share one.

As in Antalya, the coastal road is also the main thoroughfare of the town (called

Atatürk Caddesi following the western beach, and *Keykubat Caddesi* along the eastern beach); the dolmuşes can take you to any point along the beaches. There's a city bus service from the harbour up to the citadel, with stops all along the way. Alanya's *otogar* is a mile outside town, just off Atatürk Caddesi near the western beach, and as there's no dolmuş service, you'll have to take a taxi in or walk a mile to the centre.

Tourist Information

Damlataş Caddesi, across from the museum, ✆ (242) 513 1240

The Red Tower

In the harbour, beside the fish restaurants, camel rides, cruises to everywhere and terraced tea gardens, you'll find the **Red Tower**, Alanya's landmark since Alâeddin built it in 1226. The government completely restored this octagonal 115ft bastion in 1955, and now it houses a small ethnographic museum (*open daily exc Mon, 8–12, 1.30–5; adm*).

The top floor, crenellated for cannons, offers a fine view of the city; note here how the floor is sloped with channels towards the middle—the centre of the building is one great cistern. This tower, a purely functional defensive work, that nonetheless ranks among the highlights of Selcuk architecture, was constructed to protect the **Tersane** (naval dockyards) built at the same time; they are joined to the tower by a short stretch of wall now surrounded by gardens.

From the start, the Selcuk aim in seizing coastal towns was to become a force at sea as well as on land, but as they never had enough time to really get under sail, the birth of Turkish seapower was deferred until the Ottomans, some two centuries later. The enclosed dockyards, connected by archways, are a cool, quiet and interesting place to visit. Judging from the remains of an old beak-prowed fishing boat in one yard, it seems they have been in use until recent times. The other side of the yards is protected by another tower, **Tophane**, literally the 'ball house'—an arsenal.

RED TOWER
ALANYA

On Kalonoros

Besides the dockyards, the Red Tower also guarded the approaches to the citadel. From here the modern road climbs up through the **main gate** with its Selcuk inscription (in Persian, the language of Alâeddin Keykubat's court) past old Ottoman-style houses and gardens. The grandest of these, conspicuous on the lower slopes, was restored by a former American ambassador to Turkey. Where the road passes through the second level of the fortification, traces of the original Hellenistic-era wall may be seen underlying Alâeddin's work; just to the right is a small Byzantine chapel, with the walls carefully built around it.

Further on, the road skirts the **Ehmediye,** a section of old Alanya within the walls that has survived as perhaps the most charming and serene quarter in Turkey, all overgrown with plane trees and flowers among the stone walls and venerable cottages. At its centre, there is a **bedesten** and **caravanserai** built by the Selcuks (now a hotel) with an unusual tomb, the 1230 **Aksebe Türbesi** and also the fine 16th-century **Sülemaniye Mosque.** Tourism has touched the Ehmediye only slightly. Some of the more enterprising residents have set up a souvenir stand on the road offering two local specialities, lace, and gourds painted with the faces of—we can only guess—Cleopatra and Bugs Bunny. A few hundred yards further on and the road reaches the **Iç Kale** (*open daily 8–sunset; adm*), the inner fortress. Once reached, a quick look down suffices to explain why the citadel was never taken by force.

Most of the buildings around the Iç Kale have gone to ruin; some are certainly part of the palace or governor's residence that existed here; another building with extremely thick walls can only have been a magazine. Best preserved, surprisingly, is a **Byzantine Church** that may be as early as 6th century. Inside, there are still remnants of the original frescoes on the walls. The four Evangelists must have been the theme on the pendentives, for on one a lone, fading Evangelist, his attributes gone, can still be seen poring over his book.

Most of the citadel walls have been restored in recent years. In one corner, called the **Adam Atacaği,** a platform has been erected for the view; here, according to a highly improbable local legend, condemned criminals were tossed off. The Adam Atacaği looks out over a narrow spit of land extending southwest from the rock of Alanya called **Cilvarda Burnu,** on which stand the ruins of a tower, a Byzantine monastery and chapel, and a building the Turks call the Darphane, or mint. There is no way of getting there on foot, but boats in the harbour take trippers to the rock and to other spots around it: the huge **Pirate's Cave** and a **phosphorescent cave,** among others, and of course you'll be shown the little secluded beach where Cleopatra took her dip in the ocean.

One final cave, the best of all, can be reached from near the beaches to the west of the rock. **Damlataş Cave,** with its forests of stalagmites in delicate colours, was discovered only in 1948. Most visitors come just to look, but sufferers from bronchitis and other ailments find its mixture of radioactivity and high humidity to have curative properties. Not far from the cave, the **Alanya Museum** (*open daily 8–12, 1.30–5.30; adm*) in a new building contains local archaeological finds. **Market** day in Alanya is Friday, and it takes place on Tevfikiye Caddesi, north of Atatürk.

35km to the west, Alanya has spawned a new baby resort, around the broad sandy beach at **Incekum.** The Alanya tourist office is currently trying to promote the *yaylas* (summer pastures), the lovely hills north of the city as a day trip destination—if only for a picnic, as the Alanyalilar themselves are fond of doing—but there's no public transport and you'll need a car to get around. One spot that can almost be reached by dolmuş is the scenic valley of the **Dimçay;** the minibus will take you to the mouth of the stream, 6km east of town, but from there it's a trek of about 10km up to the dam, where there is swimming and restaurants. Directly north of Alanya, there are a number of lovely picnic sites in the yaylas, pine forests, and some charming villages: **Mahmut Seydi,** with an interesting Selcuk mosque, and **Türktaş Köyü,** with a little waterfall nearby.

Where to Stay

luxury/expensive

As elsewhere on the southern coast, plenty of new pleasure domes have opened in the last few years, both on the town's beaches and at Incekum. 3km west of the city, the *******Grand Kaptan**, Oba Göl Mevkii, ✆ 514 0100, ✉ 514 0092, has everything you could ask for, including Alanya's only casino, a private beach, water sports, and air-conditioned rooms with a sea view and balcony. Less expensively, there's the ******Club Alantur**, Dimçayi Mevkii, ✆ 518 1740, ✉ 518 1756, a complex of low-rise buildings by the beach with bars and lots of sports facilities.

moderate

Above all, Alanya is the land of the three-star package hotel; there are over a hundred of them. Prices are all officially about the same (about £30/$45 in season, but as elsewhere big discounts can often be managed) but there is a great difference in the amenities provided. The only exception to the rule is the **(S) Bedesten**, ✆ 512 1036, up on Kalonoros, a remodelled *han* that has been beautifully restored. No matter where else you stay, you'll never be far from a beach. If you want to be right on the beach, the *****Panorama Hotel**, Keykubat Caddesi 30, ✆ 513 1181, a 10-minute walk east of the Atatürk statue, is worth considering. Here you can stagger out of your room in the morning and plunge straight into the sea; pool, tennis and most water sports on offer. The ****Yunusgücü**, on Atatürk Caddesi, ✆ 513 9366, must be the archetypal Turkish resort hotel, from the little flags flying out front to the forgettable restaurant, but it's a good bargain, with air-conditioned rooms and a pool for about £20/$30 at most. In a more isolated setting—Konakli, 15km west of town, the *****Saphir**, ✆ 565 2525, also on the beach, offers air-conditioned rooms with satellite TV, pool and tennis. A less expensive choice nearby is the ****Galaxy**, ✆ 565 2636, a simple place with nice rooms and a pool. If all you want is a quiet room with a balcony close to the beach, the ****Ikiz**, ✆ 513 3155, off Atatürk Caddesi on the west beach, will do just fine.

There's plenty more of the same at Incekum, such as the sleek modern *****Aspendos**, Avsallar Mah, ✆ 517 1091, with a big pool, tennis courts and private section of beach. An alternative is the *****Yalihan**, also at Avsallar Mah, ✆ 517 1010, air-conditioned rooms, some with a sea-view balcony; water sports arranged.

cheap

The nicest of Alanya's cheapies, a long trek from the beach in the centre of town, is the **Günaydin**, ✆ 513 1943, on Damlataş Caddesi; decent rooms with bath and balcony, and the specific charm of being able to look down at the street life below and forget you're in a resort altogether. Not far away, on Iskele Caddesi (the street that curves around the bottom of Kalonoros), the **Baba**, ✆ 513 1032, is right in the centre of the action, fun but a little noisy. Near the west beach, on Haci Hamidoğlu Sokak, the **Saray**, ✆ 513 2811, is simple, acceptable and cheap. There are a few inexpensive pensions around the eastern beach, one being the **Yazicioğlu Pansiyon**, Güller Pinari Mah, ✆ 513 2902.

Just walk on down to the centre, between Atatürk/Keykubat Caddesi and the harbour, and you'll find dozens of places to choose from, nearly all of them good, inexpensive and simple, with very few blatantly *turistik* restaurants. The **Gaziantep Köy'in**, close to the port, grills a nice *tavuk şiş* (chicken), among a wide choice of other kebabs; about £3/$5. Deservedly successful, they've opened up a second branch around the corner. For about the same price, you can sample the liver kebabs and other Turkish soul food at the **Inegol Köftecisi**, on Izzet Azakoğlu Caddesi (the *Kordon*). There is a whole street of even cheaper kebab stands off Kalğidim Sokak, of which the **Hunkar Lokanta** will do for a quick lunch. Iskele Caddesi, along the harbour, is crammed with the usual fish restaurants, averaging £7/$11 for a three-course meal with a drink; the **Iskele** is a good one, and often has live music. Slightly more expensive, but worth it, is the **Anatolian Restaurant**, around the corner on Rihtim Caddesi, delicious seafood, including prawns and shellfish, in a lovely setting; average £8/$12 if you don't get carried away.

Further out Keykubat Caddesi, the bar/restaurant **Cemali Plaj** makes a proper pizza; £3/$5 with a beer. On Atatürk, the inexpensive **Arzum Manti Evi** offers not only *manti*, but some vegetarian dishes, a rarity in these parts. For a country outing take Keykubat Caddesi out 6km and take the turnoff left for the valley of the Dimçay; all the way up the road into the mountains are picnic spots and nice, informal restaurants under the trees that serve fresh trout and barbecue.

Like Side, Alanya is mostly a family resort, and nightlife is limited to a few discos, the occasional karaoke bar, and clubs that entertain Germans with belly-dancing displays—as *Türkische Bauchtanzerei* it doesn't seem quite so exotic. There are a few noisy bars around the harbour, including the **Pub 13** on Iskele Caddesi; others are out on Keykubat Caddesi.

Alanya to Silifke

Leaving Alanya for the east, the Cilician coast road follows the beaches for some distance before the steep slopes of the Taurus, plunging directly into the sea, compel it to climb into a spectacular corniche that runs all the way to Silifke, bordered by thick pine forests that in summer exude an almost overwhelming fragrance. The Turkish forestry service takes good care of these, the most extensive forests in the country, and no knowledge of Turkish is needed to understand the signs, posted every few hundred feet, warning about forest fires: *One tree can make a million matches, and one match can kill a million trees.* In summer, the pines will be full of cicadas, jammering away all afternoon and making an unearthly racket. The Turks are very fond of them; children keep them as pets, and it isn't unusual to see a grown man pick one off a tree and put it on his shoulder for company. In this region, towns are few, but the entire coast is littered with ruins: Byzantine buildings and churches near the shore, and crumbling fortifications of different ages on the heights.

Getting Around

If you're driving, avoid the coastal road at night. It twists and turns like a snake with St Vitus Dance and there are no crash barriers; one mistake and you're over the cliffs. Besides, during the day you can enjoy the scenery, among Turkey's loveliest. The one route inland, through the Taurus Mountains to Konya, is equally picturesque, following the Göksu valley from Silifke. Buses travel along the coast every hour or so (6½ hours from Alanya to Silifke; pack some sandwiches!). Anamur is a sprawling town and it is difficult to see all the sites in the area without a car.

From Taşucu, the car ferry to Girne (Kyrenia) in northern Cyprus leaves at midnight daily in season, Sunday–Thursday; there are also hydrofoils, daily except Saturday. British subjects may need a visa to get in, due to some political silliness, though local officials think the problem should be ironed out soon—ask in advance. If your passport is stamped in Girne, you'll need to get a new one should you ever want to go to Greece. Ask for a stamp on a separate sheet of paper instead. Officials will comply.

Tourist Information

Anamur: Bulvar Caddesi, ✆ (324) 816 7051

Silifke: Atatürk Caddesi, Veli Gürten Gözbey Caddesi, ✆ (324) 714 1151

Castles along the Shore, and Anamur

All along this wonderful drive, there are ruins to distract you, either a few km up in the hills or directly on the shore. Few of the sites really have much to show, as **Laertes**, 11km east of Alanya, or **Syedra**, another 6km after that. The next site, **Iotape**, is a little better; built on a small promontory, it has substantial ruins of a bathhouse, and a good beach below the cliffs. The best part of the drive begins at **Gazipaşa**, a fishermen's town with a beach near the ruins of an ancient town named Selinus. Twelve miles (20km) further, at the boundary between Antalya and İçel (Mersin) provinces, another undeveloped beach runs along the edge of a narrow enclosed plain full of banana fields. The village of **Kaladiran** nearby stands in the shadow of a ruined Hellenistic castle.

The first town reached of any size is **Anamur**, on a plateau of greenhouses. The town itself has little appeal, but there is a beach 3 miles (5km) south at its suburb of **Iskele**. Nearby, at the cape now called Anamur Burnu, the southernmost point of Cilicia, are the ruins of **Anemurium**, a town founded in the late Hellenistic era. Its ruins seem shabby compared with the towns of Pamphylia—not a scrap of marble, only the dark, conglomerate archaeologists call 'pudding stone'—but they are substantial: a church and the arcades of an aqueduct on the hillside, with a castle on top. Near the beach, there are towers and ruined tombs. Some of the mosaics unearthed at Anemurium can be seen in the small **museum** in Iskele. A mile or so to the east, the 12th-century **Castle of Anamur** was built directly on the shore by the kings of Little Armenia, in a peaceful, dreamy setting between two long beaches. The castle is almost completely intact, not through any virtue in its construction; the Ottomans kept it in good repair after the British occupied Cyprus, and used it as a fortress again in the First World War. The small mosque inside is still in use.

The coast road continues east, climbing ever higher up and down the edge of the Taurus. On the very clearest days, they say that the mountains of Cyprus, some 30 miles (50km) to the south, can be seen. **Softa Kalesi**, on a peak just after the holiday village of Bozyazi, was also built by the Armenians. 'Softa', in Turkish, means a student of theology, and the castle probably got its name from the chapel, still visible from the road below. On this stretch, there are several isolated beaches, but near Ovacik the road cuts inland for a while, up the forested Akdere (White Valley) and back.

When it returns to the sea, the road reaches its crescendo of scenery just before the plain of Silifke, at **Bağsak**, a pretty bay with beaches and the ruins of a medieval fort; this, and the crumbling chapel on the bay's islet, was built by the Knights of St John. While this order still occupied Rhodes and Bodrum, its fleet often gave it control of all the southern Turkish coast. **Taşucu**, an old village with a good harbour, has developed recently into a small and unpretentious beach resort; from here you can take a trip on the regular ferry to Girne in northern Cyprus.

Silifke

Like Alexander the Great, who left 'Alexandrias' all over three continents lest we ever forget him, his generals and their successors who founded the Seleucid Kingdom of Persia and Syria bedevilled mapmakers with a score of 'Seleucias' all over the Middle East. Most have fallen to ruins long ago. One survived, and almost kept its name. Ancient Seleucia ad Calycadnos, once a great, thriving city, has been whittled down by the years to plain **Silifke** on the Göksü, a piquant and humble Turkish town. There are no signs of Seleucia apart from a single standing Corinthian column with a stork on top, and traces of a theatre south of the Göksü, but the **Byzantine Castle** still peers down from the nearest crag, and on a slight rise near modern Silifke, in the east of the Göksü plain near the coastal highway, stand the ruins of a Byzantine religious complex the Turks call **Meryemlik**, with the once-great **church of Saint Thecla**.

This saint, according to the imagination of the hagiographers, was the first girl to throw over her fiancé for a life of chastity, and soon became the first female Christian martyr. Foundations of a colonnaded building that was once part of the monastery remain as well as the still-standing apse of the large basilica. Beneath it, recent excavations have uncovered a cavern, later carved into a chapel, where the early Christians hid. There are bits of mosaics and frescoes in the chapel, and the municipality has made it a small museum for architectural sculpture found throughout Silifke.

The Göksü, though a poor excuse for a river until the spring floods, once changed the course of European history. The Germans like to think of their old Barbarossa, Kaiser Frederick I of the Holy Roman Empire, as asleep under his mountain, like King Arthur. By 1190 Barbarossa had made the empire a going concern, the most powerful state in Europe; he was on his way to the Holy Land to teach the Saracens a lesson when he met his match in the Göksü. According to the chroniclers, he unaccountably fell off his horse in the stream, and drowned before anyone could reach him, in 6 inches of water. The crusade was aborted, and German unification postponed 700 years. Upstream from Silifke, a small plaque marks the spot in the lovely **Göksü gorge** along the road to Konya.

Across Rough Cilicia, there have been few opportunities to strike inland to look at the Taurus Mountains; most of the roads are unpaved and the region remains as isolated and wild as in ancient times. The Byzantines called this land Isauria, and while its barbarous natives helped wreck the urban life of the coasts in the 5th and 6th centuries, in the process they themselves were becoming Christianized. By the 8th century they were producing Byzantine emperors, like Leo III, the famous Iconoclast.

Silifke ① (324–)   **Where to Stay**

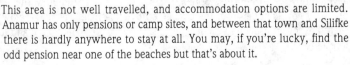

This area is not well travelled, and accommodation options are limited. Anamur has only pensions or camp sites, and between that town and Silifke there is hardly anywhere to stay at all. You may, if you're lucky, find the odd pension near one of the beaches but that's about it.

expensive

Such luxury as there is in this area is represented by the ****Vivianco on its own beach at Bozyazi, 13km east of Anamur, ℗ 851 4200, ℗ 851 2291. Nice though austere, air-conditioned rooms with satellite TV and balconies, a hamam and gym; water sports.

moderate

In Taşucu, the ***Taştur Oteli, ℗ 714 1090, is pleasant, with a pool and a better than average restaurant; it's right on the shore, though there isn't a beach. The **Kral Motel**, Atatürk Caddesi 89, offers better value for money. It has a swimming pool and rooms with fine sea views. Silifke has but one decent hotel, the **Hotel Çadir**, by the riverside on Atatürk Caddesi 8, ℗ 714 2449, with large en suite rooms and good service; £12/$18.

cheap

In Anamur you can either stay in the town or near the beach in Iskele. The average price for a pension in Iskele is £6/$9, as at the **Eser**, ℗ 814 2322, a pleasant, family-run place right by the beach. In Anamur, the **Pansiyon Ünal**, ℗ 814 2091, is cheap and cheerful, if you don't mind using the bathroom down the hall. There are two good camp sites in the vicinity, the **Yali Mocamp** in Iskele, ℗ 814 3474, on the beach and with several basic rooms to let to non-campers, and the **Pullu**, ℗ 814 1105, 4 miles (6km) out of Anamur in the forests, but still near a beach. Both sites have restaurants and mosquitoes.

In Taşucu the **Tekin Pansiyon**, Mehsuriye Mah, ℗ 714 1541, is very welcoming and has nice, if waterless, rooms for £5/$8. Silifke has very little in the way of *pansiyons* and much of what's there is grim. The **Akdeniz** on Menderes Caddesi will attract anyone nostalgic for the Turkey of a decade ago; gray-painted rooms with a bog down the hall for 65p.

Eating Out

Wherever the road meets the coast on the way to Silifke, there is sure to be a fish restaurant; often a very informal place that's nothing more than a few tables under the trees. Most are pretty good; you just peer in the cooler and select your fish. Two that have grown up into proper restaurants are the **Merreç** and the **Terizane**, both about 80km east of Gazipaşa. Both are good and quite a bit cheaper than seafood restaurants in the resorts; the Terizane also has inexpensive rooms.

Iskele has several good fish restaurants, where the prices are dependent on how good the catch was that morning. The restaurant at the **Yali Mocamp** serves tasty, if over-priced grub to the thunderous sounds of Deep Purple. Anamur has an excellent cheap *pide* parlour, the **Merhabe**, next to the bus station. Anamur's delicious tea, *ada çay*, is famous. Made from sage flowers picked on the mountains, it possesses, so they say, innumerable healing properties.

In Taşucu, the **Baba** and the **Denizkizi** are both near the harbour and more than acceptable. The restaurant at the **Çinar Hotel** is the best place to dine in Silifke (when it's open); £4/$6. Otherwise the choice is between a handful of uninspiring lokantas that tend to close early.

In ancient times, however, the furthest Greek civilization ever penetrated the Taurus was the mountain city of Olbia, founded in the 3rd century BC, known as Diocaesarea to the Romans and **Uzuncaburç** to the Turks. This is your chance for an excursion into the mountains. Not only are the ruins worth the 30km drive, but the road itself passes through a charming landscape of rolling, well-tended farm land, reminiscent of some corner of Italy. On the way are three **Roman tombs**, small temples in form, and almost entirely intact; two, at **Çifte Anit**, are visible from the road, and one of these is an unusual two-level temple with an arched vestibule and Corinthian columns.

'Uzuncaburç' means 'tall tower', referring to the two 70ft Hellenistic towers, one in the city and another on a nearby hilltop, perhaps the best-preserved examples in Turkey. It's believed there were others, forming a communications system with the coast; messages were sent by flashing the sun off polished shields in a kind of Morse code. The city itself is a much more pleasant site than any on the coast in Pamphylia, a bucolic ruin shaded with walnut and fruit trees, among vineyards and goats.

You still enter the city through the **monumental gate**, with corbels and niches for long-vanished statues, leading to the usual **colonnaded street**. Just outside the gate is the theatre, unexcavated and overgrown. The pride of the ancient city, the **Temple of Zeus Olbios** is the oldest structure yet discovered using the Corinthian order (3rd century BC). The capitals are mainly on the ground, though several columns have been re-erected; the proto-Corinthian design shows traces of the Ionic scrolls from which it evolved. An apse still stands at the east end, reminding us that the temple was later pressed into service as a church. The sculptural friezes have been gathered in the garden. Their cartoon lions, boars, bulls and leopards show a distinct decline from the best work of the Greeks, but have their charm, reminiscent of the carvings in many medieval cathedrals. From here, a crossroads of colonnaded streets will take you either to a rare, surviving arched **city gate**, or to the **Temple of Fortuna** (1st century BC), which, as fortune would have it, has now become a social club for goats. Outside the city, you may also visit the large **necropolis** of tombs, some separate, some cut into the rock, and simple sarcophagi—many with the bones still visible inside.

The Caves of Heaven and Hell

Back along the coast, a few miles east of Silifke, feverish development is under way at the beaches around **Susanoğlu**, **Narlikuyu** and **Atakent**. Narlikuyu boasts one curiosity: Turkey's smallest national museum consists only of one small room with a fountain and a famous relief of the **Three Graces**, Aglaia, Thalia, and Euphrosyne, looking much as they do in Botticelli's painting. In the 4th century, there was a Roman spa around the spring here.

The Corycian caves, **Cennet** and **Cehennem**, can be most easily and truthfully explained as two great holes in the ground. They're interesting enough for the Turks, who coined these names 'heaven' and 'hell' for them, and they so fascinated the ancients that an important sanctuary of unfathomable antiquity was maintained in Cennet; it may have hosted mysteries such as those in Eleusis, or perhaps an oracle—Delphi also had a 'Corycian Cave'. Cennet, an enormous chasm difficult of entry, can be explored with the aid of a guide; at the bottom, the remains of the old sanctuary have been incorporated into a 5th-century church. The little church was never an important site for the Christians; apparently they hoped to keep the old pagan demons deep inside by building it there, like the stopper in a bottle. The chasm, turning into a cave, continues on with an underground stream, no one knows how far; many believe the stream flows to the spring of the Three Graces.

Cehennem cannot be entered at all, except by its multitude of birds; their chirping echoes weirdly through the chasm. Like its counterpart, it is enormous and bottomless. A team of alpinists went down recently, and found only the bones of the few unfortunates who had fallen in. To the Greeks, this was the lair of Typhon, the monster of monsters spawned by Mother Earth in revenge for Zeus' defeat of the Titans. Typhon actually defeated Zeus and dragged him here, where he escaped only through the cunning of Hermes. Before succumbing to thunderbolts, however, Typhon managed to start a fine family; according to Hesiod, his offspring included the Hydra, the Chimaera and Cerberus; his grandchildren, the Sphinx and the Nemean Lion.

Kizkalesi

The growth of Kizkalesi has been secretive and stealthy; what was only a few years ago a tiny fishing hamlet is now the largest resort east of Alanya. Yet this is a resort with a difference. Foreigners are in the strict minority here and most visitors are families from the big cities of Anatolia, making Kizkalesi the most 'Turkish' of all the Turkish resorts. Those overseas visitors that do come have their chance to holiday in Turkish style, although it's worth remembering that certain Western holiday conventions—topless sunbathing for example, and excessive boozing—are simply not acceptable here. Kizkalesi has a nice beach, but there is more to the town than just sea and sand; it has two perfect Armenian castles and, within walking distance, some intriguing, barely touched, historical sites.

History: Little Armenia

In ancient days Kizkalesi was Korykos, never a large town although it's remembered as the place where Cicero spent two years of his exile from Rome. In the 11th century, however, Korykos achieved prominence along with its sister settlement **Elaiussa-Sebeste** (modern Ayas) when the Rubenid kings of Little Armenia made it their capital.

This odd state, formed by an opportunist group of refugee nobles after the Armenian homeland was overrun by the Selcuks, managed to survive for three centuries by a system of alliances, first with the Crusader states, and later, with the Ilhanli Mongols, a remnant of the empire of Genghis Khan to which many states, both Christian and Muslim, paid tribute. Life as a Christian principality surrounded by Muslims became increasingly precarious in the 14th century, though ironically it was Peter I, the French-born King of Cyprus, who contributed the most to the end of Little Armenia. The last king of any independent Armenian state, King Leon VI, went into exile in Paris, where he is buried at St Denis.

Getting Around

Kizkalesi is connected by frequent bus and dolmuş to both Silifke and Mersin. The nearest airport is at Adana. Mersin has a car ferry service to Gazimağusa (Famogusta) in Northern Cyprus three times a week (Mon–Wed–Fri), though the Tasuçu–Girne ferry is cheaper and faster.

Mersin: Inönü Bulv, near the harbour, © (324) 231 6358

Korykos

The Armenians concentrated their military forces at the **Castles of Korykos**. These two large fortifications, which also served as their port, were begun by the Byzantine Admiral Eustachius; the Armenians enlarged and improved them, using lots of stone from nearby ancient cities, including an entire Roman gate rebuilt into the new wall. The smaller castle, called locally the Kizkalesi or **Maiden's Castle**, stands romantically offshore on a small island; in the Middle Ages the Armenians joined it to the mainland with a causeway that enclosed their harbour, but today you either have to swim or hire a boat if you want to see it.

The Castle of the Sparrowhawk

Marco Polo went all the way to China, and when he came back his neighbours in Venice didn't believe a word he said; they called him 'Mr Million', for what they thought were just a lot of wild exaggerations. He might have done better just to stay at home, following the example of one of the slipperiest travel writers of all time, the author of the medieval classic *Mandeville's Travels*. Nobody even knows who Mandeville really was—maybe an Englishman from St Albans or a Frenchman from Liège—and from all evidence he never set foot outside Europe, but merely drew on the works of real travellers and classical authors. But his book, written around 1375, was popular all over Europe and translated into many languages. When the first printing presses started up a half-century later it became one of the first best-sellers. From it, many Europeans first learned about India, and the Great Khan of Cathay, and that the world was round.

As a storyteller, Mandeville is hard to beat. One of the most elegant fairytales in his *Travels* comes from one of these castles, concerning the demise of the Kingdom of Little Armenia. In that country, he relates, there is 'an old castle that standeth upon a rock, the which is cleped the Castle of the Sparrowhawk.' He locates it near the city of Ayas, and undoubtedly one of the Corycian castles is meant. In the tale, the castle held a sparrowhawk upon a perch, and 'a fair lady of faerie that keepith it'. To anyone who stayed there seven days alone without sleep, the lady would appear and grant a wish. A King of Armenia stood the trial, and when the lady appeared he boldly stated he'd had enough of power and wealth, and demanded the lady herself. For such impudence she could only curse him and his nation to unending strife and impoverishment, and Little Armenia withered ever after. Another knight, a Templar, also stood watch with the sparrowhawk, and after his vigil asked for a purse of gold that should never empty. The lady granted it, but told the knight it would mean the end of his Order, 'for the trust and the affiance of that purse, and the great pride that they should have. And so it was.' Other men fared better in the Castle of the Sparrowhawk, though Mandeville warns that any who fail and fall asleep will be forever lost.

Is the lady of this story the 'maiden' of Kizkalesi? Perhaps—though the Turks tell visitors a different, Sleeping Beauty-type story about a princess who, it was prophesied at her birth, would die of a snakebite. Her father locked her up here, but the snake came out of a basket of fruit and got her anyhow.

The **ruins of Korykos** begin from across the main road behind the land castle and continue for several miles along the coast, merging with the remains of Elaiussa-Sebeste before coming to an end in Ayas, where the apses of two large **basilicas** are clearly visible from the road. In some areas farmers have cultivated the land around the old stones; in other parts the land-scape is wild and undeveloped and there is a ghostly pleasure in exploring the ruins, identifying a house here, a cemetery there, pretending to be Heinrich Schliemann. Part of the site is given over to a huge **necropolis** dating from the 4th century AD, where there are rock tombs and ornate sarcophagi, some still with their lids, decorated with crosses, garlands and animals. In one area, some 6km north of the castles, a series of Roman-era **reliefs** is carved into the cliff—men, women, children and animals; probably this too is a funeral monument. You may chance upon these, and the necropolis, within 20 minutes of wandering, or you may search fruitlessly all day—it's that hard to find. If you're lucky, you'll meet a local who knows exactly where it is.

From Ayas, the road passes more ruins, of the ancient towns of **Kanlidivane** and **Soli**, as the coastal plain opens outwards into the flatlands of Smooth Cilicia. Kanlidivane (*open daily 9–5; adm*), which means 'court of blood', is a fascinating place, built around a natural chasm that was used as a necropolis; stairs lead down, and there are fragments of tombs and reliefs at the bottom. Nearby is a well-preserved Hellenistic tower and an expanse of Byzantine-era ruins. Soli, originally a Greek colony, was probably happy to be re-founded by the Romans and renamed Pompeiopolis, in honour of the conqueror of the pirates. Soli had long been the butt of jokes for the clumsy way the inhabitants had of speaking Greek; the town gives us the word *soloikos*, or solecism. The Turks call the site Viranşehir, or 'ruined city'—a common enough place name in this country. There is a good beach where people from Mersin come on week-ends, and plenty of ruins; as at Side, you can trace the course of a once–impressive colonnaded street down to the harbour.

Mersin

Nothing in Mersin is very old or of particular interest, but the city is well built and attractive, with a lovely park running almost the entire length of its shore. Mersin has grown from nothing into a city of 400,000 over the last three decades, as the port for the busy textile industries of Adana and Tarsus. Ironically, it is one of the oldest towns in the world; remains of a 6000-year-old culture, related to that of Çatal Höyük, have been dug from a mound called Yumuk Tepe, but from then to now, there have only been small settlements. Excavations at these have unearthed a few finds, from the Hittite to Byzantine eras, that can be seen in the town **museum**. The most astounding sight in Mersin, though, is a new 650ft luxury hotel; inexplicably thrown up in the centre of town by an American chain, it stands like a visitation from outer space. Who goes there, and what do they do?

This is as far as we go in this book, but if you're determined to press further eastwards, you'll come to the plains of 'Smooth Cilicia', known to the Turks of today as **Çukurova**, the land of cotton that feeds the textile mills of **Adana**, Turkey's fourth-largest city (and a bit of a toad-stool, though likeable enough). There are lots more castles in the region to explore, and a major Hittite site, **Karatepe**. Beyond that comes the Hatay, a mountainous finger of land that meets the Syrian border, and its capital **Antakya**—ancient Antioch, which for a while in late Roman and Byzantine times was the second-largest city in the Mediterranean world. You might find its museum worth the detour, for it contains a spectacular collection of Roman mosaics, rivalling Naples' as the best anywhere.

luxury/expensive

If by chance you should want to find out who stays in the monster, it's the *****Ramada Hotel Mersin**, Kuvay Milliye Caddesi, ☎ 336 1010, ✆ 336 0722. As in other Turkish cities, this luxury hotel has become the social centre of Mersin, with its restaurants, casino, disco, health club and so on. The ****Mersin**, Gümrük Meydani, ☎ 232 1640, is centrally located, with sea views and satellite TV.

The only top-class resort in the area is the ****Altinorfoz Banana** at Atakent beach near Silifke, ☎ 722 4211, ✆ 722 4215. Don't worry about the name; Banana is another chain, represented in other establishments such as the Banana Queen in Alanya. In a peaceful setting on the beach, this one has air-conditioned rooms, a hamam, and all water sports facilities.

moderate

Kizkalesi must have the highest density of hotels to square kilometres in all of Turkey. There is, however, nothing at the top end of the accommodation market. The town is very centralized, to the point that no one seems to bother with addresses.

The ***Kilikya**, ☎ 523 2116, boasts air-conditioned rooms with a view of the Maiden's Castle, a friendly and helpful staff, and a broad stretch of beach. If it's full, try either the **Hotel Hantur**, ☎ 523 1367, or the **Best Motel**, ☎ 523 1074, both good, both with en suite doubles for £14/$21. The **Nobel Motel**, ☎ 523 1075, is also attractively priced, bed and breakfast for two costing £9/$14. In Mersin, the **Gökhan**, Soğuksu Caaddesi, ☎ 231 6256, is a solid, unspectacular city-centre hotel; it is air-conditioned, though, which can be the most important thing here in summer.

cheap

In Kizkalesi, *pansiyons* are everywhere, ranging from the acceptable to the utterly vile. Be sure to see the room before agreeing to stay and remember that a better deal can often be obtained in some of the motels listed above. The **Erdal Pansiyon**, ☎ 523 1071, has en suite rooms that are cheap enough, though a little noisy. The **Lüx Paşa Pansiyon**, ☎ 523 1080, is quiet and clean.

Mersin has a whole street full of good, reasonably priced hotels next to the bus station, useful if you're just passing through or need to make an early start in the morning. Two particularly nice ones are the **Everdi**, Otogar Çarşisi 35, ☎ 231 5071, with en suite doubles for £5/$8, and the slightly more expensive **Derya**, Mersinli Ahmet Caddesi 28, ☎ 231 8069.

Eating Out

Kizkalesi is swamped with restaurants. Three are worth a mention: the **Plaji**, on the beach, for its views of the sea castle, £3/$5; the **Bonjour** for its inexpensive all-you-can-eat *meze* buffets, and the restaurant of the hotel **Kilikya**, for the house speciality of *tava*, a mix of meat, aubergines, spices, tomatoes and so on. A plate of *tava*, a salad and a drink costs £3/$5.

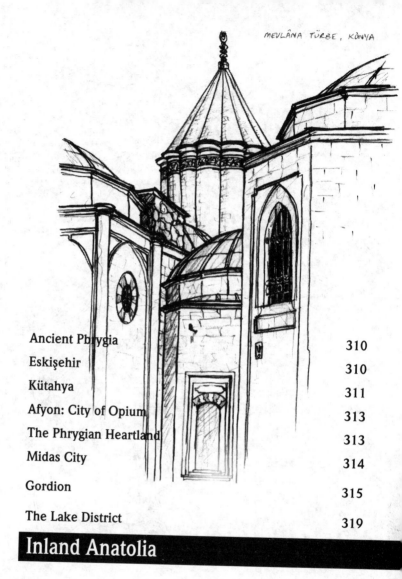

MEVLÂNA TÜRBE, KONYA

Ancient Phrygia	310
Eskişehir	310
Kütahya	311
Afyon: City of Opium	313
The Phrygian Heartland	313
Midas City	314
Gordion	315
The Lake District	319

Inland Anatolia

Eğirdir	319
Konya	325
Cappadocia	333
Central Cappadocia	339
Underground Cities	343
South and West of Göreme	344

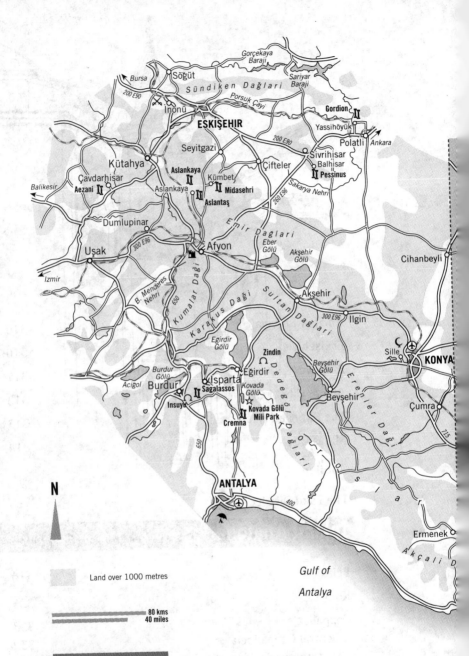

Inland Anatolia

Land over 1000 metres

80 kms
40 miles

N

Gulf of
Antalya

If you can tear yourself away from the delights of the coasts for a while, we can show you a bit of the real Anatolia: a stark, rough-edged, land, where bleak and empty vastnesses change in a twinkling to little green paradises and spectacular mountain scenery. The landscapes are more varied than you would imagine: lush, fertile plains around Kütahya and Afyon, steep granite peaks around beautiful Lake Eğirdir, the cheerless, wheat-covered steppe around Konya and the Salt Lake, and of course Cappadocia, one of the natural marvels of the Earth.

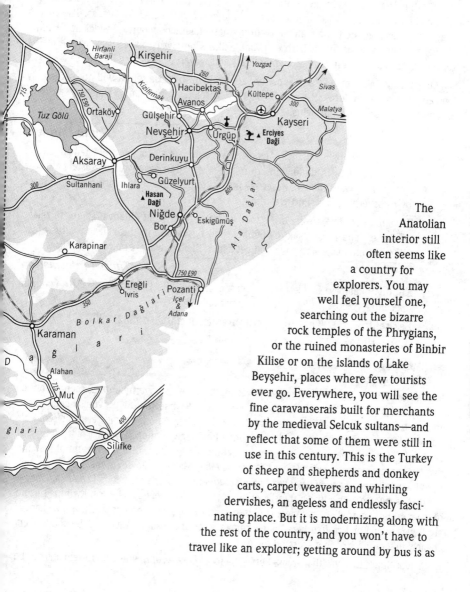

The Anatolian interior still often seems like a country for explorers. You may well feel yourself one, searching out the bizarre rock temples of the Phrygians, or the ruined monasteries of Binbir Kilise or on the islands of Lake Beyşehir, places where few tourists ever go. Everywhere, you will see the fine caravanserais built for merchants by the medieval Selcuk sultans—and reflect that some of them were still in use in this century. This is the Turkey of sheep and shepherds and donkey carts, carpet weavers and whirling dervishes, an ageless and endlessly fascinating place. But it is modernizing along with the rest of the country, and you won't have to travel like an explorer; getting around by bus is as fast and convenient as on the coasts, and there are good hotels and places to eat almost everywhere.

Ancient Phrygia: Eskişehir to Gordion

Once you get to know the Phrygians, you'll wish they were still around. They had style. Just enough of their art survives to make us wish we could see more—the way they dressed and decorated their houses. And we would love to hear some of their famous music, played on lyres, cymbals and flutes in the weird, wailing 'Phrygian mode'. Musicologists would give anything for a chance; it was the foundation of the music of the classical Greeks. The Greeks may even have learned their alphabet from these talented people. Besides music, the Phrygians were famous for their roses (Midas, like King Cyrus of Persia, was one of the legendary gardeners of antiquity), for embroidery and woven wool carpets.

The tantalizing fragments of this lost culture are well worth a visit, but it will not necessarily be easy. The three modern cities of the region—Eskişehir, Kütahya and Afyon—are all some distance away from the main sights.

Getting Around

Couldn't be simpler. Kütahya, Afyon and Eskişehir are all connected by rail and bus to Istanbul and Izmir. Stations in both cities are within easy walking distance of the centres. As always though, buses are the better deal, and again, fortunately, all three towns have *otogars* a short walk from their centres.

Çavdarhisar, with the ruins of Aizanoi, is easy to reach from Kütahya. There are village minibuses, and most Usak- or Izmir-bound buses stop in the village's *otogar* (ask beforehand to make sure you don't get left on the highway, 4km from the village).

Tourist Information

Kütahya: Fuatpaşa Caddesi, in the centre, ℗ (274) 223 1962; there is also a booth in the central Azerbaijan Park, open summer only.

Eskişehir: Vilayet Binasi (provincial government office), ℗ (222) 230 1752

Afyon: Hükümet Konaği, ℗ (272) 213 5447

Eskişehir

To make up for what nature has denied this land, the Turkish Government has spent a considerable part of its development effort here. As a result, **Eskişehir**, the provincial capital, has grown up to become one of Turkey's largest cities. It's a joke among people here that Yenişehir ('new town') to the northwest is a crumbling old village, while Eskişehir ('old town') has become a thoroughly modern city, grown wealthy enough from its manufacture of locomotives and meerschaum pipes to water its streets twice a day to keep down the dust—and they need it. This is one of a very few places on earth where meerschaum is found (*meerschaum*— German 'sea-foam'—is a direct translation from the Persian kef-i-daryâ; it's a hydrous silicate of magnesium), and when you see any of it in tourist shops elsewhere in Turkey, the chances are it was mined and crafted here. Finely carved pipes and walking sticks can be bought very cheaply in a number of shops around town.

In ancient times, this was the Greek–Phrygian city of Dorylaeum, whose scant remains can be seen around the Selcuk castle northwest of the town. Grave steles and columns of Dorylaeum, some quite interesting examples in fact, are on display at Eskişehir's **Archaeological Museum**. On the eastern edge of the city is the 16th-century **Kurşunlu Mosque**, a complex attributed to Mimar Sinan. Eskişehir is a pleasant and animated city; the Porsuk Su (Beaver Creek) and its tributaries and canals run all through it, crossed by hundreds of little bridges, but it hasn't much to show the visitor.

Kütahya

Kütahya, a prosperous and amiable city that spreads under an Ottoman castle, would be unremarkable but for its ceramics, one of the great craft traditions of Turkey. You'll notice it as soon as you arrive; the bus station is the prettiest in Turkey, with pillars tiled from floor to ceiling. Hotels, shops and even bars in the modern town have façades covered in Kütahya tiles, and all the main streets are lined with showrooms for the scores of workshops in and around the city. The first to practise the art here were Persians, brought as captives by Selim the Grim in 1514. While the art of ceramics declined in Iznik, in the 18th century, Kütahya seized the opportunity, and now makes fine china and faïence in classic Ottoman patterns, as well as architectural tiles, used in the restorations of all the old mosques. If you are looking for something besides carpets to take home, Kütahya is well worth a stop. You can window-shop conveniently or go in and have a cup of tea; quality is high and prices quite low, in everything from simple vases and plates to urns the size of refrigerators for your favourite paşa's seraglio—one very good place is Güven Çini, Fatih Sultan Mehmet Bulvari at Belediye Meydani. (Places here in the centre are a bit more expensive. Walk out Atatürk Bulvari towards the *otogar* and you'll find some good things for less; in some of the smaller concerns here you can watch the artists at work.)

Kütahya was the ancient Cotiaeum, a town several times destroyed and rebuilt, most recently by Mehmet the Conqueror; he captured it from another, more obscure Turkish tribe called the Germaniyids, for whom Kütahya served as capital. It has a few Ottoman mosques of its own,

notably the 15th-century **Ulu Cami**, in a pretty garden at the end of Cumhuriyet Meydani, the street that leads from the centre through Kütahya's bazaar district. The medrese adjoining the mosque, built by the Germaniyids, now houses Kütahya's little **museum**, a reminder that one should never pass up a provincial museum in any Turkish town, no matter how obscure. The best ones are dusty curiosity shops, like Kütahya's, that offer some genuine treasures of ancient art: surprises here include some painted geometric pots from Hacilar (some of the oldest in the world), fine grave steles with the death's door motif common on the southern coast, a big flashy Hellenistic sarcophagus with a *Battle of the Amazons*, and some unique terracotta ex-votos: weird triple-formed Hecate with torches, the underworld patroness of witches who was worshipped at Colophon and in Caria, and another, unidentified goddess fondling her flowing tresses, with a bird in her other hand, a small boy by her side, and a snake emerging from her genitals. There are several versions of her; the later ones, from Roman times, are at least decently covered.

In the older neighbourhoods, on the slopes around the Ulu Cami, are many lovely Ottoman wooden houses, some of which have been restored. One of them can be visited, the **Kossuth House**, where Lajos Kossuth, the romantic leader of Hungary's 1848 fight for independence, spent part of his subsequent exile (at the time, the Hungarians like the Poles were natural friends of Ottoman Turkey, having common enemies in Austria and Russia). Today the interior has been recreated as it was at the time Kossuth lived there. From nearby a track leads up to the ruined **castle**, begun under the Byzantines.

From Kütahya, the first slopes of a broad massif called **Türkmen Dağ** rise up over the horizon, stretching off to the east. On its opposite slope, in difficult hill country, is the source of the Sakarya River. There you will also find Midas City and nearly a dozen temple façades and tombs in the heartland of ancient Phrygia. There is no way over the mountain, unfortunately, and adventurous souls desiring to explore Phrygia must start from Eskişehir or **Afyon** to the south. Paved roads from either city will carry you 50 or 60 miles into the area, but then, if you're not driving, you will be at the mercy of whatever taxi drivers you can find in the villages of Seyitgazi or Ihsaniye.

Aizanoi's Temple of Zeus

Aizanoi (*Aezani* in Turkish), an important town in Greek and Roman times, stood 36km southwest of Kütahya, near the present-day village of Çavdarhisar (the 'rye castle'). Almost nothing remains of it—nothing except the best-preserved ancient temple in Turkey. The Temple of Zeus is also one of the largest, almost 100 feet across the bottom of its podium, and one of the last to be built—in the 2nd century during the reign of Hadrian. Despite the fashion of the day for the Corinthian order, the temple is Ionian, showing the Roman preference for tall elevations and narrow columns.

Most of these columns and half the walls of the cella still stand. Parts of the frieze connecting the tops of the columns are present as well, though the pediment and roof are long gone. This pediment had been decorated at its peaks and corners with huge *acroteria*, carved stone acanthus leaves, and bits of these lie on the ground. Hadrian's reign was one of the better times for Asia Minor and the rest of the empire, when both prosperity and building talent were still undiminished. The style of the temple may have been thought old-fashioned when it was built, and less charitable critics today may find it lacking in inspiration—with something of the air of a 1920s bank building, erected by men to whom art no longer came easily, but who did their best to strive for a quiet tastefulness. The temple's form, which you can call *pseudo-dipteral* (having open corridors behind the columns instead of a second row of columns), is a copy of the Temple of Zeus Sosipolis at Magnesia (Manisa), a work much admired in that era.

One Roman innovation, made possible by the temple's great height, is the cellar, with its barrel-vaulted roof. Zeus had to share his temple with the goddess Cybele, which is not unusual in a town so near Phrygia, although in Phrygia proper Cybele's orgiastic rites were conducted in the open air; it's difficult to say what went on in her subterranean sanctuary here. Relegation to the cellar implies no disrespect for Cybele, but it does wonderfully symbolize the state of mind of the ancient world. Zeus, representing reason, order, and light, rules the upper world, while, just below the surface, lay mystery and the unconscious bound up in the formidable personality of the great goddess. The huge acroterion on the east front was a bust of Zeus, while that on the west depicted Cybele. Here the two co-existed in a hard-earned balance that was not lost until the coming of Christianity.

Little remains of the rest of Aizanoi; if you have time you can trace the outlines of the stadium, having an unusual arrangement in which the town's theatre closes its open end. The Temple of Zeus faced an agora fronting on the now intermittent stream the Greeks called Rhyndakos, where there are still remnants of bridges and quays.

Afyon: City of Opium

Afyon's official name is *Afyon Karahisar*, which means 'opium black fortress'. That little product has been the city's name and its fame perhaps for millennia. Today, the poppies have largely been replaced by sunflowers; nevertheless, you'll still see vast expanses of poppy fields all around the city—supposedly this is strictly controlled, but Afyon still celebrates its ancient speciality with a big poppy-head fountain in the middle of town. The black **fortress** remains, on top of an enormous black rock, thrusting 741 feet into the sky. The original castle was probably Hittite, c. 1500 BC; it has been rebuilt many times since then and was used as a treasury by both the Selcuks and the Ottomans. In the old town, which is clustered round the foot of the rock, is the **Ulu Cami**, a fine Selcuk mosque built in 1273. It has a flat roof supported by 40 wooden columns with stalactite-carved capitals. Near the mosque are some well-preserved Ottoman houses with typical overhanging upper storeys. Also in the area is a **Mevlevi museum**, housed in a converted mosque; Afyon is not far from Konya and the Mevlâna's teachings soon found favour here.

In the new town, one building dominates all others, the **Gedik Ahmet Paşa Külliyesi**, built by a grand vezir of Mehmet the Conqueror. The mosque, the Imaret Camii, has a minaret decorated with Iznik tiles, but the adjoining medrese and hamam (currently closed) are squat and functional, Byzantine in design but lacking the grace of that age.

The area round Afyon is famous for its hot springs. Some not-so-hot springs near the **Gazligöl** ('Gassy Lake'), north of Afyon, supply the mineral soda water you find in little green bottles all over Turkey.

The Phrygian Heartland

Anyone seriously interested in the fascinating world of pre-Hellenic Anatolia should not be discouraged from pushing into this little-visited region. The Phrygian monuments are well preserved and quite impressive in their lonely settings, and you'll have a chance for some real exploration. No archaeological area in western Anatolia is less documented, many of the sites still being known only to the locals. Though Bursa's Uludağ and Murat Dağ, west of Afyon, are both taller, **Turkmen Dağ** and its surrounding peaks between Afyon and Eskişehir make the rooftop of western Anatolia; many important rivers, including the Sakarya and the Menderes, have their sources here. If this area was not the most populous part of Phrygia, it was at least the holiest place. The evidence suggests that the Phrygians' religion had much to do with water; each of the great temple façades was located near a spring.

Getting Around

You have a choice of bases for seeing Midas City and nearby sites, all of them inconvenient. Afyon is perhaps the best, since it is closest to the ruins and there are a number of village dolmuş lines running at least close to the sites. The village of Seyitgazi is even closer, though there is only the most rudimentary and unreliable accommodation there, and the same chance of a dolmuş that takes you more or less near the sites, and maybe, just maybe, another one to bring you back. In other words, rent a car if you're serious, or initiate some serious bargaining with taxi drivers. This is one of the few parts of western Turkey where taxis are still a relatively inexpensive option for exploration; £20/$30 for a day trip from Afyon or Seyitgazi should do it, though of course it will help if you can find a taxi driver who actually knows where the sites are and doesn't have to stop for directions every few minutes.

It's much easier visiting Gordion. From Eskişehir or Afyon, any bus bound for Ankara can leave you in the village of Polatli; dolmuş service from there to the village of Yassihöyük is regular enough, and you can walk from there.

Seyitgazi

If you go through **Seyitgazi**, stop for the **Mosque and Tomb of Seyit Battal Gazi**, the semi-legendary Arab warrior who died in battle here in 740, when the town was much more important than it is now. The tomb at the centre of this large complex was constructed in around 1200 by the mother of the Selcuk sultan Alâeddin Keykubad; Seyit Gazi lies inside a sarcophagus a full 20 feet long, next to his Greek wife Eleonora. The mosque and medrese were added in the 16th century by Selim I.

Midas City

If there's only time for one site, head for **Midas Sehri**, the so-called 'Midas City', 15 miles (25km) southeast of Seyitgazi. Here, bordering the modern village of Yazilikaya, the acropolis of a 6th-century Phrygian city, whose true name we do not know, rises up from the surrounding plains. There's little on the top, but a wealth of detail carved into its steep sides.

It was named Midas City by Captain Leake, a British traveller who discovered it in the early 1800s. At the end of the acropolis facing Yazilikaya (not to be confused with the Yazilikaya at Boğazköy) stands the largest and most striking monument, a temple façade some 70 feet high; at its top, Leake thought he could discern the letters 'MIDAI' in a long Phrygian inscription, and reported back to the world that he had found the grave of King Midas. In truth, the Phrygian language still remains something of a mystery. Most of the letters were adapted from the Greek, however, and more likely than not, some 'Midas' had something to do with it. This is no tomb, however; the experts think of it as a kind of stage background for the outdoor rites of Cybele. Her cult statue would be placed in the niche at the bottom of the monument during the festivities.

Around the niche, the precise, symmetrical maze-like pattern that covers most of the monument's face shows the odd degree of abstraction the Phrygians had reached in their religious art. The pediment suggests roof beams resting on a central ridge-pole, and it may be that the cliff façades are representations of wooden temples that no longer exist. A second, somewhat smaller façade was carved into the north face of the hill, roughly the same in form, with a frieze along the top decorated with Greek-style acanthus-leaf designs. All around the other hillsides, both above and below the bits of the original defence wall, a day's exploration will reveal any number of other niches and altars, inscriptions, underground chambers, and other features whose uses can only be guessed at.

Sites near Midas City

A third temple façade, smaller and somewhat eroded, can be seen near Yazilikaya at **Arezastis**. You can compare all three with the entire temples in the same area, one cut out of the **Gerdek Rock** near the village of Çukurca, and another at **Hisar Kale**, 5½ miles (9km) to the southwest at Yapildak village. Another site near Çukurca, perhaps the most unusual of all, is the **Doğanli Kale**, an outlandishly eroded crag of limestone, honey-combed with chambers and niches, with hollows that seem to have, at one time, held wooden beams and stairways. Again, whatever was the purpose of this lost little piece of Cappadocia is left to the imagination. Some of the work is said to date from Byzantine times, and like the similar oddities in Cappadocia may have been used as a monastery.

The road going west from Yazilikaya passes a **Phrygian tumulus** on its way to the village of **Kümbetköy**, which takes its name from a Roman-era tomb guarded by two lions in low relief, a recurring symbol in Phrygian art just as it was for the Hittites. South of here, on the way to Afyon, other Phrygian lions have given the villages of **Aslantaş** and **Aslankaya** their names. The temple façade at Aslankaya is a remarkable sight, carved out of a thin, twisted pinnacle of rock; two lions keep watch from its pediment while two other huge figures as high as the façade itself, though badly eroded, flank the monument. Both this and the smaller façade at Aslantaş are done in the same angular patterns as at Midas City.

Pessinus

Pessinus, 10 miles (16km) south of where the Eskişehir–Ankara highway passes Sivrihisar, was the religious and geographic centre of Phrygia. Almost nothing can be seen on the site, but archaeologists have found a 1st-century AD temple at the top of a broad ceremonial stair. A college of priests ruled the city; an inscription records that half were Phrygian and half Galatian. Even during the two centuries when Pessinus was under the sovereignty of the kings of Pergamon, these priests, or *galli*, ruled the city and its hinterlands as a theocratic state, and their influence spread far beyond Phrygia's borders.

The Romans put a stop to this in their usual ingenious fashion. In 204 BC, they instructed their Pergamene allies to send them the cult figure, a *baetyl* from Pessinus. King Attalos was glad to comply; the respected Sibylline Oracle had commanded it, and the *baetyl* (probably a meteorite, like the Kaaba in Mecca) was conveyed to Rome with all proper observances and placed in a temple specially built for it. The Romans expanded their power as much through this talent for taking over other people's religions, as by triumph of arms; one wonders what happened to all the statues, relics and cult objects they collected. Does the pope have them up in his attic?

In Phrygia, the worship of Cybele had much to do with bees; Greek mythographers always associated her with Aphrodite Ericyna and her golden honeycomb, worshipped at Mt Eryx in Sicily. Today, the site of Pessinus is known to the Turks as Ballihisar—the Honey Castle.

Gordion

Gordion, like Pessinus, is a site only an archaeologist could love; the early Phrygian capital contains no well-preserved buildings or fine reliefs; only parts of it have really been excavated, though enough for specialists to have drawn up a ground plan of the major palace buildings.

Much more interesting is the **Great Tumulus** on the edge of the city, which, as you might guess, everyone calls 'Midas' Tomb'. Gordion is reached from the same Eskişehir–Ankara road, 12 miles (20km) northeast of the town of **Polatli**, with yellow signs marking the route from there. Approaching the site, you see mounds of all sizes, gradually increasing in number. The largest, most likely, were for the kings, though even mere nobles apparently had the resources to build them. Few of the smaller tumuli have been excavated; the burials in them were cleverly placed off-centre to discourage grave robbers and archaeologists. One they did find yielded the remains of a five-year-old boy, with some charming toys that are now in the Ankara Museum.

The Great Tumulus

The **Great Tumulus**, now worn down to about 160ft in height, must originally have been close to 250 feet. In Turkey only the mound called King Alyattes's Tomb near Sardis is bigger, and it's difficult to think of a taller one anywhere else in the world. Whether or not the king inside was a 'Midas' or a 'Gordius' is unknown—they alternated these names the way Danish kings do with 'Christian' and 'Frederick'—but he was a small man, no more than 5 feet 2 inches, and close to 60 years of age. The tomb at the centre of the mound has been thoroughly excavated, and you can reach it through the long, lighted tunnel, recently constructed. To build this mound, the Phrygians started with a double-walled wooden house set into the ground, covered it with stones and clay, and then piled up the earth above it. The wood—great logs of cedar that must have come from Lebanon, still sound after 2600 years under the earth—is mortised at the corners like a frontier cabin. Inside, interestingly enough, no gold or silver was found; there were dozens of pots, many with inscriptions in the Phrygian alphabet, some exceedingly well-crafted furniture, now in Ankara and, inexplicably, 145 brass *fibulae*—the archaeologists' word for 'safety-pins'.

The current excavations of the city are surrounded by a fence. Having been nearly completely covered with centuries of silt from the Sakarya's floods, the site is now exposed and you can look down into the diggings and make out, at the southeastern end, the **monumental gateway**, and behind it the palace buildings and a long row, somewhat like a modern residential terrace, that belonged to the palace household. The palaces themselves consisted of a row of megaron-style structures, with a central hearth surrounded by rooms and one large hall in front serving as the entrance; it is quite likely these had façades in wood similar to the temple façades mentioned above.

Gordius and Midas

Arrian's life of Alexander mentions that the Gordian knot was kept in the Gordion acropolis. Since nothing like an acropolis exists here, the temple complex is probably what he had in mind. According to the myth as related by Arrian, Gordius was originally a poor farmer. One day an eagle perched on his wagon tongue, and Gordius, taking it as an omen, decided to visit an oracle at Phrygian Telmessus to ask its meaning. On the way, the eagle still riding along with him, he met a local priestess who instructed him in the proper sacrifices for the oracle. He married her, and she bore him a son named Midas. In the meantime, the Phrygian king had died, and the country was drifting into factional strife. The same oracle announced that a man in an ox-cart would come to bring peace to the land, and when the unsuspecting Gordius rode into the city one day, he found himself proclaimed king.

He founded the city of Gordion, the story continues, and laid up his wagon there. Over the years, a prophecy gained currency that whoever could solve the cornel-bark knot that bound the yoke to the wagon tongue would become 'master of Asia'. Much speculation has gone into the nature of this knot, although its presence here is historical fact. When Alexander passed this way—Gordion lay directly on the Persian Royal Road, the great trade and conquest route between Greece and the east—he felt obliged to fulfil the prophecy, since becoming master of Asia was exactly what he had in mind. Most commentators claim he cut the knot with his sword, which provides the most poetic solution. Robert Graves believes the knot was an alphabetic cipher, expressing the secret name of a god (Incas and ancient Britons had such devices, so why not the Phrygians?); he sees Alexander's sword stroke as a historical turning point, at which the power of blind ambition and main force broke the last barrier to the destruction of the ancient authority of religion.

Of Midas, we learn that he planted famous rose gardens and was a great musician, taught by Orpheus himself. As well as the tale of the golden touch, Midas is said to have had a pair of ass's ears planted on him by Apollo; Midas unwisely voted against the god in a musical contest with his countryman, Marsyas. His barber was supposed to keep the secret (which Midas hid from others with a conical Phrygian cap, such as was the fashion during the French Revolution) but couldn't manage to. He dug a hole in the ground near a river and whispered, 'Midas has ass's ears!' into it; most unfortunately for him, the reeds on the spot spread the message to everyone within earshot, 'Midas has ass's ears!'

Midas's name, like Gordius's, probably has a basis in history. He, or one of the kings with that name, appears in Assyrian records as 'Mita of Mushki'. This Mushki, most likely, was the Phrygians' own name for their nation. 'Phrygian' is a Greek word meaning 'free men'. As a pastoral people without a strong state, they probably were just that.

Despite the wealth that lay behind the legend of Midas' golden touch, his capital was not to endure. The Great Tumulus was built around 720 BC, and the Cimmerians came to sack Gordion only 20 years or so later. Though it revived in the 6th century, by Roman times writers were already sadly remarking that the once-great city was dwindling into a mere village.

Finds from Gordion

Whatever finds the government hasn't carried off to Ankara are on display in the small **museum**. Small bits of red, white, and black architectural ceramics give some idea of how the palaces originally looked; the rockpile that is Gordion today belies the Phrygian talent and liking for extensive decoration. Other artefacts include a wildly undisciplined geometric-pattern mosaic (from one of the megaron houses) that looks more post-impressionist than ancient Phrygian, and one perfectly serviceable pair of dice.

On your way back to Polatli, take time to notice the **Atatürk Monument** on the crest of the most prominent hill north of town. This could well be the only really successful modern memorial anywhere in Turkey; at least it's an interesting attempt at recapturing the ancient Anatolians' talent for monumental sculpture. Consisting of two long rows of marble columns of increasing height, tracing a gracefully curved silhouette over the hilltop, it's as abstract and as memorable as any work of the Phrygians.

Where to Stay

Kütahya, Afyon and Eskişehir are all towns where you will have trouble spending a lot of money on hotel rooms, with nothing at the upper end of the accommodation market. Most of the moderately priced hotels are clean and comfortable, however, even if English-speaking staff are a rarity.

expensive

To take in the hot springs, or merely to enjoy a night's luxury in this little-travelled region, on the outskirts of Afyon is the ★★★★**Termal Resort Oruçoğlu**, on the Kütahya road, ✆ (272) 251 5050, ✆ 251 5060. It's an apparition in these empty landscapes, a weird futuristic concrete spa hotel next to a big water slide in the middle of nowhere; all rooms with satelite TV, sauna and hamam, and they'll supposedly do wonders for your rheumatism and gynaecological problems.

moderate

Two modest hotels in Eskişehir have thermal baths, both next to each other on Hamamyolu Caddesi: the ★★**Has Termal Oteli** at no. 7, ✆ (221) 221 9191, and the ★**Sultan Termal Otel** at no. 1, ✆ 221 8371. After visiting the Phrygian sites you may well appreciate the warm baths. Rates average £12/$18.

In Kütahya, the best is the ★★★**Erbaylar**, near the centre at Afyon Caddesi 14, ✆ (274) 223 6960; comfortable rooms where you can watch incomprehensible Turkish films on video and plan your shopping. Less expensive ones can be found on the central Belediye Meydani: the lovely tile-covered facade of the ★**Gül Palas**, ✆ (274) 223 2325, conceals a very basic place with simple rooms with bath for about £10/$15.

Afyon's best is the ★★**Oruçoğlu**, in the centre on Bankalar Caddesi, ✆ (272) 212 0120, a well-appointed businessman's hotel; most rooms with balcony and satellite TV. The **Otel Mesut** on Dumlupinar Caddesi, ✆ (272) 212 0429, is a lot better than its rather sorry exterior would suggest; £8/$12.

cheap

In any town you will find something for under £4/$6—the basic, old reliable Turkish flophouse of a decade ago. Surprisingly, in interior towns like this there are no pretensions—you can almost always judge a place from its façade. Just don't expect much beyond a tolerably clean room looking out onto a garage, and a folkloric bog down the hall. In Kütahya, there is an exception, the well-kept **Yüksel II**, ✆ (274) 223 4567, on central Belediye Meydani. If it's full the **Otel Koşk** next door, ✆ (274) 223 0644, would just do. In Afyon there are a number of places that will do fine for an overnight stay, including the **Eroğlu**, across from the *otogar*, which also has a decent *lokanta*.

Eating Out

Restaurants are small and inexpensive and all about the same; this is not a well-travelled region. You won't starve in Kütahya, though all the restaurants in town are near the central Belediye Meydani; the inexpensive **Meşhur** ('Famous') **Iskender Salonu**, on Azerbaycan Parki next to Belediye Meydani lays on a quite nice bowl of *mercimek* (red lentil) soup and *iskender kebab*. The **Bursa Iskender** on Atatürk Bulvari is a simple kebab salon that tries hard; good cooking and a bill of about £3/$5 no matter what you order. The **Cumhuriyet Lokantasi** nearby on Belediye Meydani is just as good though slightly more expensive.

In Afyon, the place to go is the excellent **Ikbal Lokantasi** on Uzun Carşi, close to the Oruçoğlu Oteli. It's an old-style restaurant, so popular with the locals at lunch time that the waiters have to run while they serve the food. A meal here costs about £3/$5. Finish your meal with *ekmek kadayif* (bread soaked in syrup) or *visneli ekmek tatlisi* (bread soaked in cherry juice); both come topped with a slab of the rich cream for which Afyon is renowned.

The Lake District

For a change from the endless blue sky and sea and seafood and trinkets of the Mediterranean coasts, there's either the gloomy grey Marmara or Black Sea, and this seldom-visited corner of the country, which has quite a personality. There's nothing in Europe or anywhere around the Mediterranean quite like it: sparse emerald hills and craggy mountains, enclosing enormous fresh-water lakes that change colour with every mood of the weather.

Although it lies at the crossroads of routes connecting major tourist centres, the region of lakes remains relatively undiscovered; only Eğirdir has any pretensions to be a resort, and a modest one at that. The east–west road from Cappadocia and Konya to Pamukkale and Ephesus, and the north–south road from Istanbul and Bursa to Antalya and the south coast meet here. It cannot be long before the area makes better use of its position to attract tourists in greater numbers, so go now before it's too late.

Getting Around

Eğirdir, Burdur and Isparta are very accessible, being on major bus routes, though be warned that the roads are narrow and wind all over the map; whether you're travelling by bus or car it will always take longer than you expect (3½ hours from Eğirdir to Antalya and more than 4 to Konya). The Eğirdir tourist office will help to arrange taxi trips to Zindan Cave and Adada, or to Kovada; if you can find some companions, you can share the £24/$36 that is the going rate for a carful to either—lunch included. There are regular minibus services to Ağlasun, Bucak and Gölhisar, but in each case you will need a car to reach the sites. Minibuses to Insuyu leave frequently from Burdur.

Tourist Information

Eğirdir: 2 Sahil Yolu 13a, ✆ (246) 311 4388

Isparta: Hükümet Konaği, ✆ (246) 218 4438

Burdur: Cumhuriyet Meydani 4, ✆ (248) 233 1078

Eğirdir

This pretty lakeside town was called Acrotiri in the Byzantine era, meaning promontory; this changed into the Turkish name Eğridir, with the unfortunate meaning of 'it's bent'. In the mid-1980s, the residents, tired of the jokes, changed the name to Eğirdir, which has the more satisfactory meaning of 'she is spinning'. The new name fits in with a local legend. In the past, there was no lake. Up in the mountains, the queen was spinning while the young prince was out hunting with bow and arrow. He shot at a deer, but the animal ran away and the arrow hit a large stone which shattered, releasing a torrent of water which drowned the prince. Thus the lake was formed. The grieving king said to his wife, *'Eğirdir! Sen eğirdir! Oğlun öldu. Sen ne yapiyorsun hâlâ?'* ('Spinning! You are spinning! Your son is dead. Just what are you doing?').

Eğirdir sits on a small promontory jutting into the turquoise-blue waters of the lake, tucked under steep, enormous Mount Davras. The view from the Isparta road as you descend to the town is spectacular, especially in the evening. During Selcuk times, Eğirdir was part of the Sultanate of Rum and capital of the lake district. When the Selcuk hegemony was broken in the mid-13th century, Eğirdir became the seat of the powerful Hamitoğullari emirs, who had control of Antalya and were able to trade with the Aegean islands, Egypt and the eastern Mediterranean. Today, Eğirdir makes its living from its excellent red apples, and increasingly from tourism. It is a humble and almost-too-friendly and entirely too relaxing resort where people seem absolutely delighted you've come so far to visit their town. Its nightlife consists of watching the kids play football on the lighted pitch facing the harbour. Boat tours, offered around the harbour or arranged through hotels, are nothing as lavish as the ones on the seacoast—just a pleasant outing around the lake in a little motorboat. **Market day** is Thursday, when you may sample the apples and other specialities of the area, such as rose water soap from Isparta; for the perfect souvenir, if you're lucky, the man who sells dried weasel skins will be around.

One of the Hamitoğullari emirs, Felekeddin Dündar, changed the name of the town to Felekabad, and built the attractive Dündarbey Medrese, which has been restored and converted to a shopping bazaar. The magnificent stalactite gateway formerly belonged to a ruined caravansarai 3 miles (5km) from Eğirdir. Other reused stones from the caravansarai can be seen in the wall which bars the entrance to the peninsula and which connects the medrese to the earlier **Hizarbey Camii.** The minaret is unusual, in that it is not free-standing, but sits on top of this wall. Below the minaret is an arch which allows passage between the religious complex and the inner town; on the lake side of the wall you can see doors that lead to a tunnel in the wall, for use in times of trouble. The mosque has an ornate door with a wooden porch. An unusual floral pattern is carved into the stone above the door. Inside is an Iznik-tiled mihrab and a forest of wooden pillars, painted blue, which support the roof. A causeway, built in the early 1980s, joins the promontory to a small island, **Yeşilada** (Green Island). A sizeable Greek community lived here before the exchange of populations and it is possible to see old Greek buildings on the island and on the promontory, within the town's dilapidated fortress. Today the island is full of *pansiyons*.

The water in Eğirdir Lake is sweet and full of good fish, the hot item in the town's restaurants. It is possible to swim at the town beach, a 10-minute walk from the centre, though you may prefer the bigger and nicer **Altinkum** (Golden Sand) beach, 3km from the centre of town in the direction of Isparta, or **Bedre** beach, the best of all, 11km on the road to Barla.

Kovada National Park

About 19 miles (30km) south of Eğirdir Lake is the small **Kovada Lake**. The road from Eğirdir runs beside a canal connecting the two lakes and is lined by apple orchards which form the basis of the town's economy. In the summer, as you near Kovada, you can see the goat's-hair tents of nomads who have migrated to their *yayla*, summer pastures. The area round the lake is a national park, **Kovada Milli Parki**, with reputedly 70 species each of trees and animals, including wild boar. In winter hunting is possible.

Zindan Cave

If you enjoy bats and the stench of bat guano, and slithering snake-like through narrow, mud-lined passages, you will enjoy a visit to **Zindan Cave**, about 27km southeast of Eğirdir. Old clothing, stout shoes and a torch are essential. The cave is 2.4km long and it is possible to 'walk' to the end. By the entrance is a pretty stone bridge across a little stream—very convenient for washing off the mud. On this bridge, a bit of ancient relief can be made out, said to be the Titan Eurymedon, father of Promethius. Apparently the cave was a holy place in antiquity; the bridge leads to a nearby necropolis. The road passes a turning to **Adada**, where there are three almost completely preserved Roman temples, a nice forum and some Hellenistic buildings. After Aksu, the road (no longer asphalt) passes through a magnificent gorge. Beehives dot the surrounding hills.

Another possible excursion from Eğirdir is to **Yalvaç**, 65km to the north. 2km from this village are the ruins of Pisidian Antioch, a city founded in Hellenistic times that was the capital of the province under the Romans; both St Paul and St Philip passed through. There isn't a lot to see, but Yalvaç has a small museum of finds from the site.

Isparta and Burdur

Famous for attar of roses and carpets, **Isparta** is an attractive city of modern boulevards with lots of trees and little else; its old town was devastated by an earthquake at the end of the 19th century, leaving only the impressive **Ulu Cami**, built in 1417. The rose fields lie in the plains north of the town, but are not visible from the road. Out of them Isparta makes rose oil, rose water soap and shampoo, cologne, rose flavoured *lokum* (Turkish delight) and rose everything else. The carpets are for domestic consumption; you will find them not in tourist carpet shops, but on the floors of Turkish houses or in the town **museum** on Kenan Evren Caddesi. Another speciality of Isparta is Isparta kebab, made of lean roast meat—either veal or goat, but goat is tastier—wrapped in *pide* bread.

Unlike Eğirdir, **Burdur** is not directly on the lake. There is little to see in the town, apart from the **Ulu Cami**, built in the 14th century by Dündar Bey, the Hamitoğul emir. South from the main street and across a little river is a charming residential area. Here, through the open doors of the houses, you can see carpet looms being worked. Women sit on the pavements, chatting and doing their knitting, tatting, needlework and crochet-work. The **museum** is just off the main street and houses finds from **Hacilar**, a Neolithic settlement 15 miles (24km) southwest of Burdur that was one of the successors (*c.* 6600 BC) to the more sophisticated culture of Çatal Höyük. Hacilar itself is not worth a visit; you can poke about in a field and find a few shards, but that is all.

The water of Lake Burdur is saline, containing about 21 grams of dissolved salts per litre, and it supports only very small fish. There are beaches near **Cendik**, where it is possible to swim.

Insuyu Cave

Insuyu is a popular recreation spot about 9 miles (14km) east of Burdur. The cave is clean and well lit, and its length of 600m can be walked in comfort. It consists of a series of grottoes with stalagmites and stalactites. Its nine lakes contain mineral water so clear it might not be there; this water is thought to be therapeutic for diabetics.

Sagalassos

The largest towns in Pisidia were Sagalassos, Termessos and Selge. Termessos was previously thought to be Pisidia's greatest city, but recent research shows that Sagalassos was both the wealthiest and the most populous. Like the other Pisidian cities, Sagalassos lies high in the mountains between Burdur and Isparta, in a spectacular setting some 7km from the village of Ağlasun. The remains are extensive and are considered by archaeologists to be well preserved; tourists will need to be imaginative.

Alexander the Great came to Sagalassos in 334 BC and captured the city. At that time there were no city walls; to the south of the main path through the city is a small flat hill, which slopes steeply to the south and from which the Sagalassians believed they could defend them-selves. However, Alexander and his army managed to scale the hillside and thus took the city. Some walls were built much later, but Sagalassos was never enclosed by real city walls; the walls just connected the public areas, so that in times of trouble the population crowded into the centre. The city was abandoned in the early Byzantine period; there are three churches, one of which was never completed.

The older part of the city lies to the north of the main path. Among a few late Hellenistic build-ings, the best-preserved is a 1st-century BC **Doric temple** with two standing walls, but fallen columns. Southeast of the Doric temple are benches indicating a **bouleuterion**, and to the northeast, a terrace supporting a heroon. The beautiful frieze from this heroon can be seen in the fire station in Ağlasun, although there are plans for a permanent museum (other carvings currently adorn a tea garden in Ağlasun). Also in the upper city is a large, well-preserved **theatre**, approximately the same size as those at Perge and Side. The **agora** lies between the theatre and the Doric temple.

The lower city dates from Roman times. **Baths** flank the **lower agora**, to the north of which is a large 2nd-century AD **nymphaeum**. Two temples have been identified here: the **temple of Apollo Clarius**, which was transformed into a Christian basilica, and the **temple of Antoninus Pius** (AD 138–161). To the southwest of Antoninus Pius can be seen the sarcophagi of a Hellenistic and Roman **necropolis**. At the far west is a **Christian basilica** made of the remains of two Roman monuments. The cliff face to the west of the city is full of small **rock tombs** for cremated bodies, from the 2nd and 3rd centuries AD; some are decoratively carved with animal heads and garlands. A third necropolis lies to the southeast of the theatre.

Cremna

If you have time for another ruined city in an isolated, picturesque setting, there's **Cremna**, an Augustan colony about 15km from the village of Bucak, just east of the Antalya highway. The road is stabilized rather than asphalt, and winds through scented pine forests. Cremna is situ-ated on top of a steep hill; there is much climbing to do. The **city walls** to the west are well preserved; outside them lies a **necropolis**. As you approach the city from the southwest, you will come across the two arches of a **gate**, probably Hellenistic. Within the city, the **public agora** can be identified by the 20 steps which form its north side. A very large triple gateway, whose façade was a close copy of that of the library of Celsus at Ephesus, once stood at the top of these steps; although the steps remain, the gateway is scattered in ruins at the bottom. Behind where the archway should be are enormous **cisterns**. East of the public agora, the **Forum of Longus** contains the remains of a basilica, with some arches still standing, as well as a large inscribed pillar; this is a **dice oracle**, used in fortune-telling to interpret the throw of the dice. There's little else to see: a small **theatre** in the middle of the town, the excavated remains of a bath to the west, and remains of a few poorly preserved temples.

Kibyra

Kibyra is a wonderful windswept site, high on a hilltop overlooking a broad plain. The ruins are neglected save for the goatherds who bring their goats to graze on the wild thyme, producing very tasty meat ideal for Isparta kebab. Graves tumble down the hillside, which is littered with fluted columns and carved blocks of stone, some inscribed, including one on which the letters KIBYR can clearly be seen. The remains of several public buildings can be identified, including, on the eastern side of the hill, a well-preserved **theatre** and a less-well-preserved **stadium**. Next to the theatre is a large building with arches, now half-submerged in the soil.

Kibyra is about 100km from Burdur and can be reached by heading southwest via the villages of Tefenni and Çavdar ('barley') to Gölhisar ('lake castle'), the nearest village to Kibyra. The lake in question has, as a result of canalization, shrunk to a tiny size, leaving a broad, fertile plain between Çavdar and Gölhisar; crops grown here include sugar beet and aniseed, for the production of raki.

Where to Stay

moderate

In Eğirdir, there are only a few places with any pretensions among the myriad of *pansiyons*, including the old, reliable ★★★**Eğirdir**, Kuzey Sahil Yolu 2 on the lake front, ✆ (246) 311 4992. Simple rooms with a view for £22/$33. Next door, and enjoying the same views, is the smaller ★**Çinar**, ✆ (246) 311 4678, which is much better value at less than half the price. In Isparta, the most comfortable hotel is the brand-new ★★★★**Büyük Isparta Oteli**, Atatürk Caddesi 8, ✆ (246) 212 1017, with doubles for £26/$39. The ★★**Bolat** at Demirel Bul. 71, ✆ (246) 223 9001, boasts a tennis court and central heating; it is very relaxing and good value at £14/$21 for an en suite double with breakfast. Burdur can be a discouraging place to stay, but the ★★**Çendik Motel**, on Tefenni Yolu, ✆ (248) 242 8081, makes it tolerable; quiet rooms and a pool.

cheap

Eğirdir has a wide choice of *pansiyons*, sweet family-run places that in themselves can make the trip here worthwhile. The **Lale Pansiyon**, for example, near the castle, ✆ (246) 312 2406: rooms with a view of the lake, a delightful family who do everything to make you happy, and very inexpensive dinners provided (mom's an excellent cook). Another similar one, just as good, is the **Kösk**, ✆ (246) 312 3032, 1km out at Yazla Mah. near the beach with great views from most rooms. On Yeşilada Island, the **Sunshine**, ✆ (246) 311 5859, is typical of what is on offer there, small and cosy, and with a fine restaurant. Other good choices are the Akdeniz, ✆ (246) 312 2432, at the tip of the island, and the **Halley**, ✆ (246) 312 3625.

Isparta has a handful of cheap hotels and pensions, mostly around Mimar Caddesi, the main street. The **Bayram**, ✆ (246) 218 1480, is more expensive than most but a pleasing place to stay; a double room with private shower will cost £8/$12. The ★**Burdur Oteli**, Gazi Caddesi 37, ✆ (246) 233 2245, is easily the best in Burdur and suprisingly inexpensive.

The star attraction here, understandably, is fish from the lake, which is inexpensive and delicious—much more delicate than most salt-water fish, and a lot like perch from the Great Lakes in America. There are also lake crayfish.

In Eğirdir, the **Deyra Restoran** on the waterfront, opposite the Çinar Oteli, offers a large selection of cold meze and excellent fish in batter, served by waiters dressed in picturesque orange Adana *şalvar*. A meal costs about £4/$6, only slightly more than the many other fish restaurants around the lake, and on Yeşilada island. At the tip of the island, the **Melodi Restoran** is good and inexpensive.

There's nothing out of the ordinary in Isparta or Burdur—but try a goat-meat Isparta kebab, available almost anywhere in its town of origin.

West towards Konya

To get to Konya, it's a long and roundabout trip up the west side of Lake Eğirdir and then down the back side of the biggest of the region's lakes, **Beyşehir Gölü**, passing on the way the most unspellable, unpronounceable village in Turkey, ramshackle **Şarkîkaraağaç**. Just south of here a new national park has been established, the **Kizildağ Milli Parki**. To the north, **Akşehir** claims to be the home of the legendary Nasreddin Hoca; you can buy a postcard of the famous picture of him seated backwards on his donkey, and visit his tomb in a little pavilion on the town green. On the gate is a big heavy lock, though it's wide open on the other three sides.

Nasreddin Hoca

This fellow, the clever-foolish country priest (*hoca*) who goes under the name of Goha in the Arabian Nights tales, is the classic comic figure of Turkish folklore. Outwitting himself as often as the Emperor Tamerlane, at whose court he is supposed to have lived, the Hoca's adventures are still current among all Turks; you'll see souvenir pictures of him everywhere, seated backwards on his donkey. He is very much a creation of the Sufis, the mystics of Islam who condense volumes of theology into such tales. One famous story has the Hoca walking with a friend discussing the completeness of creation. The Hoca considers that it would have been better if horses had wings; thus, they would be much more helpful to mankind. Just then some pigeon droppings fall on the Hoca's turban. He reflects, 'Allah knows best!'.

Down the eastern shore of Beyşehir Gölü, 4km off the main road at **Eflatunpinari** is a Hittite relief, with figures of four kings and some mythological beasts, set by a small lagoon. **Beyşehir**, at the southeastern corner of the lake, is a bedraggled town that could be much nicer if it set its mind to it. It's a poor, out-of-the-way place, a reminder of what most Turkish provincial towns were like twenty years ago. Nevertheless, it's worth a stop for the **Eşrefoğlu Camii** and its *külliye*, built by the Eşrefoğlu emirs, who installed themselves here after the breakup of Selcuk power. The mosque has a beautiful interior of painted tiles and carved wood; adjacent is the *türbe* of the emirs, with more fine tiles, a medrese and hamam.

Neither Beyşehir nor its lake get many visitors. Facilities are generally poor—this is a corner still open to exploration. In Beyşehir or any of the little fishing hamlets around the lake you may find someone with a boat to take you around the lake's many **islands**. None seems to be inhabited now, though a few have traces of Byzantine monasteries. West of Beyşehir on the lakeshore are the ruins of **Kubadabad Palace**, the summer retreat of the Selcuk sultans. There isn't much to see, but if the finds now in Konya's Karatay Medrese are any indication it must have been a marvel. (It would have been impious to build a palace to last, so in medieval times Muslim rulers always made their pleasure domes of perishable materials: mud brick covered with painted tiles, and wood. As far as we know the only medieval Muslim palace surviving anywhere is the Alhambra in Granada. Imagine what the others must have been like!)

East of Beyşehir, on the way to Konya, the bleak scenery is interrupted by a rather incredible sight, the **Atatürk 100 Yil Ormani** (Atatürk Centennial Forest): several million trees, all recently planted in a wonderfully mad project to make a wasteland into a forest. In a century it will be truly impressive, even if now it looks like the world's biggest Christmas tree farm.

Konya

Some cities, such as Istanbul, are forced by their location to play a large role in the world's affairs; others may survive for millennia without contributing anything. Most fortunate of all, however, are the towns that at one time in their lives have a little empire of their own, and then move off history's stage into a long golden twilight. Bursa is one such Turkish city; Konya, the old Selcuk capital, is the other.

These two have other things in common; both have wonderful patrimonies of Turkish art and architecture, and both are trying hard to manage the difficult process of becoming modern and prosperous on their own terms. Turkey often advertises itself as the 'Land of Civilizations', and with the many peoples and cultural influences that have drifted through over the centuries, it is hard to isolate anything as specifically 'Turkish', until you come to Bursa or Konya, the most Turkish of the nation's cities. Konya has a reputation for being the most conservative and devout corner of Turkey; in truth, there are plenty of other candidates for that honour. This is nothing to be alarmed about; Konya is a city where culture and tolerance have always been accounted virtues. If it has a living faith to sustain it, so much the better. The spirit of the Mevlâna still protects this city, and ensures that religion shows us only its most benign face.

History

The first we hear of Konya is as a Phrygian town called Kawania; later, under the Greeks and Romans it became Iconium, capital of the province of Lycaonia. The Selcuks, with whom medieval Konya is usually associated, were not the first Turks in the neighbourhood; other warrior bands were around as early as the 9th century, and the Arabs of the Abbasid Caliphate had arrived before them, twice capturing the city from the Byzantines though they could not keep it. When the Selcuks came, in 1076 after the Battle of Manzikert gave them control of Anatolia, Sultan Süleyman Ibn Kutulmuş made Konya his capital. Not that the city had much to commend it; its only real advantage was equal distance from all possible enemies, or perhaps the broad, treeless Plain of Konya reminded the Selcuks of their ancestral home on the Asian steppe. For a time the Selcuks, strong as they were, had a hard time holding Konya. During the first Crusade, Godfrey of Bouillon occupied the city for a short while, and Frederick Barbarossa passed through in 1190 on his way to the Holy Land. Neither of these harmed either the city or the Selcuks. Like any of the early Turkish principalities, the Selcuks' Empire of Rum was hardly a modern, centralized state; the real 'capital' was the sultan's throne, and that moved with him wherever his whims or campaigns took him. Konya, however, was the residence of the sultans, and the major beneficiary of their building work and philanthropy.

Under their intelligent and tolerant regime, Konya in the 12th and 13th centuries became a refuge for artists and men of learning from all over the Middle East and Muslim Asia, fleeing the depredations of the Mongols and Crusaders. Rulers such as **Alâeddin Keykubad**, who liked to surround himself with poets and erudite dervishes, endowed a collection of mosques and schools that has made the city the equal of Istanbul and Bursa as a showplace of Turkish architecture. They had hardly begun when the Mongols came in 1243 to spoil the party; they never sacked Konya, but they did put an end to the Selcuk state, which survived for a few decades afterwards only as a much-reduced, tribute-paying vassal of the Great Khan. After the fall of the Empire of Rum, the Karamanoğullari, the Turks from Karaman, filled the vacuum but moved the capital to their own town of Ermenek. Konya declined and did not recover until the coming of the republic.

Celâleddin Rumi, the Mevlâna, one of the great mystics of Islam and founder of the 'Whirling' Mevlevi dervishes, was the most famous of all the figures of Konya's golden age (*see* **Topics**) and his spirit continues to animate the city today. Throughout the Ottoman period, Mevlevi sheikhs were often close advisers to the sultan. Even in 1919, Konya elected the sheikh (the head of the order) to represent it at the first Turkish National Assembly.

Getting Around

Konya has an airport, but flights are infrequent, with only one or two a week to Ankara, Izmir or Istanbul. Trains from Istanbul pass through Akşehir, Konya, and Karaman on their slow way to Adana. Here your best bet is the bus: as usual, there will be no problem making connections to anywhere. The train station is on Feritpaşa Caddesi, about 1 mile southwest of the Alâeddin Hill. The bus depot is equally far, but towards the northwest on Ankara Caddesi; dolmuşes to the centre are infrequent, and you might as well take a cab. Konya is a compact city, and you can easily go everywhere on foot.

Tourist Information

Mevlâna Caddesi 21, near the Mevlâna museum, ℗ (332) 351 1074 . In the museum there is a small bookstore with books in English about the city and the Mevlevis, as well as tapes of Mevlevi music.

Alâeddin Hill

Today dervishes may be less conspicuous, but the people of Konya like to joke that they're still going around in circles; any trip through the town is likely to lead through the **Alâeddin Bulvari**, the circular road around the Alâeddin Hill in the centre of the city. This little mound, all alone in the broad plain of Konya, is a 'tell', the sort of hill that grows up wherever a small town or village occupies a site continuously for thousands of years. Later cultures, including the Selcuks, simply built over the top. The **Alâeddin Kiosk**, the palace of the Selcuk sultans, or rather the last little bit of it, still stands, lovingly preserved under a modern arched pavilion; interestingly, they built their schools and religious buildings in stone and good brick, but, as at Kubatabad, expended only cheap mud brick and conglomerate on themselves.

Alâeddin Mosque

Their **Alâeddin Mosque**, begun by Sultan Rukaeddin Mesut in 1130 and finally completed by Alâeddin Keykubad in 1221, has fared somewhat better. Though well built, its position on

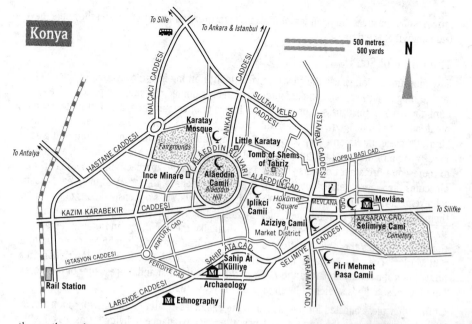

Konya

the northern slope of the unstable mound has made almost constant restoration work a necessity; they're busy on it now. The changes and additions of various sultans over those 91 years explain the unusual form of the mosque; together with its courtyard behind the great façade, it has the shape of an open book, with a large pillared hall in one corner. The plan of this hall is that of the Selcuk 'great mosques' all over Turkey, but here the neat rows of columns are marble, reused from Greek and Byzantine buildings. There are more old columns on the façade; the Selcuks apparently found them in different sizes, and cleverly arranged them in a series of arches, slanted to match the slope of the hill. At the centre of the structure are two large *türbes*. The largest, with a conical roof, contains the bodies of eight Selcuk sultans, including Alâeddin Keykubad, all in tiled sarcophagi; the adjacent *türbe* stands empty.

Karatay Medrese

The rest of Alâeddin Hill, once all part of the Sultan of Rum's palace grounds, has been rehabilitated and planted with pine trees and flower-beds among shady cafés. Just across Alâeddin Bulvari from the mosque stands another Selcuk masterpiece, the **Karatay Medrese** (*open daily exc Mon, 9–12, 1.30–5.30; adm*). Once famous for its dome of coloured tiles, this former theological school has now fittingly become a museum of Selcuk and Ottoman ceramics. Its founder, Celaleddin Karatay, was vezir to the Selcuk sultans for forty years; he is buried under the smaller dome of the medrese's mosque.

Much of this building complex, like so much else the Selcuks built, has disappeared, but fortunately the portal still stands, echoing the Alâeddin Mosque across the way, with its geometric patterns in white and blue-grey stone. Nothing symbolizes the synthesis of cultures the Selcuks tried to create better than this gate. Influences of the Arab and Persian are obvious, and the Greek declares itself in two Corinthian columns flanking the entrances; even the ancient Phrygians seem to be recalled in the geometric lattices of the lower section. This isn't too unlikely; the great Phrygian temple façades aren't very far from Konya, and they must have been known at the time.

The Dome of Stars

Few museum buildings are their own prize exhibit; nothing in the collection of this one, in fact nothing in Turkey, can compare with the Karatay's domed mosque, completely covered in miniature tiles of unsurpassed precision and intensity of colour (though unfortunately somewhat faded and damaged). These are not the large painted squares of Ottoman Iznik, but a kind of mosaic, in which every colour is fired separately for perfection of colour and glaze. These geometric stars of 24 points, set in neat rows against a deep blue background, are meant to represent a firmament of stars. This is a specifically Islamic approach; in many of Turkey's museums there are carefully detailed star charts and almanacs, the legacy of the great Muslim achievement in astronomy, but there are hardly ever actual stars or constellations depicted on them, as if the Islamic prohibition of images extended to the stars themselves. These geometric stars, with a hint of orange fire at the centre, shine like the real thing, and their interconnection demonstrates the divine pattern and meaning in a way that might never occur to a non-Muslim. The equally beautiful panel around the bottom of the dome is an inscription, in a flowering Kufic script, of part of the *Book of the Cow*, the first and longest sura of the Koran (and the most tedious stretch of inspired poetry ever written).

Of the other tiles collected for the museum, the examples of later Ottoman work look almost primitive compared to the fine Selcuk fancy; the strict avoidance of living forms was fine for theological schools, but the Selcuk princes enjoyed nothing in their art so much as the kind of birds and fantasy animals and crowned angels displayed here. One plate portrays a *simurgh*, the mythical king of the birds, the object of the mystical search in the great Persian poem *Parliament of the Birds*, which was a favourite among princes and dervishes alike in Selcuk times (and the source of Chaucer's *Parliament of the Fowles*.) Among the later work are plenty of fine ceramics from Kütahya, from 17th-century tiles to a lovely sign for a printer's shop, made in the '20s.

Across the street, sheltered under a pavilion like the Alâeddin Kiosk, you can see the portal and sparse remains of another Selcuk school, the **Little Karatay Medrese**.

Ince Minare Medrese

If any film director ever needed a backdrop for the palace of a science-fiction Emperor of Mars, he would do well to study the portal of the **Ince Minare Medrese**, three blocks down Alâeddin Bulvari. This is no insult either to the architect Keluk or to Fahreddin Ali, the Selcuk vezir who paid for it; the unique design and skilful carving of this gate can only be described as utterly bizarre. This complex too has suffered much during centuries of neglect; most of the outbuildings are gone, and the 'slender minaret' that gave the place its name, decorated in patterns of brick and blue tile like other Selcuk works in Sivas and Erzurum, was swatted down to stubbiness by a lightning bolt in 1901. The remains are now the **Museum of Selcuk Stone and Woodcarving**. As with the ceramics, many of the artefacts are from the Selcuk palace on Alâeddin Hill, and the same fantastical forms are represented.

Continuing your whirl around Alâeddin Bulvari, you pass a 19th-century French church and then, one block later, come to Alâeddin Caddesi (also often called Hükümet Caddesi), the business street of the modern town and the way to the Mevlâna's tomb; there are relics of the mystic throughout the area. On Alâeddin, the many reconstructions of the 13th-century **Iplikci Camii** have left only a plain brick barn, but this is the mosque in which the Mevlâna did much of his teaching and practised his meditations. The tomb of his spiritual guide, Shems ed-Din of Tabriz, a mysterious dervish from Persia, can be seen on a side street two blocks north. The Mevlâna's own disciples murdered this Shems under strange circumstances.

Further down, Hükümet Caddesi skirts the market district, passing through **Hükümet Meydani**, a large square with the 16th-century **Şerafettin Mosque**, a distinguished Ottoman-style work that replaced a Selcuk original destroyed by fire; around the back is the city's best hamam. The square has been redone recently, with an underground shopping mall, the **Şaraflar Yeralti Çarşisi**, full of glittering jewellery. Beyond that the street changes its name to Mevlâna Caddesi, and the famous green tiled dome of Rumi's tomb comes into view.

Mevlâna Museum

It is believed the site of the **Mevlâna Museum** (*open daily 9–6.30, Mon 10–6; adm*), formerly the central *tekke* (dervish house) of the Mevlevi order and burial place of Celâleddin Rumi, was a garden belonging to the Selcuk sultans, presented as a gift to the Mevlâna's father, Bahaeddin Veled. He was buried here in 1232, and when the Mevlâna joined him in 1273, work was immediately begun on a cylindrical *türbe*. Over the years, the buildings adjacent to the *tekke* were enlarged and expanded; the whole seems to have been reconstructed in the 15th century under the patronage of the Ottoman sultans, particularly Beyazit II. Over the nearly 700 years of the *tekke*'s existence, the *çelebis* ('inheritors'), the descendants of the Mevlâna onto whom passed the hereditary leadership of the order, were men influential not only in Konya and among the dervishes, but in the affairs of the empire as well.

By the 20th century, it seemed to many that such influence, and such easy living, had staled the original spiritual impulse, and the Mevlevi sheikhs were known to be among the most reactionary and self-serving upholders of the old order. Atatürk's inability to prevent them from interfering in the politics of his new republic was the main cause of his decree dissolving the dervish orders. In 1925, a year later, the Konya *tekke* became the first of Atatürk's new museums, with the title of 'Konya Museum of Ancient Works'.

Dervishes of the Mevlevi and other orders do still practise semi-openly in modern Turkey: as long as religion stays out of politics, the authorities are content. Even though this *tekke*, along with the others, has been secularized, most Turks still see it as a holy site; most of the visitors at the museum are not tourists, but Turks from all walks of life, good Muslims come to pray at the tomb of a man they regard almost as a saint. Lately, large numbers of pilgrims have again started coming from the former Soviet republics of central Asia; you're sure to see many exotic faces in the crowd.

Through the entrance, incongruously embellished with a ticket window, you pass into a small courtyard. The fountain on the left is the **şadirvan**, where ablutions are performed before prayer, that on the right the **Şeb'i Arus** (wedding night pool), a gift of Yavuz Selim; the Mevlâna, in his later years, always spoke of his coming death as a 'wedding', an event to be celebrated rather than mourned, and on its anniversary every 17 December (a modern adjustment from the Muslim calendar), the dervishes performed their whirling dance, the *sema*, around this fountain in remembrance. Three small *türbes* nearby with shallow domes were contributed by governors of the 16th century, when Konya was subject to the Karamanoğullari emirs, themselves also patrons of the Mevlevis.

The Green Dome

Inside the main building, beyond a hall containing exhibits of Islamic calligraphy, lie the Mevlâna, his father, his son Sultan Veled, and other notables of the order, all in elaborate sarcophagi covered with richly embroidered cloths, with the turbans of the deceased placed at the top; six of the sarcophagi belong to the 'men of Horosan' who accompanied the Mevlâna and his father in their flight to Konya. The famous green dome, Konya's most conspicuous landmark, rises over the Mevlâna's sarcophagus. On the outside, the blue band of tiles around the dome has the words of the *bismele*, the formula 'In the name of Allah, the compassionate, the merciful' that begins each book of the Koran; usually there will be pigeons, marching like sentries on the cornice above. Inside, the dome is covered with a pattern of geometric stars; the Mevlevis called it the 'Dome of the Pole'.

Anyone may feel sceptical seeing how much show and glitter have accumulated around the grave of a saintly and humble man. Rather than being any reflection on the Mevlâna, the vast array of sumptuous carpets, cloths, and other works of art show the favour the Mevlevis always enjoyed with the powerful, for almost everything here came as gifts from sultans and princes. One of the exceptions to this is the Mevlâna's sarcophagus, a triumph of Turkish woodcarving, done by an artist named Abdulvahid solely as a labour of love. Built entirely without nails, the sarcophagus is completely covered with Mevlâna's poetry, carved in different styles and patterns of calligraphy. The introductory inscription begins: 'Here lies Mevlâna, sultan of scholars ...'

His prayer carpet, said to be a wedding gift from Alâeddin Keykubad, is a work of art in its own right, but it cannot compare with another on display, a 500-year-old silk carpet from Persia, said to be the finest ever woven; it has 144 knots to the square centimetre, 2,197,000 in all— it isn't surprising it took five years to complete. Other treasures include hairs from the beard of Mohammed, in a mother-of-pearl box, huge carved rosaries that look like wooden ropes, musical instruments and books, among them the illuminated first edition of Mevlâna's great poetical work, the *Mathnawi*; another is the *April Cup*, a huge and beautifully carved crater of gold, silver, and bronze, made in Baghdad and presented to the Mevlevis by Elen Said Bahadir, the last Ilhanli Mongol ruler of Mesopotamia.

The Semahane

The **semahane**, a grand vaulted hall adjacent to the mosque and tombs, was the site of the *sema*, the whirling dance, still performed here every year in December. With its carpets and delicate chandeliers, it is as opulent as the tombs. The great chain suspended from the ceiling to balance the chandeliers was carved from a single piece of marble, link by link. Note also the separate galleries for women spectators at the *sema*; although Mevlâna himself had little use for such foolishness, later dervishes have been notoriously afraid of women, and prefer to keep them out of sight lest they be distracted.

Other parts of the museum that may be viewed are outside the complex of tomb and *semahane*. The **dervishes' cells** line parts of the compound's walls; some have been restored to their original appearance, as has the **soup kitchen** where would-be dervishes served an apprenticeship of 1001 days while learning the manners and precepts of the order. Next to the **sheikh's quarters**, now the museum office, stands the famous library of 5000 old works on the Mevlevis and Islamic mysticism. The southern gate of the outer wall leads to a dervish cemetery, the **Garden of Souls**.

Other Sights

Sultan Selim I, Yavuz Selim, of all the Ottoman rulers perhaps the most devoted to the work of Mevlâna, left behind the large **Selimiye Mosque** next to the Mevlevi House. With little of the architectural sophistication Selim could get in Istanbul, where the Selimiye is one of the finest imperial mosques, this ungainly work, in elevation a simple cube, is domed and surrounded by domed arcades.

From here, a walk down Selimiye Caddesi through the **bazaar** and Konya's southern districts will reveal some of the city's other monuments. The market district, while large and colourful, is not the same sort of attraction as Istanbul's or Bursa's. Konya is not a wealthy city, and what you'll see is mostly everyday clothing and housewares. Still, there are some surprises, and some traditional craftsmen and tailors (such as Mehmet Tekelioğlu on Kunduracilar Sokak, around the corner from the Aziziye, who can make you a nice pair of traditional ladies' baggy pants, or *şalvar*, in an hour).

Selim's reign also saw the construction of the **Piri Mehmet Pasha Camii**, built around the *türbe* of its founder. Another, more endearing mosque right at the centre of the market district is the **Aziziye Camii**, a 17th-century structure rebuilt by Sultan Abdülaziz in 1867 in the gaudiest style of Turkish Rococo, for in sober grey Konya this confection with its impossible minarets stands out like an uptown whore at a school board meeting. Continuing along Selimiye Caddesi, you pass another of the great Selcuk works, the 1258 **Sahip Ata Külliye**, founded by the famous vezir Fahrettin Ali. Its half-ruined state and out-of-the-way location have conspired to keep this complex obscure, but its brick and stone entrance portal is as fine as any in Konya. Konya's **archaeological museum** (*open daily exc Mon 9–12, 1.30–5.30; adm*), two blocks further down where Selimiye changes its name to Larende Caddesi, has an unremarkable collection, except for three well-preserved Roman sarcophagi from Pamphylia. The best known, the *Hercules Sarcophagus* (*c.* AD 260) depicts the hero gliding through all twelve of his Labours.

Just outside Konya, on a side road off the main route for Beyşehir and Isparta, you can take a brief excursion (by city bus) to the pretty, bucolic village of **Sille**; here, the **Aya Eleni** church may be as old as the 5th century, but was rebuilt in the 19th. There are paintings to see inside, if the key can be found.

Konya ℗ (332–)

Where to Stay

moderate

Three stars is as good as you're going to get in Konya, and it won't cost you much. Most of the places in this category have prices listed—about £20–30 for a double room. Currently, this is just a joke; the bargaining starts at half or two-thirds that. Adjacent to the Mevlâna museum, the very new ★★★**Balikçilar Hotel**, Mevlâna Karşisi, ℗ 350 9470, is by a nose the poshest in town, popular with tour groups; rooms are air-conditioned, with satellite TV. Most of the others in this category are located nearby on Mevlana Caddesi or adjacent Hükümet Meydani. The ★★**Hotel Konya**, ℗ 351 9212, an address of some charm and a longtime favourite, is just off Mevlâna Caddesi, a block from the museum; simple rooms but quieter than the hotels on the main street. Further down Mevlana you can be thouroughly confused by a row of very similar hotels that all begin with S: the modern ★★★**Sema**, ℗ 322 1510, with TV and refrigerator in the rooms; the less expensive **★★Sifa**, ✆ 350 4290; very well run and a good bargain; and the **★Şahin**, Hükümet Alani, ✆ 351 3350, an old-fashioned hotel with polite, old-fashioned staff; £16/$24 (officially, at least). Next door, the **★Başak Palas**, ✆ 351 1338, charges the same rates and is equally pleasant; balconies with a view over the parking lot.

cheap

Konya does have inexpensive hotels and pensions, serving the many Muslims who come to Konya on pilgrimages, but on the whole the situation is not encouraging; you might be happier splurging for a (bargained down) £8–10 room in one of the places listed above. To find the cheapest places, just look in the side streets off Mevlâna Caddesi, or around the Aziziye Mosque. On Istanbul Caddesi, the big street that crosses Mevlana, the **Çeşme**, ✆ 351 2426, is one of the better ones, with clean and airy rooms. Just beyond the Azizye Cami, the **Azizye Otel**, ✆ 351 2287, is the Tardis of Konya, seemingly tiny from the outside but massive within, with dozens of clean, well-maintained rooms along endless corridors. For what you get, it's terrific value for money; some £3/$5 rooms have baths. The toilets are down the hall and are cleaned several times a day.

Eating Out

Konya's most popular elegant restaurant is the **Fuar Lokanta** in the fairgrounds just off Alâeddin Bulvari, with a pleasant outdoor terrace and entertainment; the sweet *tel kadayif* is their dessert speciality. Meals are about £5/$8. Outside of that, don't expect anything special. Most of the tolerable restaurants (and the only ones where you can get a glass of beer) will be found along Mevlana Caddesi around the hotels. The **Sema** on Mevlâna Caddesi is that Turkish rarity, a restaurant that advertises vegetarian food (mostly the usual aubergine stews and such, on a relatively typical menu; tasty though). Next door, the **Sifa-2** offers the usual mezes and kebabs —but the cooking's quite good and they serve alcohol; both these places go for about £3/$5. Konya has plenty of even lower-priced *lokantas*, including the twin of the Sifa-2, the original **Sifa Lokanta** across the street; another one is the **Çatal** by the Mevlâna museum, good for kebabs.

Save one lunch in Konya for one of the best simple *döner* stands you'll find anywhere, the **Kervanseray**, on Alâeddin Caddesi.

The Plain of Konya

Tourist Information

Karaman: Gazidükkan Mah, Eski Buğday Pazari, ✆ (338) 212 6741

Konya province, the largest in Turkey, is also one of its most important agricultural regions. One would hardly guess this from looking at a map: the region appears a strangely empty space, stretching over 150 miles from the lake district to Cappadocia. There's really no anomaly—it looks even emptier when you're in it. Somehow, lonesome flat country is always good for wheat, and this is one of the best. Your introduction to the breadbasket of Turkey will be any of the roads east from Konya, lined with grain elevators and flour mills. Its farmers have serious faces, rosy children, and shiny new Türk Fiat tractors, and they do a lot to keep Turkey self-sufficient in food.

They were at it with much the same vigour 8000 years ago, with enough leisure left over to create one of the world's first urban cultures, at least until archaeologists find an even older one. History used to begin with Sumer. Now with the great discoveries by James Mellaart at **Çatal Höyük**, we must say it begins here on the Plain of Konya, where long before nation-states, sky-gods or warrior castes, this town, and probably dozens like it, enjoyed what seems an easy and blessedly peaceful existence in trade and agriculture, making the beautiful works of art on display in the Ankara museum. Don't bother to visit the site—all you will get there is a lesson in the archaeologist's talent for recreating a culture from the tiniest of clues.

The road that passes Çatal Höyük continues on to the Mediterranean coast at Silifke, crossing the beautiful Taurus after **Karaman**, the Larende of ancient times and capital of the Karamanoğullari Turks after the fall of the Empire of Rum. Karaman has its castle, most noteworthy for being the only one in Turkey with its name in an electric sign on top, a 14th-century Mevlevi house called Ak Tekke, and a number of other mosques built by the Karamanoğullari. Further along through the mountains, a once-great 5th-century Byzantine monastery may be seen at **Alahan**; there are many others in various states of ruin in the area the Turks, with some exaggeration, call **Binbir Kilise** (1001 churches). It isn't the easiest spot to reach, around the village of Madenşehir, on a dead-end dirt road some 45km north of Karaman. You can find someone in the village to guide you around, but from all indications little is left of what was once a substantial Cappadocian-style network of religious communities. Here also was the once-thriving city of Derbe, 30km north of Karaman, one of the places St Paul visited on his trip through Asia Minor; almost nothing of the city remains.

North of Konya, the roads to Ankara and Kayseri pass on either side of Turkey's biggest lake, **Tuz Gölü**, the Salt Lake, a soberingly dismal corner of the republic. Both these roads were important in Selcuk times, and the Sultans of Rum built a large number of elegant hans, or caravanserais, along them, free of charge to merchants and travellers. You see them particularly on the route to Kayseri, mostly in ruins, every 9 miles, the distance a caravan could cover in a day. The best preserved is at **Sultanhani**, about 60 miles (100km) northeast of Konya. Alâeddin Keykubad built it in 1229; lately it has been restored with some modern stonework as good as the Selcuks'. It has been converted into a restaurant, open mainly in summer for tour groups, and it is also open for visits (*daily 9–7; adm*).

Cappadocia

Although never a distinct nation like Lydia or Phrygia, Cappadocia was known as a kingdom as early as 600 BC—it was probably really a loose confederacy of towns or tribes united to keep the Persians out, which didn't always work. Usually reduced to a tributary state of the Persian Empire, Cappadocia's rough terrain helped it survive with a modicum of independence into

Roman times. Under the Romans it was still a client state, with kings named either Ariarathres or Ariobarzanes, ruling first at Nyssa (the modern Nevşehir), and later at Mazaca (today's Kayseri). In AD 17, Emperor Tiberius' legions invited themselves in, and Cappadocia became a Roman province. Still a backwater, it never did receive its share of theatres or aqueducts; in fact its only discernible benefit from joining the Mediterranean community was a visit from St Paul, who corralled the inhabitants for Christianity with ease. St Paul never had to rebuke the Cappadocians as he did the Galatians. So fervently did they take to the new creed that Cappadocia replaced Africa as the great stronghold of Christian monasticism. St Basil, the 4th-century prelate who laid down the rules for Orthodox monks, as St Benedict was later to do for the Christians of the West, was bishop of Caesarea (Kayseri's name in Roman times); monks following his rule made the region's peculiar landscapes the biggest monastic centre of the east, a role Cappadocia was to retain for over a millennium. Generation after generation, they hollowed out the easily-worked tufa of Cappadocia's cliffs and canyons to make cave sanctuaries, and often entire churches complete with columns and domes—in all, Cappadocia has over a thousand rock-cut churches and chapels. In the 7th and 8th centuries, the monks survived the recurring attacks of Arab armies by squirreling themselves deeper away in their mountain fastnesses. The monasteries, though much reduced, survived for over eight centuries under Turkish rule, up until the exchange of populations of 1923.

The Cappadocian Picture Show

Some 200 of Cappadocia's rock churches are decorated, though it must be said that their artistic merit is limited at best. Whether any of the works were exceptional to begin with, we will never know—many have been repainted over and over through the centuries whenever they began to fade, on up to the expulsion of the Greeks in 1923. Nevertheless, these paintings are a landmark; during the Iconoclastic troubles of the 8th century, the Cappadocian monks kept the tradition of Greek painting alive (just barely!) in this inaccessible spot, scrawling red-and-white crosses and arabesques until the whim of Empress Irene made images permissible once again.

You'll see nothing of the sophistication of the frescoes in Istanbul's Kariye here, but Cappadocia's styles, symbols and motifs provide a useful handbook to decipher a thousand years of Greek art. For example, look out for the often-repeated image of two symmetric angels in flight, holding a crown or a cross between them. Originally these were two allegorical spirits holding a laurel crown—the seal and symbol of the Roman Empire, invented in the time of Augustus and common in all the propagandist artworks of the age; the Christians took it over later to remind people how their Church was taking the place of the dying Roman state. In works from the 6th century onward, you will see important figures, such as Jesus or Constantine, dressed in stylish tunics with a design of small rectangular plaques and white dots. These represented golden plates and jewels; such costumes were nothing but precise pictures of the Byzantine court dress in fashion since the time of Justinian—if they were good enough for the Emperor and Empress, they would do for God and the saints also.

Even as simple a symbol as the cross is worked for its historical resonance; in many scenes on the arches before the main altars, the familiar *chi-rho* monogram of Christ turns into an 8-pointed star, like an asterisk. That's another old political logo, the one adopted by Alexander the Great for his short-lived empire, and maintained by his

Seleucid successors. Keep an eye out for trivial details like the fall of draperies, the kinky folds in the clothing of figures from the 10th and 11th centuries. This very strange and stylized kind of art is unmistakeable—especially to us Westerners, since it is exactly the same as in the reliefs on Romanesque churches of the early Middle Ages, heavily influenced by the Greeks.

One frequently recurring motif from that time is *Daniel in the Lions' Den*, another Byzantine obsession, as common in the churches of Cappadocia as it is in the churches of England and France (no one has a clue why it was so important). Another is *St George and the Dragon*, this one not surprisingly, since George was a native Cappadocian, supposedly a martyr under Diocletian. The saint's popularity in England is entirely a reflection of pre-Christian myth there, though in the Greek East he somehow became associated with Athanasius, the fire-breathing 4th-century orthodox Patriarch of Alexandria. George slaying the dragon allegorically meant the triumph of the Church over those who disagreed with it. In domes and apses, the common figure is *Christ Pantocrator* ('ruler of all'), sending a blessing down from heaven.

Some churches have no great pretensions, like the one near Çavuşin that shows Emperor Nicephoras Phocas on his triumphal tour through Cappadocia in the 10th century. And others are intensely spiritual, like the scene of the *Ascension* on a celestial blue background in a Göreme church. As always, it's those big, staring Byzantine eyes, eyes that look straight into your soul. No better artistic trick was ever invented for expressing the outlook of early Christianity and its transcendant God. They are eyes that ask the big questions, eyes not content with the pageantry of earthly rulers—not even of the Byzantine emperors.

The Cappadocian Landscape

The real history of Cappadocia, however, begins some 30 million years ago. In the Cenozoic era, Erciyes Dağ, Hasan Dağ and Melendiz Dağ, the three tall peaks that dominate the region, were still active volcanoes. Over millions of years, their eruptions covered the land between them with thick layers of volcanic tufa, a stone made of compressed volcanic ash that is soft and easily worked. A few million more years of erosion turned Cappadocia into the dream landscape that attracted the hermits and monks, and now entertains over 100,000 visitors each year.

Words fail the honest writer attempting to do justice to the Cappadocian landscape; landscape, in fact, does not even seem the right word, for no other corner of the earth can have anything like the twisted, billowing forms found in the rocks of Göreme or Ortahisar. What makes Cappadocia so exceedingly strange is the very domesticity of the place. When wandering through the valley of Göreme, you may run across a stack of tufa shaped like a banana sticking out of the ground, white as sugar, with a door and window cut at the base, hollowed out long ago by a hermit or just a local farmer. On the window is a potted geranium, and on the doormat will be a sleeping cat.

Getting Around

Wherever you're coming from, chances are you'll find a bus to Nevşehir, and then make a connection to Ürgüp, Göreme or the other villages from there. The bus station is on Lâle Caddesi on the northern end of town; almost all buses pass through the centre first, so if you mean to stay in Nevşehir, be alert and ask them to let you off there.

Compactness is definitely one of Cappadocia's charms. The greatest part of its attractions is contained in an area about eight miles square, marked by the triangle of villages Nevşehir–Avanos–Ürgüp, with Göreme at its centre. It's not really difficult to see a lot without a car. The very helpful tourist office in Ürgüp prints a timetable of the regular Ürgüp–Nevşehir and Ürgüp–Ortahisar bus services; there's a bus every half-hour or so in season on these lines. Less frequent services take you to the underground cities, though mini-buses (or big buses) are very frequent between Nevşehir or Ürgüp and Derinkuyu, the easiest of the underground cities to visit. But be careful planning return trips—the last ones on most lines run at 5pm, or 6 in summer.

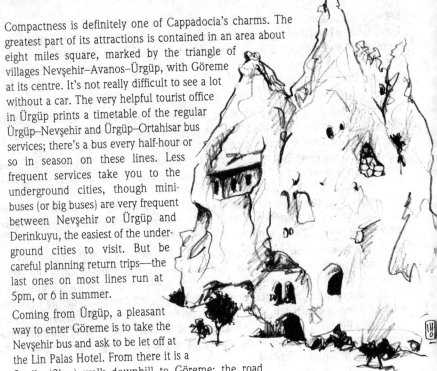

Coming from Ürgüp, a pleasant way to enter Göreme is to take the Nevşehir bus and ask to be let off at the Lin Palas Hotel. From there it is a 2-mile (3km) walk downhill to Göreme; the road passes the open-air museum. You can hire a taxi for the day for around £25/$38 or, less expensively, just use them to get around between the villages, if you can't wait for a bus. But no doubt about it, Cappadocia is Turkey's perfect spot for hiking or biking; the sights are suitably close together, and there are few tiring hills to climb. You'll find rental agencies in Ürgüp (ten of them), Uçhisar and Göreme. Horses are another popular way of sightseeing here. Several of the many travel agencies offer days in the saddle, or you can rent one at the Göreme Ranch in Ortahisar, ✆ (384) 343 3763.

Nevşehir, Niğde, and less frequently Ürgüp have regular coach services in all directions. If you're going on to Konya, you may have to change buses at Aksaray.

Tourist Information

All of these see a lot of foreign visitors, and are surprisingly well-organized and helpful by the standards of interior Anatolia, especially Nevşehir's.

Nevşehir: Atatürk Bulv, Hastane Önü, ✆ (384) 213 3659

Göreme: municipality office at the bus station, no phone

Avanos: Açik Pazar Yeri (marketplace), over the bridge from the central square, ✆ (384) 511 4360

Ürgüp: Kültür Park, ✆ (384) 341 4059

Mustafapaşa: on the central square, open irregularly in summer

Nigde: Belediye Binasi (town hall), ✆ (388) 232 3393

Kırşehir and Hacıbektaş

If you are travelling from Ankara, to reach Cappadocia you pass through towns that have nothing to do with the Greek–Christian air of the cave cities, but add an Islamic angle to the ambient piety; both were the homes of mystic Muslim sects that gained great popularity in the late Middle Ages. **Kırşehir** was the headquarters of the Ahi brotherhood, a sensible, plain-living society, widespread among the artisan guilds and workmen of central Anatolia. Following the precepts of their leader, Ahi Evran, who is buried here, the Ahis became renowned less for their mystic accomplishments than for their hospitality and good fellowship. Kırşehir's medieval monuments include the **Cacabey Mosque**, built by the Ilhanli Mongols, and the **Alâeddin Mosque**, of which only the richly ornamented portal remains. 'Alâeddin' stands, of course, for Alâeddin Keykubad, the indefatigable Selcuk sultan who contributed something to nearly every town in central Anatolia.

The Bektaşis

In the same century, the 13th, another dervish named Hacıbektaş Veli, preaching a message of moderation and discipline, founded the Bektaşi order. When he became spiritual leader of the newly founded Janissary corps, his order began its career as the most influential in the Ottoman state, surpassing even the Mevlevis. His tomb, and the former head Bektaşi *tekke*, are now a **museum** (*open daily 8–12, 1–5; adm*) in the town of **Hacıbektaş** renamed in his honour. The tomb lies behind a gilded door; nearby is the beautiful hall where the dervishes performed their rituals, and where other notables of their order lie buried alongside three unknown women, mysteriously known only as the 'Beauties of the World'. Other buildings of the complex you may visit are the soup kitchen, perhaps the most important of all for the complicated symbolism the Bektaşis and their Janissary followers built up around the eating of soup. The great cauldron hanging in the hearth is the famous 'Karakazan', the Black Kettle; the Janissaries turned it upside-down and paraded it through the streets of Istanbul to show their displeasure with the sultan whenever they felt like deposing one. A Bektaşi festival is still held in Hacıbektaş every year on 15–18 August.

Gülşehir, on the road south towards Nevşehir, is an attractive town with some remains of early Christian settlements and churches that can serve as an appetizer for the main course, at Göreme. Near the Nevşehir road is a huge area of cave dwellings, necropoli, and other remains, including the **Church of St John** and a complex called **Açiksaray** (the 'open palace'), a two-storey affair built into a hill, similar in many ways to the underground cities (*see* below). Unfortunately, both these sites have been heavily vandalized and their painted decoration is largely lost.

Nevşehir

From here, another 50km takes you to **Nevşehir**, Cappadocia's provincial capital and one of the convenient bases for seeing the region. Although the castle on the hill above the city dates from the Crusaders, Nevşehir is not an old city. Damad Ibrahim Paşa (born 1678), an Ottoman vezir of the Tulip Period, famous for attempts at reform and for introducing European art and culture into Turkey, was born in the tiny village of Muscara. His efforts earned him an assassination in Istanbul, but not before he had refounded his home village as a city (Nevşehir means 'new town'), and built mosques, schools, libraries and an aqueduct; his statue stands in the centre of the town.

The Turks, despite their many artistic talents, have never had a clue at town design. Ibrahim Paşa left Nevşehir some fine buildings, but the town itself, like all Turkish towns, is made of pointless streets that wander wherever they please. Nevşehir at least makes it easy to find your way around, tidily chopped into quarters by Lâle Caddesi, leading north to the *otogar*, and east–west Atatürk Caddesi/Yeni Kayseri Caddesi, the road to Ürgüp. The benefactor's main complex of buildings stands south of the bazaar district off Lâle Caddesi, around the **Damad Ibrahim Paşa Mosque**, with a lovely 'Turkish Baroque' interior much more subtle than Konya's Aziziye. The complex includes a a medrese and library, and also a hamam, still in operation and little changed since it was built. Behind the mosque, the narrow streets of old Nevşehir climb up to the ruined Selcuk **castle**. Nevşehir's **museum**, on Yeni Kayseri Caddesi (*open daily exc Mon, 8–12, 1.30–5.30; adm*), offers the typical mix of archaeological finds and old carpets and bric-a-brac.

Market day is Sunday, usually carrying on through Monday; it's a big affair. West of Nevşehir, another **underground city** (*see* p.343) has been discovered at Tatlarin (from the city turn left at Acigöl, 22km out; it's signposted). It isn't as impressive or as large as the ones at Derinkuyu and Kaymakli, but it's only been open a short while and you'll be one of the first to see it.

Cappadocia ℗ (384–)   **Where to Stay**

Think carefully before deciding where to base yourself in Cappadocia. If you're short on time, stay in Göreme where the open-air museum is but a stroll away; if you have longer, Ürgüp is better, being a bigger town with more facilities. For peace and quiet, Mustafapaşa and Ortahisar are perfect (*see* below for all of these towns). Nevşehir may seem the obvious choice with its good bus connections and fancy hotels, but there's no dreamy landscapes in its immediate vicinity, and staying over among the fairy chimneys is half the fun (actually, Nevşehir's charms wear out in a day or so.)

expensive/moderate

Recent years have seen a boom in hotel building in Nevşehir, waiting for a tourist boom that so far hasn't happened. As at Konya, they take what they can get, so *always* bargain. For the time being, the best is the ★★★★★**Dedeman Oteli**, 1km out of Nevşehir on the Ürgüp road, ℗ 213 9900, which looks like a state mental hospital but has all the appropriate trimmings: rooms with minibars, satellite TV and air conditioning, hamam, casino, disco, etc. Less expensively nearby, the ★★★**Orsan**, Yeni Kayseri Yolu, ℗ 213 2115 has comfortable rooms with balconies, a swimming pool and tennis courts. In the centre of Nevşehir and near the *otogar*, there is a number of overpriced three-star hotels with little to offer.

cheap

There's quite a bit of choice here, but the best bargain is probably the **Şems**, right in the centre on Atatürk Caddesi, ℗ 213 3597. Once a hotel of some pretensions, with a star or two, it's deteriorating at a modest pace, but in the meantime you can have an acceptable room with bath for about £5/$8. The very cheapest places in town cluster around the western end of Atatürk Caddesi, including the **Uçhisar**, on Aksaray Caddesi, ℗ 212 5672, and the **Ipek Palas** a few doors down, ℗ 212 1478. Both are relatively clean and rock-bottom cheap; the rest of the places in this area seem to be real dives.

Eating Out

As usual in towns like this, the place to go for a good dinner and a drink is in the town park on Atatürk Caddesi: the **Park Restoran** isn't exceptional, but you'll be glad it's there; good *böreks* and kebabs, on outside tables in the park; £5/$8. Beyond this, the city offers simple repasts at places such as the **Şen**, on Ragip Üner Sokak off Atatürk, near the Altinoz Otel: a tidy place with tasty lentil soup and roast chicken for next to nothing. Another simple *lokanta* where you won't go wrong is the **Aspava**, on Atatürk Bulvari.

Central Cappadocia

Ancient Cappadocia was a large province, but don't be dismayed; seeing its scenic marvels will not require any long or difficult travel. Most of the rock cities, as well as the valley of Göreme, are located between Nevşehir and Ürgüp, only 11 miles (18km) to the east. Halfway along this route, the triple rock of **Üçhisar** introduces you to the oddities of the region. Although the villagers of Üçhisar have long ago moved down into more modern lodgings, the peak, the largest in the area, remains laced with the tunnels and chambers they used when it served as their giant apartment house. From the top—a road leads most of the way up—there is a panoramic view of the Göreme valley, just to the east, with Mt Erciyes in the distance. Come past at night, if you can; the entire rock is illuminated, appearing like some post-impressionist skyscraper. If you mean to do any exploring in Üçhisar, *be careful*; some of the floors are weak and could collapse. Keep this caveat in mind for the rest of Cappadocia, too, though there is little danger in seeing the main attractions.

From Üçhisar to Göreme, the road passes more curiosities, including some of the famous **fairy chimneys,** tall needles of stone, often with large rocks balanced on top. Their volcanic origin is not hard to detect. As well as vast quantities of ash, Mt Erciyes would occasionally toss out some boulders of hard basalt. During the periods of erosion, these boulders protected the ash, now hardened into tufa beneath, resulting in a column that grows taller as the land around it is scoured away. Also on this road, there is a viewpoint (unmarked) to the right from which you can see one of the most remarkable corners of Göreme. By now you will certainly have been surprised at the greenness and fertility of this part of Cappadocia; if you saw pictures, you will have come expecting desert rockpiles, only to find instead rolling hills of pretty farms, olive groves and vineyards; the region is famous for its wine. Beneath the good volcanic soil are the rocks, and the narrow valleys where they have been eroded away are low-set and easy to overlook. Here, masses of glistening white tufa, blown into shapes of futuristic World's Fair pavilions, fill the valley, dotted here and there with doors and windows, with little gardens and citrus orchards in between. Some of the outcrops are shaped like lemons, and oddly enough the farmers use them for storing the lemons and oranges they grow here.

Göreme

Göreme is the real centre of Cappadocia, the village closest to the heart of the area. Ten years ago it was a peaceful, delightful place. Today, commercialized out of all recognition, boiling with *pansiyons* and carpet shops—somehow it's still fun. It isn't very big, thank goodness, and you can still walk a few minutes outside town and be lost among the marvels and jests of nature.

The attractions are a short walk away in the **Valley of Göreme**; it goes on and on, the scenes changing continuously; many visitors become entranced and spend days wandering along its quiet paths. If you haven't the time, at least visit the **Göreme open-air museum** (*open daily 8.30–5, until 7 in summer; adm*), where over two dozen churches, some with beautifully painted frescoes, make up the largest monastic complex in the region, all hewn out of the cliffs and crags and joined by stairs, paths, and tunnels. Two very distinct styles of Byzantine painting explain between them something of the Iconoclastic conflict of the 8th and 9th centuries, the bitter struggle over images (and church politics) that sent so many refugees into Cappadocia. Those painted just after the downfall of the Iconoclasts are awkward, almost primitive geometric patterns and symbols—the Greeks had forgotten how to draw. By the 10th century, however, in the surprisingly quick renaissance of art that followed, the monks of Cappadocia contributed some fine work—nothing really special, but a good indicator of the artistic trends of the day.

Most of the churches are called after some feature of the paintings; the **Church with the Apple**, for example. Many of these small churches are carved with arches, pillars, vaults, and domes, distinguishable from an ordinary church only by a lack of windows. In the Church with the Apple (currently closed for restoration), many of the frescoes have peeled away, revealing the simple post-Iconoclastic decoration underneath. Like many others, this one has been much defaced by graffiti, the oldest in Greek, the most recent in Turkish, as high up as an adolescent can reach. Only recently has the government, along with private foundations and UNESCO, spent money to protect and restore them (the area is a United Nations World Heritage Site).

Among the other noteworthy churches nearby are the **Church with the Buckle**, with painted scenes from the life of St Basil; the **Church of the Sandal**, where an imprint on the floor is said to be a cast of Jesus's own footstep, brought from Jerusalem; and the **Dark Church** with familiar New Testament scenes, in some of the best work in Cappadocia, recently restored by UNESCO. The **Church with the Snake** shows St George with his dragon, and large figures of Helen and Constantine holding the true cross. There's more fine work at the **Hidden Church**, if you can find it. Further inside the complex the **Jerphanion Church** was discovered only in 1965 and named after Guillaume de Jerphanion, the French art historian who spent his life uncovering and cataloguing the Göreme paintings; it has some of the most interesting primitive frescoes, sun symbols and interlaced crosses.

Two large, self-contained monasteries can be seen near the valley, the **Firkatan** for men and the **Girls Monastery**, accommodating some 300 nuns, a network of tunnels, cells, and churches on three floors, carved from a large crag (the Turks call it the 'Virgins' Castle'). From here, several other attractions of the Göreme valley can be reached on foot, notably the village of **Çavuşin**, a rock-fortress similar to Uçhisar. Here though, half the original rock collapsed long ago, leaving the walls and corridors of the ancient rock town open to the sky; in places, the crag is so thin you can see through it. A stairway off the Avanos road, just north of the village, leads up into the **Çavuşin Church**, guarded by frescoes of the angels Michael and Gabriel which were exposed by the collapse; inside are more fine paintings, scenes from the life of Christ. Up in the hills nearby is another exceptional painted church, the **Church of St John the Baptist**, with works from the 6th–8th centuries.

Kizilçukor and Ortahisar

Kizilçukor, a village just to the east of the Nevşehir–Ürgüp road, has been a wine-making centre since antiquity, and its **Church of the Grapes** has frescoes of scenes of the harvest and wine-making, as well as the usual saints. Three miles (5km) to the south, the crumbling crag of

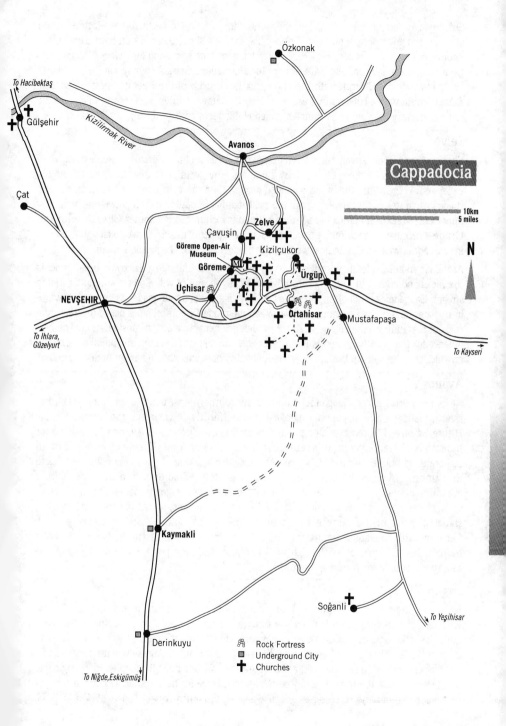

Özkonak

To Hacibektaş

Gülşehir

Kızılırmak River

Avanos

Çat

Cappadocia

10km
5 miles

N

Zelve

Çavuşin

Kizilçukor

Göreme Open-Air
Museum

Göreme

Üçhisar

Ürgüp

NEVŞEHIR

*To Ihlara,
Güzelyurt*

Ortahisar

Mustafapaşa

To Kayseri

Kaymakli

Soğanli

To Yeşihisar

Derinkuyu

Rock Fortress
Underground City
Churches

To Niğde, Eskigümüş

341

Ortahisar is perhaps the only rock in the world with sash windows; there's an electric sign on top, too, and an underground tunnel (now collapsed) to a similar complex on the village's edge. Enough of Ortahisar has been repaired so that you can climb to the top for a view of further religious complexes, fairy chimneys and strange rock formations. Several churches in the area worth visiting include the **Church with the Hare** and the **Church of the Beet** (signposted *Pancarlik Kilisesi*), both with 11th-century frescoes of New Testament scenes. West of the village are the ruins of an Armenian monastic complex, called **Halaşdere**, with an underground basilica.

Zelve

There is yet another canyon full of churches, 6km northeast of the Göreme museum at **Zelve**— a district where, in some spots, the fairy chimneys grow as thick as trees in a forest. Two old valleys converge at the site of the complex, eroded from the warm, tan rock with an outcrop shaped like a steamship between them. It is believed that St Basil himself founded one of the first important Greek seminaries here. Among the many churches is another **Church with the Grape** which has some primitive paintings. Here, too, parts of the cliffs have collapsed, exposing, in one spot, a wall lined with neatly cut compartments in rows, like pigeonholes in a post office.

At the far end of the left-hand valley, you can pick your way through a narrow natural tunnel in the rocks and come out into a beautiful isolated canyon, full of wild flowers around a running stream. Cappadocia is full of surprises like this, both natural and man-made. As times grew worse in the later days of the Byzantine Empire, when the monastic communities began to suffer from raids of marauding Turkish and Arab tribes, defence became a prime consideration. The best defence for the peaceful monks was concealment, and many of the monastic buildings are cleverly hidden in crevices in the cliff faces; undoubtedly some exist that are as yet undiscovered.

Avanos

At its northern fringes, Cappadocia touches the southernmost bend of the Kizilirmak ('red river'), the major river of central Anatolia and once (further downstream) the heartland of the Hittite Empire. The red clay along its banks has kept the potters of **Avanos** in business for thousands of years. Avanos is an attractive town, reached from Göreme or Nevşehir by an elaborate old bridge over the Kizilirmak. At the centre, a statue of a working potter testifies to the fame the Avanos work has always had in Anatolia. Traditionally painted red with a minimum of decoration, the pottery of the modern artisans is enjoying something of a revival, selling by the ton to Cappadocia's tourists. Just east of Avanos, on the old road to Nevşehir, stands another of the caravansarais built by the Selcuk Sultan Alâeddin Keykubad, the **Sarihan**, with an elaborate entrance portal. Avanos and Nevşehir form the two corners of a triangle that bounds most of the sights in the region; the third point would be at Ürgüp, the most popular base for visitors to Cappadocia.

Ürgüp

Even more than Avanos, **Ürgüp** is an exceptionally lovely town, unlike any other in Turkey, with its Belgian-block paved streets and unusual designs carved into the stone of the older buildings. Like Üçhisar and Ortahisar, it has come down from the cliffs in recent decades, and today it is the main base for Cappadocian tourism (and the only village where it's easy to find a drink after dinner). Here, however, a few of the cave houses are still occupied; one troglodyte on the edge of the town has recently added a cave-garage for his new car. Ürgüp has most of the region's hotels and restaurants, and also a small **museum** (*open daily exc Mon, 8–5.30;*

adm) in the city park. Most of the region's vineyards are on the roads just outside Ürgüp, and you can visit the **Tursan winery** just outside town and have a few samples (and buy a crate to tide you over if you're going to Konya).

Up until the exchange of populations in the 1920s, Ürgüp and its neighbouring villages had sizeable Greek communities. If you approach Ürgüp from Nevşehir, the new one-way system takes you down into town past some fine old houses, many with wooden balconies; the exit road back up the hill passes more of the same. These are the old Greek houses, several of which have been restored and converted into hotels; one is now the main office of a firm of carpet dealers. When the Greeks left, they were replaced by Muslims from Thessalonika who spoke a Macedonian dialect. You can still hear this language spoken, especially in nearby Mustafapaşa (which had been an entirely Greek village, called Sinanos), by the original settlers and their children; grandchildren understand but are not fluent, and the language will soon die out here.

South of the town, the road to Yeşilhisar passes through other towns with cave churches: **Mustafapaşa**, with irregular dolmuş service from Ürgüp, is the first. This village wants its cut of Cappadocian tourism, and a few *pansiyons*, carpet shops and restaurants are starting to appear. There is little to see, though, save the restored church of **SS. Constantine and Helen** in the centre, and the 18th-century **St Basil Church** on the northern outskirts, with some of its original frescoes. South of Mustafapaşa the landscape changes completely, into a Wild West backdrop of mesas and buttes. You can swim here, at the Damsa Reservoir, created by a dam on a tributary of the Kizilirmak. There are two tiny villages in the area, **Camil**, with yet another medieval monastic complex (some good frescoes in the **church of St Stephen**), and **Taşkinpaşa**, with a much-decayed Selcuk mosque.

There is as yet no public transportation in this part of Cappadocia, and you'll need a car or a horse or some determination on your bike to push the next 21km to one of the grandest and least-known sights the region has to offer: the valleys of **Soğanli**. Here, unlike the other sites in which churches are merely cut into the rocks, is a crag that has been sculpted into a church, with even a typical Byzantine cylindrical dome; there are frescoes inside. The locals call it the **Church with the Beret**. Some other rock-cut churches are nearby, including the **Church of the Snake**, named for a painting of St George and the Dragon. There are more churches further up the valley, some of them painted.

Another spot you'll need transportation for is **Sultan Sazliği** (Sultan Marshes), on the southern slopes of Mt Erciyes, centre of a beautiful area of lakes, of which the largest is Yay Göl (south of Yeşilhisar on the road to Niğde, turn left for Yahyali and look for the signs). The government has recently declared the area a nature reserve; it is one of the country's major nesting areas for waterfowl, as well as a major migration stopover for flamingoes, herons, cranes and dozens of other species on their way to and from Africa. The centre of the reserve is the village of **Ovaçiftlik**, a short distance from the edge of the Yay Göl marshes; it has a small museum and observation tower, as well as the only accommodation in the area.

Underground Cities

On top of all this, the most outlandish feature of the Cappadocian fun-house has not yet even been mentioned: the **underground cities**. Six have been discovered so far, and three have been excavated and lit for visitors, at least for a small part of their total extent. Each of them was capable of accommodating several thousand inhabitants, supplied with water by underground springs and air through elaborate ventilation systems.

None has been completely explored—they haven't even found the bottom of one yet. The best known, at Derinkuyu, goes down at least 15 floors, with air shafts as deep as 400 feet. At Özkonak, the top levels cover some 3½ square miles. Strangest of all, these cities are all interconnected by a network of tunnels, some as much as 6 miles long. No one knows who built them. Medieval Christians certainly occupied them, but a Roman tomb has also been found on the seventh level of one, and a Hittite-style grain mill and Hittite seals deep in another. Except for one brief mention in Xenophon, ancient and medieval authors ignore them entirely. They must have taken centuries to create; all the tunnels and corridors are narrow, and only one man at a time could have worked at digging them. It's likely that the cities were never continuously occupied, but rather served the inhabitants of the region as refuges in times of trouble.

The history of warfare has shown that there is no such thing as an invulnerable fortress, but these may be the exception. Storming them would be quite impossible; at all the entrances, and even at many points within the cities, great round 'blocking stones' were set that could seal off the passage in a minute, with no room for the enemy to work at moving them, and with plenty of slits in the walls through which the defenders could thrust in their spears. Secret entrances and hundreds of airshaft openings are scattered over miles of difficult terrain; it would be impossible for an enemy to find them all, and wonderfully easy for the people inside to send out forces to harry the attackers, or restock their supplies.

Whoever was responsible for all this, something in it smacks of a bad case of paranoia. Even if built over a period of centuries, the effort to create such prodigies of mole-work could only come from a slave empire with a large economic surplus—of which there is no record here— or an obsession on the part of some petty rulers. There were never many big towns in this part of Anatolia, and it is highly unlikely that any enemy could have been so terrible to country people as to drive them to such extremes.

You may choose which of the three to visit; **Özkonak** is on a dirt road 21km north of Avanos; the other two, **Kaymakli** and **Derinkuyu** (*both open daily 8–5, until 7 in summer; adm*) are south of Nevşehir, 20km and 30km respectively. None of the three has any special features peculiar to itself; the cities are strictly utilitarian, with no embellishment. All have 'blocking stones' and other defensive features, and churches, common dining halls, and even tombs marked out in them. All three will wear you out, climbing back up from the lower levels, but the air is surprisingly fresh, and the temperature always cool.

At Derinkuyu, a fascinating separate underground city has recently been discovered, connected to the main one by a 1.5km tunnel, now collapsed; at its centre is a kind of 'temple' with a grand hall supported by sixteen columns. In Derinkuyu you can also visit the unusual **Greek Church** of the last century, with blind arcades and lovely carvings of birds, vines, and floral crosses that hint at an Armenian influence. Locked up since 1923, it has frescoes and carved wood details inside that are deteriorating rapidly (you might ask at the village hall, or bribe the underground city guards for a visit to either of these). Other underground cities have been found at Tatlarin, west of Nevşehir (*see* above), at Çardak, south of Nevşehir (ask at the village hall for a tour), at Karacören, east of Ürgüp, and at Gülşehir; the latter two are not open to visitors.

South and West of Göreme

Ihlara

For those not sated with the rupestrian excess of the Göreme area, little bits have spilled over into the lands west and south. On the lowest slopes of Hasan Dağ, one of the region's extinct volcanoes, the **Valley of Ihlara** has another entire complex of churches, many with excellent frescoes, in a steep and picturesque valley. No public transportation runs here (except minibuses from Aksaray, the nearest city), and it's 43km west of Derinkuyu on a back road, the most distant and hardest to reach of all the sights of Cappadocia. Nevertheless, it's worth a visit for the natural beauty of its red clay cliffs, and its relative isolation; if you're around in July or August and the churches of Göreme are full of Germans videotaping the frescoes, Ihlara is the place to go.

The sights lie in a 10km stretch of the Melendiz river valley, in a rugged canyon between the villages of **Ihlara** and **Belistirma** (from *Peristrema*, the old Greek name for the valley); exploring them will be a day's work, but a day you won't regret. Really, you may walk in from anywhere, but the main entrance is off the road between the villages, at the centre of the old monastic community. Near this entrance are a number of churches, including the **Yilanli Kilise**, the 'snake church', where the paintings show the Last Judgement and some interesting tortures of the damned. To the north, towards Belistirma, you will find the **Church of St George**, with familiar scenes of the dragon-killer, and Greek inscriptions to the glory of the medieval Selcuk emirs; and the **Direkli Kilise** ('columned church') one of the prettiest in the valley, with more frescoes of St George, and the Virgin and Child. South of the entrance, the **Ağaçalti Kilise** has scenes of the Three Kings and Daniel in the Lions' Den, while more well-preserved New Testament vignettes can be seen in the **Kokar Kilise**, halfway to Ihlara.

Near Ihlara, a side road leads off to the town of **Güzelyurt**, built over and below a cliff full of caves, with another 19th-century Greek church and some houses decorated in the same style as in Ürgüp. North of Belistirma, **Selime** is one of the most charming and totally unspoiled villages of Cappadocia, surrounded by fairy chimneys and other weird formations; many of its people still live in houses partially cut out of the rock, or in old monastic cells.

Eskigümüş

To the south of Göreme, the road through Derinkuyu continues on to **Eskigümüş** ('old silver'), a former troglodyte colony with yet another Byzantine monastery cut into the cliffs; especially interesting here is the large, open courtyard carved out of the rock, completely hidden from view from the outside. Cells and corridors are carved into the sides on several levels, with sockets for beams and posts that suggest the entire space was once filled with a building of several storeys completely encased in solid rock. Frescoes in the church within, from the 7th to the 11th centuries, include some particularly well-executed figures of Christ, Mary, and the saints. To the left of the narthex, the 600-foot escape tunnel is typical of the precautions medieval monks were forced to take.

Niğde

Niğde, a quiet provincial capital west of Hasan Dağ, marks the southern limits of the land of fairy chimneys and caves. Quiet is the word, for somehow, between Selcuks and Karamanoğullari, Mongols and Ottomans, Niğde has avoided having much history. All the same, it managed to get a good building or two from most of its medieval rulers, and while none is exceptional on its own, together they make a lovely, unified cityscape. Unfortunately, it doesn't seem as if anyone cares about the place; the centre is shot to hell, while folks get on in the outlying districts manufacturing cement and breeze blocks.

Sultan Alâeddin Keykubad is represented here up in the deserted citadel, in the **Alâeddin Mosque** (1223), decorated in unusual geometric flowers and wave designs; its three domes are Niğde's landmark together with an odd minaret that looks more like a lighthouse. In the town below, the **Sungurbey Mosque** of 1335, built by and named after an Ilhanli Mongol emir, has a much more graceful, spirally fluted minaret, but the decoration of its portal and roofline, as in most works begun by the Mongols, are incomplete. Just off Bor Caddesi, the main street, the **Akmedrese** of 1409 is the Karamanoğullari contribution, having the uncommon feature of a loggia built into its façade. Other medieval mosques, as well as schools and fountains, two lovely *türbes* and a 16th-century *bedesten* in the bazaar under the citadel walls, combine to make Niğde one of the most architecturally distinguished cities of Anatolia. On the west side of town, the province keeps a small **museum** with a grave stele and handicrafts (but everyone really comes to see the Byzantine mummy).

Cappadocia ℗ (384–)	*Where to Stay and Eating Out*

 It's hard to choose between the Cappadocian villages for a base. Ürgüp is the biggest town, with the best choice in accommodation and restaurants. Avanos has a few too, but it's a bit out of the way. In Göreme and Uçhisar, you'll be out in the wilds, but so much the better for walking or bicycling and getting to know the countryside and its oddities.

Uçhisar

A favourite with backpackers, Uçhisar has a load of inexpensive *pansiyons*, most of which are quite nice, and go for about £6/$9. Some of them are built into the rock, or at least have underground breakfast rooms. Streets here are not likely to have names, but proprietors put up little signs everywhere to direct you in. One of the best is the **Anatolia**, ℗ 219 2339, simple but clean and very well run. The **Derebağ**, ℗ 219 2143, has rooms with bath for slightly more, and offers meals, a consideration in this town where the restaurants are few. One step up from these, there is the **Garden of the 1001 Nights**, ℗ 219 2293, which is as over the top as its name would suggest; rooms with panoramic views set among the fairy chimneys; there's a restaurant. Ring ahead, since some rooms are dear, others relatively inexpensive.

Göreme

It doesn't look like much from the outside, but the (S) **Ataman** in Göreme, ℗ 271 2310, is one of the most pleasant hotels in Cappadocia, a tufa construction set (rather obtrusively) among the ruins; beautifully appointed, air conditioned rooms, pool and hamam. The ★★★**Çiner**, ℗ 271 2039, is new and eager to please, with a swimming pool and satellite TV, and charges £15/$22 per person, breakfast and half-board.

Göreme is where the backpackers go and this is the place to find dozens of *pansiyons*, many of them with rooms cut out of the rock, so that you can live like a Byzantine ascetic, with or without bath. Almost all are modern, purpose built and family-run, and rates are about £5/$8 for a double room. To choose one, go to the municipality information office at the bus station (*open 5am–11pm daily*), where you will find, pinned to the walls, photographs of all of the pensions, information on the facilities each one offers, and directions on how to get to them. One of the best is the **Saksağan**, ℗ 271 2165, with pyramidal chimneys, lovely rooms and friendly people, on the Nevşehir road. The **Paradise**, near the open air museum, ℗ 271 2248, has rooms carved into the rock as does the nearby **Peri**, ℗ 271 2136, with rooms right in the fairy chimneys.

Both these places are very well kept, and have some rooms with baths. Two other nice ones: the **Esen**, ✆ 271 2278, and the **Rock Valley**, ✆ 271 2351.

There are plenty of campsites around: large, well-equipped ones like the **Dilek**, ✆ 271 2395, and the **Kapadokya**, ✆ 271 2317; both have swimming pools, and the Kapadokya also has inexpensive bungalows to rent.

The **Ataman Hotel** (*see* above) also has the best restaurant in Göreme: nothing special, but a wide choice of kebabs in a dining room cut out of the tufa; outdoor terrace in summer; £6/$9. Göreme's real *turistik restoran* is the **Mehmet Paşa**, just off the main street; as in some of the restored restaurants of Istanbul, here one goes less for the cuisine than the decor—it's a tastefully-restored 18th-century mansion with some Tulip Period frescoes inside; £9/$13. Beyond these there isn't much apart from simple *lokantas.*

Ortahisar

You may find Ortahisar a welcome alternative to Göreme or Ürgüp; it's smaller and less overloaded with tourists—a bit like those villages were fifteen years ago. A motel-style place built of native tufa, the ★★★**Burcu**, ✆ 343 3200, is nothing special; its main strength is a beautiful location close to the weird rock. There aren't a lot of *pansiyons.* In the inexpensive range, the spartan **Göreme Hotel**, ✆ 343 3005, will be adequate.

Avanos

At the northern end of the Cappadocian triangle, Avanos has its share of comfortable accommodation, thrown up in the recent speculative binge. The ★★★★**Büyük Avanos**, Kapadokya Caddesi, ✆ 511 3577, 📠 511 4863, has a pool and rooms with satellite TV, and not much else to offer; it doesn't really seem a four-star place, but then it doesn't have the rates of one either. Something a little more stylish is the (M) **Sofa**, Orta Mah, ✆ 511 4489, a charmingly furnished, stone-built motel with an accommodating, English-speaking proprietor; doubles with bath £12/$18. *Pansiyons* are spread pretty much all over the village: the **Nazar**, ✆ 511 4801, is in the centre near the bridge. The least expensive ones will be found further in, up the hillside behind the town square. Here, the **Panorama**, ✆ 511 4654, has views over the town and clean rooms with or without bath. Nearby, the **Fantasie**, ✆ 511 2947, is just as good; lots of French tourists come here. Just outside the town, the **Ada Camping**, ✆ 511 2429, is a modern facility with everything you would ask for in a campground, including a pool; it's a bit more expensive than most.

If you're coming through here, plan a lunch at the **Tuvanna Restaurant** on the main square, one of the best in the area: home-made *pide*, tasty kebabs, even omelettes and other breaks from the usual, for an average £4/$6 (not to be confused with the popular, *pide*-and-kebab **Tefanna**, nearby on the main street, Kenan Evren Caddesi). For something simpler, you can have a filling plate of *manti* at the **Çağlak**, just down the street.

Ürgüp

Ürgüp, like Nevşehir, has seen its share of speculative hotel building in recent years; most of them are nearly empty much of the time, and big discounts are more the rule than the exception. There are four big ones on the Nevşehir road west of the town. It's hard to distinguish between them, but the ★★★★**Perissia**, ✆ 341 2930, 📠 341 2288, has the best pool, also air conditioned rooms with balconies, minibar and satellite TV, and all the facilities you would expect in a four-star. The ★★★★**Mustafa**, down the road, ✆ 341 3970, is smaller and a little more intimate, but just as well-equipped.

In the middle range, a recent and unusual addition is the (S)**Alfina**, Istiklâl Caddesi, ✆ 341 4822. Like so many of the old houses here, it is built into the side of a cliff; a series of terraces of tufa-built rooms with balconies. Ürgüp has a wonderful collection of moderately and inexpensively priced hotels, several of them being old mansions that once housed the town's well-heeled. These are intriguing places to stay at, with original features like shuttered niches in the wall and decorative carving. One such is the **Asia Minor Hotel**, Istiklâl Caddesi 38, ✆ 341 2721; another is near the hamam and mosque, the Elvan, ✆ 341 4191. The **Born**, Nevşehir Caddesi, ✆ 341 3756, is a quiet hideaway set in what was once the Ottoman governor's house. All three have double rooms with bath for £8/$12. For a little extra money, you can get a hotel with a pool: the **Türkeler**, Nevşehir Caddesi, ✆ 341 8870, charges £12/$18 for a double room.

As for the rest of the pensions, Ürgüp has plenty; the tourist office there publishes a full list, with prices. Just off Istiklâl Caddesi by the central square are two more pleasant, very inexpensive places in old Greek buildings: the **Cappadoce**, ✆ 341 4714, and the **Seymen**, ✆ 341 4380. The **Dinler Camping**, ✆ 213 1428, is the serious campsite in town, with shady spots, a pool, and a restaurant/snack bar. There are a number of simpler places, including the **Pinar**, ✆ 341 4054, by the hotel of the same name, on Kayseri Caddesi.

Ürgüp has several good restaurants, notably the **Hanedan**, built into the rocks on the Nevşehir road. It's a very refined place, despite the stuffed foxes and pelicans glowering down from the ceiling, with the biggest choices of mezes you'll see outside Istanbul and a changing menu of surprising main courses; £10/$15, cheaper for the lunch buffet. The best of the simple *lokantas* is the **Kardeşler**, in the centre near the Hitit Otel, with *pides*, kebabs and just about everything else for small change. More good eating can be had at the **Kapadokya** and the **Sofa** in the centre of town.

Villages South of Ürgüp

In Mustafapaşa, part of the **Monastery Pension**, ✆ 353 5005, is carved into the rock, and a pleasant evening can be spent listening to the owner playing his sax in the cave bar. It's friendly and cheap. If you want to spend time at the 'Bird Paradise' of Sultansazliği, there is a simple but welcoming *pansiyon* campground, the **Sultan**, ✆ 658 5576, which also organizes tours and bird-watching expeditions.

Ihlara

In this last frontier of Cappadocian tourism, choices are few, but such accommodation as there is will inevitably be cheap and amiable. A wonderful place to get away from it all is the **Belediye**, ✆ 453 7242, in Ihlara village near the entrance to the valley park; very inexpensive rooms with a view, some with baths. There are other *pansiyons* in Ihlara and rudimentary campgrounds there and in the neighbouring village of Belistirma.

And if you're coming or going to Cappadocia by way of the Niğde—Mersin road to the coast, plan a lunch stop along the way at the **Topbaşlar Restoran**, in the bus service area along the highway, just north of Polatli. Surprisingly good dining in the middle of nowhere: Gaziantep-style kebabs, rich desserts, and a stuffed antelope to contemplate for about £3/$5.

Some Sentimental Reflections, with Speculation on the Origins of Pizza

Finally finishing this long run through western Turkey, an area about the size of France, makes us feel weary and a bit reflective, and so in closing we will offer a number of facetious superlatives that come to mind, entirely fitting for what, as you will agree by now, is a superlative country in every way.

Kerb height: in Turkey, unfortunately, it's every pedestrian for himself. Anyone walking in Turkish cities is liable to disappear without a trace at any moment, especially in Istanbul where shops have wells below the pavement for deliveries—without railings. The biggest sheer drop, about nine feet, is on Istanbul's Atatürk Caddesi; may you find it before it finds you.

Bus wait: arriving at the station without a ticket, you should be on your way in 15 mins, on average. Our record is three and a half hours, going from Nevşehir to Aksaray on election day. Tell a Turk about this and he'll think the world is going to hell in a handcart.

Rip-off: Marlboros, at £4/$6 the pack because of taxes. Though they're the ultimate status symbol here, you'll do better with a pack of *Samsuns*, rich and strong and possibly the finest filter smokes in the galaxy.

Bargain: in this land of bargains, the absolute best, sad to relate, is marble. If there's room in your grip you can pick up a table top, or fifty square yards of floor tiling, for next to nothing in a dozen places around the Aegean coast. Second best bargain is '50s American cars with tons of chrome trim, which can be even heavier.

Best mistranslation: the Turks aren't nearly as much fun as the Greeks, on whose tourist menus you will see offered such dishes as *lamp chops, rabbit in lesbian sauce,* and *fresh crap*. By now we hope you've tried *börekler*, the rolled-up tubes of fried pastry with fillings, one of Turkey's best snack treats. A restaurant in Bergama advertises: *Try our cigarette pie!*

Improvement (over the last ten years): no doubt about it—the plumbing.

Grandest sight: go a little further east, and see Mt Ararat jumping three miles straight up from its plain, or Mt Erciyes, visible from the centre of Kayseri with the sun behind it at noon, shining like a heavenly vision. Within the confines of this book, you won't do better than taking the boat back to Stamboul at twilight from the Asian side or the Princes' Islands, with plenty of time to look over the minarets and domes above the water and think of Justinian and Mehmet the Conqueror.

And a final thought: did you ever suppose that pizza might have been invented in Turkey? No one knows the origins of the word or the dish, but consider: Turkey is famous for its flattish loaves called *pide* (or *pita* in Arab countries), and the Turks like to put things on top, such as ground meat, onions and tomatoes for a *lahmacun pidesi*. Note the suffix there; in Turkish, which has no prepositions, the –i or –si goes on the end of a noun in place of the 'of' or 'with'. With *pidesi*, its syllables all smashed together as the Turks are wont to do in common speech, we have something that not only looks very like a *pizza*, but sounds like one. Maybe the Amalfitano traders brought it to Italy in the Middle Ages (Amalfi is very close to Naples). If you find this convincing, please ring up the Neapolitans and pass on the news. We wouldn't try it; they got very excited and irrational when people tried to tell them spaghetti came from China.

Architectural Terms

acroterion	acanthus-leaf decoration on the roofline of a Greek temple
acropolis	citadel; usually the original habitation of a Greek city
agora	market-place, public forum
ashlar	masonry with squared stones laid in even courses
basilica	a rectangular building of three aisles divided by columns: originally a Roman government building, later a form for Byzantine churches
bedesten	the inner chamber of a market, built to keep safe the merchant's most valuable goods
bouleuterion	town hall of a Greek city, the meeting place of the council
cami	Turkish for mosque
caravanserai	inn for caravans and merchants
cavea	semicircle of seats in a Greek theatre
cella	inner sanctum of a Greek temple
eyvan	in early Ottoman mosques, a chamber to the side of the main prayer hall
exedra	semi-circular recess—space contained under a semi-dome
geometric	style of early Greek pottery, roughly 900–700 BC, so called for its abstract geometric designs. Earlier, more primitive work is called protogeometric
gymnasium	Greek or Roman school
hamam	Turkish bath
han	inn for merchants
heroon	shrine of a hero—demigod or mortal
hetacomb	sacrifice of a hundred animals
hisar	a Turkish citadel or castle
kale	same as a hisar
kapi	gate
kilise	Turkish for church
külliye	complex of pious foundations (educational or charitable) around a mosque
kümbet	a türbe (see below)
medrese	old school of theology
megaron	large house from Mycenaean period
mescid	a place set aside for Muslim prayer;

	it may be anything from a small mosque in a palace or han to a simple room in a bus station
mihrab	niche in a mosque indicating the direction of Mecca
mimber	mosque pulpit
minare	a minaret
naos	the inner chamber of a temple, containing the cult image
narthex	outer porch of a church
nave	central aisle of basilica form church
nymphaion	sanctuary of nymphs or public fountain
oculus	a circular opening at the top of a dome
odeion	concert hall
orchestra	the circular space at the centre of an ancient theatre; originally the dancing ground, later the centre of the action in early Greek drama
palaestra	exercise ground of a gymnasium
pendentives	(also known as squinches) spherical sections that support a dome over a square space
proscenium	a colonnade behind the orchestra of a theatre
prytaneion	committee room of a bouleuterion (see above), locale of a city's sacred fire
şadirva:	mosque fountain
stoa	large colonnaded porch attached to another building
stele	an upright stone decorated with inscriptions or a relief, often a gravestone
stylobate	the platform supporting the columns of a temple
temenos	sacred enclosure of a temple
tholos	a vaulted, 'beehive' shaped tomb, used for important personages by the Mycaean Greeks.
türbe	a mausoleum for a ruler, political dignitary or holy man. In Turkey they are usually free-standing structures with six or eight sides, and a round or prismatic dome.

BC

c. 50,000	Neanderthal man inhabiting southwestern Anatolia
c. 8500	Oldest known urban society flourishes at Çatal Höyük
c. 5000	Neolithic cultures in southern Anatolia
c. 2500	Hatti people reach the height of their culture in the Kizilirmak valley region
c. 2000	Arrival of Hittites in Anatolia
c. 1720	Hattusas becomes Hittite capital
c. 1600	*Mursilis I (Hittite)*
1450–1400	Series of long wars, between Egypt (19th dynasty) and the Hurri-Mitanni kingdom of east Anatolia
c. 1400	Extension of literacy to Anatolia
1380–1346	*Suppiluliumas (Hittite)*
1259	Treaty of Kadesh between Hittites and Egyptians— earliest recorded peace treaty
1260–1240	*Tudhalyas IV (Hittite)*
c. 1200	Destruction of Hittite Empire
c. 1180	Fall of Troy
c. 1000	Greeks begin to colonize Aegean coast
c. 900	Anatolian wool and timber begin to enter main Mediterranean trade routes
c. 760	*Sarduri I (Urartian)*
c. 750	Sinope, first Greek town on Black Sea, colonized by Miletus
c. 700	*'King Midas' (Phrygia)*
717	Sack of Carchemish by Assyrians
690	Cimmerians raid throughout Anatolia
612	Medes conquer Urartians, Assyria
c. 600	Kingdom of Cappadocia begins

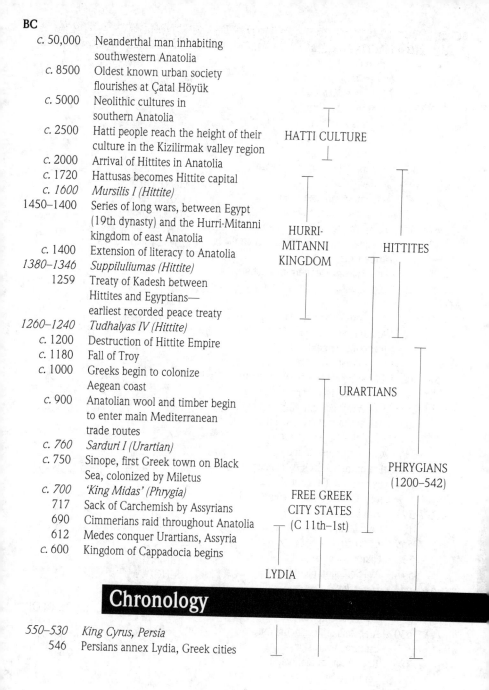

HATTI CULTURE

HURRI-MITANNI KINGDOM

HITTITES

URARTIANS

PHRYGIANS (1200–542)

FREE GREEK CITY STATES (C 11th–1st)

LYDIA

Chronology

550–530	*King Cyrus, Persia*
546	Persians annex Lydia, Greek cities

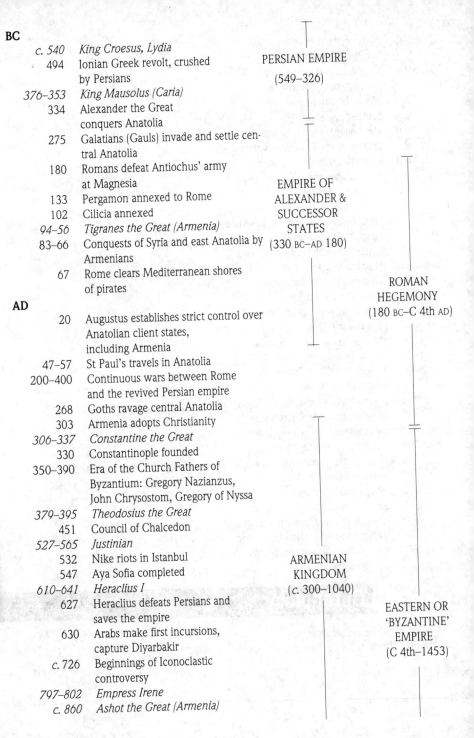

BC

c. 540	*King Croesus, Lydia*
494	Ionian Greek revolt, crushed by Persians
376–353	*King Mausolus (Caria)*
334	Alexander the Great conquers Anatolia
275	Galatians (Gauls) invade and settle central Anatolia
180	Romans defeat Antiochus' army at Magnesia
133	Pergamon annexed to Rome
102	Cilicia annexed
94–56	*Tigranes the Great (Armenia)*
83–66	Conquests of Syria and east Anatolia by Armenians
67	Rome clears Mediterranean shores of pirates

AD

20	Augustus establishes strict control over Anatolian client states, including Armenia
47–57	St Paul's travels in Anatolia
200–400	Continuous wars between Rome and the revived Persian empire
268	Goths ravage central Anatolia
303	Armenia adopts Christianity
306–337	*Constantine the Great*
330	Constantinople founded
350–390	Era of the Church Fathers of Byzantium: Gregory Nazianzus, John Chrysostom, Gregory of Nyssa
379–395	*Theodosius the Great*
451	Council of Chalcedon
527–565	*Justinian*
532	Nike riots in Istanbul
547	Aya Sofia completed
610–641	*Heraclius I*
627	Heraclius defeats Persians and saves the empire
630	Arabs make first incursions, capture Diyarbakir
c. 726	Beginnings of Iconoclastic controversy
797–802	*Empress Irene*
c. 860	*Ashot the Great (Armenia)*

PERSIAN EMPIRE
(549–326)

EMPIRE OF
ALEXANDER &
SUCCESSOR
STATES
(330 BC–AD 180)

ROMAN
HEGEMONY
(180 BC–C 4th AD)

ARMENIAN
KINGDOM
(*c.* 300–1040)

EASTERN OR
'BYZANTINE'
EMPIRE
(C 4th–1453)

AD

950–1050	Golden age of Armenian Kingdom
963–969	*Nicephorus Phocas*
990–1020	*Gagik I (Armenia)*
976–1025	*Basil Bulgaroctonus*
1040	Armenia conquered by Byzantines
1071	Battle of Manzikert; Selcuk Turks conquer most of Anatolia
1100s	Crusaders campaign in southern Anatolia
1200s	Revival of commerce and learning under Selcuks in Konya
1204	Sack of Constantinople by Crusaders
1243	Mongols invade Anatolia; defeat Selcuks at Battle of Kösedağ
1273	First appearance of Ottomans
1300s	Various Mongol and Turkish emirates contend for Anatolia
1293–1324	*Osman I*
1374–1360	*Orhan*
1324	Ottoman capture of Bursa
1346	Dynastic alliance between Ottomans and Byzantine Emperor
1360–1389	*Murat I*
1389	Battle of Kossovo: Turks conquer much of Balkans
1389–1402	*Beyazit I*
1390–1403	Tamerlane's invasion of Anatolia
1413–1421	*Mehmet I*
1421–1451	*Murat II*
1422	First siege of Constantinople
1420s–30s	Institution of the Janissary corps and the devşirme
1451–1481	*Mehmet II (the Conqueror)*
1453	Conquest of Constantinople
1460s	Conquest of Trebizond, Konya
1481–1512	*Beyazit II (the Mystic)*
1480s	Civil wars of the pretender Prince Cem
1490s	Shiite revolts in Anatolia
1512–1520	*Selim I (the Grim)*
1510s	Conquest of Egypt and the last surviving Turkish emirates
1520–1566	*Süleyman I (the Magnificent)*
1522	Crusaders expelled from Aegean coast

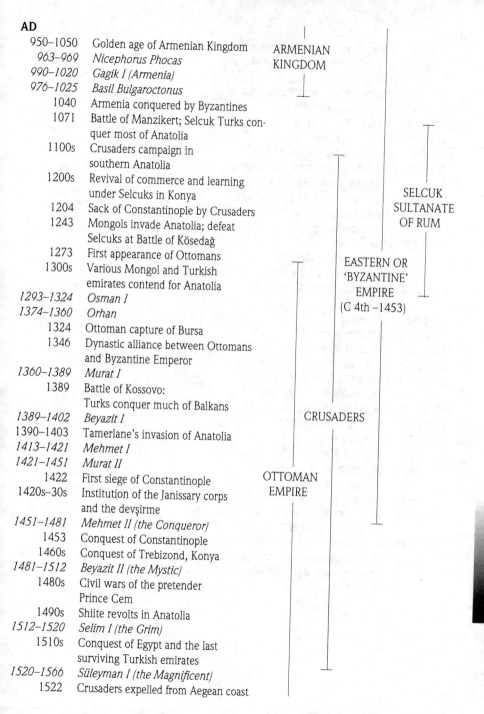

ARMENIAN
KINGDOM

SELCUK
SULTANATE
OF RUM

EASTERN OR
'BYZANTINE'
EMPIRE
(C 4th –1453)

CRUSADERS

OTTOMAN
EMPIRE

AD

1530–50	New Ottoman Navy controls much of the Mediterranean; high point of Ottoman power
1622	Murder of reforming Sultan Osman II
1683	Second siege of Vienna
1703–30	*Ahmet III*
1717–30	The 'Tulip Period'
1727	First books in Turkish published
1770	Battle of Çeşme; total destruction of Ottoman fleet by Russians
1789–1807	*Selim II*
1804–21	Greek and Serbian Wars of Independence
1808–1839	*Mahmud II*
1826	The Auspicious Incident: massacre of the Janissaries
1830	'Tanzimat' reforms; abolition of feudalism
1839–61	*Abdül Mecit I*
1853–6	Crimean War
1876–1909	*Abdül Hamid*
1876	First constitution
1909	'Young Turk' revolution
1912–13	Balkan Wars
1914–18	World War I
1919–23	Wars of Independence
1920s–30s	Atatürk's era of reforms
1938	Death of Atatürk
1939	The Hatay joins Turkey through plebiscite
1949	First free nationwide elections
1960	First of three military coups; civilian government restored in 1960
1980	Political crisis and terrorism results in third army takeover; civilian government re-established in 1983

OTTOMAN EMPIRE

TURKISH REPUBLIC

Linguists say Turkish is a member of the Ural-Altaic group, which makes it related to Finnish, Hungarian, and little else. As well as the 50 million Turks in Turkey, dialects are spoken by perhaps as many as 100 million more Turcomans, Kirghiz, Uzbeks, and others in central Asia; a Turk from Istanbul could make himself understood as far east as Manchuria. He couldn't get far, though, in Helsinki or Budapest. This is one of the truly grey areas in linguistics, but what proves these languages have a common origin is their use of *agglutination*. Turkish has no prepositions, and most of the difficulties of the language are caused by the subtleties of the infinite number of suffixes that are tacked onto words or replace them. In this book, for instance, words may often be disguised by their endings: *Yeşil Cami*—Green Mosque, but *Rüstem Paşa Camii*—Mosque *of* Rustem Pasha.

The Turks are very proud of their language, with its long and distinguished list of poets and writers, its melodious vowel harmony, and its wealth of expressive colloquialisms. There is even a slang dictionary for Turkish. The Turks love playing word games; there are palindromes, like '*Traş niçin şart?*' or 'Why get a haircut?', and long nightmares of agglutination; the longest word yet discovered in Turkish is an entire sentence:

'*Çekoslovakyalilaştiramadiklarimizdanmisiniz?*'

meaning 'Are you the people whose nationality we cannot change to Czechoslovakian?'.

Like the French, the Turks have a semi-official body concerned with keeping the purity of the language. In the 1930s, this was a hot political issue; reforming the language was one of Atatürk's pet ideas, and he replaced thousands of Arabic, Persian, and Greek words with 'Turkish' equivalents, either invented or found in use in obscure corners of the nation. The drive for reform slowed down when parents began to have trouble understanding their children—and Atatürk's speeches. The 30s was also the decade of the great Alphabet Reform. Previously, Turkish, with its eight vowels, had been shoehorned into Arabic characters, which have only three, with results such as the words for 'great' and 'dead' being written the same (*ulu, ölü*). In part for this reason, but also to make European languages accessible to the Turks, Atatürk decreed that the change must be made. Throughout the decade, he travelled to almost every large town in Turkey with chalk and a blackboard. While the people crowded around in thousands to see their nation's hero, they got their first lesson in Roman letters. Amazingly, it all worked, far better, in fact, than Atatürk ever dreamed. The changeover that was supposed to take fifteen years was accomplished in five.

Language

Learning Turkish

If you want to learn some Turkish before you go, the best book is *Colloquial Turkish* by Yusuf Mardin (Routledge & Kegan Paul). Second best is *Teach Yourself Turkish* by G. L. Lewis

(Hodder and Stoughton), a more stiff and formal approach with big grammar charts. Don't bother using a phrase book. The difficulties in pronunciation are great, and most of the phrases in such books will either perplex the Turks or make them laugh. If you can learn the numbers, and some of the words listed below, you can communicate almost all your wishes, and make your stay in Turkey infinitely more fun. Literature from the Turkish Travel Office tends to overestimate the number of people you'll find who speak English or German—which also comes in handy. Knowing just a few words will also endear you to the Turks (and probably prevent you from ever getting ripped off).

Yok is one of the essential words to know. Its meaning approximates 'There's none', but it is used much more commonly than 'no' ('*hayir*'). It is a sentence from which there is no appeal. If a Turk is at all inclined to help you out, he will exhaust all possibilities before intoning the fatal '*yok*'. Its positive counterpart is '*var*' ('There is'), always a cheering note in Turkey, although when you do get it, it may not be what you expected

Pronunciation

This is regular and logical, since the alphabet was designed to fit the language. Get to know these new letters:

â—faint 'y' sound in preceding consonant; lâleli is lyaah-leh-lee
ç—'ch' as in 'chin';
c—is pronounced like the English 'j'
ş—'sh' as in 'ship'
ğ—'silent' as the 'gh' in 'eight'; it sometimes lengthens the preceding vowel
ö—as the 'eu' in French
ü—as the 'u' in French, almost the same as 'eu'

Turkish also has an **undotted 'I'**, hardly a letter at all; its sound is half-swallowed, like the English 'e' in 'barrel' or 'packer'. For printing reasons, it is omitted in this book. All the other letters are more or less as in English except **j** which is 'zh' as in 'measure' and 'v' is more like the English 'w'. All vowels are short except 'o', which is sometimes long, and 'g' is always hard.

Something that could cause confusion is vowel harmony. There are two sorts of vowel: the 'back' vowels (a, undotted i, o and u) and the 'front' vowels (e, i, ö and ü). Genuine Turkish words contain one sort of vowel only and suffixes have their vowels changed, if necessary, to comply with the rules of vowel harmony. Words of foreign origin, like *şoför* (chauffeur) often contain a mixture of the two types of vowel.

Note: Turkish syllables almost *always carry equal weight*. If there is any stress, it will usually be at the end. Besides forgetting that 'c' is sounded like English 'j', the most common mistake foreigners make is to put accents where they don't belong. We do it naturally, but it makes Turkish words unintelligible to the Turks.

Turkish plural forms are -ler or -lar added to the end of the word, for example *adam* (man), *adamlar* (men) or *kalem* (pen), *kalemler* (pens).

Vocabulary

Because it's impossible to represent phonetically the sounds of the Turkish ü and ö, we've represented both as *eu*; pronounced as in French; they're almost the same. The sound of the Turkish undotted i is represented by *i*. See the chart above for the pronunciation of these difficult vowels. Remember that all syllables are unstressed—pronounced with equal emphasis.

Directions and Geography

Nerede? as in:	neh-reh-deh	where is?
Karakol nerede?	Kah-rah-kol neh-reh-deh	Where is the police station?
Tuvalet nerede?	Too-vah-let neh reh-deh	Where is the toilet?
Şehir	sheh-hihr	city
Su, Çay	soo, chahy	stream
Irmak, Nehir	ihr-mahk, neh-hihr	river
Kuzey	koo-zay	north
Güney	geu-nay	south
Bati	bah-tih	west
Doğu	doh-oo	east
Sol	sohl	left
Sağ	sah	right
Höyük	heu-yeuk	mound
Yayla	yay-lah	mountain pastureland
Ada	ah-dah	island
Dere	deh-reh	valley
Körfez	keur-fehz	bay
Göl	geul	lake
Kapi	kah-pih	gate
Hisar, Kale	hih-sahr, kah-leh	castle
Saray	sahr-ahy	palace
Geçit	geh-chit	pass
Tepe	teh-peh	hill
Pinar	pih-nahr	spring
Kuyu	koo-yoo	well
Orman	ohr-mahn	forest
Kilise	kih-lih-seh	church
Cami	jah-mee	mosque
Bekçi	bek-chee	caretaker (the man you'll need to find to get into many of the lesser-known sights)
Sokak, Caddesi	soh-kahk, jah-deh-sih	street
Mahalle	ma-hal-leh	city ward or district
mevki	mev-kee	place, site
Yol	yohl	road
Köy	keuy	village
Çiftlik	chihft-lihk	farm
Deniz	deh-nihz	sea
Gümrük	geum-reuk	customs
Lise	lih-seh	school
Postane	pos-tah-neh	post office
Türbe, kümbet	teur-beh, keum-beht	mausoleum
Karakol	kah-rah-kol	police station
Banka	bahn-kah	bank
Lokanta	loh-kahn-tah	restaurant
Gazino	gah-zih-noh	night club
Gar, Istasyon	gahr, ihs-tas-yohn	train station
Otogar	oh-toh-gahr	bus station

Hamam	hah-mahm	Turkish bath
Benzin istasyonu	ben-zihn ihs-tahs-yohn-oo	petrol station
Sigara içilmez	sih-gah-rah itch-il-mez	no smoking
Çeşme	chesh-meh	fountain
Çarşi	chahr-shih	market, bazaar
Vilayet	vil-ahy-eht	provincial government house
Kisa	kih-sah	short
Uzun	oo-zoon	long
Durak	doo-rahk	stop (noun)
Dur!	door	stop (imperative)
Yakin	yah-kih	near
Uzak	oo-zahk	far
Burada	boo-rah-dah	here
Şurada	shoo-rah-dah	there
Orada	o-rah-dah	over there
Meydan	may-dahn	square
Hava alani	hah-vah ah-lah-nih	airport
Liman	lih-mahn	port
Iskele	ihs-keh-leh	quay
Köprü	keu-preu	bridge
Türkiye	Teur-kee-yeh	Turkey
Akdeniz	ahk-deh-nihz	Mediterranean ('white sea')
Karadeniz	kah-rah-deh-nihz	Black Sea
Ege Deniz	eg-eh deh-nihz	Aegean Sea
Trakya	trahk-yah	Thrace
Anadolu	ah-nah-doh-loo	Anatolia
Yunanistan	yoo-nan-ih-stan	Greece
Kibris	kih-brihs	Cyprus

Time

Sabah	sah-bah	morning
Öğleden sonra	eu-le-den sohn-ra	afternoon
Akşam	ahk-shahm	evening
Gece	geh-jeh	night
Şimdi	shihm-dee	now
Ay	ahy	month
Hafta	hahf-tah	week
Yil	yihl	year
Mevsim	mev-sihm	season
Bu/Gelecek	boo/gel-eh-jek	this/next
Bugün	boo-geun	today
Yarin	yahr-ihn	tomorrow
Dün	deun	yesterday
Gelecek hafta	geh-leh-jek hahf-tah	next week
Kaç saat?	kahtch saaht	what time is it?
Kaçta?	kahch-tah	what time (will it occur?)
Ne zaman?	neh zah-mahn	when?
Saat bir	sah-at bihr	one o'clock
bir büçük	bihr beu-cheuk	one-thirty

Days

Pazar	pah-zahr	Sunday
Pazartesi	pah-zahr-teh-sih	Monday
Salı	sah-lıh	Tuesday
Çarşamba	chahr-shahm-bah	Wednesday
Perşembe	pehr-shem-beh	Thursday
Cuma	joo-mah	Friday
Cumartesi	joo-mar-teh-sih	Saturday

Months

Ocak	o-jahk	January
Şubat	shoo-baht	February
Mart	mahrt	March
Nisan	nih-sahn	April
Mayıs	my-ıhs	May
Haziran	hah-zih-rahn	June
Temmuz	tem-mooz	July
Ağustos	ah-oos-tohs	August
Eylül	ai-leul	September
Ekim	eh-kihm	October
Kasım	kah-sıhm	November
Aralık	ah-rah-lıhk	December

Numbers

Bir	bihr	one
İki	ih-kih	two
Üç	eutch	three
Dört	deurt	four
Beş	besh	five
Altı	ahl-tıh	six
Yedi	yeh-dih	seven
Sekiz	seh-kihz	eight
Dokuz	doh-kooz	nine
On	ohn	ten
Onbir	ohn-bihr	eleven
Oniki	ohn-ih-kih	twelve
Yirmi	yihr-mih	twenty
Yirmibir	yihr-mihbihr	twenty-one
Otuz	oh-tooz	thirty
Kirk	kıhrk	forty
Elli	el-lih	fifty
Altmış	ahlt-mısh	sixty
Yetmiş	yet-mish	seventy
Seksen	sek-sehn	eighty
Doksan	dohk-sahn	ninety
Yüz	yeuz	hundred
İki yüz	ihk-yeuz	two hundred
Beş yüz altmış dört	besh-yeuz-ahlt-mish-deurt	564
Bin	bihn	thousand

Bin bir	bihn-bihr	a thousand and one
Milyon	mil-yoan	million
Milyar	mil-yahr	milliard (billion)
Bin dokuz yüz doksan üç	bihn doh-kooz yeuz dohk-sahn eutch	1993

Note: for a number of objects, use the word *tane* (tah-neh) (piece, bit) in all instances after the number, e.g.: *iki tane biletler*—two tickets (not *iki biletler*).

Yarim, buçuk	yahr-ihm, boo-chook	half, *buçuk* is used after numerals
Çeyrek	chay-rehk	quarter
Yüzde ...	yeuz-deh	... per cent
Ilk, birinci	ihlk, bihr-ihn-jih	first
Onuncu	ohn-oon-joo	tenth
Yüzüncü	yeuz-eun-jeu	hundredth

Conversation

Hoş geldiniz	hohsh gehl-dihn-ihz	welcome
Hoş bulduk	hohsh bool-dook	in reply to *hoş geldiniz* (we have found well)
Anlamadim, anla- miyorum	ahn-lah-mah-dihm, ahn-lah- mih-yor-oom	I don't understand
Anliyorum	ahn-lih-yohr-oom	I understand
Anliyormusun?	ahn-lih-yohr-moo-soon	do you understand?
Evet	eh-veht	yes
Hayir	hyihr	no
Var	vahr	there is
Yok	yohk	there's none
Belki	behl-kih	perhaps
Biliyorum	bihl-ih-yohr-oom	I know
Bilmiyorum	bihl-mih-yohr-oom	I don't know
Inglizce biliyormusunuz?	Ing-leez-jeh bihl-ih-yohr- moo-soo-nooz?	Do you speak English?
Türkçe biliyormusunuz?	Teurk-cheh bihl-ih-yohr- moo-soo-nooz?	Do you speak Turkish?
Bir as	bihr ahs	a little
Tarzanca	tahr-zahn-jah	like Tarzan
Lütfen	leut-fehn	please
(Çok) teşekkür ederim	(chohk) tesh-eh-keur eh-deh-rihm	thank you (very much)
Bir şey değil	bihr shay dayl	you're welcome, not at all
Affedersiniz	ahf-feh-dehr-sih-niz	pardon, excuse me
Allahaismarladik	ahl-ahs-mahr-lah-dik	good bye ('Allah go with you')
Güle güle	geu-leh geu-leh	good bye ('smiling, smiling')

Allahaismarladik is said by the person leaving, *güle güle* is said by the person staying behind.

Merhaba	mehr-hah-bah	hello
Selâmaleyküm	sehl-aahm-ahl-ay-kum	hello ('peace be with you')
Aleykümselâm	ahl-ay-koom-seh-laahm	hello—in reply to *selâmaleyküm*
Günaydin	geun-ahy-din	good day
Iyi akşamlar	eey ahk-shahm-lahr	good evening

İyi geceler	eey geh-jeh-lehr	good night
Yavaş yavaş	yah-vahsh yah-vahsh	slow, wait!
Güzel!	geu-zehl	beautiful (all-purpose compliment)
Çok iyi	chohk eey	very good
Nasilsiniz?	nah-sıl-sın-ız	How are you?
Türkçe bilmiyorum	teurk-cheh bihl-mih-yohrum	I don't speak Turkish
Bu nedir? O nedir?	boo/o neh-dihr	What is this/that?
Ne kadar?	neh kah-dahr	How much is it?
... istiyorum	ihs-tih-yohr-um	I want ...
Niçin?	nih-chihn	how?
Bir dakika	bihr dah-kih-kah	wait a minute
Yaramaz	yahr-ah-mahz	good for nothing! useless
Ucuz	oo-jooz	cheap
Pahali	pah-hah-lıh	expensive
Çok fazla	chohk fahz-lah	that's too much
Para	pah-rah	money
Indirim	in-dih-rim	discount
Inecek var	in-eh-jek vahr	'there's a departure' (what you say to get off a bus)
Hasta	hahs-tah	sick, ill
Sicak	sih-jahk	hot
Soğuk	so-ook	cold
Eski	es-kih	old
Yeni	yeh-nih	new

Listesi	**lihs-teh-sih**	**Menu**
Ekmek	ek-mek	bread
Su	soo	water
Süt	seut	milk
Tuz	tooz	salt
Şeker	shek-ehr	sugar
Yoğurt	yo-oort	yoghurt
Tereyağ	te-re-yay	butter
Kahve	kah-veh	coffee
Kahve ala franga	... a -la frahn-ga	Western coffee (usually Nescafé)
Kizarmiş ekmek	kız-ar-mish ek-mek	toast
Meyva suyu	may-va soo-yoo	fruit juice
Reçel	reh-chel	jam
Çay	chahy	tea
Oralet	or-a-let	orange-flavoured hot drink
Maden suyu	ma-dehn soo-yoo	mineral water
Turşu	toor-shoo	pickles
Zeytinyağ	zay-tin-ya	olive oil
Sirke	sihr-keh	vinegar
Suyu	soo-yoo	juice
Salça	sahl-cha	sauce
Şarap (beyaz, kirmizi)	shar-ahp (beh-yaz, kıhr-mıh-zıh)	wine (white, red)
Bira	bih-ra	beer

Buz	booz	ice
Limonata	lihm-o-nah-ta	lemonade
Kahvalti	kah-vahl-t*ih*	breakfast
Öğle yemeği	*eu*-leh yeh-meh-ee	lunch
Akşam yemeği	ahk-shahm yeh-meh-ee	dinner
Garson	gar-son	waiter
Hesap	he-sahp	bill
Bal	bahl	honey
Salep (or *sahlep*)	sah-lep	a hot drink for winter, made from milk, sugar and salep (powdered orchid tuber)
Ada çayi	ah-dah chahy	sage tea (literally, island tea)
Elma çayi	el-mah chahy	apple tea
Poğaci	poh-ah-j*ih*	bun
Yumurta	yoo-moor-tah	eggs
Rafadan/haşlama	rah-fah-dan/hahsh-lah-mah	boiled/poached
Omlet	ohm-let	omelette
Menemen	meh-neh-mehn	scrambled eggs with tomatoes, cheese and peppers
Kaymak	kahy-mak	cream

Meze	**meh-zeh**	**Hors d'Oeuvres**
Fasulye	fah-sool-yeh	green beans (in olive oil)
Sigara Böreği	sih-gah-rah b*eu*r-ay-ee	cigarette-shaped borek, with cheese or meat
Cacik	jah-j*ik*	ground cucumber, garlic, and yoghurt
Midye plakisi	mid-yeh plah-k*ih*-s*ih*	mussels cooked in olive oil
Kisir	k*ih*-s*ih*r	bulgar with onions, pepper, and parsley
Yalanci dolma	yahl-ahn-jih dohl-mah	stuffed vine leaves
Arnavut ciğeri	ahr-nah-voot jee-ehr-ih	Albanian liver—cold, spicy fried liver
Pastirma	pahs-t*ih*r-mah	Turkish pastrami, with lots of spice and garlic
Sucuk	soo-jook	Turkish sausage
Manti	mahn-t*ih*	ravioli

Corba	**chor-bah**	**Soup**
Mercimek çorbasi	mehr-jih-mek chor-bah-s*ih*	red lentil soup
Yayla çorbasi	yay-lah ...	rice, yoghurt; egg yolks in broth
Işkembe çorbasi	ish-kem-beh ...	tripe soup with egg sauce
Şehriye çorbasi	shehr-ee-yeh ...	chicken noodle soup
Paça	pah-chah	sheep-trotters soup
Ezo gelin corbasi	e-zoh geh-lin ...	tomatoes, lentils, mint and lemon soup
Düğün corbasi	dooh-oon ...	Wedding soup—lamb soup with eggs and lemon
Et suyu	et soo-yoo	consommé (meat water)

Salata	**sah-lah-tah**	**Salads**
Tarama salatasi	tah-rah-mah sah-lah-tah-s*ih*	roe with olive oil and lemon juice
Patlican salatasi	paht-l*ih*-jan ...	mashed eggplant, olive oil, lemon juice, and mayonnaise
Çoban salatasi	cho-bahn ...	mixed vegetable salad

| Beyin salatasi | bey-ihn ... | sheep's brain salad |
| Tarator salatasi | tah-rah-tohr ... | sesame syrup, walnuts and garlic |

Et
et
Meat

Kuzu	koo-zoo	lamb
Kuzu kapamasi	koo-zoo kah-pah-mah-sih	grilled lamb cooked with vegetables
Haşlama	hahsh-lah-mah	leg of lamb with carrots and celery
Kuzu incik patlicanli	koo-zoo in-jik paht-lih-jahn-lih	lamb stew with eggplant
Et saç kavurma	et sahtch ka-voor-ma	thin slices of lamb, tomatoes, and peppers sautéed at the table
Siğir	sih-ihr	beef
Biftek	bihf-tehk	beef steak
Papaz yahnisi	pah-pahz yah-nih-sih	beef, onions, and spices
Dana	dah-nah	veal
Kiyma	kee-mah	minced meat
Köfte	keuf-teh	meatballs
Cizbiz	jiz-biz	grilled meatballs
Ciğer	jee-ehr	liver
Işkembe nohutlu	ish-kehm-beh noh-hoot-lu	tripe (with chickpeas)
Tavuk	tah-vook	chicken
Çerkez tavuğu	cher-kez tah-voo-oo	chicken in walnut sauce
Beğendili tavuk	beh-en-dih-lih tah-vook	chicken with mashed eggplant, milk, and cheese
Hindi	hin-dih	turkey
Kadin budu köfte	kah-din boo-doo keuf-teh	ladies' thighs meatballs (minced lamb and rice)

Balik
bah-lik
Fish

Hamsi	hahm-sih	anchovy
Iskorpit	ihs-kor-piht	rock fish, stone bass
Kalkan	kahl-kahn	turbot
Barbunya	bahr-boon-yah	red mullet
Kefal	keh-fahl	grey mullet
Kiliç Baliği	kihl-itch bah-lih-ih	swordfish
Lüfer	leu-fehr	blue fish
Istavrit	is-tahv-riht	mackerel
Karagöz	kahr-ah-geuz	sargus
Palamut	pahl-ah-moot	bonito
Mercan	mehr-jahn	pandora
Pisi	pih-sih	brill
Dil	dihl	sole
Pavurya	pah-voor-yah	crab
Medye	mehd-yeh	mussels
Istiridye	ihs-tihr-ihd-yeh	oyster
Kalamar	kah-lah-mahr	squid
Kerevit	kehr-ih-viht	prawn
Kiliç şiş	kihl-itch shish	swordfish kebabs
Barbunya Kağitta	bahr-boon-yah kah-it-ta	red mullet in foil
Papaz Yahnisi	pah-pahz yah-nih-sih	bonito in olive oil

Sebze	**seh-bze**	**Vegetables**
Biber	bee-behr	green pepper
Patlican	paht-lıh-jan	eggplant (aubergine)
Domates	doh-mah-tes	tomatoes
Kabak	kah-bahk	zucchini, squash
Yaprak	yahp-rahk	vine leaves

(any of the above can be *dolmasi* (dohl-mah-sıh) stuffed with rice and meat)

Enginar	en-gee-nahr	artichokes
Fasulye	fah-sool-yeh	beans
Bamya	bahm-yah	okra
Lahana	lah-han-ah	cabbage
Patates	pah-tah-tes	potatoes
Ispanak	ıs-pahn-ahk	spinach
Soğan	so-ahn	onion
Bezelye	beh-zehl-yeh	peas
Havuç	hah-vooch	carrots
Kuşkonmaz	koosh-kahn-mahz	asparagus
Marul	mahr-ool	lettuce
Zeytin	zay-tihn	olives
Mantar	mahn-tahr	mushrooms
Nohut	no-hoot	chickpeas
Fava	fah-vah	broadbeans
Bamya Etli	bahm-yah et-lih	lady's fingers with beef
Imam Bayildi	ih-mahm bay-yıl-dıh	'the imam fainted'—eggplant stuffed with onions and garlic in olive oil
Pilav	pihl-ahv	rice
İç pilav	itch pihl-ahv	rice with chopped liver, raisins and pine nuts
Bulgur Pilavi	bool-goor pihl-ah-vih	bulgar with onions and tomatoes
Firinda Makarna	fıh-rın-dah mah-kahr-nah	baked macaroni, a bit like lasagna

Meyva	**may-vah**	**Fruit**
Ahududu	ah-hoo-doo-doo	raspberries
Armut	ahr-moot	pear
Çilek	chih-lek	strawberry
Elma	el-mah	apple
Erik	eh-rihk	plum
Incir	in-jeer	figs
Karpuz	kahr-pooz	watermelon
Kavun	kah-voon	melon
Kayisi	kah-yıh-sıh	apricot
Kiraz	kih-rahz	cherry
Muz	mooz	banana
Portakal	por-tah-kahl	orange
Badem	bah-dem	walnuts
Şam fistiği	shahm fis-tee-yee	pistachios
Seftali	shef-tah-li	peach
Vişne	vish-neh	cherry

Tatli	taht-lih	Desserts/sweets
Aşure	ah-shur-eh	pudding with beans, cereals, nuts and raisins
Zerde	zehr-deh	sweet rice with saffron
Un Helvasi	oon hel-vah-sih	halvah made of flour and butter
Pasta	pah-stah	cake
Lokma	lohk-mah	round doughnuts in syrup
Kabak Tatlisi	kah-bak taht-lih-sih	slices of pumpkin in syrup
Dondurma	don-duhr-mah	ice cream
Çikolata	chik-o-lah-tah	chocolate
Peynir	pay-nihr	cheese
Krem karamel	krem kah-rah-mehl	caramel custard
Tel kadayif	tel kah-dah-yıf	shredded wheat in syrup
Ekmek kadayif	ek-mek kah-dah-yıf	bread in syrup

Pudings	puh-dings	Puddings
Muhallebi	mu-hal-le-bih	milk pudding
Sütlaç	seut-lahtch	rice pudding
Tavuk Göğsü	tah-vook geu-seu	milk pudding with chicken breasts

Verbs

If you want to try a few sentences, here are some verbs and how to use them.

The verbs 'to be' and 'to have' don't really exist. 'To be' appears as a suffix, as in, for example:

Ingilizim	*Türkün*
English—I am	Turk—you are

Var, 'there is' and *yok* 'there is not' are used in place of to have. For example:

Su var	*Su yok*
there is water	there is no water

Anlamak	ahn-lah-mahk	to understand
Bakmak	bahk-mahk	to look
Beğenmek	beh-ehn-mehk	to like
Beklemek	behk-leh-mehk	to wait
Bilmek	bihl-mehk	to know
Çalişmak	chahl-ish-mahk	to work
Dinlemek	dihn-leh-mehk	to listen
Dinlenmek	dihn-lehn-mehk	to rest
Duymak	dooy-mahk	to hear
Gelmek	gehl-mehk	to come
Gezmek	gehz-mekh	to walk
Gitmek	giht-mehk	to go
Görmek	geur-mehk	to see
Içmek	ihch-mehk	to drink
Istemek	ihs-teh-mehk	to want
Konuşmak	koh-noosh-mahk	to speak
Öğrenmek	eur-ehn-mehk	to learn
Öğretmek	eur-eht-mehk	to teach

Okulmak	oh-kool-mahk	to read
Sevmek	sehv-mehk	to love
Uyanmak	oo-yahn-mahk	to wake up
Uyumak	oo-yoo-mahk	to sleep
Yazmak	yahz-mahk	to write
Yemek	yeh-mehk	to eat
Yüzmek	yeuz-mehk	to swim

It is relatively easy to use the present continuous, future and past definite tenses. The verb root is taken, a tense marker added, followed by the suffix indicating person. The rules of vowel harmony are obeyed.

-yor- is the present continuous tense marker. After consonants, an i is inserted. Thus, using *gezmek*, we have:

geziyorum	I am walking	geziyoruz	we are walking
geziyorsun	you are walking	geziyorsunuz	you are walking
geziyor	he/she/it is walking	geziyorlar	they are walking

-ecek- is the future tense marker. Before a vowel, the k turns into a ğ.:

gezeceğim	I will walk	gezeceğiz	we will walk
gezeceksin	you will walk	gezeceksiniz	you will walk
gezecek	he/she/it will walk	gezecekler	they will walk

-d- is the past definite tense marker:

gezdim	I walked	gezdik	we walked
gezdin	you walked	gezdiniz	you walked
gezdi	he/she/it walked	gezdiler	they walked

A verb is turned into the negative form by inserting -*mi*- between the root and the tense marker. For example:

| geziyorum | gezmiyorum |
| I'm walking | I'm not walking |

A question is formed by inserting -*mi*- after the tense marker, or in the case of the past definite tense, after the whole word:

| geziyorsun | geziyormusun? |
| you are walking | are you walking? |

| gezdin | gezdinmi? |
| you walked | did you walk? |

There is no need to use the personal pronouns, except for emphasis, or if you are worried that you have got it wrong. They are:

ben	I
sen	you
o	he/she/it
biz	we
siz	you
onlar	they

Ancient History

Akurgal, Ekrem, *Ancient Civilizations and Ruins of Turkey*, Türk Tarih Kurumu, Ankara, 1983. The indispensable guide for anyone interested in exploring Turkey's innumerable archaeological sites in detail (though weak on eastern Anatolia).

Apollonius of Rhodes, *The Voyage of Argo*, translated by E. V. Rieu, Penguin, 1971. Jason's journey along the Black Sea coast.

Arrian, *The Campaigns of Alexander*, translated by Aubrey de Sélincourt, Penguin, 1971.

Bean, George, *Aegean Turkey*, 1966; *Turkey's Southern Shore*, 1968; *Turkey Beyond the Maeander*, 1971; and *Lycia*, 1978, Ernest Benn. Fine, anecdotal accounts and detailed guides to Turkey's Greek and Roman sites, by a scholar who discovered not a few of them himself.

Mellaart, James, *Earliest Civilizations of the Near East*, Thames and Hudson, 1965 and *Çatal Höyük*, Thames and Hudson, 1967. Two fascinating books by the archaeologist who uncovered the most important site in the Middle East since Schliemann.

Sandars, N. K. *The Sea Peoples: Warriors of the Ancient Mediterranean*, Thames and Hudson, 1978. The true story of the dark age that brought down the curtain on Troy and the Hittites.

Wood, Michael, *In Search of the Trojan War*, BBC, 1985. A good compilation of current thought on Troy, from the popular TV series.

Young, Rodney S, *Gordion*, Ankara, 1975. More about the Phrygians.

Byzantines and Ottomans

Barber, Noel, *The Sultans*, Simon and Schuster, 1973. The inside story.

Billings, Malcolm, *The Cross and the Crescent*, BBC Publications, 1987. A history of the Crusades.

Goodwin, Godfrey, *A History of Ottoman Architecture*, Thames and Hudson, 1971. The best book on the subject.

Lord Kinross, *The Ottoman Centuries*, Morrow, NY/Jonathan Cape, London, 1977. The best known popular history.

Rodley, Lyn, *Cave Monasteries of Byzantine Cappadocia*, Cambridge, 1986.

Runciman, Steven, *Byzantine Civilization*, Edward Arnold, London, 1933, and *The Fall of Constantinople, 1453*, Cambridge University Press, 1965. Apologist for the Byzantines, accounted for the foremost scholar in the field, these are coloured by an unfortunate prejudice against both Muslims and Turks.

Shaw, Stanford and Ezel, Kual, *History of the Ottoman Empire and Modern Turkey*, 2 vols, Cambridge University Press, 1976.

Wheatcroft, Andrew, *The Ottomans*, Penguin 1990. Anecdotal, illustrated account.

Further Reading

Modern Turkey

Garnett, Lucy M. J, *The Turkish People; their social life, religious beliefs, institutions and domestic life*, Methuen, London AMS Press NY 1909. Hard to find, but very interesting account by a turn-of-the-century traveller.

Hotham, David, *The Turks*, Murray, London, 1972. One of the best books about modern Turkey.

Kazancagil, Ali and Özbudun, Ergun, eds, *Atatürk, founder of a modern state*, Anchor Hambden, Conn, 1981.

Lewis, Bernard, *The Emergence of Modern Turkey*, Oxford Library Press, 1968.

Michaud, Roland and Sabrina, *Turkey*, Thames and Hudson, 1986. Magnificent photographs.

Mirabile, P., *The Book of the Oghuz Peoples, or Legends Told and Sung by Dede Korkut*. Quite fascinating legends of the early nomadic Turks, in a Turkish-printed paperback available in souvenir stands. A scholarly French translation rendered into English with marvellous incompetence, which somehow makes it even more fun.

Stewart, Deamond, *Turkey*, Life World Library, NY, 1965.

Volkan, Vamik D, Itzkowitz, Norman, *The Immortal Atatürk, A Psychobiography*. Unintentionally hilarious ('Little Mustafa's grandiose self was his basic character trait').

Religion and Folklore

And, Metin, *Karagoz: Turkish Shadow Theatre*, Dost, Istanbul, 1979. An excellent account of a dying art, readily available in Turkey.

Nicholson, Reynold A, trans. *Rumi: Poet and Mystic*, George Allen & Unwin, 1950. An introduction to the great Sufi teacher, the Mevlâna.

Önder, Mehmed, *Mevlâna and Mevlâna Museum*, Istanbul, 1985. Story of the Mevlâna's life in Konya.

Walker, Warren S. & Uysal, Ahmet E, *Tales Alive in Turkey*, Harvard University Press, 1966. An absorbing collection of Turkish folk tales and lore.

Travel Writers

Burnaby, Frederick, *On Horseback Through Asia Minor*, Alan Sutton, 1985. A fascinating account of a journey undertaken in the winter of 1876/7.

Glazebrook, Philip, *Journey to Kars*, Penguin, 1985.

Pereira, Michael, *East of Trebizond*, Geoffrey Bles, 1971. For those interested in Tao-Georgia.

Stark, Freya, *Alexander's Path*, Century, 1984; and *Ionia*, Century, 1988. Two beautiful, evocative accounts that bring Turkey's ancient cities to life.

Novels

Cleary, Jon, *The Fall of an Eagle*, 1964. Romantic thriller set in Cappadocia.

Dunnett, Dorothy, *Pawn in Frankincense*, Cassell, 1969, also available as an Arrow paperback. An historical adventure story featuring Süleyman, Roxelana, Dragut and others mentioned in this guide book!

Kemal, Yaşar, *Mehmed, My Hawk*, 1961; *The Lords of Akchasaz*, 1979; and *The Sea-Crossed Fisherman*, 1985, Collins and Harvill. Turkey's leading contemporary novelist. More of his books are available in English translation.

Macauley, Rose, *The Towers of Trebizond*, Futura 1981. A classic and very funny novel about a journey in Turkey with the wonderful eccentrics Aunt Dot and Father Chantry-Pigg.

Chapter titles and main page references are in **bold**; page references to maps are in *italic*.

Abydos 158
accommodation *see* where to stay
Adana, consulate 17
Adrianople, *see* Edirne
Aegean Coast, *see* North Aegean
  Coast; South Aegean Coast
Aegean Islands 185–7
Aeolia *197*, 194–201
Aeolian Greeks 46, 194
Afyon 313
agriculture 20
Ahhiyawa (Mycenaean Greeks)
  45
air travel
  internal 7–8
  international 2–3
Aizanoi 312–13
Akçay 187, 189, 190, 191
Akşehir 324
Akyar 252
Alabanda 245
Alahan 333
Alanya 294–8
  caves 296
  the Red Tower 295
Alexander the Great **48**, 61, **162**,
  316–17, 322
Alexandria Troas 187–8
Ali Ağa 201
Alibey Island 192, 193, 194
Alinda 244–5
Altinkum 231, 237, 238
Altinoluk 189, 190, 191
Altinova 192, 193, 194
Anamur 299, 302
Anatolia *308*, **309–48**
Antalya *279*, 278–84
  beaches 281
  consulate 17
  eating out 283–4
  history 278
  Karain Cave 45, 280
  the Old Town 279–80

Regional Museum 280–1
Termessos 281–2
travel 278–9
where to stay 282–3
Antiochus III 49
antiquities, shopping for 16
Aperlae 271, 274
Aphrodisias 240–1, *241*
Arezastis 315
Armenia, visas 5
Aslankaya 315
Aslantaş 315
Aspendos 287–8
Assos 188–9, 190
Atatürk Centennial Forest 66, **325**
Atatürk (Mustafa Kemal) 54,
  60–1, 98–9, 160
Attalus I 195
Attalus II 195
Attalus III 195–6
auto clubs 5, 12–13
Avanos 342, 347
Avşa Island 163, **164**
Aydin (Tralles) 239–40, 243
Ayvalik 191–4
  Çinarli Cami 191

Babaeski 155
Bafa, Lake 237–8
Bağsak 300
Balikesir 175, 189
Balkan Wars 54
Bandirma 162, 163, 164
banks 27, 29
bargaining 32, 33
bars (*meyhaneler*) 21, 63–4
Bayraktar, Nusret 127
Bayramdere beach 163
beaches
  North Aegean coast 185, 187,
    189, 192, 201
  South Aegean coast 237,
    251–2, 257

Southern Coast 264, 269–70,
  272, 281, 296, 298, 299–30,
  302
Thrace and the Marmara coast
  157, 162, 163, 175, 178
Behramkale 188, 190
Bektaşis, The 337
Belevi 227
Bergama 199–201
  Asklepieon 200
  eating out 203
  Sacred Tunnel 201
  travel and information 194
  where to stay 202–3
  see also Pergamon
Betiz 252
Beyazit I 52
Beyazit II 53, 96, 171
Beyşehir 324–5
Biga 162
Bilecik 175
Binbir Kilise 333
Black Eunuchs 95
Blegen, Carl 182
boats
  ferries 3, 8–9
  sea travel 3, 8–9
  yachting 34–5
Bodrum 248–51, *251*
  Castle of St Peter 250–1
  eating out 254–5
  entertainment and nightlife 255
  history 248–9
  the Mausoleum 251
  travel 249
  where to stay 252–4
Bodrum Peninsula 251–60
Bolayir 157
börekci 21
Bozcaada Island 185
Bronze Age 45
Burdur 319, 321, 323, 324
  Insuyu Cave 321

Index

Bursa *165*, 165–76
  Çekirge 171–2, 172–3, 174
  citadel area 168
  eating out 174–5
  Emir Sultan Camii 170
  Green Mausoleum 169–70
  Green Medrese 170
  hinterland 175–6
  market area 167–8
  Muradiye Complex 170–1
  travel 166–7
  Uludağ 165–6, **172**, 173–4
  where to stay 172–4
  Yeşil Cami 168–9
  Yildirim Beyazit Camii 170
buses
  internal travel 9–10
  international travel 4
  minibuses 13–14
Byzantine Empire **50**, 118

Calvert, Frank 182
camel wrestling 36
Çamlik 192
camping 42
Çanakkale 181, 184–7, 186–7
Çandarli 201
Cape Helles 160, 161
Cappadocia 333–44, *341*
  central 339–44
  eating out 339, 346–8
  fairy chimneys 339
  history 333–5
  landscape 335
  rock churches 334–5
  tourist information 336
  travel 335–6
  underground cities 336, 338,
    343–4
  where to stay 338, 346–8
Caria 244–51
Carians 47
carpets 30–1
cars
  accidents 11
  auto clubs 5, 12–13
  ferries 3, 8–9
  hiring 12

internal travel 10–14
international travel 5
Çatal Höyük 333
caves 35, 280, 296, 302–3, 321
Cehennem caves 302–3
Celâleddin Rumi 71–2, 329
Cennet caves 302–3
ceramics 32
Çeşme 213, 214, 215–16
Çeşme Peninsula 213–16
charter flights 2
cheese 22
children 39
Chimaera 275–6
Chios Island 215
Christie, Agatha 63
cigarettes 33–4
  customs restrictions 5
Cilicia 293–8
Cimmerians 47
Çine 245
Claros 219–20
climate 16
clothing
  buying 32
  packing 28
Cnidus 258
coffee 5, **23**
Colophon 219
Constantinople 75–6
  capture by Mehmet II 52, 61,
    76
  founding of 49
  sacking by the Crusaders 51, 76,
    102
  see also Istanbul
consulates 17
credit cards 27
Cremna 322–3
Croesus, King 47, 222, 236
Crusader States 51
Crusaders, sacking of
    Constantinople 51, 76, 102
currency controls 6
customs 6
Cyme 201
Cyrus 47

Dalaman, getting to 8
Dalyan 263–4
  beaches 269–70
Dardanelles 157–8, 159–60
Darius, King 162
Datça 257, 258, 259, 260
Delian Confederacy 47–8
Demre (Kale) 274, 276–7
Denizli 241, 243–4
Dereköy 155
Derinkuyu 344
Didyma 236, 238
Dikili 201, 202–3
disabled travellers 16–17
doctors 24
Doğanli Kale 315
dolmuş taxis 13–14
Dorians 46
Dracula, Count 123
drinks 22–3
  coffee 5, **23**
  prohibitionism 63–4
  tap water 24, 113
drugs 17

Eceabat 158
economy 58
Edincik 162
Edirne 151–5
  Adrianople Battle 155
  Ali Paşa Çarşi 153
  Archaeological and
    Ethnographic Museum 152
  Beyazit Bridge 154
  eating out 156
  Eski Cami 153
  Gazimihal Bridge 153–4
  Gazimihal Mosque 154
  Ikinci Beyazit Külliyesi 154
  imperial loge 152
  Kavaflar Arasta 152
  monuments 153–4
  mosques 153
  Muradiye 153
  Museum of Turkish and Islamic
    Art 152
  Rüstem Paşa Kervensaray 153
  Sarayiçi 154

Edirne cont'd
Selimiye Mosque 152
Sokullu Hamam 153
tourist information 152
travel 151–2
Üç Şerefeli Cami 153
where to stay 155–6
wrestlers 154–5
Yildirim Camii 154
Edremit 189, 190, 191
Edremit Gulf 189
Eflatunpinari 324
Eğirdir 319–21
eating out 324
Kovada National Park 320
travel 319
where to stay 323
Zindan Cave 321
Ekinlik Island 164
electricity 28
embassies 17
entry formalities 5–6
Ephesus 223, 223–7
along the Marble Road 225
excavations 224
history 222
House of the Virgin Mary 226–7
St Paul 223
the Seven Sleepers 226
street of the Curetes 225–6
Temple of Artemis 224
Theatre 224–5
see also Selçuk
Erdek 163, 164
Erdoğan, Tayyip 77–8, 126–7
Eski Foça 194, 201–2
Eskigümüş 345
Eskişehir 310–11, 318–19
Eşrefoğlu Camii 324
Eumenes II 195
Eurocheques 27
Euromos 244, 246
Europe
air travel from 2–3
rail travel from 3–4
EurRail 4
evil-eye medallions 61–2

ferries 3, 8–9
festivals 17–19
Fethiye 265–6, 268–9
fez, banning of 98–9
Finike 275
First World War 53–4, 159–60, 161
fishing 36
food 19–22
football 64–5
forestry service 66

Galatians 49
Gallipoli 157
Gazipaşa 299
Gelibolu 157, 161, 162
Gelibolu Peninsula 159–62
geography 23–4
Georgia, visas 5
Gerga 245
Gökçeada Island 185
Göksü gorge 300
Gönen 163
Gordion 315–17
Great Tumulus 315–16
Göreme 339–40, 346–7
Greece
cities 67–9
rail travel from 4
and Turkish history 46, 47–9, 61
Gryneum 201
Güllük 244, 247–8
Gülşehir 337
Gümbet 251–2
Gümüşlük 252
Gyllius, Petrus 101

Hacibektaş 337
Hadrian, Emperor 49, 196
hamams 36, 137
Hamdi Bey 99
harems 94–5
Harpagus, General 47
Hat Law 98–9
Hattian culture 45
health 24–5
disabled travellers 16–17

tap water 24, 113
Heracleia 237–8
Hisar Kale 315
History 44, 44–59
Alexander the Great 48, 61, 162, 316–17, 322
ancient 44, 45
Bronze Age 45
Byzantine Empire 49–50, 118
Constantinople 50, 51, 52–3, 61, 75–6
Greeks and Persians 47–8
New Nations in Anatolia 45–7
Ottoman Empire
(1300–1453) 51–2
(1454–1700) 52–3
(1700–1910) 54
Roman rule 49
Selcuks lead the Turkish invasion 50–1
sites 14
Turkey today 56–8
Turkish Revolution 54
Westernization 55
World War One 53–4, 159–60, 161
Hittites 45, 46
holiday villages 41
hospitals 25
hotels 39–42
Humann, Karl 196
hunting 36

Ibrahim the Mad 53, 91, 96
Iğneada 155
Ihlara 344–5, 348
Inegöl 176
inoculations 24
Inönü 176
insurance
car 5
medical 24–5
Insuyu Cave 321
international driver's licence 5
InterRail 4
Ionians 46, 47, 218
cities 231
Iotape 299

Ipsus, Battle of 49
Iraq 5
Iskele, eating out 302
işkembeci 21
Isparta 319, 321, 323, 324
Istanbul **73–148**, *84–5, 108, 116–17*
Adam Mickiewicz Museum 133
Adnan Menderes Bulvari 121
Ağa Cami 126
airline offices 3
airport 8
Aksaray 83–4, **114**
Alay Kiosk 100
Altimermer 121
Amcazade 114
Anadolu Hisar 132
Anadolu Kavaği 133
Anatolia Club 134
Aqueduct of Valens 112–13
Arap Cami 123
Arasta Bazaar 104
Archaeology Museum 99–100
Arnavutköy 132
Asian side 129–30
Atatürk Bulvari 112–14
Atatürk Cultural Centre 127
Atatürk Monument 100
Atik Ali Paşa Camii 106
Audience Chamber 97
Augusteion 87
Avrupa Pasaji 126
Aya Irene 93–4
Aya Sofia 88–91
Aya Sofia Baths 87
Aya Triada 126
Aya Triada Monastery 134–5
Ayvansaray 120
Bab-i-Humayun 91, **93**
Baghdad Kiosk 98
Balikpazari 126
Belgrade Forest 132
Beşiktaş 129
Beyazit Square 110
Beylerbey Palace 131–2
Beyoğlu (Pera) 83, **122–3**
Binbirdirek Cistern 103–4

Blue Mosque (Sultanahmet Camii) **91–2**, 104
Blues and Greens 101–2
Bookseller's Market 109–10
Bosphorus 131–4
Bosphorus Bridge 77, **131–2**
Burgazada 135
Burmali Minare 112
Burnt Column 105
Büyük Vakif Han 107
Büyükada 134
Cağaloğlu 105–6
Çamlica Hill 132
Carpet Sales Centre 91
Carriage Room 96
Çemberlitaş 105–6
Cerrahpaşa Camii 121
Chinese porcelain 96
church of Christ Pantepoptes 115
church of the Pantocrator 113–14
church of St Saviour in Chora 119–20
church of St Theodorus 111
Çiçek Pasaji 125
Çirağan Palace 129
Cistern of Aspar 115
clock collection 98
Column of Constantine Porphyrogenitus 102
Column of Marcian 114
construction industry 133–4
consulate 17, 126
Court of the Black Eunuch 95
Court of the Divan 94
Courtyard of the Sultan Valide 95–6
Covered Bazaar 76, 86, *108*, **109–10**
Divan Yolu 105–6
Dolmabahçe Palace 128–9
Dungeon of Anemas 120
eating out 142–7
Eminönü 106–9
Eminönü Market 108
Emirgân 132–3
Erdine Gate 120–1
Exokionion 115

Eyüp 121–2
Fatih District 114–15
Fener Quarter 115–22
Firuz Ağa Camii 103
fish market 126
Fountain of Ahmed III 91
Fountain of Mehmet II 91
Galata Bridge 83, 86, **107**
Galata Tower 123–4
Galata town 122
Galatasaray Hamam 125
Galatasaray Lisesi 125
Gate of Felicity 97
Gate of Salutations 95
Genoese castle 133
Golden Gate 121
Golden Horn 77, 83, 122
Goth's Column 100
Greek Orthodox Patriarchate 118–19
Gülhane Park 100
hamams 137
Harem 94–6
Haydarpaşa 83
railway station 130
Heybeliada 134
Hidiv Kasri 132
Hippodrome 101, 102–3
Hirka-i Saadet 98
history 75–8
hospitals 25
Imperial Museums 99–100
Istiklâl Caddesi 125
Kadiköy 83, **129–30**
Kaiser Wilhelm II Fountain 87
Kalenderhane Cami 112
Kamariotissa 134
Kanlica 132
Karaca Ahmet cemetary 130
Karaköy 123–9
Karamustafa of Merzifon Medrese 106
Kavaği 132–3
Kemeralti Caddesi 124
Kiliç Ali Paşa Camii 124
Kinaliada 135
Köprülü Kütüphenasi Library 106

Istanbul cont'd
Küçük Aya Sofia 104–5
Küçüksu Palace 132
Külliye of Koça Sinan Paşa 106
Lâleli District 114
language quiz 126
Leander's Tower 129
Library of Ahmet I 96, 97
Malta Kiosk 129
maps 82
Marble Tower 121
Martyrium of St Euphemia 103
mausoleums 90–1
Mehmet Fatih Bridge 131
Mehmet Paşa Camii 105, 106
Mehter Band 128
Mihrimah Camii 130
Mimar Sinan 110, **111**, 132
Mirelaon Convent 114
monastery of St George 134
money 82–3
Mosaic Museum 104
Municipal Museum 113
Museum of the Ancient Orient 100
Museum of Calligraphy 110
Museum of Divan Literature 124
Museum of Turkish Carpets and Kilims 91
Museum of Turkish Ceramics 100
Museum of Turkish and Islamic Arts 103
Naval Museum 129
Neve Shalom 124
Nevizade Sokak 126–7
nightlife 147–8
Nike Revolt 75, **101–2**
Nuruosmaniye Camii 106
Nüsretiye Cami 124
Obelisk of Theodosius 102–3
Old Istanbul (Stamboul) 83, **87–104**
orientation 83
Ortaköy Cami 131
Palace of Blachernae 120
Palace of the Byzantine Emperors 104

Palace of Constantine Porphyrogenitus 120
Palace Kitchens 96
Pammakaristos Church 119
Panaya Isodion 126
Paraecclesion 120
Patriarchate 118–19
Pera (Beyoğlu) 83, **122–3**
Pera Palace Hotel **62–3**, 125
Polonezköy 132–3
post offices 82, 107
Prince's Islands (Ada Günleri) 134–5
Revan Kiosk 98
Rumeli Hisar 132
Rumeli Kavaği 133
Rüstem Paşa Camii 108–9
Sadberk Hanim Museum 133
St Andreas in Crisal 121
St Benoit Chorch 124
St John in Studion 121
St Mary Mouchliotissa 119
St Stephen of the Bulgars 119
Şale Kiosk 129
Şehzade Camii 112
Selimiye Barracks 130
Selimiye Cami 130
Senate House 87
Serpentine Column 102
Seven Hills 87
Shantytown 133–4
shopping 31, **135–7**
Sirkeci **106–9**, 130
Şişhane Square 124–5
Soğukçeşme Sokak 91
Soldier's Museum 128
Spice Market 107–8
sports 137
Stamboul 83, **87–104**
Sublime Porte 100
Süleymaniye Cami 110–11
Sultan Mustafa III Cami 130
Sultan Selim Camii 115
Sultanahmet Camii (Blue Mosque) **91–2**, 104
Sultanahmet District 83–4, **104–5**
Sultanahmet Square 87

Sultan's Residence 98–9
Surp Yerrortutyun 126
Taksim Square 127
Tarabya 133
temperature 16
Theodosian Walls 120
Tomb of Barbarossa 129
Tophane Square 124
Topkapi Saray 76, **92–9**
tourist information 81–2, 87
travel 11, **78–81**
Treasury 97–8
Tulip Period 93
Tünel 124
Türbe of Sultan Mahmud II 105–6
University 110
Üsküdar 129–30
Valide Cami 114
Voyvoda Caddesi 123
water supply 100–1, **113**
where to stay 137–42
Yedikule Castle 121
Yellow Pavilion 132
Yeni Cami 107–8
Yeni Valide Camii 130
Yeniköy 133
Yeralti Cami 123
Yerebatan Sarayi 100–1
Yildiz Park 129
Zeuxippos baths 87
Izmir **205**, 203–10
bazaar district 206
consulate 17
Cumhuriyet Meydani 206
eating out 209–10
hospitals 25
Kadifekale 207
Karşiyaka 206
Kizlar Ağasi Hani 206
Konak 206
Kordon 206
Kültürpark 206
museums 207
Roman agora 207
tourist information 206
travel 204, 206
where to stay 207–8

Iznik 175, 176–8
  beaches 178
  Byzantine aqueduct 177
  Church Councils 176–7
  Istanbul Gate 177
  Lefke Gate 177
  where to stay and eating out
    178

Jason and the Argonauts 158–9
javelins (cirit) 36
jewellery 31
Justinian, Emperor 87, 88, 104

Kabatepe 161
Kadesh, Treaty of 100
Kadikalesi 252
Kadyama 266
Kaladiran 299
Kale (Demre) 274, 276–7
Kalkan 269, 270
Kanlidivane 305
Kapidaği 163
Karaada (Black Island) 252
Karaman 332, 333
Kaş 271–3
Kaunos 264
Kaymakli 344
kebab salons 21
Kekova Island 271, 273–4
Kemalpaşa 213
Kemer 266, 276–7
Keykubad, Sultan Alâeddin 51
Kibyra 323
Kilitbahir 158
Kirklareli 155
Kirşehir 337
Kizilçukor 340, 342
Kizildağ Milli Parki 324
Kizkalesi 303–4, 306
Knights of St John 249, 250, 256,
    300
Konya 325–33, 327
  Alâeddin Hill 326
  Alâeddin Mosque 326–7
  archaeological museum 331
  Aya Eleni 331
  Aziziye Camii 331

bazaar 331
Çatal Höyük 45
Dome of Stars 328
eating out 332
the Green Dome 330
history 325–6
Ince Minare Medrese 328–9
Iplikci Camii 329
Karatay Medrese 327–8
Mevlâna Museum 329
Museum of Selcuk Stone and
    Woodcarving 328
Piri Mehmet Pasha Camii 331
Plain of Konya 332–3
Sahip Ata Külliye 331
Selimiye Mosque 331
the Semahane 330
Şerafettin Mosque 329
tourist information 326
travel 326
where to stay 331–2
Korykos 304–5
Kos 252
Kovada National Park 320
Köyceğiz 263, 264–5
Küçükkuyu 189, 190–1
Kumbağ beach 161
Kümbetköy 315
Kurban Bayrami 17
Kurds 37, 57–8
Kuş Cenneti National Park
    163
Kuşadasi Bay 218–31
  Claros 219–20
  Colophon 219
  Ephesus 223, 223–7
  Kuşadasi 228–31
  Notium 219–20
  Selçuk 219, 220–2, 227–8
Kütahya 311–13
  eating out 318–19
  Kossuth House 312
  museum 311
  Temple of Zeus 312–13
  travel and information 310
  Türkmen Dağ 312, 313
  Ulu Cami 311
  where to stay 318

Kyanaea 271

Labranda 246
Laertes 299
Lagina 246
language 126, 355–66
Lapeski 157, 162
Lausanne, Treaty of 57
leather 31
Lesbos (Mytilini) island 192
Lüleburgaz 155
Lycians 47, 262–3
Lydians 46, 47, 211–12

Maender (Menderes) valley 231
Magnesia ad Maeander 239
Magnesia ad Sipylum 210
Mahmut II 53–4
Mandeville's Travels 304
Manisa 210
maps 25, 82
Marco Polo 304
Marmara, where to stay and
    eating out 164
Marmara Coast 157–78
Marmara Ereğli beach 157
Marmaris 251, 256–60
  around the town 257
  eating out 259–60
  entertainment and nightlife
    260
  history 256
  Rhodes 257–8
  travel 256
  where to stay 258–9
Medes, The 47
media 25–6
medical insurance 24–5
meerschaum pipes 32
Mehmet I 52, 168–9
Mehmet II (the Conqueror) 52,
    61, 76
Menderes, Adnan 55–6
Mersin 305, 306
metalwork 32
Mevlâna 71–2
  museum 329
meyhaneler (bars) 21, 63–4

Midas City 313, 314–15
Midas, King 316–17
Milas (Mylasa) 246–7, 248
Miletus 45, **46**, 47, **234–6**
minibuses 13–14
money 26–7
  currency controls 6
Mongols 50
mosques 70
motoring, *see* cars
mountain climbing 35
Mudanya 175
Muğla 244, 245–6, 247–8
muhallebici 21
Murat I 52, 172
Murat II 52
Murat IV 98
Mursilis I 45
museums 27–8
music 66–7
musical instruments 32
Mustafa Kemal Atatürk 54, 60–1, 98–9, 160
Mylasa (Milas) 246–7, 248
Myra 274–5
Myrina 201
Mysia 175
Myus 239

Nasreddin Hoca 324
Nevşehir 337–8
newspapers 25–6
Nicaea 176–7
  see also Iznik
Niğde 345–6
Nike Revolt 75, **101–2**
North Aegean Coast *180*, **180–216**
Notium 219–20
Nyssa 240

Olympos 275–6
Olympos, Mount 271, 275
Ören 187, 189, 190, 191, 244, 247
Orhan 52
orientation 14
  Istanbul 83

Ortahisar 340, 342, 347
Ortakent 252
Osman, Sultan 51
Ottoman Empire 51–4
Özal, Turgut **56**, 58
Özkonak 344

packing 28
Pamphylia 46
Pamukkale 242–4
pansiyons 39–41
Paşalimani Island 163–4
pastry shops 22
Patara 269–70, 214
Paul, St 223
Peloponnesian War 48
Pera Palace **62–3**, 125
Pergamon 49, **195–9**, *197*
  Acropolis 196–8
  Altar of Zeus 195, **198–9**
  Dikili 201, 202–3
  Library 198
  middle town 199
  site 196
  Theatre 198
  see also Bergama
Perge *285*, 285–7
Persia, and Turkish history 47–8
Pessinus 315
Petara, where to stay 270
Phaselis 276
Philip of Macedon 48
philosophy 235
phone cards 36
photography 28–9
Phrygia 46, **310–19**
pide salons 21
Pinara 266
PKK (Kurdish terrorists) 37, 57–8
poetry 71–2
police 29
  Trafik Polis 11
politics (from 1922) 55–8
population 71
port taxes 3
post offices 29
Practical A–Z 16–43

Priene *232*, **231–4**, 238
  Temple of Athena 233–4
prohibitionism 63–4
public holidays 29–30
Pythagoria 229

rabies 24
radio 26
rafting 35
rail travel
  internal 9
  international 4
Rakoczy, Prince Ferenc II 157
Ramazan 17, 21, **30**
Rand, Tamara 63
religion 69–71
  holidays 29–30
  revolution 54–5
Rhodes 258
road signs 12
Roman Empire
  fall of 155
  and Turkish history 49–50

Sagalassos 322
Samos 229
Sardis 211–13
Sarduri II 46
Sarimsakli 191, 192, 193
Şarköy beach 157
Sart 211–13
Schliemann, Heinrich 182
scuba diving 34
'Sea Peoples' 45
sea travel
  internal 8–9
  international 3
Şeker Bayrami 17
Selçuk 219, 220–2, 227–8
  Ephesian Artemis statues 220–2
  see also Ephesus
Selcuks 50–1
Seleucid Kingdom 48
Selge 288
Selim I 331
Selim the Sot 53, 91
Selimiye 244
Sestos 158

Sèvres, Treaty of **54**, 55, 57
Seyitgazi 313–14
shopping 30–3
  for antiquities 16
Side *289*, 288–93
  attractions near to 291–2
  city remains 290–1
  eating out 293
  history 289–90
  travel 284
  where to stay 292
Sidyma 266
Siğacik 213
Silifke 300, 301
Silivri 161
Sillyon 287
Sinan the Architect 110, **111**, 132, 152, 157
Sipylus, Mount 210–11
Sivas massacre 70–1
ski resorts 41
skiing 35–6
smoking 33–4
Smyrna, *see* Izmir
snorkelling 34
Softa Kalesi 299
Söğüt 176
Söke 231, 244
Soli 305
South Aegean Coast *218*, **218–60**
Southern Coast *262*, **262–306**
special interest holidays 6–7
sports 34–6
  football 64–5
Stratonikya 245–6
street food 22
Süleyman the Magnificent 53, 95, 112, 210, 256
Sultanhani 333
Syedra 299
Syria, visas 5

Taş Kule 202

Taşucu 300, 301–2
taxis 13
tea 23
Tekirdağ 157, 161–2
telephones 36–7
television 26
Temasalik Burnu 201
temperature 16
Termal 175
terrorists 37
Thrace *150*, **150–78**
Tiglath-Pileser III 46
time 37
Tlos 266
toilets 37
Topics 60–72
tour operators 6
tourist offices 38
Trafik Polis 11
Tralles (Aydin) 239–40, 243
Travel 2–14
  air 2–3, 7–8
  bus 4, 9–10
  car 5, 10–14
  dolmuş taxi 13–14
  entry formalities 5–6
  minibus 13–14
  orientation 14
  rail 4, 9
  sea 3, 8–9
  special interest holidays 6–7
  taxis 13
  see also under individual places
traveller's cheques 27
Troad peninsula 187–94
Troy 45, **181–4**, *183*
TTOK (Türk Turing ve Otomobil Kulübü) 5, **12–13**
Turgut Reis 252
Türk Turing ve Otomobil Kulübü (TTOK) 5, **12–13**
Turkish baths 36, 137
Türkmen Dağ 312, 313
Tuz Gölü 333

Üçağiz 274, 277
Uçhisar, where to stay and eating out 346
Uludağ 165–6, **172**, 173–4
underground cities 338, 343–4
United Kingdom
  air travel from 2
  rail travel from 4
United States, air travel from 2
Urartians 46
Ürgüp 342–3, 347–8
Uzuncaburç 302
Uzunköprü 155

visas 5
Visigoths 155

Warner Brothers 63
water, drinking 24, 113
water sports 34
where to stay 39–42
  see also under individual places
windsurfing 34
wine 22–3
World War One **54**, **159–60**, 161
wrestling 36, 154–5

Xanthus 266–7, 271
Xerxes, King 47, 158

yachting 34–5
Yalikavak 252
Yalova 175
Yeats, William Butler 61
Yeni Foça 202
Yeşil Üzümlü 266
Young Turks 53
youth hostels 42

Zelve 342
Zindan Cave 321

KT-363-973

Contents

Looking for answers 4

River floods 6

The strongest winds 8

Where the Earth shakes 10

Disaster on the coast 12

Volcano watching 14

Living with danger 16

Battle against the sea 18

Up in flames 20

Drought and famine 22

Trapped in the 'greenhouse' 24

The world's biggest disaster 26

Sites of natural disasters 28

Glossary 30

Index 32

LOOKING FOR ANSWERS

What is a natural disaster?

Earthquakes, floods, hurricanes and volcanic eruptions can all cause deaths, injuries and enormous damage. Events such as these are called natural disasters. Some natural disasters only last for a few seconds or a few hours, though the problems they cause can last for years. An earthquake, for example, can last for seconds but destroy a whole city. Other disasters take several months to happen, such as when there is too little rain and crops do not grow.

Earthquakes destroy people's homes.

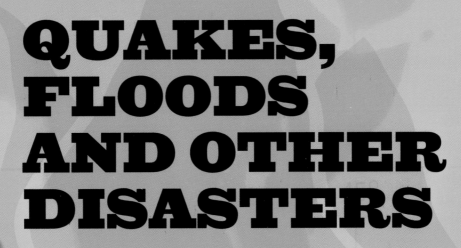

QUAKES, FLOODS AND OTHER DISASTERS

Fred Martin

Heinemann Educational Publishers
Halley Court, Jordan Hill, Oxford OX2 8EJ
a division of Reed Educational & Professional Publishing Limited

Heinemann is a registered trademark of Reed Educational & Professional Publishing Limited

OXFORD   MELBOURNE   AUCKLAND
JOHANNESBURG   BLANTYRE   GABORONE
IBADAN   PORTSMOUTH (NH) USA   CHICAGO

First published 1999

03 02 01 00 99

10 9 8 7 6 5 4 3 2 1

British Library Cataloguing in Publication Data
A catalogue record for this book is available from the British Library.

ISBN 0 435 09689 3   *Quakes, Floods and Other Disasters* single copy

ISBN 0 435 09691 5   *Quakes, Floods and Other Disasters* 6 copy pack

Photos
The National History Museum, title page and page 26. E.T. Archive, page 4. Keith Kent /
Science Photo Library, page 5. Popperfoto / Reuters, page 7. Mark Edwards / Still Pictures,
page 10. Lynette Cook / Science Photo Library, page 12. Werner Stoy / Bruce Coleman Ltd,
page 14. R. Holcomb, page 15. Sean Sprague, page 16. Robert Harding Picture Library, page
18. Richard Ashworth / Robert Harding Picture Library, page 20. A & M Breuil / Still
Pictures, page 21. Mark Edwards / Still Pictures, page 22. Anne Piantanida / Still Pictures,
page 25. Rev. Ronald Royer / Science Photo Library, page 27.

Illustrations
Illustrations by Hardlines and M2.

Designed by M2

Printed and bound in the UK

Lightning, which can start fires, is caused when an electrical spark jumps between the clouds and the ground.

Questions about natural disasters

People need to find out more about natural disasters. Some questions are easy to answer, such as where a disaster has happened and what damage has been done. It is not as easy to explain what causes a natural disaster or to predict when the next one will happen.

In the past, natural disasters were blamed on 'the gods'. Now scientists know more about the natural forces that cause them. Although these events can be a disaster for people, they are all simply part of how nature works.

Nature, however, still has many secrets. This is why it is still so hard to predict the next natural disaster, and what will happen when it begins.

RIVER FLOODS

Fighting floods in China

During the summer of 1998, people in China fought to stop their rivers from flooding. A flood is when water from a river flows over the land. The river Yangtze was one of the biggest rivers that flooded. Farmers and soldiers tried to make the river banks stronger and higher with stones and sandbags.

They were successful in some places. In others, the rivers either burst through their banks or flowed over the top. Once this happened, there was nothing to stop the water from spreading across the flat valley bottoms where people had their homes and farms.

What caused the disaster?

The main reason for the floods was that there was more rain than usual. At first, most of the rain sank into the ground. After more rain, the ground became so wet that no more rain could sink into it. It carried on raining. Next, the rainwater began to flow quickly off the ground and into the rivers. Before long, the rivers were so full that they began to overflow and flood.

Sometimes there is more than one reason for a flood. If mountain snow and ice melt in spring, at the same time as there is heavy rain, streams can quickly become raging torrents. The extra water then flows down to the lowland rivers. When this happens, people need to watch out for floods.

How a river floods its valley.

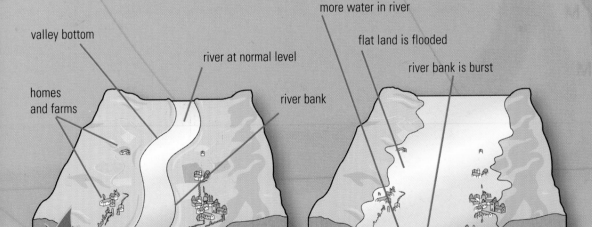

valley bottom

homes and farms

river at normal level

river bank

more water in river

flat land is flooded

river bank is burst

People made homeless by the floods in China.

THE 1998 RIVER FLOODS IN CHINA

- About 2600 people were killed during the floods.
- At least 20 million homes were washed away.
- One city was saved from flooding by blowing up the banks with dynamite and flooding farmland instead.
- The last bad floods were in 1954, when 30,000 people died.

THE STRONGEST WINDS

Measuring the wind

The wind is one of nature's most common and destructive forces. Although it is nothing more than moving air, the wind can cause enormous damage.

Wind speed is measured on the Beaufort Scale. The strongest winds on this scale blow at force 12, called hurricane force.

The fastest and most violent winds of all are in a tornado. A tornado is a very narrow funnel of air that spirals up from the ground to the sky. The wind speed can be up to 800 km per hour, which is too fast to be measured on the Beaufort Scale.

The Beaufort Scale

0	**calm** — smoke rises straight up		**6**	**strong breeze** — hard to use an umbrella	
1	**light air** — smoke starts to drift		**7**	**moderate gale** — hard to walk into the wind	
2	**light breeze** — leaves rustle		**8**	**fresh gale** — twigs break off trees	
3	**gentle breeze** — flags wave		**9**	**strong gale** — roof slates move	
4	**moderate breeze** — small branches move		**10**	**storm** — trees uprooted	
5	**fresh breeze** — small trees sway		**11**	**violent storm** — houses damaged	
			12	**hurricane** — destruction of many buildings	

air and clouds spiral out at the top

air continues to spiral upwards to form dense clouds

air rotates around the centre

hot, moist air spirals quickly upwards towards cold, dry air

more air is sucked into the low pressure area at the bottom

What makes the wind blow?

Air is made up of many tiny particles called molecules. When the air is cold, the molecules are very close together. When the air is warm, the molecules spread out. Warm air with fewer molecules is lighter than cold air that has more molecules. The scientific name for these different weights of air is air pressure. An area of high pressure is when the air is sinking. An area of low pressure is caused by rising air.

Wind occurs when warm air rises and an area of low pressure develops beneath it. Air moves in from an area of high pressure to replace the rising air. This movement of air is called the wind.

Why does a tornado cause so much damage?

The pressure in the centre of a tornado is very low. As a tornado passes a building, the air pressure outside the building suddenly becomes much lower than the pressure inside. The building is not strong enough to hold the pressure in, so windows are blown out and, in extreme cases, the whole building explodes. The safest place to be during a tornado is in a cellar under the house.

FACTS ABOUT HURRICANES AND TORNADOES

- A hurricane is also called a typhoon or cyclone.
- In the USA, a tornado is also called a twister.
- Tornadoes in the USA are mostly in the central plains, also called 'tornado alley'.
- Sometimes, there are small tornadoes in the UK.

WHERE THE EARTH SHAKES

Why do earthquakes only happen in some places?

Why is it that news reports about earthquakes always seem to be from another country? The same countries seem to suffer from earthquakes over and over again. The UK never seems to be affected.

The strongest earthquakes are in places where there are giant cracks called fault lines through the Earth's surface. These fault lines divide the Earth's outer layer, called the crust, into giant slabs called plates. Forces inside the Earth push and pull the plates, making them move. A sudden jerk along a fault line causes an earthquake.

House destroyed by an earthquake in Turkey.

Earthquake damage

A strong earthquake in some countries can cause enormous damage and kill thousands of people in seconds. In 1993, about 20,000 people died in one short earthquake in India. There are also strong earthquakes in California in the USA, but they do not kill as many people. This is because people in California have enough money to make buildings that are strong enough to survive an earthquake.

There are some earthquakes in the UK, but they are never very strong and they do not cause much damage. This is because, as shown on the map below, the UK is not near any of the major fault lines.

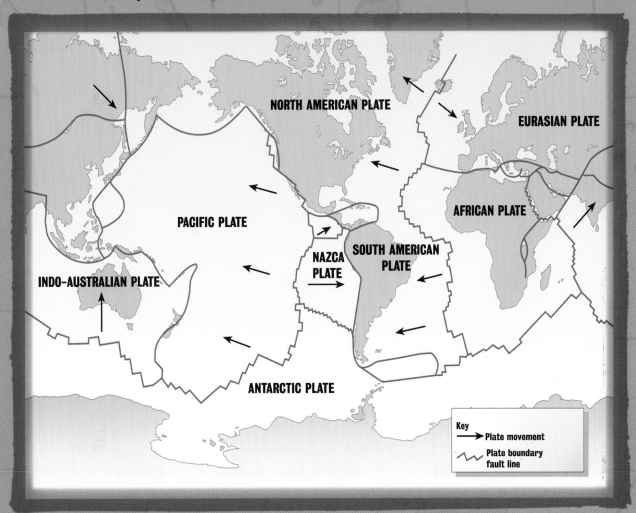

The Earth's plates and major fault lines.

DISASTER ON THE COAST

Giant waves

A tidal wave can be bigger than a two-storey house. A tidal wave is also called a tsunami (pronounced *sue-naa-me*), from two Japanese words, 'tsu' meaning a harbour and 'nami' meaning a wave.

A tsunami crashing on to the shore.

What causes a tsunami?

A tsunami can be caused by an earthquake that shakes the sea bed, sometimes hundreds of kilometres out to sea. An erupting volcano can have the same effect. The sea bed heaves, and so does the water above it. This starts a long, low wave that ripples out at great speed towards the coast. The wave can travel at several hundred kilometres per hour. As the tsunami approaches the shore, it moves over shallower water and begins to build up. It gradually becomes a roaring wall of water that crashes on to the shore.

The New Guinea disaster

A tsunami struck the north coast of Papua New Guinea in August 1998. The people had no time to get away. Homes were smashed, farmland was ruined and at least 2000 people were killed.

In time, the survivors will move back and rebuild their homes, although there is no reason why another tidal wave should not strike again. People who live near the sea in areas where there are earthquakes always live with the risk of a tsunami.

A tsunami spreads out from the centre of an underwater earthquake.

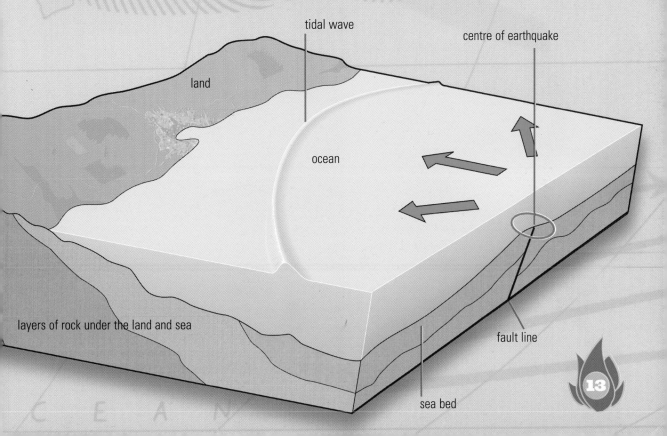

tidal wave

centre of earthquake

land

ocean

layers of rock under the land and sea

fault line

sea bed

VOLCANO WATCHING

A spectacular event

An erupting volcano is one of nature's most spectacular events. There is no way to stop it from happening. All that scientists can do to help people escape from danger is to try to predict when a volcano will erupt.

How can a volcano eruption be predicted?

Sometimes, a volcano gives clues that it is going to erupt. In the weeks and days before it erupts, hot molten rock called magma moves up into the volcano from deep inside the Earth. This makes the volcano swell. Instruments placed on the slopes are able to measure the change. Another clue is that gases sometimes start to rise from the volcano. There may also be some small eruptions and local earthquakes before a big eruption.

Lava flowing down the slopes of an erupting volcano.

Hard to predict

One problem with trying to predict an eruption is that these clues are not always evident. A second problem is that many volcanoes are in remote places where there are no scientists and no instruments, therefore the clues go unnoticed.

Scientists can study a volcano's history to try to predict what might happen when it erupts. Some erupt like an explosion, sending lumps of rock and ash high into the air. Others erupt more gently, sending rivers of molten lava down their slopes.

There is a lot more that scientists need to find out about volcanoes before they can predict exactly when and how a volcano will erupt.

Scientist studying lava flowing under a cooled lava crust

LIVING WITH DANGER

Why do people live in places where natural disasters may occur?

It is sometimes hard to understand why people live in places where there may be a natural disaster. It may just be that people find it hard to move away from their homes, but sometimes there are other reasons why people choose to live near the site of a natural disaster.

Farmers growing crops near a volcano in the Philippines.

Living near a volcano

There are some good reasons why people live near volcanoes. In Iceland, the hot rock near volcanoes heats water in the ground, and people use this hot water to heat their homes. Near some volcanoes in New Zealand, the climate acts on the volcanic deposits to produce steam, which is used to generate electricity. In Indonesia and Japan, heavy rain and strong sunlight break down lava until it becomes soil that is very good for growing crops. A volcano can also attract tourists, such as those who go to see Vesuvius in Italy.

Types of volcano

To live near a volcano, it is useful to know how often it is likely to erupt. There are three types of volcano:

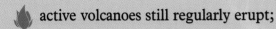 active volcanoes still regularly erupt;

dormant volcanoes have not erupted for several hundred years, but may still erupt;

extinct volcanoes will never erupt again.

People live on or near all three types, though extinct volcanoes are the only ones that are really safe.

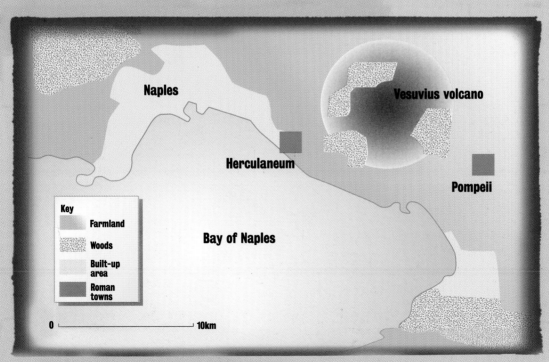

Key
- Farmland
- Woods
- Built-up area
- Roman towns

Naples

Vesuvius volcano

Herculaneum

Pompeii

Bay of Naples

0 ————— 10km

The Italian city of Naples has spread close to Vesuvius, the volcano that destroyed the Roman towns of Pompeii and Herculaneum. Vesuvius is still an active volcano.

BATTLE AGAINST THE SEA

Living by the sea

People have settled in coastal areas over thousands of years. These areas often have low, flat land that is good for growing food and for industry. Many coastal areas are also beautiful places in which to live. But the sea can be upredictable, as storms and huge waves can wreck harbours and seaside homes, and alter coastlines.

How can people protect themselves from the sea?

To protect themselves from the sea, people build stone and concrete sea walls. Building sea defences is expensive and the result can look ugly. It is for these reasons that the whole coast is not protected by sea walls. In some places where there are no defences, waves smash against the coast and wear it away, causing buildings to collapse into the sea and farmers' fields to be washed away.

Powerful waves crashing against a sea wall.

Breaking sea defences

The sea, however, is strong enough to break through any wall. Sea water can also flow over a sea wall if it is not high enough. In February 1990, at the seaside resort of Towyn in North Wales, strong winds blew from the sea towards the coast. These gale force winds coincided with high tides, with the result that ten-metre-high waves broke through and spilled over the sea walls. About 6000 holiday caravans and 3000 homes were flooded and ruined by the salt water.

Perhaps it is a waste of money to try to beat the power of the sea. The best answer may be to avoid living in places that are likely to be eroded or flooded by the sea.

"Our holiday caravan was smashed by the waves."
(Caravan owners)

"It was just bad luck that the wind came at the same time as the high tide, but it might happen again."
(Local resident)

"We did not think this would ever happen so we were not insured. Now we have nothing left."
(Local resident)

"It will cost almost £15 million to repair the damage to roads, homes and the sea wall."
(Council official)

"The flood water left mud all over our carpets, furniture and on the walls."
(Local resident)

"We had to move out of our house for months until it dried out and was repaired."
(Local resident)

UP IN FLAMES

Fire in the grasslands

Fire burns both plants and animals. One way that a fire can start naturally is when a white hot streak of lightning hits the ground.

The grassland areas of Australia and Africa have a dry season when there is often no rain for up to six months. During this season, rivers dry up and the grass becomes extremely dry. If lightning hits the ground a fire can easily start, and the slightest wind will fan the fire, quickly spreading it across large areas. Some animals survive by running away or by hiding underground, but others are not so lucky. Sometimes people are trapped in grassland fires, and lives and homes are lost.

Grassland fire.

Can a natural disaster do any good?

After the fire has died out, burnt ash from dead plants is left on the ground. When it rains again, the ash is washed into the soil, making the soil fertile so that more plants can grow. Seeds already in the ground grow quickly because the fire has cleared away the old plants. There are some plants whose seeds only begin to germinate after they have been exposed to the intense heat of a fire.

Before long, the grassland grows again with fresh young plants. The animals start to return, and eventually the landscape looks as before. Fire is one of nature's ways of helping new plants to grow and maintaining the grassland.

New plants grow quickly after a fire.

DROUGHT AND FAMINE

Rains that fail

A famine is a time when food is scarce, so people do not have enough to eat. A principal cause of famine is drought. During a drought rainfall is unusually low, so crops fail to grow.

In some parts of Africa, such as Sudan, Mali and Ethiopia, the amount of rain can vary from year to year. When the rain fails, there is a drought. As a result, crops do not grow, animals die of thirst and people go hungry.

Watering plants in a dry part of Africa.

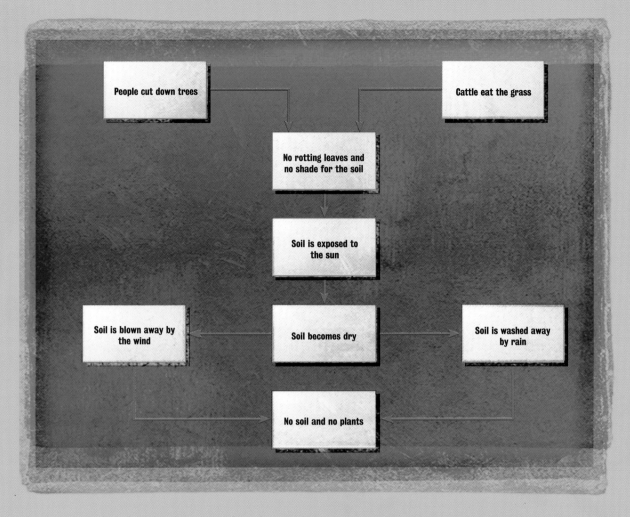

How people and their animals make a drought worse.

Can people make a natural disaster worse?

The effects of a drought can be made worse by people. This happens when people cut down trees for firewood and to get more land for farming. Without shade from the sun, and with no more rotting leaves to enrich it, the soil turns to dust that is useless for growing crops. Without trees to protect it, the soil is exposed, so it is easily washed away by heavy rain or blown away by the wind. Another problem is caused by over-grazing, when too many cattle eat the grass, making the soil dry and useless.

Wars can make a famine even worse. In recent years there have been wars in places where drought already makes it hard for people to survive.

TRAPPED IN THE 'GREENHOUSE'

Global warming

July 1998 broke all weather records. It was the world's hottest month since weather records began. Scientists believe that this is proof that the Earth is getting warmer, and have called this 'global warming'. Further evidence of global warming may be a giant sheet of ice that broke away from the Arctic Sea ice pack and floated south into the Atlantic Ocean.

What causes global warming?

It is thought that global warming is caused by the gases that people are putting into the air by burning coal, petrol and trees. These gases are known as 'greenhouse gases'. This is because they let in the sun's heat, but instead of it escaping back to space again, the gases trap the heat and keep it in the Earth's atmosphere.

Icebergs break away from an ice shelf as the air becomes warmer.

What effects will global warming have in the future?

If global warming continues, there could be many more natural disasters because of changes in the weather. In some places, there could be longer droughts. In others, the extra heat could start more hurricanes and tornadoes. There could be more rain, so there would be more flooding. As the oceans become warmer, the water will expand and cause the sea level to rise, leading to problems of flooding around the coast.

If all this happens, it will be because people have not considered how their actions affect the ecological balance of the planet.

THE WORLD'S BIGGEST DISASTER

About 65 million years ago dinosaurs were the biggest and most powerful animals on Earth. Then suddenly there was an enormous explosion as the Earth was hit by something from space. Millions of tons of rock, dust and gases were blasted high into the atmosphere. A tidal wave spread out, drowning everything in its path. Fires broke out, burning vast areas of trees and other plants. Millions of animals were instantly killed by the blast.

For the next six months, dust from the explosion blocked out the sun. Plants died and there was nothing for the plant-eating dinosaurs to eat. The Earth also became too cold for the dinosaurs. Only the small animals that lived under the ground were able to survive.

Dinosaurs were the most powerful animals on Earth.

A comet hurtling through space.

Why did this disaster happen?

Scientists have found evidence that a comet or a meteor from space collided with the Earth, causing widespread devastation. They have found the remains of a crater where the Earth was hit on the Yucatan peninsula in Mexico. They have also found a thin layer of dust just above the rocks containing the last fossils of dinosaurs. It is thought that this layer is the dust that settled back to the ground after the explosion.

It looks at last as if the puzzle of why the dinosaurs became extinct may have been answered.

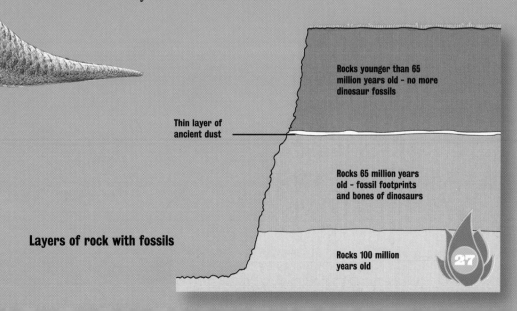

Rocks younger than 65 million years old – no more dinosaur fossils

Thin layer of ancient dust

Rocks 65 million years old – fossil footprints and bones of dinosaurs

Layers of rock with fossils

Rocks 100 million years old

SITES OF NATURAL DISASTERS

ARCTIC SEA

WALES
(Towyn)—

ATLANTIC OCEAN

UNITED STATES
OF AMERICA

(California)—

MEXICO

(Yucatan
Peninsula)

PACIFIC OCEAN

28

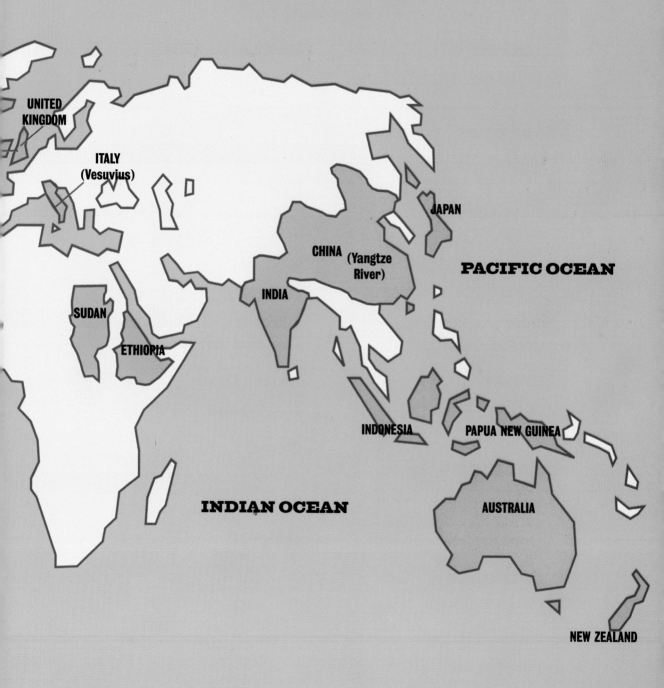

UNITED
KINGDOM

ITALY
(Vesuvius)

JAPAN

CHINA (Yangtze
River)

PACIFIC OCEAN

SUDAN

INDIA

ETHIOPIA

INDONESIA

PAPUA NEW GUINEA

INDIAN OCEAN

AUSTRALIA

NEW ZEALAND

29

GLOSSARY

active

used to describe a volcano that still erupts

air pressure

the amount of air in a space

atmosphere

the layer of gases around the Earth

Beaufort Scale

a scale used to measure wind speed

crust

the thin, hard outer layer of the Earth

dormant

used to describe a volcano that has not erupted for several hundred years

drought

a long period when there is no rain

earthquake

when the ground shakes

eruption

an explosion of a volcano

extinct

used to describe a very old volcano that will never erupt again

famine

a time when crops do not grow and people have no food

fault line

a crack through layers of rock

flood

river or sea water that flows over the land

fossils

the prints of ancient animals and vegetation in rocks

global warming

the air temperature around the Earth becoming warmer

greenhouse gases

gases that trap the Sun's heat in the Earth's atmosphere

hurricane

very strong winds and wet weather

ice pack

ice that floats over the sea

lava

hot molten rock that flows from a volcano

lightning

an electric spark between the ground and clouds

magma

rock from inside the Earth

natural disaster

a natural event that causes problems for people

plates

large slabs of the Earth's crust

sea walls

concrete and stone walls built to protect the coast from the sea

tidal wave

a large wave that comes onshore

tornado

a narrow funnel of fast-spinning air

tsunami

see *tidal wave*

volcano

a mountain that erupts with gases and rock from inside the Earth

INDEX

Africa 20, 22

air pressure 9

Australia 20, 29

Beaufort Scale 8, 30

California 11, 28

China 6, 7, 29

comet 27

crops 4, 17, 22

dinosaurs 26, 27

drought 22, 23, 25, 30

earthquake 4, 10, 11, 13, 30

Ethiopia 22, 29

famine 22, 23, 30

fault lines 10, 11, 30

fire 20, 21, 26

flood 4, 6, 7, 19, 25, 30

global warming 24, 25, 31

grasslands 20, 21

greenhouse gases 24, 31

Herculaneum 17

hurricane 4, 8, 9, 25, 31

ice 6, 24, 31

Iceland 17

India 11, 29

Indonesia 17, 29

Italy 17, 29

Japan 17, 29

lightning 5, 20, 31

Mali 22, 29

meteor 27

Mexico 27, 28

Naples 17

New Zealand 17, 29

Papua New Guinea 13, 29

plates 10, 11, 31

Pompeii 17

rain 4, 6, 20–23, 25

river 6, 7, 20

sea 13, 18, 19, 24, 25, 28, 31

sea wall 18, 19, 31

Sudan 22, 29

tidal wave 12, 13, 26, 31

tornado 8, 9, 25, 31

Towyn 19, 29

tsunami 12, 13, 31

UK 10, 11, 19, 29

USA 11, 28

Vesuvius 17, 29

volcano 4, 13–15, 17, 30, 31

war 23

wind 8, 9, 19, 20, 30

Yangtze 6, 29

Yucatan peninsula 27, 28